Praise for
Blues-Rock Explosion

"This book is an exundant tide—almost a tsunami—of information.
Plunge in and enjoy!"
— **Mark Naftalin**, formerly of the Paul Butterfield Blues Band and Mother Earth
and host of the weekly radio broadcast, *Mark Naftalin's Blues Power Hour*

"I was fascinated by the detailed reconstruction of the very early careers of artists who
didn't make their mark until years later. The unheralded connections between artists not usually
mentioned in the same breath provides a larger, and more enlightening context than I've seen
before in any textual study of sixties music. I thought I knew most of this stuff but I had no
idea how much more there was to learn. A phenomenal research job."
— **Greg Shaw**, founder of Bomp Records, former editor of *Phonograph Record Magazine*,
former publisher of *Mojo-Navigator Rock & Roll News* and *Who Put the Bomp*

"A book like this would be a valuable asset to a blues-rock fan.
Let's hope that it gets the recognition it deserves and that the facts
for once will now be the right ones. Best of luck with it."
— **Stan Webb**, Chicken Shack

"An outstanding piece of research work full of detail and pertinent information.
Essential reading for all music fans and surely a 'must acquire' for
serious aficionados of the 'sixties blues revival.'"
— **Mike Vernon**, producer and founder of Blue Horizon Records

"At last we have an important research work on how blues-based musicians
have made, and continue to make, vital musical contributions that devoted fans have
heartily enjoyed for decades. I can attest that this intensive work is put together
with the utmost care and enthusiasm. All music fans should be indebted to everyone
involved with this book. Congratulations for a job well done, and many
thanks for taking on this task before I did!"
— **Greg Russo**, author of *Yardbirds: The Ultimate Rave-Up*

"A magnificent piece of research with stuff in there that I'd forgotten
and will use whenever I eventually write an autobiography without clash of facts."
— **John Mayall**

Praise Continued . . .

"This fact-rich compilation is a music fan's treasure, full of information and insights about the artists. The helpful postscripts answer the where-are-they-now question. The discographies remind us of all that came out of this important musical moment."
— **Nadine Cohodas**, author of *Spinning Blues into Gold*:
The Chess Brothers and the Legendary Chess Records

"An indispensable reference . . . a fascinating journey back into the heyday of the blues revival, bringing to life once more, in anecdotes and great detail, those exciting American and British bands that shaped rock history."
— **Chris Welch**, a former features editor of *Melody Maker;* author of 27 books, including
Cream: Eric Clapton, Jack Bruce and Ginger Baker—The Legendary Sixties Supergroup

"Such assiduity warms the cockles of my heart."
— **Pete Frame**, author of *The Complete Rock Family Trees*, *More Rock Family Trees*
and *The Beatles and Some Other Guys (Rock Family Trees of the Early Sixties)*

BLUES-ROCK EXPLOSION

Contributors

Summer McStravick—Editor

Summer McStravick is the editor of *Readers & Writers Magazine*, an arts and literary periodical. Prior to her writing career, Summer spent two years studying music composition and theory at San Diego State University. She later graduated summa cum laude with honors from the University of California, San Diego. She resides in Southern California with her husband.

John Roos—Editor

Specializing in a variety of genres, including rock, blues, country, folk, cajun, Celtic, world, roots and alternative, John Roos has been covering the national pop music scene as a freelance writer/editor for the past 15 years. A frequent contributor to *The Los Angeles Times* and *OC Weekly*, member of the National Music Critics Association (NMCA) and graduate of the University of California at Berkeley, John resides in Orange County, California with his wife, Kitty, and their daughter, Marissa. When not immersed in music, he is an outdoor enthusiast who enjoys whitewater rafting, bodysurfing and playing softball.

Julian Barker—Archive Consultant

Described by Britain's most popular paper, *The Sun*, as "The nation's leading authority on 1960s music," Julian (who has every original record to have made the 1952–69 U.K. charts) specializes in information garnered from his thousands of 1950s and 1960s pop papers and the like. He's compiled massive databases referencing articles, pictures, record reviews, LP listings and record company advertisments, etc. Julian has supplied information to everybody from the Copyright Protection Society to a Polish oldies magazine, as well as to record companies, newspapers, writers, and (via his Web site at http://freespace.virgin.net/julian.barker) hundreds of everyday "oldies" enthusiasts.

"Jet" Martin Celmins—Contributor

After a first career in advertising media research, "Jet" Martin Celmins decided in 1991 to devote all his time to playing blues music and writing. *Peter Green—The Biography* was first published in spring 1995. It received positive reviews and Jet gradually built a friendship with Peter and has been a face on the Splinter Group scene ever since Green's return to the stage in 1996. As Jet Martin, solo guitarist and one-man band, he has been Splinter Group's regular support act on most British appearances since 1997. Martin is currently working with Stan Webb on memoirs written by the guitarist himself over the years. The book, illustrated with Stan's own memorabilia, will be published in late 2001.

Borge Skilbrigt—Contributor

Borge was the last editor of the now defunct Graham Bond fanzine *GRAMBO*. He is currently working on a new book about Bond. Besides contributing to the Graham Bond Web site (www.grahambond.net), he is also an occasional drummer.

Harry Shapiro—Contributor

Harry is the author of biographies on Alexis Korner, Graham Bond and Eric Clapton, and has written a study of the relationship between drugs and popular music called *Waiting for the Man*. His biography of Jimi Hendrix, *Electric Gypsy*, was nominated for a Ralph J. Gleason award for music books. He is a regular contributor to *Mojo*, the blues magazine *Blueprint*, and he contributes to many radio music programs. With a partner, two children, a snake called Homer and a mortgage to support, he hasn't given up the day job—working for a drugs charity in London.

Mike Stax—Contributor

Mike is the editor and publisher of *Ugly Things* magazine, which focuses on the greatest overlooked bands of the 1960s and other "wild sounds from past dimensions." Published since 1983, *Ugly Things* is considered one of the world's premiere publications about the music and culture of the 1960s. Mike has written and researched liner notes for numerous reissues, including the track-by-track liners for Rhino's highly acclaimed *Nuggets* boxed set and its companion, *Nuggets Volume 2*. His writing has also appeared in magazines such as *Discoveries*, *Your Flesh* and *Pulse*. In the tiny fragments of spare time left between writing, editing and publishing, he performs and records with his band, the Loons.

Jeff Watt—Contributor

Jeff is a frequent contributor to *Blues Matters!* magazine. His writings have also appeared in *Discoveries* and *Ugly Things*.

BLUES-ROCK EXPLOSION

Edited by

Summer McStravick and John Roos

Old Goat Publishing
Mission Viejo, California

Published by Old Goat Publishing, 23052 Alicia Parkway #H-183, Mission Viejo, CA 92692-1662,USA
Visit our Web site at: www.oldgoat.com

Publishers Cataloging in Publication Data
(Provided by Quality Books, Inc.)

Blues-rock explosion / edited by Summer McStravick and John Roos. -- 1st ed
    p. cm.
    Includes bibliographical references and index.
    LCCN 00-104616
    ISBN 0-9701332-7-8

    1. Blues musicians-Biography. 2. Rock musicians—Biography. 3. Blues (Music)-1961-1970—History and criticism. 4. Rock music—1961-1970—History and criticism. I. McStravick, Summer. II. Roos, John, 1958-

ML3521.B58 2001   781.643'092'2
                              QBI00-901369

ISBN 0-9701332-7-8

Printed in the United States of America

Photo Credits:

All photos are from the collection of Old Goat Publishing with the exception of the following:

    Duane Allman (front cover): Photo courtesy of Jon Levicke
    Fleetwood Mac at the Windsor Jazz and Blues Festival (foreword): Photo courtesy of Bob Brunning
    Artwoods (insert): Photo courtesy of Art Wood
    Black Cat Bones (insert): Photo courtesy of Stuart Brooks
    Jo Ann Kelly (insert): Photo courtesy of Pete Moody

Contents

**The original Fleetwood Mac with Bob Brunning (far right)
at the Windsor Jazz & Blues Festival.**

Foreword

It hardly seems possible that it has been over thirty years since I nervously stepped out onstage at a major U.K. blues festival with my musical colleagues Peter Green, Jeremy Spencer and Mick Fleetwood for the band's first ever concert. We were absolutely terrified, and I'm sure that it showed. Of course we didn't know it at the time, but Fleetwood Mac were just one of many bands that were part of the sixties blues and rock explosion that was taking place on both sides of the Atlantic—cast your eyes toward the chapter titles for this book to see just how many!

Virtually without exception, we all had one thing in common. We were inspired, motivated and captivated by the glorious blues music that we had heard on obscure records, hard-to-find radio stations and the (very occasional) visit to our hometowns by real blues musicians. B.B. King, Muddy Waters, Elmore James, Lightning Hopkins, Sonny Boy Williamson, Howlin' Wolf, John Lee Hooker, Robert Johnson and Bessie Smith were just some of our many heroes, and we idolized them. But many of our contemporaries were not nearly as successful in their homeland as they deserved to be. During the '60s and '70s, they were often to be found playing in small clubs for little money, and many of their careers were in decline. However, the British musical invasion of the U.S. during the same period, along with the numerous American bands extolling the virtues of the musicians in their own backyard, began to bring the attention of a new generation of music lovers to just how much fabulous blues music could be found on their own doorstep. I've lost count of the number of interviews in which I've heard U.S. bluesmen pay credit to the likes of Fleetwood Mac, the Rolling Stones, Savoy Brown, the Paul Butterfield Blues Band, Canned Heat, Stevie Ray Vaughan, Alexis Korner, Jeff Beck, the Yardbirds, Led Zeppelin, Ten Years After, the Blues Project, Eric Clapton, etc., for championing the quality, beauty and sheer power of what is arguably one of the most important musical genres ever to have emerged from the United States.

This book comprehensively explores that whole fascinating period in the recent history of popular music. A real labor of love, the detail is breathtaking. Virtually every band (and musician) on both sides of the Atlantic that had a role, however minor, in the saga will find themselves acknowledged in this book. Anecdotes abound, and the editors and contributors have made what could have been a rather dry and academic treatise into an entertaining and above all informative work. I look forward to volume two!

Bob Brunning, author of *Blues in Britain*
London, England
September 2000

Preface

Over the years, a number of publishers have released "rock encyclopedias." The first entry into the market, Lillian Roxen's celebrated *Rock Encyclopedia,* was unleashed in 1969.

"It took me eight months to complete," Roxen told *The New York Times* in 1970, "and I must have put on about 40 pounds. It was a very high price to pay. I lost my friends, my health, my looks."

In the years since, some critics have complained about inaccuracies in her book, though Roxon herself was also keenly aware of the potential for error. She acknowledged as much in her author's note in which she wrote, "Groups split even as I wrote of their inner harmony, and got themselves together just as I had acknowledged their tragic demise. Baritones turned sopranos overnight; bands expanded and contracted their personnel like concertinas; fine performers degenerated swiftly and inexplicably while supposed second-raters found their promise all too late to make our deadlines." Sadly, Roxon passed away in 1973 at the age of 41.

Subsequent attempts to issue similar reference works have been plagued with flaws. Most do not contain track listings associated with each release, which to this day has been one of the most appealing features of the original *Rock Encyclopedia.* Also, in the more than thirty years since the release of Roxon's book, most other rock reference books have tended to restrict themselves to profiling performers who have achieved significant commercial success or critical impact. The end result has been that more than half the artists covered in the original *Rock Encyclopedia* haven't been profiled in most other reference works. Worse yet, given the overly broad scope of many of these books, coverage is often superficial for those performers who do rate an entry.

We think that this trend has been a step in the wrong direction. Old Goat Publishing views the 1960s as a renaissance period for music and is dedicated to providing a series of comprehensive, A–Z reference books covering a variety of musical movements of the era. Each title in the Sixties Rock series will provide in-depth profiles, painstakingly reviewed for accuracy and detail, of groups and solo artists who defined '60s rock'n'roll. Our Sixties Rock series writers have combined exhaustive searches of 1960s and 1970s rock journalism with up-to-date personal interviews to gather new, accurate information about some of the '60s' greatest stars . . . as well as some of the most overlooked but talented bands. Readers will find everything from musicians' individual biographies to chronological histories of the evolutions and dissolutions of the bands themselves. The guiding principle behind each Old Goat release is that each title be accurate, objective, and above all, entertaining. The first issue of the series, *Blues-Rock Explosion,* contains thorough histories of 42 different solo artists and bands that made the genre *rock.*

A music writer once observed, "Compiling rock data is a thankless task. No matter how careful researchers think they are, once their work is published they'll be inundated with letters revealing hitherto preciously hoarded information." We agree with the sentiment, but by consulting experts as well as the artists themselves, we hope to have kept errors to a minimum.

Similarly, we've meticulously compiled each chapter's discography with an eye toward both accuracy and ease of use. Since *Blues-Rock Explosion* focuses primarily on recordings made through 1972, we've summarized artists' subsequent releases in the postscript, thereby keeping to the subject at hand. (Recordings made through 1972 that were only issued years later, such as "lost" recordings, live versions and various outtakes, are usually listed.) We have also provided in-text chart rankings where appropriate (i.e. "U.S. #6, U.K. #8") and the matrix number and country of issue beside obscure releases and peripheral recordings, such as those typically made by an artist prior to joining the profiled group (i.e. "U.K./Fontana TFL 5108"). And lastly, to eliminate repetition, complete track listings for albums released in both the United States and Great Britain are only listed under the U.S. portion of the discography.

Summer McStravick, Editor

Acknowledgments

It furthers one to install helpers. — I Ching

Putting together *Blues-Rock Explosion* has been a massive undertaking that would not have been possible without the assistance and contributions of many people. The editors would like to thank the following: Rene Aagaard, Nicholas Aleshin (a.k.a. Delta Nick), Bob Birnbaum, Elvin Bishop, Louis Borenius, Geoff Bradford, Stuart Brooks, Pete Brown, Bob Brunning, Casey Butler, Clem Clempson, Don Craine, Rebecca Davis, Brian and Pam Dixon, Aynsley Dunbar, Hughie Flint, Terry (Gibson) Clemson, Barry Goldberg, Arnie Goodman, Keith Grant, Nick Gravenites, Peter Green, Bob Hall, Dick Heckstall-Smith, Derek Holt, Brian Knight, Al Kooper, Andy Kulburg, Mike Lefebvre, Carlo Little, Leo Lyons, Gerald Malone, Phil May, John Mayall, Vince Mullet, Charlie Musselwhite, Tracy Nelson, Paul Olsen, Alan Pearce, Robert Phipps, Rod Piazza, Duffy Power, Tim Pratt, Rod Price, Giselle Rawlins, Randy Resnick, Brent Roberson, Greg Russo, Ezra Sidran, Corky Siegel, Kim Simmonds, John Stax, Dick Taylor, Miguel Terol, Paul Tiller, Wally Waller, Stan Webb, Clive Wicheloew, Brian Wilcock, and Art Wood.

The publisher would like to extend a special "thank you" to Pete Moody and Mark Naftalin for their continuous support and assistance.

Introduction

Detonators

If MTV accounts for your earliest memories of rock music on television, then you won't have heard of most of the bands profiled in this book. But if you're into Lenny Kravitz, Nirvana, Aerosmith or Sheryl Crow and want to know where the music you love really came from, you should read this book and check out (if you haven't done so already) some of the music that it profiles.

Before the 1980s- and 1990s-MTV wave of artists there was 1970s adult-oriented rock (AOR), and before that was the sixties blues-rock explosion. Before that was the blues . . . and the blues go back a long, long way.

You've probably heard of Fleetwood Mac—*everybody's* heard of Mac if only because back in 1992 President Bill Clinton chose their hit from the blockbuster *Rumours* album—"Don't Stop (Thinking About Tomorrow)"—as the anthem for his presidential campaign.

What is an anthem? It's a piece of music that unites, that crosses social barriers bonding young and old, the rich and not-so-rich. Now, from a rock fan's point of view, the "President Clinton-plays-Fleetwood-Mac" scenario is chock-full of irony, because at the root of the music rallying that tuxedos-only political convention is the blues of Fleetwood Mac's founder, guitarist Peter Green. At the root of Green's blues is an American subculture a million miles away from the Democrats' black-tie jamborees . . . a culture of blacks in dungarees.

Green, and other "white boy" blues contemporaries such as Eric Clapton and Jeff Beck, learned his craft back in the 1960s from recordings made by such African Americans as B.B. King, Freddie King and Otis Rush. For a long time, these artists' blues music was filed under "race records," a term that more than hinted at the complex civil rights and racial agendas underpinning the blues.

For instance, can you believe that in late-1960s America, B.B. King was playing the big hotels in Las Vegas but wasn't allowed to sleep in them? Yet when he visited Britain in 1969, rock's aristocracy turned out for his concert at London's Royal Albert Hall to declare respect for King and thank him for what he had already handed down to rock music. In other words, a musician who was regarded as royalty in England was being treated like a second-class citizen by his own country. It was this kind of irony, coupled with other weird social dynamics, which in fact conspired to push the blues forward. In order to show how, let's begin with the recent past.

WE'RE IN THE YEAR 2000 and *Riding with the King*—the new album by Eric Clapton and B.B. King—is #3 in the Billboard 200. This marks King's first ever placement in the Top Ten after a career spanning nearly fifty-five years.

Certainly the man himself has been waiting for it. He may be contented now, but only three years earlier in late 1997, it was a pensive and even somber B.B. King whom I interviewed backstage in Glasgow at the start of a short tour of U.K. arenas with Peter Green's Splinter Group as support.

Although genial company throughout, King did not try to hide his gloom when talking about the "very bad breaks" given to blues in America. "We did a survey a couple of years ago," he said with a frown, "and out of the thousands of radio stations in the U.S.—and I mean thousands—only 28 stations play blues weekly. I thought that was very sad and I still think we get a very bad break when it comes to blues music being played on the radio. Only once, a long time ago did we beat this bad break and that was with the hit 'The Thrill Is Gone.'"

He then went on to explain how this lack of media exposure for his studio output meant that he and his loyal band had no choice but to continue working those punishing tour schedules, year in and year out, just to keep their albums selling in the shops.

A surefire way to create media interest, though, is by hooking up with rock stars: On this 1997 U.K. tour (which coincided with the release of *Deuces Wild,* his duets album featuring names such as Van Morrison, Jeff Beck, the Rolling Stones and Eric Clapton) King chose to share the bill with a leading light from the 1960s blues-rock explosion—Peter Green, ex-Bluesbreakers guitarist and founder of Fleetwood Mac.

Only a decade or so earlier in the mid-1980s, B.B. King's cool collaboration with stadium-rockers U2 produced the forceful blues-rock crossover track, "When Love Comes to Town." And, as part of the Live Aid global TV marathon, B.B. King's few minutes in the spotlight probably gave him more mass exposure than all his years of performing added together.

Way back in 1962, in a "blacks-only" club in Texas, the gracious 37-year-old King gave a good break to an albino guitar player exactly half his age. That night, teenager Johnny Winter earned a standing ovation from the Raven club crowd, and Winter hasn't looked back since. Or, picture Chicago's South Side around 1960. Enter Paul Butterfield and Mike Bloomfield—brave, lone white faces soaking up the blues in blacks-only clubs. In time, they were accepted as brothers and invited up on stage to play.

What all this suggests is that once the old-time, African American blues artists and young white blues fanatics began to seek each other out, things began to change for the better. The two groups' collaborative, shared passion helped the blues evolve into all kinds of physical and cultural crossovers, and these, in a very short time, developed a new music—blues-rock. Just how this happened forms the subtext of this book.

RETURNING TO THE PRESENT and *Riding with the King*, if—as they say—every picture tells a story, then the bigger picture coming up off this CD's cover-shot is that of a journey: Cruising along in a convertible limo, a wind-swept but quietly smiling Eric Clapton is at the wheel while B.B. King relaxes with guitar in the backseat, just taking in the scenery.

In Clapton's teens, these two musicians were separated by some twenty years, an ocean, and an even wider cultural gap. And yet now, nearly forty years later, in the photo these two free spirits sit a couple of feet apart heading for the exact same spiritual place. Free spirits maybe, but happily dependent on each other as blues artists—King for half his career, and Clapton, in a sense, for the whole of his. They are interdependent in the sense that during the early 1960s, it took a blues innovator such as King to inspire Clapton and help him hone his technique to unprecedented world-class standards (for either a white or black guitarist), making the way for B.B. King to at last secure his rightful place at the top of the album charts in 2000. . . through the help

of his young protégé, Clapton. This "reversed" rise to fame (with the young Clapton paving the way for his mentor) is certainly ironic, something that Clapton alluded to in a recent interview on Sky TV's Biography Channel. Speaking about his meteoric rise in his teens and the odd feeling it gave him, he reflected, "I suppose somewhere in the back of my mind I was going to be ready perhaps when I was about forty to make a record, and that up until then I was going to be a student and trying to get it right. And it was going to be another ten or fifteen or twenty years of trying to get it right before I would have to stand up and account for what I had achieved.

"And yet here I was twenty years old and shoved into the studio—although I'm sure I was very happy to be there—with Muddy Waters and Otis Spann. And these were already, you know, men—men's men—and I was a kid with a guitar and I felt terrified and I had no idea how to conduct myself and I don't know whether I did well. It was almost like I'd blanked it out of [my] memory and these guys were wearing suits and they were men in their forties . . . They were the kings. And in a way it just didn't seem right to me . . . and it still doesn't seem right to me."

Likewise, it wasn't "right" that John Lee Hooker had to wait until his 1970 collaboration with America's most successful blues band, Canned Heat, before *Hooker 'N Heat* gave him an album that placed in the charts. But right or not and regardless of who came first, without this kind of collaboration, the immense talents of all—Canned Heat, Eric Clapton, B.B. King and even John Lee Hooker—might still be obscure today.

Black Fathers of the "New White Vaudeville"

"Those English boys want to play the blues so bad . . . And they play the blues so bad."

— Sonny Boy Williamson II talking to Robbie Robertson, having toured England with the Yardbirds in 1964

If the B.B. King/Eric Clapton *Riding with the King* example left you with a saccharine-sweet aftertaste—referring solely, as it did, to the many positive changes that have resulted from collaborations between black and white blues musicians—then Sonny Boy Williamson's infamous cutting remark, "Those English boys want to play the blues so bad . . . And they play the blues *so bad*," will cheer you.

Of course, the issue of race and American music has its ugly side as well. Not everyone saw the value in collaboration, often applying the word "co-opting" instead. The derisive phrase "the new white vaudeville," for instance, was coined in the late 1960s by the Black Students' Alliance of America.

Following the assassination of Dr. Martin Luther King in 1968, tensions between white and black musicians once again rose. Dr. King's death put a sudden stop to the gradual easing of racial separatism that had taken place during the 1960s in the music business, as well as in America in general. The mid-1960s rise of the Stax label in racially divided Memphis had embodied the spirit of camaraderie between black and white musicians, helping both move forward into uncharted territory.

But then, after Dr. King's death, young political activists such as the Black Panthers were eager to put racial barriers back up by doing things like trying to enlist the support of Jimi Hendrix—himself an icon of a future world of racial harmony. Thankfully, Hendrix did not side with the Panthers.

Still, once again skin color mattered, and so, caustically, the phrase "new white vaudeville" lampooned young white blues-rock stars like Janis Joplin and Mick Jagger who were—in the eyes of the Students' Alliance—lampooning black music and culture. But the Alliance did have a point.

The Rolling Stones and their part in the blues-rock explosion were caricatured by British writer and recent John Lee Hooker biographer Charles Shaar Murray when he described Mick Jagger's stage moves as "updated Al Jolson routines." (Here is a thing to aspire to in writing about music—a phrase made up of equal parts sensationalism *and* truth.)

Back in the late 1960s, Albert Goldman made a remark similar to Shaar Murray's, only Goldman put the spotlight on Stevie Winwood and Janis Joplin, claiming they were both singing in "vocal blackface."

To some degree, both men's assessments had merit. The musicians involved in the sixties blues-rock explosion *were* participating in a kind of respectful minstrelsy, in essence a new white vaudeville . . . but they were also participating in something much bigger.

Imagine a very skinny, very white young Jagger in the early Stones days, standing in the wings at every opportunity to watch each move that James Brown or Chester Burnett (a.k.a. Howlin' Wolf) used in order to slay their audiences.

Cleverly, Jagger modifies Brown's and Wolf's powerful moves into a repertoire of jerky but choreographed

"whitey-goes-voodoo" movements, some of which are distinctive enough to be mimicked at a million teenage parties thereafter. Then he works on imitating a black American's singing style so that when he sings a Robert Johnson tune it sounds every bit as phony as Jolson singing "My Mammy." But Jagger's take on, say, "Love in Vain," still somehow sounds cool.

Future Led Zeppelin frontman Robert Plant watched Jagger honing his moves at a Rolling Stones concert in a package tour with Bo Diddley in 1963. While Plant recognized Jagger's homage to the blues, he as much as said that he still preferred the real thing: "Diddley was superb. I was sweating with excitement! Although the Stones were great, they were really camp in comparison with Diddley—all his [Jagger's] rhythms were so sexual, just oozing, even in a 20-minute spot." Plant was right—the Stones were keen to the point of campiness.

Not surprisingly, the media at first were wary of the Stones' blues fundamentalism. Jagger was seen as just too extreme. For instance, in January 1963, the then-Rolling Stones leader Brian Jones (who at that point used the minstrel-type stage name Elmo Lewis) wrote to the BBC. He was desperate to get his band some national radio exposure performing their enthusiasts' take on—as he put it to the BBC—"outstanding exponents of Chicago blues."

But the world's flagship patron of exotic music and arts turned the hapless Jones down. The BBC's reason was that although they liked the group, "The singer [Jagger] sounds too coloured."

Now, was this a case of political correctness gone mad over at the BBC? Did the radio producer mistake the Stones' simple and honest passion for wanting to play authentic Chicago blues for a parody done "in poor taste"? (Remember, Britain was a *very* stuffy place back in the 1950s and 1960s.)

The answer is *who knows?* What it does tell us, however, is that even if the blues-rock explosion in itself had no particular agenda—other than serious respect for black music and the desire to emulate and creatively extrapolate from it—the media at the time had all kinds of racially sensitive, and even racist, agendas.

This, in turn, meant that artists and record companies had no choice but to accept these implicit constraints and simply try to work them in their favor. Early in the Stones' career, for example, American television was even more hostile and sneering than the BBC. American TV host Dean Martin greeted the Rolling Stones' cover of "Time Is on My Side" (originally sung by Irma Thomas) with redneck-style sarcasm. The year 1964 saw a single the Stones had recorded on a pilgrimage to Chicago's Chess Studios (Willie Dixon's "Little Red Rooster") banned in America because of its earthy lyrics . . . and yet it rose to #1 in the British charts.

Apparently, white British teenage audiences were hungering for the earthy lyrics and sexy rhythms that were the backbone of many blues songs such as "Little Red Rooster," even if the U.K. media, like their U.S. counterparts, were closely but somewhat more casually monitoring their exposure.

In the U.S., Berry Gordy, Jr., had sensed this trend in music as early as the late 1950s when he started to make big plans for his new indie label, Tamla. Right at the front of his mind was the word *funky* (which was originally an African American slang term for both the smell of sex and music with go-for-it sexual rhythms). But for a hungry black American record producer, *funky* was real dangerous territory: Too much funky backbeat to a song made it too controversial for mainstream television, too little and your record wouldn't even make it onto black or white radio stations' playlists. Of course, black artists of the kind Gordy wanted to sign already often appeared on U.S. television—but in order to get airtime they had to sing music that was palatable to mainstream white America, and, in the early 1960s at least, this music was definitely *not funky*.

Ironically, this tense American atmosphere was a catalyst for the British-led sixties blues-rock explosion. Like releasing a genie from a bottle, the British could tap the black Americans' legacy of funk and blues without the need to reckon with the media clamps of narrow-minded and over-protective American apple pie motherhood, making a British "invasion" the only way for things to change.

The U.S. was not entirely without its own struggling visionaries, however. The British were helped by such U.S. mavericks as Paul Butterfield and Canned Heat founder Al Wilson, who, in the early 1960s, led what began as a small American blues revival that eventually merged with and fueled the greater, intercontinental blues-rock explosion.

Yet for the most part, young Americans, both black and white, ignored the blues. White Americans wanted the Beatles or Dion while young African Americans wanted something newer than the blues of their parents, and soon found it in the shape of soul music. After all, by the 1960s, Chicago blues was well out of date if you were young, smart and black.

This weird social dynamic wherein blues was primitively "cool" in Britain and passé or socially inferior in the States was yet another cause of the 1960s blues-rock explosion.

The (Blues) *Voice of America . . . and How England Tuned In*

"The Stones came over to the United States and got Howlin' Wolf's and Muddy's face on television for the first time. White Americans were saying, 'The British are coming out with new music.' The British musicians would come and say, 'No, this is not new. This is Muddy Waters. This is Howlin' Wolf.' The Stones took their name from a Muddy Waters record. . . . Somebody else has got to come from another country to tell you what you got?

"But that's America, man. Nobody knows what they got."

— Buddy Guy talking to Donald E. Wilcock, his biographer and author of *Damn Right I've Got the Blues*

"We really thought that when we went to America and played them that music that it wouldn't work because it was their *music. We didn't realize that the white kids had never heard that music."*

— Ex-Rolling Stone Bill Wyman, interviewed by BBC2 in 1997

Buddy Guy's words—"Somebody else has got to come from another country to tell you what you got"—hit the spot. While this is a book about music with African American origins, over two-thirds of the blues-rock acts profiled in these pages are British. Only one, Taj Mahal, is a black American, but then he's a Jamaican who in the 1960s was a recent university graduate from the middle-class side of town.

Paul McCartney was in for a shock back in 1964 when the Beatles first visited America just as the British R&B boom—which led to the 1960s blues-rock explosion—was kicking off. "Don't you know who your own famous people are here?" an amazed McCartney asked a white journalist at a press conference during which the Beatles had said that they would really like to meet Muddy Waters. "Muddy Waters . . . *where's* that?" the smart-ass (or ignorant) reporter replied.

As written in Nadine Cahodas's definitive book about Chess Records, *Spinning Blues into Gold*, Muddy Waters himself said to blues researcher Robert Palmer, "When that [the blues boom] happened, I thinks to myself how these white kids was sitting down and thinking and playing the blues that my black kids was bypassing. That was a hell of a thing, man, to think about."

To get an idea of how "these white kids" began to sit down and think about blues, picture a young English beatnik called John Mayall sitting by the radio in his home studio in Manchester with the dial tuned to the *Voice of America* in the late 1950s. Studiously, Mayall tapes any blues music the station plays. Then, he meticulously catalogs it before playing the music to friends like future Bluesbreakers' drummer Hughie Flint. In ways such as this, by the early 1960s American blues had spread through Britain's musical underground, piquing the interest of a young generation of new, foreign enthusiasts.

Around the same time that John Mayall was delving deeper into the blues on his side of the Atlantic, there were also a few young Americans—Paul Butterfield, Mike Bloomfield, Charlie Musselwhite, Nick Gravenites and Harvey Mandel—who were brave enough to hang out in the kind of Chicago clubs where a white face usually only meant one thing—*the Law*. But they, too, were discovering the blues and beginning to emulate the music, reworking it with their particular rock'n'roll sensibilities.

Britain, however, less burdened by social restraints and racial tensions and, perhaps more importantly, enamored with all things American, was already slightly ahead. From the 1950s onwards, young British kids had been giving a liberator's welcome to Americana of every kind—from Big Bill Broonzy and Leadbelly-inspired skiffle music to Elvis, Eddie Cochran and Little Richard (who were already hip to the blues); from pink Studebakers with white-walled tires to blue Levis with red seam-stitching. From across the water, broadcasts on the *Voice of America* of blues and rock'n'roll, along with those pink Studebakers, together spelled the word f-r-e-e-d-o-m. To a post-war England that was tired, gray and busted, the United States was a land full of color. Sadly, to many of its own citizens, the States was still a land full of "coloreds." These two very different views on American life nonetheless would cause the blues to flourish over the ten years that followed.

What ultimately happened was the so-called "1960s crossover" that saw American blues music both cross the Atlantic and cross the tracks from its black, blue-collar origins in America to a new and incongruously cozy home—white bohemian England. As mostly white, middle-class British youth in the "underground" scene embraced the music, things began to happen—on both sides of the Atlantic.

As Bill Wyman pointed out, 1964 was "year one" of a blues-rock explosion lasting a further six or so years during which the British made music and made money by selling back to America that which they had begged, borrowed or stolen. Weirder still was that most Americans did

not feel ripped off when this happened. But there wasn't just a single fuse setting off this six-year explosion—there were several, and they were being lit on both sides of the Atlantic throughout the 1950s.

THE VERY FIRST FUSE TO BE LIT IN ENGLAND was ignited by traditional jazz. American blues in Britain began to be promoted via the 1950s U.K. "trad" jazz boom that had filtered over from the States. The notion of trad jazz promoting (as opposed to *stunting*) blues or, "The Art of the Negro" (as the BBC called it in the early 1950s), again is ironic to some—the some, in this case, being conspiracy theorists who maintain that the 1940s American trad jazz revival was really just an attempt to keep down or eclipse cutting-edge black musicians such as Lester Young and Charlie Parker.

The artistry and crazed genius of Young, Parker, Charlie Christian, Dizzy Gillespie and John Coltrane, to name but five black geniuses of modern jazz (all five were big influences on future Brit blues-rockers such as Graham Bond, Hughie Flint and Dick Heckstall-Smith), posed a threat to the established order of things Stateside, an order that artists such as Louis Armstrong would eventually bow to and honor. The talented Armstrong began as a genius of jazz and a radical, and yet ended up as something of a vaudeville caricature . . . albeit a very rich vaudeville caricature.

Likewise, for years some theorists have believed that veteran cornet player Bunk Johnson, for example, who was a crucial part of the 1940s New Orleans revival, was wheeled out by white music-biz moguls and given teeth (literally) mostly because he was a throwback to days when black musicians "knew their place"—namely, as slightly comical entertainers in medicine shows.

What is indisputable, however, is that black musicians—from jazz players and bluesmen to Tamla-Motown bands—repeatedly found themselves reluctantly or even unknowingly caught in right-wing hidden agendas, such as the one faced by Josh White in the 1950s. White—who had worked for both Blind Lemon Jefferson and Blind Blake as their "eyes"—was the first black American solo performer to tour England in 1950 under the blues banner. (Leadbelly came over in 1949 but he was more of a folk-blues artist.) Like Berry Gordy in the early 1960s, White crafted black music with white audiences in mind. Even so, doing this sometimes spelled trouble for him back home because he was more of a political folk singer than a bluesman during this U.S. era of anti-communist witch-hunts. When White sang songs about the Spanish Civil War to English audiences, for instance, the F.B.I. always heard about it and were not pleased. Nonetheless, by then White had started a new and unstoppable 1950s trend of bluesmen visiting England, where they were treated like stars.

Big Bill Broonzy soon followed White and helped to further enflame Britain's infatuation with the blues. Still giddy from the trad jazz boom, British fans were especially receptive to players such as Broonzy. In fact, one story goes that after the handsome Broonzy had played London's Kingsway Hall in September 1951, a Londoner checked into Charing Cross Hospital and seriously inquired if there were injections available that would turn his white skin black.

Broonzy returned to Britain in 1954 and then again in 1955 when he recorded thirteen tracks for the Pye label (which later would become the U.K. distributor for Chess). In those sessions, he was backed by English modern jazz players such as drummer Phil Seamen (on whom Cream's Ginger Baker would soon style himself). During this time, Broonzy met and inspired Alexis Korner and a very young clarinet player called Alvin Lee, who immediately switched to playing guitar. Very soon these blues fans formed blues bands, thereby helping spread the blues through Britain and starting the blues-rock wave that followed.

THE MOST IMPORTANT FUSE detonating the 1960s blues-rock explosion was lit by an unspectacular event in 1952 when jazz-blues guitarist Lonnie Johnson played London's Royal Festival Hall backed by Tony Donegan and his Jazz Band.

Overwhelmed and in complete awe of Johnson, overnight Tony changed his name to Lonnie Donegan and some four years later recorded the first ever white crossover "blues"—a skiffle version of Leadbelly's "Rock Island Line" that went Top Ten on both sides of the Atlantic in 1956. In the four years between, Donegan spent his time playing banjo and guitar in the Chris Barber Band.

Chris Barber, Alexis Korner, Lonnie Donegan and an astonishing Leadbelly clone and harmonica player called Cyril Davies . . . these were the real founding fathers of what became the British sixties blues-rock explosion. Just as the catalyst in America was the tense racial atmosphere that pushed the blues toward Britain, in Britain the skiffle craze that immediately followed trad jazz became the detonator for the forthcoming explosion.

Skiffle—a coarse blend of hokum and country blues—was the new English pop music of the mid-1950s. Rock'n'roll at first had to be imported from Memphis, but skiffle was homegrown. The connection between skiffle

and the blues-rock explosion that came a few years later may seem remote, but it was nevertheless a crucial musical signpost for some of blues-rock's future stars.

Brit-blues maestro Peter Green recalls hearing Lonnie Donegan's version of Leadbelly's "Alabama Bound" and thinking, "Blues." Similarly, the late great Irish bluesrocker Rory Gallagher's first guitar hero was Lonnie Donegan.

But the skiffle craze also exposed a very British trait among music fans—namely, an inborn and irresistible urge to be class-conscious about different styles of music. Brits were class-conscious about everything else, so why not music? And so they felt compelled to classify and categorize into some secure order.

As hip young America in the 1950s steeped itself in the protest song movement and had slogans on their acoustic guitars that read, "This machine kills fascists," music fans in England tossed around burning issues such as, "Is skiffle piffle?"

Cyril Davies, for one, ended up loathing skiffle, so much so that in a characteristically Celtic fit of passion he closed the very well-attended London Skiffle Club he ran during 1956 at the Roundhouse pub in Soho London and persuaded Alexis Korner to partner him in starting up the London Blues and Barrelhouse Club in that same pub on the same night of the week—Thursday.

On the opening night, three people turned up. Another five long years had to pass before these two blues musicians and promoters would run the successful Ealing Club, which opened its doors to the likes of Mick Jagger, Eric Burdon, Brian Jones, Paul Jones, Dick Heckstall-Smith and Keith Richards in early 1962.

From Blues Fans . . . to Blues Bands

"Yes, truthfully, I thought that white boys couldn't play the blues, but they were playing the hell out of the music. One of them played the harp—I think he was the leader—and they were all good on their instruments. But also them boys was as pure in the blues as many a Negro group back home. In fact there's many a player in the States couldn't keep up with them."

— Little Walter Jacobs on tour in Britain in 1964, talking to *Melody Maker* after having seen the Artwoods and Brian Knight's Blues by Six performing at London's 100 Club

"I am amazed the electric blues bands in Britain are so much better than the Americans—with the exception of Canned Heat."

— Stefan Grossman talking to *Melody Maker's* Bob Dawbarn in 1968

In the years between the Barrelhouse Club and Ealing, an enterprising band leader, trombonist, guitarist and upright bass player named Chris Barber continued the trad jazz and blues tradition of bringing U.S. musicians to the U.K., where the blues was continuing to gain momentum. Barber arranged gigs for such American bluesmen as Speckled Red, Memphis Slim, Sonny Terry and Brownie McGhee and sometimes gave them a featured spot in his own band's gigs. In the global village of the new millennium, the thought of Barber doing this back then may now seem like no big deal—professional musicians freely travel and work all around the world—but back in the 1950s it was a bureaucratic nightmare for him to pull it off.

Fueling this nightmare were musicians' trade unions and a labyrinth of restrictive practices designed to protect jobs for the boys at home. In 1958, Barber's band backed Muddy Waters and pianist Otis Spann on a controversial U.K. tour—controversial only because class-conscious, conservative English blues fans turned up to heckle Waters at the opening concert at Leeds Town Hall for no other reason than that Waters had by now gone electric.

To the British purist, acoustic blues meant art . . . while electric blues meant lowest common denominator rock'n'roll. (Some seven years after this, Bob Dylan and Mike Bloomfield—both armed with electric guitars—would provoke similar audience outrage at the 1965 Newport Jazz Festival.) With Barber's support, Muddy Waters survived this British prejudice and, soon after, Waters was able to return the favor by helping out Barber when he visited the States. Apparently, after just having arrived in Chicago, Barber and his band headed straight for Smitty's Corner club to look up their dear friend Muddy Waters. On entering the place they immediately realized that their white faces were *not* welcome by anyone except Waters. Until, that is, Chris Barber's female vocalist and partner, Ottilie Paterson (who back in England had shared concert-hall stages with gospel singer Sister Rosetta Tharp) took the stage with some of the band to sing, backed by Waters and Little Walter. The exclusively black audience loved her enough to wait in line for autographs afterward.

Meanwhile, in another Chicago club—maybe even on that very same night—American player Paul Butterfield was jamming with Big Walter "Shakey" Horton and absorbing the harmonica player's style. In this way—in an era of race riots, the Ku Klux Klan and segregation—the blues began to wobble, if not break down, some age-old social barriers in the U.S.

When Korner and Davies opened the Ealing Club in 1962 (which ostensibly gave birth to British blues-rock), even they had to contend with that old British music-snob attitude: On first hearing Korner's band, Blues Incorporated, at the club, future Cream bassist Jack Bruce dismissed them as "just a rock'n'roll band." Bruce regarded himself as a something far more highbrow and cool—a modern jazzman.

Blues Incorporated was Cyril Davies's and Alexis Korner's take on the Muddy Waters Blues Band—exciting loud R&B with some dance rhythms thrown in. But even though he was a world-class blues harp player, Davies could be stubborn and petty. When Korner brought in saxophone player Dick Heckstall-Smith, amazingly, Davies just couldn't handle the idea of a saxophone in a blues band, so he decided to leave. Korner replaced him with Graham Bond on Hammond organ and sax. Occasionally, guitarist Geoff Bradford would stand in for Korner. On one such occasion at the Ealing Club, a young blues fan called Brian Jones spoke to Bradford about forming a new band. Jones later invited Mick Jagger and Keith Richards along to rehearsals and was soon told-off by blues purist Bradford for hanging out with "a bunch of rock'n'rollers" (just another instance of yet more musical snobbishness).

Even with Geoff Bradford sometimes in the lineup, Blues Incorporated did not feature a lead guitarist in the way that, only a couple of years later, lead guitarists would become the focus and whole driving force behind the British blues-rock sound. However, Bradford was an essential part of this development in that he had sought out records by both Howlin' Wolf's guitarist, Hubert Sumlin, and T-Bone Walker and based his own style around their playing. (By the mid-1960s it was much easier to obtain what up until then had been very rare and sought-after blues records, since the Pye International label had started licensing the Chess catalog. Illegal offshore pirate radio stations around England were also R&B-friendly.)

Though only a few years older, Geoff Bradford became something of a blues father to the first wave of British guitar heroes, including Jeff Beck, Eric Clapton and Jimmy Page. All three soon would make crucial contributions to a London band that really was the spearhead of British blues-rock—the Yardbirds (which started out as the Metropolis Blues Quartet). But first Alexis Korner, Blues Incorporated, and their offshoot, the Rolling Stones, had to pave the way.

After a couple of months, in May 1962 the Ealing Club moved to the heart of London to take over Thursday nights at the Marquee nightclub. That the club managed to attract very good crowds on a normally dead evening (the day before payday) confirmed that the British R&B boom was gathering momentum. Meanwhile, Alexis Korner found a more welcoming home for his increasingly jazz-tinged blues at Soho's Flamingo Club, where Georgie Fame had been honing a Caribbean-style R&B with his resident band, the Blue Flames.

The Marquee, however, remained one of the hottest clubs, and even an early lineup of the Stones used the Marquee as a launch pad before taking their following to the Crawdaddy club in Richmond, U.K., in early 1963. In April of that year, music-biz hustler Andrew Loog Oldham spotted the Stones at the Crawdaddy, moved in quick, and soon helped catapult the Stones to pop stardom. After the Rolling Stones had left, the Crawdaddy Club manager, Giorgio Gomelsky, decided to turn his attention to the Yardbirds.

Gomelsky's early management of the Yardbirds was inspired in that, unwittingly, the advice he gave them in the autumn of 1963 as they took over the Crawdaddy residency laid some crucial foundations for British blues-rock. "We didn't want a copycat band of the Stones just to keep the [Crawdaddy] audience," Gomelsky said. "You know, I always felt that we could go further, and one element that was kind of missing in the Stones was instrumental improvisation. So we needed to get a band where there are people who can play solos." Enter 18-years old Eric Clapton, blues fanatic.

Under Gomelsky's management, the Yardbirds toured England and Europe with Sonny Boy Williamson II in 1964 and 1965. Relations between this blues father and his "sons" were frosty, mainly because, as Clapton explained to *Mojo* in 1998, they had little respect for one another at the time. "You've got to remember how arrogant teenagers can be," Clapton said. "I had already decided before I had even met him that he wasn't really one of the great blues artists. And I acted like that. Where does this young white kid get off being judgmental about a guy like that? I think he sussed it. I think he sensed my arrogance and deliberately gave me a hard time. He put me on the spot at any possible occasion—'take a solo now'—when I was least expecting it. It was just a nightmare, and I asked for it. I had it coming, no doubt about it. Apparently he went back and met up with The Band and told them what a bunch of wankers we were." Deadly wankers, if the truth were known—nonplussed blues father Williamson breathed his very final note-bending breath some ten days after his second European tour ended.

But for every Sonny Boy Williamson (who as part of his act sometimes would actually make members of the Yardbirds kneel before him on stage) there were a dozen African-American bluesmen who toured England and Europe in the 1950s and 1960s and got along just fine with their white blues brothers.

For instance, the Groundhogs became John Lee's Groundhogs when they backed John Lee Hooker on some of his mid-1960s U.K. tours that promoted his U.K. hit single, "Dimples." What's more, they would socialize. Groundhog guitarist Tony McPhee has fond memories of showing Hooker how to sign his own autograph. Being treated like a star by English blues fans was a welcome new experience for the Delta bluesman back then.

By 1963–64, the whole notion of musical "fathers and sons" was no longer based on being a generation or a half-generation apart, as it had been, say, between the reluctant Sonny Boy Williamson and the Yardbirds, Lonnie Donegan and Lonnie Johnson, or Geoff Bradford and T-Bone Walker. In Britain, the scene was moving so fast that a year's passionate study of blues guitar made you a father to someone who was still in the early stages of getting it together. The Yardbirds' soloist Eric Clapton became a musical father to future Fleetwood Mac founder Peter Green when Clapton was 18 and Green just 17.

Green first saw the Yardbirds at the Crawdaddy and immediately was hooked on the form of guitar playing he heard, as he recalled in an interview published in *Guitarist* in September 1993: "[The] guitar playing was fabulous. Wow! He [Clapton] actually played it not like The Rolling Stones and The Beatles, who were just filling in a solo, clunking along; the whole thing was a break. Do you remember that? The whole piece used to suddenly have a break, where the whole band goes into it, not just the guitar player. . . . In The Yardbirds, when there was a solo break they all went in there and all came out the other end. And it was nice, the proper thing."

In this way, guitarists and bands that followed the Stones in blues-rock's second wave—which kicked off in 1963 with the Yardbirds—were so *studied* and fanatical about blues that they soon made Jagger, Richards & Co. look like dabblers and renegades who occasionally, with albums such as *Beggar's Banquet*, would foray back to the blues for a while.

Nineteen sixty-three was also the year that John Mayall decided to go for it—moving from Manchester to London to get seriously involved in the blues scene. Within a year or two he was firmly established as a white father of

British blues, going on to mentor future blues-rock stars such as Peter Green, Mick Taylor, Jack Bruce and John McVie. But the rise of John Mayall's Bluesbreakers was soon criticized by Alexis Korner, who felt that the Bluesbreakers' hard electric urban blues amounted to their "selling out" just to get big bucks—commercialism was definitely a dirty word among certain rarefied sectors of the 1960s British music scene.

English bands such as Korner, the Yardbirds and, following in their footsteps, Fleetwood Mac, had one thing in common with their Stateside counterparts (such as Canned Heat and the Electric Flag): They all began as devotional enthusiasts. They were obsessives only just on the right side of sanity, and mimics who were at their happiest when doing their updated "Al Jolson routines." Surely the sight of Fleetwood Mac's 5'4" tall slide guitarist Jeremy Spencer up on stage singing Elmore James in a black American accent with every vocal inflection perfectly in place and every slide guitar vibe eerily resurrected was blues vaudeville. And the same applies to Chicken Shack's Stan Webb, who walked out into the audience with his guitar on the end of a great long lead—just like he'd seen Buddy Guy do.

But soon players such as Spencer and Webb progressed well beyond being just theatrical copyists harboring mojo-hand fixations. They began to really challenge traditional interpretations, injecting new lifeblood into the blues and, viewing that decade as a whole, some of them helped the Stones to give rock music its key to the 1970s highway.

By 1968, even the Beatles with their *White Album* wanted to join in the blues boom. One track from that album, "Yer Blues," may even have been a thinly veiled announcement: Psychedelia is dead, *now back to the blues*.

Preservation Versus Innovation

How did those white boys on both sides of the Atlantic get so hooked on blues back in the early 1960s, and how did the Brits soon become better players than their American peers—even better perhaps, than the likes of Paul Butterfield and Mike Bloomfield, who were just a Chicago non-segregated bus ride away from the real thing?

The British got to be better because back in the late 1950s, having met the blues and fallen in love, they then embellished the music with their own homegrown roman-

tic notions about American blues culture and the bluesman's lifestyle in a big city. Thus Brit bluesmen aggrandized the blues, making the music even more popular than in its own homeland. Their mythmaking worked wonders.

In the 1990s, Newcastle-born Eric Burdon—singer with first-wave Brit R&B band the Animals—spoke of this myth that fueled the Brit blues-rock explosion: "All these young white kids in England were into this black thing that no longer mattered to anybody anymore, especially the blacks. These guys [black bluesmen] were out of work." Out of work—or facing the wrong end of a water cannon.

Van Morrison, founding member of Belfast blues band Them, told BBC2 in the 1990s: "John Lee Hooker says blues is the truth. It is what it is. . . . You can't glamorize it . . . some days are good, some days are bad, and that's reality."

But back in the sixties, the Brits did glamorize the blues—most had a limited awareness of its heritage and no real idea of its place in the social pecking order of 1960s' America; nor were they aware of the day-to-day pressures facing black bluesmen who were just trying to get by.

Oddly enough, this gave the most talented British blues players an edge over the Americans. Once British blues students such as the Bluesbreakers' Eric Clapton, Peter Green and Mick Taylor had mastered the music's various styles, each with its own vocabulary, they then interpreted these languages in new, interesting and foreign kinds of ways. Their interpretations were often more panoramic and eclectic, drawing from a variety of blues styles that in America had remained geographically separate. Clapton's studies included Matt Murphy and Freddie King—who each held very different approaches to electric blues. Green studied, among others, B.B. King and Muddy Waters—high-class and primitive blues, respectively. Sometimes what came out of this white-boy blues melting pot was a happy accident. Take the case of teenager Danny Kirwan, regarded in 1967 as a Brit-blues boy wonder, who one year later joined Fleetwood Mac.

Kirwan's earliest influences were Otis Rush, gypsy jazz player Django Reinhardt, and Jimi Hendrix. When British blues producer Mike Vernon first heard the 16-years-old Kirwan (who at that point had been playing guitar for only a year), he told Kirwan that his guitar sound reminded him of Tulsa-born bluesman Lowell "Reconsider Baby" Fulson.

"Who's Lowell Fulson . . . never heard of him!" was young Kirwan's honest reply.

Meanwhile, the British blues players' American counterparts were very sure of their subject, often acting more like preservationists than innovators. Whereas British musicians in the 1950s were shoved in the right direction from the skiffle/folk-blues of Lonnie Donegan, in the United States, musicians such as Wilson, Butterfield and, obviously, Bob Dylan, took their lead from the folk and protest movement.

In the early 1960s, Al Wilson, Paul Butterfield, Mike Bloomfield and Ry Cooder all sought to preserve blues as a folk art in a tradition that had been started by Alan Lomax some twenty years earlier, which was the exact opposite of what their British peers were doing.

In 1941, Alan Lomax had recorded the legendary bluesman Eddie "Son" House, who would then have faded into obscurity had it not been for the dedication some twenty years after of Al Wilson, the 19-years-old future creative genius behind Canned Heat. Wilson was part of the folk music revival in Cambridge, Massachusetts, where— as Rebecca Davis eloquently captured in her *Blues Access* magazine article, "Child is Father to the Man" (Fall '98)— moves were afoot that led to Son House's rediscovery.

The central characters in the quest were young blues researchers Dick Waterman, Phil Spiro, Nick Perls and Wilson. After Delta bluesman Bukka White played a coffee-house gig in Cambridge, the gang learned to their astonishment that Son House was alive and thought to be living in Memphis.

They eventually caught up with him in Rochester only to discover that Son House no longer owned a guitar but was very willing to try to revive his blues playing despite being handicapped by a hand tremor that could only be calmed by a lot of alcohol.

At the time, Wilson was an unknown young musician who was so fanatical and so familiar with Son House's earlier recordings that he was able to demonstrate to the living legend the slide guitar technique that left the likes of Robert Johnson in awe of House back in the 1920s and 1930s.

As a direct result of Wilson's tutoring, House's manager, Dick Waterman, was able to land House a record deal with Columbia in 1965. *Father of the Folk Blues* was recorded in New York City in April of that year. Produced by the legendary John Hammond, Sr., the album featured Al Wilson on harmonica and second guitar on four of the tracks. *Father of the Folk Blues* has since been regarded as by far the most creditable rediscovery project and one in which the artist's awesome former talents are still very exposed and untarnished by the ravages of time.

The following short extract from a letter Wilson wrote to friend David Evans (as reproduced in Rebecca Davis's article) gives insight into the mindset of this blues student.

In it, Wilson describes the problems posed by Son House's hand tremor and how House tried to deal with them at a "comeback" gig in front of a small audience prior to Wilson's and House's collaboration: "At a short gig at the Unicorn when sober he was pathetic. When he was drunk he a) played some of the best blues I have heard up to the time, on occasion, b) gave the crowd 10-minute sermons which were not only nonsensical but nearly unintelligible, and c) took as long as five minutes to tune his guitar."

The letter's recipient, David Evans, today is a professor of music at Memphis State University. Back then, Evans was not altogether happy about Wilson collaborating with Son House and actually felt that Wilson "went a little too far in performing with these artists in public." Apparently, Evans's training as a folklore graduate instilled in him the need to keep blues music pure and in the hands of its folk artists. To Evans, the notion of white blues fanatics sharing a stage or studio with the music's mostly black originators amounted to no less than "contamination."

Contamination or not, over the next few years Wilson's creativity began to peak when he wrote Canned Heat's worldwide hit "On the Road Again," itself an adaptation of Floyd Jones's 1952 "Dark Road," which in itself was somewhat derivative of Tommy Johnson's 1929 "Big Road Blues."

However, to some very vociferous critics, this kind of "white-boy blues" was not valid, and was certainly not *the blues* and never could be, even though a hit single like "On the Road Again" was the product of deep and respectful study of the music. During the 1960s, blues writers such as Ralph Gleason in America and Paul Oliver in England didn't pull any punches as they tried to undermine the validity of this "white-boy" music: Without a black American's heritage of slavery and oppression, they quipped, one cannot sing the blues.

"It's the music, stupid!" was the simple and effective response to this blinkered attitude. In other words, if it sounds like good blues . . . it *is* good blues, especially once so-called white-boy blues began sounding even better than most contemporary black American blues that was meeting with the Gleason/Oliver seal of approval.

Being white or being blissfully ignorant about the racial climate Stateside, past and present, just didn't matter when it came to understanding what blues music was really all about. What mattered was that hearing old blues records struck a deep spiritual chord in a young artist like Eric Clapton, as he recalled in the late 1980s to British arts broadcaster Lord Melvyn Bragg: "I felt through most of my youth that my back was against the wall and that the only way to survive was with dignity and pride and courage. I heard that in certain forms of music and I heard it most of all in the blues, because it was always an individual: It was one man and his guitar against the world. It wasn't a company, or a band, or a group. When it came down to it, it was one guy who was completely alone and had no options, no alternatives other than to sing and play to ease his pain."

Clapton's words encompass an intuitive definition of the blues as made by an artist, as opposed to a musicological definition constructed by a precious blues archivist who is perhaps partly out to justify a lot of painstaking field research.

Clapton's approach also cut dead the "blues are black-only" attitude that is still alive and kicking today in the pages of *Living Blues,* a magazine with an editorial policy of only featuring African American blues artists.

Eric Clapton, who was in many ways emblematic of the pioneering musicians of the blues-rock movement, looked to the blues both for spiritual shelter and as an emotional outlet, just as his black mentors had done. In the blues, he found a way to cope with the pain of rejection he felt after having learned that he was illegitimate and that his "parents" in fact were his grandparents, who had no choice but to pretend otherwise because his mother had abandoned him as a toddler. Just like countless blues players before him, Clapton first picked up a guitar "to ease his pain," and also to escape a lonely childhood by making new friends, some of whom were diehard blues nuts just like him, as he explained to *Mojo* magazine in April 1998: "All through my teens I began to experience relationships through music. And I learnt how to listen to other people, to music. I saw a guy called Ted Wilton listen to Howlin' Wolf one night; he danced to it and he danced to the words and I'd never seen anybody do that before. So I was learning all the time that underneath the pop facade there were meanings and inner meanings and writing in between the lines. Music in its purest form was a sharing of life and experience—it became vital to me.

"In my early teens I wasn't sure about what was white and what was black: it all seemed two sides to the same coin. I didn't know Chuck Berry was black. I thought he was another weird-sounding white man [like Elvis Presley]. I had no idea that there was a racial thing involved. I guess Elvis must have been taking a great risk associating with guys like Bobby 'Blue' Bland or B.B. King. I never had to go through that. I had the luxury of hearing from a distance."

FOR THE BRITISH, possessing just a little knowledge turned out to be a good thing. Today it is generally known that in 1960, blues music had only been recorded for a mere forty years. Its first big turning point came in the 1940s when technology and innovation replaced cotton field workers with machines. Field workers migrated to find jobs in the heavy industry of urban centers such as Chicago, leaving to the past most of the culture underpinning acoustic country blues.

With just some scratchy 78 rpm recordings and black and white photos as artifacts, it came down to artists like Muddy Waters, John Lee Hooker and Lightnin' Hopkins to carry the blues through its first of many crossovers from the eerie peace of the Mississippi Delta to noisy cities. Urban blues wasn't the same thing as Delta blues—it was music performed in rowdy clubs, and so musicians definitely needed amplified guitars and harmonicas if they wanted to be heard.

The urban blues sound, and the sometimes murky underworld culture surrounding it, became the model for many obsessive young white guys in Britain, the majority of whom were seriously embarrassed about coming from comfortable, late 1950s boom-economy middle-class homes. Brit blues rockers such as John Mayall, Eric Clapton, Jeff Beck, Keith Richards and many others had all been art students with a lot of time on their hands to devote to extracurricular activities . . . they were not steel mill apprentices.

Being art students, young musicians such as Eric Clapton and Jeff Beck really went for the *style* of blues—as well as its content, as Clapton has since explained: "I would try to picture what an ideal blues man would live like. I would picture what kind of car he drove, what it would smell like inside. Me and Jeff [Beck] had this idea of one day owning a black Cadillac or Stingray that smelled of sex inside and had tinted windows and a great sound system."

To Clapton and Beck, Chicago blues was an erotic fantasy that in addition to the music, also encompassed fast American cars and even faster women. Clapton has readily admitted that he hadn't a clue about the everyday racism that remained the harsh reality of a black musician's life in America in the early 1960s. Not in his worst dreams could he have pictured stars in the Tamla-Motown Revue out on the road and having to make do with cold hamburgers served to them at the back entrance of whites-only restaurants.

On the face of it, the British side of the 1960s blues-rock explosion was partly propelled by a kind of inverted snobbery wherein arty middle-class rebels sick of pop music's small-town compromise and niceness found a cool cause in American blues.

Mid-1950s rock'n'roll had previously given young people the beginnings of a cool cause, but too soon record company fat cats emasculated much of what had been an exciting Memphis-centered musical revolt against "Perry Como-ism." In place of rock'n'roll wildness and trashed cinema seats came the appallingly cute and tame Frankie Avalon-type Philly pretty-boy scene.

The hipness of "Brit-blues" and the upside-down snobbery that fanned its popularity is neatly captured on the cover shot of an album that turned out to be the epicenter of the 1960s blues-rock explosion—*Blues Breakers: John Mayall with Eric Clapton*. The shot shows four Bluesbreakers against graffiti-daubed inner city decay: With only a little imagination, these guys could be four struggling bluesmen killing time on Chicago's Maxwell Street and hungry for their next gig. (In fact, the band's partially erased graffiti was to have read, "Harold Wilson [Britain's socialist Prime Minister] is a nit," but photographer David Wedgbury could see a libel suit on the horizon and so scrubbed it.)

As such, the "Beano" album (so called because of Clapton's choice of reading matter in the shot) started a fashion in Brit-blues LP sleeves. Bands such as Fleetwood Mac, Chicken Shack and the Brunning Hall Sunflower Blues Band all used the "urban-decay/back alley/street scene" image to present their music: garbage bins, empty beer bottles, and white, mostly middle-class, blues musicians dressed studiously down-at-heel.

Of course, these Englishmen had no problem with slumming it for a photo shoot before some of them would leg it back to tea and a comfortable home tended to by Mum. But their reverence was in fact genuine and hardly exploitive. They were like actors out to recapture the style—but not context—of another place and time by glamorizing Chicago's South Side and the hard times on which the blues had thrived in the 1940s and 1950s. In order to take the music forward, they had to revisit and fixate on a place and period that African Americans were by then happy to forget.

By the 1960s, urban black Americans were looking to move upscale to better jobs and better residential areas. Most of them wanted to leave the lowdown blues of Chicago's overpopulated housing projects and South Side ghettoes behind them. As black Americans became socially mobile and escaped from the oppressed underclass, American blues music likewise began to mirror a new and more diverse social climate. As Muddy Waters pointed out, while B.B. King played "high-class" jazz and gospel-tinged blues, Waters continued to perform lowdown raw blues—"I'm a *Maynn*"-style.

Eventually, any romantic notions that hip English blues-rockers such as Eric Clapton, Jeff Beck or the Rolling Stones might have had about the cool lifestyles of their blues heroes were dashed. Reality caught up with the Stones when they first met Muddy Waters on their summer 1964 visit to Chess Studios.

Allegedly, Waters, out of work and decorating the studio to earn some extra cash, greeted them at Chess. Bill Wyman recalled, "We were unloading the van, taking the equipment in, amps, guitars, mike [sic] stands etc., when this big black guy comes in and says, 'Want some help?' We look round and it's Muddy Waters. He starts helping us carry in the guitars and all that! As kids we would have given our right arm just to say hello to him and here's the great Muddy Waters helping to carry my guitar into the studio."

Keith Richards—who has often referred back to that scene in interviews—took it as a poignant lesson about how even living blues legends had to live a hard life. Author Nadine Cahodas likewise reported on the incident, writing, "Keith Richards is responsible for one of the most widely circulated myths about the Chess operation. In a well-publicized interview he claimed that when he came into the [Chess] building and went upstairs to the studio, he passed a man in overalls on a ladder painting the ceiling. Someone said, 'Oh, by the way, this is Muddy Waters.'

"'He wasn't selling records at the time,' Richards said, 'and this is the way he got treated.'"

Since then, several people who worked at Chess Records at the time have forcefully denied that any such thing ever happened. Therefore it can only be left for the reader to decide whether the incident truly occurred, or whether this is just another example of the Rolling Stones' publicity machine in overdrive, speeding to a point where Richards and perhaps Wyman were apparently happy to churn out media spin that was bound to humble their heroes.

What is not in dispute, though, is that in the mid-1960s the renowned Chess Studios was not the groundbreaking creative haven it had been during the late 1950s. The label's hardworking blues stars who plied their trade in Chicago's clubs were not allowed to stretch out creatively in the same way as visitors making pilgrimages to Chess from abroad.

When he spoke to BBC2 television in the mid-1990s, Marshall Chess was being something of a rose-tinted revisionist when he recalled the Stones' first visit and how, unintentionally, they ended up progressing the classic Chess sound. "I think that the Stones understood a certain sexual energy that was in Chess Records' music and amplified that into their own music," he said. "They wanted to mimic [the Chess Sound]—they would have loved Chess Records to be exactly like the originals [*Best of Muddy Waters* studio sound] . . . but it came out like the Rolling Stones—which was great!"

According to Cahodas, however, when the Rolling Stones first visited Chess Studios in 1964, the fans' hysteria outside 2120 South Michigan was a far cry from the vibes inside the Chess building. Cahodas writes that Chess's Dick LaPalm recalled the scene: "None of the [Chess] artists were very impressed. None of the people at Chess gave a damn who they [the Stones] were." (Ironically, only a year earlier in 1963, the Stones had done much to popularize the Chess sound on the the Richmond, U.K., R&B scene—centered in Gomelsky's Crawdaddy Club—with their rocking adaptations of funky Bo Diddley rhythms.)

Regardless of the rhetoric, what Chess studios truly had to offer British visitors like the Stones was a much dirtier, funkier and upfront rhythm-section sound—partly because of an innovative studio setup wherein the bass was directly fed into the sound desk, as opposed to via a microphone placed near an amp.

What Chess studios did *not* have to offer during the mid-1960s was creative direction—either to visitors such as the Yardbirds (who recorded "Shapes of the Things" there in 1966) or to their own artists, such as Buddy Guy.

In the same year that the Stones visited the studio, Chess artist Buddy Guy was ready to cut an album with Leonard Chess producing. By this time, in Chicago's clubs Guy was honing his very wild-sounding guitar as well as the extrovert stage moves that Jimi Hendrix would adopt as his very own just a couple of years later.

Buddy Guy's fast, fat guitar sound would soon become the root of 1960s' blues-rock, but to Leonard Chess's untutored ears this kind of guitar was "just noise." So when Buddy kicked off with his wild-man style, Chess quickly stopped the tapes and sent for Muddy Waters in the hope of bringing some tasteful restraint back to the sessions. Amazingly, Guy kowtowed to this clumsy suggestion because on the Chicago blues scene, Guy was a relatively new kid on the block compared to Muddy Waters. The result was that Buddy's ahead-of-its-time guitar sound remained one of Chicago blues' best-kept and unrecorded secrets—at least to the masses. In the same way that Tamla-Motown's Berry Gordy was cautious in his use of the "funky" factor, Leonard Chess felt uncomfortable with Guy's wild electric sounds. But once Guy traveled across the Atlantic and got away from such American conservatism, he received instant respect for his progressive blues.

Soon after that problematic recording session in February 1965, Guy went to England and was welcomed as a star. He received a good-luck telegram from the Beatles; he appeared on *Ready, Steady Go!* and was mobbed at the TV studios; and when he played at London's prestigious Marquee club, Eric Clapton was in the audience along with Rod Stewart, who was also a huge Buddy Guy fan. At the time, the young Clapton had probably the keenest ears in England and was scouting around for a new guitar sound as he played out his time with the Yardbirds. Clapton was mesmerized.

Neil Slaven, editor of *R&B Monthly* and future co-founder of Blue Horizon Records, was in the audience as well and soon reported, "Eric Clapton, seated next to me, collapsed in frustrated tears." Clearly, seeing Buddy Guy was the final straw for Clapton's career as a fledgling pop star with the Yardbirds. One month later he had left them, and after another month of manual labor at a building site, he joined John Mayall's Bluesbreakers in April 1965.

It is no exaggeration to say that what Clapton learned by watching and listening to Buddy Guy on that short U.K. tour led him to the guitar sound that was the prime force behind the whole 1960s blues-rock explosion.

First, Clapton learned that there was little point in a blues artist recording an album if it didn't capture his live sound, as was the case with Guy. Clapton had been doubly mesmerized when watching Buddy Guy live because his sound was way ahead of any of Guy's earlier Chess recordings. "I didn't think his [Guy's] guitar recorded very well," Clapton is said to have remarked. He vowed not to be tamed in the studio.

So, when his turn came, Clapton let nobody push him around when it came to defining and recording his guitar's unique voice and timbre. He spent the first couple of months in the Bluesbreakers experimenting with a sound that was a fusion of his three electric blues mentors—Guy, Freddie King and Otis Rush. Freddie King's guitar of choice was a gold-top Gibson Les Paul, and Clapton reasoned that the guitar's considerable weight—the main reason Gibson had ceased Les Paul production in 1960—might give more presence playing live. His hunch was good.

Clapton bought a secondhand Les Paul that he hooked up to a Marshall amp. In doing so, the core sound of the 1960s blues-rock explosion could first be heard. Following Clapton's lead, other young, hopeful guitar heroes soon spent their hard-earned cash on 1950s Les Pauls, including Peter Green, Jimmy Page, Paul Kossoff and Keith Richards, who later sold his to Mick Taylor.

After he had defined his live sound, Clapton found that

there were still battles to be fought in the recording studio before that same trademark intensity could be captured on tape. His first semi-successful attempt had come in the summer of 1965 when Mayall and Clapton recorded, on Immediate, the Jimmy Page-produced single "I'm Your Witchdoctor" backed with "Telephone Blues." Clapton was adamant that his guitar should be recorded at the same volume that he used in live venues.

Page was working with a studio engineer accustomed only to sorting out the sound problems of orchestras and big bands. The man insisted that Clapton was "unrecordable" at such levels and furthermore simply refused to believe that any musician actually would want to sound like that. Page himself was not entirely sure, but decided to risk the consequences anyway. The outcome, especially "Telephone Blues," marked the beginning of something completely new and revolutionary in the studio.

Meanwhile, at around the same time back in Chicago, the real creator of this new guitar style and sound, Buddy Guy, was having no more luck in convincing a stubborn Leonard Chess that there was a future in what the boss man still regarded as "just noise." Leonard's son, Marshall, was by this time loudly arguing Guy's case to his father, but Chess Senior would not budge.

In April 1966, John Mayall's Bluesbreakers went into Decca's West Hampstead, London, studios to record the "Beano" album. Once again, Clapton stood his ground against the so-called wisdom of sound engineer Gus Dudgeon. Clapton had the idea of "bleeding" the guitar amp's overdriven sound into the microphones of other instruments that were also being recorded. This was in stark contrast to the conventional sound-separation-with-baffle-boards approach. Producer Mike Vernon agreed to give it a try.

Once everyone was in the control room listening to the first playback, it became clear that, defying all technical logic, the sound was powerful, different and professionally acceptable. What none of the musicians could have known, though, was that this was a defining moment in the 1960s blues-rock explosion. Ironically, of course, the basis of this new blues sound was fostered thousands of miles across the Atlantic in London, and not in its natural home at 2120 South Michigan, Chicago.

Fast-forward about two years. Leonard Chess is in his office having a heated meeting with Buddy Guy. This time, Chess's head honcho is eating humble pie. Leonard has realized far too late that Chess and Buddy Guy have all but missed the blues-rock boat. Cahodas writes that Leonard at first berated Guy, but then mostly chided himself for not recognizing that two years ago Buddy Guy had

honed a sound and style that had since lent much to the legends of Clapton and Hendrix: "I was fucking dumb," Leonard finally admitted to Guy.

"Fucking lily-livered" is perhaps nearer the truth. Having missed the boat once, Chess then overreacted in his bid to keep up with the scene. The incongruous and psychedelic *Electric Mud* album by Muddy Waters was one sad outcome.

The truth was that Clapton, Hendrix, and others had picked up Guy's moves and sound and were raking in profits. A year earlier in autumn 1966, Jimi Hendrix came, saw, and (with the right management) eventually conquered the blues-boom in Britain with extrovert teeth-as-plectrum guitar playing and a stage presentation derived from Buddy Guy and, before him, Guitar Slim and Tommy Johnson. Hendrix's thick, distorted sound could also partly be traced back to Buddy Guy as he sounded at London's Marquee in early 1965. In fact, Guy had been experimenting with feedback since the late 1950s.

Even Eric Clapton later paid homage to Guy when he remarked, "It was such a blast to see him [Buddy Guy] live doing all that pre-Hendrix stuff which he'd always done, like playing with his teeth, on the floor and throwing the guitar around."

The big difference between Hendrix and Guy was that a stage act that began by crawling onto the stage would get Hendrix banned from England's more conservative provincial theaters and also get him a page of free publicity in the next day's *Daily Mirror*, fueling his status as a rock star. Meanwhile, the wild-man stage moves of Buddy Guy in the Chicago clubs never made headline news in the *National Enquirer*. Guy lacked a manager who possessed the vision to exploit his originality; Hendrix didn't.

Ultimately, Buddy Guy became a textbook case of management not developing heavyweight blues talent—and in *not* doing so, managing only to steer the course of blues-rock once again away from its black origins and toward the achievements of mainly white bands throughout the 1960s.

Meanwhile, on both sides of the Atlantic, Clapton's new band, Cream, was proving to be a monster money-maker as a cutting-edge blues-rock trio, even though when Clapton joined forces with Ginger Baker and Jack Bruce, he saw himself as nothing more progressive than a leader of a "Buddy Guy-type blues trio." Clapton has since acknowledged Guy as an influence in the Cream sound, as Buddy Guy was quick to explain to *Mojo* magazine in April 1998: "My favourite is 'Strange Brew.' I was really impressed by the tone he was getting, plus the way he was playing. When we became friends I asked him, 'What are you doing there?' He just said, 'I copied you!' Then he played me this tune from me and Junior Wells's record called Everything's Gonna Be Alright—I played the riff on the low strings, Eric played it on the high strings. I hadn't even noticed!"

Clearly, however, besides the liberating creative atmosphere in which to work (or if not exactly *liberating,* at least less controlled than in the U.S.), the Brits had two things on their black American brothers: They had youth, along with its irreverence, and the bands that broke through usually had top management that knew how to work the system and media in a way that they were simply not able or allowed to do for black artists in the America of the early 1960s. A good example is B.B. King, who for decades led his band in the face of huge mounting personal debts until the late 1960s when his business affairs were taken over by an astute (white) New York accountant named Sidney Seidenberg.

Likewise, Tamla-Motown had become the "Sound of Young America" by meekly deferring to the U.S. establishment and its sacred cows running the media; the Stones, on the other hand, mocked VIPs just for kicks.

Whereas Rolling Stones manager Andrew Loog Oldham was the original blues-rock spin doctor, it was Jimi Hendrix's mentor Chas Chandler—not Jimi Hendrix's music on its own—who helped establish the Hendrix legend; and it was manager Robert Stigwood who created and then—unknowingly—hastened the breakup of the most influential band of the 1960s blues-rock explosion—Cream. The Yardbirds had Giorgio Gomelsky and then Simon Napier-Bell to give them a leg up to stardom, while their late-1960s offshoot, Led Zeppelin, had the feared and respected (in that order) Peter Grant looking after them.

In Eric Clapton's case, the star-making was far less focused but nevertheless as effective: Clapton already had an eye on the big time when he was playing with the Bluesbreakers, as ex-Bluesbreaker Hughie Flint well remembered: "Eric would get into the van to go to a gig and he'd be wearing black nail varnish. John McVie would be there in the back grinning and sniggering away." Clapton himself explained his probable motives: "What I was probably doing . . . was that every now and then I'd sabotage the whole thing so that he'd [John Mayall] know that he couldn't count on me and that I was actually passing through. I don't know where I was going but I'm not staying here."

Being late for gigs, not showing up at all, going AWOL on an ill-advised Greek holiday, not delivering on stage on nights when he didn't feel like it . . . this was the saboteur's box of tricks, and yet from all this still came gold in the form of the groundbreaking "Beano" Bluesbreakers album.

Clapton's guitar was groundbreaking, but when John Mayall recalls the album today he is reluctant to elevate it in the way others have, instead preferring to remember it as simply "documenting" the Bluesbreakers' sound on a good night at a club on the so-called Ricky-Tick circuit of 1966.

For the sake of argument, if today someone played this album for the first time to untutored young ears keen on electric blues, followed straight after by Paul Butterfield's second album, *East-West* (released in the same year), would our imaginary new-to-the-blues fan be able to sense any big difference in the quality or power of blues-rock guitar coming from either side of the big pond? Moreover, does Eric Clapton's inspired playing and new sound completely overshadow Mike Bloomfield's impressive two-guitar dueling and improvising with Elvin Bishop? Probably not. And yet in the context of this book and the music covered by it, the Bluesbreakers' album over time has taken on far greater significance.

One explanation for this has something to do with Eric Clapton's painted fingernails. In other words, Britain was entering an era of the guitar hero . . . both ahead of, and far more than, America. The "Clapton is God" graffiti, which started to appear on walls around London as Clapton's stature as a pioneering soloist grew, reflected this. Furthermore, Clapton's follow-up group, Cream, couldn't have been more *big time*. Meanwhile, in their subsequent projects, Bloomfield and Bishop failed to build on the creativity of *East-West*.

Cream, on the other hand, went on to define blues-rock and explore its musical boundlessness before the three musicians found themselves burned out by the music-biz monster they themselves had created. Relevant chapters in this book document the heavy kickback that Eric Clapton had to deal with after Cream had seemingly wrenched a lifetime's creativity out of him in just two short years.

Cream's musical approach—lengthy improvisation—turned out to be the making and the breaking of the 1960s blues-rock explosion. Whereas Clapton originally saw Cream as a band with himself as the focal point of the aforementioned "Buddy Guy-type blues trio," bassist Jack Bruce and drummer Ginger Baker had other ideas: Bass solos, drum solos and guitar solos were going to be the scene. At first, this was a good thing, but in the long run this strategy showed its downside.

Jazz-style improvisation in the hands of world-class musicians such as Clapton, Bruce and Baker was more often than not good news for audiences (though Bruce and Clapton both have since pointed out that coming up with cool guitar solos night after night became an ordeal as the touring schedules became endless and exhausting). But improvisation in the hands of less experienced musicians who were going for a slice of the blues-rock action in the late 1960s could be a terminally boring experience for the audience. This spelled the beginning of the end.

The Late-1960s
Blues-rock *Implosion*

(Full-circle from the Yardbirds to Led Zeppelin—and from the Blues to Rock)

"Then other bands got drawn into it; even Jethro Tull were categorized as a blues band, but with all due respect they were never a blues band. . . . It became like anyone with a Marshall amplifier who played a few hackneyed blues licks was a 'blues' player. We were a lot more special. In terms of immediate peers there was Eric, though he was flying off at a different tangent. It was quite competitive really."

— Mick Fleetwood, interviewed by *Q Magazine*, May 1990

Mick Fleetwood's comments say it all about the late 1960s: Namely, what had begun as something special in the mid-1960s ended up as an overcrowded bandwagon with a lot of semi-pro bands latching on to the blues and blues-rock boom in order to get gigs in the many blues clubs that had sprung up. From the moment this occurred, the quality of entertainment took a dive and the boom was bound to go bust.

The Yardbirds, John Mayall's Bluesbreakers, Cream, Fleetwood Mac, Led Zeppelin, Chicken Shack and the rest of the bands in this book were the special groups that helped take Brit-blues to blues-rock during the 1960s. Meanwhile in the States, the movement was led by such musicians as Canned Heat, Electric Flag and Johnny Winter, all presenting their more eclectic take on blues music.

But toward the end of the decade, bands such as Fleetwood Mac and Led Zeppelin changed musical direction. They moved away from short, faithful interpretations of Elmore James, Howlin' Wolf, B.B. King, Buddy Guy and the Chicago blues masters and toward their own blues-based material, which consisted of longer songs with a lot of improvisation thrown in. This was a natural evolution,

inspired by Cream and also by classic Grateful Dead excursions such the acid-blues "Dark Star."

The music became known as free-form rock, and whereas "formlessness" had originally equated to musical freedom, paradoxically many blues-rock musicians soon found themselves flailing in an excess of freedom.

Drugs, especially LSD, became as essential to this music as Ecstasy became to the late 1980s' dance movement. Fleetwood Mac's Peter Green later recalled, "When I first heard Grateful Dead's jamming I thought it was a bit boring. But then if you listened to it when you'd taken some LSD you could get into it and understand what they were doing."

From 1969 onward, Peter Green—with Grateful Dead's Jerry Garcia as a mentor—led Fleetwood Mac in the free-form direction. This meant that songs like "Green Manalishi" (which had begun its life as a three- to four-minute hit single) were developed into 10- to 20-minute acid jams. Similarly, in 1969 John Mayall disbanded the Bluesbreakers and assembled a drummer-less band that was heavily into jazz-blues and improvising.

Initially, these moves paid off for both bands. *Then Play On*, Fleetwood Mac's 1969 album that augured their short-lived free-form era before Green quit, was a chart success. With half of their set devoted to jamming, Fleetwood Mac was one of the biggest live acts in Europe. Mayall's *The Turning Point* similarly sold well and his popularity peaked with his *USA Union* release.

But by 1970, the mood of the times was changing. Summer music festivals on both sides of the Atlantic had more than a few bad vibes to dispel. This may have had something to do with the bad acid that increasingly found its way to the market; it certainly had a lot to do with hapless audiences having to endure yet another 10-minute guitar or drum solo that was going nowhere.

In spite of a few enlightened reviews, Peter Green's 1970 progressive acid-rock experiment—a solo album called *The End of the Game*—was too left-field even for most left-fielders. Meanwhile, Mayall's mainstream appeal declined the more he delved into improvisation-based jazz blues. Blues-rock's heyday was fast coming to a close.

Tragically, Canned Heat's Al Wilson died in September 1970 (the same month as rock star Jimi Hendrix). It's painful even to contemplate where Hendrix might have taken his jazz-rock music had he lived on, while at the time of Wilson's death, Wilson was about to begin mixing an outstanding studio collaboration between Canned Heat and John Lee Hooker—the acclaimed *Hooker 'N Heat* double-album. Furthermore, Canned Heat without Al Wilson's genius proved to be a Canned Heat going cold: It's similarly painful even to think about the blues-rock innovation that passed away along with Wilson.

Oddly enough, by the early 1970s, an offshoot of the band that really got British blues on the road back in 1964—the Yardbirds—was suddenly poised to take blues-rock forward toward something entirely new—heavy rock and heavy metal. Led Zeppelin had risen from the still-warm ashes of the New Yardbirds in 1968 and, under the musical direction of guitar hero Jimmy Page, had an agenda all their own—what Page called "CIA" music—Celtic-, Indian- and Arabic-influenced rock.

But in the band's early days, this agenda—very loud guitar-riff-based blues-rock with an emphasis on rock and theatrical vocals, sometimes interspersed with exotic folk-rock—met with crowd resistance in Britain, but not in the States. At the 1969 Bath Blues & Progressive Rock Festival, a defiant Jimmy Page reportedly gave hecklers and doubters some peace signs in reverse as the band motored through their set. Not everybody in Britain was ready for Page's and Plant's radical showmanship.

But, as Mick Fleetwood told *Mojo* magazine much later, Led Zeppelin were simply tapping into something that was new and unique in the world of blues-rock—theatricalness—wherein the flamboyant Buddy Guy style was taken much further: "Led Zeppelin had a shtick, they had a lead singer with an image . . . We [Fleetwood Mac] would have been a less showbizzy version of what they represented—rightly or wrongly. I think some of their earlier music got overshadowed by the bulge in the pants!"

Again, rightly or wrongly, in the 1970s the festival and stadium rock world was ready for the "bulge-in-the-pants" posing, stage moves and showmanship that would become heavy metal's calling cards. The studious and wooden "stand-on-the-spot" stage presentation typified by blues-student-turned-unlikely-rock-star Al Wilson belonged to the 1960s. The future of blues-rock went to bands that could act, and Led Zeppelin and America's Z.Z. Top were among the first to pass the audition.

In the mid-1990s in a BBC2 interview, ex-Yardbird Jeff Beck confessed how much he envied rock musicians such as Hendrix who had no inhibitions about onstage theatricalness: "That's what I wanted to do but being British and a victim of the class system, whatever . . . you know, these poxy little schools you went to . . . I couldn't do it. Perhaps if I'd gone to acting class I could have done it."

The Jeff Beck Group had jammed with Page and Plant, and Zeppelin's first album was influenced by the ex-Yardbirds guitarist—both *Led Zeppelin* and Jeff Beck's *Truth* album featured Willie Dixon's "You Shook Me," and another cut from *Led Zeppelin* ("Dazed and Confused") had been part of the Yardbirds' 1967 stage act (originally called "I'm Confused," this was a Yardbirds' adaptation of ex-Youngblood Jake Holmes's song about a bad LSD experience, confusingly also titled "Dazed and Confused.")

For the blues world, there was a downside to Zeppelin taking off on such a massive scale (some of their early 1970s American tours broke box office records previously held by the Beatles). Namely, the classic pre-war blues songs that Led Zeppelin reworked and masterfully updated more often than not weren't credited to the bluesmen who actually wrote them. For instance, "Whole Lotta Love" was an obvious reworking of Willie Dixon's "You Need Love," but it took many years before Dixon received his royalties. (When Dixon was finally awarded his funds, they apparently went toward setting up the Blues Heaven Foundation.)

Musically, the emergence of Led Zeppelin at the end of the decade meant that the blues-rock explosion begun by the Yardbirds in 1963 had come full circle. Led Zeppelin were about to take rock to new heights, but in doing so they acknowledged where they had come from by continuing to include old Yardbirds' live standards such as "Train Kept A-Rollin" in their early 1970s stadium-rock repertoire.

Around 1968, Robert Plant must have sensed that it was time for something new, as he explained to BBC2: "I was trying to create a program of songs when I met Jimmy [Page] that combined very scary white rock'n'roll . . . which was a far cry from the kind of blues-rock that had been influencing me up until then. I was trying to make something extraordinary out of a very obvious clichéd vocalist approach."

Plant and Led Zeppelin's reply to outraged accusations that they had ripped off African-American bluesmen was unrepentant and bold: Blues, to Page and Plant, was a music handed down through the years among "one great big family of beggars and thieves." Stealing was essential to the development of this folk art and, anyway, all the acoustic and electric blues greats such as Robert Johnson and Elmore James were as guilty of theft as they themselves . . . if *guilty* is the right word.

While the whole question of plagiarism (with regard to folk music) can never be a clear-cut right or wrong issue, some musicians never shared Led Zeppelin's views. Eric Clapton personally saw to it that Skip James received royalties for Cream's version of James's "I'm So Glad," even though the spiritual James, reportedly, was underwhelmed by his material being updated in this manner. Then, too, there's always that inspired and inspiring Son House and Al Wilson hook-up in the early 1960s, where there was certainly a lot more giving than taking going on.

What cannot be disputed is that the product of what some purists consider artistic contamination and stealing is a genre of music that still sounds vibrant, not dated, and more than thirty years later represents a standard to which younger musicians continue to aspire.

A final word on the matter is right here in the present and comes from Texas guitar wizard Eric Johnson, who told *The Guitar Magazine* (May 2000): "I was always in love with the early Cream when Eric was playing with them. I felt that although you heard this blues thing that was happening, there was this whole new tone; he touched on something that was so much bigger than life . . . I don't think that the Cream style of playing has been exhausted, I still think there's an opportunity to take it and go somewhere else."

In Conclusion

It is my hope that this introduction to *Blues-Rock Explosion* has provided an alternative to the idea that when cultures intermix, music loses its purity and thus loses out, a view strongly held by writers such as Ralph Gleason, Paul Oliver and *Living Blues Magazine*. I hope, too, that it has shed light on how, and perhaps even why, the 1960s blues-rock explosion happened. Today, the image of Eric Clapton driving B.B. King in an open-top Cadillac is truly a heroic scene, and the album *Riding with the King* is a celebration.

This is not to say, however, that all blues collaborations between whites and blacks have succeeded in a similar way. There was the aforementioned misjudged foray by Muddy Waters into 1960s psychedelia—*Electric Mud*. There was Fleetwood Mac's *Blues Jam at Chess*. There was *The London Howlin' Wolf Sessions*. Though of obvious interest to blues fans, none of these were progressive blues projects in the way that *Hooker 'N Heat* or *Hard Again* (Muddy Waters's post-Chess Records comeback produced by Johnny Winter) most certainly were.

As to why or how the blues-rock explosion really occurred, in summary I can only say that a combination of British snobbery and blissful ignorance about the repressive politics underpinning American blues and race records allowed the music to grow so fast in Britain. Freed of its social shackles, the blues in Britain was able to move forward in a modernized form to ultimately be welcomed back in America, where only a tiny minority of musicians was already in the know about blues and its origins.

To end, here is a bit of blues imagery about the past and present, which carries hope for the future. A few years ago on several occasions I met and spoke at length with Danny Kirwan, a young musician back in the 1960s who, as part of Fleetwood Mac, delved *very* deep into the blues—with awesome results for such an inexperienced player—before taking the music much further toward blues-rock and, later on, even to pop ballads.

Sadly, Danny's fate after quitting Fleetwood Mac in 1972 has been a sad story of hard times and the real blues: Alcoholism, mental hospitals and addiction clinics have been the long-term aftereffects of his short spell as a rock star—in fact one of our meetings took place in a rehabilitation hostel where an all-pervasive and bitter-sweet odor of stale booze is something you'd rather forget.

Yet on the day in question it was a very lucid Kirwan who offered me the following food for thought with his personal take on the blues: "The blues is a black man's language . . . something that stems from the black nature of man. A white man can try and sing the blues but he might do himself damage. If you're a white man you have to learn the blues; you don't know them. It's as simple as that. The thing is . . . those black guys play the way they are, because it's their music. It's developed with them.

"But if you understand your brain content and you're a white man, you can play it if you're clever. You see, I was infiltrated to the extent that I picked up a bug—I got into the blues and it got into my system like a bug gets into your system. . . .

"My favorite bluesman? Albert King—you'd drop out of last week for Albert wouldn't you? And Otis Rush—he had a nice sting in his playing, and he had a thick timbre, that was his stamp. But you see, those guys were blacks singing and playing about what it is to be black in their country, which isn't really their country."

And when I asked whether Eric Clapton plays the blues, Kirwan's pithy reply hit the spot: "Eric Clapton? He plays what man *is*. . . ."

There you have it. In that one short sentence about Clapton, there is a whole case for the blues, while Danny's other reflections on African-American music may contain part-answers to some other big questions mentioned and discussed at far greater length in these pages.

Enjoy the book.

— Martin Celmins, May 2001

Big thanks for information and exchange of ideas go to Jeff Watt, Hughie Flint and Peter Moody. Thanks also to Nadine Cahodas, Rebecca Davis, Harry Shapiro, Pete Brown and Charles Shaar Murray, especially in his role as consultant for the mid-1990s BBC2/WGBH television series *Dancing in the Street*.

A Chronology of the Blues-Rock Explosion

Lastly, here is a brief chronology by era that encompasses all the bands and artists in the individual chapters of this book.

Britain: The 1950s

Chris Barber and the trad jazz scene promoted visiting American acoustic bluesmen. The skiffle movement promoted the guitar as a popular "easy-to-learn" instrument for teenagers, encouraging them to form groups. Many acoustic blues artists such as Jo Ann Kelly began in the skiffle culture, as did future electric guitar heroes such as Jimmy Page.

America: The 1950s

Ray Charles and R&B were forerunners of Tracy Nelson/Mother Earth's gospel-based music. The 1950s folk music protest movement, incorporating acoustic blues, influenced Bob Dylan and artists such as Ry Cooder.

This was also the zenith of Chess Records, R&B, and rock'n'roll, with stars such as Muddy Waters, Bo Diddley and Chuck Berry. The Sun Studios Memphis sound with Elvis Presley soon influenced guitar-centered bands like the Rolling Stones in England.

Britain: The Early 1960s

The Flamingo Club showcased eclectic jazz-based R&B. Jimmy Smith and Booker T. sounds were developed by British artists such as Georgie Fame and eventually by bands such as Electric Flag in America. The Ealing Club led by Alexis Korner was the birthplace of British blues-rock.

America: The Early 1960s

The coffeehouse folk/protest movement continues to promote acoustic blues. Interest in Chicago blues gathers at the hands of Paul Butterfield, Mike Bloomfield and Charlie Musselwhite.

Britain: The Mid-1960s

The jazz-blues of Alexis Korner and post-Cyril Davies Blues Incorporated lead to the jazz-blues R&B of Graham Bond. The Chicago-inspired urban electric blues of Cyril Davies and early John Mayall come to the fore.

America: The Mid-1960s

The psychedelic West Coast blues of the Grateful Dead. The electric country blues of Canned Heat. Dylan goes electric. The British invasion pop groups break through to the U.S.

Britain and America: The Late 1960s

The radical, electric guitar-centered blues-rock gives rise to the majority of bands in this book, including the Cream, Fleetwood Mac, the Allman Brothers and the Yardbirds.

• • •

The Allman Brothers

With their inventive blend of blues, rock and jazz, the Allman Brothers will long be known as the forbearers of Southern Rock, paving the way for the likes of Lynyrd Skynyrd, the Marshall Tucker Band, the Outlaws, Wet Willie, and the Black Crowes, among others. Overcoming personal tragedies, the Allman Brothers have retained a large and faithful following. The late rock critic Lester Bangs once said of their influence: "For all the white blooze bands proliferating today, it's still inspiring when the real article comes along, a white group who've transcended their schooling to produce a volatile blues-rock sound of pure energy, inspiration and love. The Allmans know what they're doing, and feel it deeply, and they communicate immediately."

The classic lineup featured the twin guitars of Duane Allman and Dickey Betts, who spearheaded the extended, inspired improvisations that cemented the Allman Brothers' reputation as a dynamic live act. It was Duane, though, who truly offered something special. Not only was he a technically gifted guitarist—particularly at bottleneck playing—but his music seemed to feed off the complexity of his character. With his mix of contradictory personality traits—self-confident yet introverted, lighthearted but introspective—Duane channeled an ever-shifting, colorful persona into some of the most emotionally charged guitar playing of his era.

Brothers Gregory Lenoir (b. December 8, 1947) and Howard Duane (b. November 20, 1946; d. October 29, 1971, Macon, Georgia) Allman were born in Nashville, Tennessee. When the boys were two and three, their father was murdered by a hitchhiker. Following the tragedy, their mother went back to school to study accounting and earned her C.P.A. degree. During their adolescence, Duane and Gregg took piano lessons for a year and a year and a half, respectively. Later, both boys joined the marching band, playing trumpets. In 1957, the family moved to Daytona Beach, Florida.

Only two summers later, Gregg bought his first guitar at age 13 from money he saved working a paper route, as he recalled to *Rolling Stone:* "Worked all summer and cleared 21 bucks. It was getting toward the end of summer, the mornings were getting colder and I was in Sears and Roebuck to get some gloves with the money when I strolled by the guitar department and fell in love with those beauties. Found one that was $21.95 and the bastard behind the counter wouldn't let me have it. I came back the next day, got it, and proceeded to wear that son of a bitch out. I wouldn't eat or sleep or drink or anything. Just play that damn guitar." The guitar led to conflicts between the two brothers. "While I was gone, he'd [Duane] grab my axe and start picking. Pretty soon we had fights over the damn thing, so when it came around to our birthdays—mine was in December and his was in November—we both got one. I got mine a little earlier than my birthday, actually. Matter of fact, I put hands on my first electric guitar November 10th, 1960, at three o'clock that Saturday afternoon. Duane's guitar got into the picture shortly after that."

Over the next few years, Duane and Gregg were both heavily influenced by R&B and traditional blues artists, such as T-Bone Walker, Elmore James, Sonny Boy Williamson, Ray Charles, B.B. King and Little Milton. The brothers played in a series of local bands in the early 1960s, including the Kings, the Y Teens and the Shufflers. In 1963, Duane and Gregg joined a racially mixed band, the House Rockers, which backed a black R&B quartet called the Untils. This caused their Southern family a great deal of consternation, but clearly established their musical allegiances. Duane later recalled this band: "We were in this mixed band called the House Rockers—we were a smoking band! Boy, I mean we set fire to a building in a second. We were just up there blowing as funky as we pleased; sixteen years old, 41 dollars a week, the big time."

The siblings later formed the Escorts, with Duane handling lead guitar and most of the vocals, Gregg on rhythm guitar, Van Harrison on bass, and Maynard Portwood on drums. The Escorts recorded several demos for club owners, including covers of "She's a Woman," "The Last Time," "Oh Pretty Woman" and "You've Lost That Lovin' Feelin'." The highlight of their early career occurred in 1965 when the Escorts opened an Easter weekend show for the Beach Boys. They performed covers of "Hitchhike," "Game of Love," "Turn On Your Lovelight" and "What'd I Say." Soon after, Van Harrison dropped out and was replaced by Bob Keller, and the band began calling themselves the Allman Joys. Duane summed up the early years to *Beat Instrumental:*

"When we first started, Gregg and me were playing rhythm and blues. We always had blues roots, but there weren't any other white groups in Daytona, Florida, and the only way we could break into the scene was to try to play black music in white clubs. It wasn't easy, because black musicians were doing black music in black clubs. Like we were all doing the same thing, so in the end we alternated with each other playing lead guitar on different nights with a black group."

By the time Gregg graduated from Sea Breeze Senior High School in 1965, the Allman Joys were ready to hit the road (Duane had became so absorbed with his six-string that he had quit high school at 15 to practice his music). Working seven nights a week, six sets a night, the band played mostly southern teen clubs. On occasion, Butch Trucks—the drummer for the Bitter End, which was touring the same circuit—would sit in with them. One night while playing at the Briar Patch in Nashville, the Allman Joys came to the attention of Buddy Killen, who signed them to his label, Dial Records. Demos were recorded at Nashville's Bradley's Barn Studios in August 1966, including seven songs that Gregg either wrote or cowrote. Only one single was initially released, which Duane discounted as a "terrible psychedelic rendition" of "Spoonful." (Other tracks recorded during these sessions would be released in 1973 as *Early Allman*.) After listening to the recorded material, Killen advised the band to "go look for a day job."

Following the failure of "Spoonful" to chart, the Allman Joys disbanded in 1966. Duane and Gregg headed off to Decatur, Alabama, where they merged with members of another fragmented outfit, the Men-its. The new band featured Duane (lead guitar), Gregg (rhythm guitar), Johnny Sandlin (drums), Paul Hornsby (keyboards) and Mabron McKinney (bass). The new lineup went through a couple of name changes before settling on the Hour Glass. Not long after, while performing in St. Louis, Nitty Gritty Dirt Band manager Bill McEuen saw their potential and offered to manage them if they relocated to Los Angeles. He offered a recording contract and the opportunity for national exposure as enticements for the move. Despite reservations, the group agreed to move to Southern California and signed with Liberty Records, whose roster at the time was dominated by saccharine pop artists such as Vikki Carr and Bobby Vee. Not surprisingly, Liberty was an uncomfortable environment for the quartet. The label controlled every aspect of the group's career, including choice of material, even curtailing live performances (which, astonishingly, they believed would "blow the whole image," something particularly distressing to Gregg and Duane).

Their first self-titled album, *The Hour Glass*, was recorded in August 1967 and released in October 1967. The album consisted primarily of pop/soul covers and one oddity—Duane's spoken word reading of Edgar Allan Poe's poem, "Bells," to which the producers later added a cacophony of psychedelic sounds. As Gregg later told *Guitar Player*, "They'd hand us a washtub full of demos and say, 'Pick out your new album.'" The band was limited to just one original composition, Gregg's "Got to Get Away."

The Hour Glass recorded a second album, *Power of Love*, in January 1968, replacing McKinney with Jesse Willard (Pete) Carr on bass. *Power of Love* was more blues-oriented than its predecessor, with Gregg contributing seven compositions. Released in the U.K. as *The Hour Glass* (the first U.S. album wasn't issued), the LP received lukewarm reviews. *Melody Maker* observed, "Exciting but unsensational. They've got it together. But so have a thousand other similar groups," while *New Musical Express* commented, "A Hollywood group, not quite up to our own standards, but interesting." Gregg himself later dismissed both albums with the quip, "Together those two records form what is commonly known as a shit sandwich."

While in Los Angeles, Duane taught himself how to play the bottleneck guitar. It took awhile for the other group members to warm up to his new passion as he recalled in a 1971 interview with *Good Times* magazine: "I heard Ry Cooder playing it about three years ago, and I said, 'Man, that's for me!' I got me a bottleneck and went around the house for about three weeks saying, 'Hey, man. 'We've got to learn the songs—the blues to play on the stage. I love this. This is a gas!' So we started doing it. For awhile, everybody would look at me, thinking, 'Oh no! He's getting ready to do it again!' And everybody would just lower their heads—as if to say, 'Get it over with—quick.' Then I got a little bit better at it, and now everybody's blowing it all out of proportion. It's just fine for me as a relief from the other kind of playing. It's just playing."

Tired of being manipulated by label management into recording material unsuitable to their ambitions, the quintet rented studio time at Rick Hall's Fame Studios in Muscle Shoals. Fame (F.A.M.E.), an acronym for Florence Alabama Music Enterprises, was the home of the original Muscle Shoals Sound Rhythm Section, a studio band that built their reputation backing such artists as Aretha Franklin, Wilson Pickett, Percy Sledge and Clarence Carter. On April 22, 1968, the band recorded several songs from their stage set, including "Ain't No Good to

Cry," "B.B. King Medley" (combining his "Sweet Little Angel," "It's My Own Fault" and "How Blue Can You Get"), and the Gregg Allman-penned "Been Gone Much Too Long." Delighted with the results, the band returned to L.A. and presented the tapes to their West Coast manager. He rejected the demos outright, calling them "terrible and useless."

The group then toured the West Coast to promote *Power of Love*, including dates at San Francisco's Fillmore (May 2–4), the Cheetah Club in Hollywood (May 10–11), the Kaleidoscope in Hollywood (May 17–19), the Avalon Ballroom in San Francisco (May 24) and the Whisky A Go-Go in Los Angeles (June 6–9). Hour Glass disbanded shortly thereafter.

As Duane later recounted to *Circus Magazine*, "I was really disillusioned and strung out with the West Coast. The group thing left a bitter taste in my mouth." Duane returned to Florida, but Gregg was forced to stay behind for a solo project. Gregg told *Guitar Player*, "I guess we were there [Los Angeles] from part of '66 until '68, and Duane finally said, 'Man, I've had it with this bullshit! I'm leaving. Why don't we take the band and go on back home where we belong, back down South.' We owed Liberty Records about 40 thou, and they said, 'Well, we'll let you all go, but we'll put a lawsuit on you. But we won't do it if he stays,' they said, pointing at me, 'to work with our studio band.' And so I stayed. The rest of them really didn't like it; they were all cussing me on the way out the door. They thought I wanted to stay there, which I did not. So there was no lawsuit, and I cut two records with their 20-piece orchestra. I hope you never heard those."

The first record, "D-I-V-O-R-C-E" backed with "Changing of the Guard," was recorded in June 1968 with Gregg backed by studio musicians. The record was released as "Greg Allman & the Hour Glass," as was the subsequent single, "I've Been Trying" backed with "Silently." Both were recorded in August 1967 with the Hour Glass. Several more solo recordings extending into February 1969 were made that later surfaced as bonus tracks on the CD reissues of the two Hour Glass albums.

When Gregg returned to Florida, the brothers hooked up again with Butch Trucks, who was by now playing with the 31st of February. Trucks was working on some demos in a Miami studio for that band's second album and invited the brothers to join the session. However, because Liberty still had Duane and Gregg in a contract that barred them from recording on their own, their studio work with the 31st

of February went uncredited. Along with Duane, Gregg and Trucks, Scott Boyer (guitar, vocals) and David Brown (bass) recorded nine tracks at TK Studios in Hialeah, Florida during September 1968. These demos were later released in 1973 as *Duane and Gregg Allman*.

While Gregg returned to L.A., Duane stayed behind in Jacksonville, Florida and hung out at a local club, the Scene. He jammed regularly with another local group, the Second Coming, which included guitarist Forrest Richard "Dickey" Betts (b. December 12, 1943; West Palm Beach, Florida) and bassist Berry Oakley (b. April 4, 1948, Chicago, Illinois; d. November 11, 1972, Macon, Georgia). As a teenager, Betts had toured the South in various club bands, including the Jokers (who were later immortalized in Rick Derringer's "Rock and Roll Hoochie Coo"). Betts had a strong electric blues background, while Oakley's influences included a mix of country and bluegrass. Both Betts and Oakley were veterans of Tommy Roe's backup band, the Roemans. The Second Coming had recorded one promo single in November 1968, a cover of Cream's "I Feel Free" backed with a cover of Jefferson Airplane's "She Has Funny Cars" (US/Steady Records HG-001). Significantly, the Second Coming employed twin lead guitars, with the second guitar slot held down by Larry Reinhardt. Twin leads became the Allman Brothers' trademark in later years. Reinhardt later went on to play with Iron Butterfly and Captain Beefheart.

Duane never became an established member of the Second Coming. Fame Studios owner Rick Hall persuaded Duane to return to Muscle Shoals as a contract session guitarist. During recordings with Wilson Picket, Pickett quickly befriended the long-haired guitarist, calling him "Skyman," a nickname that eventually evolved into "Skydog." At Duane's urging, Pickett recorded Lennon and McCartney's "Hey Jude" (U.S./Atlantic 2591). Duane's stunning work during this session, a running obligato intertwined with Pickett's impassioned vocals, established Allman's reputation as a topnotch player. Hall was so excited by Allman's performance on "Hey Jude" that he phoned long distance to Atlantic V.P. Jerry Wexler to play the song for him. Wexler wanted to sign Allman immediately, and bought the guitarist out of his contract with Rick Hall for $15,000. Wexler planned for Allman to stay at Muscle Shoals to build a reputation for himself before being added to the roster of Capricorn Records, a new label that Wexler was forming with Phil Walden. Walden had previously managed Otis Redding and in various capacities was involved with Sam and Dave, and Arthur Conley.

As the studio's primary session guitarist, Duane eventually backed artists such as Percy Sledge, Arthur Conley, King Curtis and Aretha Franklin. Duane began work on a solo album in February 1969, assisted by Berry Oakley as well as Sandlin and Hornsby from the Hour Glass. Five tracks were recorded at Fame Studios: "Goin' Down Slow," "Slip Away," "No Money Down" and "Happily Married Man." Phil Walden recalled the sessions to *Beat Instrumental:* "We went into Rick Hall's studios down there and cut an album with Duane but neither he nor I were really happy with it because it was too R&B oriented for the rock market of the day and in any case, Duane was a pretty poor singer so we bought out Rick Hall's interest in those recordings." While the album was never completed, several of the recorded tracks—all sung by Duane—later appeared on the posthumous Duane Allman release, *An Anthology*.

Armed with the Walden/Capricorn contract, Duane returned to Florida to look for musicians to form a new band. While at Muscle Shoals, Duane had met Jai Johanny Johanson (b. John Lee Johnson, July 8, 1944; Ocean Springs, Mississippi), a Muscle Shoals drummer who was also the touring drummer for Otis Redding, Percy Sledge and Joe Tex. The two had become friends, with Duane telling Johanson that whatever his next move would be, he wanted Johanson along as the drummer. So with Johanson in tow in Jacksonville, the two of them sat in on a Sunday jam session on March 23, 1969, at Butch Trucks's house with Betts, Oakley (from the Second Coming), and Trucks (who was between bands, as the 31st of February had dissolved). All participants sensed that the session was extraordinary. In fact, Trucks later recalled, "Duane got in the doorway and said, 'Anybody in this room that's not gonna play in my band, you're gonna have to fight your way out.'" Gregg's return from L.A. on March 26 rounded out the lineup.

While in L.A. and upon his return to Jacksonville, Gregg wrote many of the songs that would appear on the first album, including "Whipping Post," "It's Not My Cross to Bear" and "Dreams." Now with $80,000 in sound equipment contributed by Walden, the band rehearsed intensely and just over one month after their formation, recorded some demos at the newly formed Capricorn Studios in Macon, Georgia. The facility was not quite ready to produce finished product, so the band went to New York in September 1969 to record their debut album at Atlantic Recording Studios.

Released that November, *The Allman Brothers Band* was well received critically but only sold about 30,000 copies. In *Rolling Stone*, Lester Bangs wrote, "The album sounds like what Led Zeppelin might have been if they weren't hung-up on gymnastics." Likewise, *Melody Maker* praised the new band, noting, "Duane Allman has assembled the kind of blues band which sweeps aside any doubts about 'validity.' Roaring, virile, and convincing music with exciting vocals, guitar, and organ all the way."

Following the album, the band embarked on a touring schedule that would see them play nearly 500 dates in a two-year period from late 1969 to autumn 1971. The early tours weren't financially lucrative, but Phil Walden continued to subsidize their efforts—even as he faced financial ruin. As Butch Trucks later told *Rolling Stone*, "Phil Walden had complete faith in us, and I'll respect him forever for that. I think he sunk about $150,000 in us. He was close to bankruptcy a lot of the time, and Atlantic kept telling him we didn't have a chance. But during the first three years, Phil never once tried to change us."

The band received a big break when it was booked to play at Bill Graham's Fillmore East auditorium in December 1969, opening for Blood, Sweat and Tears. Although the group's set was met with some booing from the crowd, the perspicacious Graham was sufficiently impressed with their performance to book them for additional dates before more sympathetic audiences. Two weeks later, they were paired with B.B. King and Buddy Guy at the Fillmore West in San Francisco. A couple of weeks after that, they were back at the Fillmore East on a bill with the Grateful Dead and Love.

Duane continued his session work while between tours, cutting numerous tracks with the Muscle Shoals House Band (bassist David Hood, guitarist Eddie Hinton, drummer Roger Hawkins and keyboardist Barry Becket) while backing artists such as Boz Scaggs and John Hammond.

In February 1970, the group commenced work on their second album at the now complete Capricorn Studios, assisted by producer Tom Dowd with Thom Doucette contributing percussion and harmonica. The LP was finished at the Criteria Studios in Miami, Florida and Regent Sound Studios in New York City in July 1970 and named after the Macon, Georgia farmhouse that served as their headquarters, *Idlewild South*. Two Dickey Betts compositions provided the highlights, the flowing instrumental, "In Memory of Elizabeth Reed," and the elegant, gospel-tinged "Revival." The album also featured four tunes by Gregg, including the brooding "Midnight Rider" (which later hit the charts when re-recorded and released in 1974 as part of a solo project).

Released in September 1970, *Idlewild South* received good reviews and peaked at #38 on the U.S. album charts.

For the next release, Tom Dowd set up a remote facility to capture the group in concert. Recorded over two nights on March 12–13, 1971, *At Fillmore East* has come to be recognized as one of rock's landmark live albums. It also provided the band with a major commercial breakthrough by reaching the Top Ten. Containing only seven tracks, the original two-record set showcased the band's disciplined interaction while establishing Duane as a premier slide guitarist. Highlights include a 20-minute version of "Whipping Post" and the instrumental "In Search of Elizabeth Reed," both lengthy, flawlessly executed jams with jazzy undercurrents. Polygram's expanded 1992 release, *The Fillmore Concerts*, contains 150 minutes of music drawn from five Fillmore East performances recorded on March 12, 1971 (two shows), March 13, 1971 (two shows) and June 27, 1971. Acclaim for *At Fillmore East* was universal, with *Rolling Stone* declaring the Allman Brothers "the best damn rock and roll band this country has produced in the past five years." The Allman Brothers became the hottest concert attraction in the country, playing to sold-out audiences.

The group's reputation was further enhanced by a triumphant appearance at the Atlanta Pop Festival in July 1970 at the Middle Georgia Raceway in Byron, Georgia. The Allman Brothers played a two-hour set on the first day of the festival and received a tremendous response from the nearly 200,000 fans. The band returned on the last day of the festival to perform with Johnny Winter and Leslie West for "Mountain Jam." Two of their songs later appeared on the triple-album, *The Great Rock Festivals of the Seventies: Isle of Wight/Atlanta Pop Festival.*

In late August and early September, Duane worked on Derek and the Domino's *Layla and Other Assorted Love Songs* album. Duane explained to *Zig Zag* magazine how he became involved with the project: "Well, I was down in Miami, at Criterion Studios—they're the best—to watch them make that record, because I was so interested. I thought, 'Well now, that cat has himself a band'—I've been an admirer of Eric Clapton for a long, long time. I've always dug his playing, he inspired me a lot and I figured I'd get a chance to meet him at the same time, watch this record going down. So when I saw him, he acted like he knew me, like I was an old friend; 'Hey man, how are you,' you know. And he said, 'As long as you're here, we want you to get on this record and make it with us, we need more guitar players anyway.' So I did, and I was real flattered and glad to be able to do it."

Layla has been viewed by many as the crowning achievement of Duane's session work. Duane's gutsy slide guitar playing pushed and prodded Eric Clapton to in turn produce some of the most memorable guitar work of his career. Allman also joined the Dominos in concert on December 1, 1970 at the Curtis Hixon Hall in Tampa, Florida, and there was some speculation that he might join the outfit. However, as he explained to *Circus* magazine, "I was gonna make the whole tour, but it took like ten weeks—and I got my own fish to fry."

The Allman Brothers had been working on their fourth album, *Eat a Peach*, for over a month when Duane Allman was killed in a motorcycle accident on October 29, 1971, in Macon, just three weeks before his twenty-fifth birthday. Duane was the band's visionary leader and the catalyst that brought their sound together. His loss deprived the band of much of their spirit. Devastated, the group played at his funeral and three weeks later, on Thanksgiving, at Carnegie Hall. Dickey Betts explained to *New Musical Express:* "When Duane suddenly split [died] from the band we just didn't know what to do. It was decided that we would all take about six months off to think things over. But soon after we played at Duane's funeral, we found that we were drifting back together again. Apparently, we were all of the same mind. The best way to relieve the immense pain we felt deep inside was to get back together again as soon as possible and go out on the road."

After several performances as a five-piece, the group abandoned the two-guitar lineup in favor of adding a second keyboardist. Chuck Leavell was brought in at Gregg's suggestion, giving the group a jazzier sound, and also allowing Gregg to concentrate more on his singing. They had recorded three new songs before Duane's death and these, combined with other leftover live and studio material, were released as the double LP *Eat a Peach* in February 1972. The LP was another commercial and critical smash hit, entering the U.S. Top Ten and rising to #4 in 1972.

The band headlined the three-day Mar Y Sol festival held April 1–3, 1972, in Vega Baja, Puerto Rico, but later that year another tragic accident left the band without a member. Berry Oakley died in a motorcycle accident on November 11, 1972. Eerily, the crash occurred a mere three blocks from the spot where Duane was killed. Like Duane, Oakley was just 24 years old when he died. Lamar Williams (b. January 14, 1949, Newton, Mississippi; d. January 19, 1983) took Oakley's place.

Postscript

The band reached a commercial peak in 1973 with the release of *Brothers and Sisters*, which topped the charts for five weeks. Two more albums were issued, *Win, Lose or Draw* (1975) and *Wipe the Windows, Check the Oil, Dollar Gas* (1976) before the group split acrimoniously in 1976. A 1979 reunion produced *Enlightened Rogues* (1979) and *Reach for the Sky* (1980) before they again disbanded. The release of the four-CD career retrospective, *Dreams* (1989), revived the public's interest, leading the group to record *Seven Turns* (1990), their strongest set in many years. The addition of guitarist Warren Haynes for *Seven Turns* returned the group to the classic two-guitar lineup, and subsequent releases, including *Shades of Two Worlds* (1991), *An Evening with the Allman Brothers Band* (1992) and *Where It All Begins* (1994) solidified their comeback. In 1995, the band released *2nd Set*, their fifth live release in twenty-five years. The band continues to tour and maintain a strong following, although in May 2000 guitarist Dickey Betts was ousted from the band, as the other group members felt that he was no longer performing at his best.

Gregg Allman has released numerous solo albums, including *Laid Back*, which yielded the hit, "Midnight Rider" (1973, U.S. #19); *The Gregg Allman Tour* (1975); *Playin' Up a Storm* (1977); the dubious *Allman and Woman: Two the Hard Way*, featuring his wife at the time, Cher (1977); *I'm No Angel* (1987); *Just Before the Bullets Fly* (1988); and *Searching for Simplicity* (1997).

Dickey Betts released four solo albums: *Highway Call* (1974), *Dickey Betts and Great Southern* (1977), *Atlanta's Burning Down* (1978), and *Pattern Disruptive* (1988).

Discography

Release Date	Title	Catalog Number

U.S. Singles

Allman Joys

1966	Spoonful/You Deserve Each Other	Dial 4046

The Hour Glass

1967	Nothing But Tears/Heartache	Liberty 56002
1968	Power of Love/I Still Want Your Love	Liberty 56029
1968	D-I-V-O-R-C-E/Changing of the Guard	Liberty 56053
1968	She's My Woman/Going Nowhere	Liberty 56065
1968	Now Is the Time/She Is My Woman	Liberty 56072
1969	I've Been Trying (Version #2)/Silently	Liberty 56091

Allman Brothers Band

1969	Black Hearted Woman/ Every Hungry Woman	Capricorn C 8003
1970	Revival/Leave My Blues at Home	Capricorn C 8011
1970	Midnight Rider/Whipping Post	Capricorn C 8014
1972	Melissa/Ain't Wastin' Time No More	Capricorn CPR 0003
1972	Melissa/Blue Sky	Capricorn CPR 0007
1972	One Way Out/Stand Back	Capricorn CPR 0014

U.S. Albums

The Allman Joys

1973   *Early Allman* (recorded 1966)   Dial DL 6005
Gotta Get Away/Oh John/Street Singer/You'll Learn Someday/Old Man River/Bell Bottom Britches/Spoonful/Stalling for Time/Doctor Fone Bone/Changing of the Guard/The Forest for the Trees/Northern Boundary

The Hour Glass

1967   *The Hour Glass*   Liberty LRP-3536 (M) / Liberty LST-7536 (S)
Out of the Night/Nothing But Tears/Love Makes the World Go 'Round/I Cast Off All My Fears/I've Been Trying/No Easy Way Down/Heartbeat/So Much Love/Got to Get Away/Silently/Bells

1968   *Power of Love*   Liberty LRP 3555 (M) / Liberty LST 7555 (S)
Power of Love/Changing of the Guard/To Things Before/I'm Not Afraid/I Can't Stand Alone/Down in Texas/I Still Want Your Love/Home for the Summer/I'm Hanging Up My Heart (For You)/Going Nowhere/Norwegian Wood (This Bird Has Flown)/Now Is the Time

1992   *The Hour Glass* (CD reissue)   EMI 077-7-96059-2-7
Same as above plus the following bonus tracks: In a Time/I've Been Trying (Version #1)/D-I-V-O-R-C-E/She Is My Woman/Bad Dream/Three Time Loser

1992   *Power of Love* (CD reissue)   EMI E2-98826
Same as above plus the following bonus tracks: Down in Texas (Version #2)/It's Not My Cross to Bear/Southbound/God Rest His Soul/February 3rd/Apollo 8

The 31st of February with Duane and Gregg Allman

1973   *Duane and Gregg Allman*   Bold 33-301
Morning Dew/God Rest His Soul/Nobody Knows You When You're Down and Out/Come Down and Get Me/Melissa/I'll Change for You/Back Down Home with You/Well I Know Too Well/In the Morning When I'm Real

The Allman Brothers Band

1969   *The Allman Brothers Band*   Atco SD 33-308

I Don't Want You No More/It's Not My Cross to Bear/Black Hearted Woman/ Trouble No More/Every Hungry Woman/Dreams/Whipping Post

1970   *Idlewild South*   Atco SD 33-342
Revival/Don't Keep Me Wonderin'/Midnight Rider/In Memory of Elizabeth Reed/Hoochie Coochie Man/Please Call Home/Leave My Blues at Home

1971   *At Fillmore East* (2 LP)   Atco SD 2802
Statesboro Blues/Done Somebody Wrong/Stormy Monday/Whipping Post/You Don't Love Me/Hot 'Lanta/In Memory of Elizabeth Reed

1972   *Eat a Peach* (2 LP)   Capricorn 2CP0102
Ain't Wastin' Time No More/Les Brers in a Minor/Melissa/Mountain Jam/One Way Out/Trouble No More/Stand Back/Blue Sky/Little Martha

1989   *Dreams* (4 CD)   Polydor 839 417-2
Shapes of Things[1]/Spoonful[1]/Crossroads[1]/Cast Off All My Fears[2]/Down in Texas[2]/Ain't No Good to Cry[2]/B.B. King Medley[2]/Morning Dew[3]/God Rest His Soul[3]/I Feel Free[4]/She Has Funny Cars[4]/Goin' Down Slow[5]/Dreams[6]/Don't Want You No More[6]/It's Not My Cross to Bear[6]/Trouble No More[6]/Dreams[6]/Statesboro Blues[6]/Hoochie Coochie Man[6]/Midnight Rider[6]/Dimples[6]/I'm Gonna Move to the Outskirts of Town[6]/Revival[6]/One More Ride[6]/Whipping Post[6]/In Memory of Elizabeth Reed[6]/Drunken Hearted Boy[6]/You Don't Love Me (Soul Serenade)[6]/Blue Sky[6]/Little Martha[6]/Melissa[6]/Ain't Wastin' Time No More[6]/Wasted Words[6]/Jessica[6]/Midnight Rider[7]/One Way Out[6]/Long Time Gone[8]/Can't Lose What You Never Had[6]/Come and Go Blues[9]/Bougainvillea[10]/Can You Fool[12]/Good Time Feeling[10]/Crazy Love[6]/Can't Take It with You[6]/Just Ain't Easy[6]/In Memory of Elizabeth Reed[6]/Angeline[6]/Things You Used to Do[6]/Nancy[8]/Rain[7]/I'm No Angel[9]/Demons[9]/Duane's Tune[11]

[1] Allman Joys	[7] Gregg Allman
[2] Hour Glass	[8] Dickey Betts
[3] The 31st of February	[9] The Gregg Allman Band
[4] The Second Coming	[10] Dickey Betts and Great Southern
[5] Duane Allman	[11] The Dickey Betts Band
[6] The Allman Brothers Band	[12] Gregg Allman and Cher

1989   *Live at Ludlow Garage 1970*   Polygram 843260-2
Recorded live April 11, 1970, Ludlow Garage, Cincinnati, Ohio. Dreams/Statesboro Blues/Trouble No More/Dimples/Every Hungry Woman/I'm Gonna Move to the Outskirts of Town/Hoochie Coochie Man/Mountain Jam

1992   *The Fillmore Concerts*   Polydor
                                                        314 517 294-2
Statesboro Blues/Trouble No More/Don't Keep Me Wonderin'/In Memory of Elizabeth Reed/One Way Out/Done Somebody Wrong/Stormy Monday/You Don't Love Me/Hot 'Lanta/Whipping Post/Mountain Jam/Drunken Hearted Boy

1997   *Fillmore East 2/70*   Grateful Dead
                                                        Records 4063
In Memory of Elizabeth Reed/Hoochie Coochie Man/Statesboro Blues/Trouble No More/Outskirts of Town/Whipping Post/Mountain Jam

Miscellaneous U.S. Releases

1971   *The Great Rock Festivals of the Seventies:* Columbia
        Isle of Wight/Atlanta Pop Festival   G3X30805
Recorded live at the Atlanta Pop Festival held July 3–5, 1970, Middle Georgia Raceway, Byron, Georgia. The Allman Brothers are represented by two songs, "Whipping Post" and "Statesboro Blues."

1972   *Mar Y Sol*   Taco 705
Recorded live April 2, 1972, Mar Y Sol Festival, Vega Baja, Puerto Rico. The Allman Brothers are represented by "Ain't Wastin' Time No More."

Duane Allman

1972   *An Anthology* (2 LP)   Capricorn 2CP 0108
B.B. King Medley (The Hour Glass)/Hey Jude (Wilson Pickett)/The Road of Love (Clarence Carter)/Goin' Down Slow (Duane Allman)/The Weight (Aretha Franklin)/Games People Play (King Curtis)/Shake for Me (John Hammond)/Loan Me a Dime (Boz Scaggs)/Rollin' Stone (Johnny Jenkins)/Livin' On the Open Road (Delaney & Bonnie & Friends)/Down Along the Cove (Johnny Jenkins)/Please Be with Me (Cowboy)/Mean Old World (Eric Clapton and Duane Allman)/Layla (Derek and the Dominos)/Statesboro Blues (The Allman Brothers Band)/Don't Keep Me Wonderin' (The Allman Brothers Band)/Standback (The Allman Brothers Band)/Dreams (The Allman Brothers Band)/Little Martha (The Allman Brothers Band)

1974   *An Anthology, Vol. 2* (2 LP)   Capricorn 2CP 0139
Happily Married Man (Duane Allman)/It Ain't Fair (Aretha Franklin)/The Weight (King Curtis)/You Reap What You Sow (Otis Rush)/Matchbox (Ronnie Hawkins)/Born to Be Wild (Wilson Pickett)/No Money Down (Duane Allman)/Been Gone Too Long (Hourglass)/Stuff You Gotta Watch (Arthur Conley)/Dirty Old Man (Lulu)/Push Push (Herbie Mann)/Walk on Gilded Splinters (Johnny Jenkins)/Waiting for a Train (Boz Scaggs)/Don't Tell Me Your Troubles (Ronnie Hawkins)/Goin' Upstairs (Sam Samudio)/Come on in My Kitchen (Delaney & Bonnie)/Dimples (The Allman Brothers Band)/Goin' Up the Country (The Duck and the Bear)/Done Somebody Wrong (The Allman Brothers Band)/Leave My Blues at Home (The Allman Brothers Band)/Midnight Rider (The Allman Brothers Band)

U.K. Albums

The Allman Joys
1973   *Allman Joys*   Mercury 6398 005

Hour Glass
1968   *The Hour Glass*   Liberty
                                                        LBL 83129 (m)
                                                        Liberty
                                                        LBS 83129 (s)
Power of Love/Changing of the Guard/To Things Before/I'm Not Afraid/I Can't Stand Alone/Down in Texas/I Still Want Your Love/Home for the Summer/I'm Hanging Up My Heart (For You)/Going Nowhere/Norwegian Wood (This Bird Has Flown)/Now Is the Time

The 31st of February
1973   *Duane & Greg Allman*   Polydor 2310 235

The Hour Glass

1968	*Hour Glass*	Liberty LBS 83129

Same tracks as U.S. release, *Power of Love.*

The Allman Brothers

1970	*The Allman Brothers Band*	Taco 228 033
1971	*Idlewild South*	Taco 2400 032
1971	*At Fillmore East*	Capricorn K60011
1972	*Eat a Peach*	Capricorn K67501
1989	*Dreams*	Polydor 839 417-2
1989	*Live at Ludlow Garage 1970*	Polygram 843260-2
1992	*The Fillmore Concerts*	Polydor 314 517 294-2

Miscellaneous U.K. Releases

1972	*Mar Y Sol*	WEA K 60029

The Artwoods

Although they only achieved one minor hit single in their three-year existence, the Artwoods are the unsung heroes of London's R&B movement in the mid-sixties. Working the scene tirelessly, averaging as many as 300 gigs a year, the Artwoods were a popular London club attraction and no doubt inspired many others to follow in their path. The group released several memorable singles containing a mixture of blues and R&B with elements of jazz, but their biggest stumbling block was their lack of original compositions (they opted instead to release numerous cover versions). In fact, the Artwoods are best remembered for band members who gained greater notoriety in other groups, among them Jon Lord (Deep Purple, Whitesnake) and Keef Hartley (John Mayall, Keef Hartley Band).

Arthur Wood (b. July 7, 1941; West Drayton, Middlesex, U.K.) began singing professionally in 1958 when he formed the nine-piece Art Wood Combo. The combo played a mixture of swing and R&B music, but Wood soon became more interested in blues music, particularly the kind played by Muddy Waters and Big Bill Broonzy. By early 1962, Wood was approached by Cyril Davies to join a band that he and Alexis Korner were forming—the seminal Blues Incorporated [see **Cyril Davies, Alexis Korner**]. Wood accepted the offer and became the group's initial lead vocalist. Blues Incorporated established a residency at London's Ealing Club and soon became a leading club attraction. Wood was supposedly the band's primary vocalist, but the group performed as a sort of R&B revue that allowed many singers to share the stage, including Long John Baldry, Paul Jones (later of Manfred Mann) and Cyril Davies. This wasn't what Wood was expecting, and so with fewer and fewer numbers to perform, he decided to leave Blues Incorporated after only a few weeks and reform the Art Wood Combo as a four-piece R&B outfit. Initially, Wood wanted to employ a variable lineup for live gigs, utilizing whomever was available, but when this proved unworkable, he sought musicians for a permanent backing band. In late 1963 he hooked up with a semiprofessional jazz/R&B quartet led by Don Wilson, consisting of Wilson (a.k.a. Red Bludd) on bass and vocals, Derek Griffiths (b. June 23, 1944; Torquay, Devon, U.K.) on guitar, Reg Dunnage on drums, and Jon Lord (b. June 9, 1941; Leicester, U.K.) on piano.

Lord, having taken ten years of piano lessons as a youngster, had wanted to become a classical pianist but changed his mind after hearing Jerry Lee Lewis's "Whole Lotta Shakin' Going On." By 1962 he was a member of the Bill Ashton Combo, a jazz group featuring tenor saxophonist Bill Ashton. He left the combo in 1963 to join Don Wilson's band, which occasionally performed R&B (as Red Bludd's Blusicians) at the Flamingo in central London and at U.S. airbases. More often, however, the quartet found themselves playing at weddings, bar mitzvahs and the like as the Don Wilson Quartet. With the addition of Wood, they renamed themselves the Art Wood Combo. After Lord switched from piano to the Lowry organ, the group sometimes billed themselves as the Great Organ-ised to capitalize on their use of the instrument.

Sadly, while returning home one night from a gig, the group's van crashed into the back of a truck, breaking both of Don Wilson's legs. Wilson recovered, but he was never able to resume his musical career. Although shattered by the accident, the group was determined to stay together. They found a replacement in bassist Malcolm Pool (b. January 10, 1944; Hayes, Middlesex, U.K.) from the Roadrunners.

In early 1964, the band, now with Pool, went into the studio to cut demos of "Kansas City" and "Talkin' 'Bout You" in the hope of landing a contract. Shortly after recording the demos, the band played at a club located in Acton, outer London called the George and Dragon. While at the gig, they were approached by Johnny Jones, a booking agent with the London City Agency. Jones signed them to a management contract and, shortly thereafter, arranged for a residency at London's 100 Club and a recording contract with Decca Records.

The change from semi-pro status to full-time musician was more than Reg Dunnage had bargained for, though, as he didn't want to give up his day job. He decided to leave the band, which quickly held auditions to find a replacement. One of the hopefuls was Mitch Mitchell, later the drummer for the Jimi Hendrix Experience, but his style was found to be unsuitable and the band instead selected Keef Hartley (b. April 8, 1944; Preston, Lancashire, U.K.) as their new drummer. Hartley hadn't started playing drums until age 18, which was the same year (1962) he moved from Preston to Liverpool and replaced Ringo Starr in the Mersey group, Rory Storm and the Hurricanes. After a stint with the Hurricanes, he next joined Freddie Starr and the Midnighters. With the change in drummer, the group also changed its name to the Artwoods at the urging of Decca's Mike Vernon.

That summer, the group recorded "Hoochie Coochie Man" as a possible single release, but the track was never issued. Instead, they released a powerful version of Leadbelly's "Sweet Mary" as their debut single in October 1964. To promote it, the band made their first appearance on the first live broadcast of *Ready, Steady, Go!* The single generated a lot of interest in the band and they were soon averaging six or seven gigs a week. "Sweet Mary" also brought session work offers for Lord, who participated in the recording of the Kinks' first album. Their growing reputation brought the band in contact with Little Walter and Bo Diddley, with Walter helping them gain credibility when he told *Record Mirror*, "Truthfully, I thought that white boys couldn't play the blues, but they were playing the hell out of the music. Them boys were as pure in the blues as many a Negro group back home."

When the Artwoods returned to the studio in January 1965 for their second single, they recorded another blues song, "Oh My Love," which largely went unnoticed. Despite both singles' lack of success, the band's popularity continued to increase in clubs, where they were becoming a strong attraction. "There's little we enjoy more," Wood explained to *Melody Maker*. "The clubs are where you make your name. Now, we get a good reception wherever we go, and if we get a hit record our prices will go up and we shall have to do more stage shows. But we shall always stick to the clubs. On the whole, they're a knockout."

Although they were being hailed as one of the more authentic R&B groups in Great Britain, Wood refused to be pigeonholed, explaining his approach to *Record Mirror:* "Most of them [the clubs] want something fresh and new. And we try to cater to them. We like authentic R&B but we also like playing everything and anything else."

With their popularity climbing, the Artwoods made another appearance on *Ready, Steady, Go!* and were featured on the radio shows *Saturday Swings* and *Easy Beat* and the television show *Beat Room*. In addition, the band backed U.S. blues singer Mae Mercer on her British tour, toured England with P.J. Proby and Europe with Petula Clark, and was invited to perform at the International Beat Festival in Monte Carlo, which was hosted by Princess Grace and Prince Rainier.

By early 1965 the band was moving away from the slow blues sound and was starting to incorporate more James Brown and Otis Redding-type soul into their repertoire. Derek Griffiths explained the group's change in direction to *Melody Maker:* "Six months ago we sat down and thought what we would do when R&B went out. We were about to go pro and thought we were going to be out of work soon. Now we realize we have changed with the trends. We've dropped the slow blues, the Jimmy Reed stuff, quite unconsciously."

Their third single, "Goodbye Sisters," was an upbeat R&B number released in August 1965. Despite Billy Fury's selecting it as the "Pick of the Week" for *Melody Maker*, this single, too, was commercially unsuccessful. The group was now desperate for a hit and was further disappointed when a proposal to tour the U.S. and record with Bo Diddley fell through because the deal would have required an American band to tour in the U.K. at the same time. When one could not be found, the trip was blocked by the Musicians' Union.

In early 1966, the Artwoods toured Poland in support of Billy J. Kramer and played a series of dates in France. They recorded four tracks, including instrumental covers of "A Taste of Honey," "Our Man Flint," "These Boots Are Made for Walkin'" and a forgettable original titled "Routine." These ill-advised tracks were issued as the EP *Jazz in Jeans.* The tracks were MOR fodder, totally unsuitable for the band, and the miscalculation severely damaged the band's R&B credibility.

Rebounding, their next single was a powerful version of Sam and Dave's "I Take What I Want," which finally gave the band a minor U.K. hit. *Melody Maker* praised the effort, writing, "Great guitar and plunging bass make for a very neat overall sound." *New Musical Express* was equally enthusiastic, proclaiming, "Hey, try and catch this one, it's great. A forceful up-tempo, mainly solo voice with organ, an insidious beat, electrifying guitar and some really great bass work. Spirited and dynamic, it's really got the message."

For concert appearances, Jon Lord switched to a Hammond B3 organ, which was cut in two for transportation purposes. Utilizing the new instrument, Lord planned to integrate his love for classical music into the group's sound, but the idea was never realized with the Artwoods. Lord would revisit the idea years later as a member of Deep Purple.

The group's fifth single, "I Feel Good," was released in August 1966. Distinguished by Derek Griffiths' distorted fuzz guitar, reviews were again positive with *New Musical Express* declaring, "This is great spine-tingling, pulse quickening R&B. It's strident, raucous and fast, but it has that authentic quality." In spite of such praise, the single failed to register on the charts.

Although the group had only achieved one minor hit, they continued to book increasingly better venues. On August 22, 1966, they made their first appearance at London's famed Marquee Club. This critical gig was reviewed by *Melody Maker's* chief reporter, Chris Welch, who praised the up-and-coming group: "One of the jazzier groups on the scene, the Artwoods scored heavily with the packed audience on numbers like 'Walk on the Wild Side,' featuring their excellent organist Jon Lord."

Unable to break through on the singles front, the group pinned their hopes on their debut long player. Unfortunately, they were unable to come up with any original material, something which was becoming increasingly frowned on by critics. Their debut, *Art Gallery,* was released in November 1966, but it didn't capture the excitement of the group's stage shows and received mixed reviews. *Record Mirror* noted tersely, "Most of the songs are slightly lesser known R&B songs, all of which have been performed better by the original artists." *Melody Maker,* however, was effusive, commenting, "On the evidence of this album, they have huge potentialities musically and commercially." The weekly music news-

paper then advised the band that they needed "somebody who can get down to the hard graft of creating images and selling the end product." Wood responded to the suggestion in a letter to *Melody Maker,* writing, "We think we do have an image, but not one that relies on psychedelic gimmicks, smoke-bombs and the rest. We like to think our image is one of a musically valid, exciting group that people know will produce a solid sound."

By the end of 1966, Decca, impatient for a hit record, dropped the Artwoods from the label. The group had recorded an album's worth of material under the working title *Zena's Twigs* with the assistance of Mike Vernon, Neil Slaven and Gus Dudgeon, but these tracks are still languishing in Decca's vaults.

The group quickly found another interested label and in January signed a one-off deal with Parlophone for a single, with an option for a second release. The strong resulting single, "What Shall I Do" backed with "In the Deep End," was released in April 1967. The Artwoods performed both tracks on a radio session for the *Wayne Fontana Show* (along with two other tracks, "Steady Getting It" and "Devil with a Blue Dress On/Good Golly Miss Molly"), but the single sold poorly and Parlophone elected not to exercise its option for a followup.

Disillusioned by their lack of success, Keef Hartley left the group in April of 1967. A new drummer, Colin Martin, replaced him and the group set out for a tour of Denmark. However, when they arrived in Copenhagen, they discovered that the tour was canceled. The promoter managed to put together some last minute engagements, but the group was becoming increasingly despondent.

In mid-1967, they announced a collaboration with German composer Hans Bregel that was to result in a joint December performance with the German Symphony Orchestra—only the project never materialized. Instead, the group entered into the final and most bizarre stage of their career after signing a recording contract with Fontana Records. Mindful of the public's current obsession with gangsters—resulting from the film success of *Bonnie and Clyde*—Fontana outfitted the group as gangsters, rechristening them the St. Valentine's Day Massacre, for a single release of "Brother Can You Spare a Dime?" (originally recorded by Bing Crosby in 1932). The group original on the flip side, "Al's Party," referred to Al Capone. While the single flopped in the U.K., the group was well received in the Scandinavian countries and subsequently toured there. However, because the single was ignored in their own homeland, the group decided to call it a day and disband.

Postscript

Art Wood went on to form the short-lived Quiet Melon in 1969, consisting of Kenny Jones, Ronnie Lane, Ian McLagan (ex-Small Faces), brother Ron Wood and Rod Stewart. This lineup only recorded three tracks and played a handful of gigs (with Kim Gardner replacing Ronnie Lane on bass) before Wood dropped out and the lineup reformed as the Faces. The tracks were issued on CD in 1995. Eventually, Wood quit the music business and became a graphic designer.

After leaving the Artwoods, Hartley was hired by John Mayall and played with the Bluesbreakers for a year. He later formed the Keef Hartley Band, issuing seven albums before rejoining Mayall's Bluesbreakers. In 1974, he and Derek Griffiths formed Dog Soldier, which issued one album in 1975.

Griffiths did some session work and joined the Mike Cotton Sound before reuniting with Hartley in Dog Soldier. He went on to form his own band, the GB Blues Company, and most recently was a member of the house band for *The Rocky Horror Show*.

Malcolm Pool joined the Don Partridge Band before retiring from music to pursue a career, like Wood, in graphic design.

Colin Martin became a BBC producer.

Following the demise of the Artwoods, Jon Lord put together an *ad hoc* studio group, the Santa Barbara Machine Head. It featured Ronnie Wood on guitar, Kim Gardner on bass, and drummer John "Twink" Alder. Three tracks were recorded and have appeared on numerous Immediate anthologies. Lord joined the Flowerpot Men for one tour following the hit single, "Let's Go to San Francisco." While a member of the Flowerpot Men, he met bassist Nick Simper and the two joined forces with guitarist Ritchie Blackmore in Roundabout, which evolved into Deep Purple. As a member of Deep Purple, and later Whitesnake, Lord found huge success.

Discography

Release Date	Title	Catalog Number

U.K. Singles

The Artwoods

1964	Sweet Mary/If I Ever Get My Hands on You	Decca F 12015
1965	Oh My Love/Big City	Decca F 12091
1965	Goodbye Sisters/She Knows What to Do	Decca F 12206
1966	I Take What I Want/I'm Looking for a Saxophonist Doubling French Horn Wearing Size 37 Boots	Decca F 12384
1966	I Feel Good/Molly Anderson's Cookery Book	Decca F 12465
1967	What Shall I Do/In the Deep End	Parlophone R 5590

The St. Valentines Day Massacre

1967	Brother Can You Spare a Dime?/Al's Party	Fontana TF 883

U.K. EPs

1966	*Jazz in Jeans*	Decca DFE 8654

These Boots Are Made for Walkin'/A Taste of Honey/Our Man Flint/Routine

U.K. Albums

1966	*Art Gallery*	Decca LK 4830

Can You Hear Me?/Down in the Valley/Things Get Better/Walk on the Wild Side/I Keep Forgetting/Keep Lookin'/One More Heartache/Work, Work, Work/Be My Lady/If You Gotta Make a Fool of Somebody/Stop and Think It Over/Don't Cry No More

1983	*100 Oxford Street*	Edsel 107

Sweet Mary/If I Ever Get My Hands on You/Goodbye Sisters/Oh My Love/I Take What I Want/Big City/She Knows What to Do/I'm Looking for a Saxophonist/Keep Lookin'/I Keep Forgettin'/I Feel Good/One More Heartache/Down in the Alley/Be My Lady/Stop and Think It Over/Don't Cry No More

1995	*The Artwoods*	Repertoire REP 4533 WP

Reissue of *Art Gallery* with the following bonus tracks: Sweet Mary/If I Ever Get My Hands on You/Goodbye Sisters/She Knows What to Do/I Take What I Want/I Feel Good/What Shall I Do/In the Deep End/These Boots Are Made for Walkin'/A Taste of Honey/Our Man Flint/Routine/Brother Can You Spare a Dime?/Al's Party

Bakerloo

Never a huge commercial success, Bakerloo was instead a "could have been great" band—could have been if they'd only stayed together after issuing their one and only critically well received album, *Bakerloo*. Now highly coveted among collectors, *Bakerloo* and their one single, "Driving BacHwards," were the band's only releases. Today the short-lived Bakerloo are remembered more for being the spawning ground of guitarist Dave "Clem" Clempson, who later played with Colosseum and Humble Pie.

Initially, the Bakerloo Blues Line trio was based in Tamworth, Staffordshire, U.K. Their repertoire was a hybrid of various forms of contemporary music. Lead guitarist Clempson described the band's sound to *Beat Instrumental:* "I suppose you could say we do about thirty percent of traditional blues in our repertoire; the rest is a mixture of all sorts of things: jazz, rock, and so on."

Clem Clempson (b. September 5, 1949; Tamworth, U.K.) started playing piano at age five and studied the instrument for ten years, even spending time at the Royal School of Music in Birmingham. Eventually, he became disenchanted with what he later described as the "lack of freedom and not being allowed to express myself" he felt at the Royal School. So he quit school and, inspired by Eric Clapton's work on the *Bluesbreakers with Eric Clapton* LP, turned to guitar at age 17. Bakerloo was formed in early 1968, with an original lineup consisting of Clem Clempson (guitar/vocals), John Hinch (drums) and a bassist by the name of Dave Mason (not Traffic's Dave Mason). Shortly after the group formed, Clempson and Hinch fired Mason and recruited bassist Terry Poole, whom Clempson had met in a Birmingham discotheque after the two discovered that they had the same taste in music. The fledgling band initially called themselves the Bakerloo Blues Line to reflect their blues-based repertoire, which included many Muddy Waters covers, but they quickly broadened their set to encompass jazz and pop influences.

Clempson explained these changes to *Melody Maker:* "As well as blues numbers, we do things like our own version of 'Eleanor Rigby' as well as more jazz-based numbers like Milt Jackson's 'Bag Groove' and Ray Charles's 'I Believe in My Soul.'"

The Bakerloo Blues Line's first big break came when they were spotted by manager Jim Simpson as they performed at a Birmingham-area battle of the bands. Simpson, a musician who played jazz trumpet, arranged for an agency contract with the Harold Davidson Organization in October 1968. With the powerful agency behind them, the group played at colleges and blues clubs across England and began playing every Tuesday evening at Henry's Blueshouse in Birmingham, Warwickshire, Henry's Blueshouse attracted such local blues enthusiasts as Spencer Davis, Cozy Powell, Robert Plant, John Bonham and Jeremy Spencer, who would regularly drop by and sit in. It was also one of the first venues that Led Zeppelin and Earth (pre-Black Sabbath) played at. The connection led to the Bakerloo Blues Line supporting Led Zeppelin the night the future superstars made their Marquee Club debut on October 18, 1968. That same month, the Bakerloo Blues Line gained additional exposure when they made a radio appearance on John Peel's influential *Top Gear* show. Not long after, Bakerloo made another Marquee appearance on November 26 supporting Jethro Tull. Clempson was later invited to a nearby pub and sounded out by Tull bassist Glenn Cornick about replacing departing guitarist Mick Abrahams in Jethro Tull, an offer Clempson declined.

While their fortunes were rising, the group experienced a rapid-fire turnover of drummers. First, John Hinch was replaced by Tony O'Reilly (formerly of the Kubas/Koobas) in December 1968. In January 1969, he was succeeded by Pete York (ex-Spencer Davis Group), who in February 1969 gave way to Poli Palmer (ex-Blossom Toes), who likewise only lasted a short while. The group had hoped to recruit Ian Wallace for the drum slot when Palmer left, but he was unavailable and they found Keith Baker instead.

By February 1969, the group had shortened their name to Bakerloo in an attempt to de-emphasize their association with traditional blues. The group also began touring as part of a package promoted as "Big Bear Ffolly." Organized by manager Jim Simpson, "Big Bear Ffolly" consisted of Bakerloo, Earth, Locomotive and Tea and Symphony. Although unsigned, the trio recorded their first album around this time, produced by Gus Dudgeon. Once completed, the band aimed to release the album under the label that offered them the best deal.

Harvest Records, a progressive subsidiary of EMI, won the bidding war and signed the band to a recording contract.

The group's debut single, "Driving BacHwards" backed with "Once Upon a Time," was issued in July with the release of a self-titled album following later in the year. Upon its release, the album received widespread accolades. *Melody Maker* called it "a praiseworthy set from this blues-based group which in fact covers a wide musical spectrum," while *Disc and Music Echo* observed, "Bakerloo, a progressive British group, has one foot in the blues scene, the other on the underground," and further singled out Dave Clempson's "superb guitar work."

Shortly after the album's release, the band broke up. Clempson rehearsed a new trio consisting of bassist Dave Pegg and drummer Cozy Powell and the trio played one or more gigs as Bakerloo; but when Clempson left to replace James Litherland in Colosseum, Bakerloo was history.

Postscript

Clem Clempson recorded two albums with Colosseum before joining Humble Pie in 1972. He remained with Humble Pie until 1975, recording four albums with the hard rock outfit. He also teamed up with former Uriah Heep vocalist David Byron in Rough Diamond, which released one album in 1977. Rough Diamond evolved into Champion in 1978 with the substitution of singer/songwriter Garry Bell for David Byron. Champion released one album in 1978. Clempson also did extensive session work for numerous artists—including Roger Daltrey, Jon Anderson and Dick Heckstall-Smith.

In January 1980, Clempson backed Cozy Powell on some BBC broadcasts with other musicians including Jack Bruce on bass. Later in the year, Clempson and Bruce toured with keyboardist/guitarist David Sancious and drummer Billy Cobham.

Following the breakup of Bakerloo, Baker and Poole formed May Blitz with guitarist/vocalist James Black. Both musicians departed before the group recorded their first album. Baker then joined Uriah Heep and appeared on their *Salisbury* album. Poole appeared on Graham Bond's *We Put Our Magick on You* LP.

Discography

Release Date	Title	Catalog Number

U.K. Singles

1969	Driving BacHwards/Once Upon a Time	Harvest HAR 5004

U.K. Albums

1969	*Bakerloo*	Harvest SHVL 762

Big Bear Folly/Bring It on Home/Driving BacHwards/Last Blues/Gang Bang/This Worried Feeling/Son of Moonshine

Miscellaneous U.K. Releases

1970	*Picnic*	Harvest SHSS 1/2

Compilation album including "This Worried Feeling" by Bakerloo.

Elvin Bishop

Irony or fate? Either way, it wasn't until the 1976 success of the pop hit "Fooled Around and Fell in Love" that Elvin Bishop (b. October 21, 1942)—one of the more prolific members of the seminal Paul Butterfield Blues Band—finally achieved mainstream success [see **Paul Butterfield**]. Guitarist/vocalist/songwriter Bishop is known for his good time music, an amalgam of down home blues, gospel, country and R&B. His keen sense of humor is reflected in the homespun wit of his lyrics, and he is recognized for his considerable skills as a slide guitarist. Bishop summed up his approach to music in a 1970 *Downbeat* article when he said, "The really hard thing in music, for getting yourself together these days when you are exposed to so many different kinds of music, is just taking parts of the different stuff that you hear and only keeping the part that applies to you personally. . . . When I sing a lot of times it comes out sounding more country than bluesish, because I don't try to sound like a Negro. It's just not me. Accepting yourself as you are, and getting it to sound good, too, is another big trip . . . and people can see that you are not shucking."

This native of Glendale, California, spent his early adolescence in Elliot, Iowa. When Elvin was twelve, the Bishop family relocated to Tulsa, Oklahoma where his family lived on a farm while he attended Will Rogers High School. After school, he worked in a restaurant where he met some black youths who turned him on to the blues and Nashville-based radio station WLAC. Exposed to such giants as Jimmy Reed, Percy Mayfield and Howlin' Wolf, Bishop bought a guitar and learned how to play songs by John Lee Hooker and Lightnin' Hopkins.

A bright student, Bishop was a National Merit Scholar. Following graduation from high school, he enrolled at the University of Chicago in 1960. The young guitarist was more excited by the thriving blues scene than by his English studies, and he soon met fellow blues enthusiast Paul Butterfield. The two jammed a lot and started performing as an acoustic blues duo at parties and cafes on the town's North Side. Bishop also played at the folk clubs near the university, both solo and with Butterfield. Along with blues material, his repertoire ranged from Johnny Cash's "Folsom Prison Blues" to tunes by bluegrass legends Flatt & Scruggs. He also played with several groups including Larry & the Crowd Chasers, the South Side Olympic Blues Team and the Salt & Pepper Shakers.

Chicago's South Side was also bustling with the blues, and Bishop frequented its clubs to see such legends as Little Walter, Muddy Waters, Magic Sam, Jimmy Reed and Otis Rush. In this charged atmosphere, Bishop strapped on an electric guitar and dug in himself. After some friends—including Little Smokey Smothers—helped him expand his skills by teaching him various other blues techniques, Bishop felt adept enough to perform on stage, and he played gigs with Junior Wells, Hound Dog Taylor and J.T. Brown. In addition, as he told *Hit Parader*, "I worked in a few rhythm and blues groups that occasionally had to do a few rock and roll tunes. I liked rock and roll to a certain extent, but not as much as I loved blues."

One day, Bishop happened on a pawn shop owned by Mike Bloomfield's uncle, in the North Side of Chicago. "He [Mike Bloomfield] worked in his uncle's pawn shop on Clark Street, I was looking for something for my guitar and I went in," Bishop told *Blues Revue*. "I was fooling with a guitar and he asked me if I liked blues. I said 'sure,' and he picked up the guitar and started playing some amazing stuff. It blew my mind." The two aspiring bluesmen exchanged playing techniques, which would be the start of many years of collaboration [see **Mike Bloomfield**].

Some time later, Bishop went to New York with a friend, but became sick and his "friend" took off with all the money, leaving him broke and alone. Staying in an unheated apartment in a Puerto Rican neighborhood, he survived on beans and bacon. When Bishop finally got well enough to seek work, he found an unusual job breaking toys for a department store so they could return the damaged merchandise to the manufacturer for credit.

Bishop eventually made his way back to Chicago where he got a job at a steel mill before becoming lead guitarist in a new band being formed by Butterfield. "When I got up with Butterfield in '64 he didn't have a band," Bishop told *Hit Parader*. "There was a band at the Blue Flame Lounge that included Smokey Smothers, who's a good guitar player. They had a loose arrangement. It was a revue type thing. They'd add different singers at different times and Paul was one of them. I was working in a steel mill at the time when Paul got an offer for a job at a place called Big John's. So I quit and we worked there for almost two years." While he was initially cast in the role of lead guitarist, he moved over to rhythm guitar when Mike Bloomfield was added to the group. Both guitarists appeared on two landmark albums together with Butterfield, *The Paul Butterfield Blues Band* (1965) and *East-West* (1966). For the third Butterfield LP, *The Resurrection of Pigboy Crabshaw* (1967), Bishop moved back into the lead guitar slot now vacated by Bloomfield. The album was in fact named after Elvin's alter ego, a country bumpkin persona. The fourth Butterfield album, *In My Own Dream* (1968), would be the guitarist's last with the group. Bishop recalled his time with Butterfield to *Blues Review*: "The best it ever sounded was when Butterfield was doing the 12-bar blues," he explained. "At some point it became too much of a democracy, where it spread out and lost character. I wanted to have more say. The only way to do that is to create your own situation."

After grinding it out for three and a half years, Bishop decided he wanted a break from touring and left Butterfield's band. At the time, he told *Rolling Stone* that he planned to return to Chicago to do a series of concerts and recordings with older, unheralded bluesmen; play some dates with a jazz quartet; and eventually form a new group. Instead, he moved to Mill Valley, just north of San Francisco, where he spent a year jamming with various musicians and writing new material. One gig at the famed Fillmore West featured Bishop filling in for Mike Bloomfield during a "Super Session" concert. Bishop's set included "No More Lonely Nights," which appeared on the subsequent LP, *The Live Adventures of Mike Bloomfield and Al Kooper.*

Bishop's initial stab at forming a band involved a female folk trio he had met previously while on tour with Butterfield in Boston. He brought the trio—Jo, Janice and Mary—back to San Francisco with the idea of forming a rhythm section to support the three singers. After many rehearsals, Janice and Mary became homesick and returned to Boston. Jo Baker stayed behind and eventually became Bishop's girlfriend.

By January 1969, the newly formed Elvin Bishop Band featured Bishop on guitar and vocals with Jack "Applejack" Walroth on harmonica, John Chambers on drums and Art Stavro on bass. The aforementioned Applejack was born in Michigan and had moved to Chicago in his teens. While in the Windy City, Applejack and Bishop had occasionally played together in some shows. San Francisco-born drummer John Chambers had a jazz background, performing with John Coltrane, Don Garrett and Dewey Redman. Chambers also played with the Mystic Knights, Linda Tillery and the Loading Zone, and the folk-rock group We Five. Bassist Art Stavro, a Seattle native, had moved with his family to San Francisco when he was two. He played trombone in elementary school but switched to bass in high school. Chambers attended the same school and Stavro would sometimes sit in with his group. Prior to joining the Bishop band, he played with Jimmy Witherspoon, Albert Collins, Barry Goldberg and the Harvey Mandel group [see **Barry Goldberg, Harvey Mandel**].

With his lineup solidified, Bishop signed with Bill Graham's new label, Fillmore Records. He was also represented by Graham's management and booking agency.

With the addition of organist Steve Miller and Alberto Gianquinto helping out on piano, the group recorded their self-titled debut in 1969. Hailing from Iowa, Miller was formerly a member of Linn County, with which he had released three albums: *Proud Flesh Soothseer* (1968), *Fever Shot* (1969) and *Till the Break of Dawn* (1970). Miller had been playing keyboards for about ten years and his main influences were Earl Hooker and Ray Charles.

The Elvin Bishop Group boasted mostly blues-oriented material with Bishop singing all lead vocals, except for J.B. Lenoir's "How Much More," where he shared the vocals with Jo Baker. Among the LP's highlights were "How Much More" and the driving instrumental, "Tulsa Shuffle." "Sweet Potato" found Bishop assuming his Pigboy Crabshaw alter ego to great comic effect in a tribute to a homely woman. Bishop's vocals had character but were limited in

range, resulting in an uneven album. The group was performing regularly in Bay Area blues clubs and did several dates at the Fillmore West and the Avalon.

Following the release of their debut album, organist Steve Miller recorded a solo album that included Bishop Band members, with a few exceptions. Stavro, who dropped out of the band, was replaced by Kip Maercklein. Applejack also exited the band and was replaced by vocalist Jo Baker in the spring of 1970.

For his next release, Bishop wanted to move away from the blues in favor of rock and soul. The result was 1970's *Feel It!* As he told *Rolling Stone*, "I'm much happier with the new album 'cause I got better singers in the group now. I do a couple of things a night just to make myself feel good, 'cause I really enjoy singing. There's a few things I can put across, in between blues and comedy. But I'm very limited vocally . . . I'm about the third vocalist in the band." *Feel It!* also included backing vocals from the Pointer Sisters, who for a time performed with Bishop's band before economics forced him to drop them from the act. "I started writing music that called for horn parts," Bishop explained to *Guitar Player*. "I couldn't afford both, so I had to let the sisters go."

Rolling Stone was unimpressed with *Feel It!*, though, noting, "More cuts like the brilliant 'So Fine' (that beats the Fiestas' version to hell) and 'Years Go Passing By' would move Elvin's group out of the 'soul' limbo it's stuck in on this album, and back into what they do so well—the blues."

Bishop's years with Fillmore were commercially unrewarding and when the label closed, he signed with Epic for one Delaney Bramlett-produced album, *Rock My Soul* (1972). More lineup changes ensued as drummer Bill Meeker replaced John Chambers and vocalist/harmonica player Perry Welsh came aboard. Despite the presence of several strong numbers, particularly the up-tempo "Rockbottom" with Jo Baker's vocals; the moody, instrumental "Last Mile"; and the gospel-tinged title track, the album was not successful. "I thought *Rock My Soul* was real good," Bishop later told *Guitar Player*. "Capricorn would have made that sell. But at Columbia they'd take a look at *Billboard* to see what was selling and try to push me in that direction." Bishop felt that Columbia "never knew exactly what to do with him," and with his commercial fortunes unchanged, he was without a recording contract by the end of 1973.

Postscript

A 1973 New Year's Eve concert at San Francisco's Winterland attended by Phil Walden, President of Capricorn Records, was a turning point for Bishop. Walden signed him to his label, and Bishop's Capricorn debut, *Let It Flow* (1974), reached #100 on the album charts. This effort, his strongest to date, included the single "Travelin' Shoes," which would become one of his best-loved songs and peak at #61 on the charts. Helping out on the album were Charlie Daniels, Dickey Betts, Steven Stills and Toy Caldwell of the Marshall Tucker Band. The core group now consisted of Bishop, Phil Aaberg on keyboards, Don Baldwin on drums, Michael Brooks on bass, John Verazza on guitar and vocalist Mickey Thomas. The followup, *Juke Joint Jump* (1975), was even more successful, reaching #46 on the album charts, thereby solidifying his growing success. Bishop's third album for Capricorn, *Struttin' My Stuff* (1976), was his biggest commercially, reaching #18. The album was bolstered by the inclusion of the smash single "Fooled Around and Fell in Love" featuring Thomas's distinctive tenor. The single became an FM radio staple and skyrocketed to #3 on the charts.

Bishop continued to achieve album success with the release of *Hometown Boy Makes Good!* (1976, U.S. #70) and *Live! Raisin' Hell* (1977, U.S. #38), at which point Thomas left the band for Jefferson Starship. Subsequent albums—including *Hog Heaven* (1978) and *The Best Of* (1979), his last for the soon-to-be bankrupt Capricorn—faltered.

Bishop started the 1980s with *Is You Is or Is You Ain't My Baby,* issued on the German label Line in 1981. Then, after a seven-year recording hiatus, he returned to his blues roots, signing with Alligator Records and releasing *Big Fun* in 1988 (with Dr. John). He released four subsequent albums on Alligator: *Don't Let the Bossman Get You Down* (1990), *Ace in the Hole* (1995), *The Skin I'm In* (1998) and *That's My Partner!* (2000, with Smokey Smothers).

Through the years, Elvin made guest appearances on numerous releases by other artists, including Clifton Chenier, John Lee Hooker and the Marshall Tucker Band.

Discography

Release Date	Title	Catalog Number

U.S. Singles

1970	So Fine/Sweet Potato	Fillmore 7002
1970	Don't Fight It, Feel It/Dolores Park	Fillmore 7003
1971	I Just Can't Go On/	Fillmore 7004
	Party Till the Cows Come Home	
1972	Holler and Shout/Rock My Soul	Epic 10926

U.S. Albums

1969 *The Elvin Bishop Group* Fillmore F-30001
The Things I Used to Do/Tulsa Shuffle/Sweet Potato/How Much More/Dad Gum Ya Hide/Boy/Honey Bee/Prisoner of Love

1970 *Feel It!* Fillmore Z-30239
Don't Fight It (Feel It)/I Just Can't Go On/So Good/Crazy 'Bout You, Baby/So Fine/Party Till the Cows Come Home/Hogbottom/Be with Me/As the Years Go Passing By

1972 *Rock My Soul* Epic 31563
Rock My Soul/Holler and Shout/Let It Shine/Don't Mind If I Do/Rock Bottom/Last Mile/Wings of a Bird/Have a Good Time/Old Man Trouble/Out Behind the Barn/Stomp

1972 *Crabshaw Rising (Best Of)* Epic 33693
Rock My Soul/So Fine/Holler and Shout/Hogbottom/Party Till the Cows Come Home/Don't Fight It (Feel It)/Stealin' Watermelons/Stomp/How Much More/Be with Me

Miscellaneous U.S. Releases

1969 *The Live Adventures of* Columbia
        Mike Bloomfield and Al Kooper Records KGP-6
Appears on "No More Lonely Nights."

1972 *Fillmore: The Last Days* (3 LP) Fillmore 31390
Includes "So Fine" and "Party Till the Cows Come Home" by the Elvin Bishop Group.

1993 *Rare Chicago Blues, 1962–1968* (CD) Bullseye Blues
        CD BB 9530
Includes Elvin Bishop on the following tracks: "So Glad You're Mine" (with James Cotton), "Diggin' My Potatoes" (with James Cotton and Paul Butterfield), and "Three Harp Boogie" (with James Cotton, Paul Butterfield and Billy Boy Arnold).

With James Cotton
1994 *3 Harp Boogie* Tomato 71662
Includes five tracks featuring Bishop, Paul Butterfield and Billy Boy Arnold recorded in 1963: "Jelly Jelly," "South Side Boogie," "So Glad You're Mine," "Good Time Charly" and "Diggin' My Potatoes."

U.K. Albums

1969	*The Elvin Bishop Group*	CBS 63910
1970	*Feel It!*	CBS 64180
1972	*Rock My Soul*	Epic 65295

Miscellaneous U.K. Releases

1972	*Fillmore: The Last Days* (3 LP)	Warner Brothers K 66013
1969	*The Live Adventures of Mike Bloomfield and Al Kooper*	CBS 66216

Black Cat Bones

Perhaps the best way to digest Black Cat Bones is with a pair of headphones and a personnel directory. Plagued by numerous member changes—only brothers Stuart (bass) and Derek (rhythm guitar) Brooks stayed on board for the entire ride—Black Cat Bones is most often remembered as the band that Paul Kossoff and Simon Kirke were in before the two formed Free. However, neither musician appears on the excellent *Barbed Wire Sandwich,* Black Cat Bones' lone recorded album.

Although the band was deep into the blues, by design it was never restricted to the genre. "We all have different tastes, though generally we go for guitarists like B.B. King and Buddy Guy, and singers like Muddy Waters or Junior Wells. Being in the blues field doesn't mean you can't change and progress," said then-vocalist Paul Tiller in a 1969 *Melody Maker* article.

The Brooks brothers formed Black Cat Bones in 1965, naming the group after the hoodoo charm immortalized in Willie Dixon's "Hoochie Coochie Man." In addition to the two siblings, the initial lineup consisted of schoolmate Terry Sparks (guitar) plus two musicians, singer Roger Brearton and drummer Mick Olive, found through ads in *Melody Maker.* Typical to many bands first starting out, the first gigs they played were to small audiences in nearby youth clubs.

By early 1967, the revolving door of personnel was in full swing: Derek Robinson had replaced Roger Brearton; Terry Sparks was supplanted by Roger Montgomery, who in turn was followed by Paul Kossoff (b. September 14, 1950; d. March 19, 1976); and Andy Berenius succeeded Mick Olive.

Kossoff's father was David Kossoff, an actor, writer and broadcaster. Paul heard the Shadows and became interested in the guitar at age nine. Although his parents provided classical training for six years, he was losing interest in playing until he saw John Mayall's Bluesbreakers perform in a London club with Eric Clapton. He was awe-struck by Clapton's style, a fascination that led to his interest in other blues artists, notably Peter Green, B.B. King and Freddie King. After leaving school, Kossoff worked briefly as a musical instrument salesman before joining Black Cat Bones in 1967.

Black Cat Bones played several times at the Eel Pie Island Hotel located on a small island ten miles southwest of central London, as well as at smaller clubs and pubs. More lineup changes were in store, however. First Frank Perry replaced Andy Berenius in early 1967. Perry (b. June 25, 1948; Hampstead, London, U.K.) had previously been a member of the R&B outfit Abstract Sound. Berenius went on to join the Wildflowers with Paul Rodgers (vocals), Bruce Thomas (bass) and Mickey Moody (guitar). Berenius introduced Kossoff to Rodgers, and together Kossoff and the Wildflowers actually played a couple of tunes at a North London blues club.

The second change occurred right before an important audition with Marquee manager John Gee. The band replaced vocalist Robinson with harpist/vocalist Paul Tiller. Tiller's selection wasn't unanimous, as he told *Ugly Things* magazine: "I discovered later after my successful audition . . . that lead guitarist Paul Kossoff had wanted his pal, Paul Rodgers, as vocalist, but was outvoted by the rest of the band." Tiller had spent the previous couple of years with an Enfield-based blues/jazz band, the Lost Souls.

After a successful audition at the Marquee, the band opened for Ten Years After on October 6, 1967, as part of the club's new Friday Blues Night [see **Ten Years After**]. Their first gig went well and the band was offered a Friday night residency, during which time they supported many of the biggest rock acts, including Fleetwood Mac, the Aynsley Dunbar Retaliation, Jethro Tull, the Nice, John Mayall and Rory Gallagher/Taste [see **Fleetwood Mac, Aynsley Dunbar Retaliation, John Mayall, Rory**

Gallagher]. The band also played regularly at nearby blues clubs and colleges.

In February 1968, Simon Kirke (b. July 28, 1949; Shrewsbury, U.K.) saw the band performing with Champion Jack Dupree at the Nag's Head pub in Battersea, Surrey. He was impressed with Kossoff's ability but didn't think much of drummer Perry. During a band break, Kirke went to the bar where Kossoff was having a drink and told the guitarist his thoughts. Kossoff mentioned that Perry was getting the sack that night, and auditions for a replacement would be held the next day. Kirke showed up and successfully auditioned. Perry speculated about his being asked to leave, stating, "I couldn't pare my drumming down enough to what they wanted."

However, Kirke's tenure in the new band was short-lived, as he and Kossoff ultimately decided to break away from Black Cat Bones. Kossoff again wanted Paul Rodgers on vocals. When he tried to find him, he learned that the Wildflowers had folded and Rodgers was playing with a band called Brown Sugar at the Fickle Pickle club in North London. Kirke finally located him and persuaded him to join his new group. With the addition of bassist Andy Fraser from John Mayall's Bluesbreakers, the band was complete. Their first rehearsal was on April 19, 1968, at the Blue Horizon Club. Among those present was Alexis Korner, who gave them the name Free and agreed to use them as his opening act.

On April 22, 1968, producer Mike Vernon used Stuart Brooks, Paul Kossoff and Simon Kirke to back Champion Jack Dupree for a Blue Horizon album, *When You Feel the Feeling You Was Feeling*.

Following the departure of Kossoff and Kirke, the remaining members of Black Cat Bones, Stuart and Derek Brooks and Paul Tiller, added guitarist Bob Weston and drummer Terry Simms. Weston had previously played with Giant Marrowfat, a band that also included saxophonist Lol Coxhill.

The new Black Cat Bones built up a strong local following while playing at the Marquee, Mothers, and other major blues venues in the U.K. In addition, the band backed Eddie Boyd on his tour of Great Britain before the group toured Germany and Scandinavia in their own right. This lineup recorded "The Warmth of the Day" for a souvenir album for the maiden voyage of the Queen Elizabeth II, but while *Beat Instrumental* reported that the group was planning to record their own album in late

1968/early 1969, the LP was not released until November 1969.

By the time the recording sessions for the LP materialized, more wholesale changes had occurred as Ken Felton replaced Terry Simms (who in turn was quickly replaced by Phil Lenoir), Brian Short replaced Paul Tiller on vocals, and Rod Price (b. November 22, 1947; Chiswick, U.K.) replaced Bob Weston on lead guitar.

Price's earliest musical influences were Big Bill Broonzy, Davey Graham, Robert Johnson and Muddy Waters (although sometime later the slide guitar work of Earl Hooker and Elmore James were sources of inspiration). He had previously been a member of Shakey Vick's Big City Blues Band and their offshoot, the Dynaflow Blues Band.

The resulting album, *Barbed Wire Sandwich,* was released on the Nova label, a subsidiary of Decca. However, by the time it hit the streets the U.K. blues boom had subsided and the record foundered on the public's disinterest. The LP was critically well received. *Disc and Music Echo* said that they played "with conviction and feeling" and *Record Mirror* observed, "Solid driving blues, largely on three chords, but the consistency doesn't flinch. It pounds with twelve bar imprudence and if that isn't enough, it comes in one of the most insidious yet exciting covers yet. Very demonic." High spots included a powerful cover of Arthur "Big Boy" Crudup's "Death Valley Blues," featuring stellar guitar work by Price; a haunting, acoustic version of Nina Simone's "Four Women"; and "Feelin' Good," another excellent number that alternated between acoustic and electric guitars and featured Steve Milliner on piano.

With *Barbed Wire Sandwich* unable to find an audience, the band was again rocked by personnel changes as Price, Short and Lenoir departed the band. As had become customary, the two Brooks brothers looked for replacements. They found their new lead vocalist, Pete Ross, through an ad in *Melody Maker*. Rod Price was replaced by Rod Davies, and drummer Ken Felton rejoined the band. Not surprisingly, this lineup was very short-lived.

Pete French quickly replaced Ross as vocalist early in 1970, as Ross couldn't accompany the group on a tour of Norway and Germany. French had been a member of the Brunning Sunflower Blues Band and appeared on their first album, *Bullen Street Blues* [see **Brunning Sunflower Blues Band**]. French recruited another member of the Brunning Sunflower Blues Band, guitarist Mick Halls, while drummer Keith Young replaced Felton. French and Halls began writing most of the material, which was moving toward a heavier sound. By mid- to late-1970, Black Cat Bones had evolved into "Leafhound." The Brooks brothers stayed with Leafhound for the recording of their only album, *Growers of Mushrooms,* which later became much sought after by hard rock collectors. Prior to the album's release, the Brooks brothers dropped out and were replaced by bassist Ron Thomas (later a member of the Heavy Metal Kids) before disbanding by late 1971.

Postscript

Stuart Brooks became a member of Pretty Things in November 1971, cutting *Freeway Madness* (1973) with the band [see **Pretty Things**].

After playing in the duo Loose Ends with Don Craine, Paul Tiller joined the reformed Downliners Sect as harpist in 1977, where he remains to this day [see **Downliners Sect**].

Both Paul Kossoff and Simon Kirke would find great success with Free, recording seven albums: *Tons of Sobs* (1968), *Free* (1969), *Fire and Water* (1970), *Highway* (1970), *Free Live* (1971), *Free at Last* (1972) and *Heartbreaker* (1973). Between Free's first breakup on May 9, 1971, and their final breakup in July 1973, Kossoff and Kirke formed a studio group with Tetsu Yamauchi and Rabbit Bundrick. The foursome released one album, *Kossoff, Kirke, Tetsu and Rabbit* (1971). Kossoff released a solo album, *Back Street Crawler,* in 1973, and with the group by the same name released two additional albums, *The Band Plays On* (1975) and *Second Avenue* (1976). Kossoff died of heart failure on March 19, 1976.

Following the breakup of Free, Kirke formed Bad Company with former Free vocalist Paul Rodgers. Together, they recorded numerous gold and platinum albums.

Following their departure from Black Cat Bones, Terry Simms and Bob Weston formed Ashkan, which released one album, *In From the Cold* (1970). Weston subsequently became a member of Long John Baldry's backing band before joining Fleetwood Mac in September 1972 [see **Fleetwood Mac**]. Weston stayed with Fleetwood Mac until mid-1973, appearing on *Penguin* and *Mystery to Me.*

Brian Short cut a solo album, *Anything for a Laugh* (1971). Andy Berenius changed his name to Louis Bore-

nius in the 1970s and went on to perform with Alexis Korner, Duffy Power, Stan Webb/Chicken Shack, Dick Heckstall-Smith and many others. His current group, Coup d'Etat released a CD of his original compositions, *Last of the Aztecs* (2000).

Frank Perry went on to play jazz-oriented free-form group improvisation and pioneered the creation of meditative music using Tibetan singing bowls and Eastern sacred percussion.

Rod Price linked up with ex-Savoy Brown members Dave Peverett, Roger Earl and Tony Stevens to form Foghat in December 1970 [see **Savoy Brown**]. As a member of Foghat, Price recorded ten albums before he left the group in November 1980: *Foghat* (1973), the similarly titled *Foghat* (1973, a.k.a. *Rock and Roll*), *Energized* (1974), *Rock and Roll Outlaws* (1974), *Fool for the City* (1975), *Night Shift* (1976), *Foghat Live* (1977), *Stone Blue* (1978), *Boogie Motel* (1979) and *Tight Shoes* (1980). All of the Foghat albums from the second release until *Stone Blue* achieved gold status with *Fool for the City* achieving platinum status and *Foghat Live* reaching double platinum. The original Foghat reformed in 1996 to record *Return of the Boogie Men* and *Road Cases* (1997).

Following the breakup of Leafhound, Peter French was briefly a member of Big Bertha until joining Atomic Rooster and appearing on their *In Hearing Of* LP (1971, U.S. #167, U.K. #18). French later became a member of Cactus, appearing on the album *Ot 'N' Sweaty* (1972, U.S. #162). After Cactus, he joined the German group Randy Pie, appearing on their *Fast Forward* album, and he released a 1978 solo album, *Ducks in Flight,* issued in Germany.

Discography

Release Date	Title	Catalog Number

U.K. Singles

With Champion Jack Dupree

1968	I Haven't Done No One No Harm[1]/ How Am I Doing It	Blue Horizon 57-3140

[1] Black Cat Bones appear on A-side only.

U.K. Albums

Black Cat Bones

1970	*Barbed Wire Sandwich*	Decca Nova SDN 15

Chauffeur/Death Valley Blues/Feelin' Good/Please Tell Me Baby/Coming Back/Save My Love/Four Women/Sylvester's Blues/Good Lookin' Woman

Miscellaneous U.K. Releases

With Champion Jack Dupree

1968	*When You Feel the Feeling You Was Feeling*	Blue Horizon 63206

See My Milk Cow/Mr. Dupree Blues/Yellow Pocohontas/Gutbucket Blues-Ugly Woman/Street Walking Woman/Income Tax/Roll On/I've Been Mistreated/A Racehorse Called Mae/My Home's in Hell

Blind Faith

When Blind Faith arrived on the music scene in 1969, it was heralded as a "supergroup," a term that over the years has come to symbolize huge individual talents that come together to create something extraordinary. Unfortunately, only rarely has it translated into a rewarding, cohesive whole, and without having had adequate time to nurture their own sound, Blind Faith never lived up to the tremendous expectations and hype thrust upon them. Despite a massively successful U.S. tour and LP, the Eric Clapton/Stevie Winwood-led quartet disintegrated within a year of its formation [see **Eric Clapton**].

Blind Faith's origins can be traced to the end of 1968 and the breakup of Cream and Traffic [see **Cream**]. Eric Clapton told *Melody Maker* writer Chris Welch earlier in the year that he would like to work with singer/instrumentalist Stevie Winwood, but believed Winwood was still committed to Traffic. Winwood (b. May 12, 1948; Birmingham, Warwickshire, U.K.) first gained recognition as a member of the Spencer Davis Group, where he was the organist/vocalist/cowriter behind such monster hits as "Gimme Some Lovin'" and "I'm a Man" in the mid-1960s. In 1967 he stunned the pop world by leaving the Spencer Davis Group to form Traffic, with which he recorded two albums (*Mr. Fantasy*, 1967, and *Traffic*, 1968) before the band's initial breakup. Winwood and Clapton had previously worked together in 1966 as the Powerhouse, a studio ensemble that recorded four tracks, three of which later appeared on the compilation album *What's Shakin'*, with Winwood adopting the pseudonym Steve Anglo for contractual reasons.

Surprisingly, Traffic disbanded in December 1968, and Welch started to ruminate about the possibility of a Winwood-Clapton hookup, predicting in the December 7, 1968, issue of *Melody Maker*, "There is a strong possibility they may get a group together, or at least record."

The rumors were confirmed in the December 21 issue of *Melody Maker*, which reported that Clapton and Winwood were planning to record an album in America along the lines of the highly successful *Super Session* LP that featured Al Kooper, Mike Bloomfield and Stephen Stills. Although the article went on to emphasize that "a permanent group will not be formed," Clapton and Winwood spent some time together at Clapton's country estate of Hurtwood Edge, which fueled further rumors. Early speculation had the pair rounded out by Stax's rhythm section of Donald "Duck" Dunn and Al Jackson, both members of Booker T. and the MGs.

After the two rehearsed for a couple of weeks, Ginger Baker dropped in and was invited to join. In an interview in the February 1, 1969, issue of *New Musical Express*, Clapton replied to a question about involving other musicians in his latest project by saying, "Well, Stevie obviously. But I don't know whether I'll be doing an album of mine, or an album of mine and Stevie, or just Stevie's album." In the same interview, Clapton said, "I'm kinda stuck for a rhythm section and my immediate reaction would be to call up Jack and Ginger because they are the only two that I am familiar with. But I don't know how Stevie would feel about that." Clapton even broached the idea of Cream reforming in nine months with the addition of Winwood.

By the first week of February, it was reported that Ginger Baker was now involved with the Clapton-Winwood group and that they had spent a week living and rehearsing at Winwood's Berkshire cottage. Clapton told *New Musical Express*, "Our first intention is to get an album together. That will give us something to work from and once this has been achieved, we'd hope to commence live performances within about a month."

In February, the group started work on their debut album at Morgan Studios in London, later using Olympic Studios under the production of Jimmy Miller. The music press reported that the as-yet-unnamed group was slated to make its live debut on Saturday, June 7, in an open-air concert in London's Hyde Park. In April, sources reported that the group had recorded enough material to fill two albums and that a tour of America was likely during June and

July. In a *Melody Maker* interview, Clapton explained how this group was completely unlike Cream: "Totally different. Steve is really the focal point. He needs a lot of encouragement. I don't know what the scene was with Traffic, but the last thing I want to do is put my songs onto Steve."

By now, offers for bookings were pouring in with the asking price reported to be $20,000 against percentages of each gate, making it a multimillion dollar tour. The group was invited to appear at the Newport Jazz Festival on July 4 and at the British National Jazz and Blues Festival at Sunbury on August 10.

Then in early May, the music papers reported that bass player/electric violinist Ric Grech (a.k.a. Rick Grech) had joined the group, which had finally found a name—"Blind Faith." They also announced that the release of the debut album was being held back to allow Grech to play on some of the tracks once he returned from a U.S. tour with the group Family. Grech (b. Richard Roman Grech, November 1, 1946, Bordeaux, Fr.; d. March 17, 1990, Leicester, U.K.) was born in war-torn France but grew up in Leicester, Lancashire in England. As a child, he studied the violin and played with the Leicester Youth Orchestra, and later, while attending an arts college, started to play the guitar. In 1962, he joined the Farinas, which changed their name to Family in 1967. While with Family, Grech appeared on their first two outstanding releases, *Music in a Doll's House* (1968) and *Family Entertainment* (1969).

On June 7, 1969, Blind Faith made their live debut in Hyde Park, London, before a crowd estimated at 100,000 to 150,000. The group performed nine songs in their set, including "Presence of the Lord" (a new Clapton original), a cover of Buddy Holly's "Well All Right," an unexpected rendition of "Under My Thumb," three Winwood originals, the Ginger Baker-penned "Do What You Like" and a cover of Sam Myers's "Sleeping in the Ground." While the band was well received by the crowd, their set was criticized in the press for Winwood's domination and their apparent lack of a musical compass. *Beat Instrumental* noted, "The music was watery, airy and pleasant but lacking a solid core that made Ginger Baker in particular seem uneasy," adding, "Much of the group's new material was mediocre and Stevie was not singing at his best." Clapton-supporter Chris Welch defended the band: "It's obviously too early to start making assessments of Blind Faith—there is so much more they are going to do. As Ginger Baker said at the beginning, 'This is the first

rehearsal.'" Clapton later admitted that after reading the negative comments in the press his instant reaction was, "Well, I'm not playing here anymore"—and in fact, they didn't.

Shaken by the ragged quality of their performance, the band embarked on a short Scandinavian tour over an eight-day period in early July before starting a two-month American tour accompanied by Delaney & Bonnie and Free. (Free was scheduled to leave the tour on July 13 and Taste took over through August 10. Three days later, Free was slated to rejoin the tour until its end.)

Their initial date in the U.S. at the Newport Jazz Festival was canceled because of riots in the city. Local authorities revoked the permission for Blind Faith and Led Zeppelin to appear at the prestigious jazz festival "in the interest of public safety"—although Led Zeppelin appeared anyway in spite of the ban.

Skipping Newport, Blind Faith instead made their much-anticipated U.S. debut on July 12 at Madison Square Garden in New York before 23,000 fans. The restless crowd became violent, rioting for 45 minutes as fans rushed the stage before being physically repelled by the police. A spokesperson for the arena observed, "We have had nothing quite like this before. It was a miracle no one was hurt seriously." Robert Christgau, writing for *The New York Times,* labeled the show "a disaster" and blamed "the poor acoustics which hindered their performance," adding, "What could be heard of the music was disappointing."

The group continued on through the U.S. and Canada in support of a self-titled debut album that was issued in the U.S. in July and in the U.K. the following month. The album sparked controversy, however, with its cover depicting a topless, pubescent girl holding an airplane that some described as overtly phallic. American dealers refused to stock the release, forcing an alternative cover featuring the group posed in a rehearsal room. In spite of the controversy—or because of it—the album generated 250,000 advance sales in the U.S. and quickly ascended to the top spot on both sides of the Atlantic. The record contained only six songs, with Baker's "Do What You Like" clocking in at over 15 minutes. Highlights included Clapton's spiritually tinged "Presence of the Lord," Winwood's "Sea of Joy," and his dreamily intoxicating "Can't Find My Way Home."

The reviews were mixed. *Record Mirror* opined, "The overall sound isn't distinctive or original—the combination hasn't formed anything distinctly new—but the overall sound is perhaps better than this type of thing has ever been done before." *Melody Maker* assessed the album as a "beautiful set to put an end to doubts as to whether Blind Faith was such a good idea after all," while *Rolling Stone* only offered, "This is a decent, listenable album—I repeat, a decent album, but by no stretch of the imagination a great album."

The group concluded their U.S. tour on August 24 in Hawaii. They then made plans for a major European tour, but the schedule was scrapped shortly before a September interview in which Clapton told *New Musical Express,* "Stevie's going to do something on his own and I will do something on my own. I am inclined to say, 'Well that was THE Blind Faith tour.' We may come together again with maybe a different name."

Rumors about the band's splitting up were beginning to circulate. First their manager, Robert Stigwood, denied that Ginger Baker would be replaced by former Traffic drummer Jim Capaldi, but then Clapton himself confirmed to *Disc and Music Echo* that Blind Faith had indeed broken up. Later in September, *Disc and Music Echo* suggested that Clapton was joining Winwood, Jim Capaldi and Chris Wood in yet another group (quickly denied by Clapton's management).

Ultimately, Clapton blamed the collapse of Blind Faith on unrealistic expectations: "Instead of being able to quietly build up from scratch they already expected the ultimate from us. When anything went wrong, when some nights the whole thing didn't gel, as it often doesn't on tour, the audience felt as though we'd let them down." Clapton later told *Melody Maker*, "We were pushed to the forefront without being ready for it. I still haven't recovered from the States. I felt quite ashamed and embarrassed on that tour."

The fallout continued through November when Clapton told *Record Mirror,* "I'm not sure what is going to happen now. No one has called me since the American tour, and I don't know whether to take that as an indication that we are not going to work again or not. If someone rings me and says we have a session, I will probably go but I'm not taking it upon myself to get things together."

The phone call never came.

Postscript

In late November, Ginger Baker formed Airforce with Grech and Winwood. Grech and Winwood appeared on the first Airforce album and Grech participated in *Airforce 2* (1970).

Winwood continued to work on a solo album that became the classic Traffic album, *John Barleycorn Must Die*. He enjoyed a prolific and successful career as a member of Traffic, in collaborations with Stomu Yamash'ta and Klaus Schulze and as a solo artist. Winwood reunited with Eric Clapton a few years later for the comeback concerts in 1973 that became the *Rainbow Concert* album.

In October 1969, Grech began work on his first solo album with assistance from the other three members of Blind Faith plus Denny Laine, Graham Bond and George Harrison. Chris Welch attended a session and wrote in the November 8, 1969, issue of *Melody Maker* that Grech seemed "unenthusiastic, unsure of himself and unable to give much clue to the direction he and his fellow musicians are headed." Preliminary reports in the February 1970 issue of *Melody Maker* about a March release date turned out to be false, as the album was never issued.

Grech joined a reunited Traffic for two subsequent releases, *Welcome to the Canteen* (1971) and *The Low Spark of High Heeled Boys* (1971). In 1972, Grech coproduced Gram Parson's first solo album, *GP*. Like Winwood, he also reunited with Clapton for the *Rainbow Concert* comeback engagement (1973). During the same year, he joined the Crickets for *Remnants* (1973), *Bubblegum, Pop, Ballads & Boogie* (1973) and *Long Way from Lubbock* (1974).

Ironically, Grech's last flirtation with the big time occurred in 1975 with the offer to join another "supergroup" featuring Mike Bloomfield (guitar) [see **Mike Bloomfield**], Barry Goldberg (keyboards) [see **Barry Goldberg**], Carmine Appice (drums, ex-Vanilla Fudge) and the relatively unknown Ray Kennedy (vocals). They called themselves KGB and issued one album by that name before Grech and Bloomfield both departed. After leaving the music business, Grech became a carpet salesman in Leicester. Suffering from liver and kidney failure following a brain hemorrhage, he passed away in 1990.

See section on Eric Clapton for his subsequent activity.

Discography

Release Date	Title	Catalog Number

U.S. Albums

1969 *Blind Faith* — Atco 33 304
Had to Cry Today/Can't Find My Way Home/Well All Right/Presence of the Lord/Sea of Joy/Do What You Like

2001 *Blind Faith* (2 CD Deluxe Edition) — Polydor 314 549 529-2
Had to Cry Today/Can't Find My Way Home/Well All Right/Presence of the Lord/Sea of Joy/Do What You Like/Sleeping in the Ground (previously unreleased mix)/Can't Find My Way Home (electric version, previously unreleased mix)/Acoustic Jam (previously unreleased)/Time Winds (previously unreleased)/Sleeping in the Ground (slow blues version, previously unreleased)/Jam No.1: Very Long & Good Jam (previously unreleased)/Jam No.2: Slow Jam #1 (previously unreleased)/Jam No.3: Change of Address Jam (previously unreleased)/Jam No.4: Slow Jam #2 (previously unreleased)

Eric Clapton
1988 *Crossroads* (4 CD) — Polydor 835 261-2
Includes one non-album track, "Sleeping in the Ground," plus "Presence of the Lord" and "Can't Find My Way Home."

Steve Winwood
1995 *The Finer Things* (4 CD) — Island 314516860-2
Includes three non-album tracks: "Can't Find My Way Home (electric version) and two tracks recorded live at Hyde Park, June 1969 ("Sleeping in the Ground" and "Under My Thumb"). Also contains two album tracks ("Had to Cry Today" and "Sea of Joy").

U.K. Singles

1969 Untitled Instrumental — Island promo

U.K. Albums

1969 *Blind Faith* — Polydor 583 059

Eric Clapton
1988 *Crossroads* — Polydor 835 261-1

Steve Winwood
1995 *The Finer Things* (4 CD) — Island 314516860-2

Mike Bloomfield

Michael Bernard Bloomfield was the first American guitar hero. With a versatile touch and tremendous depth of feeling, Bloomfield (b. July 28, 1943, Chicago, Illinois; d. February 15, 1981, San Francisco, California) played a gritty, intense and authoritative style previously not heard in popular music. Whether working with his own ensembles or with Bob Dylan, the Paul Butterfield Blues Band, the Electric Flag or Al Kooper, the axman's contributions were always pivotal. In 1967, *Hit Parader* magazine proclaimed, "Currently Mike is the most influential guitarist in pop music as evidenced by the hundreds of lead guitarists in minor bands learning from him." Remembered for the emotional peaks of his performances and for his ability to assimilate the nuances of a musical genre previously the exclusive province of Black Americans (which earned him the respect of the masters of the idiom), the charismatic guitarist was also an innovator who, as a member of the Butterfield Band, pushed the boundaries of blues music.

Bloomfield once described his playing philosophy to Don DeMicheal of *Downbeat* magazine: "You must play your music as musically as possible. Every note must be related to another note, not only harmonically, not only logically, not only tone-wise, but in timbre, attack—one note soft, one note a little louder, and it all must make sense within the framework of the genre, the framework of your own playing. I hope that I'm doing that all the time now. I know I'm trying to."

Bloomfield was the son of a wealthy businessman whose career plans for his elder boy were never realized. Ever since receiving a transistor radio at his bar mitzvah, Bloomfield had had aspirations other than taking over the family-owned restaurant supply company. The radio changed his life as he listened to influential rock'n'roll artists of the late 1950s, such as Chuck Berry and Little Richard. Equally inspiring were blues artists who regularly played on Chicago's South Side, including such monster players as Muddy Waters, Little Walter and Howlin' Wolf.

Rejecting his father's desire for him to participate in sports and excel in academics, Bloomfield instead immersed himself in the authentic recordings of Sonny Terry, Brownie McGhee, Lightnin' Hopkins, Muddy Waters and John Lee Hooker. He started playing guitar at 13 and two years later was working at a club called PG's Club 7 with a band that included harpist Jim Schwall (who would later form the Siegel-Schwall Band) [see **Siegel-Schwall Band**].

At age 14, Bloomfield and his friend Roy Ruby went to "The Place," a club located at 63rd and St. Lawrence on Chicago's South Side. Guitar Junior was the draw, but it happened to be "audition night," so Bloomfield climbed onstage and was allowed to sit in with the band. The experience hooked him. Soon he was routinely taking the "L" to South Side blues clubs to watch and learn from Elmore James, Sonny Boy Williamson, Little Walter, Howlin' Wolf, Freddy King, Albert King, Lowell Fulson, Jimmy Rogers, Otis Spann and others. With such major blues labels as Chess, Vee Jay and Cobra based in Chicago's South Side, and with the numerous blues clubs catering to black audiences, the area was an electrifying hub of musical activity. The shows there made an indelible impression on the teenage Bloomfield, as he related to *Hit Parader* years later: "I really learned. Blues is just not notes. It's a whole environmental thing with nuances of song, speech and the whole personality of the people involved. It makes me feel good to understand it. It's a personal thing. I have personal attachment to the music. It's absolutely part of me."

At 18, Bloomfield temporarily favored the acoustic over the electric guitar and started concentrating on folk music, even playing with bluegrass bands where he expanded his playing technique. As his interest in blues music intensified, he became an amateur musicologist, seeking out the earlier blues artists who were still alive. He approached the owner of a floundering coffeehouse, the Fickle Pickle, and asked that he be allowed as manager to turn the place into a blues club. With interest in the blues growing, the Fickle Pickle became a popular nightclub under his guidance. Every Tuesday night, Bloomfield booked available blues artists, including Muddy Waters, Sleepy John Estes, Yank Rachell, Little Brother Montgomery and Big Joe Williams, among others, often backing them on the piano. Big Joe Williams, with whom he became especially close, later became the topic of Bloomfield's short story, *Me and Big Joe*.

Bloomfield later took up residency at Big John's, a Wells Street bar located on Chicago's Near North Side, with a band that included Big Joe Williams and harpist Charlie Musselwhite [see **Charlie Musselwhite**]. The weekend gigs proved so successful that the trio became the house band. After a short time, Williams decided to leave, so Bloomfield switched to guitar and recruited other musicians. They began calling themselves "The Group." Bloomfield and Musselwhite were the only permanent fixtures in the Group, which also included, at times, Norman Mayell on drums; Bob Wolff, Roy Ruby or Sid Warner on bass; Gaptooth Labansky or Mike Johnson on guitar; and Brian Friedman on piano. Others would occasionally sit in, including Paul Butterfield. Big John's became so successful with Bloomfield and Musselwhite that its owners were persuaded to bring in more blues acts from the South and West Sides—Muddy Waters, Howlin' Wolf, Magic Sam, Otis Rush and other black artists, some of whom were performing before predominantly white audiences for the first time. Pete Welding of *Downbeat* reviewed a Group performance at Big John's: "This group has rapidly evolved into one of the finest, fiercest-swinging rhythm-and-blues combinations in Chicago." Welding then described Bloomfield's strengths: "Bloomfield apparently has no limitations within the confines of blues guitar. He offers fleet, supercharged, modern R&B guitar pyrotechnics with the same ease with which he re-creates the insinuating, vigorous bottleneck style of Muddy Waters." He further observed that Bloomfield had a tendency to overplay and that he was not much of a singer. Several songs recorded at Big John's on October 15, 1964, were issued as a CD accompanying the 2000 oral history *Michael Bloomfield: If You Love These Blues*.

Bloomfield stayed with Big John's for about a year, but also found work playing in topless clubs with organ player Barry Goldberg and at Delmark sessions that produced albums by Yank Rachell *(Mandolin Blues)* and Sleepy John Estes *(Broke and Hungry, Ragged and Dirty Too)*.

During this time, Bloomfield also played on a demo by some long-since-forgotten singer that fortuitously came to the attention of record executive John Hammond, Sr. Hammond recognized the talent of the young guitar player in the background and flew to Chicago to investigate. He tracked Bloomfield down and after hearing him perform, made arrangements for Columbia Records to sign him.

The Bloomfield band recorded at least five songs with Columbia while they were holding down the gig at Big John's. In addition to Musselwhite and Mayell, the band featured Johnson, Warner, and Brian Friedman, with Bloomfield handling lead guitar and vocals. Of the tracks recorded, "Last Night" and "Goin' Down Slow" were soulful, hard-edged blues finding Bloomfield in top form. The tracks were released as part of the CD career retrospective, *Mike Bloomfield: Essential Blues*. After the sessions, Bloomfield asked the owner of Big John's for a raise and was promptly replaced by Paul Butterfield.

Meanwhile, Bloomfield formed a new six-piece band that included Musselwhite and Nick Gravenites. Together they played at clubs around Chicago, but were unable to establish themselves. Through happenstance, Bloomfield ended up as a member of Butterfield's band. "I was playing on the North Side with a blues band, Paul was with an all black blues band [The Little Smokey Smothers Revue] on the South Side," Bloomfield later explained to *Downbeat*. "He would come in and sing with me in Big John's, which was in this kind of Haight-Ashbury of Chicago at the time. Then I had a chance to go to this other club which was farther up north and had more bread, so I asked Paul if he wanted to take my gig. I always hated his guts and he hated mine. He got a really good band together and when they hit they were like dynamite and it was the best band I had ever seen at that time. And so we both played in our respective clubs for a little under a year and then a guy from Elektra records [Paul Rothchild] asked Paul if he wanted to make a record and Paul asked me if I wanted to play a little slide for him. I admired Paul incredibly for his singing and his music but I never liked him, so I was kind of reluctant to do it." During the sessions, Bloomfield was persuaded to become a permanent member. As part of the Paul Butterfield Blues Band, Bloomfield recorded two albums, the seminal *Paul Butterfield Blues Band* (1965) and the forward-looking *East-West* (1966).

During his tenure with Butterfield, Bloomfield also played on recording sessions backing up John Hammond, Jr.; Peter, Paul and Mary; the Chicago Loop (which included old friend Barry Goldberg) and, most significantly, Bob Dylan. Bloomfield had first met Dylan in 1963 when the folk singer was appearing at the Bear, a Chicago club. Dylan invited Bloomfield to meet him in Woodstock, New York, where they went over a few new songs before flying to New York City to record three songs—among them the epochal "Like a Rolling Stone"—on June 15, 1965. In between sessions with Dylan, Bloomfield appeared at the Newport Folk Festival with both the Paul Butterfield Blues Band and Dylan's electric backing band. Following the Butterfield Band's appearance at a Saturday afternoon blues workshop on July 24, 1965,

Bloomfield—along with Sam Lay and Jerome Arnold from the Butterfield Band plus Al Kooper and Barry Goldberg—performed with Dylan.

Bloomfield returned to the studio to take part in additional sessions with Dylan on July 29–30 and August 2 for what would become the legendary *Highway 61 Revisited* album and the "Positively Fourth Street" single. His contributions to the sessions were considered so immense that he was asked to join Dylan's band for an upcoming tour. Bloomfield declined, so Dylan hired Robbie Robertson to play guitar.

In 1967, Bloomfield left the Butterfield band to form the Electric Flag [see **Electric Flag**]. He explained his reasons for the move to *Rolling Stone:* "I was with Butter [Paul Butterfield] and I flipped out and went crazy. I didn't dig anything. Elvin [Bishop] was really dragged, he wanted to play lead. He was tired of playing second guitar. I felt it was being shitty and that was a drag. So I quit Butter, hacked around for a while and that was more of a drag. I wanted to get a band of my own. Always wanted to and so me and Barry Goldberg put a band together." While with the Electric Flag, Bloomfield wrote the score to the movie *The Trip* and recorded one album, *A Long Time Comin'* (1967). However, conflicts within the group and his aversion to touring led him to quit after only a year.

Following the Electric Flag, Al Kooper approached Bloomfield with an offer to take part in a structured jam album, inspired by jam sessions the two had previously participated in that were issued as *Grape Jam*, the bonus LP to Moby Grape's second album, *Wow*. Kooper was a former member of the Blues Project [see **Blues Project**] and the founder of Blood, Sweat and Tears. Bloomfield was reluctant to make the record as he later recounted to *Guitar Player:* "I didn't want to make that record [*Super Session*] too much. It was just a favor for Al Kooper and he said we'll make a lot of bread out of it and subsequently he was absolutely right. It made a million."

Rounding out the sessions were drummer Eddie Hoh (a member of the Mamas and the Papas), bassist Harvey Brooks and pianist Barry Goldberg on two tracks. Both Brooks and Goldberg had been members of the Electric Flag. The makeshift band recorded several songs in a marathon nine-hour session, including a cover of Curtis Mayfield's "Man's Temptation"; a Jerry Ragovoy/Mort Shuman composition, "Stop"; and a Kooper/Bloomfield-penned, slow-burning blues instrumental, "Albert's

Shuffle." The next day, Kooper awoke to discover that Bloomfield had gone home, plagued by insomnia. With the studio time already allocated, Kooper then called every West Coast guitar player he knew to join the sessions, including Steve Miller, Randy California, Jerry Garcia and Stephen Stills. Only Stills accepted, recording several tracks—including a cover of Donovan's "Season of the Witch"—that would become side two of the album. Kooper dubbed horns onto the album while mixing the tapes in New York. *Super Session* became a surprise hit, reaching #12 on the charts and earning Bloomfield his only gold album.

Rolling Stone singled out Bloomfield's contribution for praise, noting, "The Bloomfield side is particularly excellent. Michael is heard playing better than one can hear him on records ever since the early Butterfield recordings. There is a firmness, a real steady handedness, a determinedly sure feeling as to what he puts out here . . . 'Stop' features this new Bloomfield, full-blown phrases pouring out miles of tough intricate patterns. Mike handles this track-length solo with a rare tone of surefire authority." Yet in spite of the album's popularity, Bloomfield viewed it as a scam. As Kooper explained to the *Bloomfield Notes* newsletter, "I think he was embarrassed by it. Not playing-wise, but success-wise. He just wanted to be in a certain niche, and anything above that niche really embarrassed him."

Following the success of *Super Session*, Kooper was able to persuade Bloomfield to record another album staged at the Fillmore West. John Kahn was brought in to play bass and Skip Prokop (formerly with the Canadian group the Paupers) was added on drums. Three nights in September 1968 were booked at the Fillmore West and the band rehearsed for five days prior to the performance. The first two nights of the concerts went well, with the band covering a wide range of songs, including Traffic's spacey "Dear Mr. Fantasy," Paul Simon's breezy "The 59th Street Bridge Song (Feelin' Groovy)," the Band's rootsy "The Weight," Arthur Crudup's "That's All Right Mama" and Booker T. and the MGs' classic instrumental "Green Onions."

On the morning of the third show, Kooper received a phone call from Bloomfield's wife informing him that her husband had checked himself into Ross General Hospital for insomnia. Frantically, Kooper once again called all the local guitarists he knew, eventually persuading Steve Miller, Elvin Bishop and Carlos Santana to pinch-hit during that night's concert. Each of the gui-

tarists did three or four songs. Enough material was recorded to form the double album *The Live Adventures of Mike Bloomfield and Al Kooper* (1969). While permission could not be obtained from Capitol to use Steve Miller's contribution, Elvin Bishop and the then-unsigned Carlos Santana were represented by one track apiece. The album jacket featured a specially commissioned portrait of Kooper and Bloomfield painted by Norman Rockwell, who first photographed the pair at the CBS offices and then painted from the photograph at his home. *The Live Adventures of Mike Bloomfield and Al Kooper* gave Mike Bloomfield another hit album. It reached #18 on the charts, the last time his name would grace the Top 40.

Toward the end of the year, Janis Joplin's manager, Albert Grossman, asked Bloomfield and Nick Gravenites to oversee rehearsals for a new band that had been put together for her. Grossman's decision to debut the band at the Memphis Stax/Volt "Yuletide Thing" on December 21, 1968, was a strategic mistake that ended in disaster. *Rolling Stone* reported, "Janis Joplin died in Memphis, but it wasn't her fault," blaming the poorly rehearsed band on Bloomfield and observing that the band "can all play, but not blues, and who is there to teach them? Certainly not Mike Bloomfield, whose music, like Paul Butterfield's, is a pastiche of incompatible styles."

In January and February of 1969, Bloomfield—with a core band of Nick Gravenites on vocals, Mark Naftalin on piano, Ira Kamin on organ, John Kahn on bass and Bob Jones on drums (plus a horn section)—recorded *Live at Bill Graham's Fillmore West*. The work was basically another jam album that attempted to duplicate the formula and success of the earlier *Super Session* and *The Live Adventures of Mike Bloomfield and Al Kooper* albums. The album split the vocals among Bloomfield, Gravenites, Jones and Taj Mahal, who sang on one track [see **Taj Mahal**]. Curiously, the best songs performed at these shows did not appear on this release but on a subsequent solo album by Nick Gravenites, *My Labors*. Gravenites had already recorded half his album in the studio and, feeling that the material left over from *Live at Bill Graham's Fillmore West* was better than what was issued, he offered to split the recording cost if he could use the tracks on his solo LP. Of the five Fillmore West tracks appearing on *My Labors*, "Gypsy Good Time" and "Moon Tune" found Bloomfield in particularly good form.

Bloomfield next reunited with Paul Butterfield and Sam Lay in studio and live recordings backing Muddy

Waters. Studio sessions for the album were held on April 21–23, 1969, while the concert took place on April 24 at the Super Cosmic Joy-Scout Jamboree in Chicago. The double LP, *Father and Sons* (1969), peaked on the U.S. charts at #70. In July, Bloomfield temporarily filled in for Canned Heat guitarist Henry Vestine, who had quit the band after a falling-out with bassist Larry Taylor. Bloomfield played one set and was asked to join permanently, but he declined and Harvey Mandel filled the position instead [see **Harvey Mandel**].

In October, Bloomfield released his own solo album, *It's Not Killing Me*, which he later admitted was "pretty bad." *Rolling Stone* savaged the release, describing his playing as a "specimen of boring exhibitionism," and further quipping, "Bloomfield's singing should never have been released—he has a terrible voice." That same month, Janis Joplin's new album, *I Got Dem Ol' Kosmic Blues Again Mama!*, featured Bloomfield's guitar-playing on four tracks, including a Nick Gravenites song titled "Work Me Lord."

Bloomfield also found time to take part in sessions as a sideman. He contributed to a pair of Barry Goldberg albums released in 1969, *Two Jews Blues* and *Barry Goldberg and Friends*. On *Two Jews Blues*, the title suggests a collaboration with fellow Jew Bloomfield, but Bloomfield in fact contributed to just four songs and went uncredited for contractual reasons. The guitarist's work is best heard on the instrumentals "Maxwell Street Shuffle" and "Blues for Barry And." Bloomfield contributed five tracks to *Barry Goldberg and Friends* and also helped out his former colleague in the Butterfield band, Sam Lay, on his solo album, *Sam Lay in Bluesland* (1970). Bloomfield also coproduced two James Cotton albums, *James Cotton* (coproduced with Barry Goldberg and Norman Dayron) and *Cotton in Your Ears* (coproduced with Elliot Mazer), released in 1968 and 1969, respectively, as well as the 1969 Otis Rush album *Mourning in the Morning* (coproduced with Nick Gravenites).

Bloomfield kept a low profile after 1969. After the Fillmore appearances, he stopped playing in large venues, preferring smaller clubs. In 1970, he made infrequent appearances at local clubs and disbanded his group, telling *Rolling Stone,* "I don't know, I just don't know. I just can't do it. The whole commercial music scene really has me down. I don't see any gigs worth playing. Festivals, ballrooms, they're all so packed. Even clubs are getting all crowded."

In 1971, he told *Guitar Player* that he was cutting an album with Mark Naftalin and hoping to "make this my best guitar playing record of all." Later, he admitted that they had "jacked around in the studio for six weeks or so and didn't come up with anything."

Limited to session work with Woody Herman, Beaver & Krause, Tim Davis and Millie Foster, Bloomfield's recording activity became more obscure over the next couple of years.

Postscript

Bloomfield avoided the spotlight in the seventies, preferring to play low-key gigs in the San Francisco area as Bloomfield and Friends, which included Mark Naftalin and Nick Gravenites.

In 1972, he took part in sessions with other San Francisco Bay Area musicians (including Naftalin and Gravenites) that produced tracks released as *Casting Pearls* by the Mill Valley Bunch. A year later, he appeared on *Triumvirate*, which teamed him up with John Paul Hammond and Dr. John (Mac Rebennack) (U.S. #105).

Bloomfield's last scheduled album for Columbia, *Try It Before You Buy It*, was never released on that label due to poor sales of his first solo album. (It was eventually released as intended on a 1990 CD issued by One Way). In 1974, an Electric Flag reunion produced one album, *The Band Kept Playing.* Bloomfield's last shot at commercial stardom occurred in 1975 when he was coaxed into joining the "supergroup" KGB, which featured bassist Ric Grech (formerly with Family and Blind Faith), drummer Carmine Appice (formerly with Vanilla Fudge), keyboardist Barry Goldberg and vocalist Ray Kennedy [see **Blind Faith, Barry Goldberg**]. In spite of the impressive credentials of all, the whole concept was anathema to Bloomfield. The self-titled album bombed commercially, reaching only #124 on the charts.

Subsequent Bloomfield releases were issued on small labels, mostly without national distribution. The work he considered to have the most integrity was an educational record demonstrating various blues styles. Titled *If You Love These Blues, Play 'Em as You Please*, the record was issued by *Guitar Player* magazine in 1976.

Other later releases include *Analine* (1977), *Count Talent and the Originals* (1977), *Mike Bloomfield* (1978),

Between the Hard Place and the Ground (1979), *Bloomfield/Harris* (with Woody Harris, 1979), *Livin' in the Fast Lane* (1980) and *Crusin' for a Brusin'* (1981).

Bloomfield also wrote the musical scores for the films *Medium Cool* (1969), Andy Warhol's *Bad* (1971), and *Steelyard Blues* (1979), and supplemented his income by writing advertising jingles and, on occasion, doing soundtrack work for pornographic movies.

On February 15, 1981, Bloomfield was found dead in his car, apparently the victim of a drug overdose.

Though Bloomfield has been gone for over twenty years, interest in his music remains high, especially with regard to his work with the Paul Butterfield Blues Band. This work is documented on the authorized releases *Paul Butterfield Blues Band* and *East-West* (on Elektra), *Strawberry Jam* and *East-West Live* (on Mark Naftalin's Winner label) and on the bootleg recordings *Live at the Unicorn Coffee House* and *Droppin' In*.

In 2001, *Michael Bloomfield—If You Love These Blues*, an oral history by Jan Mark Wolkin and Bill Keenom, was published. A documentary film on Bloomfield is in preparation.

Discography

Release Date	Title	Catalog Number

U.S. Singles

With the Chicago Loop

1966	(When She Needs Good Lovin') She Comes to Me/This Must Be the Place	Dyno-Voice 226
1967	Richard Corey/Cloudy	Dyno-Voice 230

Mike Bloomfield, Al Kooper and Steven Stills

1968	Season of the Witch/Albert's Shuffle	Columbia 44657

Mike Bloomfield and Al Kooper

1968	The Weight/Man's Temptation	Columbia 44678

U.S. Albums

Mike Bloomfield, Al Kooper and Steven Stills

1968	*Super Session* (with Al Kooper, Steven Stills)	Columbia OS 3240

Albert's Shuffle/Stop/Man's Temptation/His Holy Modal Majesty/Really

(Bloomfield & Kooper); It Takes a Lot to Laugh, It Takes a Train to Cry/Season of the Witch/You Don't Love Me/Harvey's Tune (Stills & Kooper)

Mike Bloomfield, Taj Mahal, Nick Gravenites and Others

1969	*Live at Bill Graham's Fillmore West*	CBS CS 9893

It Takes Time/Oh Mama/Love Got Me/Blues on a Westside/One More Mile to Go/It's About Time/Carmelita Skiffle

Mike Bloomfield and Al Kooper

1969	*The Live Adventures of Mike Bloomfield and Al Kooper*	Columbia KGP6

Opening Speech/The 59th Street Bridge Song (Feelin' Groovy)/I Wonder Who/Her Holy Modal Highness/The Weight/Mary Ann/Together Til the End/That's All Right/Green Onions/Sonny Boy Williamson/No More Lonely Nights/Dear Mr. Fantasy/Don't Throw Your Love on Me So Strong/Finale-Refugee

Mike Bloomfield

1970	*It's Not Killing Me*	Columbia KH 30395

If You See Me Baby/For Anyone You Meet/Good Old Guy/Far Too Many Nights/It's Not Killing Me/Next Time You See Me/Michael's Lament/Why Must My Baby/The Ones I Loved Are Gone/Don't Think About It, Baby

1994	*Mike Bloomfield: Essential Blues 1964–1969* (CD)	Columbia/Legacy CK 57631

I've Got You in the Palm of My Hand[1]/Last Night[1]/Feel So Good[1]/Goin' Down Slow[1]/I Got My Mojo Working[2]/Born in Chicago/Work Song/Killing Floor/Albert's Shuffle/Stop/Mary Ann/Don't Throw Your Love on Me So Strong/Don't Think About It Baby/It Takes Time/Carmelita Skiffle

[1] Recorded for Columbia Records demo session December 7, 1964.
[2] Recorded March 1, 1965.

U.K. Singles

Mike Bloomfield, Al Kooper and Steven Stills

1968	Season of the Witch/Albert's Shuffle	CBS 3770

Mike Bloomfield and Al Kooper

1969	The Weight/59th Street Bridge Song	CBS 4094

U.K. Albums

Mike Bloomfield, Al Kooper and Steven Stills

1968	*Super Session*	CBS 63396

Mike Bloomfield and Al Kooper

1969	*The Live Adventures of Mike Bloomfield and Al Kooper*	CBS 66216

Mike Bloomfield

1969	*It's Not Killing Me*	CBS 63652

Mike Bloomfield, Taj Mahal, Nick Gravenites and Others

1969	*Live at Bill Graham's Fillmore West*	CBS 63816

The Blues Project

Although eventually splintering apart due to creative differences, the Blues Project brought a pioneering spirit to blues-rock by infusing elements of blues, psychedelia, jazz, folk, classical, soul and rock-'n'roll into their own musical stew. The New York band consisted of five Jewish kids with a shared love of the blues, although otherwise they had disparate musical tastes that can be traced to their diverse backgrounds. Guitarist/vocalist Danny Kalb (b. September 19, 1942; Brooklyn, New York) was a blues purist; rhythm guitarist/vocalist Steven Katz (b. May 9, 1945; Brooklyn, New York) was a one-time folkie; bassist/flautist Andy Kulberg (b. April 30, 1944; Buffalo, New York) had classical training; drummer Roy Blumenfeld (b. May 11, 1944; The Bronx, New York) was influenced by jazz; and keyboardist/vocalist Al Kooper (b. February 5, 1944; Brooklyn, New York) was into rock'n'roll.

Driven by Kalb's guitar skills and love of the blues, the band expanded the blues horizons of New York's Greenwich Village. The Blues Project, along with the Paul Butterfield Blues Band, were directly responsible for pioneering the raw, electric, urban blues sound that "turned on" a new generation to the explosive possibilities of the idiom. Their iconoclastic performances featured Kalb's brand of improvisation, a dynamic ingredient that propelled the blues far beyond its traditional borders—from folk-rock to Chicago-style electric blues to jazz, always intertwined with the band's ensemble playing. A skilled blues interpreter, Kalb combined blistering guitar leads and big, round chordal progressions with tasteful melodic solos, transcending his total range of influences in forging his own highly charged, deeply personal style.

Kalb discovered the guitar at age 13 and a few years later, in high school, joined a rockabilly quartet called the Gay Notes. Kalb was interested in the blues at an early age, particularly Josh White, Brownie McGee, Lightnin' Hopkins and Bo Diddley. Kalb was also drawn to the pop-rock of Buddy Holly, Chuck Berry and Elvis Presley. He soon discovered the thriving Greenwich Village folk scene and eventually met folk and blues artist Dave Van Ronk (b. June 30, 1936), who became his mentor. He seriously studied the guitar under Van Ronk and became one of Van Ronk's most skilled students. In 1960, Kalb enrolled at the University of Wisconsin and found an active coffeehouse folk music circuit. He met Bob Dylan and performed with the soon-to-be folk legend on July 29, 1961, during a radio broadcast from Manhattan's Riverside Church. Kalb returned to Greenwich Village the following year and was soon performing both as a solo artist and with a number of other musicians.

With jug bands becoming popular in 1963–1964, Kalb joined Dave Van Ronk's Ragtime Jug Stompers, which also included blues historian and piano player Sam Charters and guitarist Artie Traum. The group recorded one album in 1964 for Mercury, *Ragtime Jug Stompers* (U.S./Mercury SR 60864). Kalb, Charters and Traum also formed the True Endeavor Jug Band, a spin-off group that released one album for Prestige/Folklore, *The Art of the Jug Band* (U.S./Prestige Folklore FL 14022), as well as a single, "Blues, Just Blues That's All" backed with "Jug Band Blues" (U.S./Prestige 290), both issued in 1963. Since most of the True Endeavor Jug Band's members were also in the Ragtime Jug Stompers and under contract with Mercury when the album was released, they used pseudonyms for the Prestige recording.

After playing with the Ragtime Jug Stompers for four months, Kalb and Charters started performing as a duo under the moniker New Strangers. Their inspiration was the pre-war Chicago blues played by Georgia Tom Dorsey and Tampa Red. While Charters played mostly piano, he occasionally strapped on a second guitar for the gospel numbers. The pair released one album, *Meet the New Strangers,* in 1964 (U.S./Prestige Folklore FL 14027).

That same year, Kalb recorded an album with guitarist Barry Kornfeld and bassist Artie Rose as the Folk Stringers (U.S./Prestige PRLP 7371) with Sam Charters producing. Meanwhile, he also did some session work, appearing on Phil Ochs's debut album, *All the News That's Fit to Sing* (1964) and Judy Collins's *The Fifth Album* (1965). Kalb also contributed two tracks to the high-profile folk compilation *Blues Project,* issued in 1964 (U.S./Elektra EKL 264 (m)/Elektra EKS 7264 (s)). Featuring the likes of Dave Van Ronk, Geoff Muldaur, John Sebastian, Eric Von Schmidt and John Koerner, the album also found an unlikely piano man, Bob Dylan, on a track credited as "Bob Landy."

At the time, Kalb was still playing acoustic guitar, but became enthralled with the possibilities of an electric guitar after witnessing Tim Hardin perform in the Village in 1964. Hardin was using an amplified guitar and backing musicians, including bassist Felix Pappalardi. Kalb told *Hit Parader*, "The possibilities of using rhythm in a complex, more exciting way than straight rock came to me. I knew then I needed a rhythm section in back of me and I wanted to be loud." The electric side on Dylan's 1965 *Bringing It All Back Home* echoed the direction he sought.

The origins of the Blues Project can be traced to an impromptu jam session at a 1964–65 New Year's Eve party with Kalb on guitar/vocals and childhood friend Roy Blumenfeld on drums. Blumenfeld took up the drums around 1956 or 1957 and continued to play in high school and, later, with a local rock band. He was majoring in art at NYU when he linked up with Kalb at the New Year's party.

The duo played one subsequent club date before bringing in Blumenfeld's friend, bassist Andy Kulberg. Kulberg had played the string-bass in high school with dance bands, then continued playing pop music while at Boston University and later at New York University, where he was majoring in music as a classically trained flautist. Rounding out the group was guitarist Artie Traum. The new group called themselves the Danny Kalb Quartet. Their first gig was at the Free Speech Hoot, a benefit for striking students in Bloomington, Ohio, held on April 3, 1965, at the Empire Hotel in New York. The Danny Kalb Quartet performed alongside John Hammond, Jr. and Judy Roderick. Not long after, the group began performing regularly at such venues as the Gaslight Café in Greenwich Village, where they were billed simply as "Danny Kalb."

The fledgling band soon adopted the name Blues Project, replacing Traum with guitarist/vocalist Steve Katz and adding charismatic singer and frontman Tommy Flanders. Flanders had previously performed on the Cambridge, Massachusetts, rock'n'roll circuit as a member of Tom Jones and the Trolls (later shortened to the Trolls).

Katz's first exposure to show business came at age eleven when he was a regular on a local Schenectady, New York, television program called *Teenage Barn*. As a teenager he had hung around the Greenwich Village folk scene and eventually took guitar lessons from Reverend Gary Davis and, like Kalb, Dave Van Ronk. For a while, Katz had been playing coffeehouses, later becoming a member of the Even Dozen Jug Band. The Even Dozen's

lineup fluctuated from seven to fourteen people, including Stefan Grossman, John Sebastian and Maria D'Amato (soon to become Maria Muldaur). In 1964, after the group released their only album, which was titled after the group (U.S./Elektra EKL 246 (m)/Elektra EKS 7246 (s)), Katz quit the band and began to give guitar lessons. While teaching at the Fretted Instrument music store he met Kalb, who said he needed a rhythm guitarist for a couple of weeks. The Blues Project had a date at the Gaslight folk music club and he didn't know if their regular axman, Artie Traum, would be returning from Europe. Two weeks later, when Traum decided to stay abroad, Katz became a regular member of the band.

The shows at the Gaslight went well and the group came to the attention of Columbia Records. Executives at the label decided to cut a single with the group. Staff member Tom Wilson produced the session, bringing with him sessionman Al Kooper to play keyboards.

Although young, Kooper was already something of a musical veteran. In 1958 he had become a member of the Royal Teens, best known for their #3 hit "Short Shorts." The group's most popular member, Bob Gaudio, had gone on to become a founding member of the Four Seasons. At 16, Kooper started singing Twist songs with Paul Simon at society dances, and eventually started to acquire session work and develop his songwriting skills. Working with Bob Brass and Irwin Levine, he achieved some songwriting success with Gene Pitney's 1965 hit "I Must Be Seeing Things" (U.S. #31) and Gary Lewis and the Playboys' first release, "This Diamond Ring" (U.S. #1). Despite the success, however, Kooper claimed to abhor the latter record because "they turned an R&B demo into a pop record."

Kooper also got caught up in the folk boom, performing as Al Casey in the clubs and releasing a single in the U.K. in 1965 as Alan Kooper—a cover of Mose Allison's spooky "Parchman Farm" backed with "You're the Loving End" (U.K./Mercury MF 885). Kooper also released a second single in the U.S. during the same year, "New York's My Home" backed with "My Voice, My Piano and My Foot" (U.S./Aurora 164).

Kooper became acquainted with Tom Wilson through Paul Simon, and the producer invited him to observe a Bob Dylan recording session on June 15, 1965. Kooper had brought along his guitar with the hope of being allowed to join the session. Those hopes, however, were dashed when Dylan arrived with Mike Bloomfield in tow [see **Mike**

Bloomfield]. Bloomfield was the red-hot guitarist for the Paul Butterfield Blues Band, and when Kooper heard him play his six-string, he quickly realized that he was in over his head. But fate intervened when keyboardist Paul Griffin switched from organ to piano, leaving the organ stool vacant. Although Kooper claims he could barely play the instrument at the time, he approached Wilson hoping to fill the organ hole. Wilson candidly told him that he'd embarrass himself if he tried to play the instrument. Nevertheless, when Wilson left the room for a moment, Kooper sat down at the organ stool and begin playing. To Kooper's surprise, Dylan ordered that the organ be turned up, and Kooper came up with the signature riff to Dylan's biggest ever single, "Like a Rolling Stone." Dylan invited him back the next day and Kooper sat in for two more songs, "Tombstone Blues" and "Queen Jane Approximately." Since this ended the recording session, Kooper's contact with Dylan supposedly ended there as well.

However, Kooper, who planned to attend the Newport Pop Festival just as a fan, was in for a surprise. On the festival's second day he went to a workshop where he ran into Dylan's manager, Albert Grossman, who informed him that Dylan was looking for him. On the evening of July 24, 1965, Kooper met Dylan backstage, where Dylan asked Kooper to help him perform his new material the next evening with an electric backing band. The performance lineup therefore consisted of Dylan, Kooper on organ, Barry Goldberg on piano and three members of Paul Butterfield's band—guitarist Mike Bloomfield, drummer Sam Lay and bassist Jerome Arnold. Dylan performed three songs—"Tombstone Blues," "Like a Rolling Stone" and a shambling version of "Maggie's Farm." The myth that accompanied this groundbreaking performance was that the Newport crowd booed voraciously at Dylan's use of electrical instruments, causing Dylan to leave the stage in tears.

Kooper saw it differently. What happened, he countered, was that the crowd was only upset because Dylan's set consisted of just three songs. Feeling cheated by Dylan's too brief appearance, the crowd shouted for more and/or booed, prompting Dylan to return to perform "It's All Over Now Baby Blue" and "Mr. Tambourine Man," accompanied only by acoustic guitar. Nonetheless, the difficult crowds followed Kooper and Dylan to their August 28 performance at Forest Hills Tennis Stadium in New York, where the unruly audience rushed the stage and knocked Kooper and his piano bench to the ground. Kooper's final concert appearance with Dylan on September 3 at the Hollywood Bowl in Los Angeles met with a more appreciative audience, as by then "Like a Rolling Stone" resided at the #2 spot on the charts, which no doubt helped out. Between these concerts, Kooper sat in on the balance of the sessions that would comprise Dylan's classic *Highway 61 Revisited.*

Following the Hollywood Bowl concert, Kooper bowed out of the rest of Dylan's tour. His time with Dylan was well spent, however, since after the release of *Highway 61 Revisited* and the well-publicized concerts, Kooper's stature in the music world rose dramatically. He became a much in-demand session player, as both keyboardist and guitarist, so much so that Elektra Records asked Kooper take part in a compilation LP called *What's Shakin'.* Backed by Roy Blumenfeld on drums and Andy Kulberg on bass, he cut four tracks. One, titled "I Can't Keep from Crying Sometimes," was ultimately placed on the album.

Kooper returned to the studio in late 1965 to contribute to the first Blues Project recording session. The group cut two tracks, covers of Eric Anderson's "Violets of Dawn" and Willie Dixon's "Back Door Man." However, Columbia rejected the recordings and released the group from their contract. Disappointed but undaunted, the band members followed producer Wilson—who had just left the label himself—to MGM-Verve. The Blues Project signed with the label's subsidiary, Verve-Folkways. Their initial recordings were issued as singles in January 1966. *Crawdaddy* praised "Violets of Dawn" as "one of the best songs of the year" and predicted, "The single would be a big-seller if it gets airplay," a sentiment echoed by *Billboard,* which saw "possibilities of a smash folk-rocker." However, the single failed to catch fire and make the charts, a fate that befell all their subsequent single releases but one.

Prior to this, the group had received a big break when they secured a week's booking at Greenwich Village's Café Au-Go-Go in the summer of 1965. Located at 152 Bleeker Street in a basement, the Go-Go was described by the *Village Voice* as "a cavernous coffee house with an excellent sound system and good lighting." *Hit Parader* called it "one of the best places to see and hear the newest evolution of folk music and the blues." The performances were a hit and the run was extended three more weeks. Then Howard Solomon, the club's proprietor, presented a four-day concert series called the "Blues Bag" from November 24–27 at the Café Au-Go-Go. Among the participants were John Lee Hooker, Big Joe Williams, Muddy Waters, Otis Spann, and the Blues Project, which had become the house band. The Blues Project was well received, winning praise from *New York Times* critic Robert Shelton, who observed, "Of the electric bands at 'The Blues Bag,' none impressed more than the Blues Project, possibly the most incandescent group in folk-rock today. [They are] sparked by the imaginative electric guitar of Danny Kalb, the volatile electric piano of Alan Kooper and the vocal sky-rocketing of Tommy Flanders."

The Project became a mainstay at the Café Au-Go-Go, frequently playing there over the next couple of years. "Well, we got this gig at the Café Au-Go-Go, but we played there opposite various famous blues singers and always stole the show—probably because we were the highest energy band there has ever been . . . on a par with Sly Stone," Kooper later told *Zig Zag*. "There was so much fucking energy going down from the time we went on till the time we came off, and no one had ever seen anything like that. That's what made our name—and after that, we just soared like rockets."

The Blues Project's first album was slated to include material recorded during the "Blues Bag" sets, but vocalist Flanders left the band while they were performing in Los Angeles, forcing the group to return to the Café Au-Go-Go to record additional material more representative of the revised lineup. The vocals were now divided among Steve Katz, who sang lead on his own compositions; Danny Kalb, who sang Muddy Waters covers; and Al Kooper, who handled the rest of the material. Half of the subsequent release, *Live at the Café Au-Go-Go,* which came out in early 1966, was comprised of material recorded at the "Blues Bag," while the remainder consisted of material recorded during afternoon sessions at the Café Au-Go-Go. *Live at the Café Au-Go-Go* was recorded for a modest $6,000 and sold surprisingly well for a band without a hit single. It reached #77 on the Billboard charts.

The album, with its mix of blues and folk material, received mixed reviews. *Sing Out* complained, "The reworkings of Muddy Waters, Willie Dixon, Chuck Berry, and Bo Diddley are often embarrassing and irrelevant compared to the imaginative treatments afforded Eric Anderson's 'Violets of Dawn' and Donovan's 'Catch the Wind.'" *Crawdaddy,* on the other hand, noted, "The word 'incandescent' has been used to describe them; [but] an equally valid word is 'infectious': their arrangements are irresistible, and more than once on this album, they take a song out of an individualized style of music and give it a near-universal appeal. Exactly how they do it I don't

know, but they may help revolutionize modern music in the process." *Variety* said, "The group rocks with a powerful beat and projects a strong blues feeling very much attuned to the contemporary scene."

In January 1966, members of the band recorded several tracks that were included on the novelty album *Batman and Robin* (U.S./Tifton S-78002) along with Sun Ra and members of his band. Produced by Wilson and credited to "The Sensational Guitars of Dan and Dale," a single, "Batman Theme" backed with "Robin's Theme" (U.S./Tifton 45-125), was also released with the B-side probably featuring the Blues Project as well. Andy Kulberg recalled that he, Blumenfeld and Kalb played on the session, which "was done in about six hours on a Sunday in a studio on 42nd Street, New York City."

After the departure of Flanders, the Blues Project continued as a quintet, embarking on a major tour of college campuses on the East Coast, Midwest and West Coast in the spring of 1966. From June 7–19, they were back at the Café Au-Go-Go, where a performance was reviewed by the *Village Voice:* "The Blues Project are short on gimmicks because they are confident in the ability of their music to convince. And when they capture a beat, they hold it prisoner on that tiny stage and turn its energy loose upon an audience." The Project then appeared at the Manhattan club, the Phone Booth, from July 26 to August 7 and performed at three outdoor concerts in the summer of 1966—the Central Park Music Festival, the Newport Folk Festival and the San Francisco State Folk Music Festival. From September 7–15, the band headlined at the Matrix nightclub in San Francisco.

In spite of their growing stature, they were still plagued by insecurities from the loss of their frontman. The group hired a black female singer, Emmaretta Marx, to appear on stage with them for a short time during 1966. However, they let Marx go after she missed too many rehearsals (although she did sing backup on "Where There's Smoke, There's Fire," their next single).

By now, promoter Sid Bernstein had become their manager. Bernstein, who also managed the Young Rascals, pressured the group to write more original material. As he told *Billboard* magazine, "I have them writing their own material because this is the thing today. All of the great groups, the Rolling Stones, the Beatles and the Lovin' Spoonful—are doing this. I just want them to break out with some good material. That's where the future is because it would give them more independence."

During October, while in Los Angeles again working with producer Tom Wilson, the band recorded their next album, *Projections*. Kooper's four self-penned songs provided most of the highlights, including the rave-ups "Wake Me, Shake Me" and "I Can't Keep From Crying Sometimes," which featured the first recording of a new electronic instrument called the *ondioline* or *tubon* (the tubon was a condensed version of the ondioline). Manufactured by the Guild Instrument Company, the tubon was a Swedish pianofone, a precursor to the modern synthesizer, also dubbed the "Kooperfone," as supposedly Kooper was the only one who knew how to play it.

While *Crawdaddy's* Jon Landau complained that there was "a lack of unity that ultimately results in this chaotic and superficial album," *Projections* has since been recognized as the Blues Project's masterpiece. Another highlight—the spacey, improvisational "Flute Thing"—spotlighted Kulberg's talents on that instrument and received significant airplay on East Coast FM stations. For onstage performances, Kulberg electrified the flute by drilling a hole into the instrument and adding a pickup. *Projections* also yielded an intense 11-minute version of Muddy Waters's song, "Two Trains Running," which featured Danny Kalb's searing soloing.

Released at the end of 1966, the album reached #52 on the *Billboard* charts. They had also recorded a Kooper/Levine/Brass song, "Where There's Smoke, There's Fire," during the same sessions, which they released as a single. Kooper and the others predicted, "It's going to be a real zoomer. We think this one is going to put us into that top spot." In spite of their optimism, the single never took off.

In March 1967, the group participated in one of the last of the old-time package tours, this one presented by Murray "The K" Kaufman, a New York DJ. The 10-day shows held at the old RKO 58th Street Theater included some of the biggest—and soon-to-be biggest—names in rock. Each act performed for fifteen minutes several times a day. Topping the bill were the headliners Mitch Ryder and Wilson Picket, with the Blues Project near the top of the billing and relative unknowns Cream and the Who near the bottom.

The group also shared the bill at the Café Au-Go-Go with the Paul Butterfield Blues Band for one weekend early in 1967. The two bands performed onstage separately and then jammed the night away together.

At around the same time as the Murray "The K" shows, the Blues Project worked on their next single. Frustrated by their lack of hits, the group spent a whole day in the studio working on their next release, the first time they were allowed such an extravagance. The resulting release, the Al Kooper-penned "No Time Like the Right Time," was an upbeat rock'n'roll tune that horrified the blues purist Kalb and widened the existing breach within the group. "No Time Like the Right Time" provided the group with the closest thing to a hit single, reaching #96 on the *Billboard* charts.

In 1966, Kooper recorded some tracks for a projected solo album. Kooper later described the album to *Blues-Rock Explosion* as "an exploitation LP of the worst kind. Roy and Andy from the Blues Project played on it and Wally Gold produced it. Seven or so tracks were cut inexpensively before the horror of what we were doing set in and we wisely committed album hari-kari." A solo single, a cover of Phil Ochs's "Changes" backed with Richard Farina's "Pack Up Your Sorrows," was issued in late 1966 (US/Verve-Folkways 5026).

Following a nervous breakdown and a dispute with Danny Kalb and other band members over musical direction, Kooper left the band in May 1967. Kooper had written some songs emphasizing horn arrangements, but when Kalb turned him down flat he decided to leave the band to form the pop/jazz-oriented Blood, Sweat & Tears.

The Blues Project was scheduled to make an appearance on June 18, a Sunday evening, at the Monterey Pop Festival. They recruited John McDuffy on keyboards and vocals as a substitute for Kooper, who was acting as assistant stage manager and had performed a solo set on the previous day that included many songs in the Blues Project repertoire. Without Kooper, the band lacked confidence, performing a lackluster set that included "Wake Me, Shake Me" and "Flute Thing."

After the Monterey appearance, the band flew back to New York and played a few shows with the Who, but, lacking focus, they decided to take a break. During this time off, Kalb unwittingly took a strong dose of the drug STP, which incapacitated him for a while. Katz took this as an opportunity to leave the band to join Kooper in Blood, Sweat & Tears. Those remaining in the Blues Project settled in San Francisco to rest and organize a new band. Kulberg described the internal turmoil of the Blues Project to *Rolling Stone*: "It's not unusual for exceptional musicians like Al and Danny to be in constant competition during performances. This was the group's main difficulty, our music could not progress amidst the conflict." He added, "We're not going to add horns because that was done 20 years ago. Besides, the vocals can replace the effect of the horns."

During this tumultuous time, the band's third album, *Live at Town Hall*, was released in October. The title was a misnomer, since only one track was recorded at its namesake, with the rest of the live tracks recorded at a day-long blues festival held at Stonybrook University and C. W. Post College, both on Long Island. Some of the tracks weren't recorded live at all, but were actually studio tracks with applause overdubbed, including "No Time Is the Right Time," "Where There's Smoke, There's Fire," "Love Will Endure" and "Mean Old Southern." The diamond in the rough in this mixed set was a raucous version of "Wake Me, Shake Me."

The next release, *Planned Obsolescence*, came the following year and garnered minimal enthusiasm from fans. It featured a lineup of Kulberg, Blumenfeld, guitarist John Gregory, violinist Richard Green and Kalb, although Kalb's contribution was minor. The group disbanded shortly after its release.

Kulberg and Blumenfeld went to live in Mill Valley, California, to form Seatrain, which featured Gregory and Green from the *Planned Obsolescence* lineup and lyricist Jim Roberts. Meanwhile, Kalb and guitarist Stefan Grossman recorded an album, *Crosscurrents* (1969), for Atlantic Records' Cotillion label (U.S./ Cotillion SD 9007).

In 1971, Kalb and Blumenfeld revived the Blues Project, adding Seatrain alumnus Don Kretmar on bass, David Cohen (formerly of Country Joe & the Fish) on keyboards, and original vocalist Tommy Flanders. The subsequent release, *Lazarus*, sold poorly despite Shel Talmy's production work. *Rolling Stone* observed, "[*Lazarus* is] basically a low-key effort that stays . . . generally 'all right' throughout its pair of sides, a recognition of the fact that anything the Blues Project does at this point is bound to be a coda to their previous career."

They expanded in 1972 to a six-piece with the addition of Bill Lussenden on guitar. The group, now playing generic-sounding hard rock, released one album for Capitol titled *The Blues Project*.

Postscript

In 1973, Kooper reunited the original group (minus Flanders) for a one-shot concert at Central Park, captured on the double-album *Reunion in Central Park*. The same lineup in fact performed again in 1981 in a reunion concert at Bond International Casino, New York City's biggest rock club, and again in 1996 at New York's Bottom Line as part of a lineup celebrating Kooper's fiftieth birthday.

Kulberg and Blumenfeld formed Seatrain, one of the first rock bands to successfully integrate country and progressive rock. Seatrain recorded four albums, *Seatrain* (1969), *Seatrain II* (1970), *The Marblehead Messenger* (1971) and *Watch* (1973). Blumenfeld dropped out of Seatrain after their first album, and then out of the musical scene altogether, reappearing in 1994 on the Nick Gravenites album, *Don't Feed the Animals*.

After Seatrain, Kulberg did session work and, in partnership with Chris Michie, went on to score films, television shows and other media.

Following his first departure from the Blues Project, Tommy Flanders recorded one solo album, *Moonstone* (Verve, 1969) before re-emerging with *The Blues Project* in 1971. He has maintained a low musical profile since the final breakup of the group.

After the reunion album, Kalb supported himself by giving guitar lessons and all but dropped out of the music industry. He surfaced for a performance at Phil Ochs's memorial benefit concert held at the Felt Forum in 1976 and, that same year, began performing in public again with a series of dates as the Danny Kalb Trio. Kalb released his last album, *Livin' with the Blues,* on the French Legends label in 1995.

Steve Katz joined Al Kooper in Blood, Sweat & Tears, staying with the group through six albums: *Child Is Father to the Man* (1968), *Blood, Sweat & Tears* (1969), *Blood, Sweat & Tears III* (1970), *Blood, Sweat & Tears IV* (1971), *New Blood* (1972) and *No Sweat* (1973). While with Blood, Sweat & Tears, the group was awarded three Grammys, was voted best band by the Playboy Jazz and Pop Poll two years in a row, and won three major *Downbeat* awards. After leaving the band, Katz worked for Mercury Records in an artists and repertory position and eventually became a producer. His credits include three Lou Reed albums: *Rock & Roll Animal, Sally Can't Dance* and *Lou Reed Live.*

Kooper left his creation, Blood, Sweat & Tears, after their debut album, *Child Is Father to the Man* (1968), assuming an artists and repertory/producer position with Columbia Records. Still, he continued to issue recordings, collaborating with Mike Bloomfield on *Super Session* (1968, U.S. #12) and *The Live Adventures of Mike Bloomfield and Al Kooper* (1969, U.S. #18). A collaboration with Shuggie Otis, *Kooper Session: Al Kooper Introduces Shuggie Otis* (1970) was less successful, only reaching #182 on the U.S. charts.

Kooper also issued a series of solo albums including *I Stand Alone* (1969), *You Never Know Who Your Friends Are* (1969), *Easy Does It* (1970), *New York City (You're a Woman)* (1971), *A Possible Projection of the Future/Childhood's End* (1972), and his last album for Columbia, *Naked Songs* (1972). He also scored the Hal Ashby film, *The Landlord,* in 1970.

Kooper sporadically issued recordings after leaving Columbia, concentrating more on production and session work instead. His post-Columbia solo credits include *Act Like Nothing's Wrong* (1976), *Championship Wrestling* (1982), *Rekooperation* (1994) and *Soul of a Man: Al Kooper Live* (1996).

Kooper's session credits include the Rolling Stones, Jimi Hendrix, the Who, George Harrison, Paul McCartney and Ringo Starr, among numerous others. He also worked as a producer, discovering Lynyrd Skynyrd and producing their first three albums. In 1977, he published his autobiography, *Backstage Passes*. In 1997, the book was pointedly updated and retitled *Backstage Passes & Backstabbin' Bastards*.

Discography

Release Date	Title	Catalog Number

U.S. Singles

1966	Violets of Dawn/Back Door Man	Verve/Folkways 5004
1966	I Want to Be Your Driver/Catch the Wind	Verve/Folkways 5013
1966	Where There's Smoke, There's Fire/ Goin' Down Louisiana	Verve/Folkways 5019
1967	I Can't Keep from Crying/ The Way My Baby Walks	Verve/Folkways 5032
1967	No Time Like the Right Time/ Steve's Song	Verve/Folkways 5040
1967	Gentle Dreams/Lost in the Shuffle	Verve/Forecast 5063
1972	Crazy Girl/Easy Lady	Capitol 3374

U.S. Albums

| 1966 | *Live at the Café Au-Go-Go* | Verve/Folkways FT 3000 (M) Verve/Folkways FTS 3000 (S) |

Goin' Down Louisiana/You Go and I'll Go with You/Catch the Wind/I Want to Be Your Driver/Alberta/Way My Baby Walks/Violets of Dawn/Back Door Man/Jelly Jelly Blues/Spoonful/Who Do You Love

| 1966 | *Projections* | Verve/Folkways FT 3008 (M) Verve/Folkways FTS 3008 (S) |

I Can't Keep from Crying/Sometimes/You Can't Catch Me/Steve's Song/Fly Away/Wake Me, Shake Me/Cheryl's Going Home/Two Trains Running/Flute Thing/Caress Me Baby

| 1967 | *Live at Town Hall* | Verve/Forecast FT 3025 (M) Verve/Forecast FTS 3025 (S) |

Flute Thing (Electric)/I Can't Keep from Crying/Mean Old Southern/No Time Like the Right Time/Love Will Endure/Wake Me, Shake Me/Where There's Smoke, There's Fire

| 1968 | *Planned Obsolescence* | Verve/Forecast FT 3046 (M) Verve/Forecast FTS 3046 (S) |

If You Had to Make a Fool of Somebody/Calypso/The Endless Sleep/Niartaes Hornpipe/Turtledove/Mojo Hanna/Frank and Curt Incensed/She Raised Her Hand/Dakota Recollection

| 1971 | *Lazarus* | Capitol ST 872 |

It's Alright/Personal Mercy/Black Night/Vision of Flowers/Yellow Cab/Lazarus/Brown Eyed Handsome Man/Reachings/Midnight Rain/So Far So Near

| 1972 | *The Blues Project* | Capitol EST 11017 |

Back Door Man/Danville Dame/Railroad Boy/Rainbow/Easy Lady/Plain & Fancy/Little Rain/Crazy Girl/I'm Ready

U.K. Singles

| 1967 | I Can't Keep From Crying Sometimes/ The Way My Baby Walks | Verve VS 1505 |

U.K. Albums

| 1967 | *Projections* | Verve VLP 6004 (M) Verve SVLP 6004 (S) |
| 1972 | *The Blues Project* | Capitol E-ST 11017 |

Graham Bond

While this may be news to Agent 007 lovers, there's more than one Brit named Bond. While that fictional film character with the first name of James may garner the bigger audience, it is another Bond—Graham Bond—who has left a long-lasting impression with his influential music. Although many consider Alexis Korner as the father of the British blues/R&B movement, Graham Bond also deserves credit for its development. "Loud, hypnotic and neurotic" is how *Melody Maker* reporter Chris Welch once described Bond's music. "It wails, screams and tears at the senses for minutes on end, demanding either complete attention or complete rejection."

Bond was not afraid to experiment, introducing the Mellotron to British audiences as well as being one of the first on the scene to use the Hammond organ. His approach to music was also unconventional, as he boldly mixed elements of jazz into his brand of R&B, a feat unheard of at the time. "It doesn't have to be a 12-bar. Blues can be 9½ bars, or 14 bars, and in any time," he once explained to *Melody Maker*. "You can play so many different sequences, or no sequences at all. Talk about 'Free Form'—there is a tremendous parallel with the blues, because it's so free. We are playing the blues of today and I can get away with playing practically anything. There is no reason at all why you can't take the blues and put the technique of modern jazz on it."

Graham John Clifton Bond (b. October 28, 1937, Romford, Essex; d. May 8, 1974, London, U.K.) was born a chronic asthmatic and, as a child, suffered constantly from his breathing impairment. He started playing the piano at an early age. "I told my parents I wanted to play organ and they were all going to come up to the Albert Hall to watch me play," he later recalled to *Melody Maker*. "So they got me a piano and I studied from the age of seven until I was 14." He later joined the school orchestra and became proficient on the cello and oboe. Although classically trained, he developed great interest in Dixieland jazz in the early

1950s, and by 1953 he had joined some school friends in forming the Modernnaires.

At age 14, Bond took up kharma yoga (also known as "breathing yoga"), which led to his interest in the saxophone. "When I was 15 I decided to form a jazz band and because I had chronic asthma, I took up alto sax to help strengthen my lungs and breathing. Now I've got very strong lungs. My father bought me an alto, and for weeks before that I practiced fingering with the stick with the notes cut in. I've got an unconventional approach to saxophone. I never bothered with chords—I just believe in blowing!" However, as the jazz scene was gradually changing, Bond also became interested in bebop. He soon met drummer Terry Lovelock and, along with pianist Colin Wild, formed the Terry Graham Trio.

Although the group was a modern jazz outfit, they had to compromise their style and sound because the public craved dance music. With gigs hard to come by, Bond worked days as a refrigerator salesman. But, he was eager to go a step further musically and so began jamming in the London jazz scene. He met with some resistance, however, as audiences and even most musicians found his sax playing far too avant-garde for their tastes.

By mid-1957, Bond found himself working as a cocktail pianist on the Spanish isle of Majorca. Even though he initially enjoyed the Mediterranean lifestyle, he returned to England less than a year later, where he teamed up with Lovelock and various musicians as the Terry Graham Quartet.

An important meeting took place late in March 1960. Tenor player Dick Heckstall-Smith (b. September 26, 1934; Ludlow, Shropshire, U.K.) was already a pro jazz musician with lots of experience when the two met at one of Heckstall-Smith's gigs. Bond asked to sit in and was quite impressive with his alto playing, a significant development since his earlier failings on the scene. That same month he married a pianist named Diane Eton and by May had joined the Goudie Charles Quintet, playing London's suburbs. The band expanded to a sextet with Goudie on guitar, Milton James on tenor sax, Gordon Bellamy on trombone, Roy Surman on bass and Art Terry on drums, in addition to Bond on alto sax.

Bond stayed with the group for a year until he became involved with Don Rendell and his quartet through former bandmate Lovelock. Lovelock, now Rendell's drummer on leave, had advised the tenor player to check out his friend. Bond became a member of the band, or as *Melody Maker* wrote in May 1961: "The Don Rendell Four Become Five." Bass player Tony Archer and pianist John Burch comprised the rest of the quintet. In early June, just two weeks before recording their debut album for the U.S. label Jazzland (a subsidiary of Riverside), drummer Lovelock was replaced by Phil Kinorra (a.k.a. Julian Covey).

While they were recording, *Melody Maker* reported that the month-old quintet "nearly swung the tapes off the machines when they were blowing some of the wildest jazz this side of New York." A few days after the session, the Don Rendell Five left for their first provincial tour: Birmingham, Derby, Leicester, Nottingham and Leeds. This circuit would become their usual path when they later returned north. Meanwhile, in London they secured more income with gigs at the Flamingo Club, Ronnie Scott's and the Marquee club.

Although busy by night with the quintet, Bond also worked as a sales and promotion manager for Central Record Distributors. In early October, the New Don Rendell Quintet's *Roarin'* became available in retail stores on both sides of the Atlantic (U.S./Jazzland JLP 51 (M), Jazzland JLP 951S (S); U.K./Jazzland JLP 51). As the second British jazz group ever to have a release on an American label (Joe Harriott's band having the first), this was an extraordinary achievement, as U.S. labels until that point had shown little interest in overseas groups. The record was very good with its combination of soon-to-be standards and self-produced material, and the stormy interplay between the two seemingly incongruous jazz and blues styles was especially appealing.

A month later, Bond briefly joined forces with Heckstall-Smith in the Live New Departures when a New Jazz & Poetry concert—including poet Pete Brown—was staged at St. Pancras Town Hall in London.

Kicking off 1962 rather nicely, Bond's name appeared in two sections of *Melody Maker's* annual jazz poll. Apart from achieving second place in the "New Star" section (topped only by Dick Morrissey), he also secured sixth place in the "Alto" section—not bad for a guy who was brand-new to the pro scene. In May, with drummer Kinorra now replaced by Ted Pope, the group visited Belgium and performed at an international jazz show in Brussels. They were promptly invited back for TV and radio in the autumn. Summer came with the usual festivals, and apart from First West County at Taunton, Earlswood at Birmingham, and East Coast at Cleethorpes, the band also performed at the Second National Jazz Festival at Richmond for the second straight year.

In mid-September, the quintet recorded their first session for the BBC. With Heckstall-Smith as a guest player, they sounded like a small big band á la the Cannonball Adderley Sextet. The band smoked, especially when the sax section traded solos: Rendell on soprano, Bond on alto and Heckstall-Smith on tenor.

Bond was now also involved in a budget big band, the Johnny Burch Octet. Aside from Burch, Bond and Heckstall-Smith, the lineup featured Miff Moule (baritone), Mike Falana (trumpet), John Mumford (trombone), Jack Bruce (double bass) and Ginger Baker (drums). Pretty much a combination of the Rendell Band (Bond and Burch) and Alexis Korner's Blues Incorporated (Heckstall-Smith, Bruce and Baker) [see **Alexis Korner**], they started playing together on their days off. While they didn't tour (aside from a few gigs in Wales), they did secure regular nearby gigs at clubs, including Klooks Kleek, the Plough Pub located in Illford, Essex, and occasionally the Marquee.

In late October, Bond quit the Don Rendell Quintet, explaining that he had wanted a change for a while and was feeling challenged to play piano again. The chance came almost right away, when harp player/vocalist Cyril Davies left Alexis Korner's Blues Incorporated, which was suddenly moving into a direction of mixing Muddy Waters blues with horn-driven Charles Mingus jazz—something Davies very much disliked. On the other hand, this direction appealed to Bond, who gladly accepted when Korner invited him in. In addition to Korner on guitar and Dick Heckstall-Smith on tenor, the impressive Blues Incorporated roster now included Ronnie Jones on vocals, Johnny Parker on piano, Bruce on double bass and Baker on drums. Some fine black female backing singers called the Velvettes also performed with them on occasion.

Though the Rendell Quintet had worked pretty hard on the tiny circuit, Graham's new group went into a massive round of gigs. Apart from a residence at the Marquee, they also worked regularly in clubs as far away as Manchester and Liverpool.

Early in 1963, Blues Incorporated left their Marquee residency for a new spot at the Flamingo. Although both were off-license clubs, it was probably a good move for Korner because the new venue became an all-night club during the weekends. Around this time, Bond, Bruce and Baker started to play the intervals as a Hammond organ trio. (Georgie Fame has said that Bond introduced him to the organ during this period. The instrument would prove to be quite powerful in the R&B connection in the years to come). "I was the first one to be taking the Hammond around the country except for people like Harold Smart," Bond later said to *Beat Instrumental*. "I pioneered the splitting of the Hammond. It was necessary to do it to get around in those days."

Ginger Baker was hardly a stranger to Bond. Aside from playing together in the Johnny Burch Octet, the two had played the occasional gig together in various other formations. Scotsman Jack Bruce, on the other hand, was a bit younger than the other two, although still an experienced bass player. During his early teens, Bruce had studied cello before heading off to Italy with a group for a while. He returned, sat in with Heckstall-Smith and Baker at a May ball, and next popped up in Korner's band. By this point, Bond was working every night either with Blues Incorporated, the Johnny Burch Octet or his own trio. In fact, he contributed to all three combinations on some nights.

In between the tight gig schedule, Blues Incorporated also found time to do some sessions for the BBC. They appeared on both the *6.25* TV show and radio's *Jazz Club*. (Later, "Rockin'," recorded at the radio broadcast, turned up on Korner's retrospective album, *Bootleg Him*). During this period, the band also did a session for Decca at their West Hampstead studio. Recorded at night with an invited audience, Blues Incorporated performed 11 songs. Unfortunately, only "Early in the Morning" and "Night Time Is the Right Time" were ever released.

Bond also played on a session for competitor EMI. Backed by the Blues Incorporated rhythm section plus Heckstall-Smith and the Velvettes, Bond both sang and played his Hammond through the audition recording. Nothing came to fruition at the time, but the EMI link was made.

In late February, Bond's trio played in Manchester on their own, making more money than either Blues Incorporated or the Johnny Burch Octet could command per player. Bond realized that leading his own trio would be far more lucrative financially than being part of a septet, so after a heated discussion with Korner at the Flamingo, Bond left, taking Bruce and Baker with him. The rhythm section hadn't actually decided to leave, as the steady income with Korner was quite secure, but, as Baker put it, "He left for me and Jack!" Bruce would later say it took years before Korner really forgave him.

In any event, the trio were on their own and, although Bond's reputation helped a lot, they struggled to obtain

gigs. The group was now Graham's main source of income, but he still contributed to the Burch Octet and was also occasionally involved with the Live New Departures, a jazz and poetry unit that had been performing sporadically since the St. Pancras Town Hall concert in 1961. However, early in March, guitarist John McLaughlin joined the trio after leaving Georgie Fame's band, and Bond signed a five-year contract with EMI.

The band's first release was backing singer Duffy Power [see **Duffy Power**] on a Hammond-spiced version of the Beatles' "I Saw Her Standing There." Bond's own "Farewell Baby" was originally chosen as the A-side and "I Saw Her Standing There" as the B-side, but Parlophone flip-flopped the songs prior to release.

A package tour backing Power took place in April, with Joe Brown and Marty Wilde also on the bill. That same month, the Graham Bond Quartet found time to record a BBC radio session for *Jazz Club* on the twenty-fifth. Augmented by singer Bobby Breen on two songs, they played a mix of Ray Charles songs and original material and arrangements. In May, "I Saw Her Standing There" was released as a single, and during the summer months Duffy Power and the Graham Bond Quartet—as they were billed—promoted the record through two BBC radio sessions. In June, they appeared on *Saturday Club* and the following month were featured on *Pop Goes the Beatles*. During this time, another EMI session with Duffy and the Quartet produced two Ray Charles tunes, but both remain unreleased.

In August 1963, Bond appeared at the "National Jazz Festival" again, as the organizers now had chosen to include R&B in the program. Also that month, Heckstall-Smith left Blues Incorporated. He found a new place to stay when Ginger Baker fired McLaughlin in September. The reason, according to Baker, was quite simple: McLaughlin was "a miserable moaner." During his short stay, however, McLaughlin was introduced to certain things by Bond, one being the occult. Bond had been quite interested in the subject for some time and he guided McLaughlin in learning to read Tarot cards. Bond's interest in the occult eventually grew much stronger.

With Heckstall-Smith replacing the fired guitarist, the combo could experiment with two saxophones up-front, with Bond doubling on Hammond and alto. They hit the London club scene hard, playing Klooks Kleek, the Refectory and Jazzshows Jazzclub—soon to be renamed the 100 Club—and toured further north with regular gigs at places like Manchester's Twisted Wheel and Newcastle's Club a Go-Go.

By 1964, Graham had fallen from second to fourth place in *Melody Maker's* New Star poll, but he reached a high position in the "Miscellaneous" column as an organist. By April, the group changed their name from the Graham Bond Quartet to the more dynamic Graham Bond Organization (also spelled "Organisation"). However, their earlier EMI deal hadn't really pleased the band, so the members auditioned for Decca at its West Hampstead facilities. The group played a good, live studio session that was marred only by Graham's tiring voice. They nevertheless secured a deal and recorded their first single, "Long Tall Shorty" backed with "Long Legged Baby," for their new label that May.

New Musical Express found the release "a driving, insidious 12-bar shaker" and observed, "'Long Tall Shorty' introduces Decca's Graham Bond Organization—an apt name because organ is strongly featured. Graham supplies the ravin', shoutin' vocal, with harmonica added for topical effect and a steady beat is maintained throughout."

By the end of the month, the group had recorded another four songs. Bond and the rhythm section also backed Jamaican guitarist Ernest Ranglin on a Black Swan session in the spring. Released as Ernest Ranglin and the GB's, the results were something unexpected—smooth cocktail jazz. A new chance to see the countryside arose when the Organization—with Long John Baldry & the Hoochie Coochie Men, among others—joined Memphis Slim for a month-long tour. The Graham Bond Organization now played more or less every day, with Dick Heckstall-Smith insisting that they played an incredible 50 gigs in 54 days.

By August, the band was back in the studio recording three new songs for Decca. At the same time, Decca released the album sampler, *Rhythm and Blues,* of which half the tracks were Bond-related. Apart from five belonging to the Organization, two tracks were from a Blues Incorporated session from the previous January. Sometime that autumn, the band also became involved in the film *Gonks Go Beat.* The convoluted plot involved emissaries from planet Gonk who prevented a war between "Beatland" and "Ballad Isle." Although the group came away from it with honor—miming to the song "Harmonica"—the movie itself was inane.

An article appearing in an October issue of *Melody Maker* gave Bond an opportunity to discuss his group's development: "The Organisation is a co-operative group in that there is no star and everybody is indispensable. I think the visual thing is extremely important, but the point about both our musical policy and presentation is that at least 90 per cent is completely improvised. At first things were very hard because our sound was too way out at that time. Then groups like the Stones, Beatles, Animals and Manfred Mann helped the transition which made young people able to appreciate the sort of blues and gospel things we do."

The Organization backed Motown singer Marvin Gaye on a TV show during his first U.K. visit in November 1964. Augmented by John Baldry's Hoochie Coochie Men, the Organization added punch to "How Sweet It Is (To Be Loved By You)" and "Baby Don't You Do It." In December, their collaboration with EMI also resumed as the group started working on their first album for EMI's Columbia label. The sessions continued between gigs throughout January and February. On the last day of 1964, the Organization was featured on the BBC-TV 2 *Beat in the News* show.

The band spent most of January 1965 participating in the second British Chuck Berry tour, which encompassed two shows a night for nearly a month. In addition, Columbia issued the single "Tammy" from the group's forthcoming album. *New Musical Express* described the track as having "a blues-flecked solo voice treatment with organ and brass backing and an insistent beat." The next month, Columbia brought out the group's first proper LP, *The Sound of '65.* Although it did not chart, the record was outstanding, as it effectively mixed U.S. standards with original numbers. It was, as *Record Mirror* wrote, "a first-rate record. One to be studied." *Disc Weekly's* reviewer also gave it favorable marks, writing, "It sounds like nothing else I've heard, and it's really musical in spite of the raw instrumental sounds achieved." *New Musical Express* proclaimed, "Way-out blues sounds, weird at times, but always fascinating. Plenty of wailing harmonica and raving vocalistics."

Similar to other hardworking groups of the era, the Organization was quite prolific, and the next single, "Tell Me (I'm Gonna Love Again)," hit the airwaves on April 2, 1965. *Disc Weekly* again approved the release, calling it "a real swinger from this very good group," and adding, "Far more commercial than anything they've done before, yet they still retain that gravelly quality." April also saw the issuing of Winston G's single, "Please Don't Say," with backing by Bond and Baker (U.K./Parlophone R 5266).

Their involvement likely stemmed from their sharing the same manager, Robert Stigwood, with Winston.

By late July, the Organization was featured on ITV's weekend show, *Ready Steady Go!*, on which they promoted their new single, "Lease on Love." Bond also used the opportunity to demonstrate his newfound keyboard, the Mellotron. The Mellotron resembled an organ but was able to emulate strings, brass and woodwind, giving Bond command of a mini orchestra. As Bond explained to *Melody Maker,* "The Mellotron uses pre-recorded tapes of other instruments. For example, every note in the register of the trumpet is recorded—and I can play it on the organ keyboard getting the real sound." The instrument created a minor sensation when Bond first publicly used it at the Marquee. However, they soon suspended its use in shows because, as Dick Heckstall-Smith told *Blues-Rock Explosion*, "It went out of tune the whole bloody time. It was also very big." "Lease on Love" may have been the first recording to feature the Mellotron, and the song garnered outstanding reviews. A *New Musical Express* critic noted, "Here's a good one that I can confidently recommend: 'Lease On Love' by the Graham Bond Organisation. What I like about this group is that the soloist has an inherent R&B feeling, and this is particularly noticeable with the persistent organ blues riff behind him." *Disc Weekly* asserted, "Graham is singing better than ever with a hush-coloured voice and oodles of feeling."

With autumn came the fifth festival at Richmond under the new name of The National Jazz & Blues Festival. The festival, featuring the Organization's wild version of "Hoochie Coochie Man," was taped for U.S. television.

In September, following several disagreements with Baker, Bruce was sacked from the band. However, he continued to return for gigs as he felt it was his group as well. When Baker finally pulled out a knife and told him, "If you show up again, this goes in you," Bruce left for good. The group then brought in Nigerian trumpet player Mike Falana, who had previously played with some Organization members while in the Burch Octet. Although the new lineup cut some strong recordings, only one track was ever released, a supreme version of "Wade in the Water," which made its way onto a U.S. single B-side.

Columbia released the Graham Bond Organization's second album, *There's a Bond Between Us,* in December. The material on it, which was divided between original and cover tunes, had been recorded by the original lineup over the summer. The reviews were generally positive, with *New*

Musical Express observing, "Here's a restless, wailing rhythmic and sometimes overpowering sound, both vocally and instrumentally from organist Graham Bond, who augments his music with a Mellotron." But *Record Mirror* noted a disparity between the live and studio settings, commenting, "Perhaps the atmosphere of his live performances is lacking."

On January 3, 1966, Bond joined the Trevor Watts Quintet for a gig at the Little Theatre Club at London's West End. Having recently been taken over by free-minded musicians, the club soon became an oasis for experimental jazz. Later the same month, both Baker and Bond contributed to a Marquee gig organized by the ESP label. *Melody Maker* called the proceedings "an evening of spontaneous avant garde music." Also that month, the whole Organization recorded a radio session for the BBC, this time for *Jazz Beat.*

Aside from releasing "St. James Infirmary," the group's fourth single for EMI, the band spent February on a short tour supporting the Who. The tour proved quite important, as the next month the Organization recorded an exclusive session for an upcoming Who record. The Who had decided to join Robert Stigwood's newly formed Reaction label. A planned single for their former label, Brunswick, was scrapped and it was announced that their first single for Reaction, "Substitute," would be issued in March. The single was released backed with a Pete Townshend song credited as "Instant Party" but actually titled "Circles." Reaction issued the single a second time with the B-side correctly named, but by March 11, their former producer, Shel Talmy, successfully obtained an injunction against the Reaction release, arguing that "Instant Party" infringed on his copyright. Since the Who were legally barred from recording until April 4 when the case could be heard, the Graham Bond Organization, credited as the Who Orchestra, was brought in to record a new B-side, "Waltz for a Pig" (the pig referred to Talmy) so that sales of the single could continue.

Although the single can today be found with three different B-sides, "Waltz for a Pig" is in fact the most common as most countries used that combination (U.K./Reaction 591001). Even so, the pseudonymous Who collaboration didn't really do much to spur further commercial interest in the Organization.

Despite playing more than ever, the Graham Bond Organization still lacked charting records and well-paid gigs. Even worse, most of the band members had become immersed in drugs and alcohol. As part of the hip crowd, Bond had used drugs recreationally, but he went a step further by becoming hooked—along with Baker—on heroin. With drug addictions, records that went nowhere commercially, and the breakup of Bond's marriage, the Organization began to unravel.

The unending struggle led Baker to look for something better. With a new band in mind, he approached guitarist Eric Clapton, who was fed up with endless one-nighters with John Mayall's Bluesbreakers. Clapton was interested, but suggested Jack Bruce as bass player to round out a power trio. Despite his and Bruce's former acrimony, Baker swallowed his pride, asked Bruce to join, and Cream was born [see **Cream**].

By the time Baker left the Organization, a new drummer was already waiting in the wings: Jon Hiseman. Hiseman (b. June 21, 1944; London, U.K.) was a former member of both the New Jazz Orchestra and pianist Mike Taylor's combo. Hiseman proved to be an ideal drummer for Bond and the Organization, especially in his interplay with Bond. With Bond laying down chords on the Hammond with his left hand, soloing with his right and adding bass patterns with his feet, the two sounded like a whole band when Hiseman joined in on percussion. Although most of the gigs were now out of town, the Graham Bond Organization still occasionally played the London circuit at the Ram Jam Club and various Ricky-Tick venues.

Fortunately, while on a boat trip in Ireland, Bond finally decided to kick his heroin addiction. By October he had done so, and although emotionally spent following a period of going cold turkey, he immediately joined the band on the road. However, by autumn the lineup was reduced to three, as the others had decided to let Falana go, due primarily to economic considerations: It was simply cheaper to operate as a three-piece than as a quartet. Just after the trumpet player departed, the trio went into Olympic studios to cut tracks for a planned Polydor album. Recording more or less their stage repertoire, the live, in-studio session mixed old favorites with newly produced material. The music was excellent, but Bond had spent Polydor's entire advance payment, leaving no money to pay Olympic. With the studio time unpaid for, the music sat in the vaults until 1970, when it was included on the retrospective album *Solid Bond*. The Polydor deal then fell through, so the Graham Bond Organization decided to sign with the Page One label.

In January 1967, the trio played their first BBC session. Broadcast on *Rhythm & Blues,* their set mixed old and new songs, including their upcoming single, "You've Gotta Have Love Babe." Released the following month, the single was panned by a *Disc Weekly* critic, who noted, "Someone's gone mad. 'You've Gotta Have Love Babe' is one of the oddest, messiest noises I've heard in a long time. To learn it was the Graham Bond Organisation was a shock." The Organization by then had an EP and two albums in the works with Page One, but "You've Gotta Have Love Babe" sold only modestly and the planned records were aborted.

On April 29, the group appeared at the multi-group event billed as the "14-Hour Technicolor Dream," an all-night rave at North London's Alexandra Palace. The Velvet Underground and the Mothers of Invention failed to appear, but the happening was quite successful with appearances by Pink Floyd, Soft Machine, Pretty Things and dozens of other acts. By now, Bond—like practically everyone else—was involved in the burgeoning psychedelic scene. Aside from playing at Central London's UFO club (UFO was an acronym for Unlimited Freak Out) with the Organization, he often sat in at the club with other artists, including the Crazy World of Arthur Brown.

That summer, guitarist John Moorshead joined the group for a brief spell, but the lineup changed once again as soon as Hiseman split for Georgie Fame's band. Fed up with the chaos of drugs and the ever-present need for money, he left when Fame offered the gig. Soon afterwards, Heckstall-Smith departed as well to join John Mayall's Bluesbreakers [see **John Mayall**].

Once again, Bond assembled a new band, this time with Ray Russell (guitar) and Alan Rushton (drums). In mid-August, they toured the south of France with the Soft Machine. The Russell/Rushton lineup, however, ended up being the last stable ensemble. After they, too, left, Bond's band was henceforth usually promoted under the Organization banner, but he began featuring different musicians continuously. Of the musicians Bond used during this period, singer/drummer Philamore Lincoln is worth a special mention. Bond later appeared, uncredited, on Lincoln's *The North Wind Blew South* album (U.S./Epic BN 26497).

During the winter of 1968, Bond met Diane Stewart, a fellow believer in magic who by 1970 became his second wife. At the same time, he was involved with a Dutch designer group called the Fool. Though the Fool's members could hardly play a single instrument, the band's association with the Beatles, among others, secured them a recording contract with Mercury Records. A session was arranged in America and they apparently invited Bond along for some musical stability. Since gigs had by this point become limited more or less to residencies at Klooks Kleek and the Pied Bull pub, Bond grabbed the chance.

Although Bond had seemingly kicked the heroin habit in 1966, he had subsequently slid into addiction once again. Hoping to repeat his previous success in overcoming the drug's hold on him, he arranged for another boat tour of Ireland before he left for the States, but the trip went badly from the beginning. The boat wasn't in the best condition, and when they left for Dublin, the roof leaked during a rainstorm, adding to Graham's misery. Graham said he needed rest, so his wife Diane found a hospital that she thought suited him. It was, however, a mental institution, so Bond soon left it to return to London alone. Diane and her daughter had stayed at a nearby hotel during Bond's hospitalization, but with no money and Bond back in England, they had to leave without paying the bill.

Even though Bond wasn't fully recovered, he and the Fool left for the U.S. Since the group had no experience playing and no studio practice at all, the sessions for *The Fool* album went horribly. They somehow managed to complete the project, but the release was certainly one of the worst records that Bond ever associated himself with (U.S./Mercury SMCL 61178). However, during his stay on the East Coast, he met up with Jimi Hendrix for a session at New York's Record Plant studio. Through 1968, the two continued to jam both onstage and in the studio, but no recordings ever surfaced.

By this time, Bond, Diane, and her daughter, Erica, had moved across the country to Los Angeles. Although Bond lacked a work visa, he soon appeared in recording sessions all over town. In addition to contributing to Harvey Mandel's *Christo Redemptor* album [see **Harvey Mandel**], he was also heard on Screaming Jay Hawkins's *What That Is!* (U.S./Philips PHS 600 319). Under the moniker Wade and the Renegades, he and members of Jefferson Airplane got together for a special session. The recording was originally planned as a Christmas gift for friends, but they were so pleased with the result that they kept it themselves. Bond also jammed with the Grateful Dead, but it's unclear if anything was ever committed to tape.

Bond began working on his own album for Mercury's spin-off label, Pulsar. With session drummer Hal Blaine helping out, he recorded all new songs with the exception of three titles dating back to the Korner and Organization era. Released as *Love Is the Law* in the U.S., its lyrics and song titles now reflected Graham's heavy involvement with magic (or "magick" as Bond preferred to call it) and the teachings of Aleister Crowley. The album was roundly ignored both critically and commercially.

Along with a drummer and a reed player, Bond rehearsed for the next Pulsar album soon after. However, the album's producer wanted to use session players to cut another record, the U.S.-only release, *Mighty Grahame Bond*. The album sounded quite stiff, not surprisingly, since the musicians were unfamiliar with the material. Bond is rumored to have been involved in other Pulsar releases as well. He stated several times that he had recorded a third album for the label, but this has never been confirmed.

With their visitor visas about to expire, Bond and his family next headed for Jamaica, where Diane had relatives. They had hoped to sort out their problems and return later to the States, but they instead found themselves stranded there without money. Nevertheless, they had a pleasant life in Jamaica, as Bond enjoyed the climate . . . and the local substances. After some time, Bond reluctantly accepted Englishman Barrie Hawkins's offer to help his family return to Britain.

The plane had barely touched down at London's Heathrow airport in August when Bond undertook auditions for his new group, the Graham Bond Initiation. Now based in Cambridge with Hawkins and the Rufus Manning Associates, he had originally hoped to include Jimi Hendrix's drummer Mitch Mitchell in his new outfit. Instead, he found an impressive young drummer in Keith Bailey. As a lot of gigs were already booked, other unknown but highly qualified musicians were set to join the band. Percussion was covered by Dave Sheen, and in Dave Usher, Bond found a tenor player who could double on most instruments, including trumpet and guitar. Dave Howard contributed saxophone, sitar and bass, and spouse Diane played some additional percussion and danced along with the band.

Rehearsals went well and the new group's debut was slated for the Midnight Court at the Lyceum, London, on September 12, 1969. However, equipment difficulties led to their canceling the gig and the following show at Groovesville, Epping. Then, surprisingly, they had to postpone another show when Bond was arrested on a two-year-old bankruptcy charge amounting to £2,500. Following a rehearsal at London's Country Club, he was taken to Pentonville Prison, where he remained in custody until Jack Bruce helped bail him out. The Graham Bond

Initiation finally debuted on Saturday, September 26 at the Pantiles Club in Bagshot. During the last few months of 1969, the band played over 50 concerts up and down the British countryside.

A special appearance for Bond during this period was staged at London's Royal Albert Hall on October 17. Although the concert didn't really explode into a big reunion event as some thought it would, it did offer evidence that Bond was indeed back.

The Initiation's first BBC session was aired in January 1970. Bringing together old and new songs, the band performed "Walking in the Park," "Wade in the Water" and a version of "Love Is the Law" that ended with presenter John Walters roaring, "The astounding Graham Bond!" Many fans felt that Graham Bond's new band played as well as the original Organization a half decade ago.

Although the Initiation were in fine form, Bond had also become involved in a new project called Airforce that Ginger Baker had been organizing since the previous November. With Baker's latest band, Blind Faith, on hold, Baker wanted to bring together friends for a more informal project [see **Blind Faith**]. He announced an all-star lineup that included fellow Blind Faith members Steve Winwood and Ric Grech, plus Harold McNair, Chris Wood, Phil Seamen, Remi Kabaka, Denny Laine, Jeannette Jacobs and Graham Bond. After a Dutch gig fell through and a London concert was postponed, Airforce finally took off in Birmingham on January 12. But just after the show, Bond was again arrested on the same charges that had been brought against him the previous September.

Nevertheless, three days later, Airforce, along with Bond, played London's Royal Albert Hall. Recorded under the supervision of Jimmy Miller, the concert was documented in a double-LP set released in May called *Ginger Baker's Airforce*. A month later, Bond had his own archive compilation, *Solid Bond,* in the shops. Divided between a 1963 live recording with the Quartet and a later Organization session with Heckstall-Smith and Hiseman, the album was outstanding.

The Graham Bond Initiation played constantly throughout the winter, even giving a very brief performance in the film *The Breaking of Bumbo*. But as Airforce's popularity began to soar, the Initiation faded more and more into the background. One of their last shows was documented in a stunning concert recorded for BBC's Radio 1 in March 1970, featuring guitarist Kevin Stacey.

In the early part of the year, Polydor released the Airforce single "Man of Constant Sorrow" (U.K./Polydor 56380). By spring the group had become involved in sessions for a full studio album. Steve Winwood and Chris Wood had left for a re-formed Traffic following the Royal Albert Hall concert, and Airforce's lineup began fluctuating constantly. When a U.S./Canadian summer tour fell through, Baker went to Africa and Bond took the opportunity to start working on a new solo album.

Tentatively titled *Reunion*, the LP was eventually released as *Holy Magick* at the end of the year. Bond brought together old cohorts to record the album, which was divided between a suite and shorter tracks that reflected his obsession with the occult. *Holy Magick* was widely blasted by the music press, with a *Beat Instrumental* reviewer commenting, "Reluctant as we are to pan Graham—who is an excellent and creative musician—this type of album is singularly unimpressive . . . I make no comment upon his beliefs, but I have my doubts that this boring album will convert many others to the Great Wisdom." *Disc and Music Echo* likewise quipped, "*Holy Magick* is entirely involved with the occult and the mysteries of the Higher Powers . . . And if you buy records for musical enjoyment, you won't get much here." *Sounds* concurred, stating, "*Holy Magick* is obviously the product of extreme sincerity but its appeal will be on a limited scale."

By that autumn, Airforce had found a more stable crew to tour both Ireland and the continent. Studio sessions for their second album continued through September and October. Released in December, the *Airforce II* album was a hodgepodge affair. Although Bond was impressive on his featured numbers, the whole album lacked direction. The LP was also released in Norway, Germany, New Zealand and Australia, albeit with different tracks. In addition to including a different version of "We Free Kings," Polydor substituted four new songs, but the new edition wasn't any better than the original.

After the lackluster album, Airforce fell apart. They played their final concert at Sutton Coldfield's Belfry in late February 1971.

Bond again rebounded, once more assembling a new group that this time included a few ex-Airforce members. The new band, Graham Bond with Magick, debuted in April. With upcoming gigs and a brand new Vertigo single forthcoming, everything looked bright. A Vertigo showcase tour in June, including among others Gentle

Giant and May Blitz, also helped promote the new group. Still, even with the imminent release of their debut album, *We Put Our Magick on You,* the band split up during the summer.

Bond crossed paths with Jack Bruce once again and gradually became involved with his new band, which included guitarist Chris Spedding, drummer John Marshall and occasionally Art Themen on tenor sax. Billed as Jack Bruce and Friends, the group debuted at London's Hyde Park in early September, although the band had in fact already appeared on BBC Radio 1's *In Concert* and made an appearance for Granada TV. Their set, which mixed songs from Bruce's recent album, *Harmony Row,* with older tracks, garnered great reviews. Soon a U.K. tour followed in October and November. But, after playing in Italy, it became clear that conflicts spurred by drugs and some of Bruce's more tightly arranged songs were creating unbearable tensions, so Bond was fired.

Bond spent December jamming with Pete Brown's Piblokto! But the band was foundering and their breakup made the combination of Graham Bond and Pete Brown possible again. They had worked together in the jazz and poetry scene a decade before, and Bond had also once invited Brown into a late Organization lineup as a singer (he had declined).

After playing two Christmas shows the previous year, Bond & Brown were ready for the 1972 New Year. Lisle Harper on bass, Ed Spevock on drums and Bond's wife Diane completed the ensemble. Dave Thompson even contributed soprano sax during some initial performances. The new band went directly into the gig circuit and played for the next three months, in addition to doing their first BBC radio session in March. In addition, Bond helped his old friend Dick Heckstall-Smith with his solo album, *A Story Ended* (U.K./Bronze ILPS 9196). Another record set hit the shops that spring—an archive release from late 1964, *Rock Generation Vol. 3* and *Vol. 4.* Recorded live at London's Klooks Kleek and initially released in France, it arguably presented a truer version of the Organization, one not apparent on their albums or singles. The playing was outstanding and although the sound quality was rough, it became the only Bond recording that has been continually available since its release.

By June, Bond & Brown had expanded to a sextet when guitarist Derek Foley joined. They continued record-

ing in the studio (although without Foley), resulting in the July release of the *Lost Tribe* EP. In the autumn, they taped a second BBC broadcast before the band returned to the continent, which this time included a stint in Holland. Between touring and taping, the group somehow found time to also supply music for the film *Maltamour.* A bit later, Lisle Harper left the band, and Steve York substituted before a replacement could be found in Tom Duffy.

Outwardly, Bond & Brown seemed to be faring well, supported by numerous shows and frequent studio sessions. However, growing personal trouble was tearing the band apart from the inside. To begin with, their manager wanted Diane out of the band, and so she was finally let go. She and Bond then separated when she discovered that Bond had sexually abused her daughter, Bond's stepdaughter. Under intense stress, Bond began behaving erratically. And so by December, although their debut album, *Two Heads Are Better Than One,* was by now in the record shops, Bond & Brown had completely disbanded.

Despite his personal troubles, Bond finished out the year with a role in the rock'n'roll nostalgia film *That'll Be the Day,* which featured among others David Essex, Ringo Starr and Keith Moon. Apart from his role as a sax player, he also contributed to the "who's who in rock" lineup of the movie's soundtrack.

Postscript

Records involving Bond continued to surface after 1972. Virgin issued *Manor Live,* a good time rock'n'roll session recorded by a cast of thousands. The *That'll Be the Day* soundtrack was also released in the spring. Ironically, the work on this album gave Graham his first #1 entry in the charts. He was also involved with the John Dummer Blues Band [see **John Dummer Band**]. Apart from the odd gig with them, he additionally recorded a still unreleased session for the Vertigo label at Rockfield Studios in Wales. In October, he teamed up with singer/violinist Carolanne Pegg and her new band, Magus. But the outfit, which also included guitarist Brian Holloway, bass player Pete McBeth and drummer Paul Olsen, broke up soon afterwards.

Bond's unpredictable behavior, including his obsession with magic and drug abuse, led him to become involved in bizarre situations. After cheating drug dealers, he was beaten up and had to hide for security in a police station, where he was taken into custody for possession of marijuana. When the police checked his mental stability, he convinced a psychiatrist that he was a taxi driver. Nonetheless, the authorities kept him in prison for nearly a month while awaiting his transfer to a mental hospital.

Even while taking prescription antidepressants, Bond became more depressed than ever after leaving the hospital in early March 1974. While staying with John Hunt in north London, he went for a walk on May 8 and never returned. A couple of days later, Hunt and Pete Brown were informed by the police that Bond had been killed by a tube train at Finsbury Park station. According to a witness, he had jumped in front of a passing train; yet the day before he died, he had called a music newspaper to schedule an interview.

Although Bond's personal behavior was erratic and ultimately self-destructive, by mixing jazz, blues and R&B in innovative ways, his profound influence on the early British music scene cannot be discounted, and his legacy lives on.

Discography

Release Date	Title	Catalog Number

U.S. Singles

The Graham Bond Organization

1966	St. James Infirmary/Wade in the Water	Ascot 2211 Promo only

Grahame Bond

1969	Love Is the Law/The Naz	Pulsar 2405 Promo only
1969	Moving Towards the Light/ Crossroads of Time	Pulsar 2409 Promo only
1969	Water, Water/Stiffnecked Chicken	Pulsar 2415 Promo only

U.S. Albums

Grahame Bond

1969 *Love Is the Law* Pulsar AR 10604
Love Is the Law/Moving Towards the Light/Our Love Will Come Shining Through/I Couldn't Stand It Anymore/Sun Dance/Crossroads of Time/Bad News Blues/Strange Times, Sad Times/The Naz/The World Will Soon Be Free

1969 *Mighty Grahame Bond* Pulsar AR 10606
Water, Water/Oh Shining One/Pictures in the Fire/Baroque/Sisters and Brothers/Stiffnecked Chicken/Freaky Beak/Walk onto Me/Magic Mojo/Brothers and Sisters

Graham Bond

1970 *Solid Bond* Warner Bros.
  2LS 2555
Archive album including Graham Bond Quartet live at Klooks Kleek, London, June 26, 1963 and an autumn 1966 studio session with the Organization.
Green Onions/Springtime in the City/Can't Stand It/Only Sixteen/Last Night/Long Legged Baby/Walking in the Park/It's Not Goodbye/Neighbour Neighbour/Ho Ho Country Kicking Blues/The Grass Is Greener/Doxy

1970 *Holy Magick* Mercury SR 61327
Meditation Aumgn/The Qabalistic Cross/The Word of the Aeon/Invocation to the Light/The Pentagram Ritual/Qabalistic Cross/Hymn of Praise/12 Gates to the City/The Holy Words Iao (These Are the Words)/Aquarius Mantra (in Egyptian)/Enochian (Atlantean) Call/Abrahadabra the Word of Aeo/Praise City of Light/The Qabalistic Cross Aumgn/Return of Arthur/The Magician/The Judgement/My Archangel MIKAEL

Graham Bond with Magick

1971 *We Put Our Magick on You* Mercury
  SRM-1-612
Forbidden Fruit Part 1/Moving Towards the Light/Ajama/Druid/I Put My Magick on You/Time to Die/Hail, Ra-Harakhite/Forbidden Fruit Part 2

U.K. Singles

The Graham Bond Organization

1964	Long Tall Shorty/Long Legged Baby	Decca F 11909
1965	Tammy/Wade in the Water	Columbia DB 7471
1965	Tell Me (I'm Gonna Love Again)/ Love Come Shining Through	Columbia DB 7528
1965	Lease on Love/ My Heart's in Little Pieces	Columbia DB 7647
1966	St. James Infirmary/Soul Tango	Columbia DB 7838
1967	You've Gotta Have Love Babe/ I Love You	Page One POF 014

Graham Bond

1970	Walking in the Park/ Springtime in the City	Warner Bros. WB 8004

Graham Bond with Magick

1971	Twelve Gates to the City/Water Water	Vertigo 6059 042

U.K. EPs

Bond & Brown

1972	Lost Tribe/Macumbe/ Milk Is Turning Sour in My Shoes	Greenwich GSS 104

U.K. Albums

The Graham Bond Organization

1965	*The Sound of '65*	Columbia 33SX 1711

Hoochie Coochie Man/Baby Make Love to Me/Neighbour, Neighbour/Early in the Morning/Spanish Blues/Oh Baby/Little Girl/I Want You/Wade in the Water/Got My Mojo Working/Traintime/Baby Be Good to Me/Half a Man/Tammy

1965   *There's a Bond Between Us*   Columbia
                                                33SX 1750
Who's Afraid of Virginia Woolf/Hear Me Calling Your Name/The Night
Time Is the Right Time/Walkin' in the Park/Last Night/Baby Can It Be
True?/What'd I Say?/Dick's Instrumental/Don't Let Go/Keep a' Dri-
vin'/Have You Ever Loved a Woman?/Camels and Elephants

1977   *The Beginning of Jazz-Rock*   Charly CR 300017
Recorded live at Klooks Kleek, London, October 26, 1964.
Wade in the Water/Big Boss Man/Early in the Morning/Person to Person
Blues/Spanish Blues/Introduction by Dick Jordan/The First Time I Met
the Blues/Stormy Monday Blues/Train Time/What'd I Say

Graham Bond
1970   *Solid Bond*   Warner Bros.
                                                WS 3001
1970   *Holy Magick*   Vertigo 6360 021
1972   *This Is . . . Graham Bond—*   Philips 6382010
           Bond in America
Stiffnecked Chicken/Walk Onto Me/I Couldn't Stand It Anymore/Oh
Shining One/Moving Towards the Light/Crossroads of Time/Baroque/Freaky
Beak/Strange Times, Sad Times/Love Is the Law

Graham Bond with Magick
1971   *We Put Our Magick on You*   Vertigo 6360 042
Forbidden Fruit Part 1/Moving Towards the Light/Ajama/Druid/I Put My
Magick on You/Time to Die/Hail, Ra-Harakhite/Forbidden Fruit Part 2

Bond & Brown
1972   *Two Heads Are Better Than One*   Chapter 1
                                                CHS R 813
The CD issue (See for Miles SEE 345) includes the *Lost Tribe* EP and
Maltamour movie soundtrack.
Lost Tribe/Ig the Pig/Oobati/Amazin Grass/Scunthorpe Crabmeat Train
Sideways Boogie Shuffle Stomp/C.F.D.T. (Captain Frights' Dancing
Terrapins)/Mass Debate/Looking for Time

Miscellaneous U.K. Releases

Singles

Duffy Power with the Graham Bond Quartet
1963   I Saw Her Standing There/Farewell Baby Parlophone R 5024

Ernest Ranglin and the GB's
1964   Swing-A-Ling Pt. 1/Swing-A-Ling Pt. 2 Black Swan WI 417
1964   Just a Little Walk Pt. 1/   Black Swan IEP 704
           Just a Little Walk Pt. 2/So-Ho

Albums

1964   *Rhythm & Blues*   Decca LK 4616
Various artists LP including "High Heeled Sneakers," "Long Legged
Baby," "Hoochie Coochie Man," "Little Girl" and "Strut Around" with
Graham Bond Organization and "Early in the Morning" and "Night
Time Is the Right Time" with Alexis Korner's Blues Incorporated.

1965   *Blues Now*   Decca LK 4681
Various artists LP including "Wade in the Water" with the Graham Bond
Organization.

The Graham Bond Organization
1965   *Gonks Go Beat* (movie soundtrack)   Decca 4873 (U.K.)
Includes "Harmonica" with the Graham Bond Organization.

Foreign Releases

1972   *Rock Generation Vol. 3* (France)   BYG 529.703
Record shared with Sonny Boy Williamson and the Animals.
Wade in the Water/Big Boss Man/Early in the Morning/Person to Person
Blues/Spanish Blues

1972   *Rock Generation Vol. 4* (France)   BYG 529.704
Record shared with Sonny Boy Williamson and the Animals.
Introduction by Dick Jordan/The First Time I Met the Blues/Stormy
Monday Blues/Traintime/What'd I Say

Brunning Hall Sunflower Blues Band

The Brunning Hall Sunflower Blues Band was just one of hundreds of semi-pro blues acts that surfaced in the late 1960s. In fact, they weren't even really an established group, as both of their principal members, bassist/vocalist Bob Brunning and pianist/vocalist Bob Hall, continued to hold down full-time day jobs during the group's existence. For them, the recordings were a side project utilizing whatever other musicians they could round up to take part in the sessions. The presence of these supporting musicians, however, has since made their recordings quite collectable, as these players happened to have been some of the heavyweights of the British Blues scene, including Peter Green and Jo Ann and Dave Kelly.

While attending the Marjons College of Education in Kings Road, Chelsea, London, to become a teacher, Brunning played bass in Five's Company. While with Five's Company, he recorded three singles, each issued in 1966 on Pye Records: "Sunday for Seven Days" backed with "The Big Kill (U.K./Pye 7N 17118), "Some Girls" backed with "Big Deal" (U.K./Pye 7N 17162) and "Session Man" backed with "Dejection" (U.K./Pye 7N 17199).

Following graduation, Brunning auditioned for Fleetwood Mac in July 1967 and was chosen for the position [see **Fleetwood Mac**]. He played with Fleetwood Mac long enough to record three songs in the studio, two of which were used as their first single. However, his spot in the group was understood as temporary while the group waited for John McVie to leave the Bluesbreakers [see **John Mayall**]. When McVie joined Fleetwood Mac in November, Brunning quickly landed a spot in the Savoy Brown Blues Band [see **Savoy Brown**]. However, he only stayed in Savoy Brown long enough to record one single before being fired for questioning their manager, Harry Simmonds, too closely about the band's finances. By this time, Brunning—who was married and desired a more stable career—had already decided to make teaching his main vocation and keep music as a hobby. It was as a member of Savoy Brown that Brunning first encountered part-time piano player Bob Hall.

Bob Hall was born in a nursing home (a residual effect of the bombing taking place during World War II) on June 13, 1942, in West Byfleet, Surrey. Following the end of the war, his mother returned to London, where Hall was raised. He grew up in a musical environment, taking inspiration from his piano-playing father. In the early 1950s, Hall discovered boogie-woogie and his early influences were female boogie-woogie piano player Winifred Atwell, Johnny Parker, and Clarence Lofton & the Boogie Woogie Trio.

Hall also became interested in the blues after hearing Howlin' Wolf and John Lee Hooker records and blues programs on *Voice of America* radio. His first band was the Bob Hall Quintet, which debuted in 1956 at the Dulwich Baths, South London. While attending Durham University, Hall visited London as frequently as possible to go to clubs, taking in Alexis Korner and Cyril Davies playing blues with Chris Barber at the Marquee, the Yardbirds backing Sonny Boy Williamson, and other significant blues gigs.

Late in 1963, Hall answered an ad for a piano player in *Melody Maker* that led to an audition with a band calling themselves the Dollar Bills, featuring guitarist Tony McPhee. Hall joined the band, which soon thereafter changed their name to the Groundhogs, a tribute to John Lee Hooker's "Ground Hog Blues." The group recorded a single for producer Mickie Most but the record was not released. Ironically, the group's first break came in July 1964, when they were asked to back Hooker for a week. That successful stint led to regularly playing the London blues circuit, further tours with Hooker and Jimmy Reed,

and gigs with Little Walter, Memphis Slim and Champion Jack Dupree. Hall stayed on for a few months before leaving the group to fulfill his responsibilities as a full-time patent attorney.

Keeping his hand in music, though, Hall started to gig with Jo Ann Kelly at the Star Club in Croydon [see **Jo Ann Kelly**]. The two met through Bob Glass, who did odd jobs at the Swing Shop in Streatham, South London. The Swing Shop, the only record store in South London at the time that carried American records, routinely had aspiring musicians hanging out for hours to soak up the latest American releases. Hall backed Kelly on several tracks that were subsequently issued on various compilations on Immediate Records.

After leaving the Groundhogs, Hall joined other short-lived bands, including Blues By Six, before answering another classified ad that led him to the John Dummer Blues Band in early 1966 [see **John Dummer Band**]. Hall took part in some demo recordings made with the Dummer Band, but did not participate in sessions for their first album. While with the Dummer Band, Hall was also a founding member of the Savoy Brown Blues Band. He played on their sessions for Immediate and their first four albums for Decca, and continued to perform with them when needed.

In January 1968, after Brunning started his teaching career, he contacted Saga Records—a label introducing a new series of bargain-priced releases—to propose a release of a blues album by "his band," which didn't actually exist. Somewhat to his surprise, the label agreed and Brunning had to put a band together in short order. Brunning contacted Bob Hall and recruited him into the studio project. Brunning also brought in guitarist Colin Jordan (whom he knew from his earlier college band, Five's Company) along with Jeff Russell on drums, Mick Halls on guitar and Peter French on vocals. Halls and French, cousins who drifted through a series of local bands including the Switch, Joe Poe, and Erotic Eel, were in the process of auditioning bassists for their new band when Brunning approached them. While ostensibly auditioning for them, Brunning managed to recruit both French and Halls into his own band.

The band went into Saga Studios and cut an album's worth of material in one day. Saga issued the recordings in 1968 as *Bullen Street Blues* under "Brunning Sunflower Blues Band." ("Big Sunflower" was a pseudonym used by Hall after a fake blues singer from the 1920s that was invented as a practical joke. Eventually, "Big Sun-flower" acquired a biography and a discography that was published in at least one reputable jazz book at the time). *Bullen Street Blues* was a solid offering of British blues, from the moody title track to the stomper "Shout Your Name and Call It." It received encouraging reviews, with *Melody Maker* opining that it was "not over-inspiring, but enthusiastic." However, French was unhappy with the project and when he saw an advertisement in *Melody Maker* for a vocalist, he jumped at the opportunity and joined Black Cat Bones, as did Mick Halls [see **Black Cat Bones**].

In the meantime, with the promise of a U.S. tour, Savoy Brown tried to lure Brunning back into the group in November 1968, but he declined, deciding to stay with his teaching job and keep music as a hobby rather than a primary vocation.

The following year was busy for Bob Hall: he recorded with Savoy Brown for their *Blue Matter* and *A Step Further* albums; appeared on the John Dummer Band's eponymous second album and Dave Kelly's first solo album, *Keeping It in the Family*; recorded miscellaneous tracks that appeared on various blues anthologies; and reconvened with Bob Brunning for two more projects.

In their first joint venture of 1969, Hall and Brunning recorded the second Brunning Sunflower Band album, *Trackside Blues*, for Saga. Again with Colin Jordan on guitar, they were rounded out by Peter Banham on drums and Brunning's friend from Fleetwood Mac, Peter Green (who for contractual reasons was credited as "Peter G___"). Green was featured on guitar and vocals on three tracks, "Ride with Your Daddy Tonight," "It Takes Time" and "If You Let Me Love You." Highlights included the slow blues, "If You Let Me Love You," which featured some nice interplay between Green and Bob Hall on piano, Hall's Boogie Woogie "Sunflower Shuffle" and Brunning's haunting "I Met This Bird in Playboy."

Their second collaboration that year was an *ad hoc* studio ensemble. Peter Eden, of Southern Music, invited them to put together a band to record an album. Brunning, Hall and writer Dennis Cotton started composing material for the project and invited several prominent acquaintances to take part in the recordings. Brunning again asked Peter Green to participate; Green declined. However, Mick Fleetwood and Danny Kirwan accepted the offer and the lineup was bolstered by the addition of Dave Kelly and his sister Jo Ann [see **Dave Kelly**].

They recorded the album in just three days and released it on Music Man as *Tramp*, a name they chose because, as Brunning explained, "We wanted a name in which we could utilize the skills of any musician who felt interested enough to work with us." The Kellys were credited as "Little Brother Dave" and "Memphis Lil" for contractual reasons. *Melody Maker* found the album "interesting with some nice solos from Hall and Kirwan."

In 1970, Brunning and Hall recorded their third album, *I Wish You Would*, with assistance from Dave and Jo Ann Kelly, Steve Rye (harmonica), Mel Wright (drums) and John Altman (sax, flute, clarinet). Peter Green also appeared on the album with "Uranus," a guitar instrumental left over from their previous Saga recording date. Dave Kelly provided two of the highlights—his compositions "Broken Hearted" (in which he was supported by his sister Jo Ann on backing vocals) and the moody "Bad Luck." Jo Ann also sang a duet with Dave on "Broken Hearted." Steve Rye contributed the spirited "All Right with Me," singing the lead vocals and blowing some mean harp. Following *I Wish You Would* in 1970, Hall and Dave Kelly recorded a joint album, *Survivors*, in Milan (Italy/Appaloosa AP 001).

Brunning and Hall recorded one more album, *The Brunning Hall Sunflower Blues Band* (1971), released by Gemini Records this time, with distribution by President. The first sessions included Keith Nelson on electric banjo and Barry Guard on drums, with Jo Ann Kelly and Bob Hall on the vocals. The sessions went badly, and additional musicians were recruited. Guitarist Pat Grover, formerly of Stackhouse, took over on guitar and vocals and Leo Manning contributed on drums. Highlights on the release were "Put a Record On," featuring Jo Ann Kelly on vocals, and the Pat Grover composition "Now Your Crying" (mistitled as "Dirty Old Blues" on the sleeve), which featured Grover on vocals and guitar.

Atypically, none of the prior Brunning Sunflower Band's lineups had ever performed live together, so for a remedy Brunning and Hall took over the club Studio 51 in London on Sundays, transforming it into an R&B showcase featuring their own lineups as well as other blues artists. The gigging band now consisted of Hall, Brunning, Grover and drummer John Hunt, another alumnus of Stackhouse. Several blues legends appeared at the club at various times, including Howlin' Wolf, whom Hall had met when they both played with the Chris Barber Band.

The Brunning Sunflower Blues Band backed American guitar/harmonica player Eddie "Guitar" Burns during both his appearance at the 1972 Lanchester Arts Festival and the recording of his album, *Bottle Up and Go* (U.K./Action ACMP 100). That same year, the band supported another American bluesman, J.B. Hutto, on his *Live in London* recording (U.K./Flyright LP 502).

Then in 1972, American songwriter/harmonica player/vocalist Johnny Mars joined the group. The band had backed Mars on his first album, *Blues from Mars* (U.K./Polydor 2460168). Mars, formerly a member of the Burning Bush, had moved in the mid-1960s to San Francisco, where he had previously formed the Johnny Mars Band.

By this time, the band had begun advertising themselves under a variety of names, including Brunning Hall, Sunflower Boogie Band, and Johnny Mars's Sunflower Band.

Postscript

During the early to mid 1970s, Bob Hall and Bob Brunning played frequently at the 100 Club and the Marquee in London, either supporting an American visitor or showcasing one of their own lineups.

Hall has appeared on nearly 100 albums throughout the years. In 1974, he and Brunning put together another Tramp album, *Put a Record On*. Returning for the Tramp sessions were past collaborators Jo Ann and Dave Kelly, Mick Fleetwood and Danny Kirwan.

In 1979, Hall joined Dave Kelly in the Blues Band. While with the Blues Band, he played on several albums, including the *Official Blues Band Bootleg Album* (1979), *Itchy Feet* (1981), *Back for More* (1989), *Fat City* (1991) and *Homage* (1993).

Hall played with the late Alexis Korner for several years, and they recorded a single, "Pine Top's Boogie Woogie," in 1978. They also formed a big band, initially called the Bob Hall George Green Boogie Woogie Band, in 1977. This band made a live album, without Korner, in the same year. Later the band changed their name to Rocket 88, which included Hall, Korner, Jack Bruce, Charlie Watts and Ian Stewart. Rocket 88 released one self-titled album in 1981 on Atlantic.

In 1981, Hall and Brunning formed the De Luxe Blues Band and issued several albums: *The De Luxe Blues Band* (1981), *A Street Car Named De Luxe* (1981), *Urban De Luxe* (1983), *Motorvating* (1988) and *De Luxe Blues Band* (1988).

Hall continues to tour with his present partner, bassist Hilary Blythe, with whom he has recorded several CDs, the latest being *Don't Play Boogie* on Indigo (2000).

In 1994, Brunning reactivated the De Luxe Blues Band and issued one album, then called it a day in 1997. Not satisfied, Brunning had soon recruited five more musicians and again brought back the De Luxe Blues Band, who continue to tour and record today.

Brunning also runs a blues club called BB's in the Colorhouse Theatre in Southwest London every Thursday and Sunday night. A related record label has released three CDs to date: *Live at B.B.'s Club, Vol. 1*; *Live at B.B.'s Club, Vol. 2*; and *The Boogie Band*.

Brunning has written numerous books, including *Blues in Britain* and *Behind the Mask*, the latter a biography of Fleetwood Mac.

Discography

Release Date	Title	Catalog Number

U.K. Albums

Brunning Sunflower Blues Band

1968 *Bullen Street Blues* Saga FID 2118
Gone Back Home/Hit That Wine/Bullen Street Blues/No Idea/Shout Your Name and Call It/Take Your Hands Off Me/'Fore Time Began/Something Tells Me/Big Belly Blues/Sunflower Boogie/Rockin' Chair

1969 *Trackside Blues* Saga EROS 8132
Ride with Your Daddy Tonight/Tube Train Blues/Sunflower Shuffle/Simple Simon/I Met This Bird in Playboy/Ah' Soul/It Takes Time/Baby You're the Real Thing/If You Let Me Love You/North Star/Closing Hours

1970 *I Wish You Would* Saga EROS 8150
I Wish You Would/On the Road/Checking On My Baby/I'm a Star/Broken Hearted/Bob's Boogie/Mean Old 57/Uranus/Bad Luck/All Right with Me/C & W Blues/Good Golly Miss Kelly

The Brunning Hall Sunflower Blues Band

1971 *The Brunning Hall Sunflower Blues Band* Gemini GM 2010
Call Me/Gotta Keep Running/Put a Record On/Once Upon a Time/Be Satisfied/Now Your Crying/Bogey Man/Feel So Bad/Rolling Down the Highway/Waiting for You/Too Poor to Die/Things Are Getting Better

Tramp

1969   *Tramp*   Music Man
                                                             SMLS 603

Own Up/Same Old Thing/What You Gonna Do When the Road Comes
Though/Somebody Watchin' Me/Too Late Now/Baby What You Want Me
to Do/Street Walkin' Blues/On the Scene/Month of Sundays/Hard
Work/Another Day

The Paul Butterfield Blues Band

As leader of the groundbreaking ensemble, Paul Butterfield (b. December 17, 1942; d. May 4, 1987)
was enormously influential as an ambassador of the
blues by introducing the music to a new and broader generation of fans. The racially integrated Paul Butterfield
Blues Band was in the vanguard of a musical revolution
that sparked a blues revival in the mid-1960s, in the process
bringing greater attention and recognition to the black
pioneers who had inspired them. The band built their reputation by touring and became one of the hottest live acts
in America, with a level of musicianship superior to virtually all of their contemporaries.

Butterfield and Chicago cross-town rival Charlie Musselwhite [see **Charlie Musselwhite**] were considered two
of the leading blues harmonica players in America during
the 1960s. Butterfield's albums contained an amalgam of
jazz, soul, rock and blues, as he continuously experimented
with new styles throughout his career.

Butterfield grew up in Chicago with his older brother,
Peter, in a musical environment. Their dad was an attorney,
while their mother worked in the registrar's office at the
University of Chicago. At an early age, Peter took up the
clarinet and Paul played the flute. By high school, Paul was
studying with the first-chair flautist from the Chicago
Symphony. Paul was also a star athlete on the soccer and
track teams and had been offered a track scholarship to
Brown University (this plan was derailed by a knee injury).

By 16, he became obsessed with the blues, listening
to Muddy Waters, Lightnin' Hopkins, Little Milton, Bobby
Bland and B.B. King. Within a few months of his knee
injury, he took up the harmonica and spent hours practicing by himself. He was strongly influenced by the blues
master Marion Walter Jacobs, better known as Little Walter, who pioneered the use of the amplified harmonica.

While in high school, Butterfield joined the Folklore
Society, where he met University of Chicago student
Nick Gravenites, who was four years his senior [see **Nick
Gravenites**]. Performing as Nick and Paul, the pair played
at the Blind Pig, a small club on Wells Street in Old
Town, with Nick on acoustic and electric guitar and Paul
on harmonica. The duo also played a couple of folk fes-
tivals and started to frequent the blues clubs on Chicago's
South Side. Gravenites spent time at Fradder's Jukebox
Lounge and was occasionally allowed to sing, performing Lightnin' Hopkins songs accompanied by Butterfield on harp. The first club Butterfield had ever ventured
into was Smitty's, at 35th and Indiana, to see Muddy
Waters perform. He soon spent all of his free time going
to clubs to see artists such as Junior Parker, B.B. King and
Howlin' Wolf. These venues catered to an all-black audience and the shows typically ran like revues, offering
members of the audience an opportunity to perform with
the house band. At Smitty's, Butterfield sat in with the
band to the delight and amusement of an audience unaccustomed to the sight of a white boy singing the blues.
Muddy Waters was particularly encouraging to Butterfield. He allowed him to sit in during some sets, an experience that led to frequent appearances with Waters while
he performed at Pepper's Lounge at 503 E. 43rd Street.
Butterfield also sat in with other major blues artists,
among them Magic Sam, Buddy Guy, Otis Rush, Little
Walter and Howlin' Wolf.

While ostensibly still in college, Butterfield continued
to spend more and more time at the clubs, hanging out at
places like Pepper's, Smitty's and Trocadero's, sitting in
at every opportunity. In the autumn of 1960, Butterfield met
University of Chicago student Elvin Bishop [see **Elvin
Bishop**]. The guitar-playing Bishop, a National Merit
Scholar who could attend the school of his choice, chose
the University of Chicago because of his love for the
blues. Butterfield and Bishop jammed a lot together at
parties, eventually becoming a fixture of the Wednesday
night "twist" parties held by University students and locals.
During the day, they hung out at the Fret Shop, a 57th Street
music store where all the folkies congregated.

Butterfield went to live in California in 1962 with his terminally ill girlfriend. They lived with her family near Los Angeles until her death. While in Los Angeles, he traveled north to San Francisco to visit Nick Gravenites. Gravenites arranged a gig for the two of them at a folk music coffeehouse in Berkeley called the Cabal. After their set, Elektra Records producer Paul Rothchild offered Butterfield the opportunity to cut a record. Although interested, Butterfield told him that he didn't have a band and wasn't ready to record, so the producer told him that he would record him whenever Butterfield was ready.

Following the death of his girlfriend, Butterfield returned to Chicago in 1963 and was walking down the street playing harmonica in the rain when guitarist Smokey Smothers, leader of the Little Smokey Smothers Revue, spotted him. Smothers was intrigued and invited him to start playing with his group at the Blue Flame. The rhythm section consisted of bassist Jerome Arnold—the brother of Billy Boy Arnold—and drummer Sam Lay, both longtime members of Howlin' Wolf's band. Butterfield became a regular of Smothers Revue, typically playing harp and singing on four or five songs during the set. At this time, Butterfield made his first recordings with the band, which were issued in 1972 as one side of the album, *An Offer You Can't Refuse*. (The other side consisted of recordings made by Walter Horton.) Butterfield also sat in with local bands at other clubs, including the 1015 Club.

In the winter of 1963, Butterfield visited Gravenites, who was in Lake Hiawatha, New Jersey, and tried to persuade him to go to New York City to line up some gigs. They went to Greenwich Village and visited four or five folk clubs, but made little headway.

Butterfield had better luck in his hometown of Chicago, where his years spent playing with local blues musicians began paying off. In 1963, the owner of a club on Chicago's North Side, called Big John's, offered him a regular gig if he could put a band together. The owner had let his last house band go (which had included Mike Bloomfield on guitar and Charlie Musselwhite on harp) after Bloomfield had asked for a raise [see **Mike Bloomfield, Charlie Musselwhite**].

Butterfield recruited Elvin Bishop, Sam Lay and Jerome Arnold, and the first lineup of the Paul Butterfield Blues Band was born. Located at North Avenue and Wells Street in Old Town, Chicago (near their old venue—the Blind Pig), Butterfield found himself once again heating up Wells Street as Big John's became the hottest club in the

city. Butterfield first played weekends—then soon four nights a week, six sets a night and even seven on weekends. On Butterfield's nights off, Big John's booked Howlin' Wolf, Little Walter and other legends from Chicago's South Side. Influential *Downbeat* correspondent Pete Welding praised the band as "a tight, disciplined, cohesive unit that sets up a strong rhythmic undertow that furnishes the singer all the support he could ask for. The musicians are all first-rate blues men."

Then, after a few months of tremendous success at Big John's, Butterfield received an untimely draft notice. He frantically contacted all of his female acquaintances to find someone to marry him in a hurry in order to claim a marriage exemption to the draft. He finally located a high school friend who agreed to marry him, thereby narrowly escaping the draft and the threat to his career.

Butterfield had been at Big John's for almost a year when he again came to the attention of producer Paul Rothchild. Rothchild had been at a New Year's Eve party in Cambridge on December 31, 1964, when he received an enthusiastic call from Fritz Richmond, washtub bassist with Jim Kweskin & the Jug Band, raving about the Butterfield band. Rothchild left the party, flew out to Chicago to catch their last set at Big John's, and was impressed enough to offer them a contract—but recommended that they add a second guitarist. Sam Lay suggested that they catch Bloomfield playing after-hours over at Magoo's with a six-piece band that included Musselwhite and Gravenites. Rothchild liked Bloomfield enough to suggest that Butterfield enlist him in the lineup. Butterfield was skeptical, believing that Bloomfield wouldn't want to leave his band, but after twenty minutes, Rothchild persuaded him to come on board. Money was not a factor: Bloomfield was heir to a fortune from the family business, which allowed him to concentrate on his passion—playing blues guitar.

Shortly after signing, the band entered the Mastertone recording studio in New York to record their first album, with Paul Rothchild producing. From these sessions, they produced an album and had 25,000 finished copies sitting in a New York warehouse awaiting shipment when Rothchild and the band suddenly had a change of heart—they decided to scrap the whole release. Understandably, Elektra boss Jac Holzman was not pleased, but he eventually relented and agreed to give the band another opportunity to record their debut. The band's main concern with their initial recording was that their performances sounded too tentative and lacked the firepower of their live shows.

Elektra later released these sessions in 1995 as *The Original Lost Elektra Sessions*, although an early take of Gravenites's "Born in Chicago" appeared on the 1965 sampler album, *Folk Song '65,* and five other tracks appeared on the 1966 sampler, *What's Shakin'*. Most of the songs they recorded at these sessions came from the songbooks of Tampa Red, Willie Dixon, Little Walter, Big Joe Turner, Big Boy Crudup, and the Sonny Boy Williamsons I and II; but the three originals stood out. Butterfield wrote two of these: "Lovin' Cup," which initially appeared on the *What's Shakin'* compilation, and an instrumental, "Nut Popper #1," which is one of the few tracks in which Bloomfield unleashed his fiery guitar work.

The inclusion of "Born in Chicago" on the budget sampler album *Folk Song '65* caused quite a stir when the release sold ten times more than expected. This convinced Holtzman that he had a hit band on his hands and he was anxious to get some product out to capitalize on their popularity. With the disappointing initial studio sessions behind them, it was decided to tape the band live at the Café Au-Go-Go, located on Bleecker Street in Greenwich Village. Although four nights were recorded, again the band and Rothchild felt that the performances were not up to standard. When informed, Holtzman was once again livid, but he nonetheless agreed to give the band one final shot at the studio.

Before the upcoming recording session, however, Bloomfield participated in the June 15, 1965, sessions with Bob Dylan that produced the landmark track, "Like a Rolling Stone."

Rothchild initially managed (as well as produced) the band, getting them dates at the Philadelphia and Newport Folk Festivals, but soon realized that the task would be beyond his capabilities. He contacted Albert Grossman, the powerful manager of Bob Dylan and Peter, Paul and Mary, and asked if he would be interested in managing the band. Grossman saw the group at Café Au-Go-Go and reportedly told Rothchild, "I'll see them at Newport."

The Newport Folk Festival was held on July 24–25, 1965, amid a simmering controversy over the use of electric instruments. The controversy was fueled by headliner Bob Dylan's use of such instruments on one side of his latest album, *Bringing It All Back Home,* as well as on his latest single, "Like a Rolling Stone." The latter was #16 on the *Billboard* charts the week of the festival, and would later peak at #2. Folk purists objected to the electric instru-

ments played by both the folk and blues artists who were scheduled to perform. Set against this backdrop, the Butterfield Blues Band opened the first night's show while the audience was still arriving. Their set was generally well received and Grossman decided to manage the band.

The very next day, the band was scheduled to appear at an afternoon blues workshop. Alan Lomax gave them a condescending introduction, posing the question, "Can a white man play the blues?" As he walked off the stage an enraged Grossman confronted him, demanding an explanation. The two bulky men started scuffling in the dirt and throwing punches. In spite of the off-stage altercation, the band turned in a fine performance, with Gravenites joining in to sing three songs. One song, "Mellow Down Easy," appeared on the 1965 compilation *The Newport Folk Festival—1965,* while three additional songs—"Blues with a Feeling," "Look Over Yonders Wall" and "Born in Chicago" appeared on the 1993 CD *Blues with a Feeling.*

Dylan's aforementioned decision to perform with an electric backing band led him to recruit Al Kooper on organ, three members of Paul Butterfield's band—Bloomfield on guitar, Lay on drums and Arnold on bass—and Barry Goldberg on piano. (Goldberg had hoped to play organ with the Butterfield band until Rothchild nixed the idea.) The under-rehearsed ensemble performed only three songs, garnering a mixed reception from the audience, which booed mercilessly, perhaps because of their unhappiness with the short duration of the headliner's set, or Dylan's use of electric instruments, or both.

Following Newport, Bloomfield played for additional Dylan sessions that appeared on the *Highway 61 Revisited* album. Dylan even asked him to become a permanent member of his band. However, Bloomfield declined the tempting offer, preferring to remain a member of the Butterfield Band.

Following the festival, the band returned to Mastertone Studios to try again to record their debut album. Finally released in October 1965, *The Paul Butterfield Blues Band* was a hard-hitting mixture of originals and covers of songs by Little Walter, Willie Dixon, Muddy Waters and Sonny Boy Williamson. The album contained several outstanding cuts, including the opening number; a reworking of the previously issued "Born in Chicago"; covers of two Little Walter tracks—"Blues with a Feeling" and "Last Night"; and the Bishop-Butterfield composition "Our Love Is Drifting."

Although the band was racially mixed, some critics argued that the release proved that white musicians could perform in and even front blues bands, which had been a traditionally Black American sound. Influential columnist Ralph Gleason made this analogy, which was telling of the racial stereotyping of the era: "It is as if a Negro sharecropper from Mississippi were suddenly to be an expert in Gaelic song." *New York Times* critic Robert Shelton noted, "Paul Butterfield's harmonica sorties against the surging, heavily amplified rhythm of drums, electric guitar, organ and bass are without parallel in blues or jazz." *Melody Maker* applauded the release, saying it "shows that there is a lot of spirit and talent on board." The record did have its detractors, however, with journalist Julius Lester attacking the album as "a watered-down version of the blues," infuriating Bloomfield and prompting a meeting between the two men.

During the recording, the group had taken a sixth member, organist Mark Naftalin. Naftalin had previously played with Butterfield and Bishop at college parties and had sat in with the band at Café Au-Go-Go. A University of Chicago graduate, he was previously a member of the Minneapolis band Johnny and the Galaxies, and was studying composition at the Mannes College of Music. He turned up at a recording session one day and sat in with the band on Hammond organ for what became "Thank You Mr. Poobah." They invited him to stay on organ as the session unfolded, and he became a member of the band before the night was out. He ultimately appeared on eight of the album's eleven tracks. While the album failed to make the Top 40 (U.S. #123), it did help to establish the group as a popular underground attraction, playing the East Coast, Detroit and Chicago. In 1997 the Blues Hall of Fame inducted the album as a "classic of blues recording."

In addition to the album, they released a single by lifting two tracks from the LP: "Mellow Down Easy" and "I Got My Mojo Working." *Crawdaddy* looked favorably on the single and predicted big things for the band, printing, "Butterfield definitely has the best sound of all the blues groups, including the Rolling Stones. Sooner or later this band is sure to record a #1 hit song. I don't think this is it, however."

While performing in Boston, drummer Sam Lay became ill with pneumonia and pleurisy in late 1965 and had to be replaced. The band recruited Billy Davenport, a jazz drummer who had played with Otis Rush and Little Walter. They played several dates at the Golden Bear in Huntington Beach, California, and while the shows were sparsely attended, Bay Area promoters Chet Helms and John Carpenter (who were then partners with the legendary Bill Graham) were in the audience and decided to book them for three gigs at the Fillmore. The March 25–27, 1966, dates were hugely successful, drawing a record 7,500 on the three nights and causing Graham to break away from his partners and book the band separately for their next Bay Area appearances. This caused deep resentment in the other two men, who felt that Graham went behind their backs. Graham developed a deep respect for Butterfield and Bloomfield, and at their urging he booked more blues and R&B artists, including Otis Redding, Muddy Waters, B.B. King, Otis Rush, Albert King and others.

While on tour, the band started to play an extended instrumental initially called "The Raga." Constructed around a Nick Gravenites bass line lifted from a song titled "It's About Time," the track was based on a drone with a series of solos using modal scales influenced by Ravi Shankar and John Coltrane. Butterfield, Bishop and Bloomfield each contributed some inspired soloing to this landmark track that was radically different from anything else that had been attempted in popular music. The song was later renamed "East-West" and became the title track of the band's next album.

The *East-West* LP provided an adventurous mix of blues numbers coupled with extended instrumentals that closed each side. The B-side instrumental, "Work Song," also successfully incorporated jazz influences into the music and again allowed the soloists plenty of room to stretch out. The rest of the album offered more straightforward blues, although one surprise track was a cover of "Mary, Mary," which was penned by Monkees' member Mike Nesmith. Davenport proved himself a more versatile drummer than Lay and was ideally suited for the flexibility demanded by these more intricate pieces. *Record Mirror* proclaimed that "the 'feel' that this band creates is exciting and authentic," while *Mojo Navigator* discounted "the ridiculous version of 'Two Trains Running'" (adding, though, that the rest of the album was "top quality music by any standard"). Jon Landau, writing an extended analysis for *Crawdaddy,* found the album disappointing, arguing, "There is an overall lack of unity both in terms of the musicians' playing with each other and in terms of the musicians' getting into their music." Although he acknowledged Mike Bloomfield as the "best lead guitarist I've heard in any rock band," he criticized the direction of the group and suggested that the title track should have been more appropriately titled "Fooling Around with Indian Sounds." Released in August 1966, the album reached

#65 on the charts. Jac Holzman told *Blues-Rock Explosion* he considered the chart placement a "miracle," adding, "No white blues band had accomplished that."

The band played numerous college dates, the Fillmore, and toured England in November 1966 as part of a Georgie Fame/Chris Farlowe package. They also appeared on the British TV show *Ready Steady Go!* They released a radio-friendly single, "Come On In" backed with "I Got a Mind to Give Up Living," to gain some commercial attention, but the gutsy B-side was much stronger. Nonetheless, neither song took off in the charts. However, while still in England, Butterfield recorded an EP with John Mayall's Bluesbreakers [see **John Mayall**]. Even though the EP reflected a high-caliber lineup, the results were surprisingly lackluster.

Mike Bloomfield's decision to leave the band in 1967 fundamentally altered the direction of the group. Butterfield himself tried to persuade the guitarist to change his mind, but Bloomfield left with the intention of fronting his own group, which he did with Electric Flag [see **Electric Flag**].

Bishop's role in the group was redefined with Bloomfield's departure, and he and Butterfield decided to move the band in a different direction. Bishop had been listening to jazz artists such as Archie Shepp and John Coltrane and was jamming with members of the Association for the Advancement of Creative Musicians (AACM), a loose consortium of Chicago's jazz musicians who frequently played with blues musicians. Rather than replacing Bloomfield with another guitarist, the band added a horn section consisting of Keith Johnson on trumpet and David Sanborn and Gene Dinwiddie on alto and tenor saxes, respectively.

Johnson was discovered in New York playing jazz in the East Village at night; he had a daytime job as a truck driver. Sanborn had studied music at Northwestern University and played in local clubs with R&B great Gil Evans. Dinwiddie was a member of the AACM who also drove a truck during the day.

Rehearsals began in New York and the lineup made their debut at the Monterey Pop Festival on July 17, 1967. From this set, five tracks surfaced on the 1992 Rhino Records boxed set, *The Monterey International Pop Festival.* Bishop ably took over the lead guitar slot and the festival presented the band in fine form.

Before they could record their next album, more changes were in store for the group. Jerome Arnold left for family reasons and because of road fatigue, and was replaced by Bugsy Maugh on bass. Maugh, who had previously played with Wilson Pickett, was from St. Joseph, Missouri, and was hired on the recommendation of drummer Buddy Miles.

Shortly thereafter, Billy Davenport quit to get off of the road and return home to Chicago. He was replaced by drummer Phillip Wilson (b. September 8, 1941, St. Louis, Missouri; d. April 1, 1992, New York City, New York), who came through the recommendations of Dinwiddie and Bishop. (Wilson's murder was reported on the TV show *America's Most Wanted* a few years ago.)

The new album, *The Resurrection of Pigboy Crabshaw,* was released in November 1967. Produced by John Court, the album title referred to Elvin Bishop's nickname. By this time, Bishop, Butterfield and Naftalin were the only original members left. This release eschewed the virtuoso soloing that distinguished the previous effort in favor of ensemble playing. While veering toward soul, some moments of fine blues were still in evidence, especially Otis Rush's "Double Trouble" and "Born Under a Bad Sign," a song associated with Albert King. *Rolling Stone* wrote, "*Resurrection* may not show the group to best advantage, but it provides plenty of evidence that these musicians are the most venturesome and exciting players of blues-based rock around." *Beat Instrumental* also praised the band: "Paul Butterfield is undoubtedly the most genuine white blues artist on the scene at the moment, and his brass-augmented band is one of the finest around." The album reached #52 on the *Billboard* charts, which would be Butterfield's highest position ever.

Elektra lifted two tracks from the album, "Run Out of Time" and "One More Heartache," and released them as a single. *Rolling Stone* wrote somewhat favorably of the A-side: "Paul Butterfield has successfully worked the brass into his band in a way that is fairly original and not imitative. . . . The song is nice, but the solo experiments have been made at the cost of the rhythm section."

Their performances were likewise hits with the press. *Downbeat* raved over a show at New York's Carnegie Hall with Albert King and Odetta, asserting, "Butterfield has assembled a group that is one of the finest musical units around. The obligatory vocal sections (good as they are) almost seem to be gotten over as quickly as possible so that the group, Butterfield included, can dig into gutsy, session-style improvisation."

In the April 6, 1968, issue of *Rolling Stone,* it was reported that Bishop planned to leave the band to play some dates with a jazz quartet and eventually form his own band, although he would stay with the band for a few more months. Prior to Bishop's departure, the fourth album, *In My Own Dream,* was recorded. The band suffered another loss during the recording when Mark Naftalin left and was not replaced. The band wrote six of the album's seven songs—all except "Just to Be with You." Al Kooper contributed organ to two tracks, "Drunk Again" and "Just to Be with You." Butterfield took lead vocals on only three songs, while Maugh, Wilson and Bishop performed the balance. *Rolling Stone* singled out "Just to Be with You" as the standout track, stating that the song was a "stone, absolute 100% knockout. It is really the blues, pungent and imaginative, classic in its strength as a Bluebird 78 and modern as a Marshall amp." The title track was almost as good, with Butterfield singing lead and playing guitar while Dinwiddie picked the mandolin and Sanborn soared on a marvelous soprano sax solo. Reviews were glowing: *Melody Maker* called it "another powerful, uncompromising set from one of the finest white blues-pop groups." *Disc and Music Echo* said that they should be regarded as "the finest white blues group anywhere." Released in September 1968, the album reached #79 on the U.S. charts.

By the time of the album's release, the band had relocated to Woodstock, New York. The group searched for a replacement for Bishop and finally held auditions at a New York practice hall. The band auditioned over 20 guitarists before settling on an unlikely choice, 19-year-old Buzz Feiten. Feiten had studied the French horn at the Mannes College of Music, but wasn't committed to it and instead started to play the guitar. He had auditioned with Elvin Bishop's group to play bass but, although Bishop liked his playing, he didn't think it was suitable for him and recommended him to Butterfield. While Feiten had never played with a horn section before and had only played one professional gig in his life, his playing was so distinctive that he snagged the position.

The next single, "Where Did My Baby Go" backed with "In My Own Dream," received an enthusiastic write-up from *New Musical Express,* which called the A-side "an invigorating R&B track from the progressive Butterfield Band. The soul-charged vocal is supported by wailing harmonica, raucous twangy guitar, chanting, scorching brass and a funky, mid-tempo beat. Very little is recognizable to it, but a powerful performance by any standards. They don't call it a blues band for nothing!" In spite of such praise, the single fell flat in both the U.S. and the U.K.

The band closed out the year by appearing at the Newport Pop Festival on August 4, 1968, and the Miami Pop Festival on December 29, 1968. The group brought in Feiten's friend, trumpeter Steve Madaio, and ex-Aretha Franklin bassist Rod Hicks around this time. *The New York Times* reviewed a performance of the new lineup in April 1969, with the observation, "The change has brought the horn section together more solidly than it was during previous New York performances."

For his next project, Butterfield reunited with Mike Bloomfield and Sam Lay to support Muddy Waters in live and studio recordings. The concept was to give some of the younger blues musicians whom Waters had mentored an opportunity to back him for some recordings. A friend of Butterfield's, Norman Dayron, who was a young, white staff producer at Chess Records, produced the sessions. The live side was recorded on April 24, 1969, at the Super Cosmic Joy-Scout Jamboree in Chicago. A reviewer for *Downbeat* wrote, "On 'Losin' Hand,' a slow blues (his meat), Butterfield sang with remarkable intensity and feeling. After the first vocal, he showed why he is, for my money, the best blues harmonica man around." Later, *Downbeat* interviewed Butterfield, Waters and Otis Spann about the sessions, with Spann noting: "I had more feeling in the session than I've had in a long time. It's a funny thing, the people say the white kids can't play blues, but that's wrong." The resulting album, released as *Fathers and Sons,* peaked on the U.S. charts at #70—making it Waters's most commercially successful release ever.

The Paul Butterfield Blues Band continued playing through several major festivals during 1969, including the Atlanta Pop Festival on July 4, the Atlantic City Pop Festival on August 3 and the Woodstock Festival on August 17. "Love March" appeared on the original *Woodstock* album, while "Everything's Going to Be Alright" is on *Woodstock II.*

For the band's next recordings, Elektra, still impatient for a hit album, made arrangements for respected R&B producer Jerry Ragovoy to oversee the project. Ragovoy had built his reputation as a first-rate songwriter, penning numerous R&B/soul classics, including "Cry Baby," a #1 R&B hit for Garnet Mimms; "Time Is on My Side," recorded by Irma Thomas and the Rolling Stones; and several songs recorded by Janis Joplin, including "Piece of My Heart" and "Try." At the same time, he was also achieving success as a producer and was responsible for Lorraine Ellison's stunning "Stay with Me" (which he co-wrote) and several sides for Garnet Mimms and Howard

Tate. The band initially lined up Gil Evans, arranger for jazz great Miles Davis, to write the chart arrangements. When he couldn't accommodate the band's recording schedule, however, they replaced him with Ted Harris, an arranger/pianist who had recently worked with Tony Bennett. Baritone saxophonist/arranger Trevor Lawrence also joined the group.

During the sessions, tensions were generated by Ragovoy's vision of creating a radio-friendly product, which conflicted with the band's desire to move in a jazzier direction. That, coupled with the tight recording schedule, ultimately contributed to the album's malaise. Ragovoy offered to withdraw from the sessions, but Elektra chief Jac Holzman persuaded him to stay on. Consequently, the resulting album, *Keep on Moving*, lacked direction and was an uneasy mixture of jazz, gospel, soul and rock that suffered from cloying horn arrangements. *Rolling Stone* pointed out that the album was "the farthest thing from the blues that Butterfield has ever done." Despite the LP's shortcomings, *Melody Maker* credited the album with ranking "with all the other great U.S. epic album jobs with some hot flute, trumpet and saxophone blowing alongside the lead guitar." Released in October 1969, *Keep On Moving* reached #102 on the U.S. charts.

A far stronger effort was *The Paul Butterfield Blues Band Live*. Produced by Todd Rundgren and released at the end of 1970, the album was recorded at the Troubadour in Los Angeles. The group was now comprised of Ralph Walsh on guitar, George Davidson on drums, Rod Hicks on bass and vocals, Ted Harris on keyboards, a horn section of Gene Dinwiddie and Trevor Lawrence, and backing vocalists Clydie King, Merry Clayton, Venetta Fields and Oma Drake. The two-record set contained live recordings of material culled from their preceding three albums, plus three tracks that had not previously appeared in the Butterfield catalog: "Number Nine," "Get Together Again" and "The Boxer." The best songs on the album included "Driftin' and Driftin'," "Born Under a Bad Sign" and "Everything's Going to Be Alright." *Beat Instrumental* lauded the release as a "brilliant album" and *Rolling Stone* reflected, "The simple fact of the matter is that Butterfield is superb in person (true for most blues bands) and this two volume set allows plenty of stretching-out space and saves any tunes from being truncated in the studio." The album reached #72 on the *Billboard* charts.

The Paul Butterfield Blues Band next released *Sometimes I Just Feel Like Smilin'* in 1971 (U.S. #124). For this recording, Dennis Whitted replaced George Davidson on drums and Bobby Hall and Big Black contributed congas and bongos, respectively, but otherwise the lineup was the same as for the previous live album. This release saw the Butterfield Band move away from the free-form improvisation of the last couple of albums and return to the more formally structured blues compositions of earlier efforts. All the songs were originals except for "Pretty Woman," a tune identified with Albert King, and the Ray Charles-associated "Drown in My Own Tears." Original producer Paul Rothchild reunited with Butterfield for this critically acclaimed effort. *Record Mirror* called it "powerful drive-along stuff from the well-established band" and *Beat Instrumental* stated, "Definitely a good album for any collection." *Sometimes I Just Feel Like Smilin'* would be the last release by the Butterfield Blues Band before the group broke up.

Postscript

Original members Mike Bloomfield and Mark Naftalin reunited with Butterfield in January 1972 for two nights, opening the Fenway Theater, a new music hall in Boston.

Butterfield's next project was forming Better Days in 1972 with Geoff Muldaur. Better Days issued two albums on Albert Grossman's Bearsville label, *Better Days* (1973) and *It All Comes Back* (1973). Butterfield's output for the rest of his career was sporadic—*Put It in Your Ear* (1976), *North-South* (1981) and *The Legendary Paul Butterfield Rides Again* (1986). On May 4, 1987, Butterfield died in his apartment at age 44.

Sam Lay issued a solo album in 1970, *Say Lay in Bluesland,* and has appeared in numerous sessions with others. In late 1969, he joined the Siegel-Schwall Band and still continues to perform with them on occasion [see **Siegel-Schwall Band**]. Lay has issued numerous recordings, including *Shuffle Master* (1992) and *Sam Lay Live* (1996) on the Appaloosa label, *Stone Blues* (1996) on Evidence Records, *Rush Hour Blues* (2000) on Telarc and *Live on Beale Street* (2000) on Blue Moon.

Mark Naftalin arranged, coproduced and played on the Mother Earth album, *Living with the Animals* (1968), and later played piano on Brewer and Shipley's Top Ten hit "One Toke Over the Line." Presently, Naftalin hosts the weekly broadcast *Mark Naftalin's Blues Power Hour* on San Francisco's KALW-FM. After his stint with the Butterfield Band, he settled in the San Francisco Bay Area and embarked on a career that has included playing with and leading bands; solo concerts; playing on blues and rock recording sessions (over 100 to date); producing festivals, concerts and shows; cofounding and heading the Blue Monday Foundation; songwriting and composing; and producing records for his own label, Winner Records. From the late 1960s through the mid-1970s, Naftalin played in the Bay Area and around the country (and on a number of recordings) with Mike Bloomfield, sometimes as a duo, but most often as a band called Mike Bloomfield and Friends.

Discography

Release Date	Title	Catalog Number

U.S. Singles

1965	Mellow Down Easy/	Elektra 45016
	I Got My Mojo Working	
1967	Come On In/I Got a Mind to	Elektra 45609
	Give Up Living	
1967	Run Out of Time/One More Heartache	Elektra 45620
1967	In My Own Dream/Love Disease	Elektra 45643
1968	Where Did My Baby Go/	Elektra 45658
	In My Own Dream	
1969	Love March/[B-side unknown]	Elektra 45692

U.S. Albums

1965   *The Paul Butterfield Blues Band*   Elektra EKS-7294
Born in Chicago/Shake Your Money-Maker/Blues with a Feeling/Thank You Mr. Poobah/I Got My Mojo Working/Mellow Down Easy/Screamin'/Our Love Is Drifting/Mystery Train/Last Night/Look Over Yonder Wall

1966   *East-West*   Elektra EKS-7315
East-West/Walkin' Blues/Get Out of My Life, Woman/I Got a Mind to Give Up Living/All These Blues/Work Song/Mary, Mary/Two Trains Running/Never Say No

1967   *The Resurrection of Pigboy Crabshaw*   Elektra EKS-74015
One More Heartache/Driftin' and Driftin'/Pity the Fool/Born Under a Bad Sign/Run Out of Time/Double Trouble/Drivin' Wheel/Droppin' Out/Tollin' Bells

1968   *In My Own Dream*   Elektra EKS-74025
Last Hope's Gone/Mine to Love/Just to Be with You/Get Yourself Together/Morning Blues/Drunk Again/In My Own Dream

1969   *Keep on Moving*   Elektra EKS-74053
Love March/No Amount of Loving/Morning Sunrise/Losing Hand/Walking By Myself/Except You/Love Disease/Where Did My Baby Go/All In a Day/So Far, So Good/Buddy's Advice/Keep On Moving

1970   *The Paul Butterfield Blues Band Live* (2 LP) Elektra 7E-2001
Everything's Going to Be Alright/Love Disease/The Boxer/No Amount of Loving/Driftin' and Driftin'/Intro/Number Nine/I Want to Be with You/Born Under a Bad Sign/Get Together Again/So Far, So Good

1971   *Sometimes I Just Feel Like Smilin'*   Elektra EKS-75031
Play On/1000 Ways/Pretty Woman/Little Piece of Dying/Song for Lee/Trainman/Night Child/Drown in My Own Tears/Blind Leading the Blind

1972   *Golden Butter (Best Of)*   Elektra EKS-7E-2005
Born in Chicago/Shake Your Money-Maker/Mellow Down Easy/Our Love Is Drifting/Mystery Train/Look Over Yonder Wall/East-West/Walking Blues/Get Out of My Life Woman/Mary, Mary/Spoonful/One More Heartache/Last Hope's Gone/In My Own Dream/Love March/Driftin' and Driftin'/Blind Leading the Blind

1995   *The Original Lost Elektra Sessions* (CD)   Elektra R2 73505
Good Morning Little School Girl/Just to Be with You/Help Me/Hate to See You Go/Poor Boy/Nut Popper #1/Everything's Gonna Be All Right/Lovin' Cup/Rock Me/It Hurts Me Too/Our Love Is Drifting/Take Me Back Baby/Mellow Down Easy/Ain't No Need to Go No Further/Love Her with a Feeling/Piney Brown Blues/Spoonful/That's All Right/Goin' Down Slow

1995   *Strawberry Jam* (CD)   Winner 446
Just to Be with You[1]/Mystery Train[2]/Tollin' Bells[3]/Cha Cha in Blues[2]/Rock Me[4]/One More Heartache[4]/Strawberry Jam[5]/Come on in This House[3]/Born in Chicago[3]
  [1] Whisky A Go-Go, Hollywood, California, winter 1966
  [2] The Golden Bear, Huntington Beach, California, spring 1967
  [3] The Golden Bear, winter 1967
  [4] New Penelope, Montreal, summer 1967
  [5] JD's, Tempe, Arizona, winter 1968

1996   *East-West Live* (CD)   Winner 447
Three live versions of "East-West." Version 1 recorded at Whisky A Go-Go, Hollywood, California, winter 1966. Version 2 recorded at Poor Richard's, Chicago, spring 1966. Version 3 recorded at the Golden Bear, Huntington Beach, California, winter 1967.

Miscellaneous U.S. Releases

1965   *Folk Song '65*   Elektra S8
Contains an alternative take of "Born in Chicago."

1965   *The Newport Folk Festival 1965*   Vanguard VRS-9225
Includes "Mellow Down Easy" by the Paul Butterfield Blues Band.

1966   *What's Shakin'*   Elektra EKS-74002 (S)   Elektra EKL-4002 (M)
Various artists album containing five tracks by the Paul Butterfield Blues Band: Spoonful/Off the Wall/Lovin' Cup/Good Morning Little School Girl/One More Mile.

1969   *You Are What You Eat* (movie soundtrack)   Columbia OS-3240
Includes one song by the Paul Butterfield Blues Band, "Teenage Fair."

1970 *Woodstock* (3 LP) Cotillion SD 3-500
Includes "Love March" by the Paul Butterfield Blues Band.

1971 *Woodstock II* (2 LP) Cotillion SD 2-400
Includes "Everything's Going to Be Alright" by the Paul Butterfield Blues Band.

1992 *The Monterey International* Rhino R70596
     Pop Festival (4 CD)
Includes "Look Over Yonders Wall," "Mystery Train," "Born in Chicago," "Double Trouble" and "Mary Ann" by the Paul Butterfield Blues Band.

1993 *Blues with a Feeling* (2 CD) Vanguard
     VCD2-77005
Recordings made at the Newport Folk Festivals including three tracks recorded at the 1965 festival with the Paul Butterfield Blues Band: "Blues with a Feeling," "Look Over Yonders Wall" and "Born in Chicago."

1993 *Rare Chicago Blues,* Bullseye Blues
     1962–1968 (CD) CD BB 9530
Includes Paul Butterfield on the following tracks: "Wild Cow Moan," (with Big Joe Williams), "Diggin' My Potatoes" (with James Cotton and Elvin Bishop) and "Three Harp Boogie" (with James Cotton, Elvin Bishop and Billy Boy Arnold).

Butterfield with Muddy Waters, Otis Spann and Mike Bloomfield
1969 *Fathers and Sons* (2 LP) Chess 127
Includes Muddy Waters, Otis Spann, Mike Bloomfield and Paul Butterfield.
All Aboard/Mean Disposition/Blow Wind Blow/Can't Lose What You Ain't Never Had/Walkin' Thru the Park/Forty Days and Forty Nights/Standin' Round Crying/I'm Ready/Twenty-Four Hours/Sugar Sweet/Long Distance Call/Baby Please Don't Go/Honey Bee/The Same Thing/Got My Mojo Working (Part 1)/Got My Mojo Working (Part 2)

Paul Butterfield and Walter Horton
1972 *An Offer You Can't Refuse* Red Lightning
     RL 008
Contains recordings made in 1963.
Everything's Gonna Be Alright/Poor Boy/I Got My Mojo Working/Last Night/Loaded/One Room Country Shack

U.K. Singles

1966 Come On In/I Got a Mind London HLZ 10100
     to Give Up Living
1967 All These Blues/Never Say No Elektra
     EKSN 45007
1967 Run Out of Time/One More Heartache Elektra
     EKSN 45020
1968 Get Yourself Together/Mine to Love Elektra
     EKSN 45047
1968 Where Did My Baby Go/ Elektra EKSN
     In My Own Dream 45069
1970 Love March/Love Disease Elektra 2101-012

U.K. Albums

1966 *The Paul Butterfield Blues Band* Elektra
     EKL 294 (m)
     Elektra
     EKS 7294 (s)

1966 *East-West* Elektra EKL 315 (m)
     Elektra
     EKS 7315 (s)
1968 *The Resurrection of Pigboy Crabshaw* Elektra
     EKL 4015 (m)
     Elektra
     EKS 74014 (s)
1968 *In My Own Dream* Elektra
     EKL 4025 (m)
     Elektra
     EKS 74025 (s)
1969 *Keep On Movin'* Elektra EKS 74053
1970 *The Paul Butterfield Blues Band Live* (2 LP) Elektra 2001
1971 *Sometimes I Just Feel Like Smilin'* Elektra K 42095

Miscellaneous U.K. Releases

1967 *John Mayall's Bluesbreakers* Decca DFER 8673
     with Paul Butterfield (EP)
All My Life/Ridin' on the L&N/Little By Little/Eagle Eye

1970 *Woodstock* (3 LP) Atlantic 2663001
1971 *Woodstock II* (2 LP) Atlantic 2657003
1997 *The Monterey International* Ode Sounds &
     Pop Festival (4 CD) Visuals 72825

Paul Butterfield and Walter Horton
1972 *An Offer You Can't Refuse* Red Lightning
     RL 008

Foreign Releases

1999 *I Blueskvarter* Jefferson
     (In the Blues Quarter) (2 CD) SBACD12655
Recorded in Chicago in 1964 for Olle Helander's Swedish Radio blues show. Includes six tracks recorded with Butterfield, Abraham "Little Smokey" Smothers (guitar), Sam Lay (drums) and Jerome Arnold (bass): "Help Me," "Going Back Home," "Poor Boy," "Everything's Gonna Be Alright," "Last Night," "Got My Mojo Working," plus selections from other artists.

Canned Heat

Canned Heat rose to fame because their knowledge and love of blues music was both wide and deep. Drawing on an encyclopedic knowledge of all phases of the genre, the group specialized in updating obscure old blues recordings. Applying this bold approach, the band attained two worldwide smash hits in 1968, "On the Road Again" and "Going Up the Country," inspired interpretations of late 1920s blues by Tommy Johnson and Henry Thomas, respectively. However, the success of this formula was short-lived as they were only able to reach the Top 40 one more time in 1970 with a cover of Wilbert Harrison's R&B classic "Let's Work Together."

Much of Canned Heat's legacy stems from these three classic early recordings, which featured two unique talents, both of whom died young: Alan Wilson (b. July 4, 1943, Boston, Massachusetts; d. September 3, 1970, Topanga, California), a gifted slide guitarist, harmonica player, songwriter and vocalist with a high tenor reminiscent of Skip James; and Bob Hite (b. February 26, 1945, Torrance, California; d. April 6, 1981, Venice, California), a blues shouter whose massive physique earned him the nickname "The Bear," which was matched only by his equally massive knowledge of blues music.

Canned Heat was conceived at Bob Hite's home during a meeting of record collectors in November 1965. Collectors Hite, Mike Perlowin, John Fahey and Alan Wilson were present, and by the meeting's end these blues devotees had decided to form their own jug band, with the first rehearsal soon to follow. The initial configuration was comprised of Perlowin on lead guitar, Wilson on bottleneck guitar, Hite on vocals, Stu Brotman on bass and Keith Sawyer on drums. Perlowin and Sawyer dropped out within a few days of the rehearsal, so guitarist Kenny Edwards (a close friend of Alan Wilson) stepped in to replace Perlowin, and Ron Holmes agreed to sit in on drums until they could find a permanent drummer.

Bob Hite was born into a musical family in Torrance, California. His mother was a singer and his father had played in a dance band in Pennsylvania. Hite remembered hearing his first blues record, "Cruel Hearted Woman" by Thunder Smith, when he was only eight. As a young man, he became obsessed with records and he used to purchase old jukebox records for 9¢ each, regardless of who the artist was. By the time he reached the fifth grade, he had amassed more records than the rest of his classmates put together. He soon expanded his collection to include 78 r.p.m. blues records, which later influenced his vocal technique of "shouting the blues." Spending his teenage years hanging around record stores, Hite would later manage a store that specialized in old records, making many useful contacts with fellow collectors and musicians as part of his job.

Alan Wilson grew up in Boston, Massachusetts, where he became a music major at Boston University and a frequent player in the Cambridge coffeehouse folk-blues circuit. He also found time to write two lengthy analytical articles on bluesmen Robert Pete Williams and Son House, which *Downbeat* described as "among the most significant contributions to modern blues scholarship, representing the first important musicological analysis of blues style." In fact, when Son House was "rediscovered" in 1964 by Phil Spiro, Dick Waterman and Nick Perls, Wilson ended up spending hours with the elderly bluesman, teaching him how to play his own songs again, as House had not even owned a guitar for several years. Waterman managed House and got him a recording contract with Columbia, and Wilson assisted House in recording his 1965 album, *Father of the Folk Blues*, and provided harmonica or guitar on three songs (two of which— "Empire State Express" and "Levee Camp Moan"—were included on the album).

Wilson was an excellent harpist, slide guitarist and vocalist with a unique high tenor style. His friend Mike Bloomfield [see **Mike Bloomfield**] introduced him to Charlie Musselwhite [see **Charlie Musselwhite**] as "the best goddamn harp player there is. He can do things that you never heard before." Wilson occasionally worked for his father's construction firm laying bricks but, thankfully, he preferred laying down unforgettable riffs to hard physical labor. Wilson's nickname, "Blind Owl," was bestowed upon him by friend John Fahey and was a reference to the extra-thick lenses Wilson wore to compensate for his poor vision. Later Fahey, while researching a book on bluesman Charlie Patton, invited Wilson out to California to help with the project.

Through Fahey, Wilson (a blues scholar) met Hite (a record collector), which led to the collectors' meeting at Hite's house where Canned Heat originated. The group decided to take their name from "Canned Heat Blues," an obscure 1928 track by bluesman Tommy Johnson that described the drug high achieved through drinking the household product Sterno. While Sterno was intended to be used for unclogging drains and its ingestion could lead to death, when mixed with soda it was a cheap way to "get high" . . . and Johnson reportedly died prematurely doing just that.

The new group quickly landed a gig at the Ash Grove on Melrose Avenue in Hollywood, and Hite invited his friend Henry Vestine to attend. Vestine liked what he heard and asked if he could join the band, so Vestine was added while keeping Edwards on temporarily. They all soon realized that three guitars were overkill, so they let Edwards go. (He went on to form the Stone Poneys with Linda Ronstadt.) At around the same time, Frank Cook came in to replace Homes as their permanent drummer.

In 1957, Henry Vestine (b. December 24, 1944, Washington, D.C.; d. October 21, 1997, Paris, Fr.) moved with his family to Los Angeles where he spent his teenage years. Like Hite, he started collecting records and became interested in the blues. In June 1964, Vestine, Fahey and another friend tracked down the legendary and mystical blues singer Skip James. Locating the 62-year-old singer in a hospital in Tunica, Mississippi, the three blues researchers arranged for him to appear at the 1964 Newport Folk Festival. The following year, Vestine became a member of the Beans, a San Fernando Valley-based group. By 1965, he had joined the Mothers of Invention, where he stayed for only a few months.

Frank Cook had a jazz background, having performed with such luminaries as bassist Charlie Haden, trumpeter Chet Baker and pianist Elmo Hope. He also collaborated with black soul/pop artists Shirley Ellis and Dobie Gray.

Canned Heat's first year was marked by infrequent gigs and public indifference. Al Wilson later told *Melody Maker*, "The first year we were together, we worked for three weeks. We'd get a gig, play three days and get fired . . . because we refused to be a (human) jukebox." After a particularly disastrous engagement (surprisingly, this was at what became the hip Whisky A Go-Go) the group disbanded in August 1966 for the next three months.

During this period, Alan Wilson and Henry Vestine moved on to join the Electric Beavers, which lasted only a short time on a rehearsal basis only. Eventually, Canned Heat re-formed in November 1966 for a one-off gig at a Mothers concert at UCLA. The owners of the Los Angeles club Kaleidoscope were in the audience that night and, following their performance, offered Canned Heat a regular engagement at the club. The group was also picked up by the management team of Skip Taylor (formerly of the William Morris Agency) and John Hartman. Under their guidance, the band's career was revitalized. The Kaleidoscope gigs brought them to the attention of Liberty Records, and within a month they had signed that all-important recording contract with a major label.

Even though their prospects were again looking good, bassist Stuart Brotman decided not to rejoin the band. He had been playing gigs in Fresno through the summer and was developing an interest in Arabic and various other types of ethnic music. Brotman later joined David Lindley and Chris Darrow in the acclaimed world-music band Kaleidoscope. So Canned Heat replaced Brotman with bassist Mark Andes, who lasted only a couple of months because he preferred to play in a rock'n'roll band. (Andes rejoined his former colleagues in the Red Roosters, a folk-rock band that had adopted a new name—Spirits Rebellious, later shortened to Spirit.)

The group finally found a permanent bassist in Larry Taylor, a.k.a. the Mole, who joined in March 1967. Taylor (b. June 26, 1942; Brooklyn, New York) was the brother of Ventures drummer Mel Taylor. He'd had previous experience backing Jerry Lee Lewis and Chuck Berry in concert. Taylor had also been a member of the Moondogs along with James Marcus Smith (who later found fame as P.J. Proby). The Moondogs had released a couple of records in the late 1950s before dissolving. As a member of Bobby Hart's Candy Store Prophets, Taylor participated in sessions that produced the first two Monkees albums.

With Taylor, the band started recording in April. Many of these early demos—including an early version of "On the Road Again"—would surface years later on the 1994 EMI CD release, *Uncanned!* Other early recordings would appear on *Vintage Canned Heat* and the multiple-artist compilation *Early L.A.*

Without the benefit of a new record to promote, the band appeared at the Monterey Pop Festival on June 17, 1967. *Downbeat* complimented their performance in an article appearing in the August 10 issue (which featured Canned Heat on the cover): "Technically, Vestine and Wilson are quite possibly the best two-guitar team in the nation, and Wilson has certainly become our finest white blues harmonica man. Together with powerhouse vocalist Bob Hite, they performed the Chicago blues idiom of the 1950s so skillfully and naturally that the question of which race the music belongs to becomes totally irrelevant."

Recordings of the festival resulted in their spirited rendition of "Rollin' and Tumblin'" being captured in a film of the event, and a 1992 boxed CD set, *The Monterey International Pop Festival,* included "Rollin' and Tumblin'" along with "Bullfrog Blues" and "Dust My Broom."

"Rollin' and Tumblin'" backed with "Bullfrog Blues" became Canned Heat's first single, which Liberty released shortly after their Monterey appearance. It received a significant amount of West Coast airplay, but failed to break out nationally, reaching only #115 on the charts.

Canned Heat's self-titled debut was released in July 1967. The straightforward, traditional blues effort was highlighted by covers of blues standards, including Willie Dixon's "Evil Is Going On," Muddy Waters's "Rollin' and Tumblin'" and a take of the Sonny Boy Williamson classic "Help Me," with vocals by Wilson. *The Los Angeles Free Press* reported, "This group puts on a great show in person. The whole group has it. They should do well, both visually and with their recordings." *Canned Heat* fared reasonably well commercially, reaching #76 on the *Billboard* charts.

Following a one-week gig at the Ash Grove from August 22–26, the band went on their first national tour. Along with their festival appearance at Monterey, the album had significantly bolstered the group's standing with the underground. Disaster struck, however, when the group was arrested in Denver for marijuana possession. Only Wilson, a pioneer eco-warrior who had been out collecting leaves at the time, escaped arrest. Upon returning to L.A., the group held a press conference to announce that their bust had been orchestrated and that the Denver Police Department had planted the evidence used against them as part of an ongoing campaign of harassment waged against the Family Dog (the promoters) and its patrons.

Publicity aside, the members, with the exception of Wilson, ended up spending the weekend in jail before being released on bail. The arrest would have disastrous financial consequences for them in future years. Lacking the funds to mount an adequate legal defense, the band was forced to sell their publishing rights to Liberty Records for $10,000 so that they could secure the services of a top local attorney. The trial ended up with the indicted band members only receiving probation.

After being released, their first gig was a shared bill with Bluesberry Jam at the Magic Mushroom in Los Angeles. Bluesberry Jam, featuring Adolpho "Fito" de la Parra on drums, thoroughly outplayed the Heat that night. Following the gig, around 3 a.m., manager Skip Taylor asked de la Parra if he would be interested in auditioning for the band, which was looking to replace Cook. De la Parra showed up for the audition clutching albums by Buddy Guy and Junior Wells, which—along with his playing skills—made an impression on Hite. When asked by Skip Taylor if he would like to join the band, de la Parra reportedly replied, "I was born to play in Canned Heat." In a neat switch, Cook took de la Parra's spot in Bluesberry Jam, which soon evolved into Pacific Gas & Electric. De la Parra played his first gig as an official member of Canned Heat on December 1, 1967.

De la Parra had played drums professionally since he was 16 years old. He was born in Mexico City on February 8, 1946, and as he grew older had become a member of a series of Mexican rock bands—starting with Los Sparks in 1958 and including Los Juniors, Los Sinners and Los Hooligans—all of which mainly played covers of American hits. His last band earned de la Parra a Mexican gold record for the single, "Despeinada." Los Sinners evolved into Los Tequilas and released two albums in Mexico on the RCA Victor/Camden label. In 1965, the band illegally entered the U.S. to play in small clubs in the Los Angeles area.

After six months of work in small L.A. clubs such as the Troubadour, P.J.'s, the Daisy and the Lazy X, Los Tequilas were deported back to Mexico. There, de la Parra started to play in more R&B-oriented Mexican groups, including Javier Batiz & the Finks and the TJ's. While playing with the Finks in Mexico City, Frank Cook sat in with the group for a couple of numbers and invited de la Parra to visit him if he ever came to L.A. Awhile later, de la Parra married an American woman and returned to the U.S. with the intention of studying psychology at a California college. Still playing drums, he joined Larry Barnes and the Creations, which became the house band at the Tom Cat Club in Torrance, California. The Tom Cat residency enabled de la Parra to play behind some of the great R&B artists of the time, including the Coasters, Ben E. King, Mary Wells, Etta James, the Platters and Jimmy Reed. De la Parra then joined Sotweed Factor, with whom he released one 45" in 1965, "Bald Headed Woman" backed with "Say It Isn't So" (U.S./Original Sound 76). After Sotweed Factor broke up, de la Parra joined Bluesberry Jam.

Canned Heat's second single—the first to feature de la Parra—was "Evil Woman" backed with "World in a Jug" released in October 1967. Although it featured moody Hite vocals and some fine guitar work by Vestine, "Evil Woman" (not to be confused with the Crow hit of the same name) failed to take off.

However, they were at last beginning to raise their profiles with mainstream media press coverage. A December review in *Variety* (a trade publication) called the band "one of the most devastating, ear-shattering psychedelic units ever to play this 'now music,'" and described Hite as "one of the rare species floating around (and that he does) who shows promise of being singled out in this new crop as a top performer."

Even though much of the second album was recorded after de la Parra joined the band, the tracks were deemed too similar-sounding to the debut album. They were scrapped, with the exception of one cut on which Cook's drum part was erased and de la Parra's was dubbed in. These tracks probably include six outtakes that surfaced for the first time on the EMI/Liberty anthology *Uncanned!* in 1994.

De la Parra's arrival marked the beginning of Canned Heat's classic lineup. An enthusiastic reviewer in the January 1968 issue of *The Beat* wrote, "The new drummer named Fito de la Parra is completely fantastic and the equal of any of the best jazz drummers around. . . . This group is completely able to play the finest solos and yet they are a totally integrated group which functions best as a unit."

The second album, *Boogie with Canned Heat,* finally arrived in January 1968. It showed the group moving away from pure blues, instead incorporating more rock'n'roll grooves into their music. *Boogie with Canned Heat* contained a number of notable tracks, especially Hite's "Amphetamine Annie" (a tune inspired by the drug abuse of an acquaintance), which became one of their most enduring songs. Another well-known track, the group original "My Crime," was a thin rewrite of "Hoochie Coochie Man" with updated lyrics inspired by the Denver drug bust. Vestine's "Marie Laveau," a slow instrumental, featured some fine interplay between his guitar and Wilson's harmonica. The crown jewel of the set, "On the Road Again," revealed Wilson in six different capacities—three tambour parts, harmonica, vocal and guitar—all recorded at different times. His unconventional falsetto and the song's Eastern textures made the recording an instant classic.

Boogie with Canned Heat also included their first recording of the elongated "Boogie," which would reappear on future albums and become a permanent concert favorite. The 11-minute "Fried Hockey Boogie" (credited to Larry Taylor, but obviously derived from John Lee Hooker's "Boogie Chillen" riff) allowed each band member to stretch out on his instrument.

Hite acknowledged Hooker's influence in a December 1968 interview with *The Los Angeles Times:* "We were all John Lee Hooker fans, very heavy Hooker fans—especially the sound he had from 1948 through 1953, before he got his band. . . . So anyway, we got in the recording studio and decided that we had to have something long on our second album because that's what everybody else was

doing. So Alan just started to play this Hooker boogie line and we all joined in. We really got going on the boogie thing by accident."

Without a single taken from the album to promote it, *Boogie with Canned Heat* nonetheless entered the charts on February 24, 1968, but stalled at #139. Then, spurred by the strong audience response that a Texas radio station received after it started playing "On the Road Again," Liberty decided to release the song as a single on April 24, 1968. "On the Road Again" rocketed to #16 and took the entire album to the same spot in the album charts. Both the single and the album became even bigger hits in the U.K., where the single reached #8 and the album climbed to #5.

The press began universally acclaiming Canned Heat as blues innovators. The influential jazz magazine *Downbeat* ran a glowing article about the group in their June 13, 1968, issue, calling them "probably the best band of its type in the world today, playing with a power and conviction, and generating an excitement which have [sic] been matched by only the finest of the Negro bands in this idiom [early postwar blues music]. One would, in fact, have to go back to the great innovators of the genre—Muddy Waters, Howlin' Wolf, John Lee Hooker, Elmore James, Little Walter, and the like—to find groups comparable to Canned Heat in mastery, ease and inventiveness."

On August 3, the band appeared at the Newport Pop Festival in California. *The Los Angeles Times* reported, "A crowd of about 50,000 fans sweltered in the sun for nine hours to hear a succession of rock groups that played from morning to evening at the First Newport Pop Festival held on a recent weekend at Costa Mesa. The group . . . Canned Meat [sic] was the biggest hit."

Canned Heat left the following month for their first European tour, a month of concert performances and media engagements that included TV appearances on the British show *Tops of the Pops* and the German program *Beat Club* (where they capably lip-synched "On the Road Again").

In October, they released a double album, *Living the Blues*. Originally, they had wanted to call it "Living the Blues Naked," which, as Bob Hite explained to *The Los Angeles Times*, meant that the blues was a "raw, naked, ugly thing," to which he added, "it can also be a good thing." They planned to carry this "naked" theme into the album cover with a shot of the band members running naked through Palisades Park in New Jersey. Ultimately, the idea was abandoned and a less controversial cover was used.

Their new double-album gave Canned Heat the freedom to experiment musically and stretch out their style. As Bob Hite explained to *Hit Parader*, "[*Living the Blues*] is another step forward for us. Progression is what we're trying to accomplish. If a group doesn't progress they might as well hang it up."

Side one comprised traditional blues, highlighted by "Pony Blues" (a number associated with Delta bluesman Charlie Patton), "Walking By Myself" (a #14 R&B hit in 1957 by Jimmy Rogers, former guitarist for Muddy Waters), and "One Kind Favor" a.k.a. "See That My Grave Is Kept Clean" (a spooky, traditional spiritual made famous by Blind Lemon Jefferson). The most celebrated track on *Living the Blues*, "Going Up the Country," was an Alan Wilson adaptation of "Going Down South," a song first recorded in 1928 by the obscure Henry Thomas. They revised it to feature prominent flute contributions by "Tank" Harrigan, a member of Ray Charles's band. "Going Up the Country" provided Canned Heat with another smash single on both sides of the Atlantic, reaching #11 in the U.S. and #19 in the U.K.

The second side of the first disc contained a single sweeping epic, "Parthenogenesis." This song, the most ambitious track on the album, was a nine-part sound collage and fusion of blues, raga, sitar music, honky-tonk, guitar distortion and other electronic effects. While only partially successful, the track included some interesting sequences, such as Henry Vestine's instrumental "Icebag" (influenced by Albert "Iceman" Collins), Alan Wilson's wailing overdubbed harmonica on "Five Owls," and "Bear Wires" (which included some honky-tonk piano courtesy of John Mayall). Both sides of disc two in the double album were devoted to "Refried Boogie," an update of the earlier "Fried Hockey Boogie." *Downbeat* trenchantly dismissed the second disc, scoffing that it was "41 minutes long and has utterly no reason for existing." In fact, *Downbeat* awarded the album only a star and a half, citing "the tremendous discrepancy between what they are capable of, as demonstrated by their live performances and earlier recordings, and what they have accomplished in this collection."

At about the same time that the band recorded *Living the Blues,* they were also taping a live album at Kaleidoscope in Hollywood, deceptively titled *Live at Topanga Corral*. It was originally issued on the small Wand label in the early 1970s, with the venue purposely incorrectly credited in order to conceal that the recording was made while the band was still under contract with Liberty.

In an incongruous move, the band next released a Christmas single. The A-side, "The Chipmunk Song," paired Canned Heat with their Liberty labelmates, the Chipmunks. "The Chipmunk Song" was not actually the same song as the Chipmunks' similarly titled 1958 chart-topper, but it was a good-natured boogie containing humorous dialogue between Bob Hite and the Chipmunks (Simon, Theodore and Alvin). Canned Heat later recycled the A-side riff—without the Chipmunks—for use as a B-side called "Low Down (And High Up)."

Canned Heat closed out the year with a second European tour in December 1968, then returned to the U.S. in time to appear on the third day of the Miami Pop Festival on December 30. They were welcomed back by an enthusiastic crowd.

They then released a new single, "Time Was" backed with "Low Down," in February 1969, which reached #67 on the charts. The A-side was from their forthcoming album, *Hallelujah.* A few months later, the band played on the second day of the Atlanta Pop Festival, held July 4–5. The very next week *Hallelujah,* their fourth album, was released.

Melody Maker's verdict on *Hallelujah* was favorable: "Less ambitious than some of their work, this is nonetheless an excellent blues-based album and they remain the most convincing of the white electric blues groups." The album contained many strong tracks, most notably the original "Same All Over," with lyrics describing the events of the past year. The tension-filled "Get Off My Back," which featured some fine psychedelic-tinged guitar work by Henry Vestine, was similarly strong, as was "Big Fat," a reading of Fats Domino's 1950 R&B hit, "The Fat Man," which was nicely empowered by Hite's explosive harmonica playing.

Hallelujah was somewhat less successful than their previous two albums, reaching #37 on the U.S. charts and, surprisingly, not charting at all in the U.K. The week after the album debuted, Liberty released a single featuring an innocuous Alan Wilson composition, "Poor Moon," backed with "Sic 'Em Pigs," an anti-police diatribe that had previously appeared on *Hallelujah.* A harbinger of problems to come, the single only reached #119 on the U.S. charts. Furthermore, the summer was to bring some difficult personnel problems to the band.

Canned Heat's appearance at the Fillmore West in late July was hampered by severe tensions between Larry

Taylor and Henry Vestine. Taylor refused to perform on the same stage as Vestine, and soon after this quarrel Henry quit to form a band of his own, the short-lived Sun. In the first set of the Fillmore gig, Mike Bloomfield filled in for the guitarist and was asked to join the band but declined due to his dislike of touring. Harvey Mandel sat in during the next set, played well and readily accepted the offer to become a member of Canned Heat. Mandel was a veteran Chicago musician, having played with both Barry Goldberg and Charlie Musselwhite and the South Side Sound System [see **Barry Goldberg**]. His own first solo album, *Christo Redemptor,* was released earlier in the year [see **Harvey Mandel**].

With Mandel as guitarist, the group played a couple of dates at the Fillmore East before appearing at the legendary Woodstock Music Festival in mid-August. De la Parra has since contended that Canned Heat received the best ovation of the entire festival (along with Sly Stone, anyway) and that they never received proper recognition for their performance at this event. "Going Up the Country," which became the festival anthem, was included on the *Woodstock* triple album and "Woodstock Boogie" was part of *Woodstock II,* while *Woodstock: The Twenty-Fifth Anniversary Collection* added "Leaving This Town" to the band's previously released Woodstock performances.

At the end of the month, Canned Heat appeared at the Texas International Pop Festival. Three songs they performed there—"Bullfrog Blues," "Rollin' and Tumblin'" and "You Can't Do No Better"—emerged on the bootleg boxed set *Texas International Pop Festival,* issued by Oh Boy! The official release, *The Boogie House Tapes,* included "Bullfrog Blues" and "Pulling Hair Blues" from the festival. Canned Heat's appearance at the Texas International Pop Festival concluded at four in the morning with the band jamming on "Refried Boogie" for more than an hour.

In October, Liberty lifted the excellent "Get Off My Back" from the band's most recent album and put it out as a single. Liberty also released a compilation album that month, *Canned Heat Cookbook,* which found its way to #86 in the U.S. and climbed to #8 in the U.K.

In January 1970, the band embarked on another European tour that provided the tracks for *Canned Heat '70 Concert,* the bulk of which was recorded at London's Royal Albert Hall. Released in Europe that June, the album (retitled *Live in Europe*) wouldn't reach American audiences for a full twelve months. *Live in Europe* was a dis-

appointment both critically and commercially, reaching only #133 in the U.S. album charts. Again, it was more successful in the U.K., peaking at #15.

Prior to their departure for Europe, the group turned out a storming version of Wilbert Harrison's "Let's Work Together." The group considered releasing it as a single in the U.S. but abandoned the idea, as Harrison himself was achieving some chart success with the song. Instead, Liberty released the single in the U.K. to coincide with the band's tour. Unexpectedly, it became their biggest British chart hit—and a classic dance single—reaching #2.

January also brought another, more dubious, record to the stores—*Vintage Canned Heat,* a collection of early outtakes issued by Janus in the U.S. (and Pye International in the U.K.). Hite expressed his displeasure about the album to *Melody Maker:* "We are not responsible for that Pye *Vintage* album, and we are trying to stop its being sold. We aren't even playing on 'Spoonful' . . . The album was cut in three hours flat, and it really shows. It's worse than terrible, and the fact that it's made the charts in the States is a big drag as it just brings us all down."

In May 1970, Liberty brought out another single, "Future Blues." Canned Heat had recorded it earlier that year as the title track for their upcoming album. Although it featured some good vocals from Hite, the song made no headway in either the U.S. or the U.K. charts. That same month, both Harvey Mandel and Larry Taylor defected from Canned Heat to join John Mayall's Bluesbreakers [see **John Mayall**]. With Taylor gone, Henry Vestine returned on guitar, accompanied by bassist Antonio "Tony" de la Barreda. De la Barreda had played with de la Parra for five years in Mexico City and was previously a member of the group Jerome. The new lineup immediately went to the studio to back John Lee Hooker on sessions that would yield the double album *Hooker 'N Heat.* The format for the three-day sessions called for Hooker to perform a few songs accompanying himself, followed by some duets with Alan Wilson playing piano or guitar and finally, Hooker with some sympathetic backing by the group sans Bob Hite, who co-produced the album along with Skip Taylor. During the sessions, Hooker and Wilson developed a special relationship based on deep mutual respect as the elder bluesman recognized Wilson's mastery of his own music. As he told Charles Shaar Murray in his biography, *Boogie Man,* "When I got with him [Alan Wilson], he had me down, my music down like you know your ABCs. He could follow me. Ain't no way in the world I could lose him when I'm playing. He was just right on me."

Once again in Britain, the group headlined the first day of the 1970 Bath festival, held June 26–28. To coincide with their Bath appearance, U.K. Liberty released the single "Sugar Bee," a cover of an obscure single originally recorded by Cajun artist Cleveland Crochet. Featuring some excellent harmonica work by Alan Wilson, this outstanding release reached #49 in the U.K. Inexplicably, Liberty did not release the single in the U.S.

In July 1970, the band cut a superb Alan Wilson boogie, "Human Condition," which unfortunately remained unissued in its original form until it showed up on the 1994 compilation *Uncanned!* "Human Condition" featured some especially good guitar work by Vestine and vocals by Wilson.

The sweep of releases in 1970 continued with *Future Blues* in August. Lyrically, the band had moved away from traditional blues topics in favor of current issues, such as the earth's fragile ecology. Controversially, the album cover depicted five astronauts on the moon planting an upside-down American flag with the earth visible in the background, its surface plainly immersed in pollution. Some segments of the public viewed the upside-down American flag as a serious affront, causing major retailers K-Mart, Sears and Woolworth's to refuse to stock the album.

This row over the cover art (ironically, not the cover's socio-ecological message) threatened to overshadow the music, which was hailed by *The New York Times* as being "as magnificent a blues-rock album as has ever been made." Among the LP's many highlights were the A-sides of the previous three singles; the environmentally conscious boogie "So Sad (The World's in a Tangle)," which contained some exceptional guitar work by Mandel; "London Blues," with lyrics that revealed Alan Wilson's bitterness toward a female friend and, more disturbingly, the fragility of his own personality; the eerily prophetic "My Time Ain't Long"; and "Skat," which contained piano work by Dr. John, a New Orleans legend, and some fine scat singing by Wilson. In spite of its high caliber, *Future Blues* only managed to reach #59 on the U.S. charts, although, as usual, it fared better in the U.K. at #27. But a far more devastating setback was still in store for the band—a tragedy that augured the end of the band's halcyon years.

On September 3, 1970, the group landed in Berlin for a concert on what was to be the start of their fifth European tour. Alan Wilson had briefly quit the band in South Carolina a few days before, but had asked to rejoin and was supposed to meet the rest of the band at the airport to fly to Germany. Wilson missed the flight, and upon arriving in Berlin the band was stunned to learn that he had died that day of complications involving barbiturates in the backyard of Bob Hite's Topanga Canyon home.

His bandmates knew Wilson as a sensitive, devoted environmentalist and ecologist who had helped establish Music Mountain, an organization formed with the goal of preserving redwood trees in an area called Skunk Cabbage Creek. In this context, they understood how his being distraught over L.A. smog and the destruction not only of redwood forests but the environment in general, coupled with strife in his own personal relationships, had pushed him to attempt suicide on several previous occasions. He had recently undergone psychiatric care in a hospital and, upon his release, had been placed under Hite's care.

Alan Wilson's premature death, at age 27, robbed music of one of its unsung geniuses. Though praised by John Lee Hooker as "the greatest harmonica player ever," multitalented Wilson never received the recognition on the world stage that he deserved.

Stoically, the band decided to continue the tour and while in London finished mixing the album they had recorded with John Lee Hooker. To finish the tour, the band recruited guitarist/vocalist Joel Scott Hill, who had previously been a member of Jerome along with Tony de la Barreda. But without Wilson's huge talent, the quality of Canned Heat's music rapidly deteriorated. In January, the new lineup released their first single, a remake of Sam the Sham & the Pharoahs' 1965 hit "Wooly Bully." Amazingly, this unlikely choice for a single actually made it as high as #105 on the U.S. singles charts.

In February, the album recorded with John Lee Hooker entitled *Hooker 'N Heat* was finally released. The album's solemn cover shot pictured Hooker accompanied by the surviving group members in a dimly lit room with a photograph of Alan Wilson on the wall. The collaborative effort was widely praised and became Hooker's biggest charting album at the time, reaching #73 in the U.S. The album is widely credited with revitalizing Hooker's career and, to the end of his great life, it remained his personal favorite of all his recordings.

Canned Heat spent much of 1971 on the road; their schedule included tours of England and Europe with John

Lee Hooker. The tours with Hooker included individual sets from Canned Heat and Hooker as well as a joint set. One date, which Hooker missed due to illness, was taped in Finland in August 1971 and issued in 1990 as *Live at the Turku Rock Festival.*

In August, Canned Heat issued a nondescript boogie titled "Long Way From L.A." backed with "Hill's Stomp" that only accelerated the band's downward spiral, although the B-side did contain some nice guitar work by Joel Scott Hill.

The band then brought out *Historical Figures and Ancient Heads* in December, which generally received positive reviews, although *Melody Maker* tersely noted, "At times the set comes dangerously close to answering the eternal question, 'Can the white man sing the blues?'" The album contained some interesting moments, including Henry Vestine's guitar playing on "Sneakin' Around" as well as Bob Hite's duel with legendary rocker Little Richard on "Rockin' with the King," and the aforementioned "Hill's Stomp." In February 1972, Liberty issued "Rockin' with the King" as a single that became the group's last minor hit, making #88 on the U.S. charts.

In June of that year, Tony de la Barreda quit and was replaced by Larry Taylor, who rejoined his former colleagues. Joel Scott Hill departed later in the year. The rest of the 1970s saw the band's mainstream appeal fall enough for them to no longer be a major label act, and with Bob Hite's sad passing in 1981, a special era in American blues-rock came to an end.

Postscript

The band recorded one more album for Liberty, 1973's *New Age,* before being dropped by the label. *New Age* included the core group of Hite, de la Parra and Taylor augmented by Hite's brother, Richard, on bass; vocalist/guitarist James Shane; and Ed Beyer on keyboards.

Canned Heat recorded two albums in France on the Barclay label with elder bluesmen, trying to replicate the success of *Hooker 'N Heat* by producing *Gates on Heat* (1973) with Clarence "Gatemouth" Brown and then *Memphis Heat* (1975), featuring Memphis Slim. In between these releases, the group signed with Atlantic and released one album, *One More River to Cross* (1974) before also being dropped by that label. In 1981, Rhino released a live album, *Hooker 'N Heat,* which was recorded live at the Fox

Venice Theatre sometime in the mid-1970s. In 1978, the group issued *Human Condition,* their last studio recording that included Bob Hite.

Bob Hite died on April 6, 1981, suffering a fatal heart attack following a gig at the Palomino in North Hollywood. In 1995, live recordings featuring Hite were released as *King Biscuit Flower Hour Presents Canned Heat.* Recorded in Long Island, New York, on September 7, 1979, the lineup included Hite, de la Parra and Larry Taylor, plus local L.A. guitar legend Mike "Hollywood Fats" Mann on lead guitar and pianist Jay Spell.

Fito de la Parra has continued to lead various lineups of Canned Heat with occasional releases, including *Kings of the Boogie* (1981), *Infinite Boogie* (1987), *Live in Australia (Boogie Assault)* (1987), *Burnin'* (1993), *Internal Combustion* (1994), *Canned Heat Blues Band* (1998) and *Boogie 2000* (1999).

Discography

Release Date	Title	Catalog Number

U.S. Singles

1967	Rollin' and Tumblin'/Bullfrog Blues	Liberty 55979
1967	Evil Woman/World in a Jug	Liberty 56005
1968	On the Road Again/Boogie Music	Liberty 56038
1968	Going Up the Country/One Kind Favor	Liberty 56077
1968	The Christmas Blues/The Chipmunk Song (with the Chipmunks)	Liberty 56079
1969	Time Was/Low Down	Liberty 56097
1969	Poor Moon/Sic 'Em Pigs	Liberty 56127
1970	Let's Work Together/I'm Her Man	Liberty 56151
1971	Wooly Bully/My Time Ain't Long	Liberty 56127
1971	Going Up the Country/Future Blues	Liberty 56180
1972	Rockin' with the King/I Don't Care What You Told Me	United Artists 50892
1972	Sneakin' Around/Cherokee Dance	United Artists 50927

U.S. Albums

1967	*Canned Heat*	Liberty 7526

Rollin' and Tumblin'/Bullfrog Blues/Evil Is Going On/Goin' Down Slow/Catfish Blues/Dust My Broom/Help Me/Big Road Blues/The Story of My Life/The Road Song/Rich Woman

1968	*Boogie with Canned Heat*	Liberty 7541

Evil Woman/My Crime/On the Road Again/World in a Jug/Turpentine Moan/Whiskey-Headed Woman No. 2/Amphetamine Annie/An Owl Song/Marie Laveau/Fried Hockey Boogie

1968   *Living the Blues* (2 LP)   Liberty 27200
Pony Blues/My Mistake/Sandy's Blues/Going Up the Country/Walking By Myself/Boogie Music/One Kind Favor/Parthenogenesis/Refried Boogie (2 Parts)

1969   *Hallelujah*   Liberty 7618
Same All Over/Change My Ways/Canned Heat/Sic 'Em Pigs/I'm Her Man/Time Was/Do Not Enter/Big Fat/Huautla/Get Off My Back/Down in the Gutter, But Free

1969   *Canned Heat Cookbook*   Liberty 11000
Bullfrog Blues/Rollin' and Tumblin'/Going Up the Country/ Amphetamine Annie/Time Was/Boogie Music/On the Road Again/Same All Over/Sic 'Em Pigs/Fried Hockey Boogie

1970   *Future Blues*   Liberty 11002
Sugar Bee/Shake It and Break It/That's All Right, Mama/My Time Ain't Long/Skat/Let's Work Together/London Blues/So Sad (The World's in a Tangle)/Future Blues

1970   *Live at the Topanga Corral*   Wand 693
Bullfrog Blues/Sweet Sixteen/I'd Rather Be the Devil/Dust My Broom/ Wish You Would/When the Things Go Wrong

1970   *Vintage Canned Heat*   Janus 3009
Spoonful/Big Road Blues/Rollin' and Tumblin'/Got My Mojo Working/Pretty Thing/Louise/Dimples/Can't Hold On Much Longer/Straight Ahead/Rollin' and Tumblin'

1971   *Live in Europe*   United Artists 5509
That's All Right Mama/Bring It on Home/Pulling Hair Blues/Medley: Back Out on the Road—On the Road Again/London Blues/Let's Work Together/Goodbye for Now

1971   *Historical Figures and Ancient Heads*   United Artists 5557
Sneakin' Around/Rockin' with the King/Long Way from L.A./That's All Right/Hill's Stomp/I Don't Care What You Tell Me/Cherokee Dance/Utah

1994   *Uncanned! The Best of*   EMI 29165
        Canned Heat (2 CD)
On the Road Again (previously unreleased, alternate take)/Nine Below Zero (previously unreleased)/TV Mama (previously unreleased)/Rollin' and Tumblin'/Bullfrog Blues/Evil Is Going On/Goin' Down Slow/Dust My Broom/Help Me/The Story of My Life/The Hunter (previously unreleased)/Whiskey and Wimmen' (previously unreleased)/Shake, Rattle and Roll (previously unreleased)/Mean Old World (previously unreleased)/Fannie Mae (previously unreleased)/Gotta Boogie (The World Boogie) (previously unreleased)/My Crime/On the Road Again/Evil Woman/Amphetamine Annie/An Owl Song/Terraplane Blues (previously unreleased)/Christmas Blues (previously unreleased, with Dr. John, alternate take)/Going Up the Country/Time Was/Low Down (And High Up)/Same All Over/Big Fat (The Fat Man)/It's All Right (previously unreleased, with John Lee Hooker)/Poor Moon/Sugar Bee/Shake It and Break It/Future Blues/Let's Work Together (Let's Stick Together)/Wooly Bully/Human Condition (previously unreleased)/Long Way from L.A./Hill's Stomp/Rockin' with the King (with Little Richard)/Harley Davidson Blues/Rock & Roll Music

Miscellaneous U.S. Releases

1970   *Woodstock* (3 LP)   Cotillion SD 3-500
Includes "Going Up the Country" by Canned Heat.

1971   *Hooker 'N Heat*   Liberty 35002
John Lee Hooker unaccompanied: Messin' with the Hook/The Feelin' Is Gone/Send Me Your Pillow/Sittin' Here Thinkin'/Meet Me in the Bottom/Alimonia Blues/Drifter/You Talk Too Much/Burning Hell
With various members of Canned Heat: Bottle Up and Go/The World Today/I Got My Eyes on You/Whiskey and Wimmen'/Just You and Me/Let's Make It/Peavine/Boogie Chillen No. 2

1971   *Early L.A.*   Together ST-1014
Various artists compilation including "You Know I Love You" and "First Time Around" by Canned Heat.

1971   *Woodstock II* (2 LP)   Cotillion SD 2-400
Includes "Woodstock Boogie" by Canned Heat.

1992   *The Monterey International*   Rhino R70596
        Pop Festival (4 CD)
Includes "Rollin' and Tumblin'," "Dust My Broom" and "Bullfrog Blues" by Canned Heat.

1994   *Woodstock: The Twenty-Fifth*   Atlantic 82636-2
        Anniversary Collection (4 CD)
Includes "Leaving This Town" and "Going Up the Country" by Canned Heat.

U.K. Singles

1968	Rollin' and Tumblin'/Bullfrog Blues	Liberty LBF 150
1968	On the Road Again/The World in a Jug	Liberty LBF 15090
1968	Going Up the Country/One Kind Favor	Liberty LBF 15169
1969	Time Was/Low Down	Liberty LBF 15200
1969	Poor Moon/Sic 'Em Pigs	Liberty LBF 15255
1970	Let's Work Together/I'm Her Man	Liberty LBF 15302
1970	Sugar Bee/Shake It and Break It	Liberty LBF 15350
1970	Spoonful/Big Road Blues	Pye International 7N 25513
1970	Future Blues/Skat	Liberty LBF 15395
1970	Christmas Blues/Do Not Enter	Liberty LBF 15429
1971	Wooly Bully/My Time Ain't Long	Liberty LBF 15439
1971	Long Way from L.A./Hill's Stomp	United Artists UP 35279
1972	Rockin' with the King/ I Don't Care What You Tell Me	United Artists UP 35348

U.K. Albums

1967	*Canned Heat*	Liberty LBL 83059 (M) Liberty LBS 83059 (S)
1968	*Boogie with Canned Heat*	Liberty LBL 83103 (M) Liberty LBS 83103 (S)

1968	*Living the Blues* (2 LP)	Liberty
		LDL 84001 (M)
		Liberty
		LDS 84001 (S)
1969	*Hallelujah*	Liberty LBS 83239
1970	*Canned Heat Cookbook*	Liberty LBS 83303
1970	*Vintage Canned Heat*	Pye International
		NSPL 28129
1970	*Canned Heat '70 Concert*	Liberty LBS 83333
1970	*Future Blues*	Liberty LBS 83364
1971	*Historical Figures and Ancient Heads*	United Artists
		UAG 29304
1992	*The Big Heat*	EMI 0777 780275 2

Rollin' and Tumblin'/Bullfrog Blues/Evil Is Going On/Help Me/Story of My Life/The Road Song/My Crime/On the Road Again/World in a Jug/Amphetamine Annie/An Owl Song/Marie Laveau/Fried Hockey Boogie/Pony Blues/My Mistake/Going Up the Country/Walking By Myself/Boogie Music/One Kind Favor/The Chipmunk Song/Parthenogenesis/Same All Over/Change My Ways/Canned Heat/Sic 'Em Pigs/Poor Moon/Time Was/Do Not Enter/Big Fat/Get Off My Back/Down in the Gutter But Free/Sugar Bee/Shake It and Break It/That's All Right/My Time Ain't Long/Skat/Let's Work Together/Future Blues/So Sad (The World's in a Tangle)/London Blues/Sneakin' Around/Hill's Stomp/Rockin' with the King/That's All Right/Utah/Keep It Clean/Harley Davidson Blues/Don't Deceive Me/You Can Run But You Sure Can't Hide/Lookin' for My Rainbow/Rock & Roll Music/Framed/Election Blues/So Long Wrong

Miscellaneous U.K. Releases

1970	*Woodstock* (3 LP)	Atlantic 2653001
1971	*Hooker 'N Heat*	Liberty LPS 103/4
1971	*Woodstock II* (2 LP)	Atlantic 2657003
1992	*The Monterey International*	Ode Sounds &
	Pop Festival (4 CD)	Visuals 72825

Foreign Releases

| 1990 | *Live at the Turku* | Bear Family |
| | *Rock Festival, 1971* (German) | BTCD 9779 409 |

Recorded in Finland.
She Don't Want Me No More/Let's Work Together/On the Road Again/That's All Right/Hill's Stomp/Long Way from LA/Watch Yourself/Canned Heat Boogie/Late Night Blues

| 2000 | *The Boogie House Tapes* (2 CD, German) | Ruf Records |
| | | 1050 |

Recorded between 1967 and 1973.
Reefer Blues/House of Blues Lights/Sleepin' in the Ground/Caterpillar Crawl/D. Drone/These Boots Are Made For—(studio jokes)/Cherokee Dance/Harley Davidson Blues/Good Bye for Now/Chicago Bound/On the Road Again/Human Condition/My Time Ain't Long/London Blues/Future Blues/Move on Down the Road/Long Way From LA/Going Up the Country/Let's Work Together/Bullfrog Blues/Bob Speaks to the Audience/Pulling Hair Blues/You Know I Love You/I Love My Baby/Breathe Easy/Sore Back Blues/Shaken Boogie/Bring It on Home/Tu Vas Trop Vite (Keep It Clean)

Chicken Shack

In the testosterone-driven days of the British blues boom, Chicken Shack immediately stood apart from other bands in the club circuit simply because it featured a female singer/pianist, Christine Perfect. Not only did she look good on stage, but she was a trained musician and art college graduate whose soulful vocals and deft piano-playing added a unique flavor to the predominantly male-driven blues-rock scene. Perfect, this first "English lady of the blues," later married Fleetwood Mac's bass player John McVie, and from the mid-1970s onward achieved mega-stardom with the "Album Oriented Rock" *Rumours* lineup of that band [see **Fleetwood Mac**]. Even in her earliest songwriting efforts, Perfect displayed a natural talent for incorporating "hooky" chord changes into standard 12-bar blues formats—the band's third U.K. single "When the Train Comes Back" being a case in point.

Chicken Shack also had a second unique selling point on stage: namely, its leader and front man Stan Webb was a guitar hero who entertained his audiences with music hall theatricality and wowed them with his fast and furious blues soloing. (Webb has attributed his speed across the fret board as coming from being a left-hander who nonetheless learned to play the guitar right-handed). While developing his energetic and aggressive playing style and act, Webb drew inspiration from such big names of the 1950s–1960s Chicago blues scene as Buddy Guy and Freddie King. He even adopted Guy's memorable stage move of walking right out into the audience while still playing a guitar connected to his amp by a long lead (radio mics and pickups hadn't been invented yet).

Webb's showmanship contrasted neatly with Christine Perfect's sultry voice and laid-back presence at the piano, and so their first two albums for Blue Horizon—*Forty Blue Fingers, Freshly Packed and Ready to Serve* (1968) and *O.K. Ken?* (1969)—were notable for their variety of blues styles that ranged from blues-rock right through to a jazzier Mose Allison feel.

Years before forming Chicken Shack, London-born Webb (b. February 3, 1946) had left school in the Midlands (where he had also been keen on art and painting) to play in local groups such as the Strangers Dance Band, the Blue Four, and Shades Five in the early 1960s before joining Sounds of Blue early in 1964. Sounds of Blue featured Webb, vocalist Dave Yeats, drummer Rob Elcock, bassist Andy Silvester, vocalist/pianist Christine Perfect, and future Traffic member Chris Wood on saxophone. Their repertoire consisted largely of covers of American R&B artists such as Mose Allison, Bo Diddley and Chuck Berry.

In April 1965, the trio of Webb, Silvester and drummer Alan Morley splintered from Sounds of Blue to form Chicken Shack and in effect turn pro. The band clinched a residency at the Star Club in Hamburg, where they learned their playing and stagecraft skills, and it was this threesome that ultimately came to the attention of Decca staff producer and soon-to-be Blue Horizon boss, Mike Vernon. Morley then left and was replaced by Alvin Sykes (who had played drums for B.B. King) who, in turn, was soon replaced by Dave Bidwell, a versatile drummer who seemed comfortable playing jazzy shuffles—as on Freddie King's "Remington Ride"—and yet could also be a firm anchor for the band's rockier material.

With the addition of pianist/vocalist Christine Perfect in April 1967, the original and best known Chicken Shack lineup was complete. A classically trained musician, Perfect had studied sculpting at Birmingham Art College with Chris Wood. During her student days, she befriended Spencer Davis and was a familiar face on Birmingham's music scene. After graduating, she moved to London where, prior to joining Chicken Shack, she landed a job as a window dresser. Although she later placed at the top of a *Melody Maker* readers' poll in 1969, Perfect has since claimed to have been a terrible singer when she first started out. She quickly improved after what amounted to a baptism of fire for this pretty daughter of a college professor when she hooked up with Chicken Shack in order to go to Hamburg and play the Star Club three nights a week for a month. As part of her apprenticeship she also took time to listen to Freddie King records and study the blues-boogie style of King's pianist Sonny Thompson.

Chicken Shack held their London-area debut at the Seventh National Jazz and Blues Festival at Windsor on August 13, 1967. Headliners that day were Cream (whose support also included Jeff Beck, John Mayall [see **Cream, John Mayall**]) and the debut of Peter Green's Fleetwood

Mac. Chicken Shack then gigged extensively and built a sizeable following in the blues clubs of the so-called Ricky-Tick circuit. They spent months on the road, sleeping on amps in the back of the band's freezing van in order to save money. Producer Mike Vernon then brought the band to London from Birmingham and signed them to his Blue Horizon label, which he had set up with his brother Richard. They recorded the group's first single, "It's Okay with Me Baby" backed with "When My Left Eye Jumps" in 1967.

Blue Horizon issued Chicken Shack's first album, *Forty Blue Fingers, Freshly Packed and Ready to Serve,* in July 1968. *Forty Blue Fingers* featured blues covers associated with John Lee Hooker, Buddy Guy, B.B. King and Freddie King, plus two original compositions (one each from Webb and Perfect). Webb acknowledged the influence of the American blues artists in a 1969 *New Musical Express* interview: "After listening to every type of music, I decided blues was it. Blues just hit me like that. Buddy Guy's 'First Time I Met the Blues' was one of the first things I heard. Then people like B.B. King and Freddie King, who we backed at one time . . . He [Freddie King] helped me a lot."

Forty Blue Fingers was warmly received by the British public, peaking at #12 on the British charts. *Melody Maker* called the group, "Definitely one of the most inventive blues groups in the country," and noted, "Musically, Chicken Shack reach moments of high excitement, especially on Stan Webb's extended guitar solos." At the end of the year *Disc and Music Echo* published an article about Webb glowingly titled "Britain's New Fab Four." This was the era of the guitar hero and, in the public's mind, Stan Webb's name was circling alongside those of Eric Clapton [see **Eric Clapton**], Alvin Lee [see **Ten Years After**] and Peter Green. In the article, bandmate Christine Perfect made an interesting prediction about Webb's future life: "He's a blues man and nothing else. If the boom died tomorrow it wouldn't make any difference to Stan—he's only happy playing blues."

A month after the release of *Forty Blues Fingers*, Christine Perfect married Fleetwood Mac bassist John McVie and became known both professionally and personally as Christine McVie.

Following a series of club gigs, the band returned to the studio to cut their next album, *O.K. Ken?* Mostly recorded over a two-day period in October 1968, *O.K. Ken?* was released in February 1969 and again placed Chicken Shack on the U.K. charts, peaking at #9. The album contained a mixture of originals and standards, coupled with between-track, alcohol-induced impersonations of British celebrities of the day performed by the ever-theatrical Webb. Musical highlights included a tidy arrangement of the Freddie King-associated instrumental "Remington Ride," and two of the four tracks written and sung by McVie—"Get Like You Used to Be" and "A Woman Is the Blues." *O.K. Ken?* revealed yet more progress by the band as they effectively incorporated horns into their recordings, an achievement praised by *Melody Maker:* "The Chicken Shack's *O.K. Ken?* is one of the best of the new crop of British blues albums and the use of brass and reeds shows a nice piece of imagination on the part of the group."

The good sales of their second album reflected the big following that Chicken Shack had achieved by autumn 1968, mostly built by their club circuit wanderings in the U.K. Webb explained to *Melody Maker,* "We could work every night of the week if we wanted to. The crowds are getting bigger than ever. I think the blues have come into their own and are now on a par with pop music." Still, despite their packed schedule, Webb found time during the year to work with American bluesmen Champion Jack Dupree and Errol Dixon in the studio.

The group released two more singles in 1968, "Worried About My Woman" backed with "Six Nights in Seven" and "When the Train Comes Back" backed with "Hey Baby" in September and December, respectively, but without any chart success. Consequently they were even more determined to notch up a hit, and so for their next single the group spent a lot of time working on an R&B number popularized by Etta James—"I'd Rather Go Blind." Featuring strong vocals from Christine McVie, Webb told *Melody Maker,* "All the singles we've made so far have never been made for the charts, although it would be very nice ego-wise to whack one up."

Released on April 18, 1969, "I'd Rather Go Blind" reached #14 on the British charts, unexpectedly providing the group with their first hit single. This long-awaited success in the singles chart, however, was tempered by Christine McVie's departure from the band on the day of their release (although she temporarily rejoined the band to promote the single on the *Top of the Pops* weekly U.K. television show). Furthermore, the group was planning a tour of America around this time, but as McVie explained to *New Musical Express,* "John [McVie] didn't want me to go there, there are some pretty dubious characters over

there and he got worried thinking about what might happen to me. Also, Fleetwood Mac was going to America at a different time and we might have been apart for four months."

While Webb was undoubtedly always the group's showman, Christine McVie, without trying, also attracted attention on stage, and perhaps for this very reason a nonplussed Webb gave an interview to *Record Mirror* shortly after she left. In it Webb discounted any negative effect her sudden departure might have on the group's popularity, and went so far as to criticize her work: "Christine wasn't featured throughout the act anyway . . . In place of Christine, we've added Paul Raymond, who's a very fine organist. Our sound has improved a lot now." Paul Raymond had come from the pop group Plastic Penny and was Perfect's replacement on keyboards. As Raymond was an accomplished rock musician, Webb was correct in saying that the new organist upgraded Chicken Shack's overall sound, but his further assertion that without the "novelty" of a female singer in the lineup, audiences would take their music more seriously, was completely unfounded. Instead, with McVie gone, Chicken Shack never consolidated that first flush of mainstream chart success, and without her the band lost something special. Leaving turned out to be more fruitful for the prescient McVie, however, who when speaking to *Disc and Music Echo* at the height of the blues boom, had seen the writing on the wall: "[The boom is] bound to burst sooner or later and then it'll be back to the same faithful fifty fans a night in the clubs again."

Following her departure, the group scrapped the planned American tour and returned to the studio in April to work on their third album. Blue Horizon released a single from it, "Tears in the Wind," in August that reached #29 on the U.K. singles chart. The song represented an early foray by songwriter Webb into the world of the rock ballad, and upon its release the guitarist commented: "It's quite surprising and not what people expect. It's a very sad record. I'm not worried if it doesn't get in the chart. What I do care about is the album. But it would be nice if the record does get in because it means we're appealing to a wider market."

Their ensuing third album, *100 Ton Chicken,* was released in September 1969. (Around this time Stan also announced plans for Chicken Shack to perform a one-off concert at London's Royal Albert Hall backed by a 15-piece big band, but they failed to pull it together.) Like the title suggests, *100 Ton Chicken* referred to a "heavier" sound, and the band dropped the horns that were prominently featured on the previous release and produced another excellent album. Highlights included the ballad "Look Ma, I'm Cryin'" and the frenzied, organ-driven "Still Worried About My Woman," which spotlighted short staccato bursts from Webb's guitar. Despite winning critical favor, the release was unable to attract an audience, as the British blues boom—and many bands closely associated with it—was by this time dying a slow death, and albums such as theirs weren't making it on the charts any longer.

Meanwhile, to Webb it only made matters worse that the group was being overshadowed by Christine McVie who, based on her work with Chicken Shack, was voted *Melody Maker's* "Top Girl Singer" in September 1969. Spurred by the poll, Chicken Shack manager Harry Simmonds immediately began grooming McVie for an ill-fated solo career. He helped her form the Christine McVie Band, featuring ex-Yardbird Tony "Top" Topham [see **Yardbirds**] on guitar. The group went on the road prematurely for a few high-profile but disastrous U.K. gigs—disastrous only because the act was under-rehearsed. After releasing an unsuccessful solo album on Blue Horizon in early 1970, McVie announced that she intended to quit the music business that June. Then, only two months later she resurfaced and played a prominent role in the second post-Peter Green lineup of Fleetwood Mac (where she would eventually achieve superstar status in the mid-1970s with the Lindsey Buckingham/Stevie Nicks configuration).

Around the same time in July 1970, Chicken Shack released their fourth album, *Accept*. For this effort, Webb strayed from the strict blues format of previous albums. He explained this change in musical style to *Melody Maker:* "We're still a blues band, but that doesn't mean to say that we've got to play three thousand slow blues on stage. We do a lot of rock and roll now as well, as we find that's what everybody wants. Everybody is basically a rock and roll fan at heart. It depends on how you present it." At the time, Webb surprisingly told the press that he thought *Accept* was "the first real Chicken Shack record," saying to *Beat Instrumental,* "It's happened that audiences, even the hard-core blues fiends, are raving over the new stuff. I'm prepared to stake everything on the new one."

Disc and Music Echo noted, "*Accept* sets out to remind us that Chicken Shack are no longer just a blues band. There are some pretty heavy things, but the variety is such that some tracks are almost commercial. There is a pleasant instrumental called 'Sad Clown' and there

appears to be an Everly Brothers take-off—'Maudie' . . . All the same, a very fine album." The band chose "Maudie" for their next single, a tight, energetic rock'n'roll dance tune with some Beatles-inspired melodic guitar breaks in between verses and a wild Webb solo in the middle. *Melody Maker's* Chris Welch wrote that the topside was "a beautiful rock and soul sound that should quickly leap to the top." The flamenco-influenced B-side, "Andalucian Blues," was equally outstanding. However, the single's inability to chart caused frustration within the band. Paul Raymond complained to *Record Mirror:* "With 'Maudie' we tried to make a commercial single, it was far more commercial than the other Chicken Shack singles—but we couldn't get the plays. So we don't know where to go from there, there doesn't seem much point in releasing singles if they're not going to get the plugs."

Following the release of *Accept*, Chicken Shack temporarily abandoned the blues altogether. Webb began concentrating on heavy rock guitar, honing the blues-based playing that eventually led to his trademark blend of blues, heavy rock and rock ballads. Webb explained his decision to *Melody Maker:* "What we are playing now is heavy rock. There have been a few alterations in the last six months and we are not doing blues anymore. So many better people than us are entitled to do it, like B.B. King, that we are going to leave them to get on with it."

Webb was voicing what had become a common attitude at the time—that white men were inherently inferior players of Black American blues. This perspective gave rise to disillusionment and industry-wide bickering and led to occasional sharp words by both critics and players in the press. In addition to Webb, the early 1970s also saw Fleetwood Mac's Peter Green and his protégé Danny Kirwan both abandoning Chicago blues in favor of free-form jamming and heavy rock or folk-rock, despite B.B. King's compliments to both for being very fine guitarists and worthy players who had added new dimensions to the Chicago style.

In August, Chicken Shack embarked on a two-month tour of the U.S. with Savoy Brown [see **Savoy Brown**]. Upon their return, manager Harry Simmonds said that in spite of losing between $20,000 to $30,000, the tour was successful because they were well received and were able to book return engagements for higher fees. The group also embarked on a short tour of Germany in November.

In December 1970, Paul Raymond left to join Savoy Brown and the next month Webb announced that he was disbanding Chicken Shack, stating, "I personally haven't been satisfied myself during the past 18 months . . . after so long the musical format had to become confining." Webb also stated that he would use the name Chicken Shack for a new group. Both bassist Andy Silvester and drummer Dave Bidwell reunited with Paul Raymond in Savoy Brown.

By March of the following year, Webb was trying to find musicians for his new group. He brought in bassist John Glascock, organist Brian Chapman and drummer Pip Pyle, but the last two dropped out after only a few weeks, with Pyle replaced by Paul Hancox. Glascock was formerly a member of the Gods and Hancox had briefly been a member of the Mindbenders.

Webb expressed optimism that his new trio would break through, telling *Record Mirror,* "We've been doing quite a lot of work recently building up a reputation for the new trio for when we put a record out. . . . People are coming to see the trio, they like it and things are building up lovely. If you're doing an average of four encores a night and they still want more, it can't be all that bad."

Along with a new lineup, Webb acquired a new record deal—a three-year contract with Decca. He hoped to find a vocalist and bring the lineup back to four in time for the next album, but had no luck finding a suitable candidate.

The first album the new members recorded, *Imagination Lady,* was released in February 1972 on the Deram label. Although *Imagination Lady* lacked the direction of previous efforts and made no impact on the U.S. or U.K. charts, it was successful in Germany, where it reached #47. In addition, they released the single "Poor Boy," which reached #49 on the German charts.

To this day, Germany remains a strong market for Chicken Shack. Webb continues to perform there, where he enjoys his strongest and most loyal support. It seems that Christine McVie's assertion some thirty years ago still rings true: Stan Webb still lives for the blues.

Postscript

Chicken Shack's second Deram recording, *Unlucky Boy,* was issued in 1973. They also recorded a live album to be issued as *Go Live,* but they shelved it when Webb temporarily joined Kim Simmonds and Miller Anderson in a new lineup of Savoy Brown that recorded *Boogie Brothers* in 1974. Instead, *Go Live* was issued as *Goodbye Chicken Shack* in Germany in 1974 and for the first time in the U.K. (under its original title) in 1994.

Webb next formed Broken Glass with Robbie Blunt on guitar. They released one self-titled album on Capitol in 1975 before disbanding. Webb's next recordings materialized several years later under the Chicken Shack moniker: *The Creeper* (1978) and *That's the Way We Are* (1979).

Chicken Shack started off the 1980s in fine form with the live album *Roadies Concerto,* featuring ex-Ten Years After drummer Ric Lee [see **Ten Years After**]. Recordings later made at the Second Blues Festival in Bonn on September 27, 1987, were issued on a German release, *Live in Bonn 1987.* Webb also recorded a studio album in 1986, *39 Bars,* likewise only released in Germany. *39 Bars* was produced by Pete Haycock of the Climax Blues Band [see **Climax Blues Band**]. Chicken Shack closed out the decade with another live album, *Simply Live,* recorded on March 3, 1989, that was released, once again, only in Germany.

The 1990s opened with the release of *On Air* (1991), featuring vintage BBC recordings from the first four albums, although these were marred by annoying fade-outs. That same year, the German INAK label released a Chicken Shack studio album, *Changes,* and followed it with another studio album, *Plucking Good,* in 1993.

In 1995, Chicken Shack released *Stan the Man Live,* which was recorded at a club near the Merry Hill Centre in Birmingham's Brierley Hill.

In 1997, Indigo released *From the Vaults,* which featured some studio outtakes circa 1968–1969. In 2001, Indigo released the album *Webb.*

Discography

Release Date	Title	Catalog Number
	U.S. Singles	
1968	Worried About My Woman/ Six Nights in Seven	Epic 10414
1970	Tears in the Wind/ The Things You Put Me Through	Blue Horizon 100
1972	Diary of Your Life/Maudie	Blue Horizon 302

U.S. Albums

1968	*Forty Blue Fingers, Freshly Packed and Ready to Serve*	Epic BN-26414

The Letter/Lonesome Whistle Blues/When the Train Comes Back/San-Ho-Zay/King of the World/See See Baby/First Time I Met the Blues/Webbed Feet/You Ain't No Good/What You Did Last Night

1969	*O.K. Ken?*	Blue Horizon BH-7705

Baby's Got Me Crying/The Right Way Is My Way/Get Like You Used to Be/Pony and Trap/Tell Me/A Woman Is the Blues/I Wanna See My Baby/Remington Ride/Fishing in Your River/Mean Old World/Sweet Sixteen

1969	*100 Ton Chicken*	Blue Horizon BH-7706

The Road of Love/Look Ma, I'm Cryin'/Evelyn/Reconsider Baby/Weekend Love/Midnight Hour/Tears in the Wind/Horse and Cart/The Way It Is/Still Worried About My Woman/Anji

1970	*Accept*	Blue Horizon BH-4809

Diary of Your Life/Pocket/Never Ever/Sad Clown/Maudie/Telling Your Fortune/Tired Eyes/Some Other Time/Going Round/Andalucian Blues/You Knew You Did/She Didn't Use Her Loaf/Apple Tart

1972	*Imagination Lady*	Deram DES-18063

Crying Won't Help You Now/Daughter of the Hillside/If I Were a Carpenter/Going Down/Poor Boy/Telling Your Fortune/Tie Lose

U.K. Singles

1967	It's Okay with Me Baby/ When My Left Eye Jumps	Blue Horizon 57-3135
1967	Worried About My Woman/ Six Nights in Seven	Blue Horizon 57-3143
1968	When the Train Comes Back/Hey Baby	Blue Horizon 57-3146
1969	I'd Rather Go Blind/Night Life	Blue Horizon 57-3153
1969	Tears in the Wind/ The Things You Put Me Through	Blue Horizon 57-3160
1970	Maudie/Andalucian Blues	Blue Horizon 57-3168
1970	Sad Clown/Tired Eyes	Blue Horizon 57-3176

U.K. Albums

1968	*Forty Blue Fingers, Freshly Packed and Ready to Serve*	Blue Horizon 7-63203
1969	*O.K. Ken?*	Blue Horizon 7-63209
1969	*100 Ton Chicken*	Blue Horizon 7-63218
1970	*Accept*	Blue Horizon 7-6386
1972	*Imagination Lady*	Deram SDL 5
1991	*On Air*	Band of Joy CD 0002

Tired Eyes/I'd Rather Go Blind/Tears in the Wind/Night Is When It Matters/Telling Your Fortune/You Knew You Did/Midnight Hour/Hey Baby/Things You Put Me Through/Get Like You Used to Be/You Done Lost That Good Thing Now/Look Ma I'm Crying

1997	*From the Vaults*	Indigo IGOXCD 508

Midnight Hour/When the Train Comes Back/Night Life/It's Okay with Me Baby/Tell Me/Telling Your Fortune/Strange Things Happening/Side Tracked/Lonesome Whistle Blows/The Letter/Mean Old World/Tired Eyes/My Mood/You've Done Lost Your Good Thing Now/Everyday I Have the Blues/Waiting for You/San-Ho-Zay/It'll Be Mine/Hey, Hey, Hey

Eric Clapton

"**A**wesome success and achievements—but at great personal cost" would be a fitting career retrospective for this unique artist and blues pioneer. Eric Clapton, who was the first musician to be inducted into the Rock and Roll Hall of Fame *three* times (as a member of the Yardbirds and Cream in 1992 and 1993, respectively, and as a solo artist in 2000), is undoubtedly one of the most influential guitarists of modern rock [see **Yardbirds** and **Cream**].

While his time with the Yardbirds and Cream lasted less than a combined four years, Clapton's solo career has spanned over 30 years, bringing him great commercial success in the shape of numerous gold and platinum records and multiple awards, including an amazing 13 Grammys. What's more, his acclaimed and successful recent collaboration with blues elder and icon B.B. King clearly shows that, like King, Clapton is a bluesman who will never stop delivering the goods.

A world-famous star in the ascendant back in the late 1960s, Clapton was *the* catalyst who introduced blues to a much broader audience on both sides of the Atlantic. He did this by making the blues *rock*—and once the blues began to rock, it was no longer an obscure folk art hidden deep in the vaults of the Library of Congress—it became FM radio-friendly chart music.

As this transformation gathered momentum in the late 1960s, blues musicians such as B.B. King and Freddie King were the first to thank Clapton for boosting their careers (ironically, these blues greats were among Clapton's own hallowed mentors when he first took up the guitar). The reason for their gratitude was that until Eric Clapton (together with Cream) brought his masterful and progressive interpretations of old Deep South country blues and early 1960s Chicago blues over to America, blues music was mostly made by black musicians for black audiences in their smart clubs and rough juke joints. Eric Clapton's guitar playing was the opening salvo of the 1960s blues-rock explosion that changed all this, giving the music a much broader audience.

Prior to the 1960s explosion of blues-based styles, black American blues music commonly crossed over the Atlantic to Great Britain, where fanatical young white English guitarists and singers embraced and developed the sounds before exporting their versions of the blues back to America, where it was then widely accepted. For instance, Eric Clapton's blues-rock take of "Crossroads" electrifyingly raised the ghost of Robert Johnson and introduced this Delta blues guitar virtuoso's music to millions, who remain to this day happily haunted. Until then, Johnson's artistry was one of American folk music's best kept secrets.

Clapton's mastery of electric Chicago blues took place at an astonishing pace in his early twenties. When he first joined John Mayall's Bluesbreakers in 1965 [see **John Mayall**], Mayall obviously recognized massive, raw talent in Clapton but nonetheless observed, "Eric was still getting his chops together." But just one year later, Clapton's guitarwork had spelled out the 1960s blues-rock explosion's manifesto with a truly seminal album, *Blues Breakers: John Mayall with Eric Clapton.* Throughout the recording of this studio album, a pioneering and opinionated young Clapton flouted hitherto accepted conventions of sound engineering: he insisted on playing at high volume in what turned out to be a successful method for recreating the live sound of a performance in a steamy blues club, complete with feedback and distortion.

Eric Patrick Clapton was born on March 30, 1945, to Patricia Molly Clapton and his father, a Canadian soldier serving in England. Clapton was raised in the English town of Ripley, Surrey, by his grandmother and her second husband after their daughter moved to Germany. He spent much of his childhood believing that his grandparents were in fact his biological parents. However, while still a child he learned the devastating truth that he had been born illegitimate and then abandoned by his mother. Much later in life, he pointed out that learning blues guitar in his teens was the first real outlet and escape he found from that painful childhood.

Clapton started playing guitar at around age 15. Soon, inspired by *The Best of Muddy Waters,* Jimmy Reed's *Live at Carnegie Hall* and Robert Johnson's *King of the Delta Blues Singers*, Clapton persuaded his grandmother to buy him a Kay semi-hollow-body electric guitar. There is sweet irony in the anecdote that grown-up advice at the time assured the youngster that while playing guitar was a fine hobby, he'd struggle to make a living from it. So by the time he was 16, Clapton had enrolled at the Kingston College of Art to study stained glass design. He was eventually expelled for being lazy and subversive.

In early 1963, Clapton joined his first semi-pro group, the blues-oriented Roosters. Consisting of future Manfred Mann bassist Tom McGuinness (guitar), Terry Brennan (vocals), Ben Palmer (piano), Robin Mason (drums) and Clapton, the Roosters' repertoire was strictly R&B, including covers of Bo Diddley, Freddie King, Lightnin' Slim, and Fats Domino numbers. Unfortunately, the Roosters only lasted until August 1963, performing less than two dozen gigs (including one at the Marquee on June 15, 1963, as support for the Mann-Hugg Blues Brothers (which later evolved into Manfred Mann).

And so for the first but not last time, in September 1963, Clapton took up with a pop group. Following the demise of the Roosters, Clapton and McGuinness joined the pop-oriented Casey Jones and the Engineers, led by vocalist Brian Casser (formerly of the Liverpool band Cass and the Casanovas). The budding guitar hero stayed for just seven performances because the band's pop material had absolutely nothing to do with his all-consuming passion—the blues.

When Clapton joined the Yardbirds a month later in October 1963, he was hopeful that he was hooking up with a blues outfit. He was satisfied for a year. The Yardbirds were a good outlet for his fiery solos during the group's "rave-ups," and very soon he had established a reputation as the leading guitarist in Britain. But the Yardbirds had an eye on the "big time" and were looking to find continued success in the singles charts. Clapton, blues purist, had no time for this commercial attitude. He stayed with the group until March 1965, appearing on their *Five Live Yardbirds* album, only to defect after they recorded the "For Your Love" single. Apparently, the pop/blues middle section of this hit was just too corny to bear for a radical blues fundamentalist such as Clapton.

Interestingly, the flip side of the single—the bluesy instrumental "Got to Hurry"—was Clapton's first recorded composition, and also an indication of the direction he wanted to take. During his time with the Yardbirds he had acquired the nickname "Slowhand," given to him by manager Giorgio Gomelsky for two related reasons: first, Clapton was a fast guitarist (an ironic play on words), and second, the Yardbirds' audiences had picked up the habit of clapping slowly while Clapton changed his frequently broken strings.

While with the Yardbirds, Clapton had also sat in on a session for Muddy Waters's pianist Otis Spann in May 1964. The session, which included Waters on guitar, produced two tracks that Clapton played on: "Pretty Girls Everywhere" and "Stirs Me Up."

After quitting the Yardbirds, Clapton stayed with his friend Ben Palmer for a few weeks until he received a fateful call from John Mayall inviting him to join the Bluesbreakers. Although Clapton was just 20 when he left the Yardbirds, the 32-year-old Mayall was a seasoned veteran who shared Clapton's obsession with the blues. The elder bandleader told Clapton that the Bluesbreakers would be the perfect vehicle for the type of music he wanted to play. Convinced, Clapton started practicing with them in April 1965.

The Bluesbreakers' first recordings with Clapton were on April 26, 1965, for the BBC. The group made four tracks for Immediate Records, produced by Jimmy Page, which included a furious version of "I'm Your Witchdoctor" that featured a blistering Clapton solo. In early 1966, Clapton and Mayall—working as a duo for Mike Vernon's special Purdah label—returned to the studio to record the more subdued "Lonely Years" and "Bernard Jenkins." Additionally, Clapton recorded several more Page-produced tracks that subsequently surfaced on several compilation albums released by Immediate.

After a few months with Mayall, a restless and adventurous Clapton left the Bluesbreakers in August 1965 to join some musical friends for a planned trip abroad. The friends—including Ben Palmer on piano, Jake Milton on drums, vocalist John Bailey, bassist Bob Ray and Bernie Greenwood on saxophone—were collectively known as the Glands.

The touring party made it as far as Greece, where they found work at an Athens nightclub, but the adventure quickly turned into a fiasco. The Glands had neglected to secure work permits, so the club owner threatened to turn them over to the authorities unless they agreed to work under his conditions. He also seized their equipment and used that as additional leverage to get his own way. Clapton found himself being forced to work long hours with the Juniors, a Greek band who played British pop, while the rest of the Glands (for whom the club owner had no need) were informed that they could no longer work in the country. The guitarist finally had to escape from the club owner's control, sacrificing a valuable Marshall amplifier—his ransom for freedom—in the process.

When Clapton returned to England, he knew he still had a gig in the Bluesbreakers, and Mayall gladly took him back even though this meant that he had to let go of Clapton's brilliant replacement, Peter Green. Green, the last and by far the best of Clapton's deputies that summer, had only been with Mayall for a week and was bitterly disappointed about losing his place in what was then an ideal gig for him. Reportedly, Mayall had to use all his powers of persuasion to get Green back in when Clapton eventually left to form Cream.

When Clapton rejoined the Bluesbreakers in mid-November, he found that the new bass player, Jack Bruce, had a jazzier style of playing and tended to improvise much more than his predecessor, John McVie. However, Bruce stayed with Mayall for only a few weeks because he was lured away to the hit-making Manfred Mann group by the prospect of more money.

In February 1966, Clapton took part in some studio sessions backing Champion Jack Dupree; three of these tracks were issued on Dupree's *From New Orleans to Chicago* album. That same month, Clapton joined an all-star studio ensemble to record some tracks. In addition to Clapton, the ad hoc lineup consisted of Jack Bruce (bass), Steve Winwood (vocals), Pete York (drums), Ben Palmer (piano) and Paul Jones (harmonica). Three tracks from this session, credited to the Powerhouse, were later released on an Elektra compilation album, *What's Shakin'*.

Clapton's time with the Bluesbreakers culminated with the recording of the seminal *Blues Breakers: John Mayall with Eric Clapton*, a.k.a. the "Beano" album because of Clapton's choice of reading matter featured on the cover shot. Astoundingly, *Blues Breakers* reached

#6 on the British charts, with *Beat Instrumental* observing, "It's Eric Clapton who steals the limelight."

During his time with the Bluesbreakers, Clapton revolutionized the guitarist's role in a band by employing feedback, distortion and sustain. He may not have been the first musician to employ these techniques, but he was the first to become famous for doing so. John Mayall noted of his famous charge: "He was a very moody player—by that I mean he'd conjure up these incredible moods and intensity. The things he did with a slow blues—when he *felt* like playing a slow blues—could send shivers down your spine." Evidently, at that point Clapton was also quite a temperamental personality whose playing varied markedly from one night to the next.

Eventually, Clapton grew tired of the Bluesbreakers' fairly rigid musical arrangements. Much to Mayall's ire, Clapton chose to leave and form the power trio Cream (along with Jack Bruce and Ginger Baker) just when *Blues Breakers* was riding high in the charts. In fact, Mayall got angry enough to fire him before Clapton had served out his notice. Clapton was also not on the best of terms with both John McVie (who had been reinstated on bass) and drummer Hughie Flint. McVie was incensed by Clapton's temerity at putting up posters that advertised forthcoming Cream gigs at venues where Mayall's band was playing. As for Flint, Clapton had begun to feel the restrictions of Flint's relatively conservative playing style, which paled into insignificance once Clapton's guitar playing had experienced, and been inspired by, the crazy-man rhythm innovator Ginger Baker.

To Clapton, Cream offered much more freedom to improvise and weave in his soloing with the improvisational approach of bass player Jack Bruce. Their complementary playing styles created a stark contrast to Clapton's previous role as the only featured musician during the mid-song instrumental breaks of a typical Bluesbreakers performance night after night. The surly soloist the fans called "God" while in Mayall's band thus became "Captain Madman" in Cream, with a whole new and more liberated attitude to presenting his music.

Now inspired by Ginger Baker's rhythms and Jack Bruce's free-form jazz, Clapton fast developed his new improvisational style that drove Cream to superstardom. During the group's two-and-a-half-year existence, Cream became a worldwide headliner, releasing a total of four albums, *Fresh Cream* (1966), *Disraeli Gears* (1967), *Wheels of Fire* (1968) and *Goodbye* (1968). While the band's most memorable songwriting output came from Bruce and poet/lyricist Pete Brown, Cream inspired some strong original material from Clapton, such as "Tales of Brave Ulysses," as well as innovative updates of such blues classics as Robert Johnson's "Crossroads."

News of Cream had by this time spilled into mainstream media. *Newsweek* lauded Clapton's virtuosity in a March 18, 1968, story: "Both Baker and Bruce are superbly skilled musicians, but Clapton is the crème de la crème. His blues are often hard to distinguish from real delta Negro blues or his clangorous rock from the urban toughness of a Muddy Waters." In addition, Clapton had begun playing with some of the best-known musicians of the day on a variety of other acclaimed recordings and projects, such as on "Good to Me as I Am to You" on Aretha Franklin's *Lady Soul* album; "Ski-ing" on the George Harrison album *Wonderwall Music;* "The Eagle Laughs at You," the stunning "Sour Milk Sea" and other tracks on Jackie Lomax's *Is This What You Want;* "While My Guitar Gently Weeps" on the Beatles' *White* album; and four tracks on the Martha Velez album *Fiends and Angels.*

On December 10 and 11, 1968, Clapton took part in the Rolling Stones' *Rock and Roll Circus,* playing with John Lennon (vocals and guitar), Mitch Mitchell (drums) and Keith Richards (bass). Dubbed "Winston Legthigh and the Dirty Macs," they performed several tracks, two of which found their way into the 1996 CD and movie, *Rock and Roll Circus.* The tracks included a sizzling rendition of Lennon's "Yer Blues" plus a Yoko Ono abomination, "Whole Lotta Yoko" (with Ivry Gitlis on violin and Yoko Ono on vocals).

Over time, the pressure of constant heavy touring and the ongoing acrimony chiefly between Jack Bruce and Ginger Baker led to Cream's inevitable demise in late 1968. As exhaustion set in from having to endure endless money-making tours, Clapton discovered that his capacity to constantly spark off new ideas began to fail him. For the first time in what had up until then been a brilliant career, Clapton's music hit a brick wall and he found out how, in the wrong commercial context, even endless musical freedom could break down in an overly pressured environment.

In this early stage of his burnout, music critics began to comment on below-par performances and cliched guitar solos by Clapton, who soon began a descent into the first real personal crisis of his career. His attempt at Blind Faith in early 1969 with Steve Winwood, Ric Grech and Ginger Baker only increased his sense of numbness and disconnection [see **Blind Faith**]. Despite recording the best-selling album *Blind Faith* and having a successful U.S. tour, within a year the high-profile venture collapsed, partly due to the weight of the hype surrounding it but also because of the almost inevitable personality clashes within the band.

As the winter approached, Clapton began playing in a number of different sessions and in impromptu performances, trying to find new inspiration for his music. On September 13, 1969, he appeared with John Lennon at the Toronto Rock and Roll Revival Festival. The festival also featured Little Richard, Chuck Berry, Gene Vincent and Bo Diddley (with Lennon headlining as the Plastic Ono Band). Lennon had assembled Clapton, Klaus Voorman (bass), Alan White (drums) and Yoko Ono (vocals), and they rehearsed on the plane ride to the festival to work out their set, which consisted primarily of rock'n'roll standards. While the performance was ragged, it had moments of interest, particularly the renditions of "Yer Blues" (from the Beatles' *White* album) and "Cold Turkey" (which chronicled Lennon's battle with heroin addiction). Unfortunately, Yoko Ono's weird and tuneless shrieking—masquerading as the avant-garde—marred the set, especially on her own compositions, which included "Don't Worry Kyoko (Mummy's Only Looking for a Hand in the Snow)" and "John John (Let's Hope for Peace)." Clapton also assisted Lennon in the studio during the September 25–26 recording of the single, "Cold Turkey," and for the October 2–6 B-side recording of Yoko Ono's "Don't Worry Kyoko."

Earlier in the year, during Blind Faith's U.S. tour, Clapton had become acquainted with the opening act, Delaney and Bonnie Bramlett and their band. Delaney Bramlett was born on July 1, 1939, in Pontotoc, Mississippi. After his mother showed him a few chords on the guitar, he taught himself how to play. Having first served in the U.S. Navy, Bramlett then moved to Los Angeles and became a member of the Shindogs, the house band for the T.V. show *Shindig.*

Bramlett also found time to work with J.J. Cale and Leon Russell, and he released some unsuccessful solo singles. In 1967, Bramlett married Bonnie Lynn O'Farrell (b. November 8, 1944; Acton, Illinois). Bonnie grew up in East St. Louis and had worked with Albert King and Ike and Tina Turner before moving to California. There, the two formed "Delaney and Bonnie and Friends." Stax released their first album, *Home,* to very little commercial attention in 1968. However, their second album, *Accept No Substi-*

tute, released on Elektra in 1969, was critically acclaimed and started to generate some interest in their music.

While on the road, Clapton had become friends with Delaney, who in turn had encouraged the shy superstar to do more singing. Clapton also enjoyed jamming with Bramlett and his group, and for this reason, as well as to escape the hype surrounding the Blind Faith tour, Clapton ultimately fled to the Delaney and Bonnie tour. Completely tired of the superstar/guitar hero role he was now duty-bound to live up to, he tried to maintain a much lower profile as a supportive as opposed to featured musician. Concerned about Clapton's anti-superstar posturing, Eric's manager, Robert Stigwood, was quick to assure the press that the guitarist's participation on the tour did not mean he was leaving Blind Faith and that, in fact, Blind Faith would reconvene in January. It was not to be.

Clapton found some of the musicians for his next project, Derek and the Dominos, through Delaney and Bonnie. In late November 1969, "Delaney and Bonnie and Friends with Eric Clapton" went on a short, four-date tour of Germany. In addition to Clapton, the backup band supporting Delaney and Bonnie consisted of drummer Jim Gordon (who had replaced their recently departed regular drummer Jim Keltner), bassist Carl Radle, organist/vocalist Bobby Whitlock, trumpeter Jim Price, saxophonist Bobby Keys, singer Rita Coolidge, percussionist Tex Johnson and ex-Traffic guitarist Dave Mason.

In December, "Delaney and Bonnie and Friends with guest star Eric Clapton" went on a seven-date tour of the U.K., with Dave Mason continuing the tour and George Harrison joining them for one engagement. *Melody Maker's* Chris Welch reviewed a Royal Albert Hall performance: "D and B proved to be a powerful if not outstanding vocal duo following the Ike and Tina Turner tradition with country overtones." A recording of the last date of this tour, December 7, 1969, at the Fairfield Halls, Croydon, was released as the album *On Tour.*

Next, a short Scandinavian tour ensued with Clapton, Dave Mason and George Harrison in addition to the regular Delaney and Bonnie lineup. Clapton explained to *New Musical Express* that touring with Delaney and Bonnie took some of the pressure off him as a solo performer: "This is the first tour I've ever been on in my life, and I've been on a good few, where everybody has had a good time—and there are a lot of people on this tour. I just don't want it to stop . . . I could happily go on with this tour for the rest of my life."

Following the Scandinavian leg of the tour, Clapton and most of the "Friends" appeared with John Lennon and the Plastic Ono Band for the "Peace for Christmas" Charity Concert for UNICEF held at the Lyceum Ballroom, London, on December 15, 1969. Over 15 musicians took part in the performance of two songs, "Cold Turkey" and Ono's "Don't Worry Kyoko (Mummy's Only Looking for a Hand in the Snow)." The tracks were released as part of a bonus disc on the *Sometime in New York City* album. Clapton also found time in December to do some session work for Vivian Stanshall of the Bonzo Dog Doo-Dah Band.

In January 1970, Clapton and some of the "Friends" went to California to work on his first solo album. While *Eric Clapton* was ostensibly a solo effort, Delaney and Bonnie were heavy influences, as Delaney co-produced the album and Bonnie provided most of the harmony vocals with the "Friends" backing. Delaney also wrote or co-wrote several of the songs (which were credited to his wife at the time, Bonnie Bramlett, for contractual reasons), and, most important of all, Delaney encouraged Clapton to sing and forced him to overcome his insecurities about how his fans would receive his vocal work. Clapton explained to *Circus Magazine* why he worked so closely with Delaney: "With Delaney, it's the idea of what I want my music to be. We think the same way—we're very much together in what we're doing." A large contingency of "Friends" helped Clapton out on the release, including Rita Coolidge (vocals), Jim Price (trumpet), Bobby Keys (saxophone), Bobby Whitlock (organ, vocals), Leon Russell (piano), Jim Gordon (drums), Carl Radle (bass), Stephen Stills (guitar and vocals on "Let It Rain") and ex-Crickets' Sonny Curtis and Jerry Allison (vocals).

Despite all the positive teamwork that went into making it, the album received mixed reviews. Critics mainly harped that Clapton relied too much on Delaney and Bonnie and therefore failed to assert his own identity. *Beat Instrumental* caustically charged, "For the most part Eric seems content to submerge himself in the familiar sound of Delaney and Bonnie and pals." *New Musical Express* was more gentle, commenting that while the LP was "not a world beater, this is a tasteful and enjoyable album." A *Rolling Stone* critic included a small barb in his compliment, calling the album a "warm, friendly record of the kind that I haven't heard since the first Delaney and Bonnie album." The most pointed observation came from *Melody Maker*: "What is surprising and most disappointing is the extent to which Eric has submerged himself in the Delaney and Bonnie sound, to the point where it really does become a Delaney and Bonnie album featuring E.

Clapton (guitar)." Even after many such unfavorable reviews, the album reached number #13 on the U.S. charts (#17 in the U.K.) and one track from the album—a cover of J.J. Cale's "After Midnight"—was a hit (U.S. #18).

In January 1970, Clapton participated in sessions for King Curtis and appeared on the Crickets' album, *Rockin' 50's Rock'n'Roll*. (Clapton also told *Beat Instrumental* of his intention to make a tribute album to Buddy Holly featuring the lesser-heard B-sides of Holly's records. The idea never reached fruition.)

On February 2, 1970, Clapton joined Delaney and Bonnie for the start of their month-long U.S. tour. Following it, Clapton mulled over several projects and contributed to a number of other recordings over the next few months, including "It Don't Come Easy" with Ringo Starr (Clapton was at the sessions but may not have ended up on the final take); *The London Howlin' Wolf Sessions*; and the album *Jesse Davis!*

Then in May, *New Musical Express* reported that Clapton was looking for two more people for the new group he was forming, and that he had already found two West Indian musicians as the nucleus. The publication also speculated, "One of the first live appearances for the new outfit may be a charity event at London Lyceum in June." In an interview published in *Downbeat* magazine that June, Clapton specifically stated that if he could have anyone in his band, he would want the musicians in Delaney and Bonnie's band. "Well," he said, "if Delaney and Bonnie didn't have their band, I'd have them. That's the way I feel about them. Because they are really the finest musicians I've ever played with, I think—playing rock'n'roll."

Clapton soon had his "dream team," as the May 23 issue of *Melody Maker* reported that three members of Delaney and Bonnie's "Friends" would be joining Clapton—bassist Carl Radle, keyboardist Bobby Whitlock and drummer Jim Gordon. Clapton planned to contact session drummer Jim Keltner, who had played on Delaney and Bonnie's *Accept No Substitute* album, but he was apparently unavailable. The music press also reported that close friend George Harrison might complete the lineup for their initial club dates.

Radle (b. June 18, 1942; d. 1979) hailed from Tulsa, Oklahoma. He had studied clarinet and piano as a child and had taken up the electric bass when he was 15. Later, he began playing professionally in the Tulsa area with pianist

Leon Russell and drummer Chuck Blackwell (who later played with Taj Mahal). He had also played with Delaney and Bonnie and joined Joe Cocker's band during their Mad Dogs and Englishmen tour prior to joining Clapton. Whitlock (b. 1948; Memphis, Tennessee) was playing organ in a Booker T.-like soul combo in Memphis when Delaney approached him to form "Friends." Whitlock was one of the few white musicians working with the Stax record label. He stayed with Delaney and Bonnie until much of the band defected to Joe Cocker, and then decided to leave as well. While vacationing in the U.K., he met Clapton and decided to join his new band. Jim Gordon (b. 1945; Los Angeles, California) had been a successful Los Angeles session drummer before joining Delaney and Bonnie. He had started his career with the Everly Brothers and had worked with Glen Campbell, Arlo Guthrie, Tom Jones, Nancy Sinatra and many others before signing on with Delaney and Bonnie. After his time with Delaney and Bonnie, he had joined Joe Cocker for the Mad Dogs and Englishmen tour.

Clapton's new group made their performing debut on June 14, 1970, at the Lyceum Ballroom in London for a charity concert for Dr. Spock's Civil Liberties Legal Defense Fund. The band conceived the name "Derek and the Dominos" just ten minutes before they went onstage. Dave Mason joined the group for the evening's performance, but chose not to stay on because his solo album was doing well in the U.S. Clapton was pleased with the gig, telling *New Musical Express,* "We are all knocked out by the way Sunday's concert went. We only had just over a day's rehearsal and yet it was as if we had been together for months. Now we want to spend about four weeks, writing and playing together—and when we think we are ready, we will start playing in public."

The Dominos made their recording debut in sessions for George Harrison's *All Things Must Pass* album, produced by Phil Spector. The third disc of this three-record set, titled *Apple Jam,* featured the Dominos and other musicians on four long, improvised instrumentals. In June, the band made their first recordings in their own right at Apple Studios with Phil Spector: "Tell the Truth" backed with "Roll It Over." Bolstered by George Harrison and Dave Mason on the second track, the songs were issued as a single in September but withdrawn almost immediately because of their dissatisfaction with the recording. Instead, "After Midnight" backed with "Easy Now" from the first album were issued.

From August 1–22, Derek and the Dominos embarked on the first leg of their U.K. tour, which deliberately favored smaller venues. Clapton told *New Musical Express,* "We want to play clubs and such like where we can get the sound right, and get some communication going with the audiences." A reviewer for *Melody Maker* remarked about the band's Marquee gig, "The excitement in his playing, which was lacking for so long, is back again. Get along to see the band if you want to see Clapton at his best."

Following their U.K. tour, the group flew to Miami, Florida, to begin work on their first album, *Layla and Other Assorted Love Songs.* It was recorded at Criteria Studios in August and September with Tom Dowd producing, and many critics consider this album the finest work of Clapton's career. Making the record was an emotional catharsis for Clapton: he had fallen in love with Patti Harrison, wife of his good friend George, and the album reflected his anguish over unrequited love. Duane Allman of the Allman Brothers [see **Allman Brothers**] sat in and pushed the sessions into high gear. The album highlights included covers of Billy Myles's "Have You Ever Loved a Woman," Big Bill Broonzy's "Key to the Highway," and Jimi Hendrix's "Little Wing"—plus the Clapton/Gordon-penned "Layla," which became an instant FM radio staple. Allman's presence clearly invigorated Clapton, who promptly invited his fellow guitarist to join the band, but Duane declined, preferring instead to stay with the Allman Brothers.

On September 20, Derek and the Dominos started on the second leg of their U.K. tour, ending on October 11 at the Lyceum Ballroom in London. *Melody Maker* championed the last show of the tour: "A tighter unit would be hard to find. Eric, the obvious leader, takes the vocals with Bobby Whitlock, and this pair is responsible for most of the writing. Jim Gordon on drums and Carl Radle on bass provide a rhythm section which must be envied by many throughout the world."

On October 15, Derek and the Dominos started their U.S. tour, which ran through December 6. *Rolling Stone* printed a harsh review of their first gig at the Fillmore East in New York City on October 23: "Clapton is doing a disservice to his audience when he allows them to accept the kind of music Derek and the Dominos played at their Fillmore East debut—a surfeit of tail-end blues licks, mainly undigested, realizing little connection with any coherent style or with the source of its inspiration."

Still, these shows were released as *Live in Concert* (with an expanded edition released on CD as *Live at the Fillmore*) and, despite *Rolling Stone's* thumbs-down, they showed the band and Clapton in fine form. His solo on an extended version of "Why Does Love Got to Be So Sad" was particularly fluid, demonstrating awesome maturity. On November 5, the band made their American television debut on the *Johnny Cash* show with two songs broadcast, "It's Too Late" and "Matchbox." They performed two other songs that were not televised, "Got to Get Better in a Little While" and "Blues Power." Johnny Cash and Carl Perkins joined them on stage for "Matchbox."

Finally, in October 1970 the double-album *Layla and Other Assorted Love Songs* was unleashed to positive reviews. Even *Rolling Stone,* which until that point was probably Clapton's harshest critic, conceded, "Clapton's not God, but he and Skydog [Duane Allman] and the Dominos together do make for an hour or so of heaven." *Melody Maker* raved, "There's a hell of a lot more to Clapton than actually meets the eye—even though his immediate talent is undoubtedly brilliant."

The album reached #16 on the U.S. charts, but inexplicably failed to chart in the U.K. This disappointment, plus the tragic deaths of two friends in a short period of time, both of whom Clapton regarded as leading lights in the music world—Jimi Hendrix in September 1970 and Duane Allman some thirteen months later—all conspired to push Clapton into depression.

He continued to keep busy during October 1970, coproducing (and playing on) an album by Buddy Guy and Junior Wells, *Play the Blues.* He then also played on a session with James Luther Dickinson that yielded "The Judgement," a track that appeared on the LP *Dixie Fried.*

In January 1971, Clapton and the other Dominos, along with George Harrison, Jim Price (trumpet) and Bobby Keys (saxophone), contributed to the first Bobby Whitlock solo album. In an interview in *New Musical Express,* Whitlock said that he thought the group might soon become just "the Dominos." He said, "I'll do my album with Derek and the Dominos, you know, and then everybody will have their shot to do their own album. It will boil down to just the Dominos, and that will be nice." Clapton also found time in January to work with his old boss John Mayall again on his *Back to the Roots* album.

Then in April, the Dominos reconvened at the Olympic Sound Studios in London to work on a follow-up album. Unfortunately, personality conflicts—exacerbated by excessive drug use—brought the group to an abrupt end. The five songs they managed to record in this second session were eventually released on the 1988 Eric Clapton *Crossroads* boxed set.

After more than five years of astonishing productivity and creativity, with the breakup of Derek and the Dominoes, Clapton retreated from public life, now suffering from both depression and a serious addiction to heroin. Although George Harrison managed to coax him into appearing at the *Concert for Bangladesh* on August 1, 1971, Clapton's increasing personal problems and drug habit prevented one of England's greatest rock musicians from producing any substantive recordings until he re-emerged in early 1973.

Postscript

Living as rock star recluse in his mansion, with heroin and his aristocratic girlfriend (and fellow addict) Alice Ormesby-Gore to keep him company, Clapton still found solace in composing songs, even though his expensive drug habit forced him to sell many prized guitars during this time.

Finally, he began to come out of this dangerous period, helped by musician friends such as Pete Townshend and George Harrison. On January 13, 1973, Eric Clapton performed two shows at the Rainbow Theatre in London supported by Pete Townshend, who assembled the backing band. Townshend's intention was to get Clapton back into the public arena, and lending a helping hand was a stellar cast of musicians—including Jim Capaldi (drums), Ric Grech (bass), Pete Townshend (guitar and vocals), Steve Winwood (keyboards and vocals) and Ron Wood (guitar). These shows were released as *Eric Clapton's Rainbow Concert* (1973).

After recovering from the most serious aspects of his heroin addiction, Clapton released his "comeback" album, *461 Ocean Boulevard* (1974). One song was a gospel-type composition called "Give Me Strength." Perhaps this haunting prayer set to music best captures the depth and soul of this truly unique artist and blues musician. With a cover of Bob Marley's "I Shot the Sheriff" climbing to #1 in the U.S. and #9 in the U.K., *461 Ocean Boulevard* reached #1 in the U.S. and #3 in the U.K.

461 Ocean Boulevard may be viewed in retrospect as marking the advent of Clapton's more laid-back approach to making records. Eschewing songs featuring extended

The Allman Joys

The Allman Brothers

The Artwoods

Bakerloo

Elvin Bishop

Black Cat Bones

Blind Faith

Mike Bloomfield
(Bob Dylan with Mike Bloomfield)

Blues Project

Graham Bond

Paul Butterfield

Canned Heat

Chicken Shack

Climax Blues Band

DEREK AND THE DOMINOS
Eric Clapton   Bobby Whitlock   Jim Gordon   Carl Radle

Eric Clapton

Eric Clapton

Cream

Cream

Eric Clapton

Cream

Ginger Baker

John Dummer Blues Band

Fleetwood Mac

guitar workouts in favor of a greater emphasis on vocals (where Clapton was frequently joined by Yvonne Elliman and/or Marcy Levy on backup vocals), these post-*Layla* works brought Clapton his greatest commercial success. Although each pop-tinged album placed in the Top 40, this was little consolation to his long-term blues- and jam-oriented fans.

Although by then Clapton had kicked his heroin habit, he had almost immediately become addicted to alcohol, which plagued him until 1987. Several spells in rehabilitation clinics eventually cured him of his alcoholism and in the mid-1990s, he became the founder of the Crossroads Center for Addictions in Antigua, graciously selling his large collection of vintage guitars to help raise funds for the project.

By the release of *461 Ocean Boulevard*, Clapton had assembled a steady band that included guitarist George Terry and bassist Carl Radle. Clapton continued issuing successful albums, including 1975's *There's One in Every Crowd* and *EC Was Here*, 1976's *No Reason to Cry*, 1977's *Slowhand* (which included the hit single "Lay Down Sally" (#3, 1978) and the radio-friendly cover of J.J. Cale's "Cocaine"), and 1978's *Backless*, which featured the single "Promises" (#9, 1979).

In December 1979, Clapton put together an all-English band to record *Just One Night* (1980) and *Another Ticket* (1981). He continued releasing successful albums into the 1980s, including 1983's *Money and Cigarettes*, 1985's *Behind the Sun* (which contained U.S. single #26 "Forever Man"), 1988's career retrospective *Crossroads* and 1989's *Journeyman*.

Clapton joined Jeff Beck and Jimmy Page in 1983 for a series of concerts for ARMS (Action Research in Multiple Sclerosis) benefiting Ronnie Lane. Shortly thereafter in 1985, he sought treatment for alcoholism.

In January 1987, Clapton played three dates at the Royal Albert Hall in London, the first of what would become an annual series of multi-night concerts at the venerated venue (eventually featuring four different lineups in one concert series). Released in 1991, *24 Nights* documented the 1990–91 Royal Albert Hall series. Then in December 1991, Clapton and his touring band backed George Harrison on his first solo tour since the mid-1970s. The shows were documented in the double live album *The Japan Tour*.

Tragedy faced Clapton on August 26, 1990, when a helicopter crash killed Stevie Ray Vaughan along with Clapton's agent and two roadies following a concert in which they shared billing. Even more devastating, on March 20, 1991, Clapton's young son, Conor, died after plunging some 50 stories from a window in his mother's Manhattan apartment.

In 1991, Clapton's "Bad Love" earned him his first Grammy Award for Best Male Rock Vocal; the following year he appeared on MTV's "Unplugged" and the resulting album topped the charts and garnered six Grammy Awards, including Album of the Year. The set included reworkings of "Layla" (U.S. #12) and the U.S. #2 "Tears in Heaven," a heartfelt tribute to his late son. He was also inducted into the Rock and Roll Hall of Fame as a member of the Yardbirds.

In 1993, Clapton was inducted into the Rock and Roll Hall of Fame for a second time as a member of Cream. He was then inducted for the third time (this time as a solo artist) on March 6, 2000, thereby becoming the Hall of Fame's first "triple inductee."

Clapton released the all-blues album *From the Cradle* in 1994, which topped the U.S. charts and won two awards, a Grammy for the Best Traditional Blues Album and a Handy Special Recognition Award for a crossover artist.

In 1996, the boxed set *Crossroads 2: Live in the Seventies* was released, and the following year Clapton received Grammy Awards for Record of the Year and Best Male Pop Vocal Performance for "Change the World," a collaboration with R&B artist/producer Babyface.

That same year, under the byline "x-sample," Clapton engaged in a collaboration with keyboardist/producer Simon Climie. Billing themselves as T.D.F. (Totally Dysfunctional Family), the pair released an album of ambient New Age music, *Retail Therapy*. He followed this with another solo album in 1998, *Pilgrim,* which placed in the Top Ten, buoyed by the success of the single, "My Father's Eyes," for which he won yet another Grammy—this one for Best Male Pop Vocal Performance. In 2000, he collaborated with 74-year-old blues icon B.B. King on *Riding with the King*.

Clapton has also been heavily involved in soundtracks over the years, including *Edge of Darkness* (1985), *Lethal Weapon* (1987), *Homeboy* (1988), *Lethal Weapon*

2 (1988), *Rush* (1992), *Lethal Weapon 3* (1992), *The Van* (1996), *Nil by Mouth* (1997) and *Lethal Weapon 4* (1998).

In addition to recording, Clapton continues to tour regularly.

Discography

Release Date	Title	Catalog Number

U.S. Singles

Eric Clapton

| 1970 | After Midnight/Easy Now | Atco 6784 |
| 1972 | Let It Rain/Easy Now | Polydor 15049 |

Derek and the Dominoes

1970	Tell the Truth/Roll It Over	Atco 45-6780 (Withdrawn)
1971	Bell Bottom Blues/Keep On Growing	Atco 6803
1971	Layla/I Am Yours	Atco 6809
1973	Why Does Love Got to Be So Sad?/Presence of the Love	RSO 400

U.S. Albums

1970   *Eric Clapton*   Atco SD-33-329
Slunky/Bad Boy/Lonesome and a Long Way from Home/After Midnight/Easy Now/Blues Power/Bottle of Red Wine/Lovin' You Lovin' Me/I've Told You for the Last Time/I Don't Know Why/Let It Rain

1972   *The History of Eric Clapton*   Atco SD-2-803
I Ain't Got You/Hideaway/Tales of Brave Ulysses/I Want to Know/Sunshine of Your Love/Crossroads/Sea of Joy/Only You Know and I Know/I Don't Want to Discuss It/Teasin'/Blues Power/Spoonful/Badge/Tell the Truth/Tell the Truth (Jam)/Layla

1988   *Crossroads* (4 CD)   Polydor 835 261
Boom Boom[1]/Honey in Your Hips[1]/Baby What's Wrong[1]/I Wish You Would[1]/A Certain Girl[1]/Good Morning Little Schoolgirl[1]/I Ain't Got You[1]/For Your Love[1]/Got to Hurry[1]/Lonely Years[2]/Bernard Jenkins[2]/Hideaway[3]/All Your Love[3]/Ramblin' On My Mind[3]/Have You Ever Loved a Woman[3] (live)/Wrapping Paper[4]/I Feel Free[4]/Spoonful[4]/Lawdy Mama[4] (previously unreleased)/Strange Brew[4]/Sunshine of Your Love[4]/Tales of Brave Ulysses[4]/Steppin' Out[4] (previously unreleased)/Anyone for Tennis[4]/White Room[4]/Crossroads[4]/Badge[4]/Presence of the Lord[5]/Can't Find My Way Home[5]/Sleeping in the Ground[5] (previously unreleased)/Comin' Home[6]/Blues Power/After Midnight (previously unreleased alternate mix)/Let It Rain/Tell the Truth[7]/Roll It Over[7]/Layla[7]/Mean Old World[8]/Key to the Highway[7] (live)/Crossroads[7] (live)/Got to Get Better in a Little While[7]/Evil[7]/One More Chance[7]/Mean Old Frisco[7]/Snake Lake Blues[7]/Let It Grow/Ain't That Lovin' You (previously unreleased)/Motherless Children/I Shot the Sheriff (previously unreleased)/Better Make It Through Today/The

Sky Is Crying/I Found a Love (previously unreleased)/(When Things Go Wrong) It Hurts Me Too (previously unreleased)/Whatcha Gonna Do (previously unreleased)/Knockin' on Heaven's Door/Someone Like You/Hello Old Friend/Sign Language/Further on Up the Road (previously unreleased)/Lay Down Sally/Wonderful Tonight/Cocaine/Promises/If I Don't Be There By Morning/Double Trouble/I Can't Stand It/The Shape You're In/Heaven Is One Step Away/She's Waiting/Too Bad/Miss You/Wanna Make Love to You/After Midnight (new version)

[1] The Yardbirds	[5] Blind Faith
[2] John Mayall	[6] Delaney and Bonnie
[3] John Mayall's Bluesbreakers	[7] Derek and the Dominos
[4] Cream	[8] With Duane Allman

Derek and the Dominoes

1970   *Layla and Other Assorted Love Songs* (2 LP)   Atco SD-2-704
I Looked Away/Bell Bottom Blues/Keep On Growing/Nobody Knows You (When You're Down and Out)/I Am Yours/Anyday/Key to the Highway/Tell the Truth/Why Does Love Got to Be So Sad?/Have You Ever Loved a Woman/Little Wing/It's Too Late/Layla/Thorn Tree in the Garden

1973   *Derek and the Dominoes Live in Concert* (2 LP)   RSO 2-8800
Why Does Love Got to Be So Sad?/Got to Get Better in a Little While/Let It Rain/Presence of the Lord/Tell the Truth/Bottle of Red Wine/Roll It Over/Blues Power/Have You Ever Loved a Woman

1990   *The Layla Sessions: 20th Anniversary Edition* (3 CD)   Polydor 847 083-2
I Looked Away/Bell Bottom Blues/Keep on Growing/Nobody Knows You (When You're Down and Out/I Am Yours/Anyday/Key to the Highway/Tell the Truth/Why Does Love Got to Be So Sad?/Have You Ever Loved a Woman/Little Wing/It's Too Late/Layla/Thorn Tree in the Garden/Jam I/Jam II/Jam III/Jam IV/Jam V/Have You Ever Loved a Woman/Have You Ever Loved a Woman/Tell the Truth/Tell the Truth/Mean Old World/Mean Old World/Mean Old World/(When Things Go Wrong) It Hurts Me Too/Tender Love/It's Too Late

1994   *Live at the Fillmore* (2 CD)   Polydor 314 521 682-2
Got to Get Better in a Little While/Why Does Love Got to Be So Sad?/Key to the Highway/Blues Power/Have You Ever Loved a Woman/Bottle of Red Wine/Tell the Truth/Nobody Knows You When You're Down and Out/Roll It Over/Presence of the Lord/Little Wing/Let It Rain/Crossroads

Miscellaneous U.S. Releases

1966   *What's Shakin'*   Elektra EKL-4002 (M)
Tracks by the Powerhouse include "I Want to Know," "Crossroads" and "Steppin' Out."

1968   *An Anthology of British Blues*   Immediate Z12 52 006
Includes "I'm Your Witchdoctor" (John Mayall and the Bluesbreakers with Eric Clapton) plus the following tracks credited to Clapton: "Snake Drive," "Tribute to Elmore" and "West Coast Idea."

1968   *An Anthology of British Blues Vol. 2*   Immediate
Z12 52 014

Includes "On Top of the World" (John Mayall and the Bluesbreakers with Eric Clapton) plus the following tracks credited to Eric Clapton and Jimmy Page: "Draggin' My Tail," "Freight Loader" and "Choker."

1968   *The Beginning of British Blues*   Immediate
Z12 52 018

Includes "Miles Road" credited to Eric Clapton and Jimmy Page.

Delaney and Bonnie and Friends with guest star Eric Clapton
1970   *On Tour with Eric Clapton*   Atco SD 33-326
Things Get Better/Poor Elijah—Tribute to Robert Johnson/Only You Know and I Know/I Don't Want to Discuss It/That's What My Man Is For/Where There's a Will, There's a Way/Coming Home/Little Richard Medley

U.K. Singles

Eric Clapton
1970   After Midnight/Easy Now   Polydor 2001 096

Derek and the Dominoes
1970   Tell the Truth/Roll It Over   Polydor 2058 057
(Withdrawn)
1970   Layla/Bell Bottom Blues   Polydor 2058 130

U.K. Albums

1970   *Eric Clapton*   Polydor 2383 021

Derek and the Dominoes
1970   *Layla and Other Assorted Love Songs*   Polydor 2625 005
1973   *Derek and the Dominoes Live in Concert*   RSO 2659 020

Miscellaneous U.K. Releases

With the Powerhouse
1966   *What's Shakin'*   Elektra EUKS 7260

1967   *Blues Anytime Volume 1*   Immediate
IMCP 014
Same tracks as the U.S. release *An Anthology of British Blues.*

1967   *Blues Anytime Volume 2*   Immediate
IMCP 015
Same tracks as the U.S. release *An Anthology of British Blues Vol. 2.*

1968   *Blues Anytime Volume 3*   Immediate
IMLP 019
Same tracks as the U.S. release *The Beginning of British Blues.*

Delaney and Bonnie and Friends with guest star Eric Clapton
1970   *On Tour with Eric Clapton*   Atlantic 2400013

The Climax Blues Band

Hailing from Stafford, Great Britain, the pop-leaning Climax Blues Band achieved worldwide popularity in the mid-1970s with the hit singles "Gotta Have More Love," "I Love You" and "Couldn't Get It Right." The Climax Blues Band, in its various incarnations and under shifting band names, is one of the few 1960s blues-rock bands to carve out an enduring career. The distinctive-sounding group was founded by Colin Richard Francis Cooper (b. October 7, 1939; Stafford, Staffordshire, U.K.), who is the only remaining original member. The Climax Blues Band continues to tour to this day.

Cooper taught himself the harmonica when he was 12 and switched to the clarinet at 16. Within a couple of years, he changed again to the saxophone and before long was playing with a jazz band. His early bands included the Climax Jazz Band in 1964 and the Hipster Image in 1965. Before disbanding, the Hipster Image recorded one single produced by ex-Animal Alan Price, "Can't Let Her Go" backed with "Make Her Mine" (U.K./Decca F 12137). In 1966, Cooper joined the short-lived group the Gospel Truth, a soul band whose membership included 16-year-old guitar prodigy Peter Haycock. Peter John Haycock (b. April 4, 1952; Stafford, Staffordshire, U.K.) started playing the harmonica at age nine, and by 11 had learned the guitar. He was playing in his first band, the Mason Dixon Line, by age 14.

In 1967, Cooper and Haycock decided to form a blues band. "We started playing blues for fun," Haycock later told *Melody Maker*, "and the thing sort of turned round on us; it became serious. Originally we got so cheesed off with soul bands we decided we would do something we would enjoy, so we moved into blues. The odd thing is that the blues band has been bigger than anything we have ever been in." The group's original name, the unwieldy Colin Cooper's Climax Chicago Blues Band, was quickly shortened to the Climax Chicago Blues Band. The new band consisted of Cooper on vocals, harmonica and saxophones, and Haycock on guitar and vocals, along with bassist Richard Jones, keyboardist Arthur Wood, rhythm guitarist Derek Holt (b. January 26, 1949; Stafford, Staffordshire, U.K.), and drummer George Newsome (b. August 14, 1947; Stafford, Staffordshire, U.K.).

By 1968, the sextet had signed with EMI's Parlophone label. The band recorded their eponymous debut LP in just two days, September 27 and November 5, at Abbey Road Studios. Between sessions, Richard Jones left the band to continue his university studies and Derek Holt moved over to bass. Released in February 1969, the album contained a mixture of blues covers and originals written in the style of Chicago Chess blues. Highlights included "Looking for My Baby" and "Insurance," both spotlighting Haycock's excellent slide work, and "Wee Baby Blues," a folksy, harmonica-accented number featuring the dual vocals of Haycock and Cooper. The album received praise from *New Musical Express,* which called it "catchy music, almost trad jazz at times . . . and at other times, jazz blues."

In June 1969, the band recorded their second album, *Plays On.* The record, a conscious effort to move away from restrictive blues structures for a more progressive sound, included the use of a mellotron. Bringing elements of jazz into the mix, the album's best tracks were two instrumentals—the smoky, sensual "Flight," which featured Cooper on alto and tenor saxophone, and a snazzy cover of Graham Bond's "Little Girl." The album received mixed reviews. *Melody Maker* dismissed the album with the observation: "Although there is very little loose playing throughout the album, the band fails to display sufficient versatility to make this one a winner." On the other hand, *Rolling Stone* extolled the long player, calling *Plays On* "strictly professional." The magazine, singling out Haycock as the group's instrumental star, noted, "He fills more than one song on this album with imaginative leads and his straight blues work," and added that the group manifested "a natural feeling for the music that makes his playing all the more admirable." *Disc and Music Echo* also gave the LP high marks, calling it "a really outstanding album . . . [which] offers brilliant musicianship, variety and very professional production."

The band also released their first single, "Like Uncle Charlie" backed with "Loving Machine." Although barely cracking the Top 200 (*Plays On* reached #197 on the U.S. charts) the band members (with the exception of school-teacher Wood) felt encouraged enough by its reception to quit their day jobs and go professional.

In 1970, Climax Chicago switched labels to Harvest, EMI's progressive label. Over just four days in August, they recorded their third album, with Humpty Farmer helping out on keyboards. Released in the U.K. as *A Lot of Bottle,* the album was arguably their most cohesive collection, marking a return to basic blues. Haycock described their approach to *Disc and Music Echo:* "Musically we're not really trying to do very clever things. We've got this sort of progressive tag from some people but all we are really is a stomping band." *Rolling Stone* gave the album passing marks: "The good moments easily outnumber the bad ones and guitarist Haycock cuts loose with some really fine licks here and there." And *Disc and Music Echo* approved of the effort: "Climax Chicago Blues Band has a fine, funky album out called *A Lot of Bottle.* Blues may be going out of fashion, and the pundits may shake their heads at another blues band trying to make it, but this one really has all the requirements and more. Their compositions are good, they use their instruments well, and they're exciting." The album was released in the U.S. as simply *Climax Blues Band,* with the tracks resequenced and an added song, the single, "Like Uncle Charlie."

The band was now becoming a popular club attraction. A reviewer for *Melody Maker* saw a Marquee performance and observed that in spite of technical issues, "The band finally overcame the glut of problems, and slammed into a great set that was howling and extremely satisfying. They are a tight band, delicately influenced by Mayall, and with a great sense of purpose and perfection."

While the band was rising in popularity, the blues wave in Britain had faded and the group felt that they had become stereotyped by their name. Peter Haycock told *Melody Maker,* "We've got a feeling that we are missing out on a large percentage of audiences because of our very name. 'The Blues Band' bit doesn't really attract the people we'd like to have there." So on their next U.K. release, they called themselves "Climax Chicago," while in the U.S. they continued to use the name adopted on their prior album there, "Climax Blues Band." They recorded their next album in May and June of 1971, which was tentatively titled "Come Stomping." Released in October 1971 as *Tightly Knit,* the album contained a hodgepodge of styles, from the menacing undertone that lurked in "Shoot Her If She Runs" and the groove-heavy riffs of "St Michael's Blues" to the percolating if spooky "Who Killed McSwiggen," which one critic described as a "mind-chilling, blues *cum* jazz rave-up."

In September and October of 1971, the Climax Blues Band coheadlined a 34-date British tour along with Argent and Satisfaction. They were then scheduled to go on their first American tour in June 1972, but trouble obtaining visas and work permits forced the trip to be postponed.

In August, the band recorded their fifth LP, *Rich Man*. The Climax Blues Band were now reduced to a four-piece, as George Newsome and Arthur Wood both left. Newsome was replaced on drums by John Cuffley, who had previously played in Cooper's old group, the Gospel Truth. While all of the previous efforts had been produced by Chris Thomas, for these sessions the band switched to American producer Richard Gottehrer. Gottehrer, as one-third of the production team of Feldman-Goldstein-Gottehrer, was responsible for a series of singles by various artists, most notably the Angels ("My Boyfriend's Back") and the McCoys ("Hang on Sloopy"). The trio even recorded themselves as the Strangeloves, achieving a #11 hit in the summer of 1965 with the infectious "I Want Candy" (covered years later by Bow Wow Wow).

Rich Man veered away from the jazz and blues leanings of their past albums and was the group's most commercial effort to date, particularly the single "Mole on the Dole." Still, the single attracted little attention, and the album only reached #150 on the U.S. charts. As a live act, however, the group continued to gain popularity and in 1972 developed a foothold with American audiences during their first stateside tour.

Postscript

Following the release of *Rich Man*, the band switched to Polydor, where they released *FM/Live* (1973, U.S. #107), which was recorded live at the New York Academy of Music. Released as a double album in the U.S., the album was reduced to a single disc in the U.K. That same year, a planned studio album titled *Reaching Out* was scrapped as the band felt that the sessions were rushed. They continued to release successful albums into the decade: *Sense of Direction* (1975, U.S. #37); *Stamp Album* (1975, U.S. #69), which marked the return of original member Richard Jones; *Gold Plated* (1976, U.S. #27, U.K. #56), which included their first big single, "Couldn't Get It Right" (U.S. #3, U.K. #10); *Shine On* (1978, U.S. #71), which saw Richard Jones leave the band for a second time; and *Real to Reel* (1979, U.S. #170), which included contributions from new full-time keyboardist Peter Filleul.

The recordings continued with *Flying the Flag* (1980, U.S. #75), which included the Derek Holt-penned ballad "I Love You" (U.S. #12); *Lucky for Some* (1981), which was the last album to include Cuffey and Holt (both left soon after its release); *Sample and Hold* (1983), the last album to feature Haycock (who left the following year); *Drastic Steps* (1988); and *Blues from the Attic* (1993).

After leaving the band, Derek Holt went on to score music for film and television. He also owns a live music bar in Stafford, England, called the Grapes, which showcases his extensive collection of memorabilia from his days with the Climax Blues Band. In 1989, he took part in the IRS album *Night of the Guitar—Live!,* which featured numerous guest guitarists including former band mate Pete Haycock, Randy California, Steve Howe, Robby Krieger, Alvin Lee and Leslie West. In 1997, he released a solo album, *After the Climax,* on HTD Records. Teaming up with guitarist Dave Day the following year, Holt and Day released the album *East Liverpool.*

Following his departure from the Climax Blues Band, Haycock formed Pete Haycock's Climax. This group released two albums, *Total Climax* (1985) and *The Soft Spot* (1986). In 1988, Haycock released an instrumental solo album, *Guitar and Son,* on IRS records. He has also recorded more than a dozen soundtracks since 1988 for film composer Hans Zimmer. In 1989, Haycock joined Electric Light Orchestra Part II for the recording of *Electric Light Orchestra Part II* (1991) and *Electric Light Orchestra Part II Performing ELO's Greatest Hits Live* (1992). In 1992, he released *Drastic Steps* with the Pete Haycock Band.

Discography

Release Date	Title	Catalog Number

U.S. Singles

The Climax Blues Band

1971	Reap What I've Sowed/Spoonful	Sire 351
1972	Hey Mama/That's All	Sire 358

U.S. Albums

The Climax Chicago Blues Band

1969	*The Climax Chicago Blues Band*	Sire SES 97013

Mean Old World/Insurance/Going Down This Road/You've Been Drinking/Don't Start Me Talkin'/Wee Baby Blues/Twenty Past One/A Stranger in Your Town/How Many More Years/Looking for My Baby/And Lonely/The Entertainer

1970   *Plays On*   Sire SES 97023
Flight/Cubano Chant/Mum's the Word/So Many Roads/Crazy 'Bout My Baby/Hey Baby Everything's Gonna Be Alright, Yeh, Yeh, Yeh /Little Girl/Twenty Past Two—Temptation Rag/City Ways

The Climax Blues Band
1971   *Climax Blues Band*   Sire SI-4901
Country Hat/Everyday/Reap What I've Sowed/Brief Case/It's Alright Blue—Country Hat Reprise/Seventh Sun/Please Don't Help Me/Like Uncle Charlie/Louisiana Blues/Cut You Loose

1972   *Tightly Knit*   Sire SI-5903
Hey Mama/Shoot Her If She Runs/Towards the Sun/Come On in My Kitchen/Who Killed McSwiggen/Little Link/St Michael's Blues/Bide My Time/That's All

1972   *Rich Man*   Sire SES-7402
Rich Man/Mole on the Dole/You Make Me Sick/Standing by a River/Shake Your Love/All the Time in the World/If You Want to Know/Don't You Mind People Grinning in Your Face

U.K. Singles

1969	Like Uncle Charlie/Loving Machine	Parlophone R5809
1970	Reap What I've Sowed/Spoonful	Harvest HAR5029
1971	Towards the Sun/Everyday	Harvest HAR5041
1972	Mole on the Dole/Like Uncle Charlie	Harvest HAR5065

U.K. Albums

The Climax Chicago Blues Band
1969	*The Climax Chicago Blues Band*	Parlophone PCS 7069 (S) Parlophone PMC 7069 (M)
1969	*Plays On*	Parlophone PCS 7084
1970	*A Lot of Bottle*	Harvest SHSP 4009

Same tracks as the U.S. release *Climax Blues Band* except with added songs "Morning Noon and Night" and "Long Lovin' Man," and deleted track, "Like Uncle Charlie."

Climax Chicago
| 1971 | *Tightly Knit* | Harvest SHSP 4015 |
| 1972 | *Rich Man* | Harvest SHSP 4024 Elektra EKS-74002 (S) |

The Cream

During the less than three years of Cream's existence, the group epitomized what three virtuoso musicians could achieve onstage, in essence defining the concepts "power trio" and "blues-rock improvisation." Though firmly grounded in electric Chicago blues, the group's excursions into free-form improvisation and extended solos revolutionized rock music and blazed a trail for others to follow, and often lesser talents attempted to do so—at their own peril. The group's moniker, originally suggested by Eric Clapton, served to put others on notice of the high caliber of the members' instrumentation skills. In a sense, Cream was to mid-1960s blues-rock what Robert Johnson was to late-1930s Delta blues. Both pushed the music forward by introducing a jazz player's virtuosity to the current state of the blues, thereby lifting it to a new level.

Formed in June 1966, it took less than two years for the unique musical freshness that was Cream to turn sour. What hastened this group's inevitable though drawn-out demise was simply the business of the music business. In other words, they became victims of their own success. Looking back, guitarist Eric Clapton [see **Eric Clapton**] now especially points out how the heady times that catapulted the band to top billing on the world stage also left them spiritually scarred for many years after the party was finally over.

For Clapton, the end came when the revered *Rolling Stone* magazine dubbed him "master of the blues clichés"; meanwhile, bass player Jack Bruce wanted out after the band played Madison Square Gardens on a corny revolving stage; likewise, Ginger Baker found such cavernous venues a totally unsuitable showcase for his intricate polyrhythmic style of drumming.

But by then—1968—it was as if their unique music had become secondary to the spectacle. The final straw, as far as the band was concerned, was that their fans' adulation persisted no matter how badly they played. For instance, Ginger Baker remembers the critically acclaimed farewell concerts at London's Royal Albert Hall in October 1968 as sadly mediocre affairs from a musical point of view. Still, the ovations echoed on into the night.

When they first came together, all three men were already highly accomplished musicians and refugees from other British R&B lineups: Eric Clapton was a former Yardbird and at the time of Cream's formation was enjoying tremendous success as lead guitarist in John Mayall's Bluesbreakers [see **Yardbirds**, **John Mayall**]; bassist Jack Bruce and drummer Ginger Baker were former members of Alexis Korner's Blues Incorporated and the Graham Bond Organization [see **Alexis Korner, Graham Bond**].

From the very start, the chemistry of Cream was destined to be volatile. Previously, Baker had conspired to fire Bruce from the Graham Bond Organization and in the end had to resort to real threats of violence to persuade him to leave. In mid-1965, Bruce then spent a short time in John Mayall's Bluesbreakers, where he first met and played alongside Clapton, who was astonished by the bass player's versatility.

But the fuse for the two-year musical firework display that was Cream at their best was lit when Clapton and Baker jammed together at a Bluesbreakers gig in Oxford in the spring of 1966. Afterwards, when Baker drove Clapton back to London in his car, the two young blues-rock virtuosos made plans: they both wanted to take electric blues into the future and make money in the process. Ironically, these two objectives sowed the seeds for not only the band's rise, but also for its sad, early demise when the moneymaking took over.

Another irony about that fateful car journey and one that would also hasten the end of the band some two and a half years later was Clapton's adamancy about having Bruce as their bass player. A few days later, an apologetic Baker went to visit old enemy Jack Bruce, who was by then a member of the pop group Manfred Mann. After Baker pleaded for forgiveness for forcing him out of the Graham Bond Organization, Bruce was ready and willing to forget past acrimonies, but theirs would forever be a difficult relationship, even when the music soared.

John Simon Asher Bruce was born May 14, 1943, in Bishopbriggs, Scotland, located three miles north of Glasgow. He started his musical education by studying cello and piano as well as by singing in the choir. Many years later, he discussed his childhood with *Melody Maker:* "When I was a young schoolboy I always wanted to play the bass—but was put on cello because I just wasn't big enough to handle the monster. At 15, having grown, I realized my first ambition, and played bass in the school orchestra, afterwards studying at the Royal Scottish Academy of Music in Glasgow."

His stay there was brief, however, because at 17, discouraged by his professors' lack of support for his interest in jazz and blues, he left the academy. Bruce had already begun gigging at jazz clubs, and he felt that that was more important to his development as a musician than studying classical harmony.

Bruce traveled to Italy, where he played double bass in the Murray Campbell Big Band before going to England to join Jim McHarg's Scotsville Jazz Band. While in Cambridge, Bruce made a strong impression when he sat in on a gig with sax player Dick Heckstall-Smith and drummer Ginger Baker. This led to Heckstall-Smith inviting him to sit in with Blues Incorporated, and he became the group's permanent bassist in May 1962. The two lobbied for Ginger Baker to join Blues Incorporated too, and by June, Baker had replaced Charlie Watts as the group's drummer. Watts, a future member of the Rolling Stones, was a fan of Baker's playing and so graciously gave up his place so that Baker could have a regular gig.

Peter Edward "Ginger" Baker was born on August 19, 1939, in Lewisham, London. As a teenager, he was a competitive bicyclist. He also became interested in jazz, particularly Dizzy Gillespie. When he was 14 he played trumpet, and he later performed in the Air Training Corp band. He switched to drums at 15 and turned professional within a few months.

At age 16, Baker answered an advertisement in *Melody Maker* for a drummer and joined the Storyville Jazz Men. During his first rehearsal with the band, he was provided with a set of instructional drumming records by famed New Orleans drummer Warren Dodds, a.k.a. Baby Dodds, that enormously aided his development. Dodds was an innovative drummer who introduced the concept of the one-man drummer to the jazz combo. Prior to his innovation, the percussion section typically consisted of three players, but he arranged the drums and cymbals in a way that allowed one person to play them all. His legacy includes recordings with Jelly Roll Morton's Red Hot Peppers and Louis Armstrong's Hot Seven. Other drummers who made an impression on the fledgling Baker included Zutty Singleton (who led his own band and also played with Louis Armstrong, Fats Waller and Roy Eldridge) and Buddy Rich (whose incredible drum solos earned him the title of "the world's greatest drummer"). While with the Storyville Jazz Men, Baker took part in studio recordings on September 19, 1957, with clarinetist Acker Bilk that were issued years later as *Acker's Early Days.* Saxophonist Dick Heckstall-Smith also took part in these sessions. Baker and Heckstall-Smith played together frequently in the succeeding years.

In August 1958, Baker left the Storyville Jazz Men to join Terry Lightfoot's Trad Band. However, his radical style of playing the heavy offbeat got him canned in short order. So in 1959, he went on a three-month tour of Copenhagen backing guitarist Diz Disley, and then made a tour of Scandinavia as support for American gospel singer Sister Rosetta Tharpe.

Although Baker was progressing as a musician, his fiery personality, heroin habit and radical style of playing limited his opportunities, and for a while he even considered quitting music altogether. However, England's legendary jazz drummer Phil Seamen saw him perform at the Flamingo and, recognizing his potential, encouraged him to continue. Baker continued to play for outfits and by 1961 was playing three or four nights a week with Dick Heckstall-Smith in a number of bands, including the Johnny Burch Octet and the Bert Courtley Band. He finally found a comfortable fit, at least temporarily, when Dick Heckstall-Smith invited him to sit in with Alexis Korner and Blues Incorporated, eventually replacing drummer Charlie Watts in June 1962.

The lineup of Blues Incorporated was fluid; between June and August 1962 it included Alexis Korner on guitar and vocals, Cyril Davies on harp and vocals, Jack Bruce on bass, Ginger Baker on drums, Dick Heckstall-Smith on saxophone, and several additional singers, including Paul Jones, Ronnie Jones and Mick Jagger. Sadly, no recordings from this period were ever released. In November 1962, sax player Graham Bond, formerly of the Johnny Burch Octet, joined and immediately settled in.

In February 1963, Bond handed Korner his resignation. Bond then formed his own band, taking Baker and Bruce with him and later adding guitarist John McLaughlin. By September 1963, McLaughlin departed after the rest of the band grew tired of his tendency to grumble and moan about the rigors of life as a musician. Dick Heckstall-Smith replaced him, and the classic lineup of the Graham Bond Organization was born. Together they issued two albums in 1965, *The Sound of '65* and *There's a Bond Between Us*, but they never achieved a commercial breakthrough.

Jack Bruce stayed with the Organization for over two years until Ginger Baker ousted him in mid-1965. Baker informed the rest of the band that they would be better off without Bruce's "disturbing influence." The two were frequently at odds, and even brawled on stage on one occasion. After Baker had fired him, Bruce still turned up at several gigs and demanded to play. In the end, Baker had to threaten Bruce with a knife for Bruce to realize that it was preferable to be alive without a band as opposed to being a fatally wounded member of the Organization.

After finally realizing that his tenure was over with the Organization, Bruce became a member of John Mayall's Bluesbreakers from October to December 1965, where he met Eric Clapton and played alongside Peter Green for a couple of gigs. While no studio recordings were made, this lineup can be heard on *Primal Solos*, a collection of primitive live recordings that includes five tracks said to have been recorded at the Flamingo Club. Another Flamingo track, "Stormy Monday," is on the John Mayall compilation *Looking Back*. Bruce left the Bluesbreakers to join the more commercially successful Manfred Mann in December 1965. He also released a solo single, "I'm Getting Tired (of Drinking and Gambling)" backed with "Rootin' Tootin'" (U.K./Polydor BM 56036).

In early 1966, Bruce took part in a session organized by Manfred Mann vocalist Paul Jones. Participants in the ad hoc lineup included Jones on harmonica, Eric Clapton on guitar, Ben Palmer on piano, Pete York on drums and Steve Winwood (using the pseudonym Steve Anglo for contractual reasons) on vocals. Three tracks recorded at this session ("I Want to Know," "Crossroads" and "Steppin' Out") appeared on the Elektra compilation album *What's Shakin'*, issued under the group name "Eric Clapton and the Powerhouse." Oddly, the last two tracks became Cream staples. In a *Guitar Player* interview, Clapton referred to an additional track recorded at these sessions, a slow blues, but it has yet to surface.

In effect, Cream began to be formed during a Bluesbreakers gig at Oxford in April 1966 when Baker asked if he could sit in with the band. Baker's playing energized Clapton, and after the gig Baker broached the idea of forming a band together. Clapton discussed the event with *Beat Instrumental*: "I had thought about a tie-up with Jack and Ginger for months but I thought it wasn't likely to come off. For a start I thought that Ginger was just too good for me to play with; too jazzy. Then he approached ME, and to my surprise I found that he was really a solid rock drummer at heart. Jack? Well, he's always been a blues man." Clapton, apparently unaware of the acrimony between Baker and Bruce, said he would join only if Bruce came in as well. So Baker took the proposal to Bruce, who found it intriguing, and the two decided to put their differences aside.

From the band's inception, Clapton and Bruce saw Cream as a moneymaker as well as a creative step up from what they had done before. Both musicians were impressed by the Rover car that Baker owned and drove to early band meetings; Baker had bought it with money made from writing the B-side of the Who single "Substitute." Both Clapton and Bruce were by now disheartened by the subsistence wages they had received for years of working long hard hours on the blues circuit.

Musically, Clapton reportedly envisioned a blues trio in the style of Buddy Guy, with himself as the frontman. Any such thoughts were quickly dispersed during rehearsals, though, when Bruce brought in his own compositions. Baker invited *Melody Maker* reporter Chris Welch to a secret rehearsal at a school hall in Willesden, and Welch broke the story in the June 11, 1966, issue of the magazine under the headline "Eric, Jack & Ginger Team Up." The article announced, "A sensational new 'Group's Group' starring Eric Clapton, Jack Bruce and Ginger Baker is being formed," then further revealed, "It is expected that they will remain as a trio with Jack as featured vocalist."

Since neither Clapton nor Bruce had given notice yet to their respective bands, this premature announcement put them in an awkward position, particularly Clapton, who was the featured performer on the upcoming Mayall album, *Blues Breakers: John Mayall with Eric Clapton.* Mayall was far from pleased about the way in which Clapton left.

A follow-up article in the June 25, 1966, issue of *Melody Maker* announced that the group would call themselves "the Cream" and would be managed by Robert Stigwood, who had signed them to his Reaction label. In the subsequent issue of the music weekly, the group discussed how they intended to approach their music. "It's blues ancient and modern," Clapton said, while Bruce called their music "sweet and sour rock and roll." Ginger Baker revealed that the group was working on building material for their set. "At the moment we're trying to get a repertoire up for all the gigs we've got to do. We're digging back as far as we can, even 1927." Clapton also indicated his awareness of what others expected: "Most people have formed the impression of us as three solo musicians clashing with each other. We want to cancel that idea and be a group that plays together."

The band played a warm-up gig at the Twisted Wheel in Manchester on July 29, 1966, before making their official debut at the Sixth National Jazz and Blues Festival held at the Balloon Meadow, Windsor Racecourse, on July 31. Cream appeared on the final day of the three-day festival and were enthusiastically received by the audience. Clapton candidly assessed the group's performance for *Record Mirror:* "We were a bit ragged at Windsor. It'll take about two months before we're okay. We've got four good numbers and a few standards."

The group briefly flirted with the idea of using props during their performances, including live turkeys. "I had a concept, yeah, it was ridiculous at the time. It was a throw over of my art school scene, something like Dada," Clapton explained to *The Los Angeles Times.* "The Cream was originally going to be a stage presentation as well as the music, like happenings on stage. We did one gig, the first one we did and we had a gorilla on stage, a stuffed one. And we had a lot of strange little things happening like this and it didn't work, nothing happened 'cause we were so involved in music that we just forgot about all these things."

Following their success at Windsor, the group honed their style on the British blues club circuit. Their second club date on August 5, 1966, was held at the Cooks Ferry Inn, Edmonton, London, and was covered by *Melody Maker.* The magazine declared, "Enthusiastic shouting and cheering were reserved for the second half of their act when they dropped their nerves and reduced the gap between numbers. Solos from Eric, Ginger and Jack had the audience in raptures, calling for more." The review predicted big things for the group: "Although the Cream are still in the experimental stage, they are striving for a perfection which, when it does come, will be little short of sensational."

The group found time during their busy club schedule to record tracks for their initial single and album at Rayvik Studio (Chalk Farm, London). To help out with the lyrics, they brought in poet Pete Brown. Baker had shared the stage with Brown at St. Pancras town hall in London a few years earlier at some jazz and poetry evenings.

Their first single, "Wrapping Paper" backed with "Cat's Squirrel" (released in October 1966), stunned their fans. The A-side, a soft-shoe bluesy number composed by Jack Bruce with cinema-imagery lyrics added by Pete Brown, was quite unexpected and immediately put the group on the defensive. Bruce told *Melody Maker,* "I must admit that we wanted to shock people, there was a feeling of that." The flip side was a gutsy blues instrumental more in tune with what the fans wanted. The single peaked at #34 on the U.K. charts.

During their appearance on the BBC radio show *Saturday Club,* the show's affable host Brian Mathew queried Clapton about their unexpected single, especially the topside.

Mathew: Now Eric, you have a large and growing fan following here in Britain and I think that they expect a certain kind of music from you, a kind that they didn't get on your hit record "Wrapping Paper," would you agree?

Clapton: Ah yeah, I would agree because we did want to surprise them in a way because we didn't want them to sort of just you know accept us as a blues band. We want to be something more than that you know.

Mathew: Yeah, well you certainly did.

To *Disc and Music Echo*, Clapton reiterated the band's financial ambitions: "We want to make money. I've been working too hard for too little for too long and I thought it's time I did something about it." Clapton also confessed to *Melody Maker*, "I don't believe we'll ever get over to them [audiences]. People will always listen with biased ears, look through unbelieving eyes, and with preconceived ideas, remembering what we used to be, and so on."

While fans might have been surprised by the single, it was the Bruce/Brown songwriting credit for "Wrapping Paper" that left Ginger Baker stunned. Even today, he still insists that the whole group contributed to the writing of the song in the rehearsal studio. This misunderstanding became just one more bit of acrimony that Baker and Bruce would nurse between them in the future.

Cream simultaneously released their second single and their first album, *Fresh Cream,* on December 9, 1966. The single, "I Feel Free" backed with "N.S.U.," was a vast improvement over their initial release, and this time the critics were far more appreciative. *Melody Maker* wrote, "The Cream have stopped fooling around single-wise and come up with an excellent production . . . exciting, groovy and original." The title of the flip side was an acronym for non-specific urethritis, a form of venereal disease. Penned by the now prolific songwriting team of Jack Bruce and Pete Brown, "I Feel Free" soared to #11 on the U.K. charts, though it stalled at #116 in the U.S. *Fresh Cream* was also a hit record, reaching #6 in the U.K. and #39 in the U.S.

Fresh Cream was a mixture of blues standards and original material that most critics rated highly. *Melody Maker* proclaimed it a good album and predicted, "There's sensational things to come from the Cream yet," while *New Musical Express* advised, "If you want something r-and-b way out, this is it." Jon Landau, writing for *Craw-*

daddy, observed, "The three men in the group are individually exceptional," but he also mused, "There is too much chaff, too much unfulfilled experimentation, to make this a really first-rate album."

In February and March of 1967, the Cream toured Germany, Northern Ireland, Sweden and Denmark before returning to the U.K. for a few additional dates. Then from March 25 to April 2, 1967, Cream flew to the U.S. for the first time to participate in a concert series dubbed "Music in the Fifth Dimension." Promoted by deejay Murray Kaufman (a.k.a. Murray "The K"), these shows featured a variety of pop acts, including the Lovin' Spoonful, the Who, Mitch Ryder, Wilson Picket, the Chicago Loop, and the Blues Project, with each act performing one or two songs per show at New York's RKO Theater on 58th Street. Initially, Cream performed "I Feel Free" and "I'm So Glad," but as the show started to run over, their set was pared down to just one song. Later, Clapton told *Melody Maker*, "We took the actual show as a joke. There was no chance for Ginger to play his solo and we had to use the Who's equipment because we couldn't take any with us and there was none provided—as usual."

In his book *Disraeli Gears*, author John Platt concludes that Cream went into Atlantic Studios in New York on April 3, 1967, to record. However, Atlantic's log indicates that two songs, "Hey Lawdy Mama" and "Strange Brew," were delivered to their tape library on April 4.

The band then flew back to England, where they played a series of club dates. *Melody Maker* reported on May 8 that the band was again planning to fly back to New York. Presumably, over the next 10-day period, the trio recorded their next album before flying to Germany on May 19. Cream then played a series of European and U.K. dates.

Although Cream was gigging heavily, they had yet to achieve the breakthrough success they were looking for. A wistful Bruce told *Beat Instrumental*, "We've reached a strange stage as a group. We're not sure exactly where we are going now. All we want to do is carry on playing the music we like. I suppose we pay very little attention to the charts."

Reaction released Cream's third single, "Strange Brew" backed with "Tales of Brave Ulysses," in June 1967. "Strange Brew" was written by Clapton, Felix Pappalardi and Pappalardi's wife, Gail Collins. Pappalardi basically took the previously recorded "Lawdy Mama" and grafted new vocals with different lyrics over the backing track. Clapton, who handled the vocals on the A-side and cowrote the flip side along with Oz graphic designer Martin Sharp, introduced some superb wah-wah pedal to his arsenal of tricks. A *New Musical Express* reviewer was charmed with the release, writing, "Yep, I can see the Cream doing nicely with this! It's moody, mean and raw—with a nagging insistent beat that gnaws at the brain and almost hypnotizes you. The lyric is absorbing, and it's sang [sic] in high-pitched tones, carried on a wave of reverberating twangs." However, Lulu, reviewing the release for *Disc and Music Echo,* was unmoved over what she saw as Clapton's too obvious similarity to Jimi Hendrix. "Hairy Clapton really HAS gone all Hendrix, hasn't he? He's great in his own right, but all I can hear is Jimi Hendrix."

Clapton was hurt by the comment and responded to the magazine, "It's a big bring down for me to be in this country at the moment. Everybody's obsessed with Jim Hendrix—and if anybody else dares to play a blues guitar phrase they're accused of copying him!" Clapton expanded on his concerns in the August issue of *Beat Instrumental:* "This comparison is unfortunate. I think that it has started because Jimi is more in the public eye than I am. I haven't changed at all. Also, the British scene is so small. Everybody knows what everyone else is doing and the whole thing thrives on competition. Some nights after a good gig, I think, 'Well, after that no one could possibly compare me with Jimi Hendrix,' but I always get someone coming up and saying that I sound like him."

Clapton himself greatly preferred the single's flip side, telling *Disc and Music Echo,* "'Strange Brew' is quite nice but it has nothing to do with our musical progress. Even the B-side, 'Tales of Brave Ulysses,' is a lot better."

Clapton's comment was a foretaste of many ego and personality clashes still to come. His lukewarm praise for "Strange Brew" must have further irked Bruce, who was already annoyed because without his being consulted, the wrong bass line had been used on the A-side of the single, presumably to save studio time and money. Nevertheless, "Strange Brew" reached #17 on the U.K. charts.

By now, Felix Pappalardi had become their producer ("by arrangement with Robert Stigwood") and the legendary Tom Dowd began engineering their sessions. (Although, interestingly enough, Robert Stigwood and Ahmet Ertegun received credit for the production of the

"Strange Brew" single.) The band was much happier with the American studios, explaining to *Disc and Music Echo,* "The engineers there are so incredibly knowledgeable musically that they're just like another member of the group. They're musical wizards—not just engineers."

On August 13, Cream played at the Seventh Annual Jazz and Blues Festival held at Windsor. Later that month, the band embarked on their second U.S. tour, playing the Fillmore Auditorium in San Francisco. After selling out the initial five nights, they were booked for a total of 12 shows between August 22 and September 3, 1967. For the first five nights, they shared the bill with the Paul Butterfield Blues Band and Charlie Musselwhite and the Southside Sound System, and for the final six nights they shared the bill with the Electric Flag and Gary Burton. The group was starting to create a sensation, about which *The San Francisco Chronicle* reported: "The most exciting rock group to hit S.F. since the whole scene began is the Cream. The only rock group from afar which lives up to its publicity. They have stage presence and showmanship in addition to their excitement." Clapton told Jan Wenner, writing for *Melody Maker,* "We seem to be a lot more popular here than I had imagined. I knew that we had been heard of through the underground thing, yet I didn't imagine we'd be this popular."

Following the Fillmore engagements, the band played three dates in Los Angeles at the Whisky A Go-Go. *The Los Angeles Free Press* reported, "They are very impressive. One guitar begins where the other leaves off, in well-calculated, brilliant improvisation. The reason for this professionalism is probably that none of the cats is on that—well—ego trip. They are so tight and all together."

Following the Whisky A Go-Go engagement, the band played dates throughout the country, including the Psychedelic Supermarket in Boston, Massachusetts; the Café Au-Go-Go in New York City; and the Grande Ballroom in Dearborn, Michigan, where the tour ended on October 15. *Time Magazine* described Cream's tour as "the biggest musical jolt out of England since the Beatles and the Rolling Stones." While in America, the group also spent some more time in the studio recording.

Reaction released Cream's long-awaited second album, *Disraeli Gears,* in November 1967. Given the tremendous success that the group had already enjoyed in the States, it's surprising that Atlantic Records took five months to release the LP. But Jack Bruce recalls protracted and heated discussions with "the powers that be" who, astonishingly, were at first of the opinion that much of his original Bruce/Brown material just wasn't "happening." The record executives couldn't have been more mistaken. Packaged in a psychedelic Day-Glo cover designed by Martin Sharpe, *Disraeli Gears* emerged as the breakthrough record they were looking for. Today, the album easily ranks as one of the classics of the decade, containing such highlights as both sides of Cream's previous single as well as "S.W.L.A.B.R." (originally titled "She Was Like a Bearded Rainbow"), with abstract Pete Brown lyrics; the stunning "We're Going Wrong," a Jack Bruce composition; and "Sunshine of Your Love," a smash hit credited to Bruce, Brown and Clapton that reached #5 on the U.S. singles charts when released in February 1968.

Ironically, Clapton had declared war on singles during the previous November, telling *Melody Maker*, "It's not definite that we won't ever release a single again. The main reason for not wanting to do them is we are very anti the whole commercial market. The whole nature of the single-making process has caused us a lot of grief in the studio."

Much of the credit for the success of *Disraeli Gears* belonged to producer Felix Pappalardi and engineer Tom Dowd. The sound quality was greatly improved, and reviewers almost unanimously praised the album. *Disc and Music Echo* said it was a "beautiful record which shows the completely individual way the group is developing from their early blues days." *Beat Instrumental* called it a "brilliant LP," while *Melody Maker* effused, "This is the creation of pure energy—from the top, the center, the bottom, all the way through—the Cream." *New Musical Express* declared, "After you have recovered from the gaudy sleeve designs, you get the meaty, original sounds of the Cream." *Rolling Stone* saw things differently, however, writing, "Unfortunately, the album does not totally hang together, marred by some poor material." *Disraeli Gears* reached #4 in the U.S. and #5 in the U.K. and earned the group their first gold record. In December, the band returned to the U.S. to play a few dates at the end of the month.

In January and February, the band spent some time in Atlantic's recording studios working on their next LP. A year-end survey published in the February 1968 issue of *Beat Instrumental* recognized all three Cream members as 1967's top musicians on their respective instruments.

On February 23, the band started their next U.S. tour, which they extended until June due to their massive pop-ularity. They were now commanding a $20,000 guarantee plus a percentage of the gate, which sometimes pushed their share of revenues over $60,000 per concert. *Newsweek* ran a favorable article on the group in its March 18 issue.

Within the band, however, relations between Baker and Bruce were strained to a breaking point, with Clapton very unhappy and feeling caught in the middle. Clapton later described the tour as "such a harrowing experience that we split from one another during it. We would hang out on our own with friends we had acquired in the cities that we were in. We weren't living as a group at all; there was a lot of conflict."

In May, the band appeared on the *Smothers Brothers* TV show, where they performed a live version of "Sunshine of Your Love." Clapton also lip-synched to "Anyone for Tennis," undoubtedly a humiliating experience because he actually hated the song, although it had been his contribution to the soundtrack of the biker film *The Savage Seven*. This violent motorcycle-gang drama was instantly forgettable but ironically starred none other than Duane Eddy, a guitar hero from a previous era. Such was Cream's popularity that when this mediocre song was released as a single, it scraped into the U.K. charts.

Everyone knew that this kind of hype couldn't go on forever, especially with the tension between Bruce and Baker tearing at the band's cohesion. *Rolling Stone* was the first to launch a media assault on the band that effectively derailed them. The May 11, 1968 issue published an interview with Eric Clapton along with a Cream concert review written by Jon Landau. The review was highly critical of Clapton, accusing him of being "a master of the blues clichés of all the post-World War II blues guitarists" and "a virtuoso at performing other people's ideas."

"That was an event in my life. I can't believe it even to this day," Clapton told *Hit Parader* a few months later. "I was reading that [the *Rolling Stone* article] in Boston. I opened it, I read the whole thing and it was all ego, ego in the interview, coming on really strong. And I turned the page and looked at the review and at that particular moment I just completely crashed inside, everything I believed fell to bits and I passed out later that evening in a restaurant and was taken home. A nervous breakdown scene. The motivation behind it seems to be very destructive. He [Jon Landau] said that I am the master of the cliché. That's what he called me. That was one of the reasons I thought, 'I'm getting out of all this.' I just thought of quitting."

Rumors started to spread of an imminent breakup. Yet an article that ran in the July 6 issue of *Rolling Stone* quoted Clapton as saying, "All rumors of a breakup are denied." But then the July 13 issue of *Melody Maker* confirmed the rumor under the headline "Cream Split Up." The article stated that the group planned a farewell tour beginning in mid-October that would last five weeks and culminate in a return to London for a farewell concert at the Royal Albert Hall. Manager Robert Stigwood announced, "This parting is completely amicable, as all three members of the Cream now want to follow their own musical policies." Clapton likewise explained the breakup to *Melody Maker:* "The reason it is breaking up is a change of attitude among ourselves more than anything. Also, we have been on the road a long time, before Cream even started."

At the time of the announcement, the group had released their third album, *Wheels of Fire,* which entered the U.S. charts at #54 and within five weeks held down the top spot. Released in the U.K. in July, the LP reached #3. *Wheels of Fire* was a double-album containing a studio LP and a live LP recorded at the Fillmore West and Winterland in San Francisco.

The studio LP contrasted sharply with the live LP, which contained extended workouts on "Spoonful" and "Toad" that each lasted more than 15 minutes. The live LP also contained the shorter "Traintime"—a Jack Bruce *tour de force* carried over from his Graham Bond days, and an electric version of Robert Johnson's "Crossroads" that received heavy airplay (and when released as a single in the U.S. reached #28). The studio LP, on the other hand, showed the band experimenting with a variety of instruments, including cello, glockenspiel, trumpet, viola, organ and bells. Some of the studio tracks were more straightforward blues, such as covers of Howlin' Wolf's "Sitting on Top of the World" and Albert King's "Born Under a Bad Sign," as well as an original composition called "Politician."

Critics widely heralded *Wheels of Fire. Beat Instrumental* warned, "Buy this or live in misery for the rest of your days." *Record Mirror* insisted that the album was "a definite must for everyone's collection." *Disc and Music Echo* proclaimed it "the best material the Cream have ever put on record. It's a very fitting—and at times superb—memorial to what headlines call 'Britain's best live group.'" *Melody Maker* dubbed it "an exciting and rewarding set, and one of the great records of the year." *New Musical Express* agreed, stating, "The numbers are varied in the extreme, from briskly paced songs to slow,

morbid ones. Everything sounds good." Only *Rolling Stone* once again crucified the album, with publisher Jan Wenner charging, "Cream is good at a number of things; unfortunately, songwriting and recording are not among them." In his review, Wenner belittled Bruce's singing and harmonica playing as well as what he called Baker's "tendency to be sloppy." Oddly, Wenner also wrote that "White Room" was "practically an exact duplication of 'Tales of Brave Ulysses'" and he wondered "why they would want to do this again." This bludgeoning by *Rolling Stone* had little, if any, impact on record-buyers. "White Room" was issued as a single in October and reached #6 on the U.S. charts and #28 in the U.K.

On October 4, Cream started their final U.S. tour at the Oakland Coliseum Arena in California. The farewell trek ended on November 14, 1968, at the Veterans Memorial Auditorium in Des Moines, Iowa. Along the way, the trio also played the Madison Square Garden in New York on November 2, where they received a platinum record for *Wheels of Fire.* This was the same venue where, reportedly, Jack Bruce had at some point decided that enough was enough.

Even so, Robert Stigwood remained hopeful that he could persuade the three not to split up. In fact, *Melody Maker* ran a front-page story on October 12, "Cream Not to Split Up," that claimed that the group was not likely to split and that Stigwood was flying to America to "talk over again their plan to disband at the end of the year." However in the October 26 issue of *Melody Maker*, Stigwood conceded that negotiations to keep the group together had broken down.

Exactly a month later on November 26 at London's Royal Albert Hall, Cream played their last date, with Yes and Taste as opening acts [see **Rory Gallagher**]. They added a second show after the first one sold out in only two hours. *New Musical Express* reported, "A sell-out crowd of 5,000 rose to their feet at the end and stomped and clapped themselves silly for more. They got more, and demanded still more." Uncharacteristically, *Rolling Stone*—under the headline "God Save the Cream"—gave the second show a rave review. The shows were filmed by Tony Palmer and later broadcast by the BBC. And yet Clapton, Baker and Bruce remember these concerts as musically undistinguished affairs.

On vinyl, at least, the ghost of Cream hovered into the New Year. In March 1969, Cream's farewell album, *Goodbye*, was released. It included three studio tracks recorded in October: "Badge" (written by Clapton and George Harrison and credited as "L'Angelo Misterioso"), "Doing That Scrapyard Thing" and "What a Bringdown." These were rounded out by three live tracks recorded on October 19 at the Forum in Los Angeles: "Politician," "I'm So Glad" and "Sitting on Top of the World." *Goodbye* reached #2 in the U.S. and #1 in the U.K. Readers of *Melody Maker* voted it the top album of the year. A single from the album, "Badge" reached #18 in the U.K. but only #60 in the U.S.

The first of two volumes of the retrospective album *Live Cream* was released in June 1970. A few months earlier in March, *Melody Maker* had run the headline "Cream Return for One Concert," reporting that there was a good chance that the group would re-form to play at the Isle of Wight Festival that summer. However, the promoters of the festival then sheepishly acknowledged that they had not actually approached the individual members about appearing before they dared to leap into print with the big-promise headline. In other words, sensation and hype of one sort or another plagued the band to the very end.

And finally, a more recent and haunting epilogue about Cream from Eric Clapton reveals a lot about just how deep his emotions ran for that band: Clapton likens the ending to a "blackout" where he still doesn't recall any of them actually ever saying that it was over. What he does remember, though, is feeling full of hatred and self-resentment in the aftermath. In other words, the ultimate *blues*.

Postscript

Shortly after Cream disbanded, Baker and Clapton formed the ill-fated Blind Faith, which also featured Steve Winwood and Ric Grech. The short-lived quartet disbanded by October 1969 [see **Blind Faith**].

Following the collapse of Blind Faith, Baker put together an ad hoc group of musicians that included Ric Grech, Steve Winwood, Graham Bond and Denny Laine to play a couple of gigs at the Birmingham Town Hall and the Royal Albert Hall in London. Encouraged by the success of these concerts, Baker released a double album, *Ginger Baker's Airforce* (1970, U.S. #33), which consisted of eight tracks recorded at the Royal Albert Hall. That same year, *Airforce II* was released, albeit with a different lineup. Baker shifted gears in 1971, releasing *Live*, a collaboration with African artist Fela Ransome Kuti, and *Stratavarious,* a mixture of jazz and rock combined with African influences.

In 1974, Baker teamed up with Paul and Adrian Gurvitz, formerly of the power trio Gun, to form the Baker Gurvitz Army, with which he released three albums: *The Baker Gurvitz Army* (1974), *Elysian Encounter* (1975) and *Hearts on Fire* (1976), the last two with an expanded lineup. In 1977, Baker recruited guitarist Chris Spedding and others to record *Eleven Sides of Baker*.

In September 1980, Baker joined Hawkwind and appeared on their *Levitation* album (1980). Baker's next release, *From Humble Oranges* (1982), was credited to "Baker and Band" and featured Baker, guitarist Douglas Brockie and bassist Karl Hill. That same year, Baker released *In Concert* with a completely different cast of musicians. In 1985, Baker played on *Album* (1986), a release by Johnny Rotten's post-Sex Pistols group, Public Image Ltd., which also featured bassist Jonas Hellborg. Baker and Hellborg toured Europe and the U.S. together in various ensembles.

Baker's next release, *Horses and Trees* (1986), continued his excursions into African percussion sounds, though by 1987 he returned briefly to jazz with the album *No Material*, featuring Sonny Sharrock (guitar), Jan Kazda (bass), Nicky Scopelitis (guitar) and Peter Brötzmann (saxophones). Baker then continued his explorations into African percussion on *African Force* (1987) and *Palanquin's Pole* (1987), the latter credited to African Force.

In 1988, Baker appeared on Jonas Hellborg's *Bass* album and Hellborg returned the favor by playing on Baker's *Middle Passage* (1990). The pair also recorded *Unseen Rain* (1992) along with pianist Jens Johansson.

In 1992, he released *Ginger Baker's Energy*, and in 1994, he reunited with Jack Bruce for the short-lived BBM, which also featured guitarist Gary Moore. BBM released one album, *Around the Next Dream* (1994). Baker also recorded the jazz album *Going Back Home* with guitarist Bill Frisell and bassist Charlie Haden. He then worked with Frisell and Haden again for the 1995 release, *Falling off the Roof*.

In 1999, Baker teamed up with trumpeter Ron Mills and bassist Artie Moore to form the Denver Jazz Quintet-to-Octet. The first album by the DJQ2O, *Coward of the County*, was issued in 1999.

Jack Bruce recorded his first solo album, the jazz-flavored *Songs for a Tailor,* in 1969 and toured the U.S. with his first band, which consisted of guitarist Larry

Coryell and drummer Mitch Mitchell. While in America, Bruce met drummer Tony Williams and joined his fusion band Lifetime, which included guitarist John McLaughlin and organist Larry Young. Lifetime released *Turn It Over* (1970) with Jack Bruce on bass on three tracks. That same year, Bruce released *Things We Like* with old friends McLaughlin, Dick Heckstall-Smith (saxophone) and Jon Hiseman (drums).

Following the breakup of Lifetime, Bruce recorded *Harmony Row* (1971) with guitarist Chris Spedding and percussionist John Marshall. The lineup of Bruce, Spedding and Marshall was rounded out by Graham Bond (vocals, Hammond organ, piano, alto saxophone) and Art Themen (tenor saxophone) for a live performance taped for the BBC at the Paris Theater, London, on August 19, 1971, that was released as *BBC Live in Concert* (1995).

Bruce then regrouped with guitarist Leslie West and drummer Corky Laing, both formerly of Mountain, to form the trio of West, Bruce and Laing. Their first release, *Why Dontcha* (1972) made #26 on the U.S. charts. Their second album, *Whatever Turns You On* (1973), was less successful, and a final live album, *Live'n' Kickin'* (1974), was unceremoniously issued before the group disbanded.

In 1974, Bruce appeared on Frank Zappa's *Apostrophe* album (1974) and issued another solo record, *Out of the Storm*. In 1975 he formed the Jack Bruce Band with members Carla Bley (keyboards) and Mick Taylor (guitar). Several tracks recorded for television on June 6, 1975 were released as *Live on the Old Grey Whistle Test* (1998).

In November 1976, Bruce recorded *How's Tricks* (1977) with Simon Phillips (drums), Hugh Burns (guitar) and Tony Hymas (keyboards, vocals). He then took a hiatus from recording, emerging again with *I've Always Wanted to Do This* (1980), on which he was supported by Clem Clempson (guitars), Billy Cobham (percussion) and David Sancious (keyboards).

In 1981, Bruce teamed up with Robin Trower and drummer Bill Lordan to form the power trio B.L.T. They recorded two albums, *B.L.T.* (1981) and *Truce* (1982), the latter with Reg Isidore replacing Bill Lordan. Then in 1983, Bruce released *Automatic* before taking another hiatus from recording.

He returned in 1989 with *A Question of Time,* which featured numerous guests (including Ginger Baker on two songs). By 1993, Bruce released *Somethin Els*, which included Eric Clapton on three tracks. In November of that year, he celebrated his fiftieth birthday by giving two concerts in Cologne, Germany, with Ginger Baker, Gary Moore, Clem Clempson and Dick Heckstall-Smith. The concerts were released as *Cities of the Heart* (1993). This led to BBM re-forming with Ginger Baker and Gary Moore.

On January 13, 1993, Cream was inducted into the Rock and Roll Hall of Fame. They performed "Sunshine of Your Love," "Born Under a Bad Sign" and "Crossroads" at the induction ceremony.

In 1995, Jack Bruce released *Monkjack (*1995), and his latest effort, *Shadows in the Air* (2001), reunited Bruce with Eric Clapton on two tracks, covers of the Cream classics "Sunshine of Your Love" and "White Room."

Discography

Release Date	Title	Catalog Number

U.S. Singles

1967	I Feel Free/N.S.U.	Atco 6462
1967	Strange Brew/Tales of Brave Ulysses	Atco 6488
1967	Spoonful/Spoonful, Part 2	Atco 6522
1967	Sunshine of Your Love/S.W.L.A.B.R.	Atco 6544
1968	Anyone for Tennis/	Atco 6575
	Pressed Rat and Warthog	
1968	White Room/Those Were the Days	Atco 6617
1969	Crossroads/Passing the Time	Atco 6646
1969	Badge/What a Bringdown	Atco 6668
1969	Sweet Wine/Lawdy Mama	Atco 6708

U.S. Albums

1967	*Fresh Cream*	Atco 33-206 (M)
		Atco SD-33-206(S)

I Feel Free/N.S.U./Sleepy Time Time/Dreaming/Sweet Wine/Cat's Squirrel/Four Until Late/Rollin' and Tumblin'/I'm So Glad/Toad

1967	*Disraeli Gears*	Atco 33-232 (M)
		Atco SD-33-232 (S)

Strange Brew/Sunshine of Your Love/World of Pain/Dance the Night Away/Blue Condition/Tales of Brave Ulysses/S.W.L.A.B.R./We're Going Wrong/Outside Woman Blues/Take It Back/Mother's Lament

1968	*Wheels of Fire*	Atco SD-2-700

White Room/Sitting on Top of the World/Passing the Time/As You Said/Pressed Rat and Warthog/Politician/Those Were the Days/Born Under a Bad Sign/Deserted Cities of the Heart/Crossroads/Spoonful/Traintime/Toad

1969   *Goodbye*   Atco SD-7001
I'm So Glad/Politician/Sitting on Top of the World/Badge/Doing That Scrapyard Thing/What a Bringdown

1970   *Live Cream*   Atco SD-33-328
N.S.U./Sleepy Time Time/Sweet Wine/Rollin' and Tumblin'/Lawdy Mama

1972   *Live Cream Volume 2*   Atco SD-7005
Deserted Cities of the Heart/White Room/Politician/Tales of Brave Ulysses/Sunshine of Your Love/Steppin' Out

1997   *Those Were the Days* (4 CD)   Polydor 539 000
Disc 1 (studio)
Wrapping Paper/I Feel Free/N.S.U./Sleepy Time Time/Dreaming/Sweet Wine/Spoonful/Cat's Squirrel/Four Until Late/Rollin' and Tumblin'/I'm So Glad/Toad/Lawdy Mama (previously unreleased, version 1)/Strange Brew/Sunshine of Your Love/World of Pain/Dance the Night Away/Blue Condition/Tales of Brave Ulysses/S.W.L.A.B.R./We're Going Wrong/Outside Woman Blues/Take It Back/Mother's Lament

Disc 2 (studio)
White Room/Sitting on Top of the World/Passing the Time (alternate take)/As You Said/Pressed Rat and Warthog/Politician/Those Were the Days/Born Under a Bad Sign/Deserted Cities of the Heart/Anyone for Tennis/Badge/Doing That Scrapyard Thing/What a Bringdown/The Coffee Song/Lawdy Mama (version 2)/You Make Me Feel (previously unreleased, demo version)/We're Going Wrong (previously unreleased, demo version)/Hey Now Princess (previously unreleased, demo version)/S.W.L.A.B.R. (previously unreleased, demo version)/Weird of Hermiston (previously unreleased, demo version)/The Clearout (previously unreleased, demo version)/Falstaff Beer Commercial (previously unreleased)

Disc 3 (live)
N.S.U. (previously unreleased, unedited version)/Sleepy Time Time/Rollin' and Tumblin'/Crossroads/Spoonful/Tales of Brave Ulysses/Sunshine of Your Love/Sweet Wine

Disc 4 (live)
White Room/Politician/I'm So Glad/Sitting on Top of the World/Stepping Out/Traintime/Toad (previously unreleased, extended version)/Deserted Cities of the Heart/Sunshine of Your Love (from *The Glen Campbell Show*, previously unreleased)

Miscellaneous U.S. Releases

1968   *The Savage Seven* (movie soundtrack)   Atco SD-33-245
Includes "Anyone for Tennis" (*The Savage Seven* theme).

U.K. Singles

1966	Wrapping Paper/Cat's Squirrel	Reaction 591007
1966	I Feel Free/N.S.U.	Reaction 591011
1967	Strange Brew/Tales of Brave Ulysses	Reaction 591015
1968	Anyone for Tennis/ Pressed Rat and Warthog	Polydor 56 258
1968	Sunshine of Your Love/S.W.L.A.B.R.	Polydor 56 286
1969	White Room/Those Were the Days	Polydor 56 300
1969	Badge/What a Bringdown	Polydor 56 315

U.K. Albums

| 1966 | *Fresh Cream* | Reaction 593 001 (M) |
| | | Reaction 594 001 (S) |

Spoonful/N.S.U./Sleepy Time Time/Dreaming/Sweet Wine/Cat's Squirrel/Four Until Late/Rollin' and Tumblin'/I'm So Glad/Toad

1967	*Disraeli Gears*	Reaction 593 003 (M)
		Reaction 594 004 (S)
1968	*Wheels of Fire*	Polydor 582 031/2 (M)
		Polydor 583 031/2 (S)
1968	*Wheels of Fire: In the Studio*	Polydor 582 033 (M)
		Polydor 583 033 (S)
1968	*Wheels of Fire: Live at the Fillmore*	Polydor 582 040 (M)
		Polydor 583 040 (S)
1969	*Goodbye*	Polydor 583 053
1970	*Live Cream*	Polydor 2383 016
1972	*Live Cream Volume 2*	Polydor 2383 119
1997	*Those Were the Days* (4 CD)	Polydor 539 000

Cyril Davies and the R&B All-Stars

Cyril Davies was known as a hard man who refused to compromise his musical approach to cater to prevailing tastes. A forceful and passionate advocate of the music he loved, he was a key personality behind the rise of the blues in England. Remembered as undoubtedly one of the finest blues harmonica players that Britain has ever produced and leader of one of the top London R&B club acts, the greatest tragedy of his sudden death at age 32 is that he was just starting to achieve real success. Although he can only be heard today on a handful of tracks, he and his band, the R&B All-Stars, inspired legions of others to follow in their footsteps.

Many imitated Davies but none could replicate his sound. He preferred faithful re-creations of Chicago-style blues without embellishments, and once told *Melody Maker,* "If you like, I'm a purist. I don't like to see the music messed about. I like it straight." With his partner Alexis Korner, he formed Blues Incorporated, the first electric blues band in the U.K., and later formed his own band, Cyril Davies and the R&B All-Stars.

While many of his contemporaries on the scene were college educated (or more often college dropouts), Davies was strictly blue collar, working as a car panel beater in a garage before eventually opening his own auto body business. He approached the blues with *attitude,* meaning he felt that if you want to *sound* like Leadbelly you have to *live* like Leadbelly. Leadbelly, who was born Hudson "Huddie" Leadbetter (b. January 29, 1885, Mooringsport, Louisiana; d. December 6, 1949, New York, New York), was incarcerated at Louisiana State Penitentiary for attempted murder when folk music researcher John Lomax "discovered" him there in 1933. Leadbelly was a master of the 12-string guitar and claimed a repertoire of 500 songs, but was also well known as a braggart, boozer, womanizer and brawler whose explosive temper often led to violent conflicts.

Cyril Davies was born in 1932 in Buckinghamshire, England, and as a child he learned to play the banjo and ukulele. After leaving school, he found work in an auto body shop, learning the skills he would use to later open his own repair business in South Harrow. While working days, he continued to play his music, putting in four years playing banjo in a traditional or "trad" jazz band, Steve Lane's Southern Stompers.

In 1955, Davies and others opened the London Skiffle Club, located upstairs at the Roundhouse pub in Soho. While there, he took up the 12-string guitar and became obsessed with American blues, particularly the music of Leadbelly.

He met fellow blues enthusiast Alexis Korner at the Roundhouse, and in 1957 they made a few recordings (with Terry Plant on bass and Mike Collins on washboard) that were issued on the tiny 77 label as *Blues from the Roundhouse* by Alexis Korner's Breakdown Group Featuring Cyril Davies. Later that year, Davies and Korner decided to transform the Skiffle Club into a blues club, renaming it the Blues and Barrelhouse Club. The small venue slowly became a stylish blues nightclub, hosting such visiting American performers as Big Bill Broonzy,

Muddy Waters, Sonny Terry, Memphis Slim and Champion Jack Dupree. The Blues and Barrelhouse Club also became known as a nurturing ground for homegrown talent. Davies and Korner performed there as a blues duo with Davies on 12-string guitar and Korner on six-string guitar and mandolin. As the shows progressed, they began inviting others onstage to perform in on-the-fly ensembles.

Korner and Davies, along with other musicians, returned to the studio in 1957 to record a few songs for Tempo, a subsidiary label of Decca. This time calling themselves the Alexis Korner Skiffle Group, they recorded four tracks, including a chugging, folksy rendition of Sleepy John Estes's "I Ain't Gonna Worry No More." Tempo released these tracks as *Blues at the Roundhouse Volume 1,* then issued an EP the next year called *Blues at the Roundhouse Volume 2,* credited to Alexis Korner's Blues Incorporated. Of the EP's four tracks, three were credited to Leadbelly.

While at the Roundhouse, Davies came into contact with many musicians who would feature prominently in his future. Guitarist Geoff Bradford (b. January 13, 1934) and pianist Keith Scott teamed up, performing Leroy Carr/Scrapper Blackwell-style duets. As a teenager, Bradford became interested in boogie-woogie through the music of Meade Lux Lewis, and had learned to play the piano. Like many young British musicians of the time, his attraction to skiffle came through the music of Lonnie Donegan. He later became influenced by American blues artists Big Bill Broonzy, Josh White and Bo Diddley. When Bradford placed a classified ad in *Melody Maker* for other blues musicians, art student Keith Scott responded and the pair became frequent performers at the Roundhouse from 1958 to 1961.

Vocalist Long John Baldry (b. January 12, 1941; Haddon, Derbyshire, U.K.), so named because of his 6'7" frame, was another Roundhouse regular. Baldry started out in the London folk scene in the late 1950s as a member of the Thameside Four. He tried to hold down a day job as a commercial artist, but the strain of working two jobs was too much. "The choice was inevitable," he later told *Music Maker.* "I turned professional in 1960 and have been professional ever since." He toured Denmark with the Bob Cort Skiffle Group and by July 1961 had joined Ken Sim's jazz band. He was also freelancing with Chris Barber, Acker Bilk and others.

Though Davies and Korner played regularly, Korner frequently failed to show up for gigs—sometimes for months at a time—and other guitarists would stand in for him, including Davy Graham. When he wasn't playing with Scott, Geoff Bradford would become Davies's most frequent partner, actually playing the "real thing"—a National Steel guitar—against Davies's 12-string.

By the late 1950s, Davies began to switch his orientation to Chicago blues after hearing the explosive amplified electric blues of Muddy Waters. Using amplifiers was highly controversial among British folk-blues purists, who actually heckled the Muddy Waters Band for that very reason. Davies also met with resistance from his pub landlord, who eventually forced him to close the club.

Meanwhile, Korner was in the process of forming a larger blues ensemble to play during the intervals of the Chris Barber Jazz Band's club gigs at the Marquee. Trombonist Barber had led his own bands since 1948 and was one of the leaders of the Trad Jazz movement (but also a strong advocate of the blues). Along with his manager Harold Pendleton, who had a controlling interest in the Marquee, Barber organized jazz concerts under the banner of the National Jazz Federation.

On January 3, 1962, Davies and Korner took the Marquee stage for their supporting slot (accompanied by trumpeter Pat Halcox) as "Blues Incorporated" and received a favorable write-up in *Jazz News and Review,* as did a second date supporting Acker Bilk on January 19. Bolstered by this positive response, Korner and Davies decided to try their hand at running another club instead of just playing during set breaks at the Marquee. Vocalist Art Wood [see **Artwoods**] knew of the Ealing Club in West London, which was located in a basement below the ABC Tea Shop. The Ealing Club was a Trad Jazz venue, and after Korner and Davies looked it over, they struck a deal with the owner. Their first gig took place in March 1962, and soon the place had been nicknamed the "Moist Hoist" because of the condensation that dripped from the ceiling onto a tarpaulin that had been installed to prevent the electrocution of performers.

In addition to Korner and Davies, the Blues Incorporated lineup included vocalist Long John Baldry, saxophonist Dick Heckstall-Smith, drummer Charlie Watts, vocalist Art Wood, bassist Andy Hoogenboom and pianist Keith Scott.

By May, the Marquee owners offered Blues Incorporated a Thursday night residency at the club, which was by now no longer an all-jazz venue. The band accepted, and they began recording again the following month for a Blues Incorporated album to be released on another subsidiary of Decca, the Ace of Clubs label. Issued in November 1962, *R&B from the Marquee* sold surprisingly well. However, just as the album was released, Davies left Blues Incorporated to form his own band. "We started at the Marquee and everything was going well, but then Alex had different ideas," he explained to *Melody Maker.* "He was after a sort of jazz-blues sound and wanted Graham Bond on sax and organ. It was just not my meat with the two saxes."

For the initial lineup of "The Cyril Davies Blues Band," Davies recruited former members of Screaming Lord Sutch's backing group, the Savages: Carlo Little on drums, Rick Brown (a.k.a. Fenson) on bass and Nicky Hopkins on piano. Future Yardbird and Led Zeppelin founder Jimmy Page was the Cyril Davies Blues Band's first fleeting guitarist, soon replaced by ex-Savages guitarist Bernie Watson.

Little (b. December 17, 1938; Wembley, Middlesex, U.K.) had formed the Savages with David Sutch in 1960, and just two years later the group—known for their outrageousness—had become one of the top club attractions on the circuit. Little's tenure with the Savages was broken up by a stint with Dougie Dee and the Strangers, a semi-professional band, from June 1960 to April 1961. Rick Brown also quit the Savages in June 1960, only to rejoin in September 1961. Nicky Hopkins (b. February 24, 1944, London, U.K.; d. September 6, 1994) was another original member. He and Bernie Watson left the Savages in May 1962 to join Cliff Bennett and the Rebel Rousers for a residency in Hamburg, Germany, only to be let go by October 1962—just in time to join Davies's new outfit. Coincidentally, around the same time that Hopkins and Watson were in Hamburg, vocalist Baldry decided to leave Blues Incorporated to pursue his music in Germany. He left in July 1962 for a German tour with the Swiss Storyville Hot Six and other groups, including the Melbourne N.O.J.B.

Meanwhile, *Jazz News and Review* reported that the newly named Cyril Davies and the R&B All-Stars' first outing at Colyer's in November 1962 was "a rave."

Propelled by Little's powerful drumming and Davies's emotionally charged harp playing, the All-Stars quickly established themselves as the top R&B act on the burgeoning London circuit, with residencies at the Railway Hotel, the Roaring Twenties and the Piccadilly Club. The group's set consisted of Chicago blues-type numbers, both originals and such covers as "I've Got My Mojo Working," "Hoochie Coochie Man," "Chicago Calling," "Country Line Special," "C.C. Rider" and Chuck Berry's "Blue Feeling." The last number went down particularly well with the audience, although Davies had initially required much persuasion from the group to undertake it.

The band also took over the prestigious Thursday night slot at the Marquee on January 3, 1963, and Korner, with the rest of Blues Incorporated, moved over to the Flamingo. During the first month at the Marquee, the Rolling Stones played during the band's set breaks. The Stones were promptly sacked at the end of the month when they asked for more money. Little and Brown even played a few gigs with the Stones in December 1962 and January 1963. Brian Jones asked Little to stay on, but with the All-Stars on the rise and the Stones struggling to find gigs, he threw in his lot with Davies.

In the meantime, *Jazz News and Review* was keeping track of Baldry, reporting in the December 12, 1962, issue, "Long John Baldry is alive and shouting over in Germany . . . still in great demand by many R&B groups." Both Alexis Korner and Cyril Davies wanted Baldry in their bands—so much so that Korner even paid for Baldry's fare back from Germany. (Baldry had been a member of Blues Incorporated from February through July before leaving for Germany.) As *Jazz News and Review* had predicted, upon his return he was heavily wooed by both Korner and Davies, appearing with both groups before committing to the All-Stars by the end of January 1963.

Besides Baldry, Davies also added the Velvettes—three female South African singers who had been touring in the musical *King Kong*—to the act. The women had formed the group and started appearing at English jazz clubs after *King Kong* had finished its run and the cast dispersed.

Reviewers found the resulting collaboration mesmerizing. Baldry was tall, lean and youthful, and could sing with the soulful edge of Ray Charles, contributing a charisma that the older, stockier Davies lacked. In its January 16, 1963, issue, *Jazz News and Review* enthusiastically reported, "Velvet Excitement was caused at the Marquee on Thursday and at the Roaring Twenties on Friday when Peggy Phango and her girls from the *King Kong* cast joined Cyril Davies and his All-Stars in two

evenings of Rhythm and Blues entertainment unsurpassed so far in London."

Ever since the All-Stars had replaced Blues Incorporated at the Marquee, comparisons between the two groups had been inevitable. In its January 24, 1963, issue, *Jazz News and Review* reported, "Marquee versus Flamingo on Thursday evenings . . . Cyril Davies packed in 800 at the Marquee, holding the audience for Thursdays to a normal extent . . . Alexis Korner gaining around 200 for the Flamingo with a gradual increase showing . . . we all hope both locations continue to do well . . . Cyril Davies has a lead in the friendly 'war' up to now."

With the All-Stars packing in crowds at the clubs, both the Decca and Pye labels expressed interest in signing the band to a record contract. In mid February, the music press reported that Davies had chosen Pye because the label was introducing a new subsidiary focusing on R&B. (Soon Pye also became the U.K. outlet for Chess Records.)

By the end of the month, the group had recorded two Davies originals for their first single, "Country Line Special" and "Chicago Calling," at Pye's Marble Arch Studio. The A-side was a hot, up-tempo stage favorite that took 13 takes to perfect. Released to rave reviews a couple of months later, *Record Mirror* noted, "From the Marquee's top man comes a wailing, fast tempo R&B number with a catchy flavor and genuine blues feel about it. It's fast and ferocious with an extremely commercial quality about it. It's the sort of thing to go really wild to—we reckon it'll be a hit of some sort. Very well performed too we may add." *Disc Weekly* commented, "Cyril Davies leads his All-Stars down the 'Country Line Special' as if he'd been born and raised in the rhythm 'n' blues country instead of Denham, England. There's a lonely, haunting quality about this side which could make it a very big seller indeed." Despite these glowing reviews, the release did not catch on with listeners and sell as well as predicted.

In April, their old "support" band, the Rolling Stones, managed to get an audition on *Jazz Club*, a BBC R&B radio show. They enlisted Carlo Little and Ricky Brown to pinch hit when Charlie Watts and Bill Wyman had to work at their day jobs, but the Rolling Stones were ultimately rejected. Brian Jones was later advised by BBC music organizer Donald MacLean that they were rejected because Mick Jagger "sounded too black."

In May 1963, the All-Stars suffered an interruption when Nicky Hopkins became seriously ill and had to be hospitalized. Keith Scott, who had left Blues Incorporated and was then a member of Blues By Six (another popular club attraction led by vocalist/harpist Brian Knight, who worked for Davies at his auto body shop) replaced him. On May 22, the All-Stars landed their first TV appearance on *The Six-Twentyfive Show*. Later that month, they became the set band for a new television show, *Hullabaloo*, Britain's first folk-music series. The All-Stars appeared on five episodes filmed on May 30 and June 8, 15, 22 and 29. They continued their media campaign into June, with appearances on the TV show *Thank Your Lucky Stars* and the BBC radio show *Saturday Club*.

However, all was not well within the group. Ricky Brown left to rejoin Lord Sutch and the Savages in June, and Carlo Little rejoined him shortly thereafter. Bernie Watson also left to join John Mayall's Bluesbreakers [see **John Mayall**].

Cliff Barton, Mickey Waller and Geoff Bradford replaced Brown, Little and Watson, respectively, giving the group a total of four new members in the space of only a few months. Baldry remembers that Jimmy Page returned to the band very briefly after Watson's departure; however, when Page's mother insisted that he continue his studies, they brought in Geoff Bradford instead. Bradford had also been a member of Blues By Six and had briefly attended rehearsals for the Rolling Stones, but didn't join them because they were heading in a Chuck Berry-flavored direction rather than for the straight Chicago blues that he preferred.

Continuing to gig, the new All-Stars lineup took a slot on the first pop all-nighter on July 5 at Alexandra Palace, London. They shared the bill with Gene Vincent, Craig Douglas, Shane Fenton and the Fentones, the John Barry Seven, Screaming Lord Sutch, the Barron Knights and others. When questioned about taking part in a pop package tour, Davies told *Melody Maker*, "On pop tours I shall still play the same way—I can't play any other. You have to try to bend the public, not the music."

In August 1963, the All-Stars recorded Robert Johnson's classic "Preachin' the Blues" and Leadbelly's "Sweet Mary" as a single. "Sweet Mary" included backing vocals by Madeline Bell and Alex Bradford from the musical show *Black Nativity*. *Record Mirror* gave Davies a glowing review: "The harmonica sound on the latest from the British R&B king is a fast-paced shouter with loads of good vocal work and a more commercial approach than on his last disc."

On August 11, the group appeared at the National Jazz Festival at Richmond Athletic Grounds. Chris Barber, the Graham Bond Quartet, Georgie Fame and the Blue Flames, Acker Bilk, and the Rolling Stones were all on the billing. "The R&B tent played to capacity business through most of the festival," *Melody Maker* reported, "and the Cyril Davies All-Stars with the Velvettes and Long John Baldry created as much excitement as anyone throughout the two days." That same month, the band also appeared in two pop package concerts held on boats, along with Gerry and the Pacemakers, Billy J. Kramer and the Dakotas, and other incongruous acts.

However, the All-Stars—with Johnny Parker now replacing pianist Keith Scott and Bob Wacket replacing drummer Mickey Waller—found themselves having to progressively accommodate Davies, who had begun to suffer from pleurisy, an inflammation and irritation of the pleura (the thin, two-layered membrane that encloses the lung and lines the inside of the chest). Drinking excessively to ease the pain, Davies continued his demanding though now curtailed schedule rather than following the advice of doctors to simply rest. He passed away on January 7, 1964.

Tributes were immediate and heartfelt: Alexis Korner told *Melody Maker*, "Despite musical differences which caused us to split about a year ago, I never ceased to consider Cyril by far the finest blues harmonica player in Britain. He was one of the really strong, driving forces behind the R&B movement over here." Graham Bond told *Melody Maker*, "It's very hard to know what to say. The whole band was completely hung up when we heard about it. We all worked with him a great deal and we all feel a personal sense of loss."

Postscript

Following the death of Davies, Long John Baldry took over the All-Stars and rechristened them the Hoochie Coochie Men, adding Rod Stewart on vocals and Ernie O'Malley on drums. They issued one single and album, *Long John's Blues,* before disbanding.

Baldry later formed Steampacket with Rod Stewart, Julie Driscoll and Brian Auger, which despite an impressive roster, went nowhere. His next band was Bluesology, which featured keyboardist Reginald Dwight (who would later find fame as Elton John). Baldry's greatest success came with the lush pop ballad "Let the Heartaches Begin," which reached #1 in the U.K. in 1967. He continued to record, returning to the blues on the 1971 release *It Ain't Easy*, coproduced by the now famous Rod Stewart and Elton John.

Bradford stayed with the All-Stars when they became Long John Baldry & the Hoochie Coochie Men and played on *Long John's Blues* before quitting the music business for a while to take a day job. Through the years, he has continued to perform acoustic traditional blues and has issued band and solo albums, including *Return of a Guitar Legend*. Bradford has also been featured on the various-artists album *Blues Britannia* and a U.K. television special, *Living with the Blues*.

Rick Brown stayed with Screaming Lord Sutch until January 1964. He has since played with Brian Auger, Steampacket and Georgie Fame.

Little stayed with the Savages until briefly rejoining Baldry in the Hoochie Coochie Men in May 1964. In August 1965, Little and the All-Stars regrouped and cut some tracks for the Immediate label. Consisting of Nicky Hopkins on piano, Cliff Barton on bass, Little on drums, and Jeff Beck and Jimmy Page sharing guitar, the group recorded six tracks that became staples of numerous anthology albums issued by Immediate.

Little later performed with Neil Christian and the Crusaders, Lord Sutch and the Roman Empire, and the Flower Pot Men, among others. He continues to perform today with a new lineup of All-Stars featuring vocalist Art Wood.

Nicky Hopkins was hospitalized from May 1963 through December 1964. Following his release from the hospital, he went on to become perhaps the most famous session player of the 1960s, appearing on albums by the Who, the Kinks and the Rolling Stones before joining the Jeff Beck Group in 1967. Hopkins appeared on *Truth* (1968) and *Beck-Ola* (1969) before leaving the Beck camp to record an album with Jon Mark (who later joined John Mayall) called *Sweet Thursday* (1969).

Hopkins continued his session work with Quicksilver Messenger Service for their album, *Shady Grove* (1970). He ended up joining Quicksilver for their *Just for*

Love (1970) and *What About Me* (1971) albums. Hopkins also issued three solo albums: *The Revolutionary Piano of Nicky Hopkins* (1966), *The Tin Man Was a Dreamer* (1973) and *No More Changes* (1975).

Bernie Watson joined Bluesbreakers in July 1963 and remained until April 1964. He has since kept a low musical profile.

Discography

Release Date	Title	Catalog Number

U.K. Singles

Cyril Davies and the R&B All-Stars

1963	Country Line Special/Chicago Calling	Pye International 7N 25194
1963	Preachin' the Blues/Sweet Mary	Pye International 7N 25221

U.K. EPs

Cyril Davies and the R&B All-Stars

1964	*The Legendary Cyril Davies*	Pye International NEP 44025

Country Line Special/Preachin' the Blues/Chicago Calling/Sweet Mary

U.K. Albums

Alexis Korner's Breakdown Group Featuring Cyril Davies

1957	*Blues from the Roundhouse*	77 LP 2

Leaving Blues/Rotten Break/Alberta/Roundhouse Stomp/Skip to My Lou/Good Morning/Boll Weevil/Ella Speed

Alexis Korner's Blues Incorporated

1970	*The Legendary Cyril Davies with Alexis Korner's Breakdown Group*	Folklore F-LEUT 9

Leaving Blues/Roundhouse Stomp/Rotten Break/K.C. Moan/Skip to My Lou/It's the Same Old Thing/Alberta/Hesitation Blues/Ella Speed/Good Morning/Boll Weevil/Short Legs Shuffle

Miscellaneous U.K. Releases

1969	*Blues Anytime Volume 3*	Immediate IMLP 019

Various artists includes "Someday Baby" by Cyril Davies and His Rhythm and Blues All-Stars.

The Downliners Sect

The Downliners Sect were among the first—and least appreciated—of Great Britain's rhythm-and-blues groups. Between 1964 and 1966, the band released three albums and a multitude of fine singles, but ultimately the Sect players were outcasts—too young, too uncouth and just a tad too eccentric to be accepted by the masses. Today, however, particularly to fans of raw, vital punk and R&B, the Downliners Sect are a cult classic, revered above many of their tamer, more famous U.K. beat contemporaries.

Guitarist Don Craine (born Mick O'Donnell) formed the group in 1962 in Twickenham, Middlesex. Originally they were simply "The Downliners," taking their inspiration from Jerry Lee Lewis's "Down the Line." By early 1963 they had essentially turned pro, and their classic lineup began to fall into place when drummer John Sutton and bassist/vocalist Keith Grant (born Keith Evans) joined the group. Terry Gibson (born Terry Clemson) replaced the original lead guitarist, a student named Melvin, in mid-1963.

By this time, the four-piece Downliners had added "Sect" to their title and were almost exclusively playing R&B, specializing in the music of such artists as Bo Diddley, Jimmy Reed and, especially, Chuck Berry. They played at a dilapidated old hotel on Twickenham's Eel Pie Island and at the Studio 51 club (also referred to as Ken Colyer's Jazz Club), at the time a cramped, sweaty Soho basement perfect for nurturing the Downliners Sect's brand of primitive, sweaty rhythm-and-blues.

In January 1964, Contrast Sound, a tiny independent label that normally specialized in sound effects records, released the Downliners Sect on a four-track EP, *At Nite in Great Newport Street*. The raw-sounding EP captured the band live at Studio 51, belting out crude but appealing versions of "Beautiful Delilah," "Shame Shame Shame," "Green Onions" and "Nursery Rhymes."

Not long after the EP, the Downliners Sect added a fifth member, harmonica player Ray Sone. With R&B earmarked as the newest teen music fad, the group easily secured a deal with Mike Collier, an independent producer who landed the band a deal with Columbia Records.

The Downliners Sect released their first single in June 1964, a cover of American bluesman Jimmy Reed's "Baby What's Wrong" backed with an original, "Be a Sect Maniac." In an article published in *Record Mirror*, Don Craine explained to Jimmy Reed why they recorded his song: "We've always played a lot of your numbers in our stage act, Jimmy, and it just seemed a natural thing to record one of them." Reed approved of other groups recording his material, but commented, "I figure it would have been much better for everybody though if I could have been sitting there just playing along with them."

"Be a Sect Maniac" was the first of a string of songs playing on the band's name, which also included "Sect Appeal," "The Leader of the Sect" and "Insecticide." This self-effacing humor, along with Don Craine's ever present deerstalker hat, was a key ingredient in the group's unique image.

Record Mirror described the effort as "a fairly authentic approach to a pungent blues song. Somewhat way-out commercially," while *Beat Instrumental* called the single "a foot-thumper" and commented that it "could do well." With the positive critical reception of "Baby What's Wrong," the group began to travel regularly to other U.K. cities, working almost constantly. They released a follow-up single, a rocking version of the Coasters' novelty tune, "Little Egypt," in September. *Record Mirror* called it "a good tune, a compulsive sound and a heavy throbbing beat," further complimenting it with, "It grows on you, and the vocal work is excellent."

The single created a small buzz in the U.K. and became a minor sensation in Sweden, where it climbed to the upper reaches of the charts. In future years, the Downliners Sect remained hugely popular in Sweden, touring there several times, often playing huge arenas. At one performance at the Stockholm Ice Hockey Stadium, police had to stop the band after only three numbers when close to 15,000 excited Swedes tried to take over the stage. The band begged to continue, but when they began playing "Little Egypt," the intensity level proved too much—the place erupted into a riot and the band was forced to flee for safety.

In November 1964, the quintet released another single, "Find Out What's Happening" backed with "Insecticide." This seemed to offer their best shot yet at a breakthrough in the U.K. A reviewer for *Disc Weekly* predicted, "The Sect must hit the upper brackets soon," describing the single's "very steady boppity blues which they perform almost casually, but without allowing any sloppiness to creep into their work." Craine told *Record Mirror*, "We think it's the best thing we've done in the eighteen months we've been together." Even though Columbia gave the single a big promotional splash, broadcasters ignored it. Nonetheless, "Find Out What's Happening" solidified their position as an up-and-coming young R&B group.

They followed up the single in December with their first LP, *The Sect*. *Melody Maker* reviewer Ray Coleman bashed the album: "If this is British rhythm-and-blues, then may we be preserved from much more. It sounds like crude, third-rate Rolling Stones, and though it might conceivably be reasonable background beat in a basement, it takes a lot of consuming for 14 tracks." *New Musical Express* was cautiously positive: "All the jangle of [R&B] comes through here, specially [sic] when the five break in between Keith Grant's monotone singing. Ray Sone's harmonica playing brews up the right excitement." But their fans loved the album, and the record sold respectably well. Today, it is regarded as something of a masterpiece of punk R&B. Among its highlights are rough versions of Inez and Charlie Foxx's "Hurt by Love," Chuck Berry's "Our Little Rendezvous," and Willy Dixon's "I Put a Tiger in Your Tank."

Craine looked to his skiffle roots for the group's next single, "Wreck of the Old '97," issued in March 1965. Ray Sone's harp gave the track a bluesy feel, about which *New Musical Express* remarked, "[The song] bounces along jauntily with a sort of railroad rhythm, with two voices duetting the sad saga of the ill-fated engine." But with its country-and-western twang, the song was an odd choice for a single.

The Downliners Sect continued to play pure R&B onstage, but they continued their experiments with country-and-western in the studio. They released the country novelty song "I Got Mine" as a single in June, soon followed by a full album, *The Country Sect*. *The Country Sect* was a strange mix of mostly tongue-in-cheek C&W material with a few bluesy gems thrown in. *New Musical Express*, which had been sympathetic before, wrote well of both the single and album. Of the single, the music newspaper declared, "It's a happy record, toe tapping and infectious—with a chorus you can join in." As for the

album, they wrote, "The group has a smooth instrumental unity, and this experiment—the marrying of skiffle with blues—is quite a success." Some fans reacted to the LP with confused head-shaking, but today Sect loyalists make a reasonably convincing argument that with this album, the Downliners Sect invented "country rock" several years before Gram Parsons and the Byrds *et al*.

Prior to *The Country Sect*, Sone departed from the band after an argument with Craine. Pip Harvey replaced him on harmonica, lasting only a few months before departing abruptly when the police came looking for him.

Concurrent with their C&W flirtations, the Downliners Sect let their unusual obsession with B-movie humor and horror run amok on *The Sect Sing Sick Songs*. The four-song EP—filled with ghoulish references to car accidents, murder and necrophilia—was instantly banned from BBC airplay. Still, it garnered much-needed publicity and assured the group's fans that the group hadn't permanently "gone country."

Released in October, their next single—the Don Craine and Keith Grant-penned "Bad Storm Coming"—was a haunting protest number that won over the reviewers at *Disc Weekly:* "It's very gentle with some lovely deep guitar work and . . . a simple and direct quality about it." However, it saw no chart action, and neither did their tough version of Rufus Thomas's "All Night Worker," which kicked off 1966 with a howl of fuzz guitar and thumping bass and drums.

As the months wore on, innovation was the mood of the day and the Downliners Sect floundered for direction, still belting out Chuck Berry songs without any inclination either to grow artistically or to pander to commercial tastes. *The Rock Sect's In* (1966), their third album, went against the grain once again. Although it contained some powerful band originals, including Keith Grant's "Outside" and "Everything I've Got to Give," it also mixed in then-unfashionable rock'n'roll favorites such as Little Richard's "Hey Hey Hey" and Vince Taylor's "Brand New Cadillac." The eclectic LP also included such sarcastic, semi-novelty material as "He Was a Square," the rocking R&B tunes "I'm Lookin' for a Woman" and "Don't Lie to Me," and a fuzz guitar-driven stomper called "Why Don't You Smile Now" that was a pre-Velvet Underground collaboration by then-unknowns Lou Reed and John Cale. If the Downliners Sect were out of step with the blues-rock scene at the time, the players didn't seem to care in the least. They saw *The Rock Sect's In* as a statement of their down-to-earth approach to music. "*The Rock Sect's In* was an attempt at fundamentalism," says Craine, "to get away from the more poppy melodic thing that was beginning to manifest itself."

They distilled that statement of raw, anti-pop intent perfectly into the A-side of their next single, released in June 1966. "Glendora," a song about a love obsession with a shop window mannequin, combined a snarling Terry Gibson fuzz guitar lead with a relentless smashing beat and deliciously black-humored lead vocals from Keith Grant. *New Musical Express* found this release to have a "great R&B sound going" but "Glendora" would be the original Sect members' last release. The band members were frustrated with the changing musical climate and diminishing gigs. The final blow for Craine came after a gig in Leicester when he discovered that there wasn't enough available floor space in Gibson's tiny Ford van to entertain an old girlfriend. The band agreed that this was a sign that the end of the line had truly been reached. They went their separate ways right there and then—at an anonymous service station somewhere on the M1 Motorway.

Still, another Downliners Sect single appeared in the autumn of 1966. "The Cost of Living" was a Graham Gouldman composition that featured Craine's and Grant's vocals over a backing track of session players.

By the end of 1966, Craine and Grant had regrouped as Don Craine's New Downliners Sect and released a single on Pye coupling a cover of the Remains' "I Can't Get Away from You" with an original titled "Roses." Soon afterward, Craine decided he'd had enough and left to pursue other interests, among them Irish folk music. Grant kept the New Downliners Sect name alive for another year (releasing several tracks on jukebox EPs in Sweden), but by the end of 1968 the Downliners were spent—at least for a while.

Postscript

After the Downliners split up, Don Craine (now using his real name, Mick O'Donnell) first busied himself with an Irish folk duo, Finnegan's Wake, with Mick Smith. He then took over a folk club at the White Bear in Hounslow, Middlesex, and formed an acoustic folk-blues duo, Loose End, with Paul Tiller [see **Black Cat Bones**].

Keith Grant joined Punchin' Judy, releasing an album on Transatlantic Records in 1972. He later played with Magnet, touring the United States in 1975 and releasing one single.

After playing in the J.J. Sound (a soul group that at one point backed Edwin Starr) and Tales of the City, Terry Gibson joined the Houseshakers at the end of 1969. The group spearheaded a rock'n'roll revival in Britain at the turn of the decade by releasing an album and backing Gene Vincent on two of his European visits. They also served as the backing group for Chuck Berry and Bo Diddley for the Wembley Rock & Roll concert in August 1972. Along with Houseshakers' singer Graham Fenton (later of the rockabilly group Matchbox), Gibson next formed the Hellraisers, which released one album on Contour Records in 1976. He also backed Screaming Lord Sutch as one of the Savages on numerous occasions throughout the 1970s.

John Sutton, the Downliners Sect's original drummer, pursued his love of 1920s jazz with the prolific Pasadena Roof Orchestra.

In 1977, feeling a resurgence of interest in their music and a kinship with the energy and attitude of punk rock, Craine, Grant and Gibson reformed the Downliners Sect with Paul Tiller on harp and Paul Holm (ex-Syndicats and Bluesology) on drums. (John Sutton had been involved in the early stages, but dropped out to continue with the Pasadena Roof Orchestra.) They released a strong punk single, "Showbiz" (backed with "Killing Me"), on Raw Records in November 1977. A full-length LP, *Showbiz,* followed in early 1980 on a German label, Sky, by which time Rod De'Ath (ex-Killing Floor and Rory Gallagher) had replaced Holm on drums.

The Downliners Sect played sporadically on the pub rock circuit throughout the 1980s. A typical set has been documented on the *Live in the 80's* album, which shows the group's rockin' R&B sound relatively unchanged since their 1960s heyday. By 1989, Rod De'Ath had disappeared and Terry Gibson decided to bow out.

The group continued, however, with Del Dwyer on guitar and Alan Brooks on drums. Both had once been members of the 1960s "freakbeat" band the Barrier (Brooks had also been in Punchin' Judy with Grant). The band stepped into high gear in the 1990s, keeping a full gig schedule as well as involving themselves in numerous recording projects. They recorded three new Downliners Sect albums that decade: *Savage Return* (1991), *A Light Went Out in New York* (1993) and *Dangerous Ground* (1998).

Craine and Grant were also a part of the British Invasion All-Stars, along with Eddie Phillips (of the Creation),

Jim McCarty (the Yardbirds) and Ray Phillips (the Nashville Teens). They released two CDs, *Regression* (1990) and *United* (1991)—the latter with guest appearances from Procol Harum's Matthew Fisher and the Pretty Things' Phil May and Dick Taylor.

Another band, Thee Headcoats, emerged in the 1990s with a sound distinctly resembling the Downliners Sect, with band members similarly clad in deerstalker hats as they churned out loud punk R&B. They collaborated with Craine on a 1990 EP as *Thee Headcoat Sect*, adding Grant to the lineup for the album *Deerstalking Men* (1996). They released a second joint Headcoat Sect LP, *Ready Steady Go*, in 2000 and were supported by a tour of Japan. The Downliners Sect, meanwhile, continued to be active, touring Sweden the same year.

Discography

Release Date	Title	Catalog Number

U.S. Singles

Downliners Sect

1964	Little Egypt/Sect Appeal	Smash 1954

U.K. Singles

Downliners Sect

1964	Baby What's Wrong/Be a Sect Maniac	Columbia DB 7300
1964	Little Egypt/Sect Appeal	Columbia DB 7347
1964	Find Out What's Happening/Insecticide	Columbia DB 7415
1965	Wreck of the Old '97/Leader of the Sect	Columbia DB 7509
1965	I Got Mine/Waiting in Heaven Somewhere	Columbia DB 7597
1965	Bad Storm Coming/Lonely and Blue	Columbia DB 7712
1966	All Night Worker/He Was a Square	Columbia DB 7817
1966	Glendora/I'll Find Out	Columbia DB 7939
1966	The Cost of Living/ Everything I've Got to Give	Columbia DB 8008

Don Craine's New Downliners Sect

1967	I Can't Get Away from You/Roses	Pye 7N 17261

U.K. EPs

1964	*At Nite in Great Newport Street*	Contrast Sound RBCSP 001

Beautiful Delilah/Shame Shame Shame/Green Onions/Nursery Rhymes

1965	*The Sect Sing Sick Songs*	Columbia SEG 8438

I Want My Baby Back/Leader of the Sect/Midnight Hour/Now She's Dead

U.K. Albums

1964	*The Sect*	Columbia 33SX 1658

Hurt By Love/One Ugly Child/Lonely and Blue/Our Little Rendezvous/Guitar Boogie/Too Much Monkey Business/Sect Appeal/Baby What's on Your Mind/Cops & Robbers/Easy Rider/Bloodhound/Bright Lights/I Wanna Put a Tiger in Your Tank/Be a Sect Maniac

1965	*The Country Sect*	Columbia 33SX 1745

If I Could Just Go Back/Rocks in My Bed/Ballad of the Hounds/Little Play Soldiers/Hard Travelin'/Wait for the Light to Shine/I Got Mine/Waiting in Heaven/Above and Beyond/Bad Storm Coming/Midnight Special/Wolverton Mountain

1966	*The Rock Sect's In*	Columbia SCX 6028

Hang on Sloopy/Fortune Teller/Hey Hey Hey/Everything I've Got to Give/Outside/I'm Hooked on You/Comin' Home Baby/Why Don't You Smile Now/Don't Lie to Me/May the Bird of Paradise Fly Up Your Nose/He Was a Square/I'm Looking for a Woman/The Rock Sect's in Again/Brand New Cadillac

The John Dummer Band

Begun as an extension of their leader's hobby, the John Dummer (Blues) Band persevered through commercial indifference, ever-changing lineups, and several name changes before finally achieving a 1970 Top Ten single in France with the instrumental "Nine by Nine." While the group's albums have become highly coveted among collectors, they only enjoyed limited success when initially released. Individual members John Dummer, Iain "Thumper" Thompson and Dave Kelly would find greater fame following the breakup of the Dummer band, when Dummer and Thompson became members of the pop group the Darts and Kelly became a fixture of the long-running Blues Band.

Dummer's bands leaned toward rural, country blues rather than the big city blues favored by most of his contemporaries. As he explained to *Melody Maker*, "We think the city blues bands have lost a lot of the rhythm thing of the early country blues. We are trying to get back to the real early country things. We want to take the early vocal stuff and retain the rhythmic feel and full melody of it while doing it in a band. Canned Heat has done this to a certain extent, but nobody else seems to try."

John Dummer (b. November 14, 1944; Kingston, Surrey, U.K.)—then known as Tony Dummer—grew up listening to country blues and such modern jazz artists as Gerry Mulligan, John Coltrane and Stan Kenton. In 1964, Dummer fronted a Georgie Fame-style band known as Lester Square & the G.T.'s, whose lineup included former Yardbird Tony "Top" Topham [see **Yardbirds**]. Topham dropped out of the band before the G.T.'s went abroad to tour Germany. Upon their return to the U.K., Dummer, responding to a *Melody Maker* ad seeking a blues vocalist, auditioned.

The new band being formed consisted of Dave Bidwell (formerly of the Muskrats) on drums, Peter Moody (formerly of the Grebbels) on bass, and Roger Pearce (previously a member of both the Muskrats and the Grebbels) on guitar. (The Muskrats, which included Peter Green on bass, folded in the autumn of 1965. Later, after switching to lead guitar, Green found fame with the Bluesbreakers and Fleetwood Mac [see **John Mayall**, **Fleetwood Mac**].) Dummer passed the audition and a second advertisement yielded pianist Bob Hall, an early member of the Groundhogs and later of the Brunning Hall Sunflower Blues Band [see **Brunning Hall Sunflower Blues Band**]. Alto saxophone player Chris Trengrove also frequently dropped by to join in.

The new lineup rehearsed and began to play some gigs as the John Dummer Blues Band. Drummer Dave Bidwell left to join Chicken Shack in December 1965 [see **Chicken Shack**], and Dave Elvidge, who had once been a member of the Nightshift (a band that briefly included Jeff Beck before he became a Yardbird), took his place. Elvidge stayed only briefly, leaving in January 1966, at which point Dummer replaced him at the drum stool while continuing to handle the vocals. The band played regularly, with gigs at Eel Pie Island in Twickenham and at the Harvest Moon Club in Guildford.

A few months later, bassist Moody left in March 1966, succeeded by Tony Walker. The band now consisted of Pearce (guitar), Hall (piano), Walker (bass) and Dummer (drums and vocals). They then recorded a few tunes with

Walker's 14-year-old sister, Regine, during the autumn of 1966. The recordings surfaced on the 1995 CD reissue of *Nine by Nine*.

Further changes took place in late 1966 and early 1967. Hall left to join Savoy Brown [see **Savoy Brown**] and two temporary players—a pianist remembered as "Gill" and a drummer whose name has been lost with time—filled in and allowed Dummer to concentrate on vocals. "Gill" then dropped out and Bob Hall rejoined (though he maintained his presence in Savoy Brown and held on to his day job). The unknown drummer also left, forcing Dummer back onto the drum stool.

More changes were in store as bassist Walker departed, explaining that he lacked enthusiasm for the Chicago/country blues direction the band was taking. Guitarist Pearce also departed sometime later in the year. (The pair later formed the group Tricycle.) Dummer found replacements in Iain "Thumper" Thompson on bass and Dave Kelly on guitar [see **Dave Kelly**]. Thumper met the band while working as a booking agent, having secured a gig for them at Kingston Poly (where he was attending college at the time). His subsequent invitation to join the group was largely based on the misconception that he owned a van.

Steve Rye on harmonica quickly replaced by John O'Leary (formerly of Savoy Brown), rounding out the new John Dummer Blues Band. Rye became a member of the Groundhogs and appeared on their first album, *Scratching the Surface*. He later teamed up with Simon Prager to form the country blues duo Simon and Steve and "The All-Star Medicine Show," a trio that also included Bob Hall on piano and mandolin.

After these extensive changes, the new group began to build their reputation by playing at the upstairs club located at the Nag's Head in Battersea. Aside from the John Dummer Blues Band, the Nag's Head featured other blues bands on the scene, including Savoy Brown, Shaky Vick's Blues Band, the Dynaflow Blues Band (with Rod Price) and the Cross Ties Blues Band (with Dave Peverett and Chris Youlden). Producer Mike Vernon took over the club in early 1968, renaming it the Blue Horizon Club and using it to showcase the bands on his roster. Dummer later recounted to *Beat Instrumental*, "We were playing semi-blues things . . . it was just a simple basic band which we started because of the interest the music held for us. We were just playing at this club [the Blue Horizon] for our own amusement, but gradually it became more important to us."

Over time, additional weekly Sunday sessions at Ken Colyer's Studio 51 club began to raise the band's profile, leading to the group's signing a recording contract with Mercury Records. With Kelly playing mostly bottleneck, the band felt that they needed an additional "proper" lead guitarist to record with, so they persuaded Tony "T.S." McPhee to join them. Interestingly, McPhee had previously turned down a chance to replace Eric Clapton in John Mayall's Bluesbreakers, having gained a solid reputation while backing John Lee Hooker, Jimmy Reed, Little Walter and Eddie Boyd.

With Mercury Records now behind them, they released the first John Dummer Blues Band single, "Traveling Man" backed with "40 Days," in July 1968. *New Musical Express* described the A-side as "meaty Chicago-type blues with a pounding, 'walking' bass, infectious beat and raucous twangs. Then it suddenly slows right down to a mean and soulful 12-bar blues. British, but authentic!" *Disc and Music Echo,* however, had reservations and called the release "tiringly bluesy."

Following the single, Mercury scheduled their first LP for release in September 1968, but then pushed it back until January of the following year. By the time it came out, John O'Leary and Tony McPhee had both left the band, with McPhee planning to reform the Groundhogs and start his own blues label. Guitarist Adrian Pietryga (a.k.a. "Putty") from the Bristol-based band the Deep replaced McPhee.

Wanting something unique, Dummer named the band's first LP *Cabal* after reading books on European witchcraft and devil-worshiping. It consisted of a mixture of blues covers (including Leiber and Stoller's "Hound Dog," Muddy Waters's "Sitting and Thinking," Little Walter's "Just a Feeling," and Willie Dixon's "Young Fashioned Ways"), and originals, including three songs penned by Dave Kelly, and a band arrangement of a Robert Johnson song. McPhee, Kelly and Kelly's sister Jo Ann (as guest vocalist) divided vocals between them. The album's high points included the energetic "I Need Love," featuring Dave Kelly on lead vocals; "Low Down Santa Fe," with the dual lead vocals of the Kelly siblings propelled by John O'Leary's stunning harmonica; and "After Hours," featuring McPhee on vocals.

Cabal was well received by the British music press. *New Musical Express* wrote, "[The group] really gets an exciting, pulsating rhythm going, and the vocalist, Dave Kelly, really gets out his message. Great party maker." *Melody Maker* said, "The band achieves just the right balance and swing, handling even the difficult slow-medium tempo well," but added, "Though they have mastered the [blues] idiom, their influences are too obvious and they lack vocal flexibility."

The band, including Bob Hall for part of the tour, was gigging heavily by midyear. Their schedule included a two-week tour backing Howlin' Wolf in England. (The booking agent reneged on payment, but the band got some consolation when they were awarded the agent's furniture in the subsequent court case.) While many of their contemporaries were experimenting with other styles, Dummer told *Melody Maker* that they were "still playing pure blues," emphasizing, "Our early influences were country blues and we've stayed fairly close to that. We have no intention of becoming a 'progressive' group."

The group's second single, "Try Me One More Time," continued in the same vein and was recognized by *Record Mirror* for its "good and prominent vocal work" and "excellent specialist's blues work . . . with interesting use of the violin in the main backing work."

Following the release of the single, their second album was issued in October 1969 and simply titled *John Dummer Band.* This release again received mixed reviews. *Melody Maker* called it "a lively collection of British-type blues and allied songs which gets away from the contemporary image," although *Disc and Music Echo* was once again critical, with the observation, "It's all competent enough but so many people are doing more original things."

By the time of the second album's release, Dave Kelly had tired of the constant touring and felt that the band had run their course. He later told *Melody Maker,* "The trouble with the Dummers was that we ran out of ideas. The group was booked for two weeks in Scandinavia and we became stagnant. I hadn't written any songs for about three months and couldn't put any enthusiasm into the vocals." The fed-up Kelly finally left the band after looking forward to a two-week vacation that had instead been filled with gigs.

Kelly himself recommended Nick Pickett as his replacement, and with Pickett's help, the group survived the loss of their main songwriter and vocalist. Pickett, a songwriter who also played fiddle, guitar, harmonica, piano and vibes, led the group away from the blues. Early in 1970, the band told *Melody Maker* that their upcoming album, tentatively titled *Sausage Grinder,* would be very different from their previous LP: "We've obviously benefited from the so-called blues boom, but have also suffered as a result of it." To emphasize their departure from the blues, the group renamed themselves John Dummer's Famous Music Band. Issued on Philips, the self-titled album failed to generate any interest in the U.K., and the group disbanded shortly after its release. However, one of the album tracks, a violin-driven instrumental titled "Nine by Nine," unexpectedly became a Top Ten hit in France when Philips released it as a single.

Following "Nine by Nine's" surprise success, the Famous Music Band lineup reunited and signed with Vertigo for another album, *Blue* (1972). Now billing themselves as the John Dummer Band Featuring Nick Pickett, the group issued another violin-instrumental single from the album, titled "Medicine Weasel." Presumably made for commercial reasons (to cash in on the success of their previous single), the tune was structured around an American Indian chant.

Blue received varied reviews from the British press, with *New Musical Express* commenting, "There are some truly excellent tracks like 'Medicine Weasel' and 'Time Will Tell,' which feature Nick Pickett playing violin as only he knows how. 'If I Could Keep from Laughing' is just beautiful—a steady rock number with great twin guitar playing in parts by Pickett and Adrian Pietryga." *Melody Maker* was less enthusiastic: "At its worst, it's ordinary. Undoubtedly, the saving grace of the album is Nick Pickett, who has written all the material, plays guitar and violin and sings the lead. His songs make use of a few memorable and imaginative ideas, but generally speaking, these are stretched to their limits and padded out with uninspiring riffs." *Blue* fell flat and the group disbanded again—but not for long.

In August 1972, the John Dummer Band reunited, this time calling themselves by the unwieldy name "John Dummer's Oobleedooblee Band." Consisting of Dave Kelly, "Thumper" Thompson, "Putty" Pietryga and Dummer, the band issued a single, "Oobleedooblee Jubilee," from an album of the same name. Both releases fared poorly commercially, despite critical praise from *Disc and Music Echo*, which wrote about both band and label, "With the help of the excellent and very talented Dummer band, Vertigo could become a household name."

In September 1972, Pietryga left to join Jo Ann Kelly in Spare Rib. A second John Dummer Band album—featuring guests Pete Emery (guitar), Graham Bond (organ and

sax) and Pete Richardson (drums)—was recorded but never released. During this time, Dummer left the group to work full time at MCA, and other lineup changes ensued as the band added Emery, Pick Withers (later of Dire Straits) on drums and pianist Colin Earl (ex-Mungo Jerry) before disbanding permanently in early 1974.

Postscript

John Dummer remained in the music business, working as a press officer and record plugger. He reunited with Thompson in a 1950s revival band, the Darts, in the mid-1970s. Between 1977 and 1980, the Darts scored eight U.K. Top 40 hit singles (including six in the Top Ten) and four albums: *Darts* (1977, U.K. #9), *Everyone Play Darts* (1978, U.K. #12), *Amazing Darts* (1978, U.K. #8) and *Dart Attack* (1979, U.K. #38). In 1980, he formed True Life Confessions, releasing three singles for A&M and two for Speed Records. In 1982, Dummer's single, "Blue Skies," a vocal duet with Helen April, reached #54 on the U.K. singles charts.

Iain "Thumper" Thompson worked with Dave Kelly in Rock Salt from February to August 1972, then joined the reformed John Dummer Band. Following the final breakup of the John Dummer Band, Thompson followed Dave Kelly into the Dogs, a pub band that played during 1974 and 1975. After the breakup of the Dogs, he joined the Jive Bombers (which evolved into the Darts).

Guitarist Adrian Pietryga joined Spare Rib—a supporting band for Jo Ann Kelly, which included drummer Bruce Rowlands (who had previously played with Joe Cocker) and Roger Brown (who would go on to form Stealers Wheel with Gerry Rafferty)—in 1972. Spare Rib lasted about a year and issued no recordings.

Discography

Release Date	Title	Catalog Number

U.K. Singles

The John Dummer Blues Band

1968	Traveling Man/40 Days	Mercury MF 1040
1969	Try Me One More Time/ Riding at Midnight	Mercury MF 1119

John Dummer's Famous Music Band

1970 Nine by Nine/Going in the Out   Philips 6006 111

1971 Medicine Weasel/The Endgame   Phillips 6006 176

John Dummer's Oobleedooblee Band

1972 Oobleedooblee Jubilee/   Vertigo 6059 074
      The Monkey Speaks His Mind

U.K. Albums

The John Dummer Blues Band

1969 *Cabal*   Mercury
                                             SMCL 20136

I Need Love/Just a Feeling/No Chance with You/Young Fashioned Ways/Sitting and Thinking/Low Down Santa Fe/When You Got a Good Friend/Welfare Blues/Hound Dog/Blue Guitar/After Hours/Daddy Please Don't Cry

John Dummer's Blues Band

1969 *John Dummer Band*   Mercury
                                             SMCL 20167

Few Short Lines/Bullfrog Blues/Try Me One More Time/Money and Fame/Reconsider Baby/Riding at Midnight/Ain't Gonna Work No More/Big Feeling/Memphis Mini/Birds and Booze Blues/Skin Game

John Dummer's Famous Music Band

1970 *Famous Music Band*   Philips 6309 008

Lady Luck/Changes/Love Ain't Nothing But Sorrow/Run Around/Yes Sir, She's My Baby/Boogie-Woogie Lullaby/Coming Home/Searching for You/Nine by Nine/Move Me, Don't Leave Me/Going in the Out/No Chance Now/Fine Looking Woman/Green Leaves

1972 *Nine by Nine*   Philips 6382 039

Nine by Nine/Move Me, Don't Leave Me/Going in the Out/Fine Looking Woman/Few Short Lines/Searching for You/Money and Fame/Reconsider Baby/I Need Love/Just a Feeling/No Chance with You/Young Fashioned Ways

1972 *Try Me One More Time*   Philips 6382040

Lady Luck/When You Got a Good Friend/Love Ain't Nothing But Sorrow/Run Around/Riding at Midnight/Ain't Gonna Work No More/Big Feeling/Memphis Mini/Traveling Man/Low Down Santa Fe/After Hours/Hound Dog

1995 *Nine by Nine* (CD)   Indigo Records
                                             IGOCD 2021

The World's in a Tangle/Soulful Dress/Let Me Love You Baby/Screaming and Crying/Big Feeling Blues/New Skin Game/No Chance Now/Reconsider Baby/Down Home Girl/I Can't Be Satisfied/Nine by Nine/I Love You Honey/Riding in the Moonlight/Walkin' Blues/Lovin' Man/Statesboro Blues/Monkey Speaks His Mind/Young Blood/Be Careful What You Do/Shame, Shame, Shame/Walking the Dog

1996 *Cabal . . . Plus* (CD)   See for Miles
                                             SEECD 456

Same tracks as LP plus the following bonus tracks: "Travelling Man," "40 Days," "Nine by Nine," "Going in the Out," "Medicine Weasel," "The Endgame," "Dooblee Dooblee Jubilee," and "Monkey Speaks His Mind."

The John Dummer Band Featuring Nick Pickett

1972 *Blue*   Vertigo 6360 055

If I Could Keep from Laughing/Medicine Weasel/Rambling Boy/Me and Your Boogie/Time Will Tell/The End Game/Me and the Lady

Foreign Releases

1968 Nine by Nine/Move Me,   Fontana 6007 027
      Don't Leave Me (France)

The Aynsley Dunbar Retaliation

Aynsley Dunbar kept both good time and company while "working the skins," playing alongside such notables as John Mayall, Jeff Beck, Rod Stewart, Peter Green and Frank Zappa. During his long career, Dunbar has been awarded over 30 gold and platinum records from the over 110 albums he has played on. But the progressive-minded, jazz-tinged drummer also sought a sound and identity of his own. He realized that ambition with the blues-based Aynsley Dunbar Retaliation, which he formed in late 1967, issuing four albums before disbanding in 1970.

Dunbar once described the group's approach to music to *Record Mirror:* "There is not enough feeling in what's being played in pop music today—when you play you've got to feel and mean it. And there are some people about who don't do this."

Aynsley Dunbar (b. January 10, 1946; Liverpool, Lancashire, U.K.) started playing the violin at age nine but by 12 had switched to the drums. He left school at age 15 and immediately formed a trio with a saxophonist and a keyboard player to play at dances. At 16, he joined the Merseysippi Jazz Band, which played Dixieland music (or "trad" jazz as it is called in England). His early influences were mostly jazz drummers: Art Blakely, Max Roach, Elvin Jones, Louie Bellson, Joe Morello (of the Dave Brubeck Quartet), Gene Krupa and Buddy Rich. In August 1963, Dunbar joined Derry Wilkie and the Pressmen. Wilkie had formerly been a member of Howie

Casey and the Seniors, with whom he recorded *Twist at the Top* (U.K./Fontana TFL 5108). This 1962 release was the first album issued by a Liverpool beat group.

In January 1964, the Pressmen splintered; Dunbar stayed with four of the band members who renamed themselves the Flamingos. The name was no doubt designed to capitalize on the goodwill built by the popular group Faron's Flamingos, whose members had abandoned the name as they pursued other endeavors. Before long, Dunbar went to Germany with the Flamingos to play at the Tanz Club in Hamburg. While there, they recorded a single for the German market, "Gluecklich Wie Noch Nieu" backed with "Mein Beatle Baby" (D/Vogue DV 14158).

Upon their return to the U.K., the Flamingos teamed up with singer Freddie Starr in April 1964 and became his backing group. Starr had also been with Howie Casey and the Seniors when they recorded *Twist at the Top,* and his previous backing band, the Midnighters, had included drummer Keef Hartley. Freddie Starr and the Flamingos returned to Germany and stayed together for a few months, but fell apart toward the end of 1964, although Dunbar didn't stay behind for the final breakup. During this time, he was also involved with a fairly inconsequential group called the Excheckers.

Dunbar's next project brought him in touch with higher caliber musicians. The Mojos were one of the more popular "Merseybeat" groups, with three singles reaching the U.K. charts in 1964: "Everything's Alright" (#9), "Why Not Tonight" (#25) and "Seven Daffodils" (#30). Even with the successful singles, personality clashes and artistic bickering left the original lineup splintered by late 1964. Disputes over who would continue to use the band's name kept the group out of the limelight for a couple of months, but ultimately vocalist Stu James and guitarist Nicky Crouch regrouped with a new set of Mojos, which now included Dunbar and bassist Lewis Collins. Dunbar stayed with the group, now called "Stu James and the Mojos," until September 1966, recording two singles with the band: "Comin' On to Cry" backed with "That's the Way It Goes," and "Wait a Minute" backed with "Wonder If She Knows." While with the Mojos, Dunbar relocated to London, but when the group went into a slow decline, he left them and was out of work for a couple of weeks. Alexis Korner [see **Alexis Korner, Cyril Davies**] invited him to sit in during one of his gigs and even though the engagement didn't go well, John Mayall was in the audience and invited Dunbar to sit in with the Bluesbreakers [see **John Mayall**]. Even though Dunbar had never heard of Mayall at the

time, he accepted the invitation to sit in and became a Bluesbreaker the next day.

The Bluesbreakers at the time of Dunbar's joining consisted of Mayall, John McVie (bass) and Peter Green (guitar). While with the Bluesbreakers, Dunbar first became interested in the blues, although he still incorporated jazz influences into his playing. "John Mayall put me into the blues thing," Dunbar later recounted to *Beat Instrumental.* "It built me up, because I was playing with good musicians, and hearing all types of blues. When I heard about him, I was told he was playing just country blues. I thought 'Jesus, here we go.' But it wasn't like that. It was good— solid and full."

While with the Bluesbreakers, Dunbar auditioned for the Jimi Hendrix Experience. After both Dunbar and Mitch Mitchell jammed with Hendrix and bassist Noel Redding, manager Chas Chandler and Hendrix were unable to decide between the two drummers. However, Dunbar asked for £30 a week and the gig paid £20, so the position went to Mitchell.

Dunbar's recordings with the Bluesbreakers consisted of two singles; "Looking Back" backed with "So Many Roads," and "Sitting in the Rain" backed with "Out of Reach"; as well as an LP (*A Hard Road*) with John Mayall; and an EP, *John Mayall's Bluesbreakers with Paul Butterfield.* During his time with the Bluesbreakers, Dunbar also appeared on the Eddie Boyd album, *Eddie Boyd & His Blues Band,* which featured the other members of the Bluesbreakers as well. Other tracks he recorded with Mayall appeared on the LPs *Raw Blues* and *Thru the Years,* a collection of rare tracks.

Despite Dunbar's considerable skills as a drummer, Mayall let him go in March 1967 because his style was "too advanced" for what Mayall wanted in the Bluesbreakers. The parting was amicable, however, as Dunbar later recalled, "I was grateful to John. He introduced me to the musicians I wanted to play with, although I eventually got the sack for playing too advanced. He wanted me to sit in the background and just play away. I didn't think I would progress until I left."

Dunbar rebounded to join the Jeff Beck Group in mid-April 1967. This astonishing lineup included Beck on guitar, Ronnie Wood on bass, Rod Stewart on vocals and Dunbar. He stayed with the Jeff Beck Group long enough to record the single "Tallyman" backed with "Rock My Plimsoul," which they released in July. Dunbar wasn't satisfied playing in other people's bands behind other people's vision, though, and in the first step to forming his own group, he gave his notice to the Jeff Beck Group the same month that the single came out, but agreed to stay on until they had found a replacement.

Even before he gave notice of his departure, Dunbar had been trying to discover his own "sound" and had been searching for like-minded musicians to help. He told *Beat Instrumental* what he envisioned for the group he had in mind: "My group will still be playing the Chicago style of blues but we'll be moving towards a more modern rhythm. Not towards jazz, we have to stay commercial. That's very important."

In mid-1967, Dunbar staged a recording session with Rod Stewart on vocals, Peter Green on guitar and Jack Bruce on bass. Produced by Mike Vernon, this session yielded a cover of Buddy Guy's "Stone Crazy"—a track that would be released much later on Sire's *History of British Blues*.

After giving notice to Beck, Dunbar began pulling together other players, finally coming up with Victor Brox on vocals, keyboards, cornet and violin; John Moorshead (also known as Jon Morshead) on guitar; and Keith Tillman on bass.

Brox had previously been fronting his own group, the Victor Brox Blues Train, which he had formed in 1964. The band played mainly in clubs and colleges in northern England. Blues Train had a high turnover, but included his future wife Annette Reis on vocals and bassist Tillman. In addition, Brox and Reis performed as a folk-blues duo and Fontana issued a single of the newly wed duo in 1965: "I've Got the World in a Jug" backed with "Wake Me and Shake Me" (UK-Fontana TF 536).

After graduating with a degree in philosophy from Manchester University, Brox had held down a teaching job while still running Blues Train. He then gave up his teaching position to work as a duo with Alexis Korner for nine months until the early part of 1968. During this time, *Melody Maker* hailed him as "one of the most underrated people around." Only three tracks recorded with Korner have ever been issued—"Corina Corina" and "The Love You Save (May Be Your Own)" on *Bootleg Him—Alexis Korner*, and "Louisiana Blues" on *Alexis Korner And*. All three tracks were recorded on November 13, 1967, after Brox became a member of the Retaliation.

John Moorshead's first known band was the Moments, which he joined in August 1964, replacing John Weider (who had joined Johnny Kidd's Pirates). The Moments consisted of Moorshead on guitar, Steve Marriott on guitar and vocals, Jimmy Winston on bass and Kenny Rowe on drums. They recorded one single that was released in America in 1964 (probably with Weider in the group), a cover of the Kinks' "You Really Got Me" backed with "Money Money" (US-World Artist 1032). At the end of 1964, the Moments broke up. By September 1965, Moorshead had found his way into Johnny Kidd and the Pirates, again replacing John Weider (who would reunite with Jimmy Winston in Jimmy Winston's Reflections). Moorshead stayed with Johnny Kidd until April 1966, when he and two other Pirates left their frontman to forge an identity in their own right. As simply "the Pirates," they recorded one single, "Shades of Blue" backed with "Can't Understand" (Polydor BM 56712), but disbanded after only three months, at which point Moorshead joined Shotgun Express (replacing Peter Green on guitar). He stayed with Shotgun Express, whose lineup included Rod Stewart on vocals, until November 1966, when he left to join Julian Covey and the Machine. Covey, better known as Phil Kinorra, was a founding member of the Brian Auger Trinity. During Moorshead's stint with the Machine, one single was issued in 1967, "A Little Bit Hurt" backed with "Sweet Bacon" (U.K./Island 6009). Moorshead, who co-authored the B-side, was with the Machine until he joined the Aynsley Dunbar Retaliation.

Keith Tillman had formerly been a member of Stone's Masonry, which had issued one single on Mike Vernon's Purdah label in early 1967, "Flapjacks" backed with "Hot Rock" (U.K./Purdah 3504). Stone's Masonry disbanded when their guitarist, Martin Stone, left to join Savoy Brown [see **Savoy Brown**].

The Aynsley Dunbar Retaliation made their debut at the Seventh National Jazz and Blues Festival at Windsor on August 12, 1967. Dunbar also made his last appearance with the Jeff Beck Group at this festival, after which Mickey Waller took his place.

The next month, the Aynsley Dunbar Retaliation recorded their first single, "Warning" backed with "Cobwebs," produced by Mike Vernon for Blue Horizon Records. At around this time, Alex Dmochowski (a.k.a. Alex Paris) replaced Tillman on bass, who had left them for the Bluesbreakers. The Polish-born Dmochowski had briefly been a member of Neil Christian's Crusaders in 1965—at the same time as Mick Abrahams (Jethro Tull,

Blodwyn Pig) and Carlo Little [see **Cyril Davies**]—and was also part of Jimmy Winston's Fumbs. Dmochowski played on the Jimmy Winston's Fumbs single "Real Crazy Apartment" backed with "Snow White" (U.K./RCA 1612), which was issued in July 1967.

In the liner notes to *History of British Blues*, Mike Vernon writes that he made three unsuccessful attempts to record the Aynsley Dunbar Retaliation live at the Blue Horizon Club in South London's old Battersea area. Each attempt was marred by difficulties that ultimately pushed their first LP release all the way to the following July.

The band signed a recording contract with Liberty Records, which assigned Ian Samwell as producer and Victor Gann as engineer for the record. Of the nine tracks on the 1968 album, *The Aynsley Dunbar Retaliation*, seven were composed by the group or individual members, while only two were outside compositions.

The reviews were encouraging. *New Musical Express* wrote that the Aynsley Dunbar Retaliation provided "some most attractive blues music, especially in the jerky, fascinating instrumental track, 'Sage of Sydney Street,' and the long 'Mutiny' track, with some dynamic drumming. There's some soulful singing on 'My Whiskey Head Woman' (with dominant trumpet), and 'Memory Pain.'" *Record Mirror* called attention to the "progressive and beautifully varied material," and wrote, "It demands close attention; if it gets it, this album will sell exceptionally well." *Melody Maker* focused on Dunbar himself, exclaiming, "An exceptional debut of the ex-John-Mayall drummer who obviously is not afraid of experimenting within the structure of blues. Very recommendable."

Liberty paired the lead track on the album, "Watch 'n' Chain," with another album track, "Roamin' and Ramblin,'" and issued it as the group's next single. The atypical "Watch 'n' Chain" was propelled by an Afro-Cuban percussive rhythm over inflected vocals. *Beat Instrumental* saw the single as "a very unusual and really rather clever performance. Lots of off-beat drumming early on; a sort of African atmosphere, and then whistling and good singing," pragmatically adding, "Even if it doesn't make it as a single then it will help boost the album named after the group."

The players also received a boost when John Mayall, Dunbar's blues mentor, told *Melody Maker*, "The Retaliation are a fine band. They are one of the few British groups playing contemporary blues music reflecting the world today, and not just reproducing blues from years ago that the audience have on record at home." More accolades came from *Beat Instrumental*, which observed, "The group has now developed into one of the most meaningful and original blues groups in England."

During this time, Dunbar was invited to join the Yardbirds during the latter part of their existence [see **Yardbirds**]. As he explained in an interview with *Modern Drummer* magazine, "I had an offer to join the Yardbirds, with Jimmy Page, when they did their last tour, but I'd just started Retaliation. I couldn't leave the people in my band just to do some wandering around the country, although it would have led to the Led Zeppelin gig, which was offered to me as well."

The band released their second album, *Doctor Dunbar's Prescription,* in November 1968. Again Ian Samwell produced, this time using Phillip Wade as engineer. Despite several strong tracks—notably "The Fugitive" and "Call My Woman"—the album received mixed reviews. *Beat Instrumental* called the album "another set of driving white blues," and mentioned that the band was "much more together now, with individuality [starting] to show heavily." And while *Record Mirror* gave the release five stars, *Melody Maker's* Chris Welch expressed disappointment with the record, calling it "unmoving," then criticizing the British blues scene in general by challenging "all bands who are going to associate themselves with blues to listen hard to themselves, maybe buy each other's LPs, and ask themselves if they are going to be content with a scene that is rapidly becoming one of the biggest bores of the day." Curiously, six of the album's ten compositions were attributed to "Hickley" as author or co-author. As it turned out, "Hickley" was a pseudonym for Victor Brox.

In spite of Chris Welch's admonition, *Melody Maker* gave heavy coverage to the British blues movement, even sponsoring a one-day festival held on November 16, 1968, at the London Royal Festival Hall. Dubbed "The Blues Scene '68," the concerts were co-headlined by Muddy Waters and John Mayall and featured Champion Jack Dupree and the Aynsley Dunbar Retaliation. The Blues Scene '68 was hugely successful, with the 3,000-seat auditorium selling out quickly and hundreds of fans turned away. *Melody Maker* writer Tony Wilson described the Aynsley Dunbar Retaliation's performance: "Drummer-leader Dunbar laid down a solid base for Victor

Brox, vocals and organ, John Moorshead on guitar and Alex Dmochowski to build on. Brox led the group through 'Low Down Man,' 'Call My Woman,' featuring John Moorshead on guitar and vocals on his own composition, [and] 'I Tried,' all from the new *Dr. Dunbar's Prescription* album, and 'Double Loving.' An exciting 'Everyday I Have The Blues'—with Brox taking a solo on pocket cornet and Dmochowski also taking a break—brought the Retaliations' part of the evening to an end."

With the success of the Blues Scene '68, *Melody Maker* cosponsored a six-date package tour of top U.S. and U.K. blues artists in February 1969. Touring as the Blues Scene '69, the lineup consisted of John Lee Hooker, Champion Jack Dupree, Jo Ann Kelly, the Groundhogs and the Aynsley Dunbar Retaliation.

In March 1969, the group went on a six-week tour of the U.S., which included four gigs at the Fillmore West from April 10–13 in support of Country Joe and the Fish. Organist Mick Weaver (also called Wynder K. Frogg) accompanied the group. However, Mick's membership was short-term and upon the group's return to England, he was replaced with Tommy Eyre. Eyre was best known for his work with Joe Cocker's Grease Band and for having played on the "With a Little Help from My Friends" hit. This addition allowed Victor Brox to concentrate on vocals, electric piano, 12-string guitar and pocket cornet.

On August 9, the Aynsley Dunbar Retaliation took part in the Ninth Jazz and Blues Festival at Plumpton, Sussex. Chris Welch covered the event for *Melody Maker*, conceding, "British blues bands have been knocked a lot recently, and it must be admitted that the sound has palled. In the hands of groups like Aynsley Dunbar and Chicken Shack, it retains a lot of power and authority, but neither group was outstanding." Ending on a positive note, he credited the band for playing "a hard, aggressive set, sparked by some fine drumming."

That same year, the group also backed veteran bluesman Champion Jack Dupree for some sessions that were eventually issued in 1972 on the French BYG label as *The Heart of the Blues Is Sound.*

Even though both albums were selling well, Dunbar told *Melody Maker* that their next album would "be more advanced," explaining, "It's a struggle because in England the blues fans expect you to just bang away, or it's not blues. In America, you've got to be advanced. Perhaps

the fans here will like it more in the end." Liberty issued the album, *To Mum from Aynsley and the Boys,* in September. The cover depicted the band in flashy 1950s attire and pompadours. Produced by John Mayall, *To Mum* received favorable reviews, with *Disc and Music Echo* commenting, "Dunbar's third LP for Liberty is undoubtedly his best . . . despite the limited eight tracks, there's something for every type of blues fan, from the very r-n-b 'Sugar On The Line' to the pseudo-classical 'Journey's End,' which starts with a mock-Bach organ fugue." *Melody Maker's* reviewer wrote that it was a "great improvement on his previous albums . . . with better recording quality and more original ideas. Generally quite satisfying for lovers of heavy blues."

In November 1969, Dunbar and Eyre unexpectedly left the group to form Aynsley Dunbar's Blue Whale. Dunbar explained the reasons for the breakup years later to *Modern Drummer:* "The band's ego got too much for me to cope with and I had to dump them. They couldn't see any further than where they were at. They thought that because we had got to the point where we were selling out everywhere and making quite a bit of money, that we had reached stardom. No way could I tell them that they had just reached the first step and we had a lot more steps to go. They were already acting like stars. So I decided it was time to get rid of that band and start another one."

Dunbar also wanted to integrate a brass section into the arrangements, and by January 1970 he believed he'd found the right combination of players for Blue Whale, which consisted of himself, Tommy Eyre (piano and organ), Paul Williams (vocals), Ivan Zagni (lead guitar), Roger Sutton (bass), Pat Hicks (trumpet), Norman Leppard (saxophone) and Edward Reay-Smith (trombone). The group embarked on a five-day Scandinavian tour beginning on January 1, 1970, appeared on Belgium television, then made their London debut at the Marquee on January 20. The combination of players proved unstable, however, and before their second month, Peter Friedberg had been added on bass, Roger Sutton had moved over to second guitar, Charles Greetham had replaced Norman Leppard on saxophone, and Pat Hicks had dropped out. However, the combination never really gelled and so Dunbar broke up the band after barely two months to join Frank Zappa and the Mothers at the end of February 1970. He told *Melody Maker* that one of the primary reasons for disbanding the group was "difficulties in finding brass players." In their short amount of time together, they recorded one album, *Blue Whale*, which Warner Brothers released after the breakup. *Disc and Music Echo* harpooned the LP, complaining, "Most of the tracks are long, boring jams round nauseatingly poor arrangements." In stark contrast, *Record Mirror* called the record "inventive and comparatively fresh."

In 1970, Liberty released one last album, *Remains to Be Heard*, under the Aynsley Dunbar Retaliation name. Produced by Victor Brox, it consisted wholly of outtakes, with Dunbar appearing on only four of the ten tracks with the balance made up of more recent recordings of the remaining trio and Annette Brox.

Postscript

Aynsley Dunbar remained with Frank Zappa until the end of 1972, recording six albums. He also established a reputation as a top session drummer, working with the Bonzo Dog Doo Dah Band, Flo and Eddie, Nils Lofgren, Lou Reed, Poco, David Bowie, Mick Ronson and Sammy Hagar, among others.

In 1974, future arena rockers Journey persuaded him to join them, an association that lasted for four years and four albums, until he was asked to leave just prior to the band's achieving mega-stardom. The acrimonious parting caused Dunbar to sue his old bandmates for $3.25 million, claiming "breach of employment and intentional interference with contractual relationships." Dunbar quickly found new employment, replacing John Barbata in Jefferson Starship, where he remained until 1982.

Dunbar's next major project was appearing on Whitesnake's 1987 self-titled release, which rocketed to #2 on the U.S. album charts and remains the band's best-selling album to date. He has also worked with Pat Travers and Mogg/Way, a band led by Phil Mogg and Pete Way, two founding members of UFO. In 1996, Dunbar joined vocalist Eric Burdon, guitarist Alvin Lee and other veteran British blues musicians for a tour entitled "Best of British Blues." He then joined Eric Burdon and the New Animals and still continues to tour with them today.

Following the breakup of the Aynsley Dunbar Retaliation, Victor Brox formed a new band, the short-lived Ring of Truth, which broke up in the spring of 1970. He subsequently reformed the Victor Brox Blues Train with his wife, Annette. He appeared on the original studio

recording of *Jesus Christ Superstar*, singing the part of Caiaphas the High Priest. (His wife also had a part in the recording, performing the part of the Maid by the Fire.) In 1974, the Broxes issued the album *Rollin' Back*. In 1983, Victor Brox appeared on the LP *The International Blues Rock Revue,* issued by the band Main Squeeze, whose players included Dick Heckstall-Smith.

Moorshead's and Dmochowski's next venture was the mysterious "Heavy Jelly," a fictitious group whose imaginary album was reviewed in the November/December 1968 issue of the underground magazine *Time Out*. The review, which said that the American quartet had "turned on to the acid-rock sound that was sweeping the country from the West Coast," contained detailed descriptions of all the tracks—including "a gentle country number called 'Journey to the Bottom of your Mind' (with an electric sitar), a raving version of the Alvis John's classic 'Dust Between My Toes' and a sound collage of street/crowd noises entitled 'Bottle-Top Serenade.'" This was followed in the next issue by a full-page advertisement for the imaginary group with a photo showing John Moorshead and some friends at the Chelsea Antique market.

Although intended as jokes, the review and ad generated so much interest in "Heavy Jelly" that two competing factions formed groups to capitalize on the favorable publicity. One group, the Island Records formation (actually the band Skip Bifferty), issued a single, "I Keep Singing the Same Old Song" (backed with "Blue"), but was legally blocked from issuing more recordings by the other group, the Head Records formation (an ad-hoc studio band with John Moorshead on lead guitar, Alex Dmochowski on bass and Carlo Little on drums), who had registered the name "Heavy Jelly." The latter group released a single of their own, "Time Out Chewn In" backed with "The Long Wait," in July 1969. Toward the end of the year, vocalist Jackie Lomax and former Animals drummer Barry Jenkins joined Heavy Jelly, which was rounded out by Dmochowski and Moorshead. One album was recorded and a promo issued, but the band broke up and the album was never officially released.

Alex Dmochowski joined John Mayall's Bluesbreakers in February 1970. He subsequently did session work for Graham Bond (*Holy Magick*), Peter Green (*The End of the Game*) and Frank Zappa (*Waka/Jawaka* and *The Grand Wazoo*). On the Zappa albums, which saw him reunited with Aynsley Dunbar, Dmochowski was credited as "Erroneous."

John Moorshead also did session work for Graham Bond (*Holy Magick*) as well as Denny Laine (*Aah Laine*).

Discography

Release Date	Title	Catalog Number

U.S. Albums

1968   *The Aynsley Dunbar Retaliation*   Blue Thumb BTS 4
Watch 'n' Chain/My Whiskey Head Woman/Trouble No More/Double Lovin'/See See Baby/Roamin' and Ramblin'/Sage of Sidney Street/Memory of Pain/Mutiny

1969   *Doctor Dunbar's Prescription*   Blue Thumb BTS 6
The Fugitive/Till Your Lovin' Makes Me Blue/Now That I've Lost You/I Tried/Change Your Low Down Ways/Call My Woman/The Devil Drives/Low Gear Man/Tuesday's Blues/Mean Old World

1970   *To Mum from Aynsley and the Boys*   Blue Thumb BTS-16
Don't Take the Power Away/Run You Off the Hill/Let It Ride/Journey's End/Down, Down and Down/Unheard/Sugar on the Line/Leaving Right Away

Miscellaneous U.S. Releases

1973   *History of British Blues*   Sire SAS 3701
Includes "Stone Crazy" by the Aynsley Dunbar Retaliation.

U.K. Singles

1967	Warning/Cobwebs	Blue Horizon 57-3109
1968	Watch 'n' Chain/Roamin' and Ramblin'	Liberty LBF 15132

U.K. Albums

1968	*The Aynsley Dunbar Retaliation*	Liberty LBL 83154 (M) Liberty LBS 83154 (S)
1969	*Doctor Dunbar's Prescription*	Liberty LBS 83177
1969	*To Mum from Aynsley and the Boys*	Liberty LBS 83223
1970	*Remains to Be Heard*	Liberty LBS 83316

Invitation to a Lady/Blood on Your Wheels/Downhearted/Whistling Blues/Keep Your Hands Out/Sleepy Town Sister/Fortune City/Put Some Love on You/Bloody Souvenir/Toga

Aynsley Dunbar's Blue Whale
1970   *Blue Whale*   Warner Brothers K 46062
Willing to Fight/Willie the Pimp/It's Your Turn/Days/Going Home

The Electric Flag

Guitarist Mike Bloomfield formed the Electric Flag as a vehicle for showcasing a wide range of American musical influences, particularly the horn-driven Stax-Volt recordings coming out of Memphis. As Mike Bloomfield explained in the liner notes to their first album, *A Long Time Comin'*, "The Electric Flag is an American Music Band. American music is not necessarily music directly from America. I think of it as the music you hear in the air, on the air, and in the streets; blues, soul, country, rock, religious music, traffic, crowds, street sounds and field sounds, the sound of people and silence." [See **Mike Bloomfield**.]

Many considered Bloomfield to be America's first great guitar hero and expectations were high for his hand-picked group of musical veterans. However, while the group achieved some commercial success with their first album reaching a respectable #31 on the U.S. charts, their potential was never realized as the collective setting proved to be highly combustible, which led to the group's demise after only a pair of albums and some soundtrack work. *Hit Parader* was on point when they predicted that the Flag "will happen" only if "their superstar egos continue to think as one," concluding with the caveat, "Groups do have a bad habit of breaking up, you know."

By the end of 1967, Mike Bloomfield had already established his reputation as a formidable blues guitarist during his two-album stint with the Paul Butterfield Blues Band [see **Paul Butterfield Blues Band**]. Now on his own, Bloomfield managed to assemble his own impressive group of musicians by winter of that year, with the support of his manager, Albert Grossman, and keyboardist Barry Goldberg [see **Barry Goldberg**].

For vocals, he initially chose Mitch Ryder, who had enlisted both Bloomfield and Goldberg to play on his 1967 LP release, *What Now My Love*. (Goldberg also performed on Ryder's #4 hit single, "Devil with the Blue Dress On.") When Ryder declined the lead vocal slot, Nick Gravenites got the job [see **Nick Gravenites**]. Gravenites was best known for penning "Born in Chicago," the Paul Butterfield Blues Band's signature song. A veteran of the Chicago folk and blues scene, he had once been part of a harmonica/acoustic guitar duo with Paul Butterfield that called themselves "Nick and Paul." In 1965, he and a friend opened the Burning Bush, a Chicago club, and formed the Chicago Folk Quintet. But the club folded and the group soon disbanded, and in late 1966 Gravenites moved to Marin County, north of San Francisco. He was taken in by Ron Polte, manager of the Quicksilver Messenger Service. When Gravenites accepted Bloomfield's offer to join the Electric Flag, he rented a house in Mill Valley, where he awaited the arrival of the band's soon-to-be-determined other musicians.

Bloomfield next recruited Harvey Brooks (born Harvey Goldstein) for bass. Bloomfield had met Brooks while working on Dylan's *Highway 61 Revisited* album. Brooks was also a veteran of sessions with Richie Havens, Judy Collins, Phil Ochs, the Drifters, Eric Anderson and numerous others. Brooks led them to drummer Buddy Miles, whom he discovered playing behind Wilson Pickett at an Easter show hosted by New York deejay Murray Kaufman (a.k.a. Murray "the K"). The shows ran from March 25 to April 2 at the R.K.O. Theater in New York. The performances featured an outstanding roster of musicians, including Simon and Garfunkel, the Lovin' Spoonful, the Blues Project, Mitch Ryder, Smokey Robinson and the Miracles, the Chicago Loop (Barry Goldberg's old group), and—making their first U.S. appearances—the Who and Cream. Each act only played for five to eight minutes—but they played six times a day. Impressed by Miles's powerhouse performance, Brooks invited Bloomfield and Goldberg to listen to the 20-year-old drummer. The sight of the behemoth percussionist with his huge pompadour flailing away at the drums won them both over, and they persuaded Miles to leave Pickett and join their new group.

Miles started performing at age 12 by playing drums in his father's band, the Bebops. He went on to play in other jazz and R&B groups including Ruby & the Romantics, the Delfonics and the Ink Spots before meeting up with Wilson Pickett.

Bloomfield completed the ensemble with Peter Strazza on tenor saxophone and trumpeter Marcus Doubleday (who was referred by jazz guitarist Larry Coryell).

The band's first opportunity to record was not for making a single or an album, but for composing and recording the soundtrack to a Roger Corman film titled *The Trip*—even before they had ever played a single live gig. Written by Jack Nicholson and starring Peter Fonda, Dennis Hopper, Susan Strasberg and Bruce Dern, the plot—such as it was—centered around an LSD experience of the Fonda character. The band temporarily moved to Los Angeles where they composed the soundtrack—a montage of various types of music. Peter Fonda described the movie soundtrack to *Downbeat*: "The group [Electric Flag] covered the realm of music. There are three r&b numbers, a disco-dance sequence, and the last love scene is into heavy rock. There is some straight jazz and some symphonic effects. They're not into one bag. And we didn't have just a bunch of studio cats playing; we had a bunch of cats creating." Released on the Sidewalk label, the soundtrack made an interesting period piece.

Bloomfield added Herbie Rich to the lineup on baritone saxophone in time for the group's debut appearance at the Monterey Pop Festival. Advance publicity billed the group as "The Mike Bloomfield Thing," later changed to the Electric Flag. Given Bloomfield's enormous stature, the festival-goers eagerly anticipated the performance. Before the band began their set, John Phillips introduced Bloomfield as "one of the two or three best guitarists in the world." Gravenites and Miles shared vocals and Miles went over particularly well with the predominantly white audience. For a first performance, it seemed to go well and their set was well received, but the band expressed disappointment with their performance nonetheless.

Following the festival, manager Albert Grossman negotiated with Columbia Records to sign three artists—the Quicksilver Messenger Service, the Steve Miller Blues Band and the Electric Flag—in a package deal for $100,000. However, the deal fell through when Grossman was unable to secure the managerial rights to Quicksilver or Steve Miller, so Columbia signed the Electric Flag separately for $50,000.

The band had already begun recording their first album, *A Long Time Comin'*, just prior to Monterey. They continued recording for the balance of 1967 and into January of 1968, at the same time gigging constantly, performing regularly at the Fillmore West and the Carousel Ballroom, as well as other selected venues outside the San Francisco Bay Area.

While Bloomfield may have been the star performer in the group, he did not consider himself the leader. He described his understanding of his role in the band to *Hit Parader:* "I don't like to be leading anything. I just want my music to get exposure. I don't dig to keep those tight reigns on everything like Frank Zappa does. He keeps his cats under control. I don't dig that at all. I'm too messed up myself to control other people's minds."

In October 1967, Bloomfield, Brooks, Goldberg and Gravenites were all arrested on drug charges at a Huntington Beach motel near the Golden Bear, a crusty but appreciated club where they had been playing a 10-day gig. The following month, they traveled to New York for gigs and recording sessions, making their New York debut at Greenwich Village's Bitter End, where they played a five-day engagement. *The New York Times* reviewed a performance, observing, "With an expert brass section and musicians like Barry Goldberg who creates his own aurora borealis at the organ, and Harvey Brooks, whose bass guitar sends out earth tremors as he scowls with his Benjamin Franklin face, Mike Bloomfield has minted a commercialized pop version of the old big-band sound."

Also in November, the Electric Flag released their first single, "Groovin' Is Easy" backed with "Over-Lovin' You," in the U.S. (U.K. fans had to wait until July 1968 for the single.) The Gravenites-penned "Groovin' Is Easy" (credited to Ron Polte) featured his smooth vocals against prominent brass lines. Bloomfield explained to *Rolling Stone* why they had chosen it as a single: "We did 'Groovin' because 'Groovin' . . . well for several reasons: One because I had a really groovy arrangement in mind for it; number two, because groovin' was the thing for a pop record, grooving all over the place. I figured well we got a pop record. In my opinion, 'Groovin'' is a great pop record, a really pop record from beginning to end. The horns, the guitar, the drums. I think the voice is a little old-timey, but it's a pretty groovy record and that's why we chose it." *Rolling Stone* reflected on a different aspect of the single, describing it as "powerhouse Memphis style blues," concluding that the best word for the record was "heavy." *New Musical Express* was equally enthusiastic, citing that the record "generates an urgent, attacking drive. Great!" Despite winning critical favor, the single failed to find an audience.

A Long Time Comin' was finally released in the early spring of 1968 and climbed to #31 on the album charts. The opening cut, a version of Howlin' Wolf's "Killing Floor," was driven by a horn section and Bloomfield's spirited guitar leads. "Texas," a slow blues tune, showcased more of Bloomfield's adept guitar work and Miles's soulful vocals. Goldberg's splendid ballad "Sittin' in Circles" provided another horn-spiced yet gritty highlight. Bloomfield had augmented the band with other musicians on many tracks, including Mike Fonfara on keyboards, Richie Havens on sitar and Paul Beaver on Moog synthesizer. Most reviewers in the music industry gave the release the thumbs up. *Rolling Stone* pronounced, "The album is not spectacular. It's good . . . truthful. The Flag are honest imitators as well as innovators. Nothing they do can be attributed to any one singular source." At the same time, *New Musical Express* called the album "varied and enjoyable" and *Guitar Player* raved, "All in all, Bloomfield is great and the band rocks."

Respected *Rolling Stone* columnist Ralph J. Gleason, however, was deeply disappointed with the LP. In an essay titled "Perspectives: Stop this Shuck, Mike Bloomfield," Gleason blasted the guitarist: "No matter how long he lives and how good he plays, Mike Bloomfield will never be a spade. You can count on that." He also noted that the band was "trying to sound like Wilson Pickett's and Otis Redding's bands. And it is a drag . . . They ought to sound original and ought to be a gas . . . but they are really only a good white band playing black music." Gleason ended his lacerating diatribe by writing, "Originality is the key. If this nonsense continues, Michael Bloomfield, one of the best guitar players in the world when he is playing guitar, will end up being the Stan Getz or Chet Baker of rock."

Writing for *Crawdaddy*, Jon Landau echoed the criticism, noting, "The album is superficial because the collective has no identity. The group goes from style to style without any continuity. They don't play any one thing long enough so that nuances and subtleties of style can be firmly developed." Landau concluded, "I fail to see a single good reason why anyone should want to listen to this record when he can listen to Otis, B.B., Albert or any good Motown artist instead."

Gleason's essay prompted a response from Gravenites, who observed, "Mike [Bloomfield] doesn't have to play with a mixed band or play a lot of black music. He just wants to. Many times in his career, he was told that by getting rid of the black members of his band, or his band altogether, he could make a lot more money, play a lot more gigs. Mike would rather have a band that played good music together than be a 'star.'"

Buddy Guy also rose to Bloomfield's defense in an interview with *Guitar Player:* "You don't have to be black, red, yellow, or green to play the blues. The music is learned and I think anybody can learn it. I wasn't born playing the guitar . . . I learned it. I don't think I could be Mike Bloomfield and I don't think he could be me . . . I can't be Clapton or B.B. and they can't be me. I'll tell you one thing, though, these kids are great, and I know Mike can play."

Criticism from the press was not the only thing hurting the band. Internal conflicts, exacerbated by drug abuse, splintered the Electric Flag. Goldberg was the first to leave. Bloomfield followed shortly thereafter, as his chronic insomnia made it difficult for him to continue. At Bill Graham's insistence, he agreed to play one more gig with the group at the Fillmore East on June 8, 1968. Following the regular set, Jimi Hendrix appeared onstage to accompany Buddy Miles, a precursor of things to come for Miles in the Band of Gypsies.

Bloomfield later told *Guitar Player* about some of the conflicts within the band: "We were really good a lot of times live, but a lot of times, well, we just had troubles. Buddy [Miles] was success crazy, he was absolutely insane to make as much money as he could as fast as he could and he would spend incredibly exorbitant amounts of money to buy giant cars. And we had junkies in the band. There were just horribly diverse factions which can break any band up." Then, lamenting the music industry's overt commercialism, Bloomfield continued, "Most of all, I found myself being a product, just a stone product. And if I had just a little more control, it wouldn't have been so bad. I don't mind being the product if I can also be the manufacturer. If somebody had taken control of the group, we would be together now. We'd have been even more beautiful."

Without Bloomfield or Goldberg, the band had to find replacements. Previously, they had already added Stemsy Hunter (saxophone and vocals) and saxophonist/keyboardist Herbie Rich (who switched to keyboards to replace Goldberg) to the remaining original members—Miles, Brooks, Gravenites and Doubleday. Virgil Gonsalves was brought in on baritone sax, guitarist Hoshal Wright replaced Bloomfield, Terry Clements joined on tenor sax and Roger Troy helped out on bass. In addition, producer John Simon sometimes played piano. The new crew released one album, *An American Music Band.* The

LP, dominated by Buddy Miles, was on overall disappointment and the Electric Flag disbanded.

Rumors circulated that the Electric Flag were reuniting in early 1970. Gravenites told *Rolling Stone* of their plans to record as the Electric Flag and possibly tour. Although Buddy Miles agreed to rejoin, the recordings never took place.

In a 1971 interview with *Guitar Player,* Bloomfield reflected on his experiences with the band: "Well, you know the Flag was a good band, but it got incredibly pushed. . . . And we never had time to mature as a band, dialectically, or even as people. The thing that made us close together was our obligation: we had to make this, we had to make that, we had to write."

Postscript

In 1974, Bloomfield, Gravenites, Miles, Goldberg and bassist Roger "Jellyroll" Troy recorded an album called *The Band Kept Playing* under the Electric Flag banner for Atlantic Records. As with the Electric Flag's prior album, it did not find commercial success and no further recordings were forthcoming.

Following the breakup of the Electric Flag, Buddy Miles wasted little time in forming a new group, the Buddy Miles Express, which he modeled after the Electric Flag. The Buddy Miles Express brought over four members of the Electric Flag—Herbie Rich (organ), Gonsalves, Clements and Doubleday—along with guitarist Jimmy McCarty (formerly with the Siegel-Schwall Band [see **Siegel-Schwall Band**] and Mitch Ryder's Detroit Wheels), bassist Billy Rich and tenor saxophonist Bob McPherson.

The Buddy Miles Express released one album, *Expressway to Your Skull* (1968), followed by a second with a reshuffled lineup, *Electric Church* (1969). *Electric Church* included four tracks produced by Jimi Hendrix, and following its release Miles left the Express to join Hendrix and Billy Cox in the short-lived Band of Gypsies, which released an eponymous live album. In addition, Miles's album releases include *Them Changes* (1970), *We Got to Live Together* (1970), *Message to the People* (1970), *Live* (1971), *Carlos Santana and Buddy Miles Live!* (1972), *Chapter VII* (1973), *All the Faces of Buddy Miles* (1974), *More Miles Per Gallon* (1975), *Bicentennial Gathering* (1976), *Sneak Attack* (1981), *Hell & Back* (1994), *Tribute to Jimi Hendrix* (1997) and *Miles Away from Home* (1997).

From 1987 to 1990, Miles also played drums and sang on albums released by the cartoon band "the California Raisins" that was inspired by the successful television campaign by the Raisin Growers Association.

Harvey Brooks returned to session work after the breakup of the Electric Flag, which included the *Bloomfield/Kooper/Stills Super Session* and dates with Richie Havens, Miles Davis, and the Doors. In 1972, he formed the Fabulous Rhinestones with keyboardist Martin Grebb (formerly of the Buckinghams). Brooks appeared on three albums issued by the Rhinestones: *The Fabulous Rhinestones* (1972), *Freewheelin'* (1973), and *The Rhinestones . . . Just Sunshine* (1975).

Discography

Release Date	Title	Catalog Number

U.S. Singles

1967	Peter's Trip/Green and Gold	Sidewalk 929
1967	Groovin' Is Easy/Over Lovin' You	Columbia 44307
1967	Sunny/Soul Searchin'	Columbia 44376

U.S. Albums

1968 *A Long Time Comin'* Columbia CS-9597
Killing Floor/Groovin' Is Easy/Over Lovin' You/She Should Have Just/Wine/Texas/Sittin' in Circles/You Don't Realize/Another Country/Easy Rider

1968 *An American Music Band* Columbia CS-9714
Soul Searchin'/Sunny/With Time There Is Change/Nothing to Do/See to Your Neighbor/Qualified/Hey, Little Girl/Mystery/My Woman that Hangs Around the House

1995 *Old Glory: The Best of* Legacy/Columbia
the Electric Flag (CD) CK 57629
Killing Floor/Groovin' Is Easy/She Should Have Just/Goin' Down Slow/Texas/Sittin' in Circles (alternate version)/You Don't Realize/Movie Music Improvisation/Another Country/Easy Rider/Soul Searchin'/See to Your Neighbor/With Time There Is Change/Nothing to Do/Hey Little Girl/Drinkin' Wine (Live—Monterey Pop Festival)/The Night Time Is the Right Time (Live—Monterey Pop Festival

Miscellaneous U.S. Releases

1967 *The Trip* (movie soundtrack) Sidewalk T-5908 (M) Sidewalk ST-5908 (S)
Peter's Trip/Joint Passing/Psyche Soap/M-23/Synethesia/A Little Head/Hobbit/Inner Pocket/Fewghh/The Other Ed Norton/Green and Gold/Flash, Bam, Pow/Home Room/Peter Gets Off/Practice Music/Fine Jung Thing/Senior Citizen/Gettin' Hard

1969 *You Are What You Eat* Columbia OS-3240
(movie soundtrack)
Includes one song by the Electric Flag, "Freakout."

1994 *Monterey Pop Festival* (4 CD) Rhino R2 70596
Includes two songs by the Electric Flag, "Groovin' Is Easy" and "Drinkin' Wine."

U.K. Singles

1969	Groovin' Is Easy/Over Lovin' You	CBS 3584
1969	Sunny/Soul Searchin'	CBS 4066

U.K. Albums

1968	*A Long Time Comin'*	CBS 62394
1969	*The Electric Flag—An American Music Band*	CBS 63462
1983	*Groovin' Is Easy*	Thunderbolt THBL 1006

Live recordings that the liner notes suggest were made in the '60s.
Spotlight/I Was Robbed Last Night/I Found Out/Never Be Lonely Again/Losing Game/My Baby Wants to Test Me/I Should Have Left Her/You Don't Realize/Groovin' Is Easy

Miscellaneous U.K. Releases

1997 *The Monterey International* Ode Sounds &
Pop Festival (4 CD) Visuals 72825

Fleetwood Mac

In a career that spanned over 30 years, Fleetwood Mac evolved from a blues purist spin-off group of John Mayall's Bluesbreakers to one of the top mainstream pop-rock act of the 1970s that continues to be successful. While later lineups of Fleetwood Mac achieved unprecedented album sales and international superstar status, the first three years of the band's existence under the stewardship of Peter Green holds the most interest for fans of hard-edged, innovative blues-rock.

Fleetwood Mac was founded in 1967 by the gifted yet troubled songwriter/guitarist/vocalist Peter Green (b. Peter

Alan Greenbaum, October 29, 1946; Bethnal Green, London, U.K.). Green was born in London's East End and was first drawn to the blues after hearing Muddy Waters's "Honey Bee" at age 14. Before that he was also a big fan of 1950s American rock'n'roll; his first guitar hero was the Shadows' lead player (and Buddy Holly look-alike) Hank Marvin. The young Green first picked up a guitar at age 10, and within a couple of years he was strumming such classic Shadows' instrumentals as "Apache" at family gatherings, accompanied on rhythm guitar by his elder brother Michael. The first amateur band he played with was the Strangers—a skiffle group that played school dance halls and youth clubs for fun.

Green's early semi-professional days saw him switch to bass guitar and play in a succession of local bands, including Bobby Dennis and the Dominoes, the Tridents, the Diddlios, and the R&B-influenced Muskrats. Prompted by Eric Clapton's increasing popularity as featured guitarist in the Yardbirds, Green switched back to guitar in 1965 [see **Eric Clapton**]. One of his first gigs as a guitarist was to temporarily fill in for Clapton—a Bluesbreaker at the time—during a few dates in August 1965 [see **John Mayall**]. He also had a very short-lived stay in a jazzy blues ensemble called Errol Dixon and the Honeydrippers.

Then, in February 1966, Green joined Peter B's Looners (later the Peter B's), a Stax-styled instrumental band led by keyboardist Peter Bardens that featured drummer Mick Fleetwood (b. June 24, 1947; Redruth, Cornwall, U.K.). Fleetwood had previously played in such London R&B bands as the Cheynes and the Bo Street Runners. While with the Cheynes, Fleetwood had appeared on three singles: "Respectable" backed with "It's Gonna Happen to You" (U.K./Columbia DB 7153), "Goin' to the River" backed with "Cheyne-Re-La" (U.K./Columbia DB 7368) and "Down and Out" backed with "Stop Running Round" (U.K./Columbia DB 7464)—released in 1963, 1964 and 1965, respectively. Fleetwood had also appeared on the Bo Street Runners' single, "Baby Never Say Goodbye" backed with "Get Out of My Way" (U.K./Columbia DB 7640), issued in 1965.

Fleetwood (a seasoned pro compared to the very green Green) was decidedly unimpressed by the guitar-playing talents of his future Fleetwood Mac boss when Green auditioned for the Peter B's spot. But, together the group recorded one single, "If You Wanna Stay Happy" backed with "Jodrell Blues" (U.K./Columbia DB 7862), released in March 1966. The single was not a commercial success, but it gave Green his first studio experience, and his fea-

tured guitar on the B-side today sounds in parts like a sincere tribute to his mentor, Eric Clapton.

In May 1966, the Peter B's added vocalists Rod Stewart and Beryl Marsden and changed their name to Shotgun Express. Green and Marsden became romantically involved, and soon after she declined his marriage proposal, he quit the band in July 1966 to replace the Cream-bound Eric Clapton as a permanent member of the Bluesbreakers. Shotgun Express lasted ten months, releasing two singles without Green, "I Could Feel the Whole World Turn Round" backed with "Curtains" (U.K./Columbia DB 8025) and "Funny 'Cos Neither Could I" backed with "Indian Thing" (U.K./Columbia DB 8178), issued in 1966 and 1967, respectively. Both singles featured Fleetwood at the drum stool.

Green joined the Bluesbreakers, which at the time consisted of Mayall, bassist John McVie and drummer Hughie Flint (who was soon replaced by Aynsley Dunbar [see **Aynsley Dunbar Retaliation**]. This incarnation of Mayall's Bluesbreakers recorded an EP with Paul Butterfield, two singles, and an album (*A Hard Road*) released in February 1967. Eric Clapton must have been one of the hardest acts to follow in the entire history of British blues-rock, but Green kept his nerve in the face of occasional taunts from diehard Clapton fans at Mayall gigs. This attitude, along with the commercial success of *A Hard Road* and Green's increasingly self-assured performances at gigs, elevated his stature and fast made him one of the most prominent guitarists in the country.

Mayall politely asked Dunbar to leave the Bluesbreakers in April 1967 because his drumming was getting too technical and busy for Mayall's liking, so Dunbar left to join the Jeff Beck group. When Mayall then asked Fleetwood—to his complete amazement—to replace Dunbar in the Bluesbreakers, the nucleus of Fleetwood Mac was unwittingly formed. (Since the demise of Shotgun Express, Fleetwood had spent his time starting an interior design business.)

But Fleetwood's stay in the Bluesbreakers was short-lived: it only took five weeks for Mayall to realize that, as was the case with John McVie, Fleetwood's need for boozed-up good times at gigs was greater than his need to keep good time on the drums. So by May 1967, Fleetwood was out and Keef Hartley was in. Still, during his short spell as a Bluesbreaker, he contributed some characteristically solid drumming on a single they released, "Double Trouble" backed with "It Hurts Me Too." An instrumental track recorded at the same mid-April 1967 session was a precursor of things to come in that it was recorded without Mayall and credited to the Bluesbreakers alone.

The track in question—"Fleetwood Mac"—was driven by McVie's chugging bass lines and Green's guitar and train-whistle harmonica. To Green, the music (inspired by Johnny Young's "Slamhammer") sounded like an American express train at high speed—and the name "Fleetwood Mac" (Mac referring to McVie) sounded like the name of a train. Although none of the musicians knew it (at the time, the song was just another enjoyable and vaguely structured studio jam), blues-rock history was made that day, April 19, 1967.

In what was a surprise move at the time, Green left Mayall's Bluesbreakers on June 15, 1967, after less than a year with the band. The main reason was the increasingly jazzy feel of some of the band's material. Mayall was beginning to use a horn section, and some of the arrangements were not to Green's liking. In particular, today Green remembers "Leaping Christine" on the *A Hard Road* album as being like a "bad joke."

At the time of his departure, Green had no clear plans for the future. He was considering going to Chicago to check out the blues scene at the street level, but work-permit and visa hassles shelved the idea. Instead, he sat in on a London session organized by Aynsley Dunbar that included Jack Bruce on bass and Rod Stewart on vocals. The session produced one track, a cover of Buddy Guy's "Stone Crazy," which surfaced on the 1973 Sire compilation, *History of British Blues*.

At this point, Green was still in touch with *A Hard Road* producer Mike Vernon, then a Decca house producer who, along with his brother Richard, also operated Blue Horizon, a small blues specialty label. But the Vernon brothers had bigger things in mind for Blue Horizon. Mike tried unsuccessfully to persuade Decca to distribute the label—but then met with success at CBS. In doing so, he dealt himself out of his salaried job at Decca and became an independent producer concentrating all his efforts on Blue Horizon. Naturally, he was hoping to add a Peter Green-led band to the fledgling label's roster of artists.

The precise timing and sequence of events leading to Blue Horizon's signing of Fleetwood Mac have become blurred over time, but it's likely that some of the planning was already going on while Green was still playing with Mayall. Vernon arranged for guitarist Jeremy Spencer (b.

July 4, 1948; West Hartlepool, Durham, U.K.) to watch one of Green's last gigs with Mayall at Le Metro club in Birmingham. Green may even have heard a demo tape of this frontman and his mediocre Birmingham blues trio, the Levi Set, beforehand. But Spencer certainly did have an informal jam with Green after the Metro gig, and Green was impressed by the "conviction" Jeremy put into his interpretations of Elmore James- and Homesick James-style slide guitar playing.

By hiring Spencer, from the very start Green began resisting the pressures of being the sole frontman. He insisted on having a second guitarist to share the spotlight and, some say, to be a warm-up artist playing upbeat R&B before Green took over and performed his quieter and darker blues. Very soon after this initial introduction, Spencer moved to London and became a member of the band.

Spencer's interest in music had begun at age nine when he had started taking piano lessons. Initially, he had been influenced by the music of Buddy Holly, Cliff Richard and the Shadows, and later Jerry Lee Lewis and Ray Charles. Blues music didn't begin appealing to him until he was 16, when he had an epiphany after hearing a recording of Elmore James on a compilation album. A year later, after breaking his leg, Spencer acquired one of James's albums and spent his time recuperating by mastering James's electric slide guitar technique.

Mick Fleetwood abandoned the paintbrush and ladders of his interior design business altogether in early June to commit to the new band, but the opening for the group's bass player proved much more difficult to fill. After John McVie (b. November 26, 1945; Ealing, Middlesex, U.K.) declined the spot, various bass players on the London scene came to audition, including Ric Grech and Dave Ambrose (who had been Green's and Fleetwood's colleague in the Peter B's). They eventually found Bob Brunning by placing an ad in *Melody Maker* [see **Brunning Hall Sunflower Blues Band**]. Green and the others told him that he was strictly a temporary replacement until they could persuade McVie to leave Mayall's Bluesbreakers.

Now that they had filled all their positions, they scheduled their debut performance at the Windsor Jazz and Blues Festival on August 13, 1967. Because the festival was less than a month away, the band started rehearsals immediately in a pub on Fulham Road called the Black Bull. Billed as "the debut of Peter Green's Fleetwood Mac," the group made their first live appearance before an audience of 30,000 at the Windsor Festival. Their 20-minute set was well received, despite some technical glitches. Later that night they played a more relaxed, hour-long set at a remote fringe venue on the festival site.

Following Windsor, Fleetwood Mac's next gig was at London's Marquee Club on August 15, 1967. (A primitive recording of this show was released in 1992 on the CD *Live at the Marquee*.) After the Marquee date, the band began gigging continuously, building up a strong reputation on the blues-club circuit, which was thriving at the time. They performed at least four nights a week at dates that included the Saville Theatre in London and an open-air festival in the Midlands.

On September 9, 1967, Fleetwood Mac went into the studio to record the two tracks that would comprise their first single, "I Believe My Time Ain't Long" backed with "Rambling Pony," released in November 1967. The A-side of the single was a Jeremy Spencer cover of an Elmore James song, while the flip side consisted of a Peter Green rewrite of the Hambone Willie Newbern standard, "Rollin' and Tumblin'." On the same day, a news item in *Melody Maker* announced, "Former Zoot Money bass guitarist Paul Williams [has] joined John Mayall's Bluesbreakers, replacing John McVie who is leaving to join Peter Green's Fleetwood Mac."

And so the initial Fleetwood Mac studio session proved to be Bob Brunning's swan song after just one month and a handful of gigs. After sitting on the fence, John McVie finally decided that even the security of a regular and fat paycheck with Mayall wasn't worthwhile when he didn't enjoy the music he was playing. Mayall was determinedly heading in a free-form jazz direction, much to McVie's boredom and displeasure.

Now with McVie, the band returned to the studio in November to record mostly blues covers for their debut album, *Peter Green's Fleetwood Mac*. Recorded in just over three days in two different studios, the LP has sometimes been referred to as the "dog and dustbin" album because of the cover, which artfully depicted the squalor of an urban alleyway in Battersea (London's answer to a run-down South Side Chicago housing project).

The material on the LP consisted of a mixture of classic blues songs and original material, with Green and Spencer sharing the vocals equally among the tracks. Highlights included a powerful rendering of Elmore James's "Shake Your Moneymaker" and two Green originals—

the moody and unsettling "I Loved Another Woman" and the fiery, harmonica-powered "Long Grey Mare" (inspired by Howlin' Wolf's "Killing Floor").

Released in the U.K. in February 1968, the album became a surprise hit, reaching #4 on the British charts and staying in the charts for 37 weeks. This previously unheard-of phenomenon—a blues album riding high in the pop charts—reflected the band's massive pulling power on the blues-club circuit. The year 1968 also saw the peak of the British blues boom; subsidiaries of major labels and majors themselves were frantically signing up new blues-rock acts. Yet within two years, attendance at clubs fell heavily and the boom went bust.

Peter Green's Fleetwood Mac came out on Epic in the U.S. not long after but only reached #198 on the U.S. charts. It nevertheless garnered a semi-favorable review from *Rolling Stone*, which printed, "On this, their first recorded effort, Fleetwood Mac have established themselves as another tight English blues band." But the magazine also described a lack of identity: "[Fleetwood Mac] know what they're doing, they dig the music they're playing and that's great, but the drawback here is that they don't put enough of themselves into it instead of what they've heard from the original artists."

This criticism was echoed by *Jazz & Pop*, which implored, "Fleetwood Mac is too good a group to see slavishly copying somebody else's music. They could do so much more if they would only free themselves a bit and look to other styles—perhaps they might even play some British music, who knows." In Britain, however, the critics embraced the new group. *Beat Instrumental* called the album "the best English blues LP ever released here." And a *New Musical Express* reviewer declared, "I wondered where the early Animal and Stones music had gone . . . well, here it is." (Outtakes from the first album—including two strong Green originals that were further developed later, "Fool No More" and "Leaving Town Blues"—were released by CBS in 1971 as *The Original Fleetwood Mac*.)

With the recording of their next single, "Black Magic Woman," released in March 1968, Peter Green emerged as Fleetwood Mac's dominant creative force. Featuring his confident vocals and economical, reverb-laden guitar, the song peaked at #37 and marked the group's first entry into the British singles charts.

With ongoing gigs, Fleetwood Mac began to solidify their album and single success. A club date they recorded during this period eventually came out on a 1986 British CD, *London Live '68*. Recorded in April 1968, this primitive recording contained only two songs from their first album, "Got to Move" and "The World Keep on Turning." They never even released six of the eight songs they performed that night, including two associated with B.B. King—"Buzz Me" and "How Blue Can You Get."

Also not included on this release were some of the rock standards that the band had started to incorporate into their act, such as "Ready Teddy" and "Lucille." Eventually, they augmented their blues set with several rock'n'roll numbers. During these, Spencer would flourish as an extroverted showman, often with an alarming vulgarity that alienated the more earnest blues purists. This penchant for onstage pornography even got the group banned from the Marquee club in London.

In July 1968, following a brief exploratory tour of the U.S. West Coast, the band issued their next single, a cover of Little Willie John's "Need Your Love So Bad." This exquisite, nearly flawless single featured Green's most soulful vocals to date coupled with a tasteful string arrangement scored by Mickey Baker (formerly of Mickey and Sylvia). Remarkably, though one of the finest singles of the era, the record only managed to reach a disappointing #31 on the British charts.

At first, Vernon and Green wanted to release the seven-minute take (now available on Sony's 6 CD boxed set *The Complete Blue Horizon Sessions*) as a double A-side. But eventually they chose "Stop Messin' 'Round," a hard-driving 12-bar blues song featuring Green, for the flip side. The use of horns and pianist Christine Perfect on "Stop Messin' 'Round" indicated the direction of the next album. At that time, Perfect was becoming well known as the keyboard player and vocalist with label-mates Chicken Shack [see **Chicken Shack**]. She was also John McVie's wife. The couple had met at the 1967 Windsor Festival—where their respective bands both made their official British debut appearances—and were married within a year.

Blue Horizon issued the group's second album, *Mr. Wonderful*, in August 1968. Augmented by a horn section and Christine McVie (Perfect) on piano, *Mr. Wonderful* was an inconsistent LP, but had moments of brilliance. One outstanding track was the Green composition "Love That Burns," hailed by *Rolling Stone* as a candidate for the "finest white recording of the blues ever made."

Other highlights included "Rollin' Man," which featured some exciting interplay between Green and the horn section; an alternate take of "Stop Messin' 'Round"; and "Lazy Poker Blues." Unfortunately, all of the strong material came from Green, whereas Spencer's endless recycling of Elmore James riffs bogged the album down. *New Musical Express* quipped that *Mr. Wonderful* was "unadventurous British Blues that seems rather dull after recent albums by Ten Years After and the Cream." However, *Beat Instrumental* was enthusiastic, calling the album "just about brilliant, all round." The high expectations that resulted from the surprising success of their debut LP made the follow-up album's climb to a mere #10 in the British charts somewhat disappointing.

Following the release of *Mr. Wonderful*, the band startled the pop world by drafting a third guitarist into the lineup—Danny Kirwan. Until then, three lead guitarists in one band had been unheard of. The move was Mick Fleetwood's idea.

Already, just one year in, Mick Fleetwood was naturally assuming the player/manager role he later would formalize in the *Rumours* lineup. With Spencer failing to progress, Fleetwood was anxious to find another guitarist to share front-line responsibilities and be there for Green to bounce ideas off. Spencer was also a liability in that he refused to learn any of Green's songs and therefore didn't participate in their recording or performance.

The new guitarist, Kirwan (b. May 13, 1950; South London, U.K.) first started to play guitar at age 15 and became interested in the blues after hearing John Mayall with Eric Clapton. He also had eclectic tastes that encompassed many eras of popular music, from Big Band to 1950s pop ballads.

Kirwan's first band was the Boilerhouse, in which he played lead guitar along with his friends David Terry on drums and Trevor Stevens on bass. Their first gig was at the Blue Horizon Club, located in the upstairs club of the Nag's Head in Battersea, London, where they supported Fleetwood Mac. Green was impressed with Kirwan and arranged for his band to play at the Marquee in December 1967. However, Fleetwood and Green didn't think that the rest of Boilerhouse was up to par, so they first tried to find suitable musicians to build a band around Kirwan. In an article that ran in the July 1968 issue of *Beat Instrumental*, Green praised Kirwan and Duster Bennett as "the only guys in this country who could make me say 'Yeah,' when I listen to them." After they placed ads in *Melody Maker* and still couldn't find an acceptable rhythm section to support Kirwan, they abandoned the idea in favor of adding 18-year-old Kirwan to the Fleetwood Mac lineup.

Kirwan's joining Fleetwood Mac was not the unanimously welcome move that Fleetwood Mac legend has suggested. The other band members—Green included—had their doubts, but soon Mick Fleetwood's intuition was validated.

Adding Kirwan paid immediate dividends with their next single, "Albatross." Released in mid-November 1968, "Albatross" was a laid-back instrumental with a Hawaiian guitar feel that surprisingly took the song to the top of the British singles charts in early January 1969. This marked the start of a new Fleetwood Mac sound—twin-guitar harmonies sometimes reminiscent of the Allman Brothers. While the success of "Albatross" alienated many of the band's hard-core followers (who cried "sellout") the single catapulted the group to top British-pop-attraction status almost overnight. The B-side, "Jigsaw Puzzle Blues," was a Django Reinhardt-influenced instrumental that Kirwan had written.

In December 1968, Fleetwood Mac began their second American tour. When the band opened for Muddy Waters in Chicago, they learned that the famed Chess Records studio was going to be closed down in 1969, and so trusted producer Vernon arranged for the band to record there in January. They invited various blues legends to the two-day sessions, including Muddy Waters's piano player, Otis Spann; Walter "Shakey" Horton on harp; guitarist Honeyboy Edwards (who knew Robert Johnson); Elmore James's tenor saxophonist, J.T. Brown; S.P. Leary on drums; and the legendary Willie Dixon on bass. Buddy Guy also made a cameo appearance using the pseudonym Guitar Buddy. The very loosely structured sessions yielded a double album, *Blues Jam at Chess*, issued a year later by Blue Horizon.

While this "fathers-and-sons" concept made for some interesting listening, a disgruntled Green later commented, "We didn't record enough songs for a double album. Therefore, it can't be a Fleetwood Mac album." The group, minus Mick Fleetwood, also backed Spann on his album, *The Biggest Thing Since Colossus*—an album featuring some of Green's most fluent and tasteful blues guitar.

Fleetwood Mac's contract with Blue Horizon expired in early 1969. Due to an appalling administrative oversight, the label failed to take up its option for a further year,

so the group's manager, Clifford Davis, announced that they were leaving Blue Horizon—something Green was unhappy about. Andrew Oldham's Immediate label ended up issuing the beautiful and haunting "Man of the World" single in April 1969, even though Mike Vernon had initially begun to produce it at Tempo Studios in New York that January.

The song's introspective lyrics suggested that despite his massive success, Green was not entirely happy with his life and this was perhaps the first indication that Green had developed certain antipathies for the music business. The single's flip side was a Jeremy Spencer rock'n'roll pastiche, "Somebody's Gonna Get Their Head Kicked in Tonight," credited to "Earl Vince and the Valiants."

"Man of the World" reached #2 on the British charts—an achievement that was helped along by some radio plugs financed by the astute Clifford Davis. Following the release of the single, the band was temporarily without a recording contract. Although Apple Records was a rumored contender, Fleetwood Mac ultimately signed a deal with Reprise, a new subsidiary of Warner Brothers.

In April 1969, the band started work on their next album, which they recorded over a four-month period. Rather than using an outside producer, they elected to produce the album themselves with the assistance of recording engineer Martin Birch.

In June, Green told the press that he favored releasing Kirwan's yet-to-be-recorded "When You Say" as their next single. However, they had to delay recording the ballad while engineer Birch recovered from a car crash. As things turned out, the track did not become a single, but Christine McVie recorded it as her first solo single and Kirwan's version went on the forthcoming Fleetwood Mac album, *Then Play On*.

Then in July, Green and Spencer announced ambitious plans for an "orchestral-choral LP" that would tell the story of Jesus. Some speculate that around this time Green's interest in religion began to engulf him. As he explained to *New Musical Express,* "I had a strong feeling that I was walking and talking with God. I was drawing away from music into just being a Christian person and it made me such a very, very happy person." Eventually Green abandoned the idea.

Meanwhile, in a calculating move designed to preempt their debut release on Reprise and cash in on the band's escalating fame, Blue Horizon issued a compilation album, *The Pious Bird of Good Omen*, which reached #18 on the British charts. Reprise then released *Then Play On*, the first release for the label, a month later. Recorded from April through July 1969, *Then Play On* was a transitional effort, with Green in some ways abdicating his leadership by composing just five tracks compared to Kirwan's seven. They rounded out the album with two instrumentals, "Searching for Madge" and "Fighting for Madge." These guitar feasts were highlights from extended jams that Green had then painstakingly edited. They were also Green's covert declaration of where he wanted the band to go musically, which was into extended free-form jams in the style of the Grateful Dead. Spencer, McVie and Fleetwood were not happy with his vision. Whereas Green was able to improvise freely, free-form did not suit their playing styles, and so they weren't able to contribute much. A little less than a year before Green finally left Fleetwood Mac, the cracks had begun to show.

The band had intended for *Then Play On* to include a bonus Jeremy Spencer EP of parodies, "The Milton Schlitz Show," that included wicked impersonations of Alexis Korner and John Mayall, however Reprise vetoed the idea. These recordings—in parts very funny—emerged much later on the 1998 CD, *The Vaudeville Years of Fleetwood Mac*. Having been edged out by Kirwan and then having had his parodies nixed, in effect Jeremy Spencer didn't have any part in *Then Play On*.

Released in September 1969, the album received positive reviews from the British press. *Melody Maker* enthused that the release was "a great leap forward for the Mac" while *Beat Instrumental* described it as "Fleetwood Mac, at their very, very best," continuing with, "Peter Green's characteristic guitar playing is evident throughout, and this LP can only add to his fast-growing stature as one of the best guitarists in Britain." In America, *Rolling Stone* was typically less enthusiastic, describing the album as "slow and wandering—instrumentals in search of an idea."

While their latest LP release garnered mixed reviews, Fleetwood Mac's next double A-side single released the same month, "Oh Well Parts 1 & 2," received universal acclaim, even though both Fleetwood and McVie had serious doubts about whether or not the left-field combination of progressive rock, rap, and classical guitar was commercial enough to make it a good single. *New Musical Express* described "Oh Well" as "a record of startling contrasts—assaulting your ears at the outset, then suddenly switching to a charming Spanish guitar theme with a fla-

menco quality." *Melody Maker* gave it high marks as "an extraordinary project which succeeds on all levels," promising that it would "undoubtedly give the group their biggest hit to date—if there is any justice." Justice in fact prevailed as the scorching yet complex single reached #2 on the British charts. (Later U.S. pressings of *Then Play On* included "Oh Well" as an added track.) Yet at one point prior to the single's release, Green had seriously considered bringing "Oh Well" out as solo release because of his colleagues' lukewarm embrace of the songs, which was a further indication of mounting dissension within the band. There was already talk around this time of Green quitting, but manager Davis dissuaded him for the sake of the others.

In November, the group embarked on what they called their second (not third) U.S. tour. (Apparently they never regarded their first brief excursion in the summer of 1968 as a proper tour.) According to some, during this three-month trek Green's behavior became increasingly erratic. He had become deeply interested in both Buddhism and Christianity, even renouncing his Jewish faith. He often wore long white robes and caftans with a big crucifix hung around his neck. Although media focus was often on Green, some music press reports also suggested that Kirwan also wanted out of the band as soon as they returned to England.

During the U.S. tour, Fleetwood Mac recorded some concerts at the Boston Tea Party club for a projected live album that was eventually scrapped. Some of the concert recordings appeared on the 1984 Shanghai Records release, *Live in Boston*, which contained about 35 minutes of material. In 1985, Shanghai issued another 95 minutes of material as a double album. Eventually, just over two hours of material from the Boston Tea Party tapes were issued in various packages on several different labels.

These Boston tapes indicate that despite the group's inner turmoil, they were still a top band performing at their peak. Highlights included a tight "Oh Well"; "Black Magic Woman"; the slow-building, ominous "Jumping at Shadows"; and Kirwan's "Like It This Way" (featuring some exciting six-string interplay between Kirwan and Green). One-third of the songs were rock'n'roll standards, mostly performed by Jeremy Spencer, who by now displayed complete mastery (or mimicry) of the Homesick James/Elmore James slide guitar idiom on blues such as "Got to Move." In retrospect, *Live in Boston* became an essential recording of the classic three-guitar lineup. Poorer sounding live recordings from their January 4, 1970, Fillmore West appearance were released on the 1994 German CD, *The Original Fleetwood Mac Blues Band.*

Fleetwood Mac were at the peak of their initial popularity by the end of 1969. The band even topped the Beatles in *Melody Maker's* Most Popular Artists poll that year, which was based on the number of weeks a band's record releases had spent in the charts.

During this time, Jeremy Spencer took the opportunity to record a self-titled solo album in which he explored his love of 1950s music. It featured Fleetwood Mac as his backing band (with Peter Green playing banjo on just one track) and was released in November 1970. An homage to 1950s rock'n'roll, the album was well received by the British music press. *Melody Maker* said it was "required listening for all" and *Record Mirror* optimistically declared, "It's really gonna be number one! Well, it'd better be—or else rock'n'roll is dead." The single from the album, "Linda," sounded like it was derived from Tommy Roe's "Sheila," which itself was derived from Buddy Holly. In spite of the favorable press, both the single and the album met with public disinterest.

Spring arrived and the band left for a European tour that began in March 1970—a tour that augured the end of the original Fleetwood Mac. When the group reached Munich, Green hooked up with some rich young hippies "blissed out" on a definitively 1960s bohemian trip. Legend has it that the hippies dosed Green with LSD continuously for three days until Mick Fleetwood and road managers Dennis Keen and Dinky Dawson rescued him.

What happened next, according to Mick Fleetwood's autobiography, was that Green "told [the band] he was finished. He said he was in a panic, that he couldn't handle the money, that he was just a working-class person, "The was going to leave Fleetwood Mac as soon as possible." After a protracted negotiation, they persuaded Green to return to the hotel and join the rest of the band. Years later, Dawson wrote in his memoir, *Life on the Road.* "The person we brought back to the hotel would never again be the man I'd known. One moment he'd express mellow sentiments of 'peace and love,' the next second he'd hurl a torrent of screams and curses at anything." Mick Fleetwood and John McVie both contend that this Munich encounter irreparably skewed Green's grasp on reality.

Both Green and Dennis Keen have a different take on what happened in Munich. They contend that it wasn't a three-day LSD binge; Green stayed just one night. He also

wasn't "dosed"—he was offered and gladly accepted the drug, as did his minder at the house party, Dennis Keen, who himself suffered no nasty after-effects from the stuff.

Perhaps the most significant and least often mentioned aspect of Green's Munich experience is Green's recollection of the next night's gig in Nuremberg. He said that his ability to improvise had become better than ever in the afterglow of the LSD, which took him down a musical road that can be heard today on various bootlegs of concerts where he performed before leaving the band in May. He developed an extended live version of his forthcoming hit single, "The Green Manalishi (with the Two-Prong Crown)," which ended with Green improvising on guitar and six-string bass accompanied by Fleetwood on kick drum and high-hat cymbals. His melodic ideas and fluency when performing in this format were exceptional, but Green now wryly remembers that Fleetwood's response was to point out that Green's playing sounded like he was "mad." On the tour bus in Sweden, Green broke the bad news of his plans to leave to manager Clifford Davis, who recalled that the reason Green gave him for deciding to quit was that the rest of the band were "just not cutting it."

And so in April, Peter Green, deeply disappointed that his band couldn't or wouldn't follow his new musical vision, stunned the pop music world by announcing his intention to leave Fleetwood Mac. Besides the musical schism, Green had been further alienated by his friends' differing religious and political beliefs, especially since his own beliefs were becoming more pronounced. For instance, he wanted the band to contribute some of the money they earned from gigs to worthwhile charities, an idea the others rejected.

Green explained his decision to leave to *New Musical Express*, saying, "There are many reasons; the main thing being that I feel it is time for a change. I want to change my whole life because I really don't want to be part of the conditioned world, and as much as possible, I am getting out of it. I am always concerned with what is right with God and what God would have me do . . . that is the most important thing to me . . . that dominates every thought in my head." The music press generally portrayed him as having become something of a religious fanatic.

Reprise released one final Peter Green single in early May, "The Green Manalishi (with the Two Prong Crown)." Green said that this heavy rock song was inspired by a nightmare he'd had some months earlier in which he had died and become isolated from the real world by all the money he was making. The "Green Manalishi" was a reference to greenbacks (dollar bills). The single reached #10 on the British charts.

Green's last live gig with the band occurred at the end of May at the Bath City football stadium. Soon afterward, the band recorded one final TV show for the BBC. Dinky Dawson remembers this time as a sad era in which Green, the departing leader, was hardly on speaking terms with the others.

Without Green, and after much soul-searching, the group elected to continue as a four-piece and regrouped at a property they'd rented known as Kiln House, located in Alton, a rural village in Hampshire. Jeremy Spencer shifted the band's direction back to vintage 1950s rock'n'roll and rockabilly, alternating with Danny Kirwan's characteristically eclectic bag of heavy rock, pop and country ballads, and instrumentals. Their subsequent album, *Kiln House,* reflected these disparate tastes.

Released in September 1970, *Kiln House* contained many fine moments, particularly Spencer's Elvis take-off, "This Is the Rock," and Kirwan's "Station Man," which featured his strong guitar work and a tasteful arrangement.

Christine McVie assisted the band by singing and playing on some of the tracks as well as drawing the cover art. *New Musical Express* commented, *"Kiln House* is a fine album with a character of its own and promises well for the band's future." The album reached #39 on the British charts and became the first album to break into the American charts, where it reached #69. Inspired by its U.S. chart action, the group decided to embark on an American tour.

To fill out the band's sound, the others asked Christine McVie to formally join the band. She had left Chicken Shack in April 1969 for a solo career that had fizzled. Despite being voted Top British Female Singer in the *Melody Maker* Pop Poll for 1969, a poorly received solo album and inadequately rehearsed debut tour pushed her into semi-retirement in April 1970.

Invigorated by Christine's presence and the U.S. audience's positive response to *Kiln House,* the band began their two-month U.S. tour in August 1970. With Christine, the band once again had three "front stars," each of whom had featured spots in the set. Toward the end of the year, the band members together purchased a vintage, lavish country house known as Benifold. Located near the rural

southwest village of Haslemere in England, the mansion became the new Fleetwood Mac communal retreat and rehearsal studio.

What had been a highly traumatic year ended on an even keel with the band playing successful shows at English clubs and European festivals. Before returning to the U.S. in February 1971 for a scheduled eight-week tour, the band released their first post-Green single in England. The A-side, "Dragonfly," was penned by Kirwan, as was the flip side, "The Purple Dancer." The release floundered despite being very well received by the music press.

While responsibility for the band's recorded output fell squarely on Kirwan's shoulders, Spencer's already popular rock'n'roll segment remained a mainstay of their live act—enough to warrant a mid-show costume change: he left the stage dressed down in jeans and T-shirt, and returned all done up in a Las Vegas-style gold lamé jacket, with hair coiffed into a high pompadour.

Then, just when the whole band—and Spencer in particular—were receiving uniformly rave reviews, Spencer temporarily disappeared—just ten months after Green's shocking departure.

On the day the band arrived in Los Angeles, Spencer vanished only hours before their scheduled appearance at the Whisky A Go-Go. He had been approached in the street by members of a religious cult called the Children of God, and based on its doctrine, he suddenly decided to completely reject rock'n'roll in favor of Jesus. When police intervention and S.O.S. calls over the radio failed to locate his whereabouts, the Whisky date had to be canceled.

Four days later they discovered him with the cult, his hair shorn and his name changed to Jonathan. Spencer indicated that he no longer wanted to play rock'n'roll and that his new purpose was to serve Jesus and God. While all this came as a near disastrous setback for the band, it was clear to both Clifford Davis and Dennis Keen, who visited him at his new home, that he was confident and happy about the dramatic change he had so abruptly made.

Still, with six weeks of contracted gigs to complete and fearing the financial repercussions of a canceled tour, in desperation they contacted Peter Green and asked if he would be willing to join them for the balance of the tour. Out of loyalty to his old bandmates, Green—whose eccentric and commercially unsuccessful first solo album, *End of the Game,* was in many parts an LSD-fueled free-form jam—agreed to fly over, but only on two strict conditions: first, the only song he would play from his old repertoire was "Black Magic Woman" and the balance of the night had to be free-form jamming, and second, he would be accompanied by his friend and conga player Nigel Watson, who would perform with the band. In spite of these restrictions, the tour went well. Even so, following the final date, their ex-leader again left the band (this time for good) and the rest of them returned to England to regroup.

Christine McVie and Kirwan both wanted a third writer to share the burden, so they began to search for a guitar player who could also sing and write. They held auditions, but finally found their player, Bob Welch, through an old friend named Judy Wong.

Welch was a struggling musician who had grown up in Beverly Hills and was now living in Paris. In 1964, he had joined a multiracial six-piece R&B band from Oregon known as Ivory Hudson and the Harlequins. The group played the Pacific Northwest circuit before relocating to Los Angeles and eventually landing a permanent spot at Maverick's Flat, a trendy black nightclub. Following a European tour, the band returned to Los Angeles, where they rechristened themselves the Seven Souls. The Seven Souls had become a popular nightclub attraction in Europe, where they had released several singles and an album. They released a few singles in the U.S., but these went nowhere and the group disbanded in Hawaii in 1969. Welch and two other members relocated to Paris, where they formed an R&B trio, Head West, which recorded one album for Disque Vogue before breaking up. Welch was in Europe when he received the call from Judy Wong in the spring of 1971.

Welch met with the band several times over the period of a month before they asked him to join. They made it immediately apparent to him that they wanted him to be a front-line member, contributing as much material as anyone else. Together, they spent June and July of 1971 touring the British club circuit (in venues several notches below those they'd played in their glory days with Green), then they entered the recording studio to record their next album, *Future Games*, which they released in September 1971.

Future Games was a relaxed, West Coast-influenced album that contained some fine moments, notably Welch's "Future Games" (which received strong FM airplay), Christine McVie's upbeat "Show Me a Smile," and Kirwan's "Sands of Time."

A reviewer for *Rolling Stone* panned the album, commenting, "*Future Games* is a thoroughly unsatisfactory album. It is thin and anemic-sounding and I get the impression that no one involved really put very much into it. If Fleetwood Mac have tried to make the transition from an energetic rocking British blues band to a softer more 'contemporary' rock group, they have failed." In spite of the sour review, Fleetwood Mac's U.S. tour in support of the album was their most successful in the U.S. to date and the album reached the lower rungs of the charts.

Having recorded their fifth album, *Bare Trees*, early in the year, the group spent most of 1972 touring the U.S. and Europe. Continuing in the same direction as its predecessor, *Bare Trees* included Welch's best-known track, "Sentimental Lady" (which also achieved substantial FM airplay), and Christine McVie's "Spare Me a Little of Your Love" (which remained a concert staple for years to come).

Rolling Stone singled out Kirwan's contributions for praise, noting, "With his multiple skills, Kirwan can't help being the focal point. It is his presence that makes Fleetwood Mac something more than another competent rock group. He gives them distinctiveness, a sting. He makes you want to hear these songs again." Very soon, the band was to discover that Kirwan was far from happy with the pressure of being the band's focal point.

Bare Trees reached #70 on the American charts, but just when the group seemed to have consolidated their U.S. following, what was becoming known as "the Fleetwood Mac curse" struck yet again. All that year, Kirwan had been drinking heavily, and he was having trouble getting along with the other band members. Finally, in an angry and inebriated outburst before a concert in August 1972, he smashed his vintage Les Paul Black Beauty guitar against a restroom wall and then refused to go onstage with the group. The remaining band members performed without him as he drunkenly heckled from the soundboard. Following the show, they decided to sack Kirwan. The group canceled the remainder of the tour and returned to England to regroup yet again.

Postscript

In late 1972, with ex-Savoy Brown singer Dave Walker as frontman and guitarist Bob Weston joining in, Fleetwood Mac began a downward spiral. The three lackluster albums they made during this period were mostly produced in trying and weird situations. The Walker/Weston sextet lasted for just one album—*Penguin* (1973). Walker was fired before the band recorded *Mystery to Me* (1973).

While touring America and promoting that album, Bob Weston began an affair with Mick Fleetwood's wife, Jenny Boyd. When Fleetwood found out, he immediately fired Weston and yet another Fleetwood Mac U.S. tour ground to a very dramatic and abrupt halt.

As with the Munich incident, myth and reality overlap with regard to what happened next. One version of events is that, completely without the band's knowledge, a Fleetwood Mac imposter (consisting of musical nobodies) suddenly went on the road in America and played a few dates before being exposed as frauds and forced off the stage by flying beer cans.

Another and very different take on the "fake Fleetwood Mac" saga is that everybody in the real band knew what was about to occur. Suddenly aborting the *Mystery to Me* U.S. tour had left hapless manager Clifford Davis facing financial ruin as aggrieved promoters threatened to sue him for breach of contract. Once Mick Fleetwood was over the worst of his marital problems in late 1973, some allege that he agreed to help Davis out of the mire by forming the "New Fleetwood Mac."

Initially, the existing band members were happy with the idea, because both John and Christine McVie as well as Welch actually wanted out in order to do their own thing. This left Fleetwood with the responsibility of trying to help out their manager.

Supposedly, Davis devised a plan to recruit seasoned musicians in England to fill in for the others. He held rehearsals in London, with a temporary drummer, for a Fleetwood Mac Greatest Hits show. For name credibility, Fleetwood was scheduled to take over once the band arrived in the U.S. to start the tour in January 1974. For reasons that remain a mystery, the plan went awry. Audiences rejected the lineup and demanded the "real" band.

Once safely back in England, some members of the doomed New Fleetwood Mac formed a band called Stretch and wrote a song, dedicated to Mick Fleetwood, about the whole bogus fiasco; the soul-funk "Why Did You Do It?" was a U.K. hit.

This episode also meant that the true Fleetwood Mac members spent most of the next year locked in a legal battle with Davis, now their former manager, over who owned the rights to the band's name. Eventually the matter was settled out of court and the remaining foursome—Fleetwood, the McVies and Welch—recorded *Heroes Are Hard to Find* (1974), their least inspired work, which ironically was their best U.S. seller to date (reaching #34 on the charts).

Bob Welch—suddenly but understandably suffering from burnout—quit Fleetwood Mac at the end of 1974 and was replaced by guitarist/vocalist/songwriter Lindsey Buckingham, whom Fleetwood had spotted while checking out a Los Angeles, California studio. Although at first interested only in Buckingham, the band agreed to hire both him and his partner and collaborator, singer/songwriter Stevie Nicks. This revamped lineup achieved superstardom with their next release, *Fleetwood Mac*, which climbed to #1 and remained on the American pop charts for an astounding 148 weeks. Subsequent releases—*Rumours* (1977), *Tusk* (1979), *Fleetwood Mac Live* (1981), *Mirage* (1982), *Tango in the Night* (1987) and *Greatest Hits* (1988)—all became huge sellers.

Buckingham's exit from Fleetwood Mac was set against the kind of drama that fans had come to expect of their fabulously theatrical band: a worldwide tour to promote the very accomplished and commercial new *Tango in the Night* album had been completely organized when at the last minute Buckingham announced that he couldn't go ahead with it. By now used to this kind of last minute defection, the rest of the band swiftly replaced him with guitarists Billy Burnette and Rick Vito (an ex-John Mayall Bluesbreaker) [see **John Mayall**]. *Behind the Mask* (1990) was the first release by the new lineup. More changes ensued shortly thereafter, leaving only Fleetwood and John McVie left from their core period. Their next release, *Time* (1995)—which featured Traffic's Dave Mason and Bonnie Bramlett's daughter Bekka—met with commercial indifference; the group was by now creatively adrift. Buckingham, Nicks and Christine McVie all rejoined for the 1998 reunion album, *The Dance*, which included some masterful reworkings of this lineup's classic songs. John McVie and Mick Fleetwood are set to record a new album with the Rumours lineup minus Christine McVie in late 2001.

Peter Green released an album of instrumental jams in November 1970 titled *The End of the Game*. He then retreated from music for most of the decade (with the exception of his short stint filling in for Jeremy Spencer during Spencer's unexpected departure). Green was expected to appear with Stone the Crows, filling in for the late Les Harvey during their 1972 appearance at the Lincoln Festival. He rehearsed with the band for six weeks but bowed out just two days before the festival and was replaced by Steve Howe. Later, in an effort to return to his roots, he gave away some of his earnings and his guitars and worked in a series of ordinary jobs.

Green released a few subsequent albums, including three recorded with Kolors, his unexceptional early-1980s band: *In the Skies* (1979), *Little Dreamer* (1980) and *Whatcha Gonna Do* (1981). With the notable exception of *In the Skies* (which charted), these albums showed little of the spark of his earlier works. Green's erratic behavior meant that he was becoming increasingly disoriented. He gave away many of his prized possessions and eventually vanished from the music scene in 1984, along with all hope that he would ever return. Green acknowledged that the use of hallucinogenic drugs harmed his mental heath.

Unflagging interest during the mid-1990s in his early achievements, combined with a return to better health, prompted Green to form Splinter Group in 1996 with Nigel Watson. To date, Green has made six albums with Splinter Group: *Peter Green Splinter Group* (1997), *Robert Johnson Songbook* (1998), *Soho Session* (1999), *Destiny Road* (1999), *Hot Foot Powder* (2000) and *Time Travels* (2001). In a warm turn of events, Green won a W. C. Handy Award for "Comeback Album of the Year" for his 1998 Robert Johnson tribute album.

Following Fleetwood Mac, Danny Kirwan issued three unsuccessful solo albums in the 1970s: *Second Chapter* (1975, with ex-Chicken Shack members Andy Sylvester and Paul Raymond backing), *Danny Kirwan* (1977) and *Hello There, Big Boy* (1979).

Jeremy Spencer issued an album in 1973, *Jeremy Spencer and the Children,* and an Atlantic album, *Flee,* in 1979. He then disappeared from the music scene. He remains a member of the religious group known as the Children of God and divides his creative time between playing guitar and art.

Bob Welch formed Paris and issued two unsuccessful albums under the moniker before achieving solo stardom with the release of his 1977 album, *French Kiss,* which included the Top 40 hits "Sentimental Lady" (which he had previously recorded with Fleetwood Mac) and "Ebony Eyes."

Discography

Release Date	Title	Catalog Number

U.S. Singles

1968	Black Magic Woman/Long Grey Mare	Epic 5-10351
1968	Need Your Love So Bad/No Place to Go	Epic 5-10386
1969	Albatross/Jigsaw Puzzle Blues	Epic 5-10436
1969	Rattlesnake Shake/Coming Your Way	Reprise 0860
1969	Oh Well (Part 1)/Oh Well (Part 2)	Reprise REP0883
1970	The Green Manalishi/World in Harmony	Reprise REP0925
1971	Jewel Eyed Judy/Station Man	Reprise REP0984
1971	Sands of Time/Lay It All Down	Reprise REP1057
1972	Sentimental Lady/Sunny Side of Heaven	Reprise REP1093

U.S. Albums

1968   *Peter Green's Fleetwood Mac*   Epic BN26402
My Heart Beat Like a Hammer/Merry Go Round/Long Grey Mare/Hellhound on My Trail/Shake Your Moneymaker/Looking for Somebody/No Place to Go/My Baby's Good to Me/I Loved Another Woman/Cold Black Night/The World Keep on Turning/Got to Move

1968   *English Rose*   Epic BN26446
Stop Messin' 'Round/Jigsaw Puzzle Blues/Doctor Brown/Something Inside of Me/Evening Boogie/Love That Burns/Black Magic Woman/I've Lost My Baby/One Sunny Day/Without You/Coming Home/Albatross

1969   *Then Play On*[1]   Reprise RS6368
Coming Your Way/Closing My Eyes/Show-Biz Blues/My Dream/Under Way/Although the Sun Is Shining/Rattlesnake Shake/Searching for Madge/Fighting for Madge/When You Say/Like Crying/Before the Beginning

    [1]Second U.S. release omitted "When You Say" and "My Dream" and added "Oh Well Parts 1 & 2" to LP.

1969   *Blues Jam at Chess Volume 1*   Blue Horizon BH4803
Watch Out/Ooh Baby/South Indiana (Take 1)/South Indiana (Take 2)/Last Night/Red Hot Jam/I'm Worried/I Held My Baby Last Night/Madison Blues/I Can't Hold Out/I Need Your Love/I Got the Blues

1969   *Blues Jam at Chess Volume 2*   Blue Horizon BH4805
World's in a Tangle/Talk with You/Like It This Way/Someday Soon Baby/Hungry Country Girl/Black Jack Blues/Everyday I Have the Blues/Rockin' Boogie/Sugar Mama/Homework

1970   *Kiln House*   Reprise RS6408
This Is the Rock/Station Man/Blood on the Floor/Hi Ho Silver/Jewel Eyed Judy/Buddy's Song/Earl Gray/One Together/Tell Me All the Things You Do/Mission Bell

1971   *Future Games*   Reprise RS6465
Woman of 1000 Years/Morning Rain/What a Shame/Future Games/Sands of Time/Sometimes/Lay It All Down/Show Me a Smile

1971   *Fleetwood Mac in Chicago*   Blue Horizon
                                           BH3801
Reissue of both volumes of *Blues Jam at Chess Volumes 1 and 2.*

1971   *The Original Fleetwood Mac*   Sire SR 6045
Drifting/Leaving Town Blues/Watch Out/A Fool No More/Mean Old
Fireman/Can't Afford to Do It/Fleetwood Mac/Worried Dream/Love That
Woman/Allow Me One More Show/First Train Home/Rambling Pony
No. 2

1972   *Bare Trees*   Reprise MS2080
Child of Mine/The Ghost/Homeward Bound/Sunny Side of Heaven/Bare
Trees/Sentimental Lady/Danny's Chant/Spare Me a Little of Your
Love/Dust/Thoughts on a Grey Day

1985   *Jumping at Shadows*   Varrick Records
                                     VR020
Recorded live at the Boston Tea Party club in Boston, Massachusetts dur-
ing a 1969 U.S. tour.
Oh Well/Like It This Way/World in Harmony/Only You/Black Magic
Woman/Jumping at Shadows/Can't Hold On

1998   *Live at the BBC*   Castle EDFCD297
Rattlesnake Shake/Sandy Mary/Believe My Time Ain't Long/Although
the Sun Is Shining/Only You/You Never Know What You're Missing/Oh
Well/Can't Believe You Wanna Leave/Jenny Lee/Heavenly/When Will
I Be Loved/When I See My Baby/Buddy's Song/Honey Hush/Preachin'
Blues/Need Your Love So Bad/Long Grey Mare/Sweet Home Chicago/
Baby Please Set a Date/Blues with a Feeling/Stop Messing Around/
Tallahassie Lassie/Hang On to a Dream/Linda/Mean Mistreating
Mama/The World Keep on Turning/I Can't Hold Out/Early Morning
Come/Albatross/Looking for Somebody/A Fool No More/Got to
Move/Like Crying, Like Dying/Man of the World

1998   *Live at the Boston Tea Party Part 1*   Original Masters
                                                      155552
Recorded at the Boston Tea Party, Boston, Massachusetts on February 5–7,
1970.
Black Magic Woman/Jumping at Shadows/Like It This Way/Only You/
Rattlesnake Shake[1]/I Can't Hold Out/Got to Move[1]/The Green Manalishi
    [1] Previously unreleased.

1999   *Live at the Boston Tea Party Part 2*   Original Masters
                                                      155562
World in Harmony/Oh Well/Rattlesnake Shake/Stranger Blues/Red Hot
Mama/Teenage Darling/Keep-a-Knocking/Jenny Jenny/Encore

1999   *Shrine '69*   Ryko 10424
Recorded January 25, 1969, at the Los Angeles Shrine Auditorium.
Tune Up/If You Be My Baby/Something Inside of Me/My Sweet
Baby/Albatross/Before the Beginning/Rollin' Man/Lemon Squeezer/Need
Your Love So Bad/Great Balls of Fire

1999   *The Complete Blue Horizon*   Sire 73003
        Sessions 1967–1969 (6 CD)
Collection of recordings made for Blue Horizon, including the albums
*Fleetwood Mac; Mr. Wonderful; The Pious Bird of Good Omen; Blues Jam
in Chicago, Volumes 1 and 2;* and *The Original Fleetwood Mac* coupled
with studio outtakes and unreleased material.

Disc 1: *Fleetwood Mac*
My Heart Beat Like a Hammer (take 2, master version with studio
talk)/Merry Go Round (remix, take 2, master version with studio
talk)/Long Grey Mare/Hellhound on My Trail (remix, take 1, complete
master version)/Shake Your Moneymaker (master version with studio
talk)/Looking for Somebody/No Place to Go/My Baby's Good to Me/I
Loved Another Woman/Cold Black Night/The World Keep on Turn-
ing/Got to Move/My Heart Beat Like a Hammer (previously unreleased,
take 1)/Merry Go Round (previously unreleased, take 1, incomplete)/I
Loved Another Woman (takes 1–6)/Cold Black Night (takes 1–6)/You're
So Evil (previously unreleased)/I'm Coming Home to Stay (previously
unreleased)

Disc 2: *Mr. Wonderful*
Stop Messin' 'Round (remix, take 4, master album version with studio
talk)/I've Lost My Baby/Rollin' Man/Dust My Broom/Love That
Burns/Doctor Brown/Need Your Love Tonight/If You Be My
Baby/Evenin' Boogie/Lazy Poker Blues/Comin' Home/Trying So Hard
to Forget/Stop Messin' 'Round (takes 1–3)/Stop Messin' 'Round (remix,
take 5, master single version)/I Held My Baby Last Night (previously
unreleased)/Mystery Boogie (previously unreleased)

Disc 3: *The Pious Bird of Good Omen*
I Need Your Love So Bad (remix, take 4, complete master version)/
Rambling Pony (remix, complete master version)/I Believe My Time
Ain't Long (remix, master version with studio talk)/The Sun is Shining/
Albatross/Black Magic Woman/Jigsaw Puzzle Blues/Like Crying
(previously unreleased)/Need Your Love So Bad, version 1(takes 1–3)/
Your Love So Bad, version 2 (takes 1–2)/Need Your Love So Bad
(previously unreleased, take 3)/Need Your Love So Bad (previously
unreleased, U.S. version)

Disc 4: *Blues Jam in Chicago Volume One*
Watch Out/Ooh Baby/South Indiana/South Indiana/Last Night/Red Hot
Jam (previously unreleased, take 1, with studio talk)/Red Hot Jam (take
2, master version)/I'm Worried/I Held My Baby Last Night/Madison
Blues/I Can't Hold Out/Bobby's Rock (previously unreleased)/I Need
Your Love (previously unreleased, take 2, master version with studio
talk)/Horton's Boogie Woogie (previously unreleased, take 1)/I Got the
Blues (previously unreleased, master version with false start)

Disc 5: *Blues Jam in Chicago Volume Two*
World's in a Tangle/Talk With You/Like It This Way/Someday Soon
Baby/Hungry Country Girl/Black Jack Blues/Every Day I Have the
Blues/Rockin' Boogie/My Baby's Gone/Sugar Mama (previously unreleased, take 1, incomplete)/Homework/Honeyboy Blues (previously
unreleased, incomplete)/I Need Your Love (previously unreleased, take
1, incomplete)/Horton's Boogie Woogie (previously unreleased, take
2)/Have a Good Time (previously unreleased)/That's Wrong (previously
unreleased)/Rock Me Baby (previously unreleased)/Rock Me Baby (previously unreleased)

Disc 6: *The Original Fleetwood Mac*
Drifting/Leaving Town Blues (remix, previously unreleased, take 5,
master version with false start)/Watch Out (remix, take 2, complete master version)/A Fool No More (takes 1–8)/Mean Old Fireman (takes
1–2)/Can't Afford to Do It/Fleetwood Mac/Worried Dream (remix, previously unreleased, take 1, incomplete)/Love That Woman (alternate
original mix)/Allow Me One More Show (alternate original mix)/First
Train Home/Rambling Pony No. 2 (alternate original mix)/Watch Out

(previously unreleased, take 1, incomplete)/Something Inside of Me/ Something Inside of Me (previously unreleased, take 2)/Something Inside of Me (previously unreleased, take 3)/One Sunny Day (remix, master version)/Without You/Coming Your Way (previously unreleased, take 6)

2000   *Live at the Boston Tea Party Part 3*   Original Masters
                                                15599

Jumping at Shadows[1] (version 2)/Sandy Mary/If You Let Me Love You[1]/Loving Kind/Coming Your Way[1]/Madison Blues/Got to Move (version 1)/The Sun Is Shining[1]/Oh Baby/Tiger[1]/Great Balls of Fire/Tutti Frutti/On We Jam[1]

   [1] Previously unreleased.

U.K. Singles

Fleetwood Mac

1967	I Believe My Time Ain't Long/ Rambling Pony	Blue Horizon 3051
1968	Black Magic Woman/The Sun Is Shining	Blue Horizon 57-3138
1968	Need Your Love So Bad/ Stop Messin' 'Round	Blue Horizon 57-3139
1968	Albatross/Jigsaw Puzzle Blues	Blue Horizon 57-3145
1969	Man of the World/Somebody's Gonna Get Their Head Kicked in Tonight	Immediate IM 080
1969	Need Your Love So Bad/No Place to Go	Blue Horizon 57-3157
1969	Oh Well (Part 1)/Oh Well (Part 2)	Reprise RS 27000
1970	The Green Manalishi/World in Harmony	Reprise RS 27007
1971	Dragonfly/The Purple Dancer	Reprise RS 27010
1972	Spare Me a Little of Your Love/ Sunny Side of Heaven	Reprise K 14194

Christine Perfect

1969	When You Say/ No Road Is the Right Road	Blue Horizon 57-3165
1970	I'm Too Far Gone/Close to Me	Blue Horizon 57-3172

Jeremy Spencer

1970	Linda/Teenage Darling	Reprise RS 27002

U.K. Albums

Fleetwood Mac

1968	*Peter Green's Fleetwood Mac*	Blue Horizon 7-63200
1968	*Mr. Wonderful*	Blue Horizon 7-63205

Stop Messin' 'Round/I've Lost My Baby/Rollin' Man/Dust My Broom/Love That Burns/Doctor Brown/Need Your Love Tonight/If You Be My Baby/Evenin' Boogie/Lazy Poker Blues/Coming Home/Trying So Hard to Forget

1969	*The Pious Bird of Good Omen*	Blue Horizon 7-64315

Need Your Love So Bad/Coming Home/Rambling Pony/The Big Boat/I Believe My Time Ain't Long/The Sun Is Shining/Albatross/Black Magic Woman/ Just the Blues/Jigsaw Puzzle Blues/Looking for Somebody/Stop Messin' 'Round

1969	*Then Play On*	Reprise RSLP 9000

Coming Your Way/Closing My Eyes/Fighting for Madge/When You Say/Show-Biz Blues/Under Way/One Sunny Day/Although the Sun Is Shining/Rattlesnake Shake/Without You/Searching for Madge/My Dream/Like Crying/Before the Beginning

1969	*Blues Jam at Chess*	Blue Horizon 7-66227

Watch Out/Ooh Baby/South Indiana (Take 1)/South Indiana (Take 2)/Last Night/Red Hot Jam/I'm Worried/I Held My Baby Last Night/Madison Blues/I Can't Hold Out/I Need Your Love/I Got the Blues/World's in a Tangle/Talk with You/Like It This Way/Someday Soon Baby/Hungry Country Girl/Black Jack Blues/Everyday I Have the Blues/Rockin' Boogie/Sugar Mama/Homework

1970	*Kiln House*	Reprise RSLP 9004
1971	*The Original Fleetwood Mac*	CBS 63875
1971	*Future Games*	Reprise K 44153
1971	*Fleetwood Mac Greatest Hits*	CBS 69011

The Green Manalishi/Oh Well (Part 1)/Oh Well (Part 2)/Shake Your Money Maker/Dragonfly/Black Magic Woman/Albatross/Man of the World/Stop Messin' 'Round/Love That Burns

1972	*Bare Trees*	Reprise K 44181
1984	*Live in Boston*	Shanghai HAI 107

Same as U.S. *Jumping at Shadows.*

1985	*Cerulean*	Shanghai HAI 300

Recorded live on at the Boston Tea Party club in Boston, Massachusetts, during 1969.

Madison Blues/Sandy Mary/Stranger Blues/Great Balls of Fire/Jenny Jenny/Got to Move/Oh Baby/Teenage Darling/Loving Kind/Tutti Frutti/Rattlesnake Shake/Keep a Knocking/Red Hot Mama/Green Manalishi

1986	*London Live '68*	Thunderbolt THBL 1-038

Recorded in April 1968.

Got to Move/I Held My Baby Last Night/My Baby's Sweet/My Baby's a Good 'Un/Don't Know Which Way to Go/Buzz Me/The World Keep on Turning/How Blue Can You Get/Bleeding Heart

1992	*Live at the Marquee* (CD)	Receiver Records RRCD 157

Recorded live in 1967 at the Marquee club in London.

Talk to Me Baby/I Held My Baby Last Night/My Baby's Sweet/Looking for Somebody/Evil Woman Blues/Got to Move/No Place to Go/Watch Out for Me Woman/Mighty Long Time/Dust My Blues/I Need You, Come On Home to Me/Shake Your Moneymaker

1998	*The Vaudeville Years of Fleetwood Mac 1968–1970* (2 CD)	Receiver Records RDPCD 142

Intro/Lazy Poker Blues[1]/My Baby's Sweeter[1]/Love That Burns[1]/Talk to Me Baby[1]/Everyday I Have the Blues 1[1]/Jeremy's Contribution to Doo Wop[2]/Everyday I Have the Blues 2[1]/Death Bells[1]/(Watch Out for Yourself) Mr. Jones[1]/Man of Action[2]/Do You Give a Damn for Me[1]/Man of the World[1]/Like It This Way[1]/Blues in B Flat Minor[1]/Someone's Gonna Get Their Head Kicked in Tonight[3]/Although the Sun Is Shining[1]/Showbiz Blues[1]/Underway[3]/The Madge Sessions 1[3]/The Madge Sessions 2[1]/(That's What) I Want to Know[2]/Oh Well (alternate version)/Love It Seems[2]/Mighty

Cold[2]/Fast Talking Woman Blues[1]/Tell Me From the Start[2]/October Jam 1[1]/October Jam[2] (instrumental)/The Green Manalishi[1]/World in Harmony[1]/ Farewell (unissued demo)

[1] Unissued version.

[2] Previously unissued.

[3] Full-length version.

| 1999 | *The Complete Blue Horizon Sessions 1967–1969* (6 CD) | Sony Music 494641-2 |
| 2000 | *Showbiz Blues 1968–1970 Volume 2* (2 CD) | Receiver Records RDPCD 12 |

Soul Dressing[2] (instrumental)/If You Want to be Happy[1]/Outrage[2] (instrumental)/The Sun is Shining[1]/Don't Be Cruel[2]/I'm So Lonely and Blue[2]/How Blue Can You Get?[3]/My Baby's Sweeter[3]/Long Grey Mare[1]/Buzz My Baby[3]/Mind of my Own[2]/I Have to Laugh[2]/You're the One[2]/Do You Give a Damn for Me[1]/Him and Me[2]/Show Biz Blues[1]/Fast Talkin' Woman Blues[1]/World in Harmony[1]/Leaving Town Blues[1]/Black Magic Woman[1]/ Jumpin' at Shadows[1]/Rattlesnake Shake-Underway[1]/Stranger Blues[1]/ World in Harmony[1]/Tiger[1]/The Green Manalishi[1]/Coming Your Way[1]/Great Balls of Fire[1]/Twist and Shout[2]

[1] Unissued version.

[2] Previously unissued.

[3] Unissued studio version.

Christine Perfect

| 1970 | *Christine Perfect* | Blue Horizon 7-63860 |

Crazy 'Bout You/I'm On My Way/Let Me Go (Leave Me Alone)/Wait and See/Close to Me/I'd Rather Go Blind/When You Say/And That's Saying a Lot/No Road Is the Right Road/For You/I'm Too Far Gone (To Turn Around)/I Want You

Jeremy Spencer

| 1970 | *Jeremy Spencer* | Reprise RSLP 9002 |

Linda/The Shape I'm In/Mean Blues/String-a-Long/Here Comes Charlie (With His Dancing Shoes On)/Teenage Love Affair/Jenny Lee/Don't Go, Please Stay/You Made a Hit/Take a Look Around Mrs. Brown/Surfin' Girl/If I Could Swim the Mountain

| 1973 | *Jeremy Spencer and the Children* | Columbia KC 31990 |

Can You Hear the Song/The World in Her Heart/Joan of Ark/The Prophet/When I Look to See the Mountains/Let's Get on the Ball/Someone Told Me/Beauty for Ashes/War Horse/I Believe in Jesus

Foreign Releases

| 1994 | *The Original Fleetwood Mac Blues Band* (German) | Eagle Records- EA-R-90601 |

Can't Stop Loving/Like It This Way/Got a Mind to Give Up Living/Stop Messing Around/Loving Kind/Please Set a Date/Rattlesnake Shake/Oh Well/Madison Blues/Jenny Jenny/Oh Suzanna/Twist & Shout/Long Tall Sally

Rory Gallagher (Taste)

Rory Gallagher will be remembered as an uncompromising musician and one of the finest slide guitar players in the world. In addition to his mastery of the dynamics of a Fender Stratocaster in overdrive, Gallagher excelled on the Dobro, mandolin, mandola, harmonica and saxophone.

Gallagher became one of Ireland's first real rock stars while fronting the power trio Taste, a promising group that essentially imploded due to ego conflicts and internal tensions. Rising above the turmoil in 1970, Gallagher went on to launch a prolific solo career steeped in rock, jazz and blues. During the twenty or so years that followed, the guitar-slinging Irishman sold 30 million records and toured extensively worldwide. Gallagher attained fantastic commercial success in Europe and mounted no fewer than 25 full-scale United States tours over the years. Overseas, he played at numerous major blues and rock festivals, including Kempton Park, Sunbury (with Taste) in 1968, and the Reading Festival, at which he performed more times than any other act. Gallagher developed an image as an adventurous yet direct bluesman who eschewed commercialism in favor of musical integrity.

"When I listen to something I like, I like to be taken out of my seat and thrown across the room," Gallagher once said. "I like guts, a good drive, which can include gentle stuff too. If it sounds good and feels good, that's it."

Quotes like that, coupled with the intensity of most of his music, might lead one to think that Rory Gallagher was a fierce character, a mean ball of energy likely to explode into action at a moment's notice. Surprisingly, Gallagher was almost the complete antithesis of his aggressive music, as he was known for being quiet, friendly, soft-spoken and eager to please.

Gallagher (b. March 2, 1948, Ballyshannon, Co. Donegal, Ir.; d. June 14, 1995) grew up in the city of Cork and, as a young boy in the 1950s, listened to skiffle musician Lonnie Donegan (who popularized folk-blues), bluesmen such as Leadbelly, and other the rock'n'roll stars of the period, including Eddie Cochran, Chuck Berry, Jerry Lee Lewis, Fats Domino and Buddy Holly.

At age nine, Gallagher acquired his first acoustic guitar, which he taught himself to play using tutorial books. By the following year, the young Gallagher was performing in public, entering local talent competitions and playing at school functions and other social events. He formed a skiffle band with his brother, Donal, on washboard, and another friend on tea-chest bass.

When he was 12, Rory won a talent competition at Cork City Hall and his picture was published in the local newspaper. That same year, he got his first electric guitar, a Rosetti Solid VII. He formed his first band the next year, but gigs were hard to find and they only played a couple of dates at the Cork Boat Club in Blackrock before disbanding. Gallagher tried unsuccessfully to form other bands, but at the time there was little demand for teenage rock'n'roll bands in Cork. Undaunted, he continued playing, and by the time he was 15, he purchased the famous 1961 Sunburst Fender Stratocaster that became his trademark, paying a small fortune of £100.

In 1964, frustrated by his inability to get a band together, Gallagher responded to an advertisement for a guitarist in the *Cork Examiner* that led to his becoming a member of the Fontana Show Band. "We played all over Ireland, toured Spain and did a couple of English gigs," Gallagher once recounted. "It turned out to be great fun. We were luckier than most show bands; the drummer wanted to do Jim Reeves stuff but the rest of us wanted to play 'Nadine' and 'A Shot of Rhythm and Blues.'"

While not a fan of show bands, Gallagher was attracted to the idea of performing before an audience while plugged into an amplifier. Show bands dominated the Irish concert landscape in the early 1960s. Basically Irish dance bands, show bands would perform a mixture of Irish music, country and western, comedy numbers and Top 20 hits. Gallagher was eager to perform rhythm and blues and rock numbers, but he had to cater to public expectations and perform the popular hits of the day, including some dreaded novelty numbers. He was eventually allowed to perform covers of Chuck Berry songs and other rock'n'roll numbers as well as a couple of his own

compositions. The Fontana Show Band played in large dance halls a couple of nights a week around Cork, Kerry and Limerick, averaging 2,000 people at each show. They performed regularly at the Arcadia in Cork, where they would play the interval slots for headlining show bands and visiting British "beat" groups such as the Searchers and the R&B-oriented Animals.

While the Fontana Show Band was touring Britain in 1964, Gallagher would spend his off-duty nights checking out the groups playing at the Marquee Club in London. Blues-driven beat music was becoming wildly popular and Gallagher was influenced by the Beatles and the Rolling Stones, particularly Stones' guitarist Brian Jones— the first musician he ever saw play the slide guitar. Gallagher also liked the Big Three, a trio from Liverpool that favored obscure American R&B numbers played in a wild, raucous style. He was particularly impressed by their guitarist, Brian "Griff" Griffiths.

In an attempt to shed the band's image, the Fontana Show Band changed their name to the Impact, with the intent of evolving into a beat group. In April 1965, the Impact appeared on the Irish TV show *Pickin' the Pops*, a program where a guest panelist predicted which records would chart. Gallagher and the Impact were expected to perform a Buddy Holly number, "Valley of Tears," which they had rehearsed. At the last minute, Gallagher decided to perform the Larry Williams rocker "Slow Down," much to the consternation of the show's producers but to the delight of an audience unaccustomed to the sight of a long-haired musician.

Later that year, the group secured a six-week summer residency at an American air base located near Madrid, Spain. Although they still had to continue to perform the hits of the day, they played a lot of Chuck Berry and rock'n'roll numbers, including several originals penned by Gallagher. But by the time the group returned to London in late 1965, Gallagher was becoming increasingly disillusioned with the band. The Impact split up shortly afterward and their manager approached Gallagher about forming a new band to honor some of the Impact's dates in Hamburg, Germany. Gallagher recruited the Impact's former bassist, Oliver Tobin, along with a drummer named Johnny Campbell, to follow through on the three-week engagement.

Other than the Big Three, a three-piece lineup was virtually unprecedented at the time. Since promoters expected a minimum of four musicians, the group had publicity photos taken with a friend posing with an organ. Upon arriving at the gigs, they would tell club managers that the fourth member had appendicitis and couldn't make the trip. Each night the trio performed six grueling 45-minute sets with 15-minute breaks, and it was here that Gallagher first experienced the pro guitarist's occupational hazard—getting "blisters on blisters" on his hands. After returning to Ireland in late 1965, even this hardy trio decided they'd had enough.

Following the breakup of his first three-piece band, Gallagher formed another in Cork with bassist Eric Kitteringham and drummer Norman D'Amery, both formerly of the Axels Show Band. Gallagher had played with both musicians while they were still with the Axels, filling in for their guitarist on some remaining dates before they disbanded. The new band called themselves Taste.

Gallagher had by now taken a strong interest in the blues, particularly the music of Muddy Waters, Jimmy Reed and other American bluesmen. Early Taste played a mixture of R&B, blues and rock'n'roll. While the group continued to perform covers, such as Booker T. and the MGs' "Green Onions" and songs from the Chuck Berry catalog, they also wrote and played their own material.

By 1966, beat music had found its way to Cork and a more active club scene emerged. Gallagher's new band found work at local clubs but encountered opposition to their three-piece lineup from the Federation of Irish Musicians. The Federation, whose membership was comprised largely of show band musicians, had strict rules regarding the minimum number of players required for each performance—usually seven or eight—and it actively enforced the minimum quota. The issue came to a head during Taste's first booking at the Arcadia in Cork when the Federation attempted to prevent the trio from performing. Eventually, the Federation offered a compromise: If Taste would audition for the union, the union would consider giving approval to the performance. The three members of Taste, however, were seasoned veterans of show bands and refused to subject themselves to an audition. Ultimately, Taste prevailed and the union backed down. The group proceeded with their performance, and in doing so also established a precedent for other beat groups that followed.

During early 1967, the group found work in Cork and Dublin, and Gallagher also returned to Hamburg with the band. Taste relocated to Belfast and obtained a residency at the Maritime Hotel, which had a 200-capacity ballroom. Three years earlier, Van Morrison and Them had been the house band for the Maritime before the band relocated to London. Taste made a few recordings at the Maritime Hotel that were issued in 1974 as *In the Beginning, 1967: Early Taste of Rory Gallagher.*

While in Belfast, the group supported many visiting British groups, including John Mayall's Bluesbreakers, the Aynsley Dunbar Retaliation and more significantly, Cream, the premier blues trio of the day. This led to work and a few gigs in London, particularly at the famed Marquee, where all the up-and-coming groups performed. London was a hotbed of blues-rock activity, so the group decided to move there in May 1968. Sometime during or after the move, the original Taste split up and by August, Gallagher found new supporting musicians: Richard McCracken on bass and John Wilson on drums. Both were Irish musicians who had met each other in the Derek and the Sounds Show Band, and Wilson had also briefly been a member of Them.

While in London, the band performed regularly at the Speakeasy nightclub and quickly landed a weekly spot at the Marquee, playing their first gig there on February 10, 1968. "We got the residency after doing a few there and we built up a following. It gave us the chance of competition and solid work every Tuesday night—it was a real morale booster," Gallagher later recalled. Ariola issued recordings of the band's October 25, 1968, Marquee gig in 1987.

Taste also generated a buzz on their first visit to Denmark in late 1968. *The Danish Daily* praised the band for their originality: "Taste does not belong to the purists and stylists. They do not belong to the introspective self-pawing and oh-so-emotional vegetables who torture the British blues with their despairing elegies. They belong to the few greats who have made the blues their very own—and their times'—expression." The review went on to predict that by the following year, Taste "with no difficulty whatsoever will inherit Cream [stature] and make themselves one of the biggest and best phenomenons beat music has ever experienced."

Taste, along with Yes, supported Cream during Cream's farewell concert on November 25, 1968, at Royal Albert Hall. Chris Welch, reviewing the show for *Melody Maker*, was not particularly impressed: "The Taste proved a personal disappointment although they were well-received (apart from somebody laughing heartily during a particularly passionate blues ditty). Perhaps they were nervous, but the lead guitarist seemed to be playing a lot of dodgy chords and 'Summertime' did not convince."

The group recorded their eponymous first album live on a rudimentary eight-track machine. Released in April 1969 on Polydor Records, *Taste* contained several strong tracks, including "Blister on the Moon," "Leaving Blues," "Born on the Wrong Side of Time" and "Same Old Story," but reviews were mixed. *Melody Maker* declared, "What they lack in style they make up in energy and enthusiasm," while *New Musical Express* stated, "This LP tends to be overbearing . . . but there's some goodness there as well."

While the album went unnoticed in the U.S. and U.K., it reached the Top Ten in Holland. To coincide with the release, Major Minor Records issued an old recording (made by the previous lineup) as a single. It consisted of "Blister on the Moon" backed with "Born on the Wrong Side of Town." Both sides of the single were early versions of songs appearing on the first LP, although the B-side was re-titled "Born on the Wrong Side of Time" for the album.

Taste soon became major headliners in Europe, and in the summer of 1969 they received even greater exposure when they toured the U.S. with Blind Faith [see **Blind Faith**]. Gallagher started to incorporate jazz influences into his music and the group's live performances offered band members an opportunity to stretch out and improvise while still maintaining a blues base. Gallagher told *Hit Parader*, "We work things out as we go. We don't want to ever play it safe . . . it may fall really flat some nights, but you will be sure never to hear the same thing twice." He also commented on his progression to *Melody Maker:* "We listen to jazz but we're not wrapped up in the jazz thing. Obviously, the numbers are becoming more complex but that doesn't stop me from taking up the bottleneck and taking it back to something very traditional and simple."

In January 1970, Taste released their second album, *On the Boards,* to unanimous critical acclaim. *Beat Instrumental* declared, "For sheer variety alone, the album is first class, and should make a substantial contribution towards giving Taste the success they deserve." *Melody Maker* commented, "Taste have matured; that is the basic difference between their debut album of last year and this collection of Rory Gallagher songs." In its review of the album, *New Musical Express* compared Taste to the icons of British blues: "Taste isn't quite a blues group and it wouldn't be right to describe them strictly as progressive, but they have an original bluesy style that is good and gutsy and reminiscent of the Stones or the Yardbirds circa 1964 in formation." Lester Bangs, writing for *Rolling Stone,* distinguished Taste from other blues bands by observing,

"The band as a whole is so tight and compelling, the songs so affecting, and the experiments and improvisations so clearly thought-out, that it seems a shame to even suggest that Taste be classed in any way with that great puddle of British blues bands. Everybody else is just wood shedding, Taste have arrived."

On the Boards reached #18 on the British charts and #33 in Germany. With a successful album behind them, the band's reputation spread fast and it seemed that Taste were poised for a big breakthrough. *Beat Instrumental* predicted, "The year of the Taste may well be 1970, on the strength both of their current album and of a return tour of the States."

While the second U.S. trek in fact never came about, the band did tour Europe, including Scandinavia. However, by the time they played the Isle of Wight Festival on August 28, 1970, relations between Gallagher and the other two members of the band had become strained to the point where they refused to speak to one another. Despite this tension and lack of communication, they put on a competent performance that was captured on an album released two years later. (A film about the festival—one beset by crowd control problems—captured a shapely girl in the audience who became so moved and excited by Gallagher's Telecaster slide guitar during "Sinner Boy" that she stripped naked and then streaked in front of the stage. Nonplussed backstage security staff at once forcefully removed her as the crowd roared their displeasure at this over-zealous "police state" spectacle.)

In the fall, Polydor Records sponsored Taste's first major tour of Britain, with support from Scottish group Stone the Crows and American singer Jake Holmes. During this tour, the sense of uneasiness grew among the band members with Gallagher effectively isolated from his rhythm section. Such friction inevitably affected their performances, as noted by this review in *Melody Maker:* "Taste swept into exciting yet totally unkempt and direction-less blues." The magazine then acknowledged, "Taste did have some good moments, but once into them, they musically took the easy way out, and for some totally inexplicable reason, for the talent IS there."

While on the verge of breaking up, the band ironically saw their popularity reach massive proportions. In the article called "Is Fan Worship Coming Back?" published on September 12, 1970, *Melody Maker* grouped Taste with some of the biggest names of the day: "TASTE, Moody Blues, Free and Ten Years After—their musical policies may differ tremendously, but they all have something strikingly in common—they are today's hell raisers. They are today's front-line bands who are creating something we had almost forgotten existed—HYSTERIA." That same issue carried the front page headline, "Taste Fight Split," which reported, "Taste narrowly averted a split last week when disagreements between themselves threatened to wreck the group."

Finally, mercifully, the group disbanded the following month. *Melody Maker* reported in its October 17, 1970, issue, "Taste will split on Saturday night and that's final." Taste's manager, Eddie Kennedy, explained some of the tensions to the magazine: "Gallagher was under the impression that HE employed Wilson and McCracken, and had in fact always been under this impression. They were purely working for HIS purposes." Moreover, drummer John Wilson complained in the same article, "The matter became absurd just before the start of last month's Polydor tour, when Gallagher demanded that he be given all tour earnings, so he could seemingly pay us whatever he felt like paying us. That was just going too far. We couldn't carry on." Wilson also remarked, "We wanted to be recognized as equals with Rory. But instead it was Rory this, and Rory that. I just wish someone had spoken to us about things."

Melody Maker then wrote, "The tragic thing about the split is that neither Gallagher, Wilson or McCracken wanted it to happen. Already £35,000 worth of bookings have had to be canceled. The group has been causing a storm throughout Europe—and their Irish tour has brought scenes that can only be compared with Beatlemania."

For his part, Gallagher refused to talk about the breakup and it remained an extremely sensitive topic throughout his life. His brother, Donal, who was his road manager at the time, blames the breakup on financial mismanagement on the part of the group's manager.

Polydor released two posthumous albums in the U.K. after the group's demise, *Live Taste,* recorded at the Montreux Casino, and the aforementioned Isle of Wight performance. Following the breakup, Wilson and McCracken teamed up with Jim Cregan, former guitarist with Blossom Toes, to form Stud. Stud issued three albums before disbanding in 1973.

Taste's disintegration and its aftermath was a traumatic period for Gallagher, but he overcame it and created another all-Irish three-piece. This time, the rhythm section consisted of drummer Wilgar Campbell and bassist Gerry McAvoy, both formerly of Deep Joy. McAvoy was a native of Belfast, Ireland, and would become a fixture in Gallagher's bands for the next 20 years. Gallagher had met McAvoy a couple of years earlier in Belfast, and Deep Joy had subsequently supported Taste on a few shows in England.

Despite all his success, Gallagher had nothing to show for it and reportedly even had to borrow money from his mother to record his first solo album in the winter of 1970. The self-produced record, simply titled *Rory Gallagher,* was released on May 7, 1971. Consisting of ten tracks, all composed by Gallagher, the album was a varied collection highlighted by two concert favorites—"Laundromat" and "Sinner Boy." The trio was augmented by the late Vincent Crane, keyboardist in Atomic Rooster, who contributed his piano playing to two tracks.

The solo release garnered favorable reactions in the U.K. *Melody Maker* opined, "Well, this is Rory—unabridged, downhome Rory Gallagher, doing precisely what he wants to do, and it's damned good. Gallagher has all the makings, all the trimmings, all the texture to be an absolute monster, and this first album since the fall of Taste is yet another pointer in that direction." Reaction in the U.S. was less enthusiastic, and Lester Bangs greeted the release with downright hostility. Writing for *Phonograph Record*, Bangs insisted, "This is one of the most positively moribund albums to come down the pike." Bangs also commented on the breakup of Taste, reminding fans, "The other cats [John Wilson and Richard McCracken] were saying things like he [Rory Gallagher] picked up the checks and paid them at rigid scale like one-nighter Chuck Berry sidemen or something. So now a little over a year later we have this album . . . [with] his fat ego flying free and it's one of the most noticeably vacuous releases of the season." Bangs's pontificating had little sway with the British record buying public, however. The album fared reasonably well, reaching #32 on the U.K. charts. In support of it, the group went on a British tour in May, followed by an Irish tour and a stint in the U.S. in October.

Later that year, the band recorded their second album, *Deuce.* Released in November, it was another hard-edged blues collection that reached #39 on the British charts.

A tour of Europe in February and March of 1972 was documented in the highly charged album, *Live in Europe.* A mixture of blues covers ("Bullfrog Blues," "I Could've Had Religion" and "Messin' with the Kid") with original compositions, *Live in Europe* was his most successful album to date, reaching #9 in the British charts and #32 in Germany. Gallagher also found time during the year to record with his hero, Muddy Waters, on the *Muddy Waters—London Sessions* album.

In June, Gallagher formed a new lineup, retaining bassist Gerry McAvoy and adding two former members of Killing Floor, Rod De'Ath (drums) and Lou Martin (keyboards). This lineup stayed together for the next five albums spread over six years.

In its September 30, 1972, issue, *Melody Maker* published its annual poll results. The readers selected Rory Gallagher as their top guitar player, dethroning none other than Eric Clapton in the process. But perhaps the most fitting affirmation of Gallagher's stature as a rock'n'roll musician is that when Mick Taylor left the Rolling Stones in 1974, Rory's name was on the short list of probable replacements.

Postscript

Throughout the rest of his career, Gallagher stayed true to his vision and released a series of solid, blues-oriented works. With supporting musicians McAvoy, De'Ath and Martin, Rory recorded *Blueprint* (1973, U.K. #12), *Tattoo* (1973, U.K. #32), and *Irish Tour '74* (U.K. #36). *Irish Tour '74* was undoubtedly his most significant accomplishment of this period. Recorded in early 1974, the Irish concerts documented his performances at the peak of his career. The tour was filmed and became the subject of a documentary by director Tony Palmer.

In 1975, Gallagher signed to Chrysalis and recorded *Against the Grain* (1975) and *Calling Card* (1976, U.K. #32). During the sessions for *Calling Card,* which took place at Musicland Studios in Munich, he attended sessions for the Rolling Stones' *Black and Blue* album.

Gallagher embarked on his tenth American tour in 1976 and had the distinction of being the first artist to perform on a Eurovision television transmission to over 100 million people.

In 1977, he recorded an album in San Francisco but was dissatisfied with the results. He disbanded his four-piece band, keeping only bassist Gerry McAvoy, and added drummer Ted McKenna, formerly of the Sensational

Alex Harvey Band. The new group recorded the hard-driving *Photo-Finish* (1978) album in Europe, re-recording many of the same tracks previously attempted in San Francisco.

This lineup released two more albums, *Top Priority* (1979, U.K. #56) and the live album *Stage Struck* (1980, U.K. #40), before changing drummers yet again in May 1981 when Brenden O'Neil replaced McKenna on drums. Together, they then recorded *Jinx* (1982, U.K. #68); *Defender,* which included the free 7" "Seems to Me" backed with "No Peace for the Wicked" (1987); and *Fresh Evidence* (1990).

Following an American tour in 1991, McAvoy and O'Neil left Rory Gallagher's band to form Nine Below Zero. Gallagher recruited a new lineup and continued touring until late in 1994, when he fell seriously ill while touring in Europe.

Following complications from a liver transplant, Rory Gallagher died on June 14, 1995, in King's College Hospital, London.

Discography

Release Date	Title	Catalog Number

U.S. Albums

Taste
1969 *Taste*   Atco SD 33-296
Blister on the Moon/Leaving Blues/Sugar Mama/Hail/Born on the Wrong Side of Time/Dual Carriageway Pain/Same Old Story/Catfish /I'm Moving On

1970 *On the Boards*   Atco SD 33-322
What's Going On/Railway and Gun/It's Happened Before, It'll Happen Again/If the Day Was Any Longer/Morning Sun/Eat My Words/On the Boards/If I Don't Sing, I'll Cry/See Here/I'll Remember

Rory Gallagher
1971 *Rory Gallagher*   Atco SD 33-368
Laundromat/Just the Smile/I Fall Apart/Wave Myself Goodbye/Hands Up/Sinner Boy/For the Last Time/It's You/I'm Not Surprised/Can't Believe It's True

1971 *Deuce*   Atco SD 7004
Used to Be/I'm Not Awake Yet/Don't Know Where I'm Going/Maybe I Will/Whole Lot of People/In Your Town/Should've Learnt My Lesson/There's a Light/Out of My Mind/Crest of a Wave

1972   *Live in Europe*   Polydor PD 5513
Messin' with the Kid/Laundromat/I Could've Had Religion/Pistol Slapper Blues/Going to My Home Town/In Your Town/Bullfrog Blues

U.K. Singles

Taste

1968	Blister on the Moon/	Major Minor
	Born on the Wrong Side of Town	MM 560
1969	Born on the Wrong Side of Time/	Polydor
	Same Old Story	56313
1970	Blister on the Moon/	Major Minor
	Born on the Wrong Side of Time	MM 718

Rory Gallagher

| 1971 | It's You/Just the Smile/Sinner Boy | Polydor 2614 004 |

U.K. Albums

Taste

1969	*Taste*	Polydor 583 042
1970	*On the Boards*	Polydor 583 083
1971	*Live Taste*	Polydor 2310 082

Recorded live at Montreux Casino.
Sugar Mama/Gamblin' Blues/I Feel So Good (Part 1)/I Feel So Good (Part 2)/Catfish/Same Old Story

| 1972 | *Taste: Live at the Isle of Wight* | Polydor 2383 120 |

Recorded August 28, 1970.
What's Going On/Sugar Mama/Morning Sun/Sinner Boy/I Feel So Good/Catfish

| 1974 | *In the Beginning, 1967:* | Emerald Gem |
| | *Early Taste of Rory Gallagher* | GES 1110 |

Recorded July 1967 at the Maritime Club, Belfast, Ireland.
Wee Wee Baby/How Many More Years/Take It Easy Baby/You've Got to Pay/Worried Man/Norman Invasion/Pardon Me Mister

Rory Gallagher

1971	*Rory Gallagher*	Polydor 2383-044
1971	*Deuce*	Polydor 2383-076
1972	*Live in Europe*	Polydor 2383 112

Foreign Releases

Taste

| 1974 | *Taste First* (German) | BASF 20290840-0 |

Same tracks as *In the Beginning, 1967: Early Taste of Rory Gallagher.*

| 1978 | *In Concert* (German) | Arioa 25001 |

Recorded October 25, 1968, at the Marquee, London, U.K.
Movin' On/Pontiac Blues/Baby Please Don't Go/Blister on the Moon/Sugar Mama/First Time I Met the Blues/Catfish

Barry Goldberg

Journeyman keyboard player, songwriter and producer Barry Goldberg (b. 1942; Chicago, Illinois) has worked with many rock and blues legends, including Janis Joplin, Jimi Hendrix, Muddy Waters, John Lee Hooker, Neil Young, Bonnie Raitt and Bob Dylan to name a few. While Goldberg was unable to parlay his status as a preeminent sideman into an enduring career as a solo artist, he found success writing music for television and films and as a record producer.

Goldberg started playing drums as a boy, later switching to piano under the influence of his barrelhouse piano-playing mother. He discovered the blues as a teenager while listening to a radio program called *Jam with Sam,* a blues, R&B and gospel show. Other influences on young Goldberg included Jerry Lee Lewis and Little Richard.

While in high school, he was part of the house band at a teenage club appropriately named Teenland. After graduation, he appeared at clubs on Rush Street in Chicago and hooked up with the R&B group Robbie and the Troubadours, a Las Vegas-type show band that came from the Peppermint Lounge in New York. While the Troubadours' repertoire included Jackie Wilson and James Brown tunes, their stage presentation relied on gimmicks such as dying their hair a different color each night. Goldberg toured the U.S. with the Troubadours for three years—a valuable stint that honed his performance skills and his playing. When the group broke up, Goldberg returned to Chicago and later played piano in Bob Dylan's backing band at the infamous 1965 Newport Folk Festival on July 25.

That same year, Goldberg was walking by a club next to the well known Big John's and heard some remarkable blues guitar playing. He walked into the club and introduced himself to the man responsible for the heavenly racket—Steve Miller. The two soon decided to form a band. Miller (b. October 5, 1943; Milwaukee, Wisconsin) grew up in Dallas, Texas, and started playing the guitar at age five. His father was a pathologist by profession but also an avid music fan. Dr. Miller encouraged his son's interest in music, frequently bringing home such musical guests as Charles Mingus and Les Paul, players who taught the young boy his first chords. T-Bone Walker was one of his father's patients and entertained at the Miller home when Steve was just 11. At the age of 12, Miller formed a blues band, the Marksmen Combo, with his friend Boz Scaggs. The two reunited at the University of Wisconsin, forming the Ardells, later known as the Fabulous Night Trains (which also included keyboardist Ben Sidran). In 1964, Miller moved to Chicago because of its thriving blues scene.

Goldberg and Miller's newly formed band also included Roy Ruby on bass and drummer Maurice McKinnley. They later shortened the group's initial, unwieldy name, the Barry Goldberg Blues Band featuring Steve Miller, to simply the Goldberg-Miller Blues Band. The band obtained a residency at Big John's and played there for about a year. In 1965, the Goldberg-Miller Blues Band issued one single, "The Mother Song" backed with "More Soul than Soulful," on Epic. The single failed to catch the public's attention, despite the band's promotional appearance on the TV show *Hullabaloo.*

Their next break came as a four-week engagement at a New York discotheque called the Phone Booth that began on December 15, 1965. An album, *Live at the Phone Booth,* was recorded but not issued and it is unknown if any advance copies made their way to reviewers, although *Hit Parader* declared, "If you want to blow your mind without blowing your cool dig a new LP by the Goldberg-Miller Blues Band on Epic. It's great for nervous frantic dancing or soulful listening. It's predominantly blues, and blues is the news."

During this period, the band leaned toward blues improvisation, which they explained to *Hit Parader:* "We are trying to take amplified guitar city blues, like the stuff that influenced Chuck Berry, Elvis Presley, Little Richard, etc. Our feeling, without trying to do anything artificial to change it . . . to play it well and free enough and not have to worry about making these arrangements. We don't do anything the same [way] twice."

However, Miller soon left the group to return to Texas (he eventually moved to San Francisco), leaving Goldberg to assume control of the band. He renamed them the Barry Goldberg Blues Band.

With Charlie Musselwhite on harp and new guitarist Harvey Mandel [see **Charlie Musselwhite**, **Harvey Mandel**], the band went to Nashville and recorded the album *Blowing My Mind* in 1966. A mixture of rock'n'roll and blues covers ("Whole Lotta Shakin' Goin' On," "Big Boss Man" and "That'll Be the Day") with some Goldberg originals, the album wasn't able to attract much notice and the band broke up shortly after its release. Goldberg later recounted, "We were playing stone blues, but nobody knew and we were starving, so we finally broke up."

Goldberg was set to tour with Bob Dylan next, but Dylan's motorcycle accident on July 29, 1966, caused the tour to be canceled. Instead, Goldberg joined the Chicago Loop. He only stayed with the Chicago Loop for a few months, but probably appeared on at least two singles (released in 1966 and 1967, respectively): a cover of the Coasters' "(When She Wants Good Lovin') She Comes to Me" backed with "This Must Be the Place," which featured Mike Bloomfield on lead guitar on the top side [see **Mike Bloomfield**] (U.S./Dyno-Voice 226), and "Richard Cory" backed with "Cloudy" (U.S./Dyno-Voice 230). The Chicago Loop went on to issue two more singles before disbanding, although only vocalist Bob Slawson stayed around until the end.

In late 1966, Goldberg sat in on the Mitch Ryder sessions that produced the #4 single, the medley "Devil with the Blue Dress On-Good Golly Miss Molly." "Devil," propelled by Goldberg's turbocharged organ, gave Ryder the biggest hit of his career. Goldberg also appeared with Mike Bloomfield on Ryder's LP, *What Now My Love* (1967). In addition, the busy Goldberg recorded with Charlie Musselwhite for his 1967 debut album, *Stand Back!* His subdued organ-playing on the melancholy "Christo Redemptor" contributed greatly to what would become Musselwhite's signature tune.

In 1967, Goldberg joined the Electric Flag [see **Electric Flag**] and appeared on the Electric Flag's soundtrack album for *The Trip* as well as their first album, *A Long Time Comin',* before leaving the group in April 1968. Goldberg then played on the Bloomfield/Kooper/Stills *Super Session* album, a high-profile project that led to a recording contract with Buddah Records.

His first solo album, *The Barry Goldberg Reunion* (1968), included contributions from Charlie Musselwhite on harp, Harvey Mandel on guitar and drummer "Fast" Eddie Hoh. Goldberg later explained to *Hit Parader*, "The guys did it as a personal favor. They didn't care about the money. I was flipped out and sad and emotionally messed up and this album was for me, like my last chance." Goldberg composed and arranged most of the material. Critically, the album was mauled. *The Los Angeles Free Press* complained that it was "inconsistent and banal," while *Rolling Stone* lamented, "The album as a whole is frustrating . . . the right people doing the wrong stuff."

In 1968, Goldberg played on and produced Musselwhite's second album, *Stone Blues;* produced the self-titled debut album by the Rockets (which later evolved into Crazy Horse); and acted as executive producer for Mother Earth's debut album, *Living with the Animals* [see **Tracy Nelson**].

His next release, *Two Jews Blues* (1969), cofeatured Mike Bloomfield, who, for contractual reasons, was credited as "Great." Harvey Mandel and Charlie Musselwhite also added their touches to the project. They recorded some of the tracks at Muscle Shoals with session players Duane Allman [see **Allman Brothers**] and Eddie Hinton (guitars), Eddie Hoh (drums), David Hood (bass) and the horn section from the Mar-Keys. The album was highlighted by the slow blues instrumental "Blues for Barry And," which was distinguished by Bloomfield's stellar fretwork; "Maxwell's Street Shuffle," featuring a whirling blend of harp, guitar and organ punctuated by a horn section; and the gospel-tinged "Jimi the Fox." The album received varied reviews. As *Rolling Stone* pointed out, "Vocals are the album's weak point. They stink." On the other hand, *Record Mirror* praised the record as "one of the best white blues LP's for a long, long time . . . thanks to its originality as much as anything else," and *Melody Maker* charted a middle course with the racially tinged comment, "While not an outstanding album, this set manages to steer clear of the stereotyped 'White Blues' sound."

More importantly, fans were beginning to recognize Goldberg as a premier musician, with the readers of *Playboy* honoring him by voting him the seventeenth and nineteenth top jazz organist for the years 1969 and 1970, respectively.

In 1970, Goldberg—along with Charlie Musselwhite, vocalist Lynn Carey and bassist Neil Merryweather—took part in sessions that were issued on the RCA album, *Ivar Avenue Reunion.* Buddah then issued two more Goldberg solo albums, *Street Man* (1970) and *Blast from My Past* (1971), the latter a compilation album. In 1972, Goldberg issued a collection of outtakes titled *Barry Goldberg and Friends.*

Postscript

In 1973, Atlantic signed Goldberg and released one album, *Barry Goldberg,* produced by Bob Dylan and Jerry Wexler. The same year, he teamed up with legendary songwriter Gerry Goffin to achieve great success when Gladys Knight and the Pips recorded the pair's "I've Got to Use My Imagination," a #4 pop hit and #1 smash on the R&B charts. The following year, he participated in the ill-fated Electric Flag reunion.

In 1976, Goldberg reunited with Bloomfield in the short-lived supergroup KGB, which recorded one eponymous album before Bloomfield abandoned the group. Goldberg stayed on through their second and final album release, *Motion* (1976).

In addition to releasing the occasional album over the years, Goldberg has participated in numerous recording sessions, including those by former Stone the Crows vocalist Maggie Bell, Leonard Cohen, Harvey Mandel, B.J. Thomas and the Ramones.

In 1996, Goldberg produced the Percy Sledge album *Blue Night*, which received a Grammy Nomination for Best Blues Album and won a W. C. Handy Award for Soul Album of the Year.

Goldberg has scored music for over twenty feature films and over fifteen television shows, including *Murphy Brown*, *Local Heroes* and *The Marshall Chronicles*.

Discography

Release Date	Title	Catalog Number

U.S. Singles

The Goldberg-Miller Blues Band

1965	The Mother Song/ More Soul Than Soulful	Epic 9865

The Barry Goldberg Blues Band

1965	Whole Lotta Shakin' Goin' On/ Ginger Man	Epic 10033

Barry Goldberg

1968	Hole in My Pocket/Sittin' in Circles	Buddah 59
1969	Jimi the Fox/On the Road Again	Buddah 103

U.S. Albums

The Barry Goldberg Blues Band

1966   *Blowing My Mind*   Epic LN-24199 (M)
                                            Epic BN-26199 (S)
Gettin' It Down/Mean Old World/Twice a Man/Whole Lotta Shakin'
Goin' On/Put Me Down/Big Boss Man/Blowing My Mind/That'll Be the
Day/Can't Stand to See You Go/Think

Barry Goldberg

1968   *The Barry Goldberg Reunion*   Buddah BDS-5012
Sittin' in Circles/Hole in My Pocket/It Hurts Me Too/Fool on a Hill/Capri-
corn Blues/Another Day/Sugar Coated Love/Strung and Young/I Think
I'm Gonna Cry/The Answers in Your Head

1969   *Two Jews Blues*   Buddah BDS-5029
You're Still My Baby/That's Alright Mama/Maxwell Street Shuffle/Blues
for Barry And/Jimi the Fox/A Lighter Blue/On the Road Again/Twice a
Man/Spirit of Trane

1969   *Street Man*   Buddah BDS-5051
I Got a Woman/Games People Play/Bo Diddley/Sittin' in Circles/Soul
Man/Tell Mama/Hey Jude/Sittin' on the Dock of the Bay/Turn on Your
Love Light/Honky Tonk

1971   *Blast from My Past*   Buddah BDS-5081
Jimi the Fox/It Hurts Me Too/Sugar Coated Love/Maxwell Street Shuf-
fle/Blues for Barry and Michael/You're Still My Baby/Another Day/I
Think I'm Gonna Cry/Sittin' in Circles/A Lighter Blue/Tea for Two

1972   *Barry Goldberg and Friends*   Record Man
                                            CR-5105
Sweet Home Chicago/I Got to Love My Woman/Long Hard Jour-
ney/Woke Up This Morning/Mess "A Da" Blues

Miscellaneous U.S. Releases

Harvey Mandel and Charlie Musselwhite

1966   *Blues from Chicago*   Cherry Red CR5104
Tracks recorded between 1964 and 1971.
Big Boss Man/Low Down Funk/Lost Love/I'm Losin' You/You Got Me
Cryin'/Hootchie Coochie Man/Cherry Jam

1966   *Chicago Anthology*   Together ST-T-1024
Slow Down I'm Gonna Lose You/I Loved and Lost/Big Boss Man/Funk/
Aunt Lilly/You Got Me Crying/Times I've Had/Hootchie Coochie Man

Neil Merryweather, Lynn Carey and Charlie Musselwhite

1970   *Ivar Avenue Reunion*   RCA LSP 4442
Ride Mama Ride/After While/Magic Fool/Fast Train/My Daddy Was a
Jockey/Charlotte Brown/Run, Run Children/Walkin' Shoes/Toe Jam

U.K. Singles

1968   Another Day/Capricorn Blues   Pye International
                                            7N 25465

U.K. Albums

1968   *The Barry Goldberg Reunion*   Pye International
                                            NSPL 28116
1969   *Two Jews Blues*   Buddah 203 020
1971   *Blast from My Past*   Buddah 2318 038

Nick Gravenites

While Nick Gravenites (b. 1938; Chicago, Illinois) has never become a household name,
musicians and listeners alike hold his songs in
high regard. Charlie Musselwhite, the Paul Butterfield
Blues Band, Elvin Bishop, the Electric Flag, Michael
Bloomfield, Howlin' Wolf, Janis Joplin, Big Brother and
the Holding Company, James Cotton, Otis Rush, Jimmy
Witherspoon, Quicksilver Messenger Service and Tracy
Nelson have all played or recorded his tunes. His close
friend and collaborator Mike Bloomfield referred to him
as "the old granddaddy of the White Chicago blues scene."

Hit Parader once declared, "Even though as little is
known publically [sic] about him as, say is known about
Bob Dylan, Nick enjoys at least as much significance
both as a singer-musician and as a composer of the today
music." While *Hit Parader's* assessment may have been
a little over the top, it still reflects the esteem in which he
was held.

The son of working-class Greek immigrants, Gravenites grew up in a poor neighborhood on Chicago's South
Side. When his father died, an 11-year-old Gravenites
went to work at the family-owned confectionery. At 13, he
started to get into trouble with the local kids and began
stealing from relatives and engaging in petty crime. To distance him from the local environment, his mother enrolled
him at Saint John's Military Academy in Delafield, Wisconsin. The military academy instilled discipline in Gravenites; his grades showed improvement and he also participated in wrestling and football. However, after three and
a half years at the institute and just months away from graduation, he was expelled for fighting. To earn his diploma,
he enrolled at the Central Day YMCA high school, where
a teacher took an interest in him and encouraged him to
attend college. With her assistance, he entered the University of Chicago in 1956.

Gravenites later recounted his college days to *Rolling
Stone:* "I wasn't a college researcher. I was a crazy street

whitey. Lotta times I carried a pistol. The South Side was my turf. I scored a lot of reefer there, got drunk there, hung out there, listened to a hell of a lot of music and learned the lessons of life."

As a freshman, Gravenites met a physics student who taught him a few chords on the guitar. Soon he was strumming some basic calypso songs from the repertoires of Harry Belafonte and Maya Angelou. Another physics student taught him a few more chords, and he began emulating the recordings of Leadbelly, Big Bill Broonzy, Josh White, Brownie McGhee, Sonny Terry and others.

Gravenites quickly gravitated toward the thriving campus folk scene and joined the Folklore Society, an active student organization that held frequent events. At these wingdings and hootenannies, students listened to live music and mixed with other like-minded students; at one of them Gravenites met a budding 16-year-old harmonica player named Paul Butterfield, who attended nearby University High School [see **Paul Butterfield**]. The two started hanging out together and, as Nick and Paul, performed as a Brownie McGee/Sonny Terry-style duet. "Then we got more interested in electric blues, and we began hanging out together in the black clubs and thinking we may even be able to play that stuff," Gravenites recalled.

Gravenites also played solo whenever and wherever he could, including in the local coffeehouse circuit, at frat parties and at the folk music shop. Eventually, an acquaintance took him to his first blues club, the 708 Club on 47th Street, where he saw a "battle of the bands" pitting Little Junior Parker's band against the Otis Rush Band. The electrified blues he took in there, at his first live blues concert, was the loudest music he had ever heard, and although his ears hurt, the sound made an indelible impression on the college student, ultimately altering the direction of his life.

Gravenites began to regularly hang out at Pepper's Lounge and Frader's Juke Box Lounge. "Frader's was a traditional blues club where they had a floor show," Gravenites recalled to *Relix* magazine. "They would have a snake dancer and people doing specialty numbers. It was pretty wild and really great." Called to the stage one night, he performed a Lightnin' Hopkins song, "Short Haired Woman," that delighted a black audience unaccustomed to the novelty of a young white student performing an old country blues number.

Gravenites had turned 21 in 1959 and had read the classic Jack Kerouac novel *On the Road*. After inheriting some money from his father's estate, he decided to go to San Francisco with a friend to check out the scene. Once there, he became something of a beatnik, playing at area coffeehouses and living wherever he could crash. For the next five years he went back and forth between Chicago and San Francisco, where he finally settled in 1965.

One night, Paul Butterfield, who was visiting the area, performed with Gravenites at the Cabal coffeehouse in Berkeley. After their set, Paul Rothchild, a producer with Elektra Records, offered Butterfield a chance to record if he was interested. Butterfield explained that he was not yet ready, so Rothchild advised him to get in touch when he was.

In 1962, while living in Inverness, California, Gravenites received the news that a close friend had been killed in a gun accident. Spurred by the news, he returned to Chicago, where he and Butterfield, along with Gravenites's pregnant wife and two others, wound up getting arrested on a variety of charges—including drug possession, carrying a concealed weapon and possessing stolen property. Fortunately, Butterfield's father—a top local defense attorney—was able to get all of the charges dropped.

In the winter of 1963, Gravenites was living in Lake Hiawatha, New Jersey, when Butterfield persuaded him to go to New York City and revive their musical partnership. They tried four or five folk clubs in Greenwich Village, but none of the clubs expressed interest in the young blues duo.

Gravenites returned to Chicago in early 1964 and got a job at a steel mill. He and Butterfield played regularly at the Blind Pig bar on Wells Street. "Paul would play harmonica, and I would play guitar and sing," Gravenites remembered. "We were learning to play music and we played folk songs from Leadbelly, the Staple Singers— 'May the Circle Be Unbroken.' 'Tops' by Sonny Terry and Brownie McGee, that type of stuff." The two parted once again when Butterfield received an offer to replace Mike Bloomfield's band at Big John's, a club down the street from the Blind Pig. Butterfield formed his own backing band, this time without Gravenites.

In early 1965, Mike Bloomfield asked Gravenites to form a band with him and they started getting some coffeehouse gigs on Chicago's North Side, at places like the End (near Rush Street) and a bar called Magoos. With a shifting lineup that also included Charlie Musselwhite on harmonica, the band never quite gelled, and when Bloomfield left to join Butterfield, it folded.

Undaunted, Gravenites rallied enough friends together to produce a single in 1965 under the imprint of Out of Sight (which sported the legend, "THE sound of the '60s"). Both songs, "Whole Lotta Soul" and "Drunken Boat," were Gravenites compositions. The rhythm section on both sides consisted of Chicago jazz musicians Scotty Holt on bass and Steve McCall on drums. On "Whole Lotta Soul," the band also included Elvin Bishop on guitar and avant-gardists Lester Bowie (trumpet), Roscoe Mitchell (alto sax) and Julian Priester (trombone). On the extraordinarily moody "Drunken Boat," Gravenites and the rhythm section were joined by Butterfield on harmonica and Erwin Helfer on harpsichord. Only 500 copies of the single were pressed. Of those, half were lost in a warehouse.

Gravenites also became involved in managing the Burning Bush, a nightclub in Chicago's Near North Side, and he formed the Chicago Folk Quintet to play there. The band performed mostly original compositions with guitarists Bob Perry and Gilbert Moses, drummer Roger Wundershide, bassist Lou Hensley and Gravenites on vocals and guitar.

One day, while sweeping the sidewalk outside the Burning Bush, Gravenites looked across the street and recognized the members of Big Brother and the Holding Company, who had come to Chicago to gig at a club called Mother Blues. Gravenites had befriended them when he was living in the San Francisco Bay Area, so he invited them into his club for a drink and socialized with them during their stay in Chicago. Soon afterwards, Gravenites's partner at the Burning Bush was killed in an automobile accident, whereupon Gravenites decided to move to the Bay Area, where he played at such clubs as the Matrix and the Jabberwock.

In 1967, Gravenites joined the Electric Flag as writer and featured vocalist, singing three of his songs (credited to R. Polte) on the band's Top 40 debut album [see **Electric Flag**]. Unfortunately, internal friction exacerbated by members' drug use led to this promising band's premature demise after only 18 months. "There was junk in the band and it got down to 50-50, cats who were shooting and those who weren't," Gravenites later recounted to *Rolling Stone*. "That's what broke up the Flag—junk. You see the press releases talking about musical differences? Naw, man. It's the junkies versus the potheads, the same old fuckin' thing it's always been."

In February 1968, *Rolling Stone* reported that Gravenites was scheduled to make a solo album for Columbia once the last details of his recording contract were finalized. In the meantime, he kept busy as coproducer of the first album by the Quicksilver Messenger Service.

During January and February 1969, Gravenites participated in several nights of live recording at the Fillmore West with Mike Bloomfield, Taj Mahal, Mark Naftalin and other musicians. Three of the tracks that featured Gravenites as lead vocalist appeared on the album *Live at Bill Graham's Fillmore West*. Five other Gravenites tracks from these sessions appeared on his debut solo album, *My Labors* (the other songs on the album were from studio sessions with members of the Quicksilver Messenger Service). *My Labors* was described by *Circus Magazine* as "an admirable first effort, and worth listening to." Today the album is highly coveted among collectors, easily fetching upwards of $100 in mint condition.

That year, Gravenites also produced Brewer and Shipley's first album, *Weeds*; coproduced (with Mike Bloomfield) Otis Rush's Cotillion album *Mourning in the Morning;* and coproduced (with Michael Melford) Mike Bloomfield's first album, *It's Not Killing Me*. He also worked with Janis Joplin: two of his songs appeared on her *I Got Dem Ol' Kozmic Blues Again Mama!* album, and a third, "Buried Alive in the Blues," was slated to be recorded by Janis the day after she died (it appears as an instrumental on her posthumous album, *Pearl).*

In late 1969, Gravenites joined Big Brother and the Holding Company, which had just reformed after a one-year hiatus. He produced and played on their album *Be a Brother* (1970) and sang his composition "Buried Alive in the Blues" on their 1971 release *How Hard It Is.*

By 1970, Gravenites had produced Brewer & Shipley's second album, *Tarkio Road*, which included the Top Ten pop single "One Toke Over the Line."

Postscript

Gravenites continued to perform but kept a lower profile over the subsequent years. Among other projects, his talents led him to score soundtrack music for the films *Steel Yard Blues* (1973), *Blue Star* (1979, with John Cipollina) and *Junkyard in Malibu* (1980).

In 1979, he teamed up with Cipollina and a loose ensemble of musicians called the San Francisco All Stars, and he toured Europe several times with Cipollina.

Gravenites performed in the theatrical film release *Survivors* (directed by Cork Marcheschi) in 1984, with Cipollina, John Lee Hooker, Archie Shepp, Lady Bianca, Dr. John, Mark Naftalin and others.

A decade later, Gravenites recorded *Don't Feed the Animals* with his new group, Animal Mind. In 1997, he participated in a tribute to Muddy Waters that took place at Washington, D.C.'s Kennedy Center and was aired on PBS. In 1999, he released another album with Animal Mind, *Kill My Brain.*

Discography

Release Date	Title	Catalog Number

U.S. Singles

Nick Gravenites
1965   Whole Lotta Soul/Drunken Boat   Out of Sight Records

Big Brother and the Holding Company
1970   Keep On/Home on the Strange   Columbia 45284

U.S. Albums

Nick Gravenites
1969   *My Labors*   Columbia CS 9899
Killing My Love/Gypsy Good Time/Holy Moly/Moon Tune/My Labors/Throw Your Dog a Bone/As Good as You've Been to This World/Wintry Countryside

Miscellaneous U.S. Releases

Mike Bloomfield, Taj Mahal, Nick Gravenites and Others
1969   *Live at Bill Graham's Fillmore West*   Columbia CS 9893
Sings on "It Takes Time," "Blues on a Westside" and "It's About Time."

Big Brother and the Holding Company
1970   *Be a Brother*   Columbia C30222
Keep On/Joseph's Coat/Home on the Strange/Someday/Heartache People/Sunshine Baby/Mr. Natural/Funkie Jim/I'll Change Your Flat Tire Merle/Be a Brother

1971   *How Hard It Is*   Columbia C 301738
Vocals on "Buried Alive in the Blues."

Janis Joplin
1972   *Joplin in Concert* (2 LP)   Columbia C2X31160
Gravenites sings duet with Janis Joplin on "Ego Rock."

U.K. Albums

Nick Gravenites
1969   *My Labors*   CBS 63818

Miscellaneous U.K. Releases

Mike Bloomfield, Taj Mahal, Nick Gravenites and Others
1969   *Live at Bill Graham's Fillmore West*   CBS 63816

Big Brother and the Holding Company
1970   *Be a Brother*   CBS 64118
1971   *How Hard It Is*   CBS 64317

Janis Joplin
1972   *Joplin in Concert* (2 LP)   CBS 67241

Dave Kelly

A veteran British slide guitarist/singer known for his gritty vocal style and expressive bottleneck playing, Dave Kelly (b. 1947; Streatham, Surrey, U.K.) ultimately found his greatest success in the 1980s as a member of the U.K.-based Blues Band. While remaining a core member of the Blues Band for the past two decades, he has also maintained an identity outside of the group, engaging in a variety of solo and collaborative projects. He has been recognized as "Best Acoustic Artist" in the BBC polls in 1991, 1994, 1996, 1997 and 1998.

The brother of vocalist Jo Ann Kelly [see **Jo Ann Kelly**], Dave started playing the guitar, piano and trombone at a young age. Initially influenced by the skiffle of Lonnie Donegan and rock'n'roll artists such as Elvis Presley, Little Richard and Buddy Holly, he later shifted his attention toward traditional folk material. Through a local record store, he discovered American blues, a genre that greatly influenced his life. Carey's Swing Shop, located in Streatham, South London, was one of the first British record stores to import blues records. Dave and Jo Ann started hanging out there and met fellow blues enthusiast Tony McPhee, founder of the Groundhogs. Dave started listening to Leadbelly, Big Bill Broonzy and other blues artists, and saw slide guitar played for the first time in the hands of the Rolling Stones' Brian Jones during the Stones' Sunday afternoon residency at London's Studio 51. In 1965, McPhee loaned Kelly a Robert Johnson album; the recording so profoundly moved him that he became determined to make music his livelihood and started playing country blues as a solo act in folk clubs.

Kelly met John Lee Hooker through Tony McPhee, whose own group, the Groundhogs (then known as John Lee's Groundhogs) backed the American bluesman for a week in July 1964 as well as during a two-month tour of Britain the following year. Hooker told Kelly to call him if he ever traveled to the United States. So, when Kelly visited the States in 1966, he went to see Hooker in the dressing room of a New York theater. Hooker introduced the eighteen year old to his friend, Muddy Waters. Also in the dressing room were other blues legends—Otis Spann, Hubert Sumlin and Big Walter Horton. After chatting with Muddy Waters for a while, Kelly asked Waters for permission to play his (Waters's) guitar. Kelly started to play, to the laughter of all the veteran musicians in the room who were surprised that a white kid from England could play the blues so well. The other musicians picked up their instruments and a jam session took place.

Upon his return to the U.K., Kelly continued to play in folk clubs, including the Troubadour and the Bristol Blues & West. In 1967, he appeared at the Dutch Blues Festival.

Around this same period, Bob Hall called Kelly and asked if he wanted to join the John Dummer Band [see **John Dummer Band**]. Kelly had met Hall in 1963 (when Hall backed Dave's sister, Jo Ann, in jazz clubs) and agreed to join. This was his first experience both playing in a band and using an electrical instrument. For the first few months with the group in late 1967, he used his Harmony Sovereign acoustic guitar with a pickup under the end of the fret board that Tony McPhee had installed. He finally purchased a proper Gibson electric guitar and, in addition to rehearsing with the band, practiced to the records of Buddy Guy, Muddy Waters, Junior Wells and Elmore James. It wasn't long before he became proficient with it, and Kelly appeared as front-line vocalist and guitarist on two albums, *Cabal* and *John Dummer's Blues Band*. He left the group at the end of 1969.

In addition to the two Dummer albums, Kelly recorded numerous tracks spread over several blues compilations. His first solo album, *Keeps It in the Family* (1969), was a country-blues effort featuring supporting musicians Bob Hall (piano), Adrian Pietryga (vocal/guitar) and Keith Tillman (bass). Jo Ann Kelly contributed vocals to two tracks, "Finger Print Blues" and "Where's My Good Man At." *Melody Maker* observed, "The

keynote of this album is variety, which helps to sustain the interest throughout."

Kelly also found time that year to take part in sessions organized by Bob Brunning and Bob Hall [see **Brunning Hall Sunflower Blues Band**] that produced an album by Tramp (a makeshift group consisting of Brunning, Hall, Dave and Jo Ann, Mick Fleetwood on drums and guitarist Danny Kirwan, the latter two of Fleetwood Mac) [see **Fleetwood Mac**].

In 1970, Kelly appeared on the third Brunning Hall album, *I Wish You Would*, along with Jo Ann, Brunning, Steve Rye and Hall. Later that year, he started recording his second solo album, *Black Blue Kelly*, using numerous guest musicians including his sister Jo Ann, Brunning, Rye, Hall, and, on three tracks, Peter Green. Mercury Records issued *Black Blue Kelly* in 1971.

In February 1972, Kelly and Iain "Thumper" Thompson from the John Dummer Band formed the country-rock band Rock Salt. Rock Salt gigged for about six months before a French agent seeking a tour of a "Dummer" band contacted Thumper about coming to France. Rock Salt toured France successfully, which created the demand for another Dummer album. So Rock Salt collapsed in August 1972 when Kelly and Thompson reunited with Dummer and "Putty" (Adrian Pietryga) for another incarnation of the John Dummer Band, this time calling themselves John Dummer's Oobleedooblee Band. Kelly stayed with the Oobleedooblee Band until it disbanded in early 1974 following the release of one album (a second recorded album remains unissued).

Postscript

Kelly was a member of the Dogs in 1974 and 1975 prior to performing solo in folk clubs. He also took part in sessions for the second Tramp album, *Put a Record On*, in 1974. He later wrote the music for a London Theater production, *The Sport of My Mad Mother*, and participated in the performances. Kelly also wrote and performed film music, including the BBC four-part series *King of the Ghetto*.

In mid-1978, Kelly formed the Wild Cats, a pub band that lasted a few months until early 1979. Later in the year, he formed the Blues Band with Paul Jones and Tom McGuinness (both former members of Manfred Mann), plus drummer Hughie Flint and bassist Gary Fletcher. As a member of the Blues Band, Kelly appeared on the *Official Blues Band Bootleg Album* (1979, U.K. #40), *Ready* (1980, U.K. #36), *Itchy Feet* (1981, U.K. #61), *Brand Loyalty* (1982), *Bye-Bye Blues* (1983), *These Kind of Blues* (1986), *Back for More* (1989), *Fat City* (1991), *Homage* (1996), *Live at the BBC* (1996), *18 Years Old and Alive* (1996), *Brassed Up* (1999) and *Scratching on My Screen* (2001).

In addition, Kelly has toured regularly with his Dave Kelly Band and released numerous albums with the band or as a solo artist, including *Willing* (1979), *Survivors* (1979, with Bob Hall), *Feels Right* (1981), *Dave Kelly Band Live* (1983), *Mind in a Glass* (1984), *Heart of the City* (1987) and *When the Blues Come to Call* (1993).

Discography

Release Date	Title	Catalog Number

Miscellaneous U.S. Releases

| 1968 | *The Anthology of British Blues: Me and the Devil* | Imperial Records LP-12434 |

Various artists including two songs by Dave Kelly: "When You Got a Good Friend" and "Arkansas Woman," plus "Diamond Ring," a duet with sister Jo Ann.

U.K. Albums

| 1969 | *Keeps It in the Family* | Mercury SMCL 20151 |

When the Levee Breaks/Fingerprint Blues/Travellin' Blues Part 2/Hard Times/Hitch Hike Blues/I've Got My Mojo Working/Fixin' to Die Blues/Treat Me Right/Where's My Good Man At/Fred's Worried Life Blues/Double Time Night-Time/Money and Fame/Lock Your Door

| 1971 | *Black Blue Kelly* | Mercury 6310 001 |

Gotta Keep Running/No Fun for Me/Fair Theme/You Got It/The Way I Feel Today/Fields of Night/Poor Old Bill/Hello L.A., Bye Bye Birmingham/It's You/Green Winter/Brooklyn Bridge/Get Right Church

Miscellaneous U.K. Releases

| 1968 | *Blues Leftovers* | Immediate IMLP 024 |

Various artists including four songs by Dave Kelly: "New Death Matter," "Married Woman Blues," "Alabama Woman" and "All Night Long."

| 1968 | *Blues Like Showers of Rain* | Saydisc Matchbox SDM 142 |

Various artists including two songs by Dave Kelly: "A Few Short Lines" and "Travelling Blues."

| 1968 | *Me and the Devil* | Liberty LBL 83190 (M) Liberty LBS 83190 (S) |
| 1969 | *Blues Like Showers of Rain Volume 2* | Saydisc Matchbox SDM 167 |

Various artists including three songs by Dave Kelly: "No Time to Lose," "Blues Walking Like a Man" and "Six Feet in the Ground."

| 1969 | *Firepoint* | Music Man SMLS 602 |

Various artists including "No More Doggin'" by Dave Kelly.

Jo Ann Kelly

Without a doubt, a different and more ambitious attitude would have made Jo Ann Kelly into a blues-rock star, but her career turned out to be dogged by missed opportunities. She could have fronted Canned Heat during their late 1960s era of chart success; she could have shared the spotlight with the red hot Johnny Winter in the early 1970s. Instead, in a very English way, she remained devout to her vision of acoustic country blues. *Melody Maker* dubbed her the "mother of the British blues revival," but Jo Ann was also the Queen of British Purism.

The likes of Mississippi Fred McDowell, John Lee Hooker and Bonnie Raitt all praised her authentic vocals, described by *The New York Times* as "hard and rough" with phrases that "come in clumps, stubby and aggressive." Yet she never parlayed these unique qualities and peer recognition into commercial success. Quite the reverse—she repeatedly turned down recording contracts until she felt she was ready.

Tragically, Jo Ann Kelly would only live to age 46—a stage in life when many blues performers really start to come into their own. After she was diagnosed with a brain tumor in 1988, doctors gave her only two more years to live. Even so, her devotion to country blues remained unshaken and she returned to performing in 1989. Sadly, she passed away on October 21, 1990.

Kelly was born on January 5, 1944, and grew up in a musical South London environment along with her sister Susan and brother Dave [see **Dave Kelly**]. "I started playing guitar when I was about 13," she recalled to *Melody Maker*. "I played just about anything from skiffle, Buddy Holly, the Everly Brothers to Lonnie Donegan." She later formed a duet with her brother. "By the time I was 15 we were playing Everly Brothers stuff in talent competitions," she said. In the summer of 1960, the siblings again entered a talent contest, this time performing Donegan's "Rock Island Line."

When she was 19, Kelly discovered the blues at the Streatham Swing Shop, a speciality record store carrying blues and jazz titles. She became particularly fascinated with American country blues artists Son House, Charlie Patton, Snooks Eaglin and Robert Johnson.

In 1962, Jo Ann met a skillful piano player named Bob Hall [see **Brunning Hall Sunflower Blues Band**] at the Swing Shop and the two formed an acoustic blues duo. Drawing from a repertoire heavy on Bessie Smith and Sister Rosetta Tharpe songs, the two became regular intermission performers at the Star, a club located in Croydon, Surrey.

In November 1963, the soon-to-be-going-places Yardbirds [see **Yardbirds**] started a residency at the Star and Kelly would occasionally sit in and sing with the group. Kelly later recalled the first meeting: "I went down to the rehearsal and Eric Clapton was there. I had a background of Everly Brothers, and the song we did was 'Baby, What You Want Me To Do,' which is a Jimmy Reed tune. At the rehearsal I did an Everly Brothers swing while Clapton's guitar work just knocked me out."

At the Streatham Swing Shop, Kelly also met Tony McPhee, who became her friend and mentor. She explained, "Of course, I like the traditional blues—I got interested in that from hanging around the Streatham Swing Shop, which I used to do with Dave at the time he was into trad [traditional] jazz. I met Tony McPhee there, and it was he who first introduced me to the work of Memphis Minnie, who I have always thought was fantastic." (McPhee, who had joined the pop band the Dollarbills in 1962 as lead guitarist, persuaded his band to change their name to John Lee's Groundhogs partly in honor of the John Lee Hooker song, "Ground Hog Blues," and also because they were his backing band when Hooker first toured in Britain.)

Kelly made her first recordings in 1964 using an Ampex recorder with McPhee at his residence. The lo-fi results were issued on a privately pressed, limited run (99 copies) EP. The record consisted of "Long Black Hair," the heartache-a-plenty "Boyfriend Blues," "New Milkcow Blues" (an inspired reworking of Robert Johnson's "Milkcow's Calf Blues") and Memphis Minnie's "I Looked Down the Road and I Wonder."

At around this time, Kelly started performing acoustic blues sets at the folk clubs and colleges located in the London area. Her singing was reminiscent of Memphis Minnie, while her guitar playing was influenced by Mississippi Fred McDowell and Robert Johnson.

In 1965, Kelly started playing at Bunjies Folk Cellar, located at 27 Litchfield Street, London. Founded in 1954 and named after the owner's hamster, Bunjies was a mainstay of the British folk scene. At Bunjies, she met another musician, Les Bridger. Bridger encouraged her to take up the 12-string guitar, and she purchased a Framus model that she used for performing songs by Lil Green, Leadbelly and Jesse Fuller. Hall took up the mandolin to accompany Kelly, as Bunjies didn't have a piano.

Sometime around November 1965, Kelly made her first studio recording at the suggestion of producer Mike Vernon. The two resulting tracks ended up being issued on numerous compilations on the Immediate label. Unfortunately, the experience left her with a negative impression. "Mike Vernon approached me to do a couple of tracks for his Purdah label, which have since come out on the Immediate *Anthology of British Blues* albums," she later recounted. "The peeving thing about that is that I haven't had any royalties despite them selling 99,000 in the States—they must owe me about £500. Anyway, I did two tracks for Vernon, and he put me off recording for a long time. The atmosphere was all wrong, and he was very unhelpful . . . I wasn't used to studios at all, and I hated the whole thing."

The tracks she had recorded for Vernon included a strong version of Big Bill Broonzy's "I Feel So Good" at a Decca studio. The track featured Kelly, McPhee, Hall on piano, Steve Rye on harmonica, Pete Cruickshank on bass, and Vaughan Rees on drums. A short time later, Kelly recorded "Ain't Seen No Whiskey" (a Big Joe Williams song) at a studio in Bromley. This time McPhee, Dave Kelly on guitar and Rye on harmonica provided the backing. (Kelly had first met Rye, who appeared on many of her subsequent recordings, through the Streatham

Swing Shop. She had previously seen him passing by her home playing the blues harp as he walked his dog.)

In 1966 Kelly contributed two songs to the *New Sounds in Folk* LP issued on the tiny Halcyon label. Kelly's selections—her own arrangement of Sleepy John Estes's "Buddy Brown Eyes" and the chugging, harmonica-driven "Black Rat Swing"—were recorded live at the Loughton Folk Club in Essex with Rye on harmonica and Gil Kodilyne on piano.

By now, Kelly was maintaining a full date sheet with regular gigs at the Scots Hoose pub in Soho's Cambridge Circus; the Hole in the Wall at Swiss Cottage, Central London; the Surbiton Folk Club at the Assembly Halls, Surbiton, Surrey; Les Cousins in Soho, London; and at numerous other club and college gigs. Kelly also frequently sat in with John Lee's Groundhogs.

The following year, Kelly recorded two more songs for a compilation album issued on the Saydisc label: "Black Mary" and a cover of Memphis Minnie's "Nothin' in Ramblin'." During 1966 and 1967, she also sang on two tracks Hall recorded at Simon Prager's house: "Backwater Blues" and "Keep Your Hands Out of My Pocket." Both songs featured piano accompaniment by Hall.

Kelly also appeared frequently at London's famous Studio 51, also known as Ken Colyer's Jazz Club, a basement venue located at Great Newport Street. At Studio 51, she was often backed by Brett Marvin and the Thunderbolts, who played there at her invitation and soon took up the regular Sunday night spot. Kelly also sat in with John Dummer at Studio 51 [see **John Dummer Band**]. "We often get Jo Ann Kelly, Bob Hall and the Panama Limited Jug Band dropping in," Dummer told *Melody Maker*. "Jo Ann Kelly is really great, she knocks me out."

Dummer was so enthralled by Kelly's vocals that he invited her to sing on his forthcoming LP. She accepted his offer, and early in 1968 Kelly appeared on the John Dummer Band's debut album, *Cabal*. During the recording of *Cabal*, the John Dummer Band also included both McPhee and her brother Dave. (By the time the album was released, McPhee—who had broken up Herbal Mixture, the successor band to the Groundhogs—had left the group to re-form the Groundhogs). Kelly contributed vocals to two songs: "No Chance with You" and "Daddy Please Don't Cry."

Kelly continued to play at Bunjies, a venue for which she had special affection. "Bunjies has always been a place for me to introduce my newer ideas, to try out things, both for the audience and myself—a practice ground—about the only practicing I do!" Kelly said. "I've been singing there for years. I do like singing with a band though, but I wouldn't have a group of my own. There are so many hang-ups with a band. I have a lot of musician friends, like Brett Marvin and the Thunderbolts, yes, give them a plug, they're good, Bob Hall, John Dummer's Blues Band (my brother's band) and I can always jam with them when I want."

Kelly's next few recordings appeared on several compilation albums issued by Liberty Records. McPhee had secured a contract for the Groundhogs that allowed him to bring in a number of artists for compilation albums as part of the "Groundhog Series."

The first of these, *Me and the Devil*, included four tracks by Jo Ann, among them a duet with her brother Dave, "Buy You a Diamond Ring." Jo Ann was not happy with the production, which was officially credited to McPhee (although she blamed a Liberty staffer). That same month, she took part in the first National Blues Federation Convention at Conway Hall in Holborn, London. The Federation was formed for the purpose of promoting blues music in the U.K. and included a formidable lineup of blues luminaries, including Jo Ann and Dave, "Davey" Graham, Stefan Grossman, Bob Hall, Mike Cooper, Hughie Flint, Free, the Aynsley Dunbar Retaliation, Mike Vernon and Alexis Korner [see **Aynsley Dunbar Retaliation, Alexis Korner**].

By 1969, Kelly was earning accolades from her peers. Influential BBC blues disc jockey Mike Raven christened her "the mother figure of British Blues." American guitarist and blues aficionado Stefan Grossman praised the British blues scene "because it has great people like Mike Cooper and Jo Ann Kelly in it," while Chris Youlden of Savoy Brown noted, "If the blues boom ends, there will still be plenty of work around for people like Jo Ann Kelly."

With her acclaim, her next logical step would have been to sign a recording contract, a move she resisted. "I'm just not interested," she explained to *Melody Maker*. "I've never done anything good on vocally [sic]. Mind you, I enjoy working occasionally with record yet [sic]. For making money I suppose records are great. But I can earn a comfortable living from folk clubs and I would rather do that and get better as a singer than have myself on record. After all, most of the blues greats didn't record until they were over 30. By that, I don't mean you have to be a certain age, or all that codswallop about 'You've got to experience life before you can sing the blues.' But you do need experience to get into the idiom."

In January, Kelly took part in a four-hour blues marathon at London's St. Pancras Town Hall. *Melody Maker* wrote of her performance, "Following a short solo spot which showcased her powerful voice and remarkable facility on guitar, Jo Ann Kelly then brought on in succession, Steve Rye (harmonica), Bob Hall (piano), Tony McPhee (guitar) and Mike Cooper. She performed duets with each one, then finished up with everybody on stage for 'Rock Me Baby,' which provided one of the high spots of the show."

In February, Kelly took part in Blues Scene 1969, a package tour of top English and American blues artists in major British cities. Sponsored by *Melody Maker,* the program featured the homegrown talent of the Aynsley Dunbar Retaliation and the Groundhogs as well as John Lee Hooker and Champion Jack Dupree.

Jo Ann sat in with Mississippi Fred McDowell at London's Mayfair Hotel on March 8, 1969, to record a duet with the elder bluesman, "When I Lay My Burden Down." The duet, along with the rest of McDowell's set, was issued in 1984. She also took part in several studio recordings, including the second John Dummer's Blues Band album in which she contributed vocals to one track, "Birds and Booze Blues."

She performed at the Memphis Blues Festival in June, where the sight of a petite white woman belting out authentic Delta blues caused quite a stir and generated major label interest. That same month, she recorded three tracks for another Liberty compilation, *I Asked for Water . . . and She Gave Me Gasoline.* These were "Rock Me," with backing by the Groundhogs; "Oh Death," a duet with McPhee; and "Dust My Blues," with backing by Brett Marvin and the Thunderbolts. The next month, she appeared on Alexis Korner's BBC Third Programme radio show.

In September, Kelly participated in the second National Blues Convention at London's Conway Hall, where she had an informal jam with Canned Heat's Al Wilson on harmonica [see **Canned Heat**]. That same month, she and Hall sat in with Canned Heat during their

September 30 appearance at the Marquee. It was here that Bob Hite, Canned Heat's singer, approached her about joining the band and she turned him down. During a *Melody Maker* "Blind Date" column, Hite was asked to critique "Whiskey Head Woman" by Kelly. "This is Jo Ann Kelly and I love it. I really like Jo Ann . . . We played with her last time we were here. I never even considered this song as a copy as she's got the feeling more than any other chick, and this is nothing like the Tommy McCleenan original, which I possess."

Looking back in 1978, Kelly regretted passing up the opportunity with Canned Heat. "I approached the whole thing with a non-business attitude and turned them [Canned Heat] down," she told Stefan Grossman, writing for *Guitar Player.* "I now think it would have been great to do a year with Canned Heat because then I would have had the experience and made my name. I was just so much into acoustic blues—a bit of a purist, I'm afraid."

She also joined musicians assembled by Bob Brunning and Bob Hall of the Brunning Hall Sunflower Blues Band to produce the album *Tramp.* These included guitarist Danny Kirwan and drummer Mick Fleetwood [see **Fleetwood Mac**] and brother Dave Kelly on guitar and vocals. The album, released on Spark Records, proved to be the first record that Kelly really enjoyed making. (She was credited as "Memphis Lil" and her brother was credited as "Little Brother Dave.") In addition, she recorded the album *Keeps It in the Family* with her brother.

By now, Kelly had struck a deal with Yazoo and Blue Goose Records' founder Nick Perls (b. April 4, 1942; d. July 22, 1987) to record some tracks with the intention of selling them to a major label. Perls's labels specialized in 1920s and 1930s blues and drew material from rare 78 rpm recordings by such musicians as Charlie Patton, Blind Willie McTell, the Memphis Jug Band, Blind Blake and Blind Lemon Jefferson.

Perls negotiated a five-year contract with Epic, a subsidiary of CBS, for a five-figure sum. Her launch was held at a Los Angeles music-biz convention where *The Los Angeles Free Press* neatly described her as "a blues singer from England who looks Mary Hopkinish and sounds like a cross between Muddy Waters and 'Big Mama' Thornton."

CBS wanted to pair Kelly with their other hot new white blues singer, Johnny Winter, and envisioned a joint Jo Ann Kelly/Johnny Winter promotional tour [see **Johnny Winter**]. The concept was for each performer to do an acoustic set, followed by a duet, after which Winter would perform with his backing band while Kelly sat in on a few numbers. She spent four days jamming with Johnny and his brother Edgar, working on material and making plans for the joint performances. "I didn't know him, so it was a bit of a surprise to learn that Steve Paul, Johnny's manager, had enquired a few weeks ago whether I would like to spend a short time at Johnny's retreat in the hills of New York State," Kelly told *Zig Zag*. "My record company said they would pay—so off I went for four days. It was like a little holiday, because Johnny's cottage in the country is equipped with a swimming pool and several Cadillacs. Johnny and his brother Edgar, who is not an identical twin, were really nice . . . we got on well musically, and the way may be open for some performances together if all the hassles about who pays the fare to the States are resolved. I would enjoy it anyway, because we were able to do nice versions of things like 'Bullfrog Blues' and 'I'll Be Satisfied.'"

A huge pity, then, that these plans never came to anything: Kelly backed out partly because she grew uncomfortable with the electric blues-rock direction some of the repertoire was taking, but mainly because of the inadequate funding proffered by her new label for her to stay and work in America. "CBS offered me $80 a week for the tour," she later told Stefan Grossman, writing for *Guitar Player*. "I said, 'Man, that won't even take care of my plane fare, let alone my hotel.' I really didn't know what was going on—I had no idea that a manager pays for the tour, or about management of anything like a tour—I had steered clear of all that. So the tour didn't come off, largely because they weren't prepared to sink any money into it, and they expected the management to. They were lazy about the whole thing, really, and I was too ignorant to push for anything."

So instead of a tour, she was recorded live in clubs for her debut solo album—*Jo Ann Kelly*—released at the end of the year. While *Rolling Stone* gave the album a generally positive review, *Melody Maker's* assessment was lukewarm: "For those who are still not tired of hearing overworked vocal and musical clichés, Jo Ann presents a tolerable picture of the British Blues scene. Her guitar work has seldom been more than mechanical and predictable, while her voice has always been powerful and forceful." Kelly herself was disappointed with the album, commenting at the time of its release, "My own album didn't come up to my hopes—in fact I think it's pretty boring. I hope the next one will be a bit different . . . I want a more electric backing, and may have Brett Marvin & the Thunderbolts on perhaps a couple of tracks."

With Kelly lacking the money to take part in Columbia's promotional plans, the album failed to sell, and she and the label parted company.

In 1970, Kelly toured Sweden with Brett Marvin and the Thunderbolts. Both artists performed separately and then shared the stage for the final set. In addition, she also went to the United States, but apparently could only get a handful of gigs, including one at the Gaslight Café in New York City. "I had only three jobs in the States. The old spades said they liked what I did, but there again, they might just be saying it," she told *Melody Maker*. "Some of the older men in Memphis still have the feeling that they shouldn't be in the same room as a white girl, as if people expect them to rape her." A glowing *New York Times* review of her performance at the Gaslight described her as "[a] folk-blues singer and guitarist—a fine one . . . And while she occasionally hits a false bottom trying to make a bass note growl, Miss Kelly does find the spirit of the blues. When you think of girl folk singers, you tend to find sweet voices with perhaps a touch of jazz. With this girl you find an old stovepipe with a touch of rust. A fine blues singer."

The year 1970 also found Kelly taking part in sessions with the Brunning Hall Sunflower Blues Band's fourth album, *I Wish You Would*. The next year she rejoined the group for their self-titled album. She also recorded the album *Jo Ann Kelly with Fahey, Mann and Miller* (with Woody Mann, Alan Seidler, John Miller and acoustic guitarist John Fahey).

In 1972, Kelly formed her first group, Spare Rib, which lasted about a year but folded because of the high costs of keeping a band on the road.

Postscript

Kelly toured the U.S. in 1973 with Taj Mahal and Larry Coryell. In 1974, she took part in a second Tramp album, *Put a Record On*. She later met guitarist Pete Emery, formerly of the Deep Blues Band and John Dummer's Oobleedooblee Band, and the duo recorded *Do It for Red Rag* in 1976. Together they had a daughter, Ellie.

Kelly remained active for the rest of the 1970s and 1980s, recording with the Blues Band, Chilli Willi and the Red Hot Peppers, and Stefan Grossman. In 1984, she issued a solo album, *Just Restless*, on Italy's Appaloosa label.

In September 1988, Kelly underwent surgery for a malignant brain tumor. The doctors who performed the surgery gave her two years to live. She returned to performing in 1989 and died in October 1990.

Discography

Release Date	Title	Catalog Number

U.S. Albums

1969   *Jo Ann Kelly*   Epic 26491

Louisiana Blues/Fingerprint Blues/Driftin' and Driftin'/Look Here Partner/The Moon Going Down/Yellow Bee Blues/Whiskey Head Woman/Sit Down on My Knee/The Man I'm Lovin'/Jinx Blues/Come on in My Kitchen

1972   *Jo Ann Kelly with Fahey,*   Blue Goose 2009
        Mann and Miller

Pigmeat Blues/Stocking Feet Blues/Henry Miller's Dream/Hard Time Killing Floor Blues/What's the Matter?/High Sheriff Blues/Arrangement for Me Blues/Bothering That Thing/Soo Cow Soo/Jo's Mistreated Blues/Tricks Ain't Walking No More/I Want You to Know/New Mind Reader Blues

Miscellaneous U.S. Releases

1968   *An Anthology of British Blues*   Immediate
                                        Z12 52 006

Includes "I Feel So Good" and "Ain't Seen No Whiskey" by Jo Ann Kelly.

1968   *The Anthology of British Blues:*   Imperial
        Me and the Devil   LP-12434

Includes "Rollin' and Tumblin'," "Make Me a Pallet on Your Floor," "Same Thing on My Mind" and "Buy You a Diamond Ring" by Jo Ann Kelly.

1969   *I Asked for Water . . .*   Imperial 12455
        and She Gave Me Gasoline

Includes "Oh Death," "Rock Me" and "Dust My Blues."

1973   *History of British Blues*   Sire SAS-3701

Includes "Nothing in Rambling."

U.K. EPs

1964   *Blues and Gospel*   GW EP 1

Live at the Bridge House Club.

Long Black Hair/Boyfriend Blues/New Milkcow Blues/Looked Down the Line (I Looked Down the Road and I Wonder)

U.K. Albums

1969   *Jo Ann Kelly*   CBS 63841

1990   *Retrospect 1964–1972*   Document
                                        CSAPLP 101 (LP)
                                        Document
                                        CSAPCD 101 (CD)

Black Cat Swing/New Milkcow Blues/Walking Blues/Hard Time Killing Floor/Shave 'Em Dry/Ain't Seen No Whiskey/Boyfriend Blues/I Feel So Good/Try Me One More Time/When I Lay My Burden Down/Long Black Hair/Just Like I Treat You/Buddy Brown Eyes/I Look Down the Road and I Wonder

1999   *Key to the Highway*   Mooncrest
                                        CRESTCD 037

Keep Your Hand Out of My Pocket/No Chance with You/You Win Again/I've Been Scorned/Can I Get a Witness/Rolling Log Blues/Louisiana Blues/I Can't Be Satisfied/Levee Camp Holler/Two Nineteen Blues/Make Me a Pallet on the Floor/Key to the Highway/You've Got to Move/Black Rat Swing/Baby What You Want Me to Do/Louisiana Blues (Version 2)/Boyfriend Blues/Catfish Blues/Walking the Dog/Jump Steady Daddy/Put a Record On/Interview

2000   *Talkin' Low*   Mooncrest
                                        CRESTCD 045Z

Tell Me Papa (How You Want It Done)/Talkin' Low/Get Right Church (Take 1)/Get Right Church (Take 2)/I Can't Quit You Baby/No Love in My Heart/'Til My Back Ain't Got No Bone/It's Too Late for That Now/Feel Like Breaking Up Somebody's Home/You Got to Move/Big Boss Man/Come See About Me/Rising Sun Shone On/Moon Going Down/Nothin' in Rambling/Death Have Mercy/Love Blind/Where Is My Good Man At/This Is Your Last Chance

Miscellaneous U.K. Releases

1966   *New Sounds in Folk*   Halcyon HAL 1

Recorded live at Loughton, Folk Club, Essex.

Includes "Black Rat Swing" and "Buddy Brown Eyes" by Jo Ann Kelly.

1967   *Blues Like Showers of Rain*   Saydisc Matchbox
                                        SDM 142

Includes "Nothin' in Ramblin'" and "Black Mary" by Jo Ann Kelly.

1968   *Blues Anytime*   Immediate
                                        IMLP 014

Includes "I Feel So Good" and "Ain't Seen No Whiskey" by Jo Ann Kelly.

1968   *Me and the Devil*   Liberty
                                        LBL 83190 (M)
                                        Liberty
                                        LBS 83190 (S)

1969   *Blues Leftovers*   Immediate
                                        IMLP 024

Includes "Keep Your Hands Out of My Pocket" and "Backwater Blues" by Jo Ann Kelly.

1969   *I Asked for Water . . .*   Liberty LBS 83252
        and She Gave Me Gasoline

1969   *Gutbucket*   Liberty LBX 3

Includes "Rollin' and Tumblin.'"

1969   *Son of Gutbucket*   Liberty LBX 4
Includes "Oh Death."

Dave Kelly

1969   *Keeps It in the Family*   Mercury
                                            SMCL 20151

Kelly sings and plays on "Fingerprint Blues" and "Where's My Good Man At."

1971   *Black Blue Kelly*   Mercury 6310 001
Kelly sings on "Gotta Keep Running."

John Dummer's Blues Band

1969   *Cabal*   Mercury
                                            SMCL 20136

Kelly sings on two tracks, "No Chance with You" and "Daddy Please Don't Cry."

1969   *John Dummer's Blues Band*   Mercury
                                            SMCL 20167

Kelly sings on "Birds and Booze Blues."

Brett Marvin and the Thunderbolts

1969   *Brett Marvin & The Thunderbolts*   Sonet SNTF 616
Kelly was credited as "Memphis Lil" on "Shave 'Em Dry."

Tramp

1969   *Tramp*   Music Man
                                            SMLS 603

Kelly sings on "Own Up," "Baby What You Want Me to Do" and "On the Scene."

The Brunning Hall Sunflower Blues Band

1970   *I Wish You Would*   Saga EROS 8150
Kelly sings on "Broken Hearted."

1971   *The Brunning Hall Sunflower Blues Band* Gemini GM 2010
Kelly sings on "Put a Record On" and "Bogey Man."

Tony McPhee and Jo Ann Kelly

1972   *The Same Thing on Their Minds*   Sunset SLS 50209
Twelve track compilation from *The Anthology of British Blues: Me and the Devil* and *I Asked for Water . . . and She Gave Me Gasoline.*
Rock Me/Death Letter/Make Me a Pallet on Your Floor/Gasoline/Same Thing on My Mind/Diamond Ring/Rollin' and Tumblin'/Me and the Devil/Dust My Blues/Oh Death/No More Doggin'/Don't Pass the Hat Around

Mississippi Fred McDowell

1984   *Standing at the Burying Ground*   Red Lightnin'
                                            RL0053

Recorded 1969 during a British tour at the Mayfair Hotel, London. Kelly performs "When I Lay My Burden Down."

Alexis Korner

Alexis Korner was not a great musician. He didn't have best-selling records (except one), and he never embarked on lengthy money-making tours. Even so, Korner was one of the most important figures to appear on the British music scene because he had "great ears" and a keenly developed sense of freedom and rebellion. His ability to sense musical potential in others was astounding, and today he is known for having encouraged and nurtured young, talented musicians even when other people told them to get "real" jobs. The influential Korner showed a generation of struggling musicians what could be achieved through passion and commitment. His most famous protégés were the Rolling Stones—but without Alexis Korner, Free and Led Zeppelin might also have never existed.

Korner was born in Paris on April 19, 1928, the son of a Greek mother and a Jewish father. His father Emil, a businessman and former Austrian cavalry officer, moved the family to different locations all over Europe and North Africa in a series of abortive business ventures, finally settling in the U.K. in 1939. Emil, who was 55 when Alexis was born, had two sons—both much older than Alexis—by a previous marriage. With an elderly and rather old-fashioned father and no other children in the house, the young Korner was quite lonely as a child. Consequently, he grew up troublesome and rebellious. (As an adult, he would tell wild stories about his background, the most famous and best accepted being that his father had surrendered his cavalry troop to the Bolsheviks during World War I.) As a schoolboy, Korner was in constant trouble, forcing his parents to send him to a special community for boys who just couldn't seem to fit in.

Throughout his life, Korner regarded himself as a juvenile delinquent. During his teen years he shoplifted records from a London street market near his home. When he stole a copy of Jimmy Yancey's "Slow and Easy Blues," he discovered boogie-woogie and fell in love with the blues. When he tried to play boogie-woogie on the family piano, his father slammed down the piano lid and locked it, admonishing the youngster, "You don't play stuff like that on my piano." But Korner's path was set.

Korner lost both his parents during the 1940s. His Greek uncle ran a shipping company and hoped that as his nephew grew older, he would join him in the family business. There was no chance, though, as Korner wasn't a corporate man and wanted no part in a career that required his wearing a suit. Instead, he chose to play the blues.

In 1949, Korner began playing guitar in Chris Barber's band. At the time, the band was modeled after Joe "King" Oliver's New Orleans jazz ensembles, with two trumpets, piano, banjo, and guitar. In the mid-1950s, Leadbelly-inspired skiffle music was all the rage in England. Because it used homemade instruments, it gave young people the chance to make their own music for the first time. Coffee bars opened up in London, and teenagers suddenly had somewhere to congregate besides the local church hall. Barber, along with Ken Colyer, spearheaded the London skiffle scene. The Barber/Colyer Jazzmen consisted of Chris Barber on bass, Ken Colyer on guitar, Bill Colyer on washboard, Lonnie Donegan on guitar and Korner on guitar, mandolin and—for a couple of weeks—very occasional harmonica. (Korner later said, "I was one of the first and one of the worst harmonica players in the country.")

The blues scene in London during the early 1950s was tiny—just a handful of middle-class "artsy" types who eagerly searched for the very few blues import records available in the shops. One of these early fans was Roberta (Bobbie) Melville, the daughter of a famous art critic. She met the dark, handsome, exotic-looking Korner and they were soon married. She knew as much about the blues as he and helped him learn to play country-style blues guitar. He was heavily influenced in his guitar playing by Scrapper Blackwell, pianist Leroy Carr's partner.

In June 1954, Colyer formed his own band and included Korner in the skiffle sections of the band's stage repertoire. The Ken Colyer Skiffle Group recorded seven tracks over the next twelve months with Korner on guitar or mandolin.

However, Korner soon began to feel alienated from skiffle. Wanting to be a solo country blues musician, he played around the burgeoning London folk-blues scene. Unable to earn enough money to support his family, he joined the British Broadcasting Corporation (BBC) on May 31, 1955, as a trainee studio manager. (This was the

first rung on a very long ladder; in the 1960s and 1970s, he hosted some of the most pioneering music shows on British radio.)

Backing Ottilie Paterson in Barber's band, Korner met 12-string guitar player Cyril Davies, who also happened to be one of the finest blues harmonica players Britain has ever produced [see **Cyril Davies and the R&B All-Stars**]. At the time, Davies ran the London Skiffle Club, which played to a packed house every Thursday night at the upstairs pub at the Roundhouse, located on the corner of Wardour Street and Brewer Street in London's West End. By 1955, both men had tired of the skiffle scene. Nor did they want to play trad (traditional) jazz (another popular music of the day) or be part of the burgeoning pop/rock scene. They wanted to play blues.

Korner was an occasional guest at the London Skiffle Club, and one day Davies suggested that he close his skiffle club and that they reopen as a blues club. Only three people showed up for the opening of the new Soho-based Blues and Barrelhouse Club at the Roundhouse, but it soon gained a foothold. If one venue can be cited as the wellspring of the U.K. music scene—and all that came from it—then it would be the Blues and Barrelhouse Club, which is even more important than the Cavern in Liverpool because of the diversity of musical genres that can be traced back to the folk and blues musicians who played there.

Ironically, it was a trad jazz musician, Chris Barber, who arranged for a steady stream of American blues artists to play in Britain. When visiting, the performers always went down to Soho to jam at the only blues joint in town, and during this period Korner shared a stage with Big Bill Broonzy, Sonny Terry, Brownie McGhee, Memphis Slim, Champion Jack Dupree and Muddy Waters.

Korner made his first recordings on February 13, 1957, at the Roundhouse. Credited as Alexis Korner's Breakdown Group Featuring Cyril Davies, the lineup consisted of Korner (guitar and mandolin), Davies (guitar and vocals), Terry Plant (string bass) and Mike Collins (washboard). Seven tracks were issued on the 10" LP, *Blues from the Roundhouse,* including "Skip to My Lou" and "Boll Weevil." The tiny 77 label only pressed 100 copies and sold the records exclusively through Doug Dobel's Jazz Shop.

Five months later, the group (with Chris Capon on bass plus Dave Stevens on piano) returned to the studio to cut four tracks for an EP on Tempo, a specialist subsidiary label of Decca. In spite of much protest, the record company renamed the group the Alexis Korner Skiffle Group. The tracks veered much closer to blues than to skiffle, with covers of Sleepy John Estes's "I Ain't Gonna Worry No More," Leadbelly's "Easy Rider," and Big Maceo's "Kid Man" and "County Jail." Oddly, the record was titled *Blues at the Roundhouse, Volume 1.*

In April 1958, Korner returned to the studio to record *Blues at the Roundhouse, Volume 2,* which Tempo also issued. This time, the lineup consisted of Korner, Davies, Stevens, Collins and bassist Jim Bray. Together they recorded four tracks, including more traditional blues (such as "Death Letter"), which the label credited to Alexis Korner's Blues Incorporated.

In the late summer of 1961, Korner reunited with Chris Barber, who had introduced an R&B slot into his show. Following the main trad set, Barber's wife, vocalist Ottilie Patterson, sang backed by Korner during a blues segment. Barber appeared regularly at the Marquee and used the blues segment as his intermission act. Encouraged by the response, Korner decided to strike out on his own and form a band.

On December 10, 1961, Korner joined Acker Bilk onstage in Ipswich. Accompanying Korner that night were pianist/drummer Stan Grieg, vocalist Ron McKay and drummer Danny Craig—but no Cyril Davies as yet.

Then with the promise of an intermission spot at the Marquee, Davies decided to join Blues Incorporated. On January 3, 1962, Korner took the stage in his own right. The event elicited this reaction from *Jazz News and Review:* "The Marquee club last Wednesday night was the scene of great excitement when guitarist Alexis Korner combined with Barber-band trumpeter Pat Halcox on piano and harmonica player Cyril Davies to play a set of rhythm and blues numbers. Following the success of the session, Korner will make regular appearances at the Marquee. Korner's own newly formed R&B band plays a concert with the Acker Bilk Band."

The Acker Bilk concert referenced was held on January 19, 1962, at the Civic Hall in Croydon. A makeshift lineup was assembled for the show which, though later characterized by Davies as "a near disaster," provided the impetus for the formation of a gigging blues band. *Jazz News and Review* reported, "The group is not quite a group yet, but it has in Cyril Davies a very exciting harmonica

player. He also had the whole audience with him when he sang 'Hoochie Coochie Man.' Keith Scott, who has done a lot of solo work at the Colyer Club, was on piano, rolling a good mean blues sound behind his leader's percussive hit parade guitar work. Colin Bowden was on drums, and while supplying the necessary drive, created undue monotony by clamping his foot firmly on the pedal of his hi-hat cymbals and bashing away on the upper one for most of the set."

As a new decade grew older, Blues Incorporated—led by Davies and Korner—became more formalized. Later generations of musicians would call this band one of the most significant groups in the history of British music, and it was certainly the first Caucasian electric blues band in the world. However, to a landlord unconcerned with history-making music, using amplification was unacceptable at the Roundhouse, and the band had to find another venue. They decided to move to a bigger place in West London, so in March 1962 they began playing at the Ealing Club—located in the damp basement of a tea shop—with the intention of recreating South Side Chicago and the sound of the Muddy Waters Blues Band. The lineup was fluid: in addition to Korner and Davies, it featured Keith Scott on piano, Andy Hoogenboom on bass, Charlie Watts on drums, Dick Heckstall-Smith on tenor saxophone, and vocalists Long John Baldry, Art Wood [see **Artwoods**], Paul Jones and Ronnie Jones.

By this time, a number of young blues players had cropped up around the country—Keith Richards and Mick Jagger in London, Brian Jones in the west of England, and Eric Burdon in Newcastle—each thinking that he was alone in his knowledge and love of the blues. When word spread about the Ealing Club, it drew them like a magnet. The list of aspiring young musicians who stood up to jam or just watch from the audience amounted to a Who's Who of British rock, including future members of the Beatles, the Rolling Stones, the Cream, the Animals and the Who.

For this reason, Korner subsequently became known as the "father of the British blues" (he always hated the title and, ironically, didn't think that British blues was any good). Never the diplomat, he often gave harsh, opinionated interviews, and the music press published many an unkind word of his about the "British Blues Boom" of the late 1960s.

Meanwhile, in May 1962, Blues Incorporated obtained a Thursday-night residency at the prestigious Marquee

Club while continuing to play Saturday nights at the Ealing Club. On their opening night on May 3, only 127 people showed up. The following month, recordings were made for their seminal first album, *R&B at the Marquee*, the closest Korner would come to a straight-ahead R&B album. *R&B at the Marquee* was actually recorded at Decca's studios in north London on June 8, 1962, with a full complement of seasoned jazz musicians replacing many of Blues Incorporated's regular players. Davies played harmonica and shared vocals with Long John Baldry (who later played with Davies in Cyril Davies and the R&B All-Stars). Chris Barber's drummer, Graham Burbidge; John Dankworth's bassist, Spike Heatley; and pianist Keith Scott made up the rhythm section, with Dick Heckstall-Smith on sax. The players were largely jazz-oriented, but the material stayed true to the album title with songs like "Got My Mojo Working," "How Long Blues" and "Hoochie Coochie Man."

Though the intent may have been altogether serious, the recording session itself was less so. In an article for *Jazz News and Review*, Korner's friend, the critic Charles Fox, described how Teddy Wadmore took over on bass for one song so that Spike Heatley could catch up on his sleep, while Super Session guitarist Jim Sullivan joined in on background vocals through mouthfuls of ginger biscuits. Inevitably, as the session wore on, out came the alcohol. "Surrealism creeps into most human activities," wrote Fox. "This time it enters during the third take of 'Finkle's Cave,' just as the tenor sax and guitar are swapping phrases. Despite the glowing red light, the studio door opens and in walks a little girl dressed in grey. It's like Alice arriving at the Mad Hatter's Tea Party."

By September, the band was regularly drawing an audience of over 1,000 at the Marquee. To accommodate the overflow crowds, Blues Incorporated was given Monday nights as well in December, but it didn't help, as both nights were filled to capacity within 30 minutes of opening.

When *R&B from the Marquee* came out in November 1962, reviews were mixed. Apart from the pop music newspapers *New Musical Express, Melody Maker,* and the like, the only other outlet for reviews were magazines and newspapers devoted to jazz, where comments ranged from "exciting music" to the inevitable charge that "the white man" can't play the blues. As Norman Jopling noted in *New Record Mirror*, "Alexis has just had an LP issued on Decca which has been unanimously panned by the purist critics and unanimously acclaimed by the ones who can enjoy a music that occasionally strays from the beaten track."

In any case, Korner had other problems to worry about. In the same month as the debut album release, Davies left the band after an argument over the growing influence—which he detested—of jazz musicians in Blues Incorporated. First came Jack Bruce, and then Charlie Watts made way for Ginger Baker [see **Cream**]. The arrival of saxophonist Heckstall-Smith was the final straw for Davies, who left to form his own band, Cyril Davies and the R&B All-Stars. To replace Davies, Korner brought in alto saxophonist Graham Bond [see **Graham Bond**].

In January 1963, Korner moved Blues Incorporated's Thursday-night residency to the Flamingo, while Davies's new group took over the Thursday night Marquee slot, setting up a rivalry between the two bands.

Meanwhile, with a trio of albums recorded in 1963 and 1964, Korner took Blues Incorporated further away from Muddy Waters and more down a Charles Mingus/Ray Charles jazz/soul path. The first album, simply titled *Alexis Korner's Blues Incorporated* (recorded in May 1963, again for Decca on its Ace of Clubs label), called upon what was by then the band's reasonably regular lineup. Heckstall-Smith was joined on sax by a surgeon, Art Themen, and by Johnny Parker on piano, Mike Scott on bass, and one of Britain's finest drummers, Phil Seamen. Although his life was blighted by heroin addiction, Seamen was regarded as the "boss drummer," the man they all looked up to.

The arrangements for the album were all specially written for the session, mainly by Korner, who stayed up all night with arranger Heckstall-Smith so that the musicians could rehearse them at the Flamingo. The all-instrumental album, which has remained a firm favorite with Korner fans, was technically superb and contained many excellent performances, in particular Korner's homage to Thelonius Monk and Charlie Mingus, "Blue Mink," which was done as a country blues song. Arguably the best track was "Preachin' Blues," played by Korner on slide bouzouki, using a door key picked up off the studio floor as a slide, complemented by sensitive drumming from Seamen. "Mississippi blues gone Greek," as Korner remarked.

Released in early 1965, the album was important in that it demonstrated Korner's ability to take American jazz and blues beyond slavish copying. The music had its own version of hipness. Rather than just reducing the music to its simplest renditions (as many critics felt that most white British blues musicians were prone to do), Korner (and the like-minded Graham Bond) experimented with jazz phrasing and arrangements to put "music" back into the blues and make it interesting.

As with many blues bands of the day, the best way to hear Blues Incorporated was live—especially because of the sterile recording techniques then in use that tended to "sanitize" the sound. For the next album, released on the Oriole label, recording engineers took one of the very first mobile recording units to the famous Cavern club in Liverpool, the Beatles' home base, to record the band on February 23, 1964. By then, the lineup had changed completely from that of a year earlier. A black American airman, vocalist Herbie Goins, had become the star of Blues Incorporated. He had excellent soul and gospel chops and had been playing with the big band jazz drummer Eric Delaney. Goins brought in Malcolm Saul on organ, Dave Castle on sax and Vernon Bown on string bass.

It appears that Korner didn't tell them that the gig was going to be recorded, because before they hit the stage, the band hit the booze. None of the band can recall much of the gig, but Goins managed to keep it together, especially with a storming version of "Hoochie Coochie Man," which was much better than the weak version on the Marquee album.

Shortly after they recorded *At the Cavern,* Korner landed another one-off deal, this time with Transatlantic, and he took yet another lineup into Olympic Studios in London to record *Red Hot from Alex.* The combination of musicians in the session revealed the way that Blues Incorporated was structured. Unlike standard blues and rock bands, Korner organized Blues Incorporated like a jazz band. The lineups were fluid; musicians might sit in just for one or two gigs, and Korner kept a very large card index by his phone, catalogued by instrument. If the drummer phoned up to say he had a gig paying more money, Korner would just flip through the index and call up somebody else, and as Blues Incorporated mainly played standards, any competent musician could come in and take over. However, it was still incredibly difficult in England to earn a living playing jazz, which partly explains why Korner played solo gigs and kept up with his radio work at the BBC. With a wife and three children to support, he didn't have much choice.

For the new album, Korner retained Goins, brought back Heckstall-Smith and Themen, and welcomed newcomers Ron Edgeworth on keyboards, Barry Howton on drums, and a real find, bassist Danny Thompson. (Thompson later became one of Britain's most sought-after bass

players, coming to fame in the late 1960s with the folk-rock group Pentangle.) "Haitian Fight Song," probably the most significant song on the album, showcased Korner's first attempt at a Mingus arrangement and it signaled a move to a more free-form style of improvisation linked to a standard blues repertoire. However, in Great Britain's current musical climate, free-form jazz/blues improvisation was virtually guaranteed to go down like a lead balloon. As *Record Mirror* noted, "They imitate nobody, and with that lineup, nobody dares to imitate them. If individuality and originality ever become the fashion in R&B circles, Alex will Korner the market."

In November 1964, Blues Incorporated released a new single, "I Need Your Lovin'" backed with "Please Please Please." Goins again sang on both sides of the release. *New Musical Express* called the single "as authentic as you can get in this country," while *Melody Maker's* Ray Coleman predicted the release would become a minor hit. When asked about his approach to making records, Korner explained to the magazine, "I'll tell you one thing: If by some very strange chance we are successful with this disc, and are called upon to make more singles, we shall try to make the next one as different as possible from this. We'd hate to think we were tied down to a type of sound. We play nothing but the blues, granted, but we'll play any good blues in any style. We don't want to be associated with one particular style."

In 1965, Korner released another single, "Little Baby" backed with "Roberta," issued on Parlophone that again featured Herbie Goins's vocals on both tracks. *New Musical Express* declared, "Both titles [are] R&B of the toe-tapping variety." Decca also finally released *Alexis Korner's Blues Incorporated* on its Ace of Clubs label.

By this time, Korner's lack of commercial success as a recording artist had become apparent by the succession of one-off deals he was having to negotiate in order to get studio time. Korner battled on, releasing another album in 1966 called *Sky High* (on account of the amount of marijuana smoked during the recording). *Sky High* was recorded by Spot at its Ryemuse Studio, located above a chemist's shop off Oxford Street. Korner brought along a young singer, Duffy Power, who had been part of Larry Parnes's roster of young, "wannabe rock'n'rollers" from which Billy Fury and Marty Wilde had emerged [see **Duffy Power**]. Being more of a blues singer, Power hadn't really fit in with Parnes's sound and had ended up living just around the corner from Korner. The two met through a mutual acquaintance, drummer Phil Kinorra. Power played

Korner some songs he had written and wound up as the vocalist on the record. A new drummer, Terry Cox, joined Danny Thompson on bass (these two went on to form the rhythm section for Pentangle). Top session brass players Alan Skidmore and Chris Pyne completed the lineup. As the studio was less than state-of-the-art, the recordings sounded thin and insubstantial, but the music had its moments, mainly provided by Power on Bill Broonzy's "Louise"; by the Skip James song made famous by Cream, "I'm So Glad"; and by Danny Thompson on the Mingus composition "Wednesday Night Prayer Meeting."

In addition to fronting the band, Korner had a career as a solo artist and a growing radio career presenting programs on a range of subjects, not just music. At one point, the BBC gave Korner a spot called "Korner's Korner," where with his immaculate, well-modulated deep voice, he was allowed to talk about anything he liked. Korner even starred in a children's TV program called *Five O'Clock Club*. He managed to bluff his way in as the show's musical director, a real coup considering that he couldn't read sheet music. He also secured an agreement that allowed him to play live one song of his own choice on each show. So once a week, Blues Incorporated fed the nation's youth a steady drip of Charlie Mingus to go with their after-school Marmite sandwiches.

Even though he had been playing to full houses at the Marquee and the Flamingo, Korner later explained to *Record Mirror* that the television work negatively affected his live gigs: "We did very few gigs as people began to regard us as a television band and thought we didn't go out on the road. On the occasional gigs we did do, [we] went out as a trio with myself, Danny Thompson and Terry Cox."

Because Korner could not land a hit album, record companies would not commit themselves beyond one-off deals. This meant they had little incentive to promote the albums, though the advances helped Korner with rent and bills. Still, he kept up the annual album pattern with *I Wonder Who*, recorded in April 1966 and released on Fontana exactly one year later. For this record, Korner reduced the lineup to a trio, his smallest ensemble yet, featuring himself with Thompson and Cox. This was probably his most "pure" blues album since *R&B from the Marquee* in 1962, with songs from Jimmy Smith, Ma Rainey, Maceo Merriweather and Jelly Roll Morton, plus Herbie Hancock's "Watermelon Man," which Korner regularly featured in his set from that point on. With no lead vocalist in the lineup, Korner assumed the role by default, and his distinctive sound was definitely an acquired taste. *Beat*

Instrumental wrote, "He's far from being another Sinatra and his grating vocal chords take some getting used to." Vocals aside, the album received positive reviews and many fans cite it as their favorite Korner record.

The trio also recorded "River's Invitation" and "Everyday I Have the Blues" at the same time as *I Wonder Who*, but the single was issued May 1966. *New Musical Express* saw this release as "possibly too morbid for the BBC and the charts, but fine authentic mid-tempo blues by this under-rated artist."

Ultimately, however, none of the singles or albums made any real impact on the British charts, and the days of Blues Incorporated were beginning to come to a close. Eventually, they dispersed with acrimony over money. It was the same old story: the musicians thought Korner was taking too much of a cut; Korner believed that as bandleader he had greater responsibility and more expenses, so he deserved the extra compensation.

For his short-lived preachin'-the-blues trio, Free at Last, formed in September 1966, Korner teamed up with drummer Hughie Flint (fresh out of the Bluesbreakers) and bassist Cliff Barton, who was soon replaced by Binky McKenzie [see **John Mayall**]. Then, in late 1967, Korner began working in a duo with Victor Brox, a much under-rated musician whose superb voice was soon to give depth and authenticity to the Aynsley Dunbar Retaliation, one of Britain's best blues bands [see **Aynsley Dunbar Retaliation**].

While Korner's career as a musician might have been faltering, he was always looking out for other talented, struggling artists. In the spring of 1968, Robert Plant was in despair. Born on August 20, 1948, he had given himself until his twentieth birthday to make it as a musician. Band after band had failed and his birthday was looming. Korner discovered Plant scuffling around the Birmingham music scene and warmed to him immediately. Here was another young man with a deep love of the blues whose family scorned his aspirations. They decided to go on the road together. Korner took Robert through his twentieth birthday, kept his faith alive and built his confidence. Jimmy Page and Peter Grant eventually spotted Plant playing in a Birmingham club, and a few days later Page invited the singer to his house. Plant's first move was to ask for Korner's advice, which was a resounding "go." The result, Led Zeppelin, made music history.

Korner also gave significant help and advice to a struggling young band called Free. Bass player Andy

Fraser had been dating Korner's daughter, Sappho, and Korner recommended the young musician to John Mayall for a brief stint in the Bluesbreakers to replace John McVie. When Free was in the process of being formed, Korner recommended Fraser to the new band and he became a member. Korner took them around the country, helping them gain wider exposure. He became their comanager and helped them secure their all-important contract with Island Records. Later, he tried to help Free guitarist Paul Kossoff as he struggled with an addiction to prescription drugs (a battle he ultimately lost in 1976).

Meanwhile, Korner had begun to give more serious consideration to his own career. Free's first comanager with Korner was Bryan Morrison, and through him Korner secured yet another one-album deal for himself, this time with Liberty Records. Although Thompson and Cox were now jamming with Pentangle, and despite all the arguments over money, Korner managed to persuade them to do the session along with a top sax player, Ray Warleigh, and piano player Steve Miller. Although fairly lightweight music compared to the contemporary blues sounds of Fleetwood Mac and the Cream, the album, *A New Generation of Blues,* contained one top song, "The Same for You." Korner's recording career was studded with gems such as these, where he was alone on acoustic guitar, singing in a range that's comfortable. These kinds of songs represent Korner's best material, and one carefully selected "Alexis Unplugged' album would be well worth the money.

With the album done, Korner laid plans for a new band featuring another eclectic mix of styles—including gospel, a sound he loved but had never explored as a musician. The band, appropriately named New Church, was a typically unlikely Korner assortment that included young, unknown bass player Nick South; Danish blues singer Peter Thorup; seasoned saxophonist Ray Warleigh from Blues Incorporated; and Sappho Korner.

New Church planned their debut gig at the Rolling Stones' free concert planned for Hyde Park in London on July 5, 1969. Since the days when Korner had helped promote the Rolling Stones, they had become one of the biggest bands in the world, but they were now going through a period of transition. They had been off the road for some time and problems were building with Brian Jones, who had been retreating into drugs in order to cope with the increasing isolation he was feeling in the band. Jagger and Richard contacted Korner about talking to Jones, who in turn phoned Korner, fearful that his band was about to replace him. When the Rolling Stones let him go, Korner and his family spent some time with Jones at his country farm as he tried to come to terms with life as an ex-Rolling Stone. Jones wanted to go out on the road with New Church, but Korner knew that would be a bad idea, feeling that Jones really needed to take some time to get himself together. Sadly, Jones never grasped that opportunity, and New Church took the stage at Hyde Park against the backdrop of Jones's tragic death just two days earlier.

In September, New Church went into Olympic Studios to lay down tracks, which, together with some live material added later, made up their one and only album, *Both Sides* (1970, Germany). For the studio sessions, Korner used his core New Church players plus a whole array of top British brass musicians (including John Surman, Henry Lowther and Harry Beckett), drummer John Marshall, and Andy Fraser and Paul Rodgers from Free. Korner, Thorup, Warleigh and world-class bassist Colin Hodgkinson (who later partnered with Korner in a duo that toured throughout Europe) recorded the live tracks in Hamburg, Germany. The songs—a mixture of soul, funk, gospel and blues—reflected Korner's eclectic intentions and included the standout tracks "Mighty Mighty Spade and Whitey" and "Funky" (a.k.a. "Soul Twist").

Korner took the band to Germany, where, as a fluent speaker of the language, he was gaining a loyal following that over the next decade would pack the halls for his concerts in numbers he could never hope to achieve in the U.K. When Korner first took New Church to Germany, the country was in the grip of a politically radical ferment, an offshoot of which was a belief that all rock music concerts should be free. New Church were due to play at a big indoor rock festival in Essen alongside Blind Faith, Pink Floyd, Free and others. The festival, however, was a total fiasco, as a torrent of forged tickets were in circulation. People with real tickets couldn't get in because of the crowds, Blind Faith didn't show up and Pink Floyd's gear was lost in transit. Eventually, the lid blew as somebody drove a van through the plate glass window at the front of the hall and created havoc. In the midst of this escalating and highly dangerous situation, Korner and Rory Gallagher went out into the foyer, now littered with broken glass, and played an impromptu concert for all those who couldn't get in [see **Rory Gallagher**]. Korner then went back into the main hall and compered the show in immaculate German.

Korner continued with his solo appearances, radio shows, and (with the help of his first professional manager) an increasing number of advertising voice-overs on TV. At the same time, he continued to draw large crowds in the

German market with New Church. After awhile, however, although he wanted to continue his working relationship with Peter Thorup, he tired of the New Church format and gradually wound the band down. Top producer Mickie Most (Animals, Herman's Hermits, Donovan, etc.) wanted to sign the pair to his RAK label, and from that came the most unlikely of outcomes—Alexis Korner had a hit record.

Korner had always said that he wanted to work with a big band and, by coincidence, one of Most's associates, John Cameron, was thinking along similar lines. They all gathered on Most's yacht in the south of France, and several bottles of wine later the idea of CCS—the Collective Consciousness Society—was born. They brought together the best of London's jazz session musicians to cut an album. But with the breathtaking audacity typical of the period, Most decided CCS's first single would be Led Zeppelin's "Whole Lotta Love." He easily obtained permission to use it, as he shared an office with Peter Grant, Zeppelin's manager. Amazingly, the improbable combination of a 40-year-old blues musician and a Danish guitarist fronting a big band of jazz musicians not only created a single that got into the U.K. Top 20, but their version of "Whole Lotta Love" was chosen as the theme song for Britain's longest running TV chart show, *Top of the Pops*. The next two singles fared even better, both getting into the Top Ten. Not without irony, after a lifetime of playing music, Korner became the archetypal overnight sensation, with his face on the front of pop magazines.

However, that same lifetime of experience gave him enough insight to know that the success would be temporary—the band was far too expensive to take on the road, and most of the musicians had regular gigs anyway. Korner also wanted another shot in the recording studio under his own name. His chance came in August 1970 when he recorded an album funded by a millionaire who was a huge Korner fan and wanted to produce the sessions. Despite being recorded in Bermuda and sporting one of Korner's best album covers, the record itself—simply called *Alexis*—was probably his worst and sank without a trace.

Bootleg Him (1972), the brainchild of Korner's manager, was a much more successful album and was meant to remind the world of Korner's legacy in rock. The double-album, with extensive sleeve notes and a very hip Roger Dean cover, comprised many unreleased tracks from Korner's past and featured everyone who had found fame and fortune after playing with Korner. Of its many highlights, it included a very rare recording with Jack Bruce, Ginger Baker and Graham Bond. One of the photos in the double-album was shot in June 1971 at Olympic Studios during the recording of B.B. King's London album. Korner was shown with King and Steve Marriott of Humble Pie. From this came an invitation for Korner and his regular partner, Peter Thorup, to support Humble Pie on their next U.S. tour.

The bill for the Humble Pie tour also included King Crimson, who were in the throes of breaking up. April Fools' Day 1972 was their last gig, and afterwards drummer Ian Wallace, saxophone player Mel Collins and bassist Boz Burrell fell in with Korner and Thorup in New Orleans. The five of them played a number of gigs across the U.S. Trading on Korner's newfound fame, they started off as "Alexis Korner and Friends," but ended up as SNAPE, an acronym for "Something Nasty 'Appens Everyday," the name of a vicious dare game played by British musicians on the road. This was Korner's first (and last) foray into straight-ahead rock. Together, they began to think they had a combination that might just work. On the strength of their live show (and German-only live album release), they had the potential to become a significant touring band, although their only studio album, *Accidentally Born in New Orleans*, had had all the guts produced out of it and the material was generally weak.

However, American promoters had become interested in SNAPE, and Korner's management hoped to persuade Korner to make a full tour of the United States. But Korner would have none of it. It's possible that he didn't want to be away from his family for too long, and touring with SNAPE would have meant at least a year away from home. Or, shrewdly, perhaps he didn't want to put all his eggs in one basket: a lengthy tour with the band would have meant turning down all his other commitments, such as radio and TV. There was also a big chance of failing in the U.S., where he wasn't well known, whereas in Europe he had a ready and enthusiastic audience. Whatever the reason, the U.S. rock'n'roll juggernaut beckoned, but Korner walked away and SNAPE folded.

Postscript

Korner still needed to consolidate his position with a strong new solo album to secure his recent commercial success. In the mid-1970s, he received a two-album deal with Polydor in Germany. The first, again called *Alexis Korner*, was essentially SNAPE plus friends (including Zoot Money and Colin Hodgkinson). The combination made a good album with some strong tracks ("Wild

Women and Desperate Men" and "Captain America") and some well-chosen covers suitable for Korner's vocal range, such as J.J. Cale's "Lies."

He had more hope for the second album, *Get Off My Cloud*, because the guests this time included Keith Richards, Peter Frampton and Steve Marriott. But despite the all-star cast and some terrific reviews, the album didn't take off. The idea was that with Keith Richards on the album, it would be released in the U.S. to tie in with the Rolling Stones' upcoming tour. Korner would go to the United States and give interviews with the band, and the record would be in the shops as the Rolling Stones went from place to place. The idea flopped because CBS mishandled the album's distribution, except in one city where 25,000 copies sold very quickly.

The breakthrough in Korner's DJ career came in 1977 when the first edition of *The Alexis Korner Blues and Soul Show* hit the airwaves. Produced by his longstanding friend and producer Jeff Griffin, the show was surprisingly successful. Korner wrote his own scripts and introduced the British public to a wealth of music—everything from Little Featto gospel to music from around the world. (This was well before anybody had coined the term "world music.")

In 1978, for Korner's fiftieth birthday, German TV producer Willie Lang decided to honor Korner by filming an all-star birthday concert for German television. Jeff Griffin added the idea of making it a "simulcast" with BBC-TV and Radio One, an idea first tried with Van Morrison back in 1974. Sadly, the BBC turned down the chance to televise a celebrity concert that celebrated one of the most influential musicians in the history of British blues and rock. Therefore, Griffin recorded the show for radio, leaving the pictures for German TV.

The German music media's esteem for Korner was demonstrated by the lavish arrangements for the birthday party/concert at no less than the Gatsby Room at Pinewood Studios, which included rivers of free booze and mountains of free food. For the show, Korner put together his current touring band of Hodgkinson and Money, along with the best of British jazz sax players (including Dick Heckstall-Smith and John Surman) standing alongside Paul Jones, Chris Farlowe and Eric Clapton [see **Eric Clapton**]. The resulting show was released as *The Party Album*.

From that highly successful and raucous evening came the idea for a new band, Rocket 88, the brainchild of the "sixth Rolling Stone," pianist Ian Stewart. He persuaded

another pianist, Bob Hall [see **Brunning Hall Sunflower Blues Band**], to become interested in the idea, and he in turn signed up Korner. Rocket 88 gained momentum, picking up Charlie Watts and Jack Bruce [see **Cream**] for the occasional gig along the way. They never intended for it to be a regular working band, but a vehicle for a group of accomplished musicians to get together, blow through some standards and generally have a good time as they touted their barroom blues around Europe.

As the 1980s dawned with Korner finally having made the transition from struggling nonentity to well-established artist, he entered a period wherein he wanted to diversify into film and television (his radio and voice-over work remained a lucrative source of income). In the early 1970s, Korner had narrated Joe Boyd's film documentary on Jimi Hendrix. Now Korner and his manager had a number of film ideas in the pipeline, including "Jody Grinder," which would explore the history of American Army marching songs; "Dream Cars," about Formula One racing drivers; and a very ambitious series on the history of rock. They had already secured interviews with Tina Turner, Paul McCartney and B.B. King when Korner's health suddenly declined.

For some time, Korner had not been feeling well. He was losing weight and complaining of headaches. On October 12, 1983, he collapsed and was taken to the hospital. Doctors diagnosed him with cancer, and his condition worsened in the coming weeks. On New Year's Day, 1984, Alexis Korner died at the age of 55.

Most of the national and major regional newspapers and all of the rock press carried substantial tributes to Korner. *Music Week* devoted five pages and the Rolling Stones took out a full-page ad in tribute. Today, Alexis Korner's legacy is locked away in memories, recalled by many different people for all sorts of reasons. Korner was an *éminence grise*, not just the Father of the Blues, but the Godfather of Good Taste.

Since his death, there has been a veritable frenzy of Korner-related activity. Many of his early recordings have been remastered and reissued on a variety of different labels. Among the long-out-of-print gems are *Sky High* and *Red Hot from Alex*.

Every year since 1994, a charity concert held in Korner's memory has taken place at Buxton Opera House in Derbyshire, deep in the English countryside. Artists appearing over the years have included Jack Bruce, Peter

Green, Eric Burdon, Chris Farlowe, Tim Rose, Mick Taylor, Aynsley Dunbar, Tony McPhee and Mick Abrahams. Robert Plant and Jimmy Page even brought their band for a full-blown session before they went on tour together for the first time since Led Zeppelin's demise.

In March 2000, the BBC produced a radio documentary about Korner presented by Tom Robinson.

Discography

Release Date	Title	Catalog Number

U.S. Albums

Alexis Korner
1972 *Bootleg Him* (2 LP) — Warner Brothers 2XS-1966

She Fooled Me/I'm a Hoochie Coochie Man/Yellow Dog Blues/I Wonder Who/Dee/Oh Lord Don't Let Them Drop That Atomic Bomb on Me/Rockin'/Honesty/I Got a Woman/Mighty-Mighty Spade and Whitey/Corina-Corina/Operator/The Love You Save/Jesus Is Just Alright/That's All/Evil Hearted Woman/Clay House Inn/Love Is Gonna Go/Sunrise/Hellhound on My Trail

SNAPE
1972 *Accidentally Borne in New Orleans* — Warner Brothers BS-2647

Gospel Ship/One Scotch, One Bourbon, One Beer/Sweet Sympathy/Rock Me/Don't Change on Me/You Got the Power/Lo and Behold/Country Shoes

U.K. Singles

Ken Colyer's Skiffle Group (with Alexis Korner)
1955 Take This Hammer/ Down By the Riverside — Decca F 10631
1956 Go Down Old Hannah/Steamline Train — Decca FJ 10711

Beryl Bryden's Back-Room Skiffle (with Alexis Korner)
1956 Kansas City Blues/Casey Jones — Decca F-J 10823

The Alexis Korner Skiffle Group
1958 County Jail/ I Ain't Gonna Worry No More — Tempo A 166

Nancy Spain with Alexis Korner and Band
1962 Up-Town/Blaydon Races[1] — Lyntone LYN 299
  [1] Credited as Blues Incorporated with Alexis Korner. This flexidisc was given away to promote the magazine *Trio*.

Alexis Korner's Blues Incorporated
1964 I Need Your Lovin'/Please Please Please — Parlophone R 5206
1965 Little Baby/Roberta — Parlophone R 5247

Alexis Korner's All-Stars
1965 See See Rider/Blues á la King — King KG 1017

Alexis Korner
1966 River's Invitation/ Everyday I Have the Blues — Fontana TF 706
1967 Rosie/Rock Me — Fontana TF 817

CCS (with Alexis Korner)
1970 Whole Lotta Love/Boom Boom — RAK 104
1971 Walking/Salome — RAK 109
1971 Tap Turns on the Water/Save the World — RAK 119
1972 Brother/Mister What You Can't Have I Can Get — RAK 126
1972 Sixteen Tons/This Is My Life — RAK 141

U.K. EPs

Ken Colyer's Skiffle Group
1955 *Ken Colyer's Skiffle Group* — Decca DFE 6286
Take This Hammer/Down by the Riverside/Go Down Old Hannah/Streamline Train

The Alexis Korner Skiffle Group
1957 *Blues from the Roundhouse, Volume 1* — Tempo EXA 76
I Ain't Gonna Worry No More/Kid Man/County Jail/Easy Rider

Alexis Korner's Blues Incorporated
1958 *Blues from the Roundhouse, Volume 2* — Tempo EXA 102
Sail On/National Defence Blues/Go Down Sunshine/Death Letter

Alexis Korner & Davy Graham
1962 *3/4 A.D.* — Topic TOP 70
3/4 A.D./Angi/Davy's Train Blues

U.K. Albums

Alexis Korner's Breakdown Group Featuring Cyril Davies
1957 *Blues from the Roundhouse* — 77 LP 2
Leaving Blues/Rotten Break/Alberta/Roundhouse Stomp/Skip to My Lou/Good Morning/Boll Weevil/Ella Speed

1984 *Alexis 1957* — Krazy Kat KK 789
Leaving Blues[1]/Alberta[1]/Roadhouse Stomp[1]/Skip to My Lou[1]/Good Morning[1]/Boll Weevil[1]/Ella Speed[1]/Streamline Train[1]/Rotten Break[2]/County Jail[2]/Doggone My Good Luck Soul[2]/Badly Mistreated Man[2]
  [1] Recorded live at the Roundhouse on February 13, 1957.
  [2] Recorded live at Burnham, Bucks on March 29, 1957.

Alexis Korner's Blues Incorporated
1962 *R&B from the Marquee* — Ace of Clubs ACL 1130
Gotta Move/Rain Is Such a Lonesome Sound/I Got My Brand on You/Spooky But Nice/Keep Your Hands Off/I Wanna Put a Tiger in Your Tank/I Got My Mojo Working/Finkle's Café/Hoochie Coochie Man/Down Town/How Long, How Long Blues/I Thought I Heard That Train Whistle Blow

1964 *Red Hot from Alex* — Transatlantic TRA 117
Woke Up This Morning/Skippin'/Herbie's Tune/Stormy Monday/It's

Happening/Roberta/Jones/Cabbage Greens/Chicken Shack/Haitian Fight Song

1964   *At the Cavern*   Oriole PS 40058
Recorded live at the Cavern, Liverpool, February 23, 1964.
Overdrive/Whoa Babe/Everyday I Have the Blues/Hoochie Coochie Man/Herbie's Tune/Little Bitty Gal Blues/Well Alright, OK, You Win/Kansas City

1965   *Alexis Korner's Blues Incorporated*   Ace of Clubs
                                        ACL 1187
Blue Mink/Rainy Tuesday/Yogi/Sappho/Navy Blue/Royal Dooji/Preachin' the Blues/The Captain's Tiger/A Little Bit Groovy/Anything for You/Chris Trundle's Habit/Trundlin'

1966   *Sky High*   Spot JW 551
Long Black Train/Rock Me/I'm So Glad (You're Mine)/Wednesday Night Prayer Meeting/Honesty/Yellow Dog Blues/Let the Good Times Roll/Ooo Wee Baby (Wee Baby Blues)/River's Invitation/Money Honey/Big Road Blues/Louise/Floating/Another 5 Miles/Daph's Dance

Alexis Korner
1967   *I Wonder Who*   Fontana TL 5381
Watermelon Man/Streamline Train/Rock Me/Come Back/Going Down Slow/2.19 Blues/I Wonder Who?/Chicken Shack Back Home/County Jail Blues/Roll 'Em Pete/Betty and Dupree/See See Rider

1968   *A New Generation of Blues*   Liberty LBL 83147
Mary Open the Door/Little Bitty Girl/Baby Don't You Love Me/Go Down Sunshine/The Same for You/I'm Tore Down/In the Evening/Somethin' You Got/New Worried Blues/What's That Sound I Hear/A Flower

1971   *Alexis*   RAK SRAK 501
Black Woman (The Wild Ox Moan)/Frankie Diamond/Clay House Inn/Stump Blues/You Can Make It Like You Want It to Be/Gold/Saturday Sun/I Don't Know/Am I My Brother's Keeper/Stop Playing Games/That's All

1971   *Bootleg Him* (2 LP)   RAK SRAK
                                        SP 51 (LP)
1986   *Alexis Korner And . . .*   Castle
        The Collection 1961–72   CCSLP 150 (LP)
                                        Castle
                                        CCSCD 150 (CD)
She Fooled Me/Hoochie Coochie Man/Oh Lord Don't Let Them Drop That Atomic Bomb on Me/I Got a Woman/Corina Corina/Everyday I Have the Blues/Operator/Rosie/Polly Put the Kettle On/I See It/You Don't Miss Your Water Till Your Well Runs Dry/Mighty Mighty Spade and Whitey/ Lo and Behold/Louisiana Blues/Ooo Wee Baby/Rock Me Baby

1994   *The BBC Radio Sessions*   Music Club
                                        MCCD 179 (CD)
Everything She Needs/(Night Time Is) The Right Time/Overdrive/Please, Please, Please/Back at the Chicken Shack/Trouble in Mind/When Will I Be Called a Man/Wednesday Night Prayer Meeting/Going Down Slow/Blue Mink/Rock Me/Louisiana Blues/Stump Blues/Jesus Is Just Alright with Me/Looking for Fun/Vicksburg Blues/Love Is Gonna Go/Bring It on Home (To Me)/Money Honey/How Can a Poor Man Stand Such Times and Live

CCS (with Alexis Korner)
1970   *CCS*   RAK SRAK 6751
Boom Boom/Satisfaction/Waiting Song/Lookin' for Fun/Whole Lotta Love/Living in the Past/Sunrise/Dos Cantos/Wade in the Water

1972   *CCS 2*   RAK SRAK 503
Brother/Black Dog/I Want You Back/Running Out of Sky/Whole Lotta Rock'n'Roll-School Day-Lucille-Long Tall Sally-Whole Lotta Love/Chaos/Can We Ever Get It Back/This Is My Life/Misunderstood/Maggie's Song/City

Miscellaneous U.K. Releases

Ken Colyer's Skiffle Group
1954   *Back to the Delta* (10" LP)   Decca LF 1196
Alexis appears on four songs, "Take This Hammer," "Down by the Riverside," "Go Down Old Hannah" and "Streamline Train."

1964   *Rhythm & Blues*   Decca LK 4616
Includes "Early in the Morning" and "Night Time Is the Right Time."

Foreign Releases

New Church and Friends
1969   *Both Sides* (Germany)   Metronome
                                        MLP15364
Mighty Mighty Spade and Whitey/Funky (a.k.a. "Soul Twist")/Wild Indian Woman/I See It/You Don't Miss Your Water Till the Well Runs Dry/Polly Put the Kettle On[1]/Worried Blues[1]/The Duo Thing[1]/Rosie[1]
    [1] Live in Hamburg, December 9, 1969.

1981   *Alexis Korner's Blues*   Decca Telde
        Incorporated (Germany)   c 6.24475
Early in the Morning/I Ain't Gonna Worry No More/Kid Man/Country Jail/Go Down Sunshine/Tiger in Your Tank/Night Time is the Right Time/I'm Built For Comfort/I Got My Mojo Working/Finkle Café/Hootchie Coochie Man/Rain Is Such a Lonesome Thing

The Mark Leeman Five

Integrating jazz and R&B influences with the blues, the Mark Leeman Five were a highly respected British band whose career was sadly cut short by the death of their leader after releasing only one single.

John Ardrey (b. April 24, 1941, Shepherd's Bush, West London, U.K.; d. June 27, 1965) attended West Kensington Central Grammar School, where he initially intended to study art. Later, he became an expert lithographer and pursued a career in the graphics field. Also drawn to music, he started to play the guitar and sing, and in September 1961, he and four musician friends formed the Mark Leeman Five. The lineup consisted of Ardrey (who at the time adopted the name Mark Leeman) on vocals and guitar, Alan Roskams on lead guitar, Terry Goldberg on organ, David Hyde on bass and Brian "Blinkie" Davison on drums.

They easily distinguished themselves from most of their contemporaries through their enthusiasm for the blues, R&B, and jazz, a combination that the band members effortlessly melded in their repertoire. However, their first demo tape, recorded in 1962, reflected none of these influences. Surprisingly, both "The Boy Who Walks All Alone" and "Chasing Shadows" were lightweight pop fare more reminiscent of Bobby Vinton than Ray Charles.

Their second demo, featuring versions of Barrett Strong's "Money" and the uncredited "Back Home," was more indicative of the band's non-pop roots and interests. Their version of "Money," which predates versions by the Beatles and the Rolling Stones, was particularly impressive.

The Mark Leeman Five first gigged at the Salutation Pub in Woolwich, then gradually expanded their territory. In an attempt to upgrade their bookings to more prestigious venues, the group financed an 11-track demo culled from their stage repertoire. Made in 1963, the recordings were remarkable in that, although primitive, they established the Mark Leeman Five as already skillful performers of R&B and blues material, such as Jimmy Reed's "Shame Shame Shame" and Willie Dixon's "You Can't Judge a Book by Looking at the Cover." At the same time, the group seamlessly switched to jazz numbers like Cannonball Adderley's "Work Song" and the instrumentals "Moanin'" and "Frenzy." The highlight of the set was their version of Nina Simone's "Forbidden Fruit," an amusing, modernized deconstruction of the Adam and Eve saga.

The quintet got their big break during a gig on January 14, 1964, supporting the red-hot Manfred Mann at St. Mary's Hall, Putney. The members of Manfred Mann (or the Manfreds as they became known) were greatly impressed by the Mark Leeman Five and advised them to get in touch with their manager, Ken Pitt. As a result, the band was soon added to Pitt's roster of artists.

The Manfreds became mentors to the Mark Leeman Five and arranged for the group to support them throughout Manfred Mann's residency at London's Marquee club. The Leeman Five's first appearance at the famed venue was on April 13, 1964, and they quickly became regulars, appearing 74 times over the next two years. The exposure at the Marquee led to dates at other venues, and a larger following started to build.

The Manfreds' sponsorship of the Mark Leeman Five extended to the studio as well. Manfred Mann formed his own production company, Manfredisc, with the intention of producing other artists. He produced the Mark Leeman Five's first single, the brooding yet snappy "Portland Town" (backed with "Gotta Get Myself Together"). Released in January 1965, the single garnered positive reviews. *New Musical Express* described the top side as "a pounding beat with organ and electronic plucking prominent. Both lyric and melody have a distinct folksy feel. There's a unison vocal and the whole effect is catchy, if only because it's so repetitive." An alternative version of "Portland Town" was released in 1972 on the French LP *Rock Generation Vol 8*.

Soon thereafter, the Mark Leeman Five were scheduled to undertake a series of 13 Sunday concerts with Manfred Mann at the Rainbow Theatre in Blackpool. The first date was on June 27, 1965, and the Mark Leeman Five went over very well. In the dressing room after the performance, Leeman discussed his next career move with his new manager, Pitt. All seemed confident that a breakthrough was imminent.

That same evening, Leeman decided to go to Blackburn to see his friend, singer Julie Grant, perform. Leeman, who didn't drive, had to catch a ride to the show, so he arranged for one of Grant's friends to drive him. While en route, the car crashed into a tree, killing Leeman and severely injuring the driver.

When the rest of the group arrived in London, they were shattered to learn of Leeman's death, but vowed to continue and keep the name Mark Leeman Five in his memory. They found singer Roger Peacock to replace him. (Peacock had previously been in the Cheynes, which had also included Mick Fleetwood and Peter Bardens. Peacock and the Cheynes cut three singles before the band folded.) The new singer's first appearance with the Mark Leeman Five was on July 2, 1965. Later that month, they played two benefit concerts for Mark's widow, Edna, at the Marquee in London. The concert included performances by Unit Four Plus Two, Manfred Mann, the Animals, and of course the Mark Leeman Five featuring Peacock.

Meanwhile, the band was approached about releasing their eleven-track demo, recorded a year earlier, as an album. Prior to the accident, they had shopped the recordings to a record company that had expressed interest but never followed through. Two weeks after Leeman's death, the company contacted manager Pitt, expressing an immediate interest in releasing the tapes. Pitt felt that issuing the recordings then would have been exploitative, and he told *Melody Maker*, "I will have nothing to do with them. We discussed this with the group and Mark's parents and we are not being phonily [sic] sentimental. The record is no better now than it was, and it's a pity they should try to cash in on it now. The rotten thing is the record has become of commercial value."

When the tapes were finally released commercially in 1991, *Record Collector* noted that they made "a clear case for rewriting the history of British rock to set the Mark Leeman Five up among the pioneers."

Terry Goldberg left the group at the end of August 1965 and was replaced by Tom Parker on keyboards. The group then released a second single that had been recorded prior to the accident. The top side, "Blow My Blues Away," had been penned by Leeman, while the song covered on the flip side, "On the Horizon," had once been the B-side of Ben E. King's smash single "Stand By Me." *New Musical Express* was impressed with "Blow My Blues Away," printing, "A self-penned title with an authentic R&B feel, it spotlights solo voice singing and blues-shouting with chanting by the other members of the Leeman Five. The mid-tempo shuffle beat is emphasized by rattling tambourine. A worthy memorial to this young artist."

For their third single, produced by Denny Cordell, the band selected "Forbidden Fruit," the song associated with Nina Simone that had long been part of their stage act. Unfortunately, the Nashville Teens also recorded a version of the song at around the same time and declared that the Mark Leeman Five had stolen the song from them. The Leeman Five responded publicly with a lengthy, somewhat humorous rebuttal. "So the Nashville Teens attacked our recording of 'Forbidden Fruit' . . . well, Stevie Winwood said: 'Mark Leeman Five—Yeah! This is all right! It's fabulous and the best thing they do on stage. It's fantastic.' But unlike the Teens, Steve is an authority on our work, having shared the Marquee stage with us for so long. He knows how 'Fruit' goes down and is accepted. Our late colleague, Mark Leeman, was singing 'Fruit' with us in

1961—just before the Nina Simone album was on sale. It's almost our signature tune—it draws ecstatic applause. When Roger Peacock joined us, we kept the number in [our repertoire]. So good was the reaction, we recorded it. We did so in October last year. We heard not a whisper of the Teens having recorded it until ours was announced in the press in January, and their manager phoned us to say they were planning a release in a few weeks. We well know 'Fruit' won't be a big seller for us, but it's been a success in other ways. We alone can judge the good it has done for us. We've got TV shows, unanimously good reviews from critics, praise and respect from knowing people and satisfied fans. We've asked around and can find nobody who knows of the Nashville Teens' association with 'Forbidden Fruit.' The only fruit they seem to be associated with is . . . SOUR GRAPES!!'"

Still, when the song lagged below the charts, it couldn't help but further demoralize the group. They issued one final single, "Follow Me," in July 1966. Hyde and Peacock wrote the B-side, "Gather Up the Pieces." Hyde had started to write material for the group and had hoped that the next A-side would be his own composition. He told *Beat Instrumental* that he favored a change in the group's style: "We're striving to do something different—not too different—but a change in arrangements and that kind of thing. We'd like to get a bit more sophisticated and get away from bashing out three chords, but we need more time and rehearsals."

However, Hyde never got his chance, as Peacock left the group for Dave Antony's Moods following the failure of "Follow Me." Vocalist Pete Hodges replaced Peacock, but the new lineup barely lasted until the end of the month. The Mark Leeman Five officially disbanded on July 29, 1966, following a gig at the Flamenco in Folkstone.

Postscript

Brian Davidson found his greatest musical success as a member of the Nice with Keith Emerson. Tom Parker briefly became a member of Eric Burdon's New Animals before joining Jimmy James and the Vagabonds. Alan Roskams became the lead guitarist in Gass; Roger Peacock became a nightclub singer in Rome; and David Hyde quit the music business.

Discography

Release Date	Title	Catalog Number

U.K. Singles

1965	Portland Town/Gotta Get Myself Together	Columbia DB 7452
1965	Blow My Blues Away/On the Horizon	Columbia DB 7648
1966	Forbidden Fruit/Going to Bluesville	Columbia DB 7812
1966	Follow Me/Gather Up the Pieces	Columbia DB 7955

U.K. Albums

1991	*The Mark Leeman Five Memorial Album*	See for Miles SEE CD 317

Portland Town/Gotta Get Myself Together/Got My Mojo Working/Green Onions/Shame Shame Shame/Work Song/Forbidden Fruit/Let the Sun Shine In/Frenzy/On the Horizon/Blow My Blues Away/Money/Back Home/The Boy Who Walks All Alone/Chasing Shadows/Moanin'/Dr. Feelgood/You Can't Judge a Book By Its Cover/Just a Little Lovin'/Going to Bluesville/Follow Me/Gather Up the Pieces/Forbidden Fruit (single version)/Portland Town (extended version)/Gotta Get Myself Together (stereo version)

Foreign Releases

1972	*Rock Generation Volume 8* (France)	BYG 529.708T

Various artists compilation album including alternative version of "Portland Town."

Taj Mahal

Taj Mahal was something of a enigma in the late 1960s—a city-born black man who almost single-handedly kept alive the 1920s and 1930s acoustic country blues music of the rural American South. By effectively resurrecting and updating obscure, older country blues material, his appeal crossed racial boundaries and found fans in both blues purists and those who were simply attracted to the electric sounds of Mahal's crack, interracial band and the charismatic personality of Mahal himself.

His hard to classify style is "an interesting blend . . . I guess I'd call it acoustic soul," Mahal told *The Los Angeles Times* in 1998. "All these different elements are part of a thread that's led me back to certain techniques and forms of traditional African music. Much of it, like fingerpickin', has influenced American guitar playing."

Born Henry Saint Claire Fredericks on May 17, 1942, in New York City, Mahal was raised in Springfield, Massachusetts, where his family moved when he was an infant. He grew up in a musically rich environment. His father, a jazz arranger and pianist who worked as a mechanic by day, was killed in a tractor accident when Mahal was 12. His mother was a classically trained pianist and gospel singer who worked as a schoolteacher. At the time of his father's death, Mahal was the oldest of five children. His mother subsequently remarried and the family expanded by four more children.

Mahal's only formal music education encompassed two weeks of piano lessons, which came to an end after his teacher told his mother that he lacked any musical aptitude. By the time he was 12 or 13, he started looking for another instrument to play and picked up the guitar. His next-door neighbor, Lynwood Perry, was a year older then Taj and an accomplished guitarist. Perry taught Taj how to play the instrument and introduced him to Southern blues. By junior high school, he had also dabbled with the trombone, clarinet and harmonica.

Growing up, Mahal listened to Charlie Parker, Coleman Hawkins, Thelonious Monk and Charles Mingus. At the same time, he discovered what would soon become an obsession—the blues. Numerous blues artists influenced him as a young man, from early country blues performers such as Charlie Patton, Robert Johnson, Garfield Akers and Kid Bailey, to the modern city blues emanating from Chicago, spearheaded by the likes of Jimmy Reed, Bo Diddley, Muddy Waters, Howlin' Wolf and the rocker, Chuck Berry.

While in high school, Mahal worked at a local dairy farm. Following graduation, he entered the University of Massachusetts at Amherst where he majored in animal husbandry and agriculture. Henry Saint Claire Fredericks also renamed himself after the famous mausoleum located in India. He explained his motives to *Hit Parader:* "My given name comes out of plantations and slavery. I took the name Taj Mahal because it's not out of that culture, my parents or my people."

Mahal joined the Folklore Society and met and played with Buffy Sainte-Marie. "This was the first time I came across white people who dug blues . . . I didn't know there were that many," Mahal later recalled to *Guitar Player.*

"Cats would lay records on me that would knock me out, and pretty soon I got hip to places like the Library of Congress, certain names or record labels, and certain record stores that had this kind of music. I listened to all these records for a few years, and I got involved by listening."

While attending college, he honed his musical skills by playing the coffeehouse and college mixer circuit, both as a solo artist and with his band, the Electras. Comprised of two guitars, piano, bass, drums and a couple of horns, the Electras played weekends at the Quonset Club and at dances. Their repertoire consisted of a cross-section of what was popular at the time: "Do You Love Me," "Twist and Shout," "What'd I Say," "Georgia on My Mind," "Searchin'," "Alley Oop" and "Misty." In addition, Mahal performed Robert Johnson and Leadbelly songs as a solo artist at a local establishment, the Salladin Coffeehouse, and made regular trips to Boston and Greenwich Village to explore the folk music scenes there.

He also spent a lot of time at the nearby Club 47 in Cambridge, Massachusetts, the legendary coffeehouse that also gave Joan Baez and Bob Dylan their start back in the early 1960s. At Club 47, he could hear and perform the music he wanted to play, and he started to acquire the recordings of the Reverend Gary Davis and Jesse Fuller, both of whom were particularly influential on him.

Following his graduation from college, where he earned his degree in Veterinary Science, he headed west in late 1964, accompanied by Jesse Lee Kincaid, a 12-string guitar player he met in the Boston clubs. Kincaid was from Detroit, but he grew up in California. The pair performed folk music as Taj Mahal and Jesse Lee Kincaid, including some well-received gigs at the prestigious Ash Grove, Los Angeles's preeminent folk and blues club.

In 1965, the United States was swept up in the folk-rock movement spearheaded by Bob Dylan and the Byrds, and Mahal and Kincaid decided to put together a folk-rock group. Their choice for lead guitarist was 17-year-old prodigy Ryland Cooder.

Born on March 15, 1947, in Santa Monica, California, Ryland Peter Cooder first started playing the guitar at age three when his father gave him a four-string Silvertone tenor guitar. Encouraged by his father, Cooder quickly learned a few simple tunes. At age ten, when his hands were big enough, his parents gave him his first proper guitar, a Martin six-string. He practiced constantly and absorbed a variety of influences, including bluegrass and country-and-western. The youngster was soon emulating the finger-picking style of Merle Travis, but his main passion would be the blues. He was particularly influenced by the guitar styles of Josh White and Son House. Other influences included Reverend Gary Davis (from whom he took lessons), Jesse Fuller, Sleepy John Estes, Doc Watson, Skip James and Mississippi John Hurt.

Cooder spent a great deal of time at McCabe's Music and the Ash Grove. Other musicians recognized his talent, and, while Cooder was still attending Santa Monica High, Jackie DeShannon hired him professionally to back her at the Ash Grove. He then briefly joined an electric blues band, King David and the Parables, whose musical director was Barry Hansen (a.k.a. Dr. Demento). He quit after only three rehearsals because he had never played electric music before and, at the time, didn't take a liking to it.

After being recruited by Mahal and Kincaid, Cooder recommended his friend, Gary Marker, as a bass player. Marker learned to play the clarinet at age nine and later took up the alto saxophone, drums, cello and double bass. He had a jazz background and had attended Boston's Berklee School of Music on a scholarship from *Downbeat* magazine. The quartet played a few gigs with Jesse Lee Kincaid moving over to the drum stool, but Marker recruited drummer Ed Cassidy, thereby freeing Kincaid to play guitar. Cassidy was Marker's former colleague in the New Jazz Trio (a combo that played New York clubs in the early 1960s) and a veteran of many jazz combos.

Naming themselves the Rising Sons, the newly formed band started to play the L.A. club scene in mid-1965, appearing at the Ash Grove, Ciro's, the Whisky A Go-Go and the Trip. Their repertoire was composed mostly of blues material, such as Muddy Waters's "I've Got My Mojo Working" and John Lee Hooker's "Crawlin' King Snake," "Jelly Jelly" and "Long Tall Shorty." They also performed the jug band-oriented "Rich Gal" and Kincaid's Beatlesque originals.

With Mahal's dynamic presence as frontman and Cooder's exemplary bottleneck playing, the band became one of Los Angeles's hottest local acts. *The Los Angles Free Press* noted, "The Rising Sons play blues, Delta blues and rhythm and blues, majority traditional material—and . . . it sounds as relevant and immediate as anything the Yardbirds or Beatles can come up with."

The Rising Sons made the Ash Grove their home-base. They began to attract major label interest and cut demos for Capitol, Warner Brothers, Elektra and Columbia before signing with Columbia in June 1965. Ed Cassidy left the band shortly after their initial sessions, as he had injured his right arm and wrist and was required to be in a cast for six weeks. He was replaced by Kevin Kelley, a first cousin of the Byrds' Chris Hillman. Kelley took up the drums at age 11, switched to guitar at 16, and reverted back to the drums after a three-year tour of duty in the Marines.

Columbia assigned ace producer Terry Melcher to work with the band, and they seemed to be on their way. Melcher, the son of Doris Day, was only 22 at the time, but was already something of a veteran in the business. As a member of the Rip Chords, along with Bruce Johnson (later of the Beach Boys), he'd released several singles and two albums on Columbia, including the single "Hey Little Cobra," which had reached #4 in 1963. Melcher and Johnson also recorded as Bruce & Terry and as the Rogues. In 1965, Melcher was red-hot as producer of both the Byrds and Paul Revere and the Raiders, two of Columbia's biggest acts. However, Melcher was unable to duplicate his success with the Rising Sons. The combination was a working mismatch as the pop savvy Melcher failed to grasp what the roots-oriented band was trying to achieve. The band and producer immediately clashed, resulting in only one release, a cover of the Reverend Gary Davis's "Candy Man" backed with Skip James's "Devil's Got My Woman." *Crawdaddy* praised the single, observing, "The Rising Sons have skillfully managed to mix Mersey rhythms and arrangements with American blues melodies, and as such have a definitely new sound." Released early in 1966, the single did not chart in spite of a spirited performance and impressive slide work by Cooder on the flip side.

Soon after, Mahal told *Hit Parader*, "We want to perform blues, rhythm'n'blues and rock with a country quality." However, an album's worth of recorded material revealed the Rising Sons to be pulling in different directions. Kincaid composed and sang his own songs, including "Spanish Lace Blues" and "Sunny's Dream." Although they were strong, the pop-oriented numbers were at odds with the blues covers that comprised the majority of the group's repertoire, which included a revved-up version of Blind Willie McTell's "Statesboro Blues," two Robert Johnson numbers, Sleepy John Estes's "If the River Was Whiskey" and Bob Dylan's then-unreleased "Walkin' Down the Line."

Hoping to help the Rising Sons make it into the charts, Columbia sent over some Brill Building demos, and the group's manager hired Cooder's old associate, musicologist Barry Hansen, to act as "musical consultant" and mediator of internal disputes. Together the band decided to work on a demo penned by Gerry Goffin and Carole King, "Take a Giant Step" (which the Monkees later recorded). Even though they managed to get the song ready for release, internal friction caused the group to disband in early 1966 and so the single remained in Columbia's vaults.

After the break-up, Columbia retained Mahal, but he was leery of a band situation after the Sons' debacle. Furthermore, Columbia wanted him to perform Stax-styled R&B numbers, while Mahal insisted on sticking with folk-blues and Chicago blues.

"I was laying low," Mahal later told *Mojo* magazine. "I had just gone through this incredible trip with the Rising Sons; it was absolutely nuts. So I was feeling like a wolf eel that had gone back into the hole, and they were still pokin' at me. If I had a chance to grab hold of your hand and inflict serious pain, I would. I was really pissed off." Occasionally sitting in with Canned Heat, Mahal eventually became amenable to forming another group after meeting and jamming with Jesse Ed Davis and other musicians out of Oklahoma.

Jesse Edwin Davis (b. September 21, 1944, Norman, Oklahoma; d. 1988), a Kiowa Comanche Native American, had taken violin lessons in the first grade, but by the sixth grade had switched to the guitar. He acquired his first electric guitar, a Silvertone, in the seventh grade. After a few lessons and constant practice, he became proficient with it, churning out renditions of rock'n'roll songs from Chuck Berry, Elvis Presley and Bill Haley. He formed a band with Mike Brewer (later of Brewer & Shipley) while in his early teens. In the tenth grade, Davis purchased a Fender Telecaster and became interested in the blues when his school's first black student turned him on to some of the old standards. Davis started frequenting a local establishment, Uncle Tom's Hickory Pit Barbecue, which had a piano bar. The resident pianist, a black musician named Wallace Thompson, took the time to teach Davis about the blues and was a major influence on the teenager. At 18, Jesse joined Conway Twitty's band on lead guitar. Two years later, in 1964, he left Oklahoma City for Los Angeles.

Mahal's first two singles with his new backing band were released in 1967. These were "Let the Good Times Roll" backed with "Shimmy Like Sister Kate" and "EZ Rider" backed with "Leaving Trunk." Columbia then released "Statesboro Blues" backed with "Everybody's Got to Change Sometime" as his third single. Mahal had initially covered "Statesboro Blues" while with the Rising Sons, but for this mesmerizing version, he slowed down the tempo. The track was bolstered by some fine slide guitar from Jesse Ed Davis, who had never seriously played bottleneck before the session.

Mahal released his solo debut album in January 1968, simply called *Taj Mahal*. The LP's eight tracks were mostly reworkings of old country blues numbers and included both sides of his second and third singles. A solid blues-rock album, the highlights included "The Celebrated Walking Blues" (featuring Ry Cooder on mandolin) and Sonny Boy Williamson's "Checkin' Up on My Baby." *Disc and Music Echo* gave the release an enthusiastic thumbs up: "[Mahal] has the music pounding in his veins and what comes out is s-o-o-o relaxed and so hard and swinging it is, to our poor little white ears, completely mind-blowing." Musicians appearing on the album included Jesse Ed Davis and Ry Cooder on guitars, James Thomas on bass, Sanford Konikoff on drums, Bill Boatman on rhythm guitar, Gary Gilmore on bass and Charles Blackwell on drums. The last two musicians joined Jesse Ed Davis as Mahal's touring band.

Gilmore (b. April 27, 1946; Salina, Kansas) moved to Tulsa, Oklahoma, in the first grade. He played the violin for a couple of years while growing up, then switched to guitar. By age 11 he had moved to bass, and by age 14 he was playing in nightclubs. Following high school, Gilmore moved to Los Angeles, where he met up with other musicians from Tulsa. He joined a group and played at the local clubs before moving to Nashville for about six months, where he played with Roger Miller. He returned to Los Angeles and joined a band with Davis and drummer Levon Helm before joining Mahal's band.

Blackwell was also from Tulsa. He had been a member of Jerry Lee Lewis's touring band before moving to California, where he worked with the Shindogs (the house band for the television show *Shindig*), which also included Delaney Bramlett.

Mahal discovered a complementary fusion of personalities with his new bandmates. "All of us had the same things in our head when we came together," he told *Guitar Player*. "It took me a long time to find the cats I wanted to play with."

Though the album, like his singles, again met with public indifference, Mahal and his band started to receive notice in the underground press and to build a local following. While performing at the Whiskey A-Go-Go, Keith Richards and Mick Jagger approached them, inviting them to perform on a TV special called *Rock and Roll Circus*. A short while later, the band received tickets to fly to London for the taping. Those involved in the TV special were rock'n'roll's most elite: the Rolling Stones, John Lennon, Eric Clapton, the Who and the up-and-coming Jethro Tull. Taj Mahal was the only American act booked for the prestigious event. The band turned in a furious version of "Ain't That a Lot of Love," but unfortunately the special didn't air because the Rolling Stones were dissatisfied with their own performance. The show was finally released in 1996.

In early 1969, Mahal released his second album, *The Natch'l Blues*, another spirited collection of blues numbers plus a cover of the 1962 William Bell hit "You Don't Miss Your Water." The core group of Mahal, Davis, Gilmore and Blackwell played on the album, plus additional musicians Al Kooper on keyboards and Earl Palmer on drums. Again, Mahal received nearly universal critical acclaim. *Beat Instrumental* declared it "a necessary record for any blues lover." *Rolling Stone* praised Davis as "easily one of the best blues guitarists around" and asserted, "Taj Mahal is an extremely engaging vocalist whose appeal is direct and immediate." *New Musical Express* wrote, "Taj Mahal is one of the best of the new American blues outfits who display a pleasantly restrained and relaxed feel through the nine tracks." *Sing Out* pronounced that Taj Mahal was "a strong blues talent that should emerge as an important figure in the field." Eric Clapton, however, was less enamored with the LP when he told *Melody Maker*: "Taj Mahal's first album was the best. On the second one they watered him down a lot." *The Natch'l Blues* reached #160 on the U.S. charts.

For his third album, *Giant Step/De Ole Folks at Home*, Mahal released two separate LPs that were packaged together as a double-album. Issued in late 1969, *Giant Step* was a group effort while *De Ole Folks at Home* was a solo album, with Mahal performing a wide array of songs on a variety of acoustic instruments, including banjo, 12-string guitar and harmonica. Mahal explained to *Rock* magazine his reasons for adding a solo album to the package: "I put out *The Ole Folks at Home* because at the time I was very disturbed about the way the electronic music was going with the band. There seemed to be a definite lack of communication and energy, and I really just wanted to put some stuff out myself and show what I was into." The release received sharply contrasting reviews from the underground press. *The Los Angeles Free Press* wrote that *Giant Step* was "the tightest and perhaps most successful studio record Taj and his band have presented. The general level of the playing is very high thanks to Taj's flawless command of contemporary blues guitar idioms and the relaxed, perfectly complementary work of his fellow musicians." *Rolling Stone* writer Ed Ward, on the other hand, was critical of the group's musicians on the first album, pointing out, "The band takes a back seat, and their parts are mostly reduced to chunka-chunka mechanical backings for Taj, who sounds like he is straining and overextending himself." Ward was equally disparaging of the choice of material, which he thought was "downright dull" aside from the title track. Ward also laid into the second disc, writing, "The instrumentals are passable, even if they do meander a bit, but the songs range from OK to terrible." *Melody Maker* also saw the release as a mixed bag that was "likely to appeal only to his greatest admirers." Even so, the double LP reached #85 on the U.S. pop charts.

Mahal and band were also becoming very popular concert attractions, touring heavily in the U.S. and Europe. After their second tour of Europe in 1970, however, the band broke up. Mahal went to Spain for six months to rest and prepare for his next move.

As Mahal felt that his existing band had run their course, he decided to try something radical. He approached tuba player Howard Johnson with the intent of creating a new horn-based band. "I always dug horns, but for me and Howard Johnson, the cat who leads my horn section, man we didn't hit it off when we first met each other, we didn't like each other at all," he told *Rock* magazine. "I was saying, 'Man, one of them snobby jazz freaks,' and he was saying, 'Man, one of them snobby ass rock freaks,' So we went through that shit [where] for a while there would be a lot of brothers who were listening to jazz who would be familiar with Johnson, and a lot of cats who were into what I had been doing, then we realized that we really had a lot of things in common and it was very interesting. The music was very challenging for him and it also gave me a chance to stretch out. I figured . . . that way maybe we could start some shit and get people listening." Johnson, who had worked with a number of prominent jazz artists including Charles Mingus, Hank Crawford, Archie Shepp, Gil Evans and Rahsaan Roland Kirk, agreed to assemble the other musicians. Johnson brought together John Simon on piano, John Hall on guitar, Bill Rich on bass, Greg Thomas on drums, percussionist Kwasi "Rocky" DziDzournu, and a contingent of four horn players: Johnson, Earl McIntyre, Joseph Daley and Bob Stewart. The nine-piece band played

an assortment of instruments, which in some configurations included four tubas.

The new ensemble started rehearsing at the beginning of January 1970 for their first engagements at the Fillmore East on January 15–16. The band stayed together for six months and went on a British tour, but the cost of supporting such a large contingent of musicians was prohibitive and Mahal had to let them go by the end of June. Still, recordings of the band at the Fillmore East were used as his next release, a double live album entitled *The Real Thing*. Containing material that was mostly written and arranged by Mahal (with Howard Johnson writing the horn arrangements and playing tuba, baritone sax, and flügelhorn), the album contained a mixture of blues, rock, jazz, ragtime and soul. Discussing the album with *Rolling Stone*, Mahal said, "My first album was live in the studio, most of the second and third albums were, and this album [*The Real Thing*] was live on stage . . . it's too often, man, that everybody's trying so hard to make this perfect thing. Man, we are not perfect, we are fucking human beings."

In a later review of the album, *Rolling Stone* took note of the imperfections, commenting that the album contained "one of the sloppiest performances ever recorded and one of the most entertaining . . . the band sounds as if they'd been together for about five minutes and had their instruments for only ten." *The Los Angeles Free Press* was also unimpressed, quipping that this release "offers nothing new or improved over the first two albums, and continues the artistic limbo of the third . . . Because of the eccentric instrumentation and sheer number of musicians (ten in all), some of the cuts sound disorganized even when they are not." Released in 1971, *The Real Thing* reached #84 on the LP pop charts, Mahal's highest placement ever.

Mahal used many of the same musicians on his next studio effort, *Happy Just to Be Like I Am*, with a couple of changes. Jesse Ed Davis returned to replace guitarist John Hall, and drummer James Charles Otey replaced Greg Thomas. Portraying an array of styles, the release was a return to form for Mahal, highlighted by "Black Spirit Boogie," a solo instrumental performed by Mahal alone on his National steel-bodied guitar. Other standouts were "West Indian Revelation"—his first excursion into Caribbean music, with Andy Narell on steel drums, a female chorus, and Mahal singing in a clipped, Caribbean dialect—and the title track with four tubas laying down the bottom. *Happy Just to Be Like I Am* was widely praised by the critics. *Disc and Music Echo* called it "a fine album. It's funky and it's gutsy, and there's splendid brass on it." *Rolling Stone* called it a "loose, riotous blues 'n roots album from Taj Mahal, who nearly alone is carrying the torch of the country blues music for other young black musicians to hear."

Mahal's next release, *Recycling the Blues & Other Related Stuff*, contained one live side and one studio side. Side one was recorded live at the Winterland in San Francisco and featured Mahal solo, performing country blues before an appreciative audience and playing kalimba (African thumb piano), banjo and his 50-year-old National steel guitar. The second side held an ambitious, four-song cycle that began with "Cakewalk into Town," an exhilarating performance of ragtime blues with Mahal on guitar and vocals accompanied only by Howard Johnson on tuba. The Pointer Sisters contributed dazzling backing vocals on two cuts, including "Texas Woman Blues," which was a swinging jazz number with Mahal on stand-up bass and scat vocals. Warmly received by the critics, the album reached #177 on the U.S. pop charts.

In 1972, Mahal scored his first movie soundtrack, *Sounder*, in which he also had a supporting role, appearing as "Ike," a friend of a family of sharecroppers in 1930s Louisiana. Based on a novel by William H. Armstrong, the movie starred Paul Winfield and Cicely Tyson, who received Academy Award nominations for Best Actor and Best Actress, respectively; the film won an Oscar for best picture.

Postscript

Following *Sounder*, Mahal released four more albums for Columbia before switching to Warner Brothers for three albums, ending with *Evolution* in 1977. Since then, he has issued numerous albums on different labels, bringing his total to over 35 releases. Over the years, it's become clear that "blue" defines only one of color of Mahal's musical rainbow. On these releases, he has covered a wide range of music, including jazz, gospel, ragtime, calypso, Caribbean, zydeco, R&B, soul, Hawaiian and world music; he has even done a variety of "music for little people" projects.

In 1997, Mahal won a Grammy award for *Señor Blues,* which was honored as "Best Contemporary Blues Album." Mahal won a second Grammy for the album *Shoutin' in Key* in 2000 for the same category.

Jesse Ed Davis went on to play on numerous sessions with George Harrison, Ringo Starr, the Pointer Sisters, Albert King, Harry Nilsson and others. He released three solo albums before his death in 1988.

Ry Cooder was utilized by Terry Melcher on sessions with Melcher's other charges, Paul Revere and the Raiders, and joined Captain Beefheart for his *Safe as Milk* album. Cooder subsequently became a successful session musician whose credits include the Rolling Stones, Phil Ochs, Randy Newman and Little Feat. He also had a stint as a member of the "supergroup" Little Village.

Kevin Kelley joined his cousin Chris Hillman in the Byrds for their *Sweetheart of the Rodeo* album before joining Fever Tree. His predecessor, Ed Cassidy, formed the critically acclaimed band Spirit. Jesse Lee Kincaid formed a country band, Jesse Kincaid and Silverado. Gary Marker formed the jazz-rock band Fusion, which released one album for Atco in 1969, then reunited with Ed Cassidy for the 1980 release by Rainbow Red Oxidiser, *Recorded Lies*.

Discography

Release Date	Title	Catalog Number

U.S. Singles

The Rising Sons

1966	Candy Man/The Devil's Got My Woman	Columbia 43534

Taj Mahal

1967	Let the Good Times Roll/ Shimmy Like Sister Kate	Columbia 44051
1967	EZ Rider/Leaving Trunk	Columbia 44405
1968	Everybody's Got to Change Sometime/ Statesboro Blues	Columbia 44476
1968	You Don't Miss Your Water/Going Down to the Country—Paint My Mailbox Blue	Columbia 44696
1969	Corinna/A Lot of Love	Columbia 44767
1969	Six Days on the Road/Light Rain Blues	Columbia 44991
1971	Diving Duck Blues/Fishin' Blues	Columbia 45419
1971	Ain't Gwine to Whistle Dixie Anymore (Part 1)/Part 2	Columbia 45455
1972	Chevrolet/Oh Susanna	Columbia 45539

U.S. Albums

The Rising Sons

1992	*The Rising Sons featuring Taj Mahal & Ry Cooder*	Legacy Records 52828

Contains tracks recorded in Hollywood, California between September 9, 1965, and May 18, 1966. Vocals tracks for "Dust My Broom," "Last

Fair Deal Gone Down" and "Baby, What You Want Me to Do?" recorded by Taj Mahal in New York, New York on June 19, 1992.

Statesboro Blues/If the River Was Whiskey (Divin' Duck Blues)/By and By (Poor Me)/Candy Man/2:10 Train/Let the Good Times Roll/.44 Blues/11th Street Overcrossing/Corrina, Corrina/Tulsa County/Walkin' Down the Line/The Girl with Green Eyes/Sunny's Dream/Spanish Lace Blues/The Devil's Got My Woman/Take a Giant Step/Flyin' So High/Dust My Broom/Last Fair Deal Gone Down/Baby, What You Want Me to Do?/Statesboro Blues (take 2)/I Got a Little

Taj Mahal

1968   *Taj Mahal*   Columbia CS-9579
Leaving Trunk/Statesboro Blues/Checkin' Up on My Baby/Everybody's Got to Change Sometime/EZ Rider/Dust My Broom/Diving Duck Blues/Celebrated Walkin' Blues

1969   *The Natch'l Blues*   Columbia CS-9698
Good Morning Miss Brown/Corinna/I Ain't Gonna Let Nobody Steal My Jellyroll/Going Up to the Country/Paint My Mailbox Blue/Done Changed My Way of Living/She Caught the Katy and Left Me a Mule to Ride/The Cuckoo/You Don't Miss Your Water ('Til Your Well Runs Dry)/A Lot of Love

1969   *Giant Step/De Ole Folks at Home* (2 LP) Columbia GP-18
Ain't Gwine to Whistle Dixie Anymore/Take a Giant Step/Give Your Woman What She Wants/Good Morning Little Schoolgirl/You're Gonna Need Somebody/Six Days on the Road/Keep Your Hands Off Her/Bacon Fat/Linin' Track/Country Blues No. 1/Wild Ox Moan/Light Rain Blues/Little Soulful Tune/Candy Man/Cluck Old Hen/Colored Aristocracy/Blind Boy Rag/Stagger Lee/Cajun Tune/Fishing Blues/Annie's Lover

1971   *The Real Thing*   Columbia 30619
Fishing Blues/Ain't Gwine to Whistle Dixie Anymore/Sweet Mama Janisse/Going Up to the Country and Paint My Mailbox Blue/Big Kneed Gal/You're Going to Need Somebody/Tom and Sally Drake/Divin' Duck Blues/John, It Ain't Hard/You Ain't No Street Walker

1972   *Happy Just to Be Like I Am*   Columbia 30767
Happy Just to Be Like I Am/Stealin'/Oh Susanna/Eighteen Hammers/Tomorrow May Not Be Your Day/Chevrolet/West Indian Develation/Black Spirit Boogie

1972   *Recycling the Blues &*   Columbia 31605
       Other Related Stuff
Conch/Kalimba/Bound to Love Me Some/Ricochet/A Free Song/Corrina/Close/Cakewalk into Town/Sweet Home Chicago/Texas Woman Blues/Gitano Negro

Miscellaneous U.S. Releases

1969   *Live at Bill Graham's Fillmore West*   Columbia Records
                                                CS-9893
Includes "One More Mile to Go" by Taj Mahal.

1972   *Fillmore: The Last Days* (3 LP)   Fillmore 31390
Includes "Jam Session: We Gonna Rock" and "Jam Session: Long and Tall" both featuring Taj Mahal, Elvin Bishop, Boz Scaggs and friends.

1972   *Sounder* (movie soundtrack)   Columbia 31944
Needed Time/Sounder/Chase a Coon/Morning Work/N'Meat's on the Stove/I'm Running & I'm Happy/Speedball/Goin' to the Country/Crit-

ters in the Woods/Motherless Children/Jailhouse Blues/Just Workin'/Harriet's Dance Song/Two Spirits Reunited/David Runs Again/Curiosity Blues/Someday Be a Change/Horse Shoes/Cheraw/David's Dream

1995   *Rolling Stones Rock and Roll Circus*   ABKCO Records
                                                1268
Includes "Ain't That a Lot of Love" by Taj Mahal.

U.K. Singles

Taj Mahal

1968	Everybody's Got to Change Sometime/ Statesboro Blues	Direction 58-3547
1969	EZ Rider/You Don't Miss Your Water	Direction 58-4044
1970	Give Your Woman What She Wants/ Further On Down the Road	Direction 58-4586
1971	Divin' Duck Blues/Fishin' Blues	CBS 7413

U.K. Albums

Taj Mahal

1968	*Taj Mahal*	Direction 8-63279
1969	*The Natch'l Blues*	Direction 8-63397
1969	*Giant Step/De Ole Folks at Home*	Direction 8-66226
1971	*The Real Thing* (2 LP)	CBS 66288
1972	*Happy Just to Be Like I Am*	CBS 64447

Miscellaneous U.K. Releases

1969	*Live at Bill Graham's Fillmore West*	CBS 63816
1972	*Fillmore: The Last Days* (3 LP)	Warner Brothers K 66013
1995	*Rolling Stones Rock and Roll Circus*	5267712

Harvey Mandel

Harvey Mandel is an innovative and distinctive guitarist who pioneered the use of modern blues-rock techniques, including the use of controlled, sustained feedback and two-handed fret board tapping. Mandel's forward-leaning, genre-bending style—mixing horns, strings and electric guitar—brought an experimental edge to much of his work, both as a solo artist and in his collaborations with Barry Goldberg, Sugarcane Harris, Charlie Musselwhite, Canned Heat, John Mayall, and the Rolling Stones.

Mandel once described his playing to *Melody Maker:* "My style is quite intricate. My solos are more melodic and I try to do other interesting things. I like to feel I have a style identifiable with me. I don't want to be regarded as just a blues guitarist. I have played with all sorts of bands in all sorts of places to gain as much experience as possible."

Mandel, a.k.a. "The Snake," was born in Detroit, Michigan, on March 11, 1945, but raised in the Chicago suburb of Morton Grove. His first musical experience was accompanying a young folk singer on bongos, but after fooling around with the singer's guitar, he decided to take it up himself. He purchased a guitar when he was 16 and began practicing day and night, working out the guitar parts to Ventures records first, then to blues recordings. Soon, he became good enough to join a rock'n'roll band as the rhythm guitarist. This led to a series of gigs with local groups until he was 18, when he met 28-year-old musician Thad Ericken. "He [Thad] and I formed a group," Mandel recounted to *Hit Parader*. "We would play at a number of hillbilly bars around Broadway. We used to sneak in and play because I wasn't 21 years old. Thad and I were the permanent members, and we'd always find different people to play along with us at each gig."

Mandel then met a black bass player, Sammy Fender, at a Broadway R&B club called Magoos. Fender became his mentor, teaching him about the blues and taking him to blues clubs. One club, Curley's Twist City, located on Madison Street on Chicago's West Side, became a favorite hangout. Mandel and Fender formed a band and played Twist City once a week. This afforded Mandel an opportunity to observe and jam with headliners such as Buddy Guy and Otis Rush, who performed frequently at the club. From Twist City, he started to frequent other blues venues, such as the Golden Peacock, the C&T Lounge and Pepper's Lounge, sitting in with the likes of B.B. King, Howlin' Wolf, Albert King and Muddy Waters.

"In Chicago I used to play every night. Guys like Mike Bloomfield, Paul Butterfield, Barry Goldberg and myself would jam with all the Chicago blues artists," Mandel later recalled. "There was sort of a friendly rivalry between the musicians to show off how good we could play. Guys would try to cut each other. You had to come up with something good every time you took a solo. It was great training."

Soon Mandel was working the blues circuit at clubs on Rush Street, performing six nights a week, sometimes until sunrise. He befriended two other white blues enthu- siasts, keyboardist Barry Goldberg and harpist Charlie Musselwhite [see **Barry Goldberg, Charlie Musselwhite**]. Goldberg began calling Mandel "The Snake" because he wore a cracked leather jacket and loved to spin out sinuous, snake-like guitar riffs.

Goldberg, a member of the Goldberg-Miller Blues Band, was recording his group's debut album when guitarist Steve Miller dropped out. Goldberg asked Mandel to replace Miller, and so both he and Charlie Musselwhite participated in the recording sessions for *Blowing My Mind*, the 1966 debut by the renamed Barry Goldberg Blues Band. The band folded shortly thereafter and Goldberg joined the Chicago Loop.

Before long, Mandel reunited with Goldberg as part of the backing band on Charlie Musselwhite's 1967 debut album, *Stand Back!* While Musselwhite favored traditional blues structures, Mandel's playing was anything but conventional. Often combining a somewhat distorted tone with multi-string bends and sustained feedback, Mandel's guitar licks were defining characteristics of the LP, but the album's initial slow sales led Mandel to return to playing gigs with the Busters, a Chicago area rock band.

However, a few months later, *Stand Back!* started getting heavy airplay on the San Francisco Bay Area's leading underground station, KMPX-FM. Abe "Voco" Kesh, a disc jockey for the station and a producer for Mercury Records, placed the album into heavy rotation and it became a local hit.

Kesh located Mandel in Chicago and invited Musselwhite and Mandel to San Francisco with the promise of work. Mandel accepted the invitation and, along with members of the Busters and Musselwhite, came to California. Calling themselves Charlie Musselwhite and his South Side Sound System, the group was immediately booked for several shows at the Fillmore West during the summer of 1967, sharing bills with the Electric Flag, the Paul Butterfield Blues Band and the Cream. After an initial flurry of work, the band, except for Mandel and Musselwhite, returned to Chicago.

Kesh secured Mandel a recording contract with Philips, a subsidiary of Mercury Records. Mandel concentrated on making his first solo album, which became the first of four LPs produced by Kesh. The sessions took place at six different Los Angeles studios and Nashville's legendary Bradley's Barn. The guitarist used a variety of musicians for the record, including bassist Art Stavro, drummer Eddie Hoh and, for the Nashville recordings, steel guitarist Pete Drake and drummer Kenny Buttrey. The resulting instrumental album, 1968's *Christo Redemptor*, was an eclectic mix of blues and rock guitar with heavy strings. Album highlights included the bluesy, chugging, harmonica-driven "The Lark" (with Charlie Musselwhite) and the slow-building, hypnotic, multilayered "Wade in the Water" (with a basic rhythm track cut live at the Avalon Ballroom in San Francisco with a band including Steve Miller from Linn County on keyboards and Armando Peraza on congas).

The album received some underground airplay, but did not make it onto the Billboard charts until almost a year later when it reached #169 on September 20, 1969. *Christo Redemptor* received mixed reviews from critics: *Melody Maker* noted that the album contained "a considerable amount of interesting progressive rock," while *Hit Parader* said, "Most of Harvey's intricate guitar work is built around the blues. After all, that was his main thing back in Chicago. It's also influenced by jazz. It's also excellent." However, *Rolling Stone* dismissed it as an "extraordinarily boring album." One person who took notice was a struggling musician named Carlos Santana: "Harvey Mandel was probably the first guy to put congas on a rock and roll album. I saw him at the Avalon one time, and I was knocked out. I learned a lot from him. I really admire guys, like Harvey Mandel, whose sound I can identify, because it takes a lot of work."

For his next solo release, *Righteous*, Mandel utilized famed jazz trumpeter/bandleader Shorty Rogers (b. Milton M. Rajonsky, April 14, 1924; d. November 7, 1994) to score the string and horn arrangements. Not surprisingly, the album contained a number of jazz-oriented tracks along with a couple of straight-ahead blues numbers. Mandel again used Stavro and Hoh, along with rhythm guitarist (and vocalist on "Love of Life") Bob Jones, keyboardist Duane Hitchings and percussionist Earl Palmer. A *Downbeat* reviewer, Heineman, gave *Righteous* only two stars with the cutting remark, "Somebody apparently told Mandel he could play jazz guitar . . . Somebody was wrong." Still, Heineman observed that Mandel was "good at playing hard blues," adding, "The only two effective tracks are '[Short's] Stuff,' which is also the longest, and 'Campus [Blues].' On the big band/R&B 'Stuff,' Mandel plays some gritty—if not particularly innovative—guitar parts. He also plays hard and well on his original blues-rocker, 'Campus.'" Released in May 1969, *Righteous* reached #187 on the Billboard charts.

In addition to working on his own album, Mandel made time in 1969 to assist Barry Goldberg on his *Barry Goldberg Reunion* release as well as *Two Jews Blues* and *Barry Goldberg and Friends*. He also played on several other musicians' albums in 1969, including Jimmy Witherspoon's *The Blues Singer* and Graham Bond's *The Mighty Graham Bond* [see **Graham Bond**].

In late July 1969, to the surprise of some, Mandel replaced Henry Vestine as the lead guitarist in Canned Heat [see **Canned Heat**]. While Mandel was watching Canned Heat perform at the Fillmore West, he was summoned to the dressing room to meet with the band. Once backstage, he was told that Vestine and bassist Larry Taylor had gotten into a big argument that had led to Vestine's departure from the band. They asked Mandel if he could fill in for the second set (Mike Bloomfield had sat in during the first). Mandel's set with Canned Heat went well and they asked him to join the group as a permanent member. He accepted, and the band left that night for a three week tour of New York, which included, in what was only Mandel's third gig with Canned Heat, their appearance at the famous Woodstock Festival. Canned Heat went over well at the festival, and Mandel quickly became integral to the band's evolving sound. During a European tour in January 1970, lead singer Bob Hite told *Melody Maker* that the difference Harvey Mandel made in Canned Heat was that "we play music now."

"They were my first real big group," Mandel later told *Hit Parader*. "I enjoyed playing with Al Wilson. He was very sensitive, a true musician. He was really into his music. But he got so depressed. He was introverted and he lived like a hermit in the woods."

Mandel appeared on what is arguably Canned Heat's finest recording, *Future Blues* (1970), as well as on the lackluster *Canned Heat '70 Concert* (which they recorded live in Europe).

In May 1970, Mandel and bassist Larry Taylor left Canned Heat to join John Mayall for his first all-American band [see **John Mayall**]. At the time, John Mayall's Bluesbreakers also included violinist Don "Sugarcane" Harris, with whom Mandel later collaborated.

Born in Pasadena, California, Don Bowman Harris (b. June 18, 1938; d. November 30, 1999) took up the violin at five or six years old and received ten years of classical training during his youth. While attending high school, he abandoned his classical aspirations and formed a doo-wop group, the Squires, featuring himself on piano and school-mate Dewey Terry on guitar. In 1955, the Squires had a regional hit with "Cindy," but Harris and Terry left the group two years later to form Don and Dewey. As Don and Dewey, they released many fine singles on Specialty, including "Farmer John," "I'm Leaving It All Up to You" and "Big Boy Pete," but never achieved any chart success. However, other artists covering their material scored hit singles, including the Premiers ("Farmer John," #19, 1964), Dale and Grace ("I'm Leaving It All Up to You," #1, 1963), and the Kingsmen, who rewrote the lyrics to "Big Boy Pete" and landed a #4 hit in 1965 with "Jolly Green Giant." Don and Dewey disbanded, only to regroup in 1964 when they cut an instrumental single called "Soul Motion," featuring Harris's violin, for Rush Records. The reunion was short-lived and Harris slipped into obscurity. Then in late 1969, when Frank Zappa decided to cut his solo album *Hot Rats*, he remembered Harris from the "Soul Motion" track and wanted him to appear on the album. Zappa found Harris playing with the Johnny Otis Revue and recruited him to perform on two tracks, including the searing "Willie the Pimp." Harris stayed with Frank Zappa to record *Burnt Weeny Sandwich* and *Weasels Ripped My Flesh* before joining Mayall's band.

Mayall's new lineup recorded *USA Union* on July 27 and 28, 1970, before embarking on a six-week American tour commencing in October. Harris dropped out of the American tour because of illness, leaving Mayall, Mandel and Taylor to tour as a trio through the rest of the U.S. and later Europe.

Mandel described to *Beat Instrumental* how Mayall wanted more subdued playing out of him: "We play at much lower volume than the average rock group. Individually, I have to play more reserved. It's not like on my albums or when I was with Canned Heat. It's not the heavy sustained ripping guitar scene—but more laid back. That's the way John wants it."

For his next solo release, 1970's *Games Guitars Play*, Mandel decided to include vocal tracks in order to gain wider airplay. He brought in Russell Dashiel, with whom he had previously worked, as vocalist and to play guitar, organ and piano. The other musicians included, once again, Taylor and Hoh. The album opened with a cover of Sleepy John Estes's country blues song "Leavin' Trunk," which they then transformed into a psychedelic workout. True to his nickname, Mandel allowed his guitar parts to characteristically "snake" through the arrangement, at times bolstered by the use of backwards tape. *Record Mirror* picked

up on his experimentation, commenting, "Harvey runs through most of the various sounds and effects obtainable from the electric guitar." *Melody Maker* viewed the LP as simply "a very bluesy set from Mandel's magnificent guitar." Nonetheless, *Games Guitars Play* made no headway in the charts, and the guitarist soon parted ways with Philips Records.

Mandel returned to an all-instrumental format for his next album, *Baby Batter*, released in 1971 on Janus Records. Reuniting with arranger Shorty Rogers, Mandel used a backing band of Taylor, Lagos, conga player Big Black, tambourinist Sandra Crouch and keyboardists Howard Wales and Mike Melvoin. *Disc and Music Echo* enthused, "Any guitarist who can hold your attention for a whole album has to have something and this is by far his best LP to date." *Beat Instrumental* found the release to be "a very good album for the punters who appreciate tasteful guitar as opposed to those who like heavy whining volume."

Mandel's next album, *The Snake* (1972), continued his exploration with a fusion sound. Utilizing various musicians—Harris (on electric violin) and Lagos, plus his former Canned Heat bandmates Taylor and drummer Fito de la Parra—he created another interesting jazz-rock album. Mandel made his first vocal appearance on "Uno Ino," which translates into "You Know, I Know." Sales once again were not forthcoming, however, as *The Snake* barely reached the Billboard Top 200, peaking at #198 on July 22, 1972.

That same year, Mandel joined a band formed by drummer Paul Lagos. The original band consisted of Lagos, Larry Taylor on bass, Don "Sugarcane" Harris on electric violin and Randy "Rare" Resnick on guitar (Resnick had developed an innovative "tapping" or "hammering" technique of playing guitar). By this time, Harris had three solo albums to his credit: *Sugarcane* (issued on Epic in 1970), *Keep on Drivin'* and *Got the Blues*, which were issued on the German label MPS in 1970 and 1971, respectively. The quartet had played at the Ash Grove in Los Angeles during 1969 before Taylor, frustrated by Sugarcane's (Harris's) constant lateness and irresponsible conduct, dropped out. Taylor was replaced by bassist Victor Conte and, to stimulate label interest, Mandel was brought in in 1972. Calling themselves the Pure Food and Drug Act, they issued one album in 1972 on Epic Records. Entitled *Choice Cuts*, the record was a collection of fusion-oriented material that mixed elements of jazz, blues and funk. The album featured an 11-minute version of "Eleanor Rigby," the classic Beatles tune, which Harris also covered on his import-only solo album, *Fiddler on the Rock*. Harris's frequent incarceration and a lack of offers brought the Pure Food and Drug Act to a premature end shortly after the release of their debut album. Mandel, however, picked up the guitar "tapping" or "hammering" technique from Resnick, employed it on his next solo release, *Shangrenade* (released in 1973), and became closely associated it.

Besides releasing *The Snake* and collaborating with Harris on *Choice Cuts* in 1972, Mandel also spent time working on a variety of other projects. He led a three-day jam session of 17 Chicago-area musicians that was released as *Get Off in Chicago*, was a featured guitarist on the Ventures' album *Rock and Roll Forever*, and some of his sessions with Canned Heat appeared on their 1972 release, *Historical Figures and Ancient Heads*.

Mandel built his reputation on the innovative playing and skillful adaptability that resulted in constant work and contributions to other musicians' records. Luminaries Canned Heat, John Mayall and other top blues-rock bands and artists have all recognized his considerable talent, but somehow Mandel's solo work has never found a wide audience. "My biggest downfall on the popular level," Mandel once told *Blues Revue*, "is that I was never a singer. Jeff Beck is one of the very, very few exceptions that can get away with a million seller on a totally instrumental album. Had I been able to be a singer on the same level as my playing, and written songs on purpose to go with some slick vocals back then, it would have made a big difference."

Postscript

Mandel released two more solo albums for Janus records, *Shangrenade*, a 1973 collaboration with "Sugarcane" Harris, and *Feel the Sound of Harvey Mandel* (1974).

He also played on Love's *Reel to Real* (1974) and the Rolling Stones' *Black and Blue*, where he contributed to two songs ("Hot Stuff" and "Memory Motel") and was considered as a replacement for Mick Taylor before they selected Ronnie Wood instead. In 1980, Mandel relocated to Florida and became a member of the house band at Ron Wood's Miami nightclub, Woody's, along with Rolling Stones saxophonist Bobby Keys.

Mandel reunited with Canned Heat for *Human Condition* (1978) and *Internal Combustion* (1994), and toured with them for the 30th Anniversary of Woodstock tour of Europe.

His subsequent releases have been sporadic and issued on small labels, including *Live Boot: Harvey Mandel—Live in California* (1990); *Twist City* (1993), *Snakes & Stripes* (1995), *Planetary Warrior* (1997), *Emerald Triangle* (1998) and *Lick This* (2000).

In addition, the guitarist has taken part in I.R.S. Records' *Guitar Speak II* and was included on a compilation CD released by Rhino Records, *Guitar Player Magazine's Legends of Guitar: Electric Blues, Vol. 1*. He has also released an instructional video for Hot Licks entitled *Harvey Mandel: Blues Guitar & Beyond*.

Discography

Release Date	Title	Catalog Number
U.S. Singles		
1968	Bradley's Barn/Christo Redemptor	Philips 40566
1968	Wade in the Water, Part 1/ Wade in the Water, Part 2	Philips 40579
1969	Campus Blues/Righteous	Philips 40607
1969	Poontang/Summer Sequence	Philips 40627
1969	Dry Your Eyes/Ridin' High	Philips 40643
1971	Midnight Sun/Baby Batter	Janus 144

U.S. Albums

1968	*Christo Redemptor*	Philips PHS 600-2811

Christo Redemptor/Before Six/The Lark/Snake/Long Wait/Wade in the Water/Lights Out/Bradley's Barn/You Can't Tell Me/Nashville 1 A.M.

1969	*Righteous*	Philips PHS 600-306

Righteous/Jive Samba/Love of Life/Poontang/Just a Hair More/Summer Sequence/Short's Stuff/Boo-Bee-Doo/Campus Blues

1970	*Games Guitars Play*	Philips PHS 600-325

Leavin' Trunk/Honky Tonk/I Don't Need No Doctor/Dry Your Eyes/Ridin' High/CAA Purange/Senor Blues/Games People Play

1971	*Baby Batter*	Janus JLS-3017

Baby Batter/Midnight Sun/One Way Street/Morton Grove Mama/Freedom Ball/El Stinger/Hank the Ripper

1972	*The Snake*	Janus JLS-3037

The Divining Rod/Pegasus/Lynda Love/Peruvian Flake/The Snake/Uno Ino/Ode to the Owl/Levitation/Bite the Electric Eel

CD CHICKEN SHACK   IMAGINATION LADY   £6.99   IGOXCD506

| 1 |

Fleetwood Mac

Rory Gallagher with Taste

Jo Ann Kelly

Taj Mahal

Harvey Mandel

John Mayall

John Mayall

Mother Earth

Pretty Things

Savoy Brown

DAVE WALKER

KIM SIMMONDS

DAVE BIDWELL

PAUL RAYMOND

ANDY SILVESTER

SAVOY BROWN

ON LONDON RECORDS
539 WEST 25th STREET
NEW YORK, N.Y. 10001

Ten Years After

The McCoys

Johnny Winter

Johnny Winter And

Yardbirds

Yardbirds

1972   *Get Off in Chicago*   Ovation QD-14-15
Check Me Out/Local Days/Highway Blues/Sweet Lynda/High Test Fish
Line/I'm a Lonely Man/Race Track Daddy/Springfield Station Theme/
Jelly Roll

Pure Food and Drug Act
1972   *Choice Cuts*   Epic 31401
Introduction: Jim's Message/My Soul's on Fire/'Til the Day I Die/Eleanor
Rigby/A Little Soul Food/Do It Yourself/Where's My Sunshine/What
Comes Around Goes Around

Miscellaneous U.S. Releases

With Charlie Musselwhite and Barry Goldberg
1966   *Chicago Anthology*   Together ST-T-1024
Mandel appears on "Slow Down I'm Gonna Lose You," "I Loved and
Lost," "Big Boss Man" and "Funk."

1973   *Blues from Chicago*   Cherry Red CR5104
Mandel appears on "Big Boss Man," "Low Down Funk" a.k.a. "Funk,"
"Lost Love" a.k.a. "I Loved and Lost," "I'm Losin' You" a.k.a. "Slow
Down I'm Gonna Lose You" and "Cherry Jam."

U.K. Albums

1968	*Christo Redemptor*	Philips SBL 7873
1969	*Righteous*	Philips SBL 7904
1970	*Games Guitars Play*	Philips SBL 7915
1971	*Baby Batter*	Dawn DNLS 3015
1972	*The Snake*	Janus 6310 210
1972	*Get Off in Chicago*	London SH-O 8426

John Mayall

With an ongoing career that spans some four decades and forty albums, John Mayall is revered on both sides of the Atlantic as the "Father of British Blues." Time after time, star performers—most notably Eric Clapton, John McVie, Peter Green, Mick Fleetwood and Mick Taylor—have passed through the ranks of Mayall's band, the Bluesbreakers, before going on to achieve much wider fame elsewhere.

But perhaps history has placed too much focus on Mayall's featured soloists and not enough on Mayall himself. Regardless of the immense musical talents he both sought out and nurtured, Mayall has always been a formidable bandleader in his own right, as well as a musical director who uses his talents as multi-instrumentalist,

vocalist, and songwriter to create bands that reflect his own changing tastes. As he once told *Goldmine* magazine, "I maintain such a strong identity in my music and playing that, when musicians join, their sole responsibility is to be creative within that context. The mood of the music has already been set. So much importance seems to be attached to these [lineup] changes, [but at the time they] didn't seem important."

What cannot be disputed is Mayall's unfailingly accurate ear for rare talent, from Davy Graham in early-1960s Bluesbreakers right through to the awesome blues-guitar master Buddy Whittington in the band's current (2001) formation.

Although Mayall has received some mixed reviews over the years, the fact that most listeners can readily identify a Bluesbreakers' tune today leaves their leader both grinning and satisfied. "Critics might put down my style from time to time," Mayall told *The Los Angeles Times* in May 1999, "but I'm very happy with it . . . it certainly has endured. It's very gratifying to me that people recognize a Bluesbreakers song when they hear one."

Richard Vernon, copublisher of the now defunct British *R&B Monthly* magazine, summed up Mayall's importance when he told *Melody Maker*, "Whatever John Mayall does, he will always be the leader of the blues in this country. People will want to know what he is doing and will follow."

Mayall was born on November 29, 1933, in Macclesfield, a small market town in the east of the county of Cheshire, outside of Manchester in the U.K. His father was an amateur guitarist whose extensive record collection exposed Mayall at an early age to such jazz greats as Charlie Christian, Louis Armstrong, Django Reinhardt and Eddie Lang.

By age 12, Mayall had taken up the guitar and ukulele, and by the time he was 13 he had started to play the piano. He had become intrigued with boogie-woogie piano through the music of Meade Lux Lewis, Albert Ammons and Pete Johnson. Other influences of this period—namely Josh White, Big Bill Broonzy and Muddy Waters—intensified his interest in the blues. When he was only 15, Mayall demonstrated his independence—and eccentricity— by moving into a tree house because he preferred living in his own place rather than with his family. He later gained national attention when *The Manchester Evening News* wrote a story about his tree-house home while he was in college. He continued to live in tree houses until the age of 22.

In 1945, Mayall enrolled in the Manchester Junior School of Art, where he honed his piano skills until 1949. After art school, he worked for a while as a window dresser before joining the British Army and serving for three years in the Korean War. While on leave in Japan, Mayall purchased his first electric guitar.

In 1954, following his stint in the military, Mayall enrolled at the College of Art in Manchester where he met a fellow musician, drummer Peter Ward. The two got together for lunchtime jam sessions that led to the formation of the Powerhouse Four in 1956. Consisting of both men plus any other musicians they could round up, the Powerhouse Four played local dances in the Manchester area. Mayall also found time to teach music at a local youth club in Wythenshawe, Manchester, where he met drummer Hughie Flint, who later played a major role in Mayall's Bluesbreakers.

Following graduation in 1959, Mayall obtained employment as a typographer and then as an art director for a graphic design company. He continued to ply his trade as an artist, working for advertising agencies while moonlighting as a musician. Ward also worked in the commercial art field and continued to play with Mayall during the evenings for a year.

While opening for Alexis Korner and Blues Incorporated at the Bodega Jazz Club one night, Mayall was befriended by Korner, who encouraged his interest in blues music [see **Alexis Korner**]. In late 1962, Mayall became a member of the Blues Syndicate, a band led by trumpeter John Rowlands whose membership included drummer Flint. The Blues Syndicate's main bookings were at the Twisted Wheel Club in Manchester. Korner continued to mentor Mayall and encouraged him to relocate to London to take advantage of the burgeoning blues scene. So, on the eve of his twenty-ninth birthday, Mayall moved to London in January 1963.

Mayall later recalled the decision to *Disc and Music Echo:* "What I always wanted to play was blues. I never had any real love for any other kind of music. It was the thing I identified with. I never came to London because it was the era of traditional jazz and there would have been no work for me. When I eventually heard that the writing was on the wall for Trad [traditional jazz] in London, I knew opportunity had knocked and I was in the wrong place."

In London, Korner introduced Mayall to other musicians looking to form bands, and soon Mayall was trying out different combinations for the new group he'd decided to call the Bluesbreakers. Many kinds of musicians passed through the ranks of the early Bluesbreakers—some staying for just a single gig—ranging from complete unknowns to guitarist Davy Graham, who is now recognized as one of the great British folk guitarists.

When Mayall discovered bassist John McVie [see **Fleetwood Mac**], however, he found a cornerstone of the Bluesbreakers for years to come, despite their on-again-off-again musical relationship. At the time, 17-year-old McVie was playing in a Shadows-style group and knew absolutely nothing about the blues, so Mayall loaned him some records to see if he could absorb the nuances of the music. Mayall's advice—to keep the bass parts as simple as possible—has helped take McVie a long way in the music business.

McVie (b. John Graham McVie, November 26, 1945; Ealing, Middlesex, U.K.) learned the trumpet as a boy, picked up the guitar at age 14 and eventually switched to bass guitar. His parents gave him a pink Fender bass like the one played by his hero, bassist Jet Harris of the Shadows. When Mayall approached him, McVie had just started his career as a tax inspector. Coincidentally, his first day of work at his new government job was also the day he played his first gig with the Bluesbreakers at the White Hart in Acton. After nine months of trying to hold down a day job while performing with the Bluesbreakers at night, McVie finally threw in his lot with Mayall and became a full-time musician.

Like many musicians, at first Mayall struggled to book gigs at local clubs. He even got thrown out of the Flamingo during one of his first shows, but persevered and was soon heavily booked on an R&B circuit that included the Ealing Club, the Six Bells, Studio 51 and, eventually, the Flamingo again, where the band played all-nighters.

His first break came when he talked Manfred Mann into giving the Bluesbreakers the intermission spot at the Marquee (supporting the red-hot Manfreds). His first Marquee gig was on November 4, 1963; after a few months, the Bluesbreakers reportedly were blowing the headliners off the stage. By now, the lineup had stabilized and included Mayall, McVie, his old friend Ward (who was able to squeeze time off from his day job) on drums, and guitarist Bernie Watson, formerly of Cyril Davies and the R&B All-Stars [see **Cyril Davies and the R&B All-Stars**].

With a repertoire consisting of Chicago blues covers, original songs and some Chuck Berry instrumentals, the band's secret weapon was Mayall's in-depth knowledge of the blues and massive record collection. As a record collector since 1949, Mayall was able to draw upon these recordings to come up with obscure numbers that were new to the others in the band and to their audiences.

Mayall soon came to the attention of Decca staff producer Mike Vernon, who besides being a blues enthusiast, was also the copublisher (with his brother, Richard, and Neil Slaven) of *R&B Monthly*. Vernon liked what he heard and recommended to Decca that they sign Mayall.

Mayall's first studio session took place on April 20, 1964, with Ian Samwell producing. By now, Ward had dropped out of the group to return to the ad agency. With Martin Hart now holding down the drum stool, two tracks were recorded: "Crawling Up a Hill" and "Mr. James." While Mayall himself discounts the A-side, it was actually a very strong debut, at least according to *Record Mirror*, which called it a "wild R&B flavoured side with a good lyric," adding, "great performance but uncommercial sound." The promising single sold a meager 500 copies and was quickly abandoned.

Soon after the sessions for the single, drummer Flint joined Mayall's band. Flint had been playing drums since he was nine. When he was in his early teens, he was an avid jazz fan, absorbing the music of Jack Parnell, Kenny Baker, Humphrey Lyttelton, Fats Waller and Lionel Hampton. At 17, he attended the Youth Club, where he discussed jazz with Mayall, who was nine years his senior. Within a couple of years, he was visiting Mayall at his home, where he was introduced to the blues.

Shortly after Flint signed on, Watson left the band to study classical music. Roger Dean, a capable guitarist with roots in Chet Atkins and country music, replaced him. In June 1964, the new lineup of the Bluesbreakers supported John Lee Hooker on a month-long club tour of the U.K. The Bluesbreakers played their set and then backed Hooker during his set. The tour was so successful that it pushed Hooker's latest release, "Dimples," up to #23 on the British singles charts.

Buoyed by this success, the Bluesbreakers recorded their own live album at Klook's Kleek on December 7, 1964. Located in West Hampstead, Middlesex, Klook's Kleek was next-door to Decca's West Hampstead studios. For the live recordings, Decca engineers ran the cables and

wires from their studios next-door to Klook's Kleek. The album, titled *John Mayall Plays John Mayall*, featured eleven of Mayall's own compositions along with covers of "Lucille" and "Night Train." Saxophonist Nigel Stanger was spotlighted on four of the tracks. Released on March 26, 1965, the album sold poorly and failed to attract critical notice.

Undeterred, the band returned to the studio on February 26, 1965, to record their next single, "Crocodile Walk" backed with a harmonica-driven instrumental, "Blues City Shakedown." Issued on April 2, the single also stiffed in spite of a spirited performance.

Their prospects for live shows continued to expand, however, as on March 3, American guitar legend T-Bone Walker flew into London and spent two days rehearsing with the Bluesbreakers before appearing with them on the television show *Ready Steady Go!* on March 5. He then went on a month-long tour of Britain supported by the Bluesbreakers. Walker praised his backing support to *Melody Maker*: "These John Mayall's Bluesbreakers I'm working with, they're dedicated to blues . . . My way's a little different, but they're good for what they do."

With three releases failing to achieve any success, Decca dropped Mayall from its roster. However, events were afoot that would change Mayall's fortunes. Eric Clapton had just quit the Yardbirds [see **Eric Clapton, Yardbirds**]. The B-side of the Yardbirds' latest release, "Got to Hurry," was an instrumental featuring Clapton. Upon hearing it, Mayall—convinced that Clapton would be a much more suitable guitarist than Dean for the Bluesbreakers—set his sights on recruiting him. Clapton joined the Bluesbreakers in April 1965 and, very soon after, the band's sound was completely transformed.

In the Yardbirds, Clapton had already begun to build a reputation as a guitar soloist, and so right from the start he was a crowd-puller at Bluesbreakers gigs. His playing was louder and far more aggressive—in a Freddy King/Buddy Guy-derived style—than anything that had been heard before in England. In effect he augured the era of the "guitar hero" wherein, for some years to come, most people in an audience would focus almost exclusively on the guitar player and his ability—or inability—to come up with imaginative and fluid solos.

On May 12, 1965, the Bluesbreakers spent a couple of hours in the studio backing Bob Dylan with Tom Wilson producing. The recordings have not been released and

Mayall later termed the session a "fiasco." Mayall also made a brief appearance in the film *Don't Look Back,* which chronicled Dylan's breakthrough visit to Britain that year.

Still without a recording contract, the band accepted an offer made by Rolling Stones manager Andrew Oldham to record a single for the maverick Immediate label. Produced by Jimmy Page, "I'm Your Witchdoctor" and the backing track, "Telephone Blues," were recorded in June 1965 and released in October. With an incendiary performance by Clapton on the A-side, the record was easily one of the best electric blues singles of the year. Nevertheless, the release sank from sight.

Then in August 1965, Mayall found himself facing something of a crisis when Clapton abruptly left the group and headed to Greece with some musician friends on what was intended to be an around-the-world working holiday.

However, Mayall had a calendar full of bookings in England, so he immediately began searching for a suitable replacement for his AWOL guitarist. Over the next few months, several guitarists stood in for Clapton, including John Weider, John Slaughter, and Geoff Krivit of Dr. K's Blues Band. Peter Green, the last guitarist to fill in, had been particularly persistent, as Mayall subsequently recalled to *Guitar Player:* "Peter, this cockney kid, kept coming down to all the gigs and saying, 'Hey, what are you doing with him; I'm much better than he is. Why don't you let me play guitar for you. Why, he's no good at all.' He got really nasty about it, so finally, I let him sit in." The brash upstart played brilliantly, but unfortunately, after just a few gigs with Green in place, Clapton returned (around November 1965) and Mayall, having previously promised to take Clapton back, was forced to let the 19-year-old Green go. His last gig with the band was on November 11 at the Mojo Club in Sheffield. Green left deeply disappointed.

Aside from Clapton's disruptive departure, Mayall had other personnel issues to contend with. McVie was fired in October for the first (but not last) time because of his excessive drinking. Teetotaler Mayall smoked cigarettes but did not tolerate any substance abuse in his band if the music suffered as a result. It was rumored that one fateful night when returning from a gig up north, Mayall ejected a vomit-prone McVie from the touring van and left him on the side of the M1 motorway, miles from anywhere. Mayall himself now recalls that this parting of ways happened more mercifully in central London. One

way or the other, it was some months before the disciplinarian bandleader agreed to give the bass player another chance. For the interim, Jack Bruce, formerly with the Graham Bond Organization [see **Graham Bond, Cream**], took McVie's place. Bruce was still playing bass when Clapton rejoined.

Sometime in late November, the band returned to the studio to record another single for Immediate, "Sitting on Top of the World." Also, a live date recorded at the Flamingo during this time yielded tracks that were later spread out on the 1969 LP *Looking Back* and the 1977 album *Primal Solos.*

Bruce stayed with the group only about six weeks, from October to December 1965, before leaving to pursue a far more lucrative gig with Manfred Mann, who were by then a successful pop group. At this point John Bradley briefly filled in on bass until McVie was allowed to return with his solemn promise to behave himself. (Which he did—for a short while, at least).

Mayall's next recording session, early in 1966, featured only himself and Clapton on a limited release single for Mike Vernon's specialist Purdah label. The single effectively captured the sound of a vintage Chicago blues record, and its run of 500 copies quickly sold out. *Melody Maker* gave the single their unconditional approval, calling it "an extraordinarily authentic sound."

With Clapton back in the fold and the Bluesbreakers now pulling large audiences into the clubs, Mike Vernon was able to persuade Decca to give the Bluesbreakers a second chance. In February 1966, Vernon used Clapton and Mayall as sidemen on a session for American bluesman Champion Jack Dupree at Decca Studios. Three tracks appear on the Dupree album *From New Orleans to Chicago* and on a various artists compilation, *Raw Blues,* both released on Decca. Also sitting in on these sessions was drummer Keef Hartley of the Artwoods, who soon thereafter played a role in the Bluesbreakers' story as well.

In April 1966, the Bluesbreakers returned to Decca Studios to record their second album, the seminal *Blues Breakers: John Mayall with Eric Clapton,* produced by Mike Vernon. The LP was recorded in just three days with the band augmented on some tracks by John Almond on baritone sax, Alan Skidmore on tenor sax and Dennis Healey on trumpet. Consisting of a mix of Mayall originals and covers—including Robert Johnson's "Ramblin' on My Mind" with vocals by Clapton, and the Otis

Rush/Willie Dixon-penned "All Your Love"—*Blues Breakers* was widely celebrated and has since been recognized as a milestone recording in British blues. Mayall had initially attempted to record one track on the album, "Double Crossing Time," prior to these sessions as the B-side to the aborted second single for Immediate. When Bruce left the group, the number was retitled "Double Crossing Mann" with the lyrics reworked by Mayall and Clapton to reflect their displeasure with Bruce's sudden departure from the Bluesbreakers for Manfred Mann. The basic track was later used to build on when the LP was recorded.

Beat Instrumental gave the LP high marks: "John Mayall's voice may not be the greatest example of blues singing there is, but he is sincere, and with blues fans that counts for a lot." The reviewer then added, "It's Eric Clapton who steals the limelight, and no doubt several copies of the album will be sold on the strength of his name." *Melody Maker* was similarly impressed, proclaiming, "No British musicians have ever sounded like this on record. It is a giant step. It is a credit to John and his musicians." And *New Musical Express* called the album a "rolling blues exciter."

Released in the U.K. on July 22, 1966, the album was Mayall's commercial breakthrough, soaring to #6 on the album charts. *Blues Breakers* would come to be affectionately known as the "Beano" album because of the cover shot capturing Clapton reading a "Beano" comic book. Two tracks—"Key to Love" and the Mose Allison-penned "Parchman Farm"—were lifted from the album and released as a single with "Parchman Farm" on the A-side, but neither found a place on the singles charts.

At the time of the album's release, Mayall was faced with yet another unplanned change in personnel. On June 25, 1966, *Melody Maker* reported that Clapton had joined forces with Jack Bruce and Ginger Baker and that this trio was about to form a new group called the Cream. Mayall was outraged and confronted Clapton. Clapton then gave notice, agreeing to stay with the group for a few more weeks until a replacement could be found. (But when he missed several gigs, he was sacked.)

With Clapton permanently gone, Mayall tried to lure Green back into the group. It was not an easy sell. For his part, Green was still angry at having been dismissed when Clapton had returned from Greece. Green was also weighing an offer from Eric Burdon to join the New Animals and go on tour in America. But while he was eager to see

America, Green loved playing pure blues more than the Animals' chart-friendly music. Finally agreeing to join (after a couple of weeks of cajoling), Green officially became a Bluesbreaker again in July 1966.

During the first few weeks in the role he had coveted for so long, Green had a difficult time. Clapton had developed his own loyal following and Green initially met with some resistance and heckling. Green even complained to *Beat Instrumental*: "I just wish people would stop comparing me with Eric. I'd just like them to accept me as Peter Green not 'Clapton's Replacement.' I've felt terribly conscious of this on stage. I can feel them listening for special phrases. They want to see how I compare with Eric. It makes my job tougher, because, just lately, I've been really trying hard all the time. Sometimes I try too hard and overplay. If I make a mistake when I'm doing this, I'm spoiled for the rest of the evening."

There was also a noticeable falloff in attendance at the band's performances. Always the astute bandleader, Mayall swiftly changed the band's repertoire around so that direct comparisons between the two guitarists became more difficult. Within a short time, the group gelled and fans began accepting Green. Mayall even told *Beat Instrumental*, "In Peter Green we have a replacement who is a young genius. He's better known than Eric was when he joined, and for my money he'll be better than Eric." Mayall then added sardonically, "Peter is more interested in playing blues than being a star. Eric's gone all 'showbiz.'" This last comment revealed more than a little bitterness on Mayall's part about the manner in which Clapton left, an uncharacteristic sentiment in the usually easygoing bandleader. In the years that followed, Mayall became far more philosophical about such defections, viewing them as inevitable and sometimes even desirable in that they promoted opportunities for musical growth and flexibility.

With the addition of Green, the Bluesbreakers underwent a period of considerable instability before things settled down. Shortly after Clapton quit, drummer Flint left as well. Flint had grown tired of the road and, reportedly, had come to be somewhat isolated within the band. "By mutual agreement" he departed and was temporarily replaced by ex-Brian Auger drummer Mickey Waller—who, in turn, then quit to join Alexis Korner. Flint now recalls with amusement the extremely matter-of-fact way in which his dismissal took place: instead of giving him a gold watch as a farewell gift, Mayall simply informed long-time colleague Flint that his final paycheck would contain five pounds less than usual (quite a sum in those days) because receipts had been down at recent gigs.

Mayall replaced Waller with Aynsley Dunbar, who joined the Bluesbreakers in September 1966 [see **Aynsley Dunbar Retaliation**]. Furthermore, McVie—whose recurrent alcoholic binges had gotten him fired again—was replaced by Steve Usher, previously of the Blue Monks. Mayall told *Beat Instrumental* that he had hoped to persuade Usher to stay on a permanent basis, but after a few weeks McVie returned (in time for the upcoming recording sessions).

The new lineup wasted little time, going into the West Hampstead Studios at the end of September to record a new single, "Looking Back" backed with "So Many Roads." The B-side was a powerful remake of "So Many Roads, So Many Trains," a song associated with Otis Rush. Mayall had earlier told *Beat Instrumental*, "We're always being asked for that ["So Many Roads"] and I'd like to get it down." Produced by Mike Vernon, both tracks featured brass backing. *Melody Maker* reacted favorably to the release, describing the A-side as a "catchy blues raver" and predicting that it would become very popular in the clubs.

The Bluesbreakers returned to the studio in mid-October to record their next single, "Sitting in the Rain" backed with "Out of Reach." Green composed the B-side, which featured his vocals and sinuous guitar solos. They also recorded material for a new album, *A Hard Road* (which had Mayall's own art on the cover). *A Hard Road* featured Green prominently and contained some strong songwriting by Mayall. Green sang lead on "You Don't Love Me" and "The Same Way" and contributed some superb guitar playing on his own "The Super-Natural" and Freddy King's "The Stumble." (His choice of the Freddy King instrumental was meant to follow Clapton's take on "Hideaway.")

Through *A Hard Road,* Green's place as Clapton's equal (and some might say superior) guitarist was now assured, and Mayall's prodigious talent was likewise showcased at its best. Critical praise for *A Hard Road* was unanimous. *Rolling Stone* said it was "by far the best album ever put out by a white blues band and should continue to be the same for quite some time." *Melody Maker* enthused, "The album's most exciting aspect is the knowledge that it is really only the first chapter in the achievements of these four very talented English bluesmen, who are gradually going to become increasingly more important in the structure of British popular music." Released on

February 17, the album climbed to #10 on the U.K. album charts.

Mayall returned to the studio in November to cut "Burn Out Your Blind Eyes" and "Milkman Strut" as solo performances. Mayall also recorded "Long Night" accompanied by the Bluesbreakers and organist Stevie Winwood (credited, for contractual reasons, as "Steve Anglo") as well as a Green/Mayall collaboration, "Evil Woman Blues."

All the tracks from this session were released on the Mike Vernon-produced *Raw Blues*, a various artists album on Decca's budget Ace of Clubs subsidary. That same month, the Bluesbreakers recorded a joint EP with American harpist Paul Butterfield, who was touring the U.K. with his band. Mike Vernon struck a deal between Decca and Elektra (Butterfield's label) that allowed Butterfield to participate, but limited distribution of the record to the U.K.

In February 1967, the three Bluesbreakers (without Mayall) recorded a single of their own, "Curly" and "Rubber Duck" (both instrumentals). The release received high marks from *Melody Maker:* "The whole record is really a climax which doesn't ease up all the way." Mayall recalls another Green instrumental jam from this session, "Greeny," as being the foundation of a blues groove that quickly evolved and soon would lead to the formation of a new British blues band, Fleetwood Mac.

The Bluesbreakers returned to the studio together in March to record a pair of songs, "Please Don't Tell" and "Your Funeral and My Trial." (These songs were not released until they appeared on the compilation album *Thru the Years* in 1971). That same month, they participated in sessions for the Eddie Boyd album, *Eddie Boyd & His Blues Band* (released in the U.S. as *I'll Dust My Broom*), produced by Mike Vernon.

In April 1967, Dunbar was ejected from the group. Dunbar's powerful and often complex style of drumming had begun to dominate the band's sound to the point where Mayall decided to replace him with someone who would play in a simpler style. Mayall later explained that when Dunbar "got too out of control, going crazy, tied up with technique and bringing down the overall thing, he had to go."

Mickey Waller stepped in for a few gigs, but ultimately Mayall brought in Mick Fleetwood—Green's former bandmate from Peter B's Looners and Shotgun Express. Fleetwood later recalled feeling deeply embarrassed about having to replace Dunbar, who was technically a far superior drummer.

With Fleetwood at the drums, the Bluesbreakers went into the studio to record their next single, "Double Trouble" backed with "It Hurts Me Too." *New Musical Express* described the disc as an "ultra-slow down-to-earth blues," observing that it was "not in the least commercial, but aimed at the specialists." The Bluesbreakers (again without Mayall) also recorded several more numbers, including the instrumental "Fleetwood Mac," an obvious precursor of things to come. Ultimately, Fleetwood's position as drummer was short-lived. After six weeks, Mayall fired him in May 1967, presumably because too often he and McVie provoked each other into drunken escapades that affected their playing. Today, Mayall simply remembers thinking at the time that Fleetwood's drumming wasn't truly suited to the Bluesbreakers.

Mayall's next recording session took place in May, when he put together a solo album in a single day. Titled *The Blues Alone*, the album—in which he's accompanied only by former Artwoods drummer Keef Hartley [see **Artwoods**] on eight of the 12 tracks—showcased Mayall's ability as a multi-instrumentalist. Released on the budget Ace of Clubs label in November 1967, *The Blues Alone* received critical laurels. *Disc and Music Echo* said it was "technically beautiful and faultlessly ethnic . . . the album's as good an example of pure blues as is ever likely to come out of Britain." *New Musical Express* said it contained "more terrific blues works of the all-rounder to end all-rounders." The disc reached #24 in the U.K. and #128 in the U.S.

To replace Fleetwood, Mayall turned to his sideman on *The Blues Alone*, Hartley. Keef Hartley (b. 1944; Preston, Lancashire, U.K.) moved to Liverpool in 1962 to join Rory Storm and the Hurricanes, replacing Ringo Starr. Two years later he moved to London, where he became a member of the Artwoods.

With the drum slot filled, Mayall then had to face a critical defection. Peter Green gave notice of his intention to leave the band in June 1967. After contemplating and then abandoning the idea of living in Chicago and working alongside up-and-coming bluesmen on the Chicago scene, Green instead decided to join Mick Fleetwood in forming Fleetwood Mac under the guidance of Mike Vernon. The name of the new group implied the involvement of bassist McVie ("Mac" Vie), but for the moment McVie was content with the security of Mayall's band. Ostensi-

bly, Green left mainly because he didn't enjoy playing the jazzy style of blues (which used horns) toward which Mayall had recently begun focusing.

Mayall's first choice to replace Green was 16-year-old Davey O'List, guitarist for the Attack. While tempted, O'List instead decided to form the Nice with organist Keith Emerson. Undaunted, Mayall found two other guitarists for the Bluesbreakers, including 19-year-old Mick Taylor.

Michael Kevin Taylor was born in Welwyn Garden City, Hertfordshire, U.K., on January 17, 1948. Taylor's vision of his future as a musician was inspired by a Bill Haley concert he attended as a young man. His uncle further exposed him to all of the great rock'n'roll heroes of the 1950s: Haley, Elvis Presley, Fats Domino, Jerry Lee Lewis and Little Richard. By the age of 11 he had started to play the guitar in earnest, and by 1962 he was in his first band, the Strangers. His next group was the Juniors, with whom he recorded one single, 1964's "There's a Pretty Girl" backed with "Pocket Size" (U.K./Columbia DB 7339).

During his early teens, Taylor discovered the blues after having come across B.B. King's classic *Live at the Regal* album. He was also greatly influenced by Freddy King. Taylor was a member of the Gods in 1965 and 1966, a group that also included future Uriah Heep keyboardist Ken Hensley on the Hammond B3 organ. During this time, Taylor attended Onslow Secondary School; later he got a job as a commercial engraver.

In June 1966, Taylor and his friends went to see John Mayall perform at a college gig in the Hatfield area. Clapton—already Cream-bound—had failed to show up for the show. Encouraged by his friends, Taylor approached Mayall after the first set and asked to sit in. With nothing to lose, Mayall decided to let him. Taylor knew the band's repertoire virtually note-by-note and performed admirably. After the gig, he disappeared before Mayall could get his name and phone number. Remembering the shy teenager's performance, Mayall sought him out by putting an ad in *Melody Maker*. Taylor responded and became a member of the Bluesbreakers.

A second guitarist, Terry Edmonds, also joined the Bluesbreakers, only to leave after a few weeks to join a group called Ferris Wheel. Mayall also recruited two saxophone players for the band, Chris Mercer and Rip Kant.

This new six-piece lineup recorded the album *Crusade* on July 11 and 12, 1967. Mayall explained the intent behind the album in his liner notes: "I have chosen to campaign for some of my blues heroes by recording one number each from their own recorded repertoires and, amongst the original compositions, I include a tribute to J.B. Lenoir, whose untimely death came as a great shock to me."

While his motivation was admirable, the record was generally disappointing. Among the conflicting reviews, *Rolling Stone* pointed out, "You can find better blues groups, white and black, by the dozens; and if you dig the material, the originals are still around. And in the case of Muddy Waters or Albert King, the originals are very much better in terms of musicianship." Still, the album contained some fine tracks, most notably Mayall's haunting tribute, "Death of J.B. Lenoir." Despite the press, the album rocketed up the U.K. charts to #8 and reached #136 in the U.S.

In the meantime, Green and Fleetwood were continuing to woo McVie to join them in their newly created Fleetwood Mac. Like Green, McVie had become increasingly put off by the jazzier direction the Bluesbreakers were taking, so in September 1967, he left the Bluesbreakers to rejoin his former bandmates. Paul Williams, formerly of the Zoot Money Big Roll Band, initially replaced him. Kant also departed and Mayall replaced him with Dick Heckstall-Smith, formerly of the Graham Bond Organization [see **Graham Bond**].

On September 14 and 15, 1967, the Bluesbreakers returned to the studio for their next single, the powerful "Suspicions" (parts one and two)—an excellent, horn-driven number that inexplicably languished beneath the charts. Although already successful several times in the album charts, Mayall had yet to be so lucky with his singles. He explained his attitude toward 45s to *Melody Maker:* "I'd like a hit record, but I'm not prepared to sell out just to get one. I'd be glad to make the chart—but only with a blues number."

Then in the October 21, 1967, issue of *Melody Maker*, Mayall came under siege from an unexpected source—his former mentor Alexis Korner. While not naming Mayall by name, Korner made the point that the Bluesbreakers contributed little of value to British blues, adding, "We blues players cannot expect plaudits just for following our chosen profession. Nobody lionizes bus conductors or even scientists unless they do something exceptional. A bluesman, let me remind you, is also judged by his performances, not his pretensions."

Mayall responded to the diatribe in the next issue of the weekly music newspaper. "We've all read it in the band, and it's obviously a very vicious and very personal attack on me. But as regards his musical reasoning, the whole thing was very confused and I can't understand it. It takes great concentration to find out what he's talking about. It seems to me he thinks there were no blues played after Robert Johnson, and that the Bluesbreakers haven't contributed anything original at all. Yet he did our first album's sleeve notes which was full of praise. I think it must be sour grapes. He doesn't even mention me by name."

The Bluesbreakers spent the duration of 1967 touring Britain, Ireland and Holland as Mayall taped the shows on a portable reel-to-reel recorder. Another lineup change occurred in October when Williams quit to join Alan Price and was replaced by Keith Tillman. At the conclusion of the tour, Mayall had over sixty hours of tape recordings (including conversations). He then assembled the highlights of the recordings into two separate albums that were issued in the U.K. as *Diary of a Band, Volumes 1 and 2*, in February 1968.

Mayall later explained the concept behind the albums to *Zig Zag* magazine: "It's a true account of a period of touring . . . a lot of memories captured on record. I think the whole thing is an in-group type thing—it would only hold real nostalgic value if you were in the band at the time. I mean, those days were really humorous, but I tried to convey to the public what it was like in a band . . . whether it came off or not, I don't know. I tried to pick things which showed everybody playing something for the first time, a little different from the usual . . . it was based around the unexpected really. They may not have been the best tracks musically, but they were the most interesting ones. It was an awkward selection to make anyway."

While the fidelity wasn't the best, the tapes effectively captured the atmosphere of a Bluesbreakers concert. *Melody Maker* had no complaints about the sound, calling the release "a remarkable collection of live performances" and further remarking, "For the first time, the creative improvising ability of a British group has been properly captured." *Volume 1* reached #27 in the U.K. and *Volume 2* stopped right behind it at #28. U.S. audiences had to wait two years before the recordings were issued in the States, but when they were finally available, *The Diary of a Band* (Volume 1) went to #93 and *Volume 2* (retitled *Live in Europe*) reached #146.

Mayall returned to the studio in December to record his next single—"Jenny" backed with "Picture on the Wall"— with Hartley and former Bluesbreaker Green. The record was not as strong as his previous singles. *New Musical Express* noted of the A-side: "It's slow and moody, with some mean guitar work off-setting the vocal. Great, but strictly for the blues connoisseur."

In January 1968, Mayall and the Bluesbreakers toured the United States for the first time, starting with a stint at the Café Au-Go-Go in New York City from January 9–23, where they broke all club attendance records. A *Billboard* reviewer said of their performance, "Musically, the group evokes an exciting sound without the loudness usually associated with blues-rock." The Bluesbreakers then moved on to the Grande Ballroom in Detroit, the Whisky A Go-Go in Los Angeles, and the Fillmore and Winterland in San Francisco. The Fillmore and Winterland gigs were awesome triple bills featuring the Bluesbreakers, Jimi Hendrix and Albert King.

Following the U.S. tour, more lineup changes occurred as Mayall ousted Tillman and replaced him with 15-year-old Andy Fraser, who came recommended by Alexis Korner and was dating Korner's daughter, Sappho. Fraser, however, left within six weeks and ended up as a member of the group Free. Tony Reeves, previously a member of the New Jazz Orchestra, replaced him. Hartley also left to form his own band, the Keef Hartley Band, and was replaced by fellow New Jazz Orchestra alumnus Jon Hiseman, who had also played with the Graham Bond Organization. Henry Lowther joined in February of 1968, bringing in his skills on cornet and violin.

In April 1968, the Bluesbreakers recorded *Bare Wires*, coproduced by Mayall and Mike Vernon. Steeped in jazz, *Bare Wires* was an altogether more complex, transitional work than previous efforts. The widely conflicting critical response included a thumbs-up from *Melody Maker*, which printed, ". . . absorbing music richer in content than any previous British group album, apart from *Sgt. Pepper* and *The Thoughts of Emerlist Davjack*." *Record Mirror* commended the album as "a remarkable showcase of one of the most inventive and authentic blues outfits on the scene." *Rolling Stone*, on the other hand, viewed the album as a "disastrous episode for Mayall" and criticized what was perceived as "sloppy orchestration and poor material." Released on June 21, 1968, the album was Mayall's most successful to date, reaching #3 in the U.K. and #59 in the U.S.

After the release of *Bare Wires*, the Bluesbreakers toured extensively until Mayall officially disbanded the group on July 14, 1968, purportedly to "work in more of a solo capacity with a small backing group." Mayall explained to *Melody Maker* reporter Chris Welch why he reduced the size of the group. "On the *Bare Wires* album, we could use the brass section properly, but in clubs, it didn't work out. There are two ways to use a section, either with arrangements, which you can get anybody to play, or to feature them all as soloists. But when you've got Jon [Hiseman] and Tony [Reeves] on bass who were front line men as well, you've got seven people queuing up for a blow, most of them standing around doing nothing. I was just one of the seven joining in a blowing session. It produced some exciting things, but it was nearer to jazz than blues, and with those people it was logical that whole evenings would be instrumental, with just a couple of vocal choruses at the beginning and end."

The new, leaner band retained only Mick Taylor and added bassist Stephen Thompson (b. October 17, 1950; Wimbledon, U.K.) and drummer Colin Allen (b. May 9, 1938; Bournemouth, U.K.), formerly of Zoot Money's Big Roll Band, Dantalian's Chariot and Georgie Fame. Hiseman, Reeves and Heckstall-Smith moved on to form Colosseum.

In August 1968, this new stripped down lineup recorded *Blues from Laurel Canyon*, a theme album conveying Mayall's impressions of Los Angeles during three weeks following the demise of the Bluesbreakers. For this, his final Decca release, Mayall elected to issue the album under his own name rather than calling it a Bluesbreakers project. Taylor blossomed on this release, particularly on the extended "Fly Tomorrow." The album received varied reviews. Surprisingly, *Melody Maker* panned it, griping, "Backed by a competent, but dull group, Mayall has come up with his least interesting album to date." *Melody Maker* had always been Mayall's biggest booster, so getting slammed by the magazine was an unpleasant surprise. In other quarters, though, the album was warmly embraced. A *Beat Instrumental* writer said, "I like this one more than anything Mayall's given us before. Spare, pruned, and a hundred percent good." *Record Mirror* observed, "This is destined to be a really big seller, and perhaps not entirely only for blues addicts. The virtuosity of voice and instrumentation really is somethin' else." A really big seller it wasn't, but the LP fared admirably, reaching #33 in the U.K. and #68 in the U.S.

In September 1968, Mayall and his new band returned to the U.S. for a successful ten-week tour. In November, Mayall flew back to London to headline Blues Scene '68, a three-day concert series at the Royal Festival Hall that also featured Muddy Waters, Champion Jack Dupree and Mayall's protégés—the Aynsley Dunbar Retaliation.

The stress of so much touring was wearing on him, however, and in late January, Mayall collapsed and was found to be suffering from "influenza and physical exhaustion." Several dates had to be rearranged and Mayall resumed touring at Brighton Dome on February 14, 1969. The band then took off for yet another American tour. Upon their return in May, Mayall again disbanded his musicians and announced a new musical policy—"blues without bashing." Inspired by avant-garde jazz composer/saxophonist Jimmy Giuffre and his soundtrack to the film *Jazz on a Summer's Day*, Mayall decided to eliminate the drums altogether and feature all of the musicians equally. Oddly enough, Taylor's dismissal opened the way for even greater fame: when Mick Jagger called Mayall and asked him to recommend a guitar player to replace Brian Jones, Mayall recommended his young protégé. Taylor officially joined the Rolling Stones on June 13, 1969. Allen then left for Stone the Crows, leaving behind bassist Thompson (who would also eventually join Stone the Crows) as the only holdover.

To implement his new vision, Mayall recruited acoustic finger-style guitarist Jon Mark and flautist/saxophonist John Almond (b. 1946; Enfield, Middlesex, U.K.). Mark was best known as Marianne Faithfull's accompanist for three years and for having been a member of the band Sweet Thursday (which included Nicky Hopkins). Sweet Thursday released one album in the U.S. on the Tetragrammoton label, but when the label went bust, the group disbanded. Almond had previously played with Zoot Money and Alan Price.

Mayall switched lineups in June during the middle of a three-week European tour. A set of Swedish dates had been canceled and Mayall took the opportunity to showcase the new acoustic-based band, which made their debut at the Paris Olympia and then went on to tour Germany before returning to England. The German promoters were so concerned about how the new band would be received that they offered to pay the airfares for both sets of musicians, but Mayall declined, telling *New Musical Express*, "If you make up your mind to do something you have to do it. If you have the responsibility of being true to your music you have to take the gamble. It's not really a risk

because obviously I must believe in it very wholeheartedly." *Melody Maker's* Chris Welch reviewed the group's first English date at the Cambridge May Ball, asserting, "They're sensational! The new Mayall 'blues without bashing' band have suddenly developed into the most original, refreshing and exciting group in Britain, nay the world."

The group then made a tour of the United States that included an appearance at the Newport Jazz Festival on July 5, 1969. Mayall was one of several blues-rock acts that appeared at the traditional jazz festival and was the surprise hit of the event, reportedly getting the biggest reception of all. Leonard Feather reported in *Downbeat* that at the end of his set, "A roar went up that could hardly have been exceeded if Mayall had announced that the Vietnam war was over."

Their July 12 appearance at the Fillmore East was then recorded for what would be their next album, *The Turning Point*. *The New York Times* reviewed the performance and declared that Mayall led "an unusually deft quartet" and that Mayall himself was "an appealing singer who could shout the blues without affectation and, when he took up his mouth organ, play it with pungent charm."

In August 1969, Decca released an album called *Looking Back* that was composed of all the singles Mayall had recorded between April 1964 and December 1967. None of the tracks on *Looking Back* had appeared in LP format before and the collection provided Mayall with another hit British album (U.S. #79, U.K. #14).

In October 1969, Mayall's new label, Polydor, released *The Turning Point*. The album contained what became his signature song, "Room to Move," which received widespread FM radio airplay. This radical departure from Mayall's prior efforts paid handsome dividends in the form of favorable reviews and the artist's first Recording Industry Association of America (RIAA) gold album award. Remarkable for a group that had only been together for four weeks, *The Turning Point* was Mayall's biggest hit yet, reaching #11 in the U.K. and his highest placement in the U.S. at #32. Some of the *Turning Point* performances were filmed and became the subject of a movie (also called *Turning Point*) produced and directed by Peter Gibson and Alex Hooper. Music from the *Turning Point* soundtrack was issued on the 1999 CD *Live at the Marquee 1969*.

Mayall was later asked by jazz critic Leonard Feather if the move toward jazz was deliberate. "Not really," Mayall replied. "If I have a band and it seems to be sagging, I just try for something fresh, and it doesn't matter what the instrumentation is or what label people put on it."

Mayall returned to the U.K. in late October and spent most of November touring the concert halls of Britain. That same month, he released the single "Don't Waste My Mind," which was enthusiastically received by *Melody Maker:* "John must hit with this cheerful country ditty featuring Mark's superb acoustic guitar and Mayall's own wow-wow harmonica and vocals."

"Don't Waste My Time" was a minor hit in the U.S., reaching #81. The British tour was a huge success: he played to packed houses and received standing ovations before returning to California, where he had made his home in Laurel Canyon.

In January 1970, Mayall went on a 30-day tour of Europe, during which bassist Thompson dropped out and was replaced by Alex Dmochowski, formerly of the Aynsley Dunbar Retaliation. In February, Mayall returned to the United States for a two-month tour. Joining forces with Mayall for the February tour was one-man band Duster Bennett. Bennett played guitar, bass drum, high-hat and harmonica (simultaneously) and recorded for Blue Horizon Records as a solo artist. Rather than being a full-fledged member of the group on tour, Bennett was to be a featured performer, doing some solo numbers and sitting in with the band on selected songs.

Mayall found time to record his next album, *Empty Rooms*, early in 1970. Utilizing guest bassist Larry Taylor, formerly of Canned Heat [see **Canned Heat**] on some tracks (Thompson plays on others), plus Mark and Almond, Mayall's second album for Polydor fared even better than its predecessor, reaching #9 in the U.K. and #33 in the U.S. Album highlights included his last single, "Don't Waste My Time," and the B-side "To a Princess," which featured some arresting electric bass lines by Larry Taylor. Reviews were positive, with *Disc and Music Echo* proclaiming the record "probably his best album to date," although *Melody Maker* complained, "The lyrics are personal and sincere, but tend to be a trifle self indulgent."

Mayall returned to the U.K. in May 1970 for a tour "featuring Duster Bennett," who had been a hit at their U.S. shows. *New Musical Express* reported, "Quite unintentionally, Duster and his one-man band set-up succeeded in stealing the show in a short spot that was nothing short of visually and musically exciting."

Following the U.K. tour, Mayall made a short European tour and then disbanded the group on June 2. For his June 27 appearance at the Bath Festival, Mayall formed a makeshift band consisting of Green, Dunbar and bassist Ric Grech.

By this time, Mayall's sense of a band had become much more fluid. His recent chart successes had shown him that recruiting musicians on a project-by-project basis allowed him to both pursue his musical vision and maintain flexibility, yielding terrific results. That year, Mayall explained his reasons for frequently replacing musicians to *Disc and Music Echo*, saying, "I don't have anybody working for me now and as far as being a band leader is concerned I'm retired. When I've got some work to do I approach certain musicians and say, 'I've got two months' work for so much money, all expenses paid, do you fancy it?'"

So for his next group, Mayall put together an all-American band consisting of Larry Taylor and lead guitarist Harvey Mandel, both formerly of Canned Heat [see **Harvey Mandel**]. Rounding out the group was violinist Don "Sugarcane" Harris, formerly of the R&B duo Don and Dewey, who was featured on the Frank Zappa album *Hot Rats*.

They made recordings in July for a new album, aptly named *USA Union*, and the lineup debuted at the Japanese Music Festival on August 11. The album received positive reviews. *New Musical Express* proclaimed it "one of the year's most important albums," though Lester Bangs, writing for *Rolling Stone,* commented that the music was "just a shade too placid." *USA Union* went to #50 in the U.K. and #22 in the U.S.

On September 11 the band began an American tour in Chicago, which Mayall followed up on November 15–25 with another ambitious recording project. Enlisting guitarist Jerry McGee and West Coast session drummer Paul Lagos, along with a number of other musicians with whom he had worked in the past (Mick Taylor, Clapton, Hartley, Almond, Larry Taylor, Sugarcane Harris, Thompson and Mandel), Mayall staged sessions in Los Angeles and London.

Mayall later explained the idea behind the sessions to *Disc and Music Echo:* "I just thought it would be a nice idea to put different combinations of musicians together to see what would result from it. There are only two tracks with Mick Taylor, Eric Clapton and Harvey Mandel, the major three guitarists used, all playing together. But there's two of them playing on other tracks and other combinations like that."

These recordings became *Back to the Roots*, a two-record set that included an elaborate color booklet with lyrics and biographies of the musicians involved. Polydor released the double album in June 1971 to the accolades of critics and fans alike. *Disc and Music Echo* wrote that it was "a must for most record collectors—a great blues record" and singled out Sugarcane Harris's contribution in particular, printing, "The crowning glory for turning a good album into an excellent one has to go to Sugarcane Harris, whose blues violin is phenomenal." *Rolling Stone* was also strongly appreciative of the album, calling it "an essential disc." A *Rolling Stone* reviewer wrote, "I only hope there's enough left from these sessions for another album at some future date." *Back to the Roots* reached #31 in the U.K. and #52 in the U.S.

Mayall, on the other hand, was never happy with the double-LP's final mix, so he partially re-recorded some of the drum tracks (using his then-current drummer Joe Yuele) and remixed certain tracks to form the album *Archives to the Eighties*, released in 1988.

On December 12, 1970, Mayall and his band, with Mandel and Larry Taylor, flew to Hawaii for the first stop of a Japanese tour. Sugarcane Harris had to stay behind due to work permit hassles. In February and March, with Sugarcane Harris and drummer Lagos in the band, Mayall toured Europe.

For his next project, Mayall utilized only Larry Taylor and Jerry McGee. McGee was born Gerald James McGee in Eunice, Louisiana, on November 17, 1937. His father, Dennis, was an influential Cajun fiddle player. Jerry started playing guitar in his early teens and in 1960 moved to Los Angeles and started doing session work. He later became a member of the Candy Store Prophets, along with Larry Taylor. The Prophets were Bobby Hart's backing band, and they also provided the instrumental support for early Monkees recordings. From 1968 to 1972, McGee was a member of the Ventures.

The trio recorded the next Mayall album, *Memories*, in July 1971. Containing introspective lyrics supported by sparse accompaniment, *Memories* only managed to reach #179 on the U.S. charts. The album received a lukewarm welcome from critics, with *Rolling Stone* chastising Mayall for the "sheer banality" of some of his lyrics.

In August 1971, Mayall produced sessions for Albert King with himself on harmonica, guitar and piano, Blue

Mitchell on trumpet, Clifford Solomon on saxophone, Ernie Watts on tenor saxophone, Larry Taylor on bass, Ron Selico on drums and Freddy Robinson on guitar. The album was not released until 1987, when it was issued as *Lost Session* on Stax.

Mayall continued to sit at the mixing board in September, producing the Shaky Jake Harris album *The Devil's Harmonica*. Later that month, he started a European tour. When Jerry McGee backed out of the tour at the last minute, Jimmy McCulloch, the young Scottish guitarist for Thunderclap Newman, stepped in. Larry Taylor and Hartley rounded out the rhythm section.

Mayall's next project took him in yet another direction. Retaining only Larry Taylor and recruiting Mitchell, Solomon, Robinson and Selico, he planned a foray into jazz. Mitchell was perhaps the best known of the new additions, having risen to prominence as a member of the Horace Silver Quintet in the early sixties. He had also recorded several solo albums and had frequently been a member of the Ray Charles Orchestra. Solomon, formerly a member of the Lionel Hampton Band, was a jazz veteran who had also played with the Ike and Tina Turner Revue. Robinson was born in Memphis, Tennessee in 1939 and had worked with Little Walter, Howlin' Wolf, Jerry Bulter and Ray Charles. In 1970, he'd had a #29 R&B hit with "Black Fox."

Together with Mayall, this new group went on a two-month tour of the United States, making live recordings in Boston and New York on November 18 and December 3 and 4, 1971. The resulting album, *Jazz-Blues Fusion,* was far more jazz-oriented than anything he had ever done, with free-flowing, wailing solos over long, improvised accompaniments. The seasoned musicians Mayall had assembled meshed brilliantly. Reviewing this lineup in performance, *Disc and Music Echo* called the show an "unqualified triumph," further expressing, "The new Mayall sound is virtually blues with a swing. It jumps rather than drives along, winding up a showcase for the individual band members." The album received altogether high marks from the critics. *Melody Maker* went as far as to say that *Jazz-Blues Fusion* was "undoubtedly John's finest band and his finest album." Released in May 1972, the album reached #64 on the U.S. charts and was Mayall's last significant hit album.

Following the U.S. tour, Mayall took the band on a tour of Australia. Selico and Larry Taylor dropped out and were replaced by Hartley and Putter Smith, respectively. Following that tour, Mayall brought in string bassist Victor Gaskin, who toured with them in Britain in April 1972. Gaskin had worked with many of the jazz greats, including Duke Ellington, Cannonball Adderley and Chico Hamilton. Mayall then took the band on a European tour.

For his next release, Mayall recorded another live album in July 1972 at the Whisky A Go-Go in Los Angeles. He again reshuffled personnel, now choosing Mitchell, Solomon, Larry Taylor, Victor Gaskin, Hartley, Robinson, Watts, flautist Charles Owen and baritone and tenor saxophonist Fred Jackson. The album, *Moving On*, was released in January 1973.

Postscript

Mayall returned to the studio for his next long player, *Ten Years Are Gone* (1973), which marked the return of Sugarcane Harris to the lineup. *Ten Years Are Gone* was produced by Don Nix. For his next release, 1974's *The Latest Edition* (coproduced by Tom Wilson), Mayall added guitarists Hightide Harris and Randy Resnick.

Following *The Latest Edition*, Mayall left Polydor and signed a three-year contract with Blue Thumb/ABC Records, where he released six albums: *New Year, New Band, New Company* (1975), *Banquet in Blues* (1975), *Notice to Appear* (1976, produced by Allen Toussaint), *Lots of People* (1976), *A Hardcore Package* (1977), and *Last of the British Blues* (1978).

In 1979, Mayall switched labels again, moving to the tiny British label DJM Records, where he released *Bottom Line* and *No More Interviews* (1979) and *Road Show Blues* (1980).

In 1982, Mayall reunited former Bluesbreakers Mick Taylor, McVie and Allen for an extensive worldwide tour. A performance on June 8, 1982, recorded at the Capitol Theatre in Passaic, New Jersey, was issued on the video *Blues Alive* in 1984. Performances recorded in the summer of 1982 at the Wax Museum were issued as *Return of the Bluesbreakers* first on AIM Records in 1985 and then on Repertoire Records (Germany) and One Way Records (U.S.) in 1994.

Mayall's next release consisted of live recordings made in Hungary featuring guitarists Coco Montoya and Walter Trout, bassist Bobby Haynes and drummer Joe

Yuele. The album, *Behind the Iron Curtain* (1986), was issued on the GNP Crescendo label. The German label Entente issued Mayall's next live album, *The Power of the Blues*, in 1987.

Mayall then signed with Island Records, where he released two albums, *Chicago Line* (1988) and *A Sense of Place* (1990) before switching to the Silvertone label, where he released three albums, *Wake Up Call* (1993), *Spinning Coin* (1996) and *Blues for the Lost Days* (1997).

In 1999, the Indigo label released *Rock the Blues Tonight*, a collection of live recordings made with the Bluesbreakers in 1970 and 1971. Two more albums of live recordings of the *Turning Point*-era Bluesbreakers were released, also in 1999, as *Live at the Marquee: 1969* and *The Masters*. The same year, Mayall released *Padlock on the Blues*. In 2001, Mayall released two CDs through his official Web site, *UK Tour 2K* and *John Mayall—Boogie Woogie Man*.

Mayall's latest album, *Along for the Ride* (2001), includes guest appearances by Mick Taylor, Mick Fleetwood, John McVie and Peter Green.

Discography

Release Date	Title	Catalog Number

U.S. Singles

1965	I'm Your Witchdoctor/Telephone Blues	Immediate 502
1966	Parchman Farm/Key to Love	London 20016
1967	All Your Love/Hideaway	London 20024
1968	Broken Wings/Sonny Boy Blow	London 20039
1968	Living Alone/Walking on Sunset	London 20042
1969	Don't Waste My Time/ Don't Pick a Flower	Polydor 14004
1970	Nature's Disappearing/Moving On	Polydor 14051

The Bluesbreakers (without Mayall)

| 1967 | Curly/Rubber Duck | London 20039 |

U.S. Albums

| 1966 | *Blues Breakers: John Mayall with Eric Clapton* | London PS 492 |

All Your Love/Hideaway/Little Girl/Another Man/Double Crossing Time/What'd I Say/Key to Love/Parchman Farm/Have You Heard/Ramblin' on My Mind/Steppin' Out/It Ain't Right

1967   *A Hard Road*   London
LL 3502 (M)
London
PS 502 (S)
A Hard Road/It's Over/You Don't Love Me/The Stumble/Another Kinda Love/Hit the Highway/Leaping Christine/Dust My Blues/There's Always Work/The Same Way/The Super-Natural/Top of the Hill/Someday After a While (You'll Be Sorry)/Living Alone

1967   *Crusade*   London
LL 3529 (M)
London PS 529 (S)
Oh, Pretty Woman/Stand Back, Baby/My Time After a While/Snowy Wood/Man of Stone/Tears in My Eyes/Driving Sideways/Death of J.B. Lenoir/I Can't Quit You Baby/Me and My Woman/Streamline/Checking on My Baby

1968   *The Blues Alone*   London PS 534
Brand New Start/Please Don't Tell/Down the Line/Sonny Boy Blow/Marsha's Mood/No More Tears/Catch That Train/Cancelling Out/Harp Man/Brown Sugar/Broken Wings/Don't Kick Me

1968   *Bare Wires*   London PS 537
Where Did I Belong/I Started Walking/Fire/Open Up a New Door/I Know Now/Look in the Mirror/I'm a Stranger/No Reply/Hartley Quits/Killing Time/She's Too Young/Sandy

1968   *Blues from Laurel Canyon*   London PS 545
Vacation/Walking on Sunset/Laurel Canyon Home/2401/Ready to Ride/Medicine Man/Somebody Acting Like a Child/The Bear/Miss James/First Time Alone/Long Gone Midnight/Fly Tomorrow

1969   *Looking Back*   London PS 562
Mr. James/Blues City Shake Down/They Call It Stormy Monday/So Many Roads/Looking Back/Sitting in the Rain/It Hurts Me Too/Double Trouble/Suspicions (Part 2)/Jenny/Picture on the Wall

1969   *The Turning Point*   Polydor 244004
The Laws Must Change/Saw Mill Gulch Road/I'm Gonna Fight for You J.B./So Hard to Share/California/Thoughts About Roxanne/Room to Move

1970   *Empty Rooms*   Polydor 24-4010
Don't Waste My Time/Plan Your Revolution/Don't Pick a Flower/Something New/People Cling Together/Waiting for the Right Time/Thinking of My Woman/Counting the Days/When I Go/Many Miles Apart/To a Princess/Lying in My Bed

1970   *The Diary of a Band*   London PS 570
Blood on the Night/Edmonton/I Can't Quit You Baby/Keef Hartley Interview/Anzio Ann/Keef Hartley Interview and John Mayall/Snowy Wood/John Mayall Interview/God Save the Queen/The Lesson/My Own Fault

1970   *USA Union*   Polydor 24-4022
Nature's Disappearing/You Must Be Crazy/Night Flyer/Off the Road/Possessive Emotions/Where Did My Legs Go/Took the Car/Crying/My Pretty Girl/Deep Blue Sea

1971   *Back to the Roots* (2 LP)   Polydor 3002
Prisons on the Road/My Children/Accidental Suicide/Groupie Girl/Blue Fox/Home Again/Television Eye/Marriage Madness/Looking at Tomorrow/Dream with Me/Full Speed Ahead/Mr. Censor Man/Force of Nature/Boogie Albert/Goodbye December/Unanswered Questions/Devil's Tricks/Traveling

1971   *Live in Europe*   London PS 589
Blues in Bb/Help Me/The Train/Soul of a Short Fat Man/Crying Shame

1971   *Thru the Years* (2 LP)   London 2PS 600
Crocodile Walk/My Baby Is Sweeter/Crawling Up a Hill (version 1)/Mama, Talk to Your Daughter/Alabama Blues/Out of Reach/ Greeny/ Curly/Missing You/Please Don't Tell/Your Funeral and My Trial/Suspicions (Part 1)/Knockers Step Forward/Hide and Seek

1971   *Memories*   Polydor 5012
Memories/Wish I Knew a Woman/The City/Home in a Tree/Separate Ways/The Fighting Line/Grandad/Back from Korea/Nobody Cares/Play the Harp

1972   *Jazz-Blues Fusion*   Polydor PD 5027
Country Road/Mess Around/Good Time Boogie/Change Your Ways/Dry Throat/Exercise in C Major for Harmonica, Bass and Shufflers/Got to Be This Way

1973   *Moving On*   Polydor PD 5036
Worried Mind/Keep Our Country Green/Christmas '71/Things Go Wrong/Do It/Moving On/Red Sky/Reasons/High Pressure Living

1977   *Primal Solos*   London 820 320-1
Maudie/It Hurts to Be in Love/Have You Ever Loved a Woman/Bye Bye Bird/I'm Your Hoochie Coochie Man/Look at the Girl/Wish You Were Mine/Start Walkin'

1999   *Rock the Blues Tonight* (2 CD)   Indigo
IGOXDCD 102 X
Canadian concert performances.
You Must Be Crazy[1]/My Pretty Girl[1]/Possessive Emotions[1]/Crying[2]/Took the Car[2]/Blue Fox[3]/Devil's Tricks[3]/Don't Bring Me Down[3]/I Took the Car[3]/Crying[3]/Possessive Emotions[3]/Won't Have to Worry[4]/Rock the Blues Tonight[4]/Goodtime Stomp[4]
[1] Recorded September 26, 1970 with Mayall, Harvey Mandel (guitar) and Larry Taylor (bass).
[2] Same date and lineup as (1) plus Sugarcane Harris (violin).
[3] Recorded April 2, 1971 with same lineup as (2) plus Paul Lagos (drums).
[4] Recorded late 1971 with Mayall, Freddie Robinson (guitar), Blue Mitchell (trumpet), Fred Clark (tenor sax), Victor Gaskin (bass) and Keef Hartley (drums).

1999   *Live at the Marquee: 1969*   Spitfire
Records 5054
Music from the original *Turning Point* film soundtrack.
Can't Sleep This Night/So Hard to Share/Don't Waste My Time/I'm Gonna Fight for You J.B./The Laws Must Change/California (1)/California (2)

2000   *The Masters* (2 CD)   Spitfire
Records 5055
Music from the original *Turning Point* film soundtrack.
Don't Waste My Time[1]/Sleeping by Her Side[1]/Room to Move[1]/Saw Mill Gulch Road[2]/Can't Sleep This Night[2]/Thoughts About Roxanne[2]/Fight for

You J.B.[2]/Fight for You J.B.[3]/California[3]/Parchman Farm[4]/An excerpt from a Mayall interview giving his reasons behind the new *Turning Point* band[5]/More interviews and a free-form instrumental workout that became "The Laws Must Change"[5]/Instrumental by Steve Thompson that became "Don't Waste My Time"[5]/ "Greensleeves Blues" and instrumental that became "I'm Gonna Fight for You J.B." Interview with Colin Allen/Instrumental workout that became "Thoughts About Roxanne"[5]/Bill Haley Lives! (spontaneous instrumental workout after a day's rehearsals)[5]/Interview with Eric Clapton and the saga of the 17-bar blues that became "Don't Pick a Flower"[5]/Mayall interview and the story of J.B. Lenoir[5]/"I'm Gonna Fight for You J.B." and excerpts from an interview with Peter Green and John McVie[5]

[1] Recorded at Civic Hall, Plymouth, June 13, 1969.
[2] Recorded at Locarno, Hull, Plymouth, June 17, 1969.
[3] Recorded at York University, June 25, 1969.
[4] Recorded by the Laurel Canyon band. Birmingham Town Hall, U.K., May 9, 1969.
[5] Filming occurred at the London home of Mayall on Billing Road, Fulham on May 27–29, 1969.

2000	*Time Capsule*	Private Stash Records STASHCD01

Featuring tracks by the Powerhouse Four and the Blues Syndicate from 1957 and 1962, respectively.

The Powerhouse Four: Introduction/Art School Boogie/The Narrow Path/Comments by John Mayall/My Old Man/I'll Be Ready/Classroom Blues/How Long, How Long/Too Close Together

The Blues Syndicate: Comments by John Mayall/Hillbilly Blues/Maudie/Twist All Night/It Hurts Me Too/The Hucklebuck/Got My Mojo Working/Soon Forgotten/Sermonette/No Rollin' Blues

Miscellaneous U.S. Releases

1968	*Raw Blues*	London PS 543

Mayall is featured on six tracks: "Burn Out Your Blind Eyes," "Long Night," "Lonely Years," "Evil Woman Blues," "Milkman Strut" and "Bernard Jenkins."

U.K. Singles

1964	Crawling Up a Hill/Mr. James	Decca F 11900
1965	Crocodile Walk/Blues City Shakedown	Decca F 12120
1965	I'm Your Witchdoctor/Telephone Blues	Immediate IM 012
1965	Lonely Years/Bernard Jenkins	Purdah 3502
1966	Parchman Farm/Key to Love	Decca F 12490
1966	Looking Back/So Many Roads	Decca F 12506
1967	Sitting in the Rain/Out of Reach	Decca F 12545
1967	Double Trouble/It Hurts Me Too	Decca F 12621
1967	Suspicions (Part 1)/Suspicions (Part 2)	Decca F 12684
1968	Pictures on the Wall/Jenny	Decca F 12732
1968	No Reply/She's Too Young	Decca F 12792
1968	The Bear/2401	Decca F 12846
1969	Don't Waste My Time/ Don't Pick a Flower	Polydor 56544
1970	Thinking of My Woman/Revolution	Polydor 2066 021
1970	Crocodile Walk/Sitting in the Rain	Decca F 13804

The Bluesbreakers (without Mayall)

1967	Curly/Rubber Duck	Decca F 12588

U.K. EPs

1967	*John Mayall's Bluesbreakers with Paul Butterfield*	Decca DFE-8673

All My Life/Ridin' on the L&N/Eagle Eye/Little by Little

U.K. Albums

1965	*John Mayall Plays John Mayall*	Decca LK 4680

Crawling Up a Hill (version 2)/I Wanna Teach You Everything/When I'm Gone/I Need Your Love/The Hoot Owl/R&B Time(Medley): Night Train-Lucille/Night Train/ Crocodile Walk (version 1)/What's the Matter with You/Doreen/Runaway/ Heartache/Chicago Line

1966	*Blues Breakers: John Mayall with Eric Clapton*	Decca LK 4804
1967	*A Hard Road*	Decca LK 4853 (M) Decca SKL 4853 (S)
1967	*Crusade*	Decca LK 4890 (M) Decca SKL 4890 (S)
1967	*The Blues Alone*	Ace of Clubs ACL 1243 (M) Ace of Clubs SCL 1243 (S)
1968	*Diary of a Band Volume 1* Same as U.S. release *The Diary of a Band.*	Decca LK 4918 (M) Decca SKL 4918 (S)
1968	*Diary of a Band Volume 2* Same as U.S. release *Live in Europe.*	Decca LK 4919 (M) Decca SKL 4919 (S)
1968	*Bare Wires*	Decca LK 4945 (M) Decca SKL 4945 (S)
1968	*Blues from Laurel Canyon*	Decca LK 4972 (M) Decca SKL 4972 (S)
1969	*Looking Back*	Decca LK 5010 (M)
1969	*The Turning Point*	Polydor 583 571
1970	*Empty Rooms*	Polydor 583 580
1970	*USA Union*	Polydor 2425 020
1971	*Back to the Roots* (2 LP)	Polydor 2657 005
1971	*Thru the Years* (2 LP)	Decca SKL 5086
1971	*Memories*	Polydor 2425 085
1972	*Jazz-Blues Fusion*	Polydor 2425 103
1983	*Primal Solos*	Decca TAB 66

Miscellaneous U.K. Releases

1967	*Raw Blues*	Ace of Clubs ACL 1220(M) Ace of Clubs SCL 1220(S)
1999	*Live at the Marquee: 1969*	Eagle EDL EAG 161-2
1999	*The Masters* (2 CD)	Eagle 6-70211-5055-2

Charlie Musselwhite

Harmonica virtuoso Charlie Musselwhite is not only one of the most recognizable names on the contemporary blues scene, he is also one of its finest talents. However, the road to the top of the blues world has not been easy for Musselwhite. Alcohol abuse hampered the early part of his career and, toward the end of the 1980s, threatened to derail it entirely. However in a remarkable turnaround, Musselwhite quit drinking in 1987 and entered the most successful phase of his career. In the 1990s, Musselwhite recorded a series of critically acclaimed albums and won W. C. Handy Awards—the blues industry's highest honor—seven times. In 1995 his band won a W. C. Handy Award for Blues Band of the Year. Today he is seen as an elder statesman for the blues, head-lining major blues festivals the world over.

Charles Douglas Musselwhite III (b. January 31, 1944) hails from the small Mississippi town of Kosciusko. When he was three, his family moved to Memphis, where his father played harp, mandolin and guitar, and his mother played the piano. As early as age three, Musselwhite was blowing into his toy harmonicas, sowing the seeds of a style that years later would blossom into something uniquely his own.

Musselwhite grew up in a neighborhood full of musi-cians, including Jimmy Griffin, Slim Rhodes and rockabilly legend Johnny Burnette, who lived just across the street from the Musselwhite family. Young Charlie listened to hillbilly and rockabilly music and, before long, developed a passion for R&B and the blues. His favorite radio station was WDIA, and he was especially fond of deejay Rufus Thomas's show. Captivated by the music, he soon started to play both the guitar and harmonica, going downtown to learn how the street musicians played.

In 1959, Musselwhite befriended several of the old-time local blues singers and players—Gus Cannon, Willie Borum and two surviving members of the legendary Mem-phis Jug Band, Walter "Furry" Lewis and Will Shade (a.k.a. Son Brimmer)—who often jammed with him, pass-ing along some of their techniques, especially on harp and slide guitar. He also visited "white" roadhouses in West Memphis that regularly featured black blues bands.

As a teenager, Musselwhite worked at various factory and construction jobs in Memphis, Arkansas, Missouri, Tennessee and Mississippi, and also ran moonshine whiskey from the country stills to downtown Memphis. In the spring of 1962, he decided to move to Chicago with his friend Gayron Turner to seek a higher paying factory job. He found his first job in the Windy City as a driver for an exterminating company, and it was this seemingly unin-spiring occupation that acquainted him with the city and led to his discovering the local blues scene. Though a fan of blues music, Musselwhite had been unaware that Chicago's South Side was a blues haven. "It didn't take long to find the blues scene up there," Musselwhite told *The Los Angeles Times.* "Here were all these people I'd been listening to on record. Every night I'd go to a different club. What a choice—should I go see Muddy [Waters] tonight, or should I go see [Howlin'] Wolf, or should I see Elmore James? And what deals! You could go to Pepper's Lounge to see Muddy Waters for 25 cents, and you got a free ticket for a free beer once you got in."

While he didn't become a professional musician by design, it wasn't long before the enthusiastic observer became an active participant in the Chicago blues scene. "I never had any dreams or goals of being a professional musician," he recalled to the *The Los Angeles Times.* "I had no vision of being on any stage anywhere. But one night this waitress that I got to know real well told Muddy that I played harmonica and I ought to sit in. He made me sit in and it was scary, but it was fun too." Musselwhite went over well with the black audience as he performed with Muddy Waters at Pepper's Lounge that night, and this led to invitations to sit in with other blues legends. "Word got around that this young white kid played harmonica. There wasn't any kids playing blues in those days. It was old men's music—out of fashion, out of style. Kids my age would be saying, 'Man, why you listening to that [stuff]?' They liked the Temptations, stuff like that. So I was always getting offers to sit in, getting offers for jobs. The musicians were flattered that I knew who they were and had their records." Musselwhite ended up playing with some of the biggest names in the field, including Howlin' Wolf, Little Walter, Big Walter Horton, Sonny Boy Williamson, Jimmy Reed, Buddy Guy and Junior Wells.

While working odd jobs, Musselwhite supplemented his income by playing for tips with guitarist/mandolinist Johnny Young at the open-air market on Chicago's

Maxwell Street (then known as "Jewtown"). The pair also played at a Mexican club, Pasa Tiempo, and later moved on to Turner's Blue Lounge and Rose & Kelly's—clubs where other bluesmen such as Big Walter, J.B. Hutto, Charlie West and Johnny Shines frequently jammed. Musselwhite picked up paid engagements with Robert Nighthawk, Sam Lay, J.B. Hutto, Homesick James and Louis Meyers.

When he wasn't playing, Musselwhite often frequented the legendary Jazz Record Mart and befriended its owner, Bob Koester. Koester also owned a record company called Delmark Records that he operated out of the basement of the store. Despite its lack of accouterments, the Jazz Record Mart was one of the prime movers behind the blues revival of the mid-1960s. Musselwhite ended up working at the store and living in the store's basement, where he shared quarters with Big Joe Williams, one of the last of the old-time itinerant bluesmen. Musselwhite and the cantankerous Williams became friends, and the seasoned blues singer provided valuable pointers in such matters as playing with feeling and not rigidly adhering to set chord changes. "Big Joe and I became friends immediately, and our friendship went far beyond surface," Musselwhite later recalled. "We had many deep philosophical conversations and hung out all the time. I absorbed a lot of life from Big Joe."

While living in the basement of the record store, Musselwhite met blues musician and aficionado Mike Bloomfield [see **Mike Bloomfield**], who had begun presenting blues artists at a small coffeehouse called the Fickle Pickle. Bloomfield arranged for Big Joe Williams to perform there regularly, backed by himself on piano and Musselwhite on harp.

Playing at the Fickle Pickle led to weekend concerts at Big John's (a Wells Street tavern on the North Side) for the trio. Williams soon left the band, but Bloomfield maintained a shifting lineup of young, white musicians known as "The Group," which held down Big John's for about a year. Meanwhile, another local bar, the Blind Pig, was enjoying success with blues programs featuring Nick Gravenites and Paul Butterfield [see **Nick Gravenites, Paul Butterfield**.]

Influential writer Pete Welding reviewed the Group at Big John's in the December 3, 1964, issue of *Downbeat*, where he observed that they had "rapidly evolved into one of the finest, fiercest-swinging rhythm-and-blues combinations in Chicago." Furthermore, he wrote, "Adding a fine blues dimension to the group's work is the idiomatic harmonica playing of Musselwhite, a young Memphis blues fan who has learned much from the bluesmen of Chicago and who has developed a convincing and earthy approach to blues harp. He and Bloomfield have worked out a number of arrangements that voice the guitar and harmonica in unison, and these are quite effective. Musselwhite is easily the most relaxed player in the group."

As the band gained attention, legendary A&R man John Hammond, Sr., invited Bloomfield to record some demos for Columbia Records. So Bloomfield, Musselwhite, guitarist Mike Johnson, pianist Brian Friedman, bassist Sid Warner and drummer Norm Mayell recorded several tracks at Hammond's behest at a Chicago studio on December 7, 1964.

Shortly after the Columbia session, Bloomfield asked for more money from the proprietor of Big John's and was promptly replaced by Paul Butterfield, who came in with his newly formed blues band. Deciding to put together another band, Bloomfield retained Musselwhite, but recruited Nick Gravenites as a vocalist and other musicians. This band found regular work at another bar, Magoo's, and at a club near Rush Street called The End. (Sadly, despite their talent, the band lacked chemistry.) Meanwhile, Butterfield's gigs at Big John's were attracting attention and the group was offered a recording contract with Elektra Records. Since Bloomfield's band was now going nowhere, Bloomfield accepted a position in Butterfield's band, breaking up his own group in the process.

Musselwhite remained active following the breakup of the Bloomfield band. In 1965, he participated in sessions for both the John Hammond album *So Many Roads, So Many Trains* and Tracy Nelson's album, *Deep Are the Roots* [see **Tracy Nelson**].

Musselwhite continued to sit in with South Side bands and became good friends with Junior Wells, often joining Wells and Buddy Guy at Theresa's, another Chicago club located at 14th and Indiana. Meanwhile, Muddy Waters and Howlin' Wolf insisted that he also sit in with their bands. A warm camaraderie developed and flourished between Musselwhite and the elder bluesmen. "Muddy and Wolf would insist that I sit in," Musselwhite told *Blues Revue Quarterly*. "If I was broke, they would give me a few bucks. It was a real warm situation. Playing with Muddy and those guys was great; I can't even tell you how excited I was . . . These guys both inspired me and gave me an incentive to work hard and develop my own sound."

Musselwhite appeared on Barry Goldberg's *Blowing My Mind* [see **Barry Goldberg**] and, as "Memphis Charlie," participated in a harp duet with Big Walter Horton on the final installment of the Vanguard blues trilogy, *Chicago/The Blues/Today! Volume 3* produced by Sam Charters. "Sam Charters would come to town and he knew that I knew where everybody was playing," Musselwhite recalled to *Bay Blues* magazine. "And he would want to go and see what was happening and I would take him around. I was his Blues guide, you know. And [I] knew everybody when we'd get somewhere, so he'd be safe, you know. I'd vouch for him, you know—'this guy's OK.'"

Charters was in turn a help to Musselwhite. "He was working for Vanguard Records," Musselwhite explained, "and Elektra, which was about the same size I guess, had come out with the Paul Butterfield album. And I guess Vanguard wanted to do a white blues harp player album. And Sam asked me if I wanted to do it and I said—'Yeah. Sure. I don't know, why not.'"

With artists like the Weavers, Joan Baez, Ian & Sylvia, Buffy Sainte-Marie and Odetta, Vanguard had established itself as the preeminent folk label of the day. With Skip James, Junior Wells and Mississippi John Hurt, the label was also in the blues market, where it hoped to increase its presence. Charters wanted to add Musselwhite to the roster, but since he didn't have a backing band, one was put together for the session that included guitarist Magic Sam, pianist Otis Spann and drummer Sam Lay. They held the first rehearsal in front of an audience at the Burning Bush club. An overly nervous Musselwhite got drunk and the session was a disaster. Musselwhite had also rehearsed some tunes with Fenton Robinson, but Robinson wasn't available for the recording. A different group of musicians was then assembled: bassist Bob Anderson (ex-James Cotton), drummer Fred Below (formerly with Junior Wells, Muddy Waters, Howlin' Wolf, Little Walter and Buddy Guy), organist Barry Goldberg and guitarist Harvey Mandel [see **Harvey Mandel**]. Recorded in a single afternoon (according to Musselwhite), his first record was issued in 1967 as *Stand Back! Here Comes Charley Musselwhite's Southside Band*. The album, a gritty collection of raw blues distinguished by Mandel's distinctive guitar and Musselwhite's powerful harp playing, included the instrumental that became Musselwhite's signature song, "Christo Redemptor." Written by Duke Pearson, "Christo Redemptor" was inspired by the statue overlooking the harbor at Rio de Janeiro. Musselwhite first came across the song (Donald Byrd's version) while working at a record store in the Old Town section of Chicago.

While awaiting the release of his album, Musselwhite continued to play in the small blues clubs on Chicago's South and West Sides, including the Hideaway, the C&J Lounge, Turner's, and Kelly's. "I wasn't getting any airplay and the only places I was playing were these little bars that hardly paid anything," he later recalled. When *Stand Back!* came out, it began receiving significant airplay on several underground radio stations in San Francisco. In August 1967, Musselwhite took a leave of absence from his factory job to go on a one-month tour of the Bay Area. A touring group—billed as the Southside Sound System and featuring guitarist Harvey Mandel, keyboardist Dave Cook, bassist Buddy Martin and drummer Sandy McKey—booked several dates at the Fillmore. The group shared the stage with the Electric Flag and Moby Grape (August 8–10), the Electric Flag and the Steve Miller Blues Band (August 11–13), and the Paul Butterfield Blues Band and the Cream (August 22–27). The shows were successful and Musselwhite saw an opportunity to earn a living playing the music he loved on the West Coast. "There was a blues scene, but mainly kind of underground in Black ghettos like Oakland, so not too many people got to hear it," he told *BBR Boogie* magazine. "Above all there was money here, plenty of clubs without the backstabbing. And it dawned on me I didn't have to get a day job! I thought this is the place to stay! So I just never went back. I came for a month and stayed."

Musselwhite released his second album, *Stone Blues,* produced by Barry Goldberg in 1968. Recorded at Paramount Studios, Los Angeles, musicians appearing on this effort included keyboardist/vocalist Clay Cotton, drummer Eddie Hoh, guitarists Tim Kaihatsu and Larry Welker and bassist Karl Sevareid. Reviews were generally positive. *Melody Maker* commented, "Musselwhite sings and plays good blues harmonica and his band performs down-to-earth 'stone' blues in the manner of the modern young urban groups." *Hit Parader* wrote that the album "swings capably and the guitar-organ solos have their shining moments when they aren't being self conscious. Some good hard stuff like 'Clay's Tune' and 'Juke.'" The most pointed observation came from *Rolling Stone:* "Musselwhite suffers by comparison to the early Butterfield recordings . . . his gravelly vocal tone seems forced and his harp playing often suffers from screechy tone and inaccurate intonation. But Musselwhite's shortcoming are more than offset by the general excellence of the rest of the band, notably organist-pianist Clay Cotton and guitarists Tim Kaihatsu and Larry Welker. Although it isn't outstanding, this album contains several fine blues and not a single poor cut."

That same year, he appeared on two tracks of the Harvey Mandel album *Christo Redemptor* and on Barry Goldberg's record *Barry Goldberg Reunion.*

Musselwhite recorded his third album for Vanguard, *Tennessee Woman*, in 1969. Although he again used Sevareid, Kaihatsu and Welker, this time he added pianist William "Skip" Rose, drummer Lance Dickerson and steel guitarist Fred Roulette. Even though it included some interesting moments, notably an extended version of "Christo Redemptor" and Musselwhite's own "Blue Feeling Today" (which included chromatic harmonica by Rod Piazza [see **Rod Piazza**]), *Tennessee Woman* was panned by *Downbeat,* which asserted that the release was "too loose, too sprawling, not clearly enough defined. Even the leader's vocals—he's usually an affecting if not sensational blues singer—are mechanical and sometimes off-pitch." However, the magazine acknowledged that Musselwhite had "no white and few black peers on his instrument when he plays as he is capable of playing" and had "a keening, unbearably painful sound, fine time and astonishing chops." *Tennessee Woman* was to be the last record Musselwhite made for Vanguard, and the label even bid him adieu in its advertising: "*Tennessee Woman*, a very heavy record, is Charlie Musselwhite's last album on Vanguard. Good-bye Charlie! It was a hassle, lots of luck with your new label!"

At about the time that *Tennessee Woman* was released, Musselwhite was involved with another album release called *Coming Home* by the Chicago Blue Stars. Musselwhite formed the Blue Stars as a gigging band consisting of Roulette, Rose, guitarist/vocalist Louis Meyers, bassist Jack Meyers (Louis's cousin) and drummer Fred Below, Jr. As Musselwhite explained to *Blues-Rock Explosion:* "My old friend from Chicago, Pete Welding, was the producer and he thought it was a good idea to record us while we had the chance. We were already in town gigging, so we just went on in the studio, too, but since I was still under contract to Vanguard, I couldn't be featured and couldn't even be in the photos." This time, Musselwhite received the thumbs up from *Downbeat,* which extolled the album as "over 34 minutes of unpretentious forceful city blues."

Musselwhite toured with the *Coming Home* musicians billed as the Charlie Musselwhite Blues Band. British record producer Mike Vernon caught one of their shows at the Golden Bear in Huntington Beach, California. Writing for *Melody Maker*, Vernon noted that Musselwhite was "still strongly rooted in the Chicago traditions, but with further working experience, a distinctive style should evolve. He was always a good harpman—and he's better now." The review went on to say that the band was "undoubtedly one of the finest on the road today." In September, the group performed at the Ann Arbor Blues Festival in Michigan, about which *Downbeat* noted, "Charlie Musselwhite, the festival's sole white leader, headed a mixed band including the first-class drummer Fred Below, pianist Skip Rose and the festival's only steel guitar player. Musselwhite is a good harpist, a pleasant singer and a sincere, ungimmicked performer. 'Help Me' and 'Long Way from Home' featured his vocals, but the emphasis throughout the set was on instrumental work. He closed with the festival's only obvious reference to jazz, a swingin' version of 'Comin' Home Baby.'"

Musselwhite appeared on two albums in 1969, Barry Goldberg's *Two Jews Blues* and Neil Merryweather's *Word of Mouth*. The following year, he appeared on another Merryweather album, the *Ivar Avenue Reunion*, and released an album for Paramount Records, *Memphis, Tennessee.* Using the same core group of musicians as heard on *Coming Home* (without Louis and Jack Meyers and with Lonnie Castille replacing Fred Below, Jr. on drums), *Memphis, Tennessee* contained some interesting tracks, especially the instrumental "Arkansas Boogie" and a cover of Little Walter's scorcher, "Temperature."

Musselwhite released another album in 1970, *Louisiana Fog*, on Cherry Red Records. For this LP, he recruited 18-year-old guitar prodigy Robben Ford and his brother Patrick on drums. *Louisiana Fog* was a fine collection with Musselwhite in excellent form on the harmonica, particularly on "Takin' Care of Business" and the jazzy instrumental "Riffin'."

In 1970, Musselwhite also played on Johnnie Lewis's album, *Alabama Slide Guitar*, on Arhoolie Records. Soon afterwards, Musselwhite himself signed to the label for his next album, *Takin' My Time* (1971). The lineup for *Takin' My Time* included Musselwhite, Rose, Robben Ford, Patrick Ford and bassist Gerald Pederson. *Rolling Stone* applauded the effort, remarking, "With the unabashed excellence of this disc Charlie Musselwhite and his tight four-piece band set the 1971 standard for white blues bands everywhere. For not since the early days of Butterfield, the Stones or Mayall have the blues and R&B echo been so pungent, exhilarating or forthright as on this release."

Postscript

Charlie released one more album for Arhoolie, *Goin' Back Down South* (1975). His subsequent releases in the 1970s were mostly one-off deals, including three more albums, *Leave the Blues to Us* (1975) on Capitol Records; *Times Gettin' Tougher Than Tough* (1978) on Crystal Clear Records; and an instructional LP, *The Harmonica According to Charlie Musselwhite* (1978), on Kicking Mule Publications (re-released by Blind Pig Records in 1994).

In 1982, Musselwhite was featured on the War Bride Records release *Curtain Call*, a live album by the Dynatones that included another rendering of "Christo Redemptor." He continued to record for small labels in the 1980s, releasing *Tell Me Where Have All the Good Times Gone?* (1984) on Blue Rock'It Records, *Mellow-Dee* (1986) on Crosscut and *Cambridge Blues* (1988) on the reactivated Blue Horizon label.

In the late 1980s, Musselwhite quit drinking alcohol, inspired by 18-month-old Jessica McClure, a little girl rescued from an abandoned water well after being trapped for two and a half days. Musselwhite later admitted, "I'd always drank. I'd never been on a stage sober in my life. But I didn't feel good; it wasn't working anymore." As a result of his sobriety, Musselwhite began the most celebrated phase of his career. He signed a deal with Alligator Records, where his three releases were all critically acclaimed: *Ace of Harps* (1990), *Signature* (1991) and *In My Time* (1993). Switching labels to Pointblank, he then put out *Rough News* (1997) and *Continental Drifter* (1999), which featured the Cuban band Cuarteto Patria.

In May 2000, Musselwhite was presented the Governor's Award for Excellence by Mississippi Governor Ronnie Musgrove.

Discography

Release Date	Title	Catalog Number

U.S. Singles

1967	Christo Redemptor/Help Me	Vanguard 35067
1968	My Buddy Buddy Friends/Everything's Gonna Be Allright	Vanguard 35078
1970	Takin' Care of Business/Just a Little Bit	Cherry Red 4503

U.S. Albums

1967	*Stand Back! Here Comes Charley Musselwhite's South Side Band*	Vanguard VRS-9232 (M) Vanguard VSD-79232 (S)

Baby Will You Please Help Me/No More Lonely Nights/Cha Cha the Blues/Christo Redemptor/Help Me/Chicken Shack/Strange Land/39th and Indiana/My Baby/Early in the Morning/4 P.M./Sad Day

1968	*Stone Blues*	Vanguard VSD-79287

My Buddy Buddy Friends/Everything's Gonna Be Allright/My Baby's Sweeter/Clay's Tune/Gone and Left Me/Cry for Me Baby/Hey Baby/Juke/She Belongs to Me/Bag Gloom Brews

1969	*Tennessee Woman*	Vanguard VSD-6528

Tennessee Woman/Blue Feeling Today/A Nice Day for Something/Everybody Needs Somebody/I Don't Play, I'll Be Your Man Some Day/Christo Redemptor/Little By Little/I'm a Stranger

1970	*Memphis, Tennessee*	Paramount PAR5012

She Used to Be Beautiful/I Got to Go/Memphis, Tennessee/One Mint Julep/Blues/The Wolf/Temperature/Arkansas Boogie/Willow Weep for Me/Trouble No More/Done Somebody Wrong

1970	*Louisiana Fog*	Cherry Red CR5102

Louisiana Fog/Takin' Care of Business/Big Legged Woman/Riffin'/Leavin'/Just a Little Bit/Fell on My Knees/Directly from My Heart/Fat City

1971	*Takin' My Time*	Arhoolie F1056

It Ain't Right/Love Me or Leave Me/Fingerlickin' Good/Two Little Girls/Up and Down the Avenue/Highway Blues/Wild, Wild Woman/Takin' My Time

1994	*The Blues Never Die*	Vanguard 153/54-2

Tennessee Woman/Stingaree/Arkansas Boogie/Temperature/Done Somebody Wrong/River Hip Mama/Help Me/Juke/Taylor, Arkansas/I Don't Play, I'll Be Your Man Some Day/Finger Lickin' Good/Blue Feeling Today/Crazy for My Baby/I'm a Stranger/Everything's Gonna Be Allright/Too Hot to Touch (previously unreleased)/Blues Got Me Again/The Blues Never Die (previously unreleased)/After While (previously unreleased)/Trouble for Everybody/Christo Redemptor

Chicago Blue Stars

1969	*Coming Home*	Blue Thumb 9

I Need Your Loving/Early in the Morning/Coming Home, Baby/She's Got a Good 'Um/Route 66/It's Your Last Time/Summertime/Black Nights/You Better Cut That Out/Walking Through the Park

    Charlie Musselwhite: harmonica, vocals
    Rod Piazza: chromatic harmonica (track 2)
    Larry Welker and Tim Kaihatsu: guitars
    Skip Rose: piano
    Carl Sevareid: bass
    Lance Dickerson: drums

Miscellaneous U.S. Releases

1966   *Chicago/The Blues/Today! Volume 3*   Vanguard
VRS-9218 (M)
Vanguard
VSD-79218 (S)

Musselwhite appears on "Rockin' My Boogie" with Big Walter Horton's Blues Harp Band.

With Barry Goldberg and Neil Merryweather

1970   *Ivar Avenue Reunion*   RCA LSP 4442
Ride Mama Ride/After While/Magic Fool/Fast Train/My Daddy Was a Jockey/Charlotte Brown/Run, Run Children/Walkin' Shoes/Toe Jam

With Barry Goldberg and Harvey Mandel

1966   *Chicago Anthology*   Together ST-T-1024
Musselwhite appears on "Slow Down I'm Gonna Lose You," "I Loved and Lost" and "Big Boss Man."

1973   *Blues from Chicago*   Cherry Red
CR-5104

Tracks recorded between 1964–1971.
Musselwhite appears on "Big Boss Man" and "Lost Love."

U.K. Albums

1969   *Stone Blues*   Vanguard
SVRL 19012

Tracy Nelson (Mother Earth)

While many predicted that Tracy Nelson would reap huge commercial rewards with Mother Earth, she has never been able to achieve widespread success. Maybe her influences and tastes were just too eclectic for mainstream rock audiences, leaving Nelson, and her band Mother Earth, often critically distinguished but commercially overlooked. Or maybe the giant shadow cast by the legendary Janis Joplin was just too far-reaching to allow Nelson to be taken on her own terms.

However, for those who savored Mother Earth, Nelson's soulful, husky voice and penchant for stormy, gospel-and country-tinged tunes was the defining ingredient that captured their attention on every album. Today, Nelson brings these same qualities to her own recently revitalized solo career.

"I always knew why I wasn't more famous," Nelson once told *The Washington Post*. "Some of it had to do with the vagaries of the business. Most of it was my personal choices—moving to Tennessee, not having much of a stage presence, not being much of a hustler, choosing certain kinds of music over others. And just being a lazy slut."

Nelson (b. December 27, 1944; French Camp, California) grew up in Shorewood Hills, Wisconsin. Exposed to folk music and blues early on, she started to play the piano at age five and by 13 had taken up the guitar. Nelson recalled her earliest musical experiences to *Hit Parader*: "My whole family is musical. My father has a great bass voice, my brother is a tenor and my mother is a fine soprano. I was doing two part harmony with my mother by the time I was six. We all sang a lot for fun."

In high school she sang with the choir and with the Fuller Woods Trio, a folk group that modeled itself after Peter, Paul and Mary.

While majoring in social work at the University of Wisconsin, Nelson performed with the Fabulous Imitations, a Madison-based R&B Top 40 cover band whose lineup included Ben Sidran on piano. As the group played at fraternity parties and area coffeehouses, even occasional Union Hall gigs, Nelson sang the repertoire of Irma Thomas, including "Time Is on My Side," "Cry On" and "I Did My Part."

When Nelson was 20 years old, noted blues authority Sam Charters came to Wisconsin and discovered her performing at a student party. Impressed, he arranged for her to record an album for Prestige Records. Produced by Charters and recorded in Chicago, *Deep Are the Roots* was issued in 1965. Harmonica player Charlie Musselwhite, who soon became her boyfriend [see **Charlie Musselwhite**], assisted in the blues-oriented effort, as did Harvey Smith on piano and Peter Wolfe on guitar. *Downbeat* loved the album, awarding it four stars and commending Nelson for her superior vocals: "To basic ease and naturalness, she adds a voice that just pours out—not in the big, overpowering fashion of Bessie Smith or Ma Rainey but with the directness and authority of a singer who knows what she's doing and knows she can do it."

Nelson recalls this period of her life with great fondness. Musselwhite, she remembers, introduced her to some of the greatest Chicago blues musicians of the time. One memorable evening, Musselwhite took her to a club and she ended up at a table with Musselwhite, Otis Spann and Muddy Waters, who dedicated "Nineteen Years Old" to her during his next set. "I was just happy all the goddamn time and walked around with this big grin on my face," she later recalled. "It was a time of pure happiness, and you don't get many of those."

In 1966, Nelson moved to San Francisco to pursue a career in music. There, Steve Miller introduced her to Ira Kamin, a keyboard player from Chicago, who was trying to put together a group with composer/vocalist/harmonica player R. Powell St. John. St. John was an alumnus of the Waller Creek Boys (an Austin-based folk group that also included Janis Joplin) and a songwriter of note—the composer of "Bye Bye Baby" (which Joplin recorded with Big Brother and the Holding Company) and (as John St. Powell) of several songs recorded by the 13th Floor Elevators. The group-in-formation was managed by Travis Rivers, the editor/publisher of *The San Francisco Oracle* and the person credited with "discovering" Janis Joplin and bringing her to San Francisco. Rivers recruited more musicians—pianist/vocalist Wayne Talbert, drummer George Rains, bassist Jance Garfat and guitarist Herbert Thomas. Naming themselves Mother Earth after a Memphis Slim song, the outfit became active on the San Francisco ballroom circuit. Occasionally, saxophonist Martin Fierro, who had his own band at the time, sat in with the group.

By 1968, Mother Earth had already shuffled through a number of musicians. John "Toad" Andrews had replaced Thomas on guitar and Bob Arthur replaced Garfat on bass. Andrews and Arthur had previously been members of the Wig, one of Austin's longest lasting (1964–1968) R&B bands, which also included Boz Scaggs, Benny Rowe and, briefly, Steve Miller. Andrews, who acquired the nickname "Toad" by hopping around onstage while playing lead guitar with his teeth, was the only group member to stay with Nelson for the life of the group.

In addition, Ira Kamin and Wayne Talbert left the group, and keyboardist Mark Naftalin (who had just left the Paul Butterfield Blues Band) was brought in to arrange the tracks and rehearse the band for their upcoming album [see **Paul Butterfield**].

With the new members in place, Mother Earth made their recording debut by contributing three songs to the soundtrack of the film *Revolution,* including a cover of Percy Mayfield's soulful "Stranger in My Home Town." Also contributing to the 1968 film were the Steve Miller Band and the Quicksilver Messenger Service.

By the time of the soundtrack's release in mid-1968, Mother Earth signed a recording contract with Mercury Records. Their first Mercury album, *Living with the Animals,* came out later in the year. Production credits included Barry Goldberg (executive producer) [see **Barry Goldberg**], Mark Naftalin (arranger and coproducer), Dan Healy (engineer and coproducer), Martin Fierro (horn arranger) and the group themselves (also listed as coproducers). *Living with the Animals* (U.S. #144) also included fiddle playing from Spencer Perskin and vocals from the Earthettes, a vocal trio consisting of Sylvia Caldwell, Linda Tillery (who fronted her own group, the Loading Zone), and Nelson, who used the name "Shalimar Samuelson."

Album highlights included Nelson's composition, "Down So Low" (her signature song, inspired by her breakup with her not-yet-famous boyfriend, Steve Miller); the piano rolls that drove "Goodbye Nelda Grebe, the Telephone Company Has Cut Us Off"; a cover of Allen Toussaint's "Cry On" (originally recorded by Irma Thomas); and the slow blues "Mother Earth" with a guest guitar solo from Makal Blumfeld (a.k.a. Michael Bloomfield) [see **Mike Bloomfield**].

Nelson sang lead on a number of additional tracks, but apparently too few to satisfy *Rolling Stone* magazine, which complained of the division of lead vocals between Nelson and St. Powell, calling it a "mixed blessing." After complimenting Nelson's powerful voice, the magazine disparaged St. John's singing as "quavery and thin," opining, "His uncertain vocal delivery mars every track on which he sings." On the other hand, *Guitar Player* gave the album an overall recommendation, dubbing it "one of the best blues albums to come out for a long time." *Hit Parader* focused on Nelson herself, writing, "Think of your favorite girl singer: Grace Slick, Mama Cass, Janis Joplin. They're good, but Tracy Nelson of Mother Earth is above them all. She's also deeper into the roots than any of them."

Following the recording of *Living with the Animals,* Mother Earth was shaken up with more personnel changes: Ronald Stallings came in on saxophone and vocals, Lonnie Castille took over on drums, and Clayborne Butler Cotton (a former member of Charlie Musselwhite's band) covered keyboards. Reviews of the new lineup's performances were glowing, with inevitable comparisons between Nelson and Janis Joplin. *Cash Box* observed, "Because of the strong and sensual voice of Tracy Nelson, one of the group's lead singers, comparison with Janis and the now-sleeping Big Brother are inevitable. Tracy is very good and possesses a voice to charm the devil, but Janis is great and, in addition to her voice, just seems to radiate total excitement. As for the rest of Mother Earth, they're far more enjoyable to hear than Big Brother, and could make a passable go at stardom by themselves, but Tracy is the icing on the cake."

Likewise, *Downbeat* honed in on the Joplin similarities in a review of a performance at the Boston Tea Party club in March 1969, predicting, "This band is going to be very, very big. It deserves to be. When it hits, it will do it initially on the strength of Miss Nelson, a powerful, tasteful rock vocalist, and the only white chick besides Janis Joplin to have assimilated the black idiom with no hint of posturing." *Downbeat* also praised the "highly competent band," singling out Castille's drumming and Stallings's "soulful" vocals.

Nelson responded by reflecting on the comparisons between herself and her more famous contemporary in the June 1969 issue of *Hit Parader:* "There will probably be critical comparisons between Janis Joplin and myself. The only thing you can say is we're both chick singers. I'd consider it a compliment if that happened though, because people would be taking me seriously and putting me up against an established singer. But that's just idle speculation because Janis and myself couldn't be more opposite. Our approaches to music are totally different. Also, we chose different material. Janis and I are not at all intellectual about our music and it's impossible to criticize what we do. Our music is extremely emotional. . . . I really hope that people keep Janis and myself separate because comparisons wouldn't be valid. Janis is close to Etta James, I think, and I'm into gospel music but not from the religious end. It's the pure emotional thing."

In the summer of 1969, the group went to Nashville to record their next album at Owen Bradley's famous Bradley's Barn studio, a few minutes east of downtown Nashville. The record, *Make a Joyful Noise* (U.S. #95), reflected the country influences surrounding its recording as well as Nelson's love of gospel music. Featuring the contributions of steel guitarist Pete Drake, dobro player Ben Keith, and fiddlers John Gimble and Shorty Lavender, the album was divided into two sides—a "country side" and a horn-laden "city" side. Reviews were positive and focused on the diversity of the effort. *Rolling Stone* said, "It's easy enough to accuse Mother Earth of being eclectic, to call them the greatest variety show on vinyl. But that's only an accusation when you can't pull it off. They can." *Record Mirror* described the album as "a kind of 'something for everybody' LP made by a group that obviously practices a lot." *Cashbox* predicted "FM play and sales" and praised the "brilliant vocal work of lead singer Tracy Nelson whose voice carries passion and vitality." And a reviewer for *The Los Angeles Free Press* wrote, "Since the comparisons with Janis are inevitable, let me say that I have never heard Janis sing as moving a blues as Tracy does on 'I Need Your Love So Bad.'"

Following the release of *Make a Joyful Noise*, Mother Earth moved to Nashville. There, the band took a break, during which time Pete Drake persuaded Nelson to cut an all-country solo album that became known as *Mother Earth Presents Tracy Nelson Country*. Scotty Moore engineered the album and, as he had on Elvis Presley's classic version of the song, played guitar on "That's Alright Mama." Other participants included Keith, Gimble and Lavender (all from the previous album), the Jordanaires vocal group, Jake Drake on string bass and another original Presley band member, D.J. Fontana, on drums. While a pioneering effort in the field of country rock, the album failed to generate significant sales.

Ironically, even with music reviewers clamoring over Nelson's exceptional voice, Nelson had steadily been sharing vocals with Stallings, St. John and Robert Arthur. As a result, Mother Earth's greatest asset—Nelson's rich blues vocals—had become diluted. Nelson eventually told *Circus* magazine, "Before, everybody wanted to sing and it got absurd because that's what I do. I sing." So following the release of *Mother Earth Presents Tracy Nelson Country*, Nelson reorganized the whole band, retaining only "Toad" Andrews. The new lineup consisted of steel guitarist Jimmy Day (ex-Hank Williams band); bassist Tim Drummond (whose credits included tours with Conway Twitty and James Brown and session work with Neil Young and Roy Buchanan); drummer Karl Himmel (who had toured with Dr. John and Brenda Lee and recorded with Bill Haley, Joe Tex, Johnny Cash, Bob Dylan, Earl Scruggs and Doug Kershaw); keyboardist Andrew McMahon; and rhythm guitarist Bob Cardwell (ex-West Coast Pop Art Experimental Band).

Still, these changes failed to alter the group's stagnating commercial prospects. Their next album, *Satisfied*, floundered both commercially and critically. For this release, the group shifted away from their recent country textures toward a gospel-infused rock approach. *Rolling Stone* commented that the album was "almost consistent to the point of melting into one long, predictable tune."

Unable to reach a wide audience with their Mercury releases, the group switched to the Reprise label. The association lasted for two albums, *Bring Me Home* (1971, U.S. #199) and *Tracy Nelson/Mother Earth* (1972). Each of the albums garnered critical acclaim—*Rolling Stone* called *Bring Me Home* "far and away the best thing they've done"—but commercial indifference ensued (neither album charted) and the label was unable to revitalize the group's career.

Postscript

Mother Earth moved to Columbia Records in 1973 for one album, *Poor Man's Paradise,* credited to Tracy Nelson/Mother Earth. It was Mother Earth's final release. Nelson then signed with Atlantic Records for the release of *Tracy Nelson* (1974), which included a Grammy-nominated duet with Willie Nelson, "After the Fire Is Gone." Her next recordings were for MCA: *Sweet Soul Music* (1975) and *Time Is on My Side* (1976). Subsequent releases, including *Doin' It My Way* (1978), *Homemade Songs* (1978) and *Come See about Me* (1980), were released on smaller labels. A 13-year recording hiatus finally ended with the release on Rounder Records of *In the Here and Now* (1993), a winner of the Nashville Music Awards "Nammy" for Best Blues Album. Subsequent recordings have also been on Rounder Records, including *I Feel So Good* (1995) and *Move On* (1996), which won a "Nammy" for Best R&B Album.

In 1998, Nelson released *Sing Out*, a Grammy-nominated collaboration with Texas firebrand Marcia Ball and gospel and R&B great Irma Thomas. Her latest album, *Ebony & Irony*, was released in 2000.

Discography

Release Date	Title	Catalog Number

U.S. Singles

Mother Earth

1968	Revolution/Stranger in My Home Town	United Artists 50303
1968	Down So Low/Goodbye Nelda Grebe, the Telephone Company Has Cut Us Off	Mercury 72878
1969	Mother Earth/I Did My Part	Mercury 72909
1969	Painted Girls and Wine/ Your Time's Comin'	Mercury 72943
1969	I Wanna Be Your Mama Again/ Wait, Wait, Wait	Mercury 72943
1969	Satisfied/Andy's Song	Mercury 73116
1970	Temptation Took Control of Me and I Fell/Soul of Sadness	Reprise 1019
1971	Bring Me Home/I'll Be Long Gone	Reprise 1041

U.S. Albums

Tracy Nelson

1966	*Deep Are the Roots*	Prestige 7393

Motherless Child Blues/Long Old Road/Startin' for Chicago/Baby Please Don't Go/Oh My Babe/Ramblin' Man/Candy Man/Grieving Hearted Blues/Black Cat Hoot Owl Blues/House of the Rising Sun/Jesus Met the Woman at the Well/Trust No Man

1969	*Mother Earth Presents Tracy Nelson Country*	Mercury SR-61230

Sad Situation/I Fall to Pieces/Stay as Sweet as You Are/Stand By Your Man/Blue Blue Day/That's All Right/I Can't Go on Loving You/You're Still My Baby/Now You're Gone/Why Why Why/I'm So Lonesome, I Could Cry

Mother Earth

1968	*Living with the Animals*	Mercury SR-61194

Marvel Group/Mother Earth/I Did My Part/Living with the Animals/ Down So Low/Cry On/It Won't Be Long/My Love Will Never Die/Good-bye Nelda Grebe, the Telephone Company Has Cut Us Off/Kingdom of Heaven (Is Within You)

1969	*Make a Joyful Noise*	Mercury SR-61226

Stop the Train/I Need Your Love So Bad/What Are You Trying to Do/Soul of the Man/Blues for the Road/You Win Again/Come On and See/Then I'll Be Moving On/The Fly/I Wanna Be Your Mama Again/Wait, Wait, Wait

1970	*Satisfied*	Mercury SR-61270

Satisfied/Groovy Way/Get Out of Here/Ruler of My Heart/Andy's Song/ Rock Me/You Won't Be Passing Here No More/This Feeling

1971	*Bring Me Home*	Reprise RS-6431

Temptation Took Control of Me and I Fell/There Is No End/Soul of Sadness/I'll Be Long Gone/Bring Me Home/Tonight, the Sky's About to Cry/Seven Bridges Road/Lo and Behold/Deliver Me

1972	*Tracy Nelson/Mother Earth*	Reprise 2054

The Same Old Thing/I'm That Way/Mother Earth (Provides for Me)/Tennessee Blues/I Want to Lay Down Beside You/Someday My Love May Grow/(Staying Home and Singing) Homemade Songs/Thinking of You/The Memory of Your Smile/I Don't Do That Kind of Thing Any More

Miscellaneous U.S. Releases

1968	*Revolution* (movie soundtrack)	United Artists UAS-5185

Includes three songs by Mother Earth: "Revolution," "Without Love" and "Stranger in My Home Town."

U.K. Singles

| 1969 | The Telephone Company Has Cut Us Off/I Did My Part | Mercury MF 1081 |
| 1971 | Temptation Took Control of Me and I Fell/I'll Be Long Gone | Reprise K 14089 |

U.K. Albums

Mother Earth

1968	*Living with the Animals*	Mercury SMCL 20143
1969	*Make a Joyful Noise*	Mercury SMCL 20173
1969	*Tracy Nelson Country*	Mercury SMCL 20179
1971	*Satisfied*	Mercury 6338 023
1971	*Bring Me Home*	Reprise K 44133

Miscellaneous U.K. Releases

| 1969 | *Revolution* | United Artists UAS 29069 |

Rod Piazza

After more than 30 years in the business, Rod Piazza has finally come to be recognized as a major force in the blues world. Piazza and his band, the Mighty Flyers, are one of the most popular attractions on the blues circuit today and have come to epitomize what is now known as the "West Coast" style of blues. "West Coast blues has more of a swingin' style, an R&B sound," Piazza told *The Los Angeles Times*. "It's more of a swingin' blues as opposed to the down-home thing, although we do play in that style too." Piazza, a charismatic frontman, is a master of the harp—particularly the chromatic.

While he and his band are perennial nominees for W. C. Handy Awards (the blues equivalent of the Grammys), he was finally recognized individually in 1998 for "Instrumentalist of the Year, Harmonica," while the Mighty Flyers received W. C. Handy awards for "Band of the Year" in 1999 and 2000. But Piazza could hardly be considered an overnight sensation and the road to the top has been fraught with disappointment.

Piazza (b. December 18, 1947; Riverside, California) started playing the guitar at age six or seven. He picked up the blues from his older brother's record collection. "I listened to my brother's records," Piazza told *The Los Angeles Times*. "He was ten years older than me. He brought home Jimmy Reed, Big Joe Turner, Earl Bostic and that kind of stuff back in the 1950s. I'd play his records when he wasn't around."

His life changed dramatically when his older brother Joe took him to see Jimmy Reed in concert. Backstage, Piazza met the famous bluesman, who gave the youngster one of his old harmonicas. Piazza thereafter concentrated on the harp, mimicking the blues he heard on his brother's records and on the radio, including such numbers as Reed's "Big Boss Man" and Slim Harpo's "Scratch My Back."

Piazza studied such harp masters as Sonny Boy Williamson, Junior Wells, James Cotton, and the two biggest influences on his career, Little Walter and George Smith. He first heard Little Walter at age 16 and was blown away by the cut, "Blues with a Feeling," found on a Checker anthology. He journeyed to nearby Los Angeles in search of Little Walter's records, and assimilated Walter's style while consciously attempting to draw out his own musical identity.

In 1965, Piazza joined his first band, the Mystics, which included drummer John Milliken and bassist Les Morrison. The Mystics evolved into the House of DBS (DBS being an acronym for Dirty Blues Sound) when they adopted a blues repertoire. The House of DBS recorded a demo single, "Mystery Train" backed with "I Wish You Would." At that point, the group consisted of Piazza (dubbed "Gingerman") on vocals and harp, Glenn Ross Campbell (formerly of the Misunderstood) on steel and slide guitars, Robert Sandell on rhythm guitar, Pat Malone on organ, Les Morrison on bass and John Milliken on drums.

The band played mostly college frat parties, but in August 1967 they played a week at the Genesis IX club in Los Angeles, which led to their first recording contract. Eileen Kaufman of *The Los Angeles Free Press* reviewed the Genesis IX gigs, predicting, "The music for the past week has been provided by a bunch of energetic youngsters from Riverside who are going to make it. The House of DBS (dirty blues sound) played to fascinated audiences for one week and was held over by popular demand. These kids are wigging out all the blues buffs with their boundless energy, funky sound and stage appearance." After watching them onstage, Lee Magid, an independent producer, approached ABC/Bluesway about getting a recording contract for the band. ABC/Bluesway signed the band to the label (whose roster already included such giants as John Lee Hooker and Otis Spann), hoping to cash in on the "white blues" boom.

Under contract to ABC/Bluesway, the band changed their name to simply the Dirty Blues Band. The first DBS release, *Dirty Blues Band*, was recorded in only two days and contained a mixture of originals and such standards as "Spoonful" and "Born Under a Bad Sign." *Hit Parader's* review was favorable: "They've got to study more styles and licks to get a good feel like [Canned] Heat; however, they fill the holes more imaginatively than Fleetwood [Mac]." *The Berkeley Barb* liked them as well, commenting that they were "better than [Paul] Butterfield's first album: the drive is there but it's not rushed."

The band toured Washington and California to promote the album, but the record failed to catch fire. In addition, several members were drafted into the military, reducing them to just Piazza and Malone.

Undaunted, the two recruited a new lineup featuring Dave Miter on drums, Rick Lunetta on guitar and Greg Anderson on bass. Augmented by a three-piece horn section, the band recorded an album in Hollywood in April 1968. Titled *Stone Dirt*, the record was another mixture of covers and originals. This release also sold poorly and the group disbanded.

Piazza still remembers those days with the Dirty Blues Band. "At that time, we were pretty optimistic, but it was too quick," he told *The Los Angeles Times*. "We weren't quite ready. When the first record came out, we were just kids and hadn't been playing long enough. I got slammed down a lot when I started. I played a whole week at the Golden Bear opening for James Cotton when I was 17. It was rough. It wasn't so much that [the crowd was] booing, but you'd finish a tune, and you wouldn't get much response. You could hear a pin drop."

Later that year, Piazza and drummer Richard Innes went to Los Angeles expecting to see Big Walter Horton at the Ash Grove. Instead, they saw George Smith filling in. While the band was setting up and the club was near empty, Piazza asked Smith if he could sit in. Piazza quickly regretted the request as the club started to fill up, and he hoped that Smith would not remember it. He told *Blues Revue* what happened next. "He came up and started blowing, and you know what he sounded like. He just wailed through that amp and the Astatic [microphone], and I'm going, 'What the hell! Damn! Oh shit! I don't wanna play!' So he comes over to

me about halfway through the set and says, 'So you're the guy who wanted to play? OK!' And he sticks the harp and mic right down in my face, like, 'OK! Take it!' And I'm thinking, 'Oh, shit. I ain't playing.' And he's like, 'C'mon! You said you can blow, so blow!'"

Piazza regained his composure, took the harp and the mic and proceeded to play. Smith pulled on the mic cord, forcing Piazza to take the stage, and he was surprised that Piazza could actually play so well. Following a couple of progressions, Smith stopped the song, shook Piazza's hand and let him return to his seat. But the trial was not over yet for Piazza as he recalled what Smith next told the audience. "'OK, we saw what he [Piazza] could do with the little one. Now let's see what he can do with Big Mama.' And he reaches down and pulls out the goddamn chromatic! And he starts this shuffle off, and I'm going, 'Oh, f——.'" I could barely make the change on a chromatic. So he comes over and does the same thing again, sticks it in my face, and I'm going, 'No, no!' And he made me take it, stood back and waited till I started blowing. And he quickly realized I could barely make the three chord changes, so he took it back and said, 'Let's give him a hand.' Everybody claps, and he lets me go."

A short time later, Piazza again shared the stage with Smith, who was at the time touring with Howlin' Wolf. Piazza said, "About two months later, I had the gig there with my band [the Rod Piazza Band]. We're opening up for Wolf. And I'm up there playing, I think I was doing 'Off the Wall' or something, and I have my eyes closed, and everybody starts to clap, and I'm thinking, 'What the hell's going on?' And I open my eyes and here's George standing next to me on stage, looking down at me, like, 'OK, I gave you your chance. Now you give me mine!' So I handed him the harp, and he just commenced to tearin' it up with my band!" Then Piazza returned to the stage and played a couple of songs together with Smith. They went over so well with the audience that Smith later broached the topic of forming a two harmonica band with him and told Piazza that he would call when he was finished with the rest of his tour with Howlin' Wolf. Piazza and Smith became fast friends and the elder bluesman served as a mentor to the younger harpist, teaching Piazza his techniques on the chromatic harmonica.

Smith was born George Washington on April 22, 1924, in Helena, Arkansas, but spent most of his youth in Cairo, Illinois. His mother, Jessie, taught her son the harmonica when he was four years old. Smith joined Early Woods's country band as a teenager and later, during 1943 or 1944, joined the Jackson Jubilee Singers, a gospel group. During the late 1940s, while working as a projectionist for a movie theater, he discovered that by using the amplifier and speaker from the film projector he could amplify his harmonica—and thus became one of the first to amplify the instrument. In 1951, Smith moved to Chicago and began performing with Otis Rush. In 1953, he briefly toured the South as a member of the Muddy Waters Band. By 1954, he had accepted a full-time gig at the Orchid Room in Kansas City. He signed with Modern Records in 1955 and released three singles on the RPM subsidiary, including the classic "Telephone Blues" backed with "Blues in the Dark" (U.S./RPM 434).

Smith's records sold well and he went on a package tour with Champion Jack Dupree and Little Willie John to promote them. He backed Dupree during the tour and, in November 1955, on four tracks recorded in Cincinnati, including "Sharp Harp" and "Overhead Blues." At the tour's end, Smith settled in Los Angeles, where he recorded for a series of small labels under a variety of names, including the Harmonica King, Little Walter Junior, and George Allen. Smith joined the Muddy Waters band for a second time in 1966 and stayed for about a year. He also found time to sit in as a sideman on Otis Spann sessions. Some of the tracks he recorded with Spann appeared on the albums *Heart Loaded with Trouble* (U.S./Bluesway 6063) and *The Blues Is Where It's At* (U.S./Bluesway BIS 6003). In 1968, he released his first solo album, *Tribute to Little Walter* (U.S./World Pacific 21887).

Upon Smith's return from the Howlin' Wolf tour, he and Piazza formed the Southside Blues Band, bringing in drummer Richard Innes, guitarist Pee Wee Crayton and bassist Lee Scallar. Their first gig together was at the Sassy Kitten in Watts. The band backed Big Mama Thornton on a nationwide tour in 1968, which was Piazza's first cross-country tour. "I never did get paid," Piazza recalled to *The Los Angeles Times*. "We were living on a shoestring, and we just barely got enough to eat. I remember living on a loaf of bread, a pepperoni, and some Cracker Barrel cheese. That's all I had for four days. That put a hurtin' on your system. It was rough. But since I was a little boy I wanted to play music."

During this same period, producer Bob Thiele utilized the group's musicians for Smith's 1969 album, *George Smith of the Blues* (U.S./Bluesway 6029).

After returning to Los Angeles, the band played mostly in the black clubs, which led to an unusual marketing slogan for Piazza: "He's white, but he's outtasight." Piazza's and Smith's new backing band was composed of Innes (drums), Jerry Smith (bass), Buddy Reed and Gregg Schaeffer (guitars).

Producer Mike Vernon saw them opening for Charlie Musselwhite at the Golden Bear in Huntington Beach and reported his impressions in *Melody Maker:* "Imagine my surprise when, returning to my seat to catch George Smith's set, my eyes rested on a bunch of youthful white musicians (all locals, it transpired) who were laying it down unlike any British band I've ever heard . . . Piazza worked a little too zealously for my liking but certainly showed a masterful technique on harp, his chromatic work was a highlight of the evening. But so was George Smith's own performance on a whole range of harps—all keys and sizes."

Vernon signed the group to his Blue Horizon label and changed their name to Bacon Fat. In November 1969, he produced their first album in Los Angeles with the addition of J.D. Nicholson on piano. The album, *Grease One for Me*, was issued in 1970. In November they also recorded tracks for another George Smith solo album, *No Time for Jive* (U.S./Blue Horizon 63856).

At the same time, the band also recorded some live tracks at Small's Paradise, located at 53rd and Avalon in Watts, where Bacon Fat had a weekend residency. The band even dedicated a track, "Small's on 53rd," to the venue on their first album. Musicians Pee Wee Crayton (backed up by Bacon Fat without Piazza), Elmon Mickle (a.k.a. Drifting Slim), and Willie D. Molette also recorded during these dates for a future album by "Bacon Fat with Friends." Unfortunately, much of the material was lost, although two Bacon Fat tracks appeared in the 1970s on the Blue Moon album *Live at Small's Paradise*.

This was a busy period for Piazza, who made time for still other sessions organized by producer Bob Thiele for a studio ensemble that included Lightnin' Red on vocals, Tom Scott on saxophone and Piazza on the harp. Coral Records released an album by this ensemble in 1970 as *The Revolutionary Blues Band*.

Bacon Fat continued to tour, backing such blues legends as T-Bone Walker and Big Joe Turner. In the main, though, they were unable to break through to the broader "white" audience and so confined their gigs to black clubs. Even so, with Vernon producing, they continued to record, laying down tracks in Los Angeles in August 1970 for the band's forthcoming album, which they supported with a tour of England three months later.

The band arrived in England in November 1970 for six weeks of engagements. *Sounds* magazine reported on their second show on November 6, 1970, at the Marquee club in London, printing, "The band's entire sound is a cast back to the early days of Chess, and the drive which made it so successful." However, Piazza was acutely aware of the U.S. music industry's seeming lack of support. He did little to conceal his bitterness when he complained to *Melody Maker*, "A lot of people in America don't really know the blues. They really don't know what you're doing if you play the real stuff. The only places where they know are the colleges and clubs. You can't get no damn work 'cause agents think the blues is all old stuff, an' everybody wants you to change it and put rock in your music." In the same interview, Innes even admitted, "We're going to have to quit if things don't get better."

While in London, the band recorded the rest of their next album, which was released as *Tough Dude* in 1971. Critical and commercial reaction was indifferent and Bacon Fat sizzled to a finish. Afterward, Piazza continued to perform under either his name or Smith's.

Postscript

In 1973, Piazza released his first solo album, *Bluesman*, on the LMI label. Toward the end of the year, his future wife, pianist Honey Alexander, joined the band. Muddy Waters wanted Piazza to join his band in 1975, but at the time Piazza was hospitalized following surgery and was unavailable for the position. Live recordings from this period—with guitarists Hollywood Fats and George Phelps, bassist Larry Taylor and drummer Innes—were issued on the 1998 Tone-Cool release, *Vintage Live 1975*. Blues music was generally in a downswing in the mid-1970s, so Piazza began a day job as a manager of a fiberglass factory to make ends meet.

In 1976, Piazza, Alexander and bassist Bill Stuve formed Rod Piazza and the Chicago Flying Saucer Band. They recorded one album in 1979 on Piazza's Gangster Records label. By the end of the decade, they had changed their name to the Mighty Flyers and were gigging continuously (which allowed Piazza to quit his day job).

Throughout the 1980s, the Mighty Flyers released a series of albums on small labels: *Radioactive Material* (1981), *File Under Rock* (1984), *From the Start to the Finish* (1985), *So Glad to Have the Blues* (1986), and *Undercover* (1988). In 1989, Piazza married Honey Alexander and the Flyers started to take off.

Signing with Black Top Records, the Flyers released four albums in the next decade: *Blues in the Dark* (1991), *Alphabet Blues* (1992), *Harpburn* (1993) and *California Blues* (1997). In addition, Big Mo Records released *Live at B.B. King's, Memphis*, in 1994. This release was recognized as Album of the Year by the National Association of Independent Record Distributors (NAIRD).

Piazza then switched labels to Tone-Cool, which released *Tough and Tender* (1997) and *Here and Now* (1999).

While the Mighty Flyers have today become leading attractions on the blues circuit, mainstream success has eluded them. "I think I've always realized that the kind of music I always loved was really specialized and not meant for the masses because of the way the world is. I made a decision early on that fortune really wasn't the name of the game I was trying to play here." That may still change. As *Billboard* magazine wrote, "Piazza is a star contemporary blues songwriter, as well as the star musician now verging on a broader breakthrough."

Piazza remained friends with George Smith throughout the elder bluesman's life. In 1983, Piazza's band backed Smith on his last recording, *Boogie'n with George*. Smith died of a heart attack on October 2, 1983.

Discography

Release Date	Title	Catalog Number

U.S. Singles

The Dirty Blues Band

1967	Hound Dog/New Orleans Woman	Bluesway 61016

U.S. Albums

The Dirty Blues Band

1967	*Dirty Blues Band*	Bluesway BLS 6010

Don't Start Me Talkin'/What Is Soul, Babe/Hound Dog/New Orleans Woman/I'll Do Anything Babe/Checkin' Up on My Baby/Shake It Baby/Worry Worry Blues/Born Under a Bad Sign/Spoonful/Chicken Shack

1968	*Stone Dirt*	Bluesway BLS 60208

Bring It on Home/It's My Own Fault Baby/I Can't Quit You Baby/Tell Me/She's the One/My Baby/Sittin' Down Wonderin'/Six Sides/You've Got to Love Her with a Feeling/Gone Too Long

Bacon Fat

1970 *Grease One for Me*   Blue Horizon 4807

Up the Line/Boom Boom (Out Go the Lights)/Small's on 53rd/She's a Wrong Woman/I Need Your Love/Juicy Harmonica/Nobody But You/Telephone Blues/You're So Fine/Too Late

1971 *Tough Dude*   Blue Horizon
                                    2431 001

Wait On It/Down the Road/Betty/Leaving on Your Mind/Jivin' the Business/Shake Dancer/Traveling South/Evil/Blues Feeling/Pool Hall Sam/Transatlantic Blues/Hurricane

The Revolutionary Blues Band

1970 *The Revolutionary Blues Band*   Coral CRL-757506

Juicy/Milkman, Milkman Leave Me Some Cream/Lanoola Goes Limp/That's the Truth, Baby/Have a Little Bit More/Take Me Back to Tennessee/Cutting the Mustard/Ring My Chimes/Funky Lady/Dirty Town Blues

U.K. Singles

Bacon Fat

1970 Small's On 53rd/Nobody But You   Blue Horizon
                                                              57-3171
1970 Evil/Blues Feeling   Blue Horizon
                                          57-3181

U.K. Albums

Bacon Fat

1970 *Grease One for Me*   Blue Horizon
                                              7-63858
1971 *Tough Dude*   Blue Horizon
                                      2431 001
Date *Live at Small's Paradise*   Blue Moon
Unknown   BMLP 1029

Various artists LP including two Bacon Fat tracks, "Everything's Going to Be Alright" and "Ode to Billie Joe."

Duffy Power

Duffy Power rates as one of the greatest British blues singers of the 1960s. No less an authority than Alexis Korner called him his favorite singer, proclaiming, "Duffy Power has influenced me an awful lot … because he's one of the most emotional singers I've ever seen or heard. He's also a very fine writer."

After an early career recording cover versions of American hit singles, Power reinvented himself as an authentic R&B-cum-jazz song stylist. Working after hours with such top musicians as John McLaughlin, Jack Bruce, Danny Thompson, Terry Cox, Ginger Baker and Phil Seamen, Power was creating what *Record Collector* later described as "some of the most enduring jazz-folk tinged blues of the 1960s." Unfortunately, this stunning cache of tracks was considered too advanced at the time and failed to capture the interest of record company executives, who viewed the tapes as lacking commercial potential. When these recordings were finally released several years after they were made, the great magnitude of his work was finally recognized and his reputation as a preeminent vocalist was established. Or, as *Record Collector* more deftly stated, "How did this man avoid becoming a superstar?"

Duffy Power (born Raymond Howard, September 9, 1941) was brought up in Fulham, South London. "I left school when I was 14 and started work when I was 15, in 1956," Power once explained to folk artist Ian Anderson writing for *Folk Roots* magazine. "I'd always been busy buying records, a Frankie Laine fanatic from the age of about ten. And then skiffle came along and I became interested in Lonnie Donegan's first thing, 'Rock Island Line.'"

Power started singing as a teenager after a friend took him to a London club called the Nucleus. His first two groups, the Amigos and the Dreamers, played skiffle music, but, by 1958, Power had started playing Elvis Presley- and Cliff Richard-influenced rock'n'roll. "I'd been turned on to the first Elvis Presley rock'n'roll album, and a combination of Elvis and my friend's sister completely changed me overnight. I went over the moon for Elvis, Chuck Berry, Little Richard, and I started singing those sort of songs." The Dreamers played at the Fulham Greyhound music pub and outside other nearby pubs, as they were all too young to perform inside. They covered an unlikely mixture of rock numbers, from Elvis Presley's "Let's Have a Party" and "I'm Gonna Sit Right Down and Cry (Over You)" to skiffle standards.

Power took his first step toward recording when his band, renamed the New Vagabonds, booked a show at Shepherds Bush Gaumont, a teenage club, in early 1959. The audience went wild over Power's performance. Fortuitously, Larry Parnes, the most successful manager and impresario in Britain at the time, was also in the audience. Parnes was in the process of building an impressive roster of male vocalists, capitalizing on his first success with his discovery of Tommy Hicks, whom he rechristened Tommy Steele. Steele achieved 17 Top 40 U.K. hits between 1956 and 1961 (including the 1956 chart-topper, "Singing the Blues") thereby becoming Great Britain's first rock'n'roll star. Parnes repeated this success with Reg Smith, who as "Marty Wilde" reached the U.K. Top 50 singles chart 13 times between 1958 and 1962, and again with his third major discovery, Ronald Wycherley, who as "Billy Fury" placed 26 singles in the U.K. charts between 1959 and 1966. By the end of the 1950s, Parnes's roster also included Joe Brown, Lance Fortune, Vince Eager, Georgie Fame, Johnny Gentle and Dickie Pride—none of whom were as successful as Parnes's first three signings. Yet Parnes saw the potential in Power (a.k.a. Raymond Howard) and signed him to a contract in early 1959, giving him the name "Duffy Power." ("Duffy" was a nickname Power had already acquired—after tough-guy actor Howard Duff—and "Power" was chosen in honor of actor Tyrone Power, who had died just that week.)

Parnes signed Power to a management contract and put him on a salary of 20 pounds a week, nearly twice what Power's own father was earning. It looked like Power was on his way, as Parnes, through his various connections, tried to groom him into a star. Teenage magazines wrote features about Power, and from 1959 to 1961 he took part in grueling package tours, including treks through Scotland with Georgie Fame. (One tour, promoted as the "Rock 'n' Trad Spectacular," had a New Orleans theme and featured an 18-piece band and professionally choreographed dancing girls in leotards.) Power was a charismatic presence on stage in his leopard-skin dinner jacket or blue and gold lamé suit.

Signing a recording contract with Fontana, Power released six undistinguished singles between 1959 and 1961. These were mostly schmaltzy arrangements of American hit songs, such as Bobby Rydell's "Kissin' Time" and Bobby Darin's "Dream Lover." When Power was allowed to record the rocker "Whole Lotta Shakin' Goin' On," the project was marred by ill-advised intervention when the producers forced the addition of the word "twist" to the lyric, believing that this touch would somehow make the record more commercial. *New Musical Express* praised Power's performance on this track as "powerful (no pun intended) and hard-hitting with an opening that shoots you out of your seat." But the ill-suited material yielded no hits, and Power's gigs began to dry up.

Power later recalled his plight to blues radio host Jean Claude Mondo for Pascal radio in France: "One night I

went to do my rock act. It included gyrating movements, the Elvis thing. This night they announced 'Duffy Power' and there was nothing—no reaction. I was there in my blue and gold lamé suit. I just thought, 'Oh God, I'd better concentrate on singing.'"

Duffy elaborated on this to *New Record Mirror:* "The trouble was I felt I wasn't getting anywhere. It took me quite a while to make up my mind what sort of singing I wanted to do . . . but once it was made up that was it."

Through his girlfriend (who turned out to be a prostitute), Power discovered the blues and started adding Ray Charles numbers to his repertoire. While at Billy Fury's flat, he heard *The Best of Muddy Waters* and was profoundly moved. But these enthusiasms were not enough to keep him from despondency and, depressed by his lack of success, he contemplated suicide. Only the hand of fate intervened with a knock on the door and the arrival of Ricky Barnes, a friend from Scotland, who showed up with his saxophone and took Power down to the Blue Gardenia, a small Soho blues club. "I went down and there was Albert Lee, Pat Donaldson, a very good drummer called Little Roy," Power told *Folk-Roots*. "For the first time I did an hour of solid blues singing, all the stuff that I'd accumulated. They all enjoyed it and I said, 'That's what I want to do.'"

Coming so close to suicide caused Power to re-examine his life, regroup, and commit himself to performing only music that was important to him. "I got myself together," he said later. "This bass player, Boot Slade, with a group called Nero & the Gladiators, was really good to me and really helped me."

By late 1961, Power had left both Fontana and Parnes and had signed with another manager, Mike Hawker, and a new label, the EMI subsidiary Parlophone. For his first EMI single, issued in February 1963, Power recorded "It Ain't Necessarily So" from *Porgy and Bess* (backed with "If I Get Lucky Someday"). He described his new approach to *New Record Mirror:* "I've listened to stars like Ray Charles, Huddie Leadbetter, Joe Williams and Big Bill Broonzy. I don't want to copy them . . . but I do want to get their 'feel' for a song."

During the transformation, Power considered changing his name a second time, explaining just after his new single was released, "I was always known as 'the wildest rock singer in the world.' At the time, this was fine. The right sort of billing to attract the customers. Recently though, I've made a complete change of style. My 'Ain't

Necessarily So,' for instance, was in the rhythm'n'blues-ballad idiom. Unfortunately, many people refuse to think of me as this type of singer. They link 'Duffy Power' with that 'Wildest' tag. Really, this is an example of when a name SHOULD be changed again. Had I realized this before the record was released, I would for sure have had second serious thoughts about adopting another stage and recording name."

New Record Mirror approved of his changeover, predicting that Power would "be lucky any day now. His improvements are enormous in voice production and technique. He is barely recognizable as the Duffy Power of the early rock days." While "It Ain't Necessarily So" missed finding a spot on the charts, it was a soulful effort that gave him significant credibility.

For his next single, Power teamed up with the Graham Bond Quartet [see **Graham Bond**] to record a version of the Beatles' "I Saw Her Standing There." They first attempted recording the song with guitarist John McLaughlin, formerly of Georgie Fame's Blue Flames. They then re-recorded the song with session guitarist Big Jim Sullivan substituting for an ailing McLaughlin, and ultimately issued this second recording as a single. While this song represented one of the first covers of a Beatles song attempted, it was not a good vehicle for Power. *Beat Monthly* explained, "Though Duffy and his friends perform it well, I don't think the song is suited to an R&B outing: still it's worth a buzz from the Graham Bond organ grooves, and Duffy's vocal escapes could make the lower deck of the charts." To plug the single, Power backed by the Bond Quartet performed the song on the BBC radio show *Pop Goes the Beatles* on July 16, 1963.

Power toured with the Graham Bond Quartet for a while before moving on to package tours. "I was never a member of the Graham Bond Organisation," Power recalled to Jean Claude Mondo. "When I met him [Bond] they were either billed as the GB Quartet or were working as a trio. I was introduced to him by my manager, a guy called Ron Richards at EMI. He suggested that I go down, meet him. I had wanted to work with someone really good on the Hammond organ. At the time, bass, organ, and vocals were a happening thing. He arranged for me to go down and sing with him at a gig to see if we liked one another. I did a number and was so knocked out. They were jazz-rooted. Jack was playing a double bass which I hadn't heard apart from on records. Though they had jazz and R&B, they were the spirit of rock'n'roll. In fact, I got such a buzz from playing with them that at the end of the

number I ran off the stage and left the building. They thought I'd quit! We started gigging around and it was billed as Duffy Power with the GB Quartet."

His next outing, "Hey Girl" backed with "Woman Made Trouble," was issued in August 1963. As *Pop Weekly* enthused, "Duffy's interpretation has all the warmth and depth to command the attention of those who like to hear the emotional strength of the R&B type song. It is a well-paced performance of strength and the exciting disc is completed by Ken Jones' backing, which is unobtrusively fascinating." While *Pop Weekly* praised the performance, they also commented on the limited commercial potential of the material. "I'm sorry to think that the disc has not got a general popular appeal. At present, Duffy is a little ahead of his time for that—but when the time does come he will be way out in front."

Power was paired with the Paramounts for the top side of his next release in March 1964, "Tired, Broke and Busted," while the flip side version of Mose Allison's "Parchman Farm" featured the support of the Graham Bond Quartet. *New Musical Express* observed, "Duffy Power shows what an improved artist he is in the foot-tapping 'Tired, Broke and Busted.' Harmonica, earthy backing and traditional 12-bar format add fuel to the fire."

Power tried a ballad for his next single, pairing "Where Am I" with "I Don't Care" issued in August 1964. A *Disc Weekly* reviewer called this release "probably the best record Duffy Power's made to date," further commenting, "He sings a very strong, pushing ballad by Peter Lee Stirling, 'Where Am I,' and could easily push himself into the charts with the performance. I like both the number and Power's first-class reading of it."

Unfortunately, while Power issued a series of classy singles for Parlophone, they were greeted with commercial indifference and at the end of 1964 he found himself without a recording contract.

Power soldiered on and recorded a self-penned ballad, "Love's Gonna Go." While the song could not secure a British release, it was released as a U.S. single in 1965 (paired with "There's No Living without Your Loving") on the Jamie label out of Philadelphia, Pennsylvania. His manager changed the credit to "Jamie Power," a name he thought would be more appealing to American consumers.

In early 1965, a demo of "Love's Gonna Go" came to the attention of Alexis Korner, who wanted to meet the vocalist [see **Alexis Korner**]. This led to Power's performing with Korner at folk clubs as a duo—and ultimately to an invitation to participate in sessions for the next Blues Incorporated album. The sessions, which took place from April to June 1965, culminated in the album *Sky High*. Power contributed his powerful vocals to "Long Black Train" (cowritten with Korner), "I'm So Glad (You're Mine)," "Ooo Wee Baby" and "Louise," as well as contributing blues harp. This Blues Incorporated lineup included bassist Danny Thompson and drummer Terry Cox, later the rhythm section of Pentangle. Power even went on the road with Blues Incorporated, but discovered that he had personality clashes with the band. As he explained, "I didn't really like the band. It was the horn section which I never really got along with."

When Korner accepted a role in the children's television show *Five O'Clock Club*, he and Power along with Thompson and Cox began performing a couple of numbers during the program. The format didn't fit Power's style, and, as he explained to Jean Claude Mondo, "I fell out with Alexis at this point. I think I'd never been a member of a band. He asked me on one of the programs to sit out during a number. I'd seen show band singers do this and actually sit on a chair, so I had this bad image in my mind. We argued and nearly came to blows over it. So, I walked away."

From 1965 to 1967, in loose collaboration with guitarist John McLaughlin (b. January, 1942; Kirk Sandall, Doncaster, South Yorkshire, U.K.) and other musicians, Power recorded numerous tracks. McLaughlin had begun taking piano lessons at age nine and had switched to guitar two years later. By 12 he had become aware of blues artists such as Big Bill Broonzy, Muddy Waters, Leadbelly and Sonny Terry. As a teenager, he was influenced by jazz guitarists Django Reinhardt and Tal Farlow. He joined his first group at age 15, and by mid-1962 he had played with Georgie Fame's Blue Flames for a few months. McLaughlin joined the Graham Bond Quartet in March 1963 and stayed with them until September. He had also played on sessions with Tony Meehan and with the Rolling Stones (three of his tracks are on the Stones' *Metamorphosis* LP).

Power's body of work with McLaughlin from this period included some of the finest jazz-blues recordings of the era. "It was done privately and on different occasions we used different people," Power told *Sounds*. "For some time beforehand, I'd been working with Jack Bruce and Graham Bond, and I knew several other people whom I just envisioned playing together; so I started getting these three piece units together. I'd have Jack on double bass with Phil Seamen on drums—and then I'd use Danny Thompson on bass with Terry Cox on drums . . . I was more interested in using different musicians than saying, 'This is the group,' and I think I got very morbid, and in the back of my mind I was doing it just for posterity."

In early 1966, the duo recruited Thompson and drummer Red Reece (later replaced by Cox) and formed Duffy's Nucleus. They recorded several songs together and released one single, "Hound Dog" backed with "Mary Open the Door," on Decca in January 1967. The label also issued a French-only EP containing both sides of the U.K. single plus "It's Funny" and "Little Boy Blue." The band played dates as Duffy's Nucleus, but disbanded when Cox and Thompson formed Pentangle.

However, Power's inability to get most of the private recordings he'd made with McLaughlin released led to his increasing frustration and mental instability. "It drove me mad for a long time," Power told *Melody Maker*. "I used to play [the recordings] to people whose opinions I valued. In a way it was a small underground package."

A sample of the tracks made with McLaughlin appeared on Transatlantic's 1971 album, *Innovations*. *Melody Maker* commented, "The music is basically blues, brash without a semblance of sophistication, and all the more absorbing for that. Duffy's voice makes any hasty generalization about rock'n'roll singers who can only shout just a trifle hasty." *Disc and Music Echo* noted, "Apart from being mono, which is rather a drag, it's a very good and well-produced blues album." Years later, *Record Collector* had this take on the record: "Few British blues men have come close to equaling the material on this album, and on tracks like 'There You Go' Power and his band are a match for any British group of the Sixties."

In 1967, Power returned to Parlophone for a one-off deal and released the single "Davy O'Brien (Leave That Baby Alone)" backed with "July Tree." The single made no headway, and no more Parlophone releases were forthcoming. Power's mental condition deteriorated further and he became a recluse, performing only occasionally at the small folk club Les Cousins. While performing there, he came into contact with producer Peter Eden, who was associated with a couple of small record companies, Music Man and Spark. In 1969, Eden recorded some demos with Power on acoustic guitar. Power was under the impression that a prominent jazz musician was going to flesh out the arrangements, but that never happened. Instead, the bare-bones recordings were released on the Spark label in 1973 as *Duffy Power*. Power also recorded two tracks that appeared on the 1969 compilation *Firepoint*.

Through connections made at Les Cousins, Duffy toured with the Blues Federation Agency as a solo acoustic act; some of these dates were with the legendary blues singer Son House. He also played harmonica on recordings with Bert Jansch (*Birthday Blues*, 1969) and Al Stewart (*Zero She Flies*, 1970).

In 1970, another opportunity arose when ex-Zombies members Rod Argent and Chris White (who were now with the band Argent) arranged for Power to receive a CBS recording contract and to tour with them and the Climax Blues Band on a 32-stop British tour from September 24 through October 13, 1971. Enough material was recorded in the studios along the way to fill an entire album, but Power was not satisfied and none of the recordings were contemporaneously released, though several tracks turned up on the 1995 CD *Just Stay Blue*.

Postscript

After releasing only one single, Power left CBS to sign with GSF, where he recorded his first contemporary solo LP, *Duffy Power* (1973), a solid effort that included contributions from Alexis Korner and King Crimson drummer Mike Giles. A *Sounds* reviewer lauded Power's "spiritual singing, his slow ballads, his jazz-tinged songs . . . they all sound great, and as a result this has quickly become one of my favorite albums even though it doesn't come near to capturing the full intensity of Duffy's performance."

Although the album garnered critical acclaim, it still met with commercial apathy, and Power returned to club gigs and the occasional session as a sideman. In 1978, he surfaced again incongruously on a disco compilation album, *Disco Round the Moon*. In 1997, he contributed a track to the *Knights of the Blues Table* CD. Power has been performing in clubs throughout the 1990s.

Discography

Release Date	Title	Catalog Number

U.S. Singles

As Jamie Power

1965	Love's Gonna Go/ There's No Living without Your Loving	Jamie 1307

As Duffy Power

1971	Hummingbird/Hell Hound	Epic EPC 7139

U.K. Singles

1959	Dream Lover/That's My Little Suzie (78)	Fontana H 194
1959	Dream Lover/That's My Little Suzie (45)	Fontana H 194
1959	Kissin' Time/Ain't She Sweet (78)	Fontana H 214
1959	Kissin' Time/Ain't She Sweet (45)	Fontana H 214
1959	Starry-Eyed/Prettier Than You (78)	Fontana H 230
1959	Starry-Eyed/Prettier Than You (45)	Fontana H 230
1960	Whole Lotta Shakin' Goin' On/ If I Can Dream	Fontana H 279
1961	When We're Walking Close/ I've Got Nobody	Fontana H 302
1961	What Now/No Other Love	Fontana H 344
1963	It Ain't Necessarily So/ If I Get Lucky Someday	Parlophone R 4992
1963	I Saw Her Standing There[1]/Farewell Baby	Parlophone R 5024
1963	Hey Girl/Woman Made Trouble	Parlophone R 5059
1964	Tired, Broke and Busted[2]/Parchman Farm	Parlophone R 5111
1964	Where Am I?/I Don't Care	Parlophone R 5169
1967	Davy O'Brien (Leave That Baby Alone) /July Tree	Parlophone R 5631
1970	Hell Hound/Humming Bird	CBS 5176

[1] With the Graham Bond Quartet.
[2] With the Paramounts.

Duffy's Nucleus

1967	Hound Dog/Mary Open the Door	Decca F 22547

U.K. Albums

1971	*Innovations*	Transatlantic TRA 229

Recorded 1965–1967.
Rosie/Leaving Blues/It's Funny/God Bless the Child/Coming Round No More/Give Me One/Mary Open the Door/Help Me/Louisiana Blues/Little Boy Blue/Exactly Like You/One Night/There You Go/Red, White & Blue

1973	*Duffy Power*	Spark SRLM 2005

Recorded 1969.
Hell Hound/Mary Open the Door/Holiday/Little Boy Blue/I Need You/Midnight Special/Gin House Blues/Fox and Geese/Exactly Like You/Fixing a Hole/Roll Over Beethoven/I've Been Lonely Baby/Lawdy Miss Clawdy/Lily/Little Man (You've Had a Busy Day)

1992   *Blues Power*   SEECD356
Contains the whole of *Duffy Power* (Spark) plus the following additional tracks: "City Woman," "Halfway," "Louisiana Blues," "One Night" and "Leaving Blues."

1992   *Little Boy Blue*   Demon 356
Rosie/Leaving Blues/It's Funny/God Bless the Child/Coming Round No More/Give Me One/Mary Open the Door/Help Me/Louisiana Blues/Little Boy Blue/Exactly Like You/One Night/There You Go/Red, White and Blue

1995   *Just Stay Blue*   Retro 802
Love's Gonna Go/There's No Living Without Your Loving/I'm So Glad You're Mine/Dollar Mamie/Little Boy Blue/Little Girl/Mary Open the Door/Hound Dog/Rags and Old Iron/Just Stay Blue/Lilly/Hell Hound/Love Is Shelter/Lawdy Miss Clawdy/Love's Prescription/ Halfway/Corrina/Song About Jesus/Lover's Prayer/Swan song/The River

Miscellaneous U.K. Releases

1960   *The Big Beat*   Fontana TFL 5080
Various artists compilation including "Kissin' Time," "That's My Little Suzie" and "Starry-Eyed."

1969   *Firepoint: A Collection of Folk Blues*   Music Man
                                               SMLS 602
Includes "Halfway" and "City Women."

Foreign Releases

Duffy's Nucleus
1967   *Hound Dog* (French EP)   Decca 457.142M
Hound Dog/It's Funny/Little Boy Blue/Mary Open the Door

The Pretty Things

The Pretty Things have been a magnet for controversy since their inception. At a time when the Rolling Stones were seen as the ultimate nonconformists, the Pretty Things made them look tame by comparison. The band members' hair was longer, their lifestyles wilder, and their music louder and more extreme. Although their commercial success was limited, the Pretty Things were able not only to survive, but to evolve from R&B punks to psychedelic vanguards to 1970s hard rockers and beyond. Born survivors, they continue to command a loyal following without ever compromising their ideals or "bad boy" image.

The roots of the band can be traced to the late 1950s when Dick Taylor (b. January 28, 1943; Dartford, Kent, U.K.), Michael ("Mick") Jagger and various school friends would meet for after-school jam sessions at Taylor's parents' house in Dartford. By 1961, the small group had adopted a blues approach and dubbed themselves Little Boy Blue and the Blue Boys. Taylor was by now attending Sidcup Art School, where he and fellow student Keith Richards, sharing a passion for blues and R&B, got together to play guitar. As it turned out, Richards was a childhood friend of Jagger, and after the pair renewed their acquaintance, Jagger invited him to join the Blue Boys. By mid-1962, they had hooked up with guitarist Brian Jones—necessitating Taylor's switch from guitar to bass—and had renamed themselves the Rollin' Stones.

The Stones' decision to go professional in late 1962 coincided with Taylor's acceptance at the London Central School of Art. At the time, rather than continuing to play a secondary instrument in a background role, he chose to bow out of the group to concentrate on his studies. "I had to start concentrating on my exams," Taylor later explained to *Rave* magazine in 1964. "We didn't have a row or anything like that. I still see the boys sometimes and get on well with them."

Taylor still had the itch to play, though, and in 1963 he teamed up with another Sidcup art student, vocalist and harmonica player Phil May (b. November 9, 1944; Dartford, Kent, U.K.) and put together a group. They brought in May's friend John Stax (born John Fullegar, April 6, 1944; Crayford, Kent, U.K.) on bass, along with rhythm guitarist Brian Pendleton (b. April 13, 1944, Wolverhampton, Warks, U.K.; d. May 16, 2001) and a succession of drummers, including Pete Kitley and Viv Andrews. The name Pretty Things was chosen with a certain sarcastic glee, in homage to Bo Diddley and as a challenge to those who would deride the musicians' long-haired appearance. The group started playing at the Dartford Station Hotel before moving on to some college dates in the city. Around this time, Jimmy Duncan spotted them playing at the Royal College of Art and decided to become their comanager along with Bryan Morrison, who had attended the Central School of Art with Taylor. Their new management team found them gigs on the art school circuit and at the Railway Station Hotel. By May 1964, the band started playing the 100 Club, located at 100 Oxford Street, London, where they quickly "built up a reputation as one of the hottest new acts on the London scene," according to *Record Mirror*.

In early 1964, the group signed with Fontana Records. The label proposed that they add Viv Prince (b. August 9, 1944; Loughborough, Leicestershire, U.K.) on drums. Although only 19, Prince was already something of a music business veteran, having played with the Dauphin Street Six and Carter Lewis and the Southerners. Reportedly, he had also once been an income tax officer in Loughborough, Leicestershire. Higher-ups at Fontana believed that Prince would bring a degree of stability and professionalism to the Pretty Things' rather undisciplined sound. Their utter misread of Prince would emerge later, but in the meantime, Prince fit perfectly into the group—his skillful, energetic drumming giving their music a powerful new engine.

For their first single, the group recorded a track penned by Jimmy Duncan. "It was very tiring at first," Dick Taylor told *Beat Instrumental*, "but it could have been worse. We tried the number out at Regent Sound originally, then did the final takes at Philips' Studios." "Rosalyn" (backed with "Big Boss Man") was released in June, and the screaming, hard-pounding A-side received encouraging reviews. "Not a great deal of melody," wrote *New Music Express*, "but ample enthusiasm, sparkle and drive." Likewise, *Record Mirror* described it as a "Bo Diddley beat, wild vocal, good song, but maybe a little too confused for the charts." An appearance on the TV show *Ready, Steady Go!* followed, and the group's long hair, frilly shirts and animalistic sound sparked sufficient press furor to propel the single into the lower regions of the charts. An American agent who had seen them on *Ready, Steady Go!* offered the group an American tour and an appearance on the *Ed Sullivan Show*, an opportunity their management failed to take advantage of.

Although together for less than a year, the Pretty Things were now touring extensively throughout Great Britain, creating mayhem both on and off stage. Such media headlines as "Adults Hate Us More Than the Stones" and "Would You Take the Pretty Things into Your Local?" became commonplace. Early articles dwelled incessantly on their appearance, particularly their long hair, with one newspaper observing, "Phil May must have the longest hair on the long-haired current pop scene."

"We simply don't care," Phil May responded to *Beat Instrumental*. "All right, people say we are copying certain other groups. We're not. We're US. We know people don't like our hair, the way we behave or the way we dress. But we've got a big fan club and our money has gone up a lot for one-nighters and that's good enough for us."

May later admitted that "the touring was dodgy," but pointed out, "At least we had the knowledge that we were always being re-booked and that our money was going up . . . but fast. We had the scenes where even the ballroom staff didn't want to help us—again because of the way we look—but the fans went wild."

Finding a suitable follow-up single was not easy. "Lots of work, not enough good material," Prince commented at the time. "And we just didn't want to come out with a load of rubbish for the sake of having a release."

May reiterated, "Eventually we'll get a lot more way-out on stage. And we'll probably work more to a folksy sort of field. But first we need a really big hit record. Must have one out for the first week in October," he joked. They considered several numbers, including a slow Jimmy Reed song called "The Moon Is Rising." Finally, they started composing their own material. "We reckon this is the best thing to do," Taylor told *Beat Instrumental*. "After all, the old authentic R&B numbers were always written from personal experience, and if we ever complete this number, it's going to be called 'Closed Restaurant Blues.'"

Phil May thought he had a better title. "The 'Long Haired Blues' would be better, because it's our mops that cause all the trouble. One look at us and taxi drivers stick the hired sign up, and, as Dick says, restaurants always close down as soon as we walk in; it's a pity because we need food to keep our hair growing!"

The group found the perfect number penned for them by Johnnie Dee, former lead singer of the Bulldogs. Dee traveled with the band to "soak up the atmosphere." "Don't Bring Me Down" backed with "We'll Be Together" was issued at the end of October 1964. The A-side's crashing, wailing tempo changes and leering, sexually provocative vocals combined to ignite more controversy—and more sales. The single smashed into the Top Ten in November, and Fontana capitalized on the group's success, recycling their first two singles on an EP by year's end. To promote the single, the group embarked on an eight-day Scottish tour on October 12, followed by TV appearances on *Ready, Steady Go!* and *Thank Your Lucky Stars*.

With the success of their first two singles, they made plans for an LP and a film, with offers coming in for an American tour. "It now looks fairly certain that they will visit the States early in the New Year, possibly for the last two weeks of January," comanager Bryan Morrison told

Record Mirror. But again, the plans fell through and the group didn't tour the States. Looking back, May felt that their not touring the U.S. until the 1970s was a mistake. He told *Ugly Things*, "The management—which was foolish really on their part—felt they were making money in Europe, and they wanted to wait for a really serious offer. Also, to some extent, our record company in America never worked very well with the singles."

"Honey, I Need" backed with "I Can Never Say" was issued in February 1965. The A-side, a raucous yet somewhat folksy number cowritten by Taylor, was another U.K. hit, peaking at #13. The Pretty Things' eponymous debut album followed in March, capturing the ferocious R&B sound of their live show on tracks like "Roadrunner" (one of four Bo Diddley covers on the LP), "Judgement Day" and "Oh Baby Doll." Meanwhile, original compositions like "13 Chester Street" and "Unknown Blues" showed the group using R&B as a form of personal expression, effectively grafting autobiographical lyrics onto traditional blues structures. *Record Mirror* aptly described *The Pretty Things* as "a lively album which although it is rough at the edges proves the Things to have a great deal to offer." The album was a strong seller, climbing to #6 in the U.K. that spring.

In March, the *Midland Beat* reported that the "unkempt look" of the Pretty Things was going out of style and contrasted their appearance unfavorably to local band Pete Tierney and the Nighthawks. "The 'smart look' is on the way back. There is no doubt that the public are getting fed up [with] groups with unruly, unkempt hair and disheveled dress," the newspaper's readers were informed. "Take a look at our photograph of the Pretty Things. Then study Jim Simpson's picture of the popular Birmingham group, Pete Tierney and the Nighthawks. The Brum boys' 'uniforms' give them a much more professional appearance than the Pretty Things."

Ironically, while the group was being bashed for their fashion sense, they were making plans to open a woman's boutique called the "Penny Halfpenny" near London's Portobello Road. Said May, "Designing for girls will be especially interesting when we get round to it. I think girls should dress to suit their personality—not the terrible fad of following fashion. I would design with a particular girl in mind. I think you've got to. Actually the most marvelous thing I ever saw was Anita Ekberg wearing a wet dress."

In April 1965, the Pretty Things made their first visit to Holland, where they had amassed a fanatical fan base.

A riotous concert in Blokker was shown live on Dutch TV, but the broadcast was terminated midway through the band's third song after outraged viewers called the television station to complain.

While the press reported that their next single might be a Donovan composition, the Pretty Things instead decided to use "Cry to Me," a track found on a Solomon Burke LP. Said Taylor at the time, "This has been something of an eye-opener for us. We weren't at all sure we could do it without the results turning out sounding like somebody copying a Solomon Burke record. But I think it is identifiable [as] us." Released in July 1965, the soulful ballad offered a change in direction. The B-side, "Get a Buzz," was a fuzz guitar-driven studio jam recorded in just one take. In an interview in *Disc Weekly*, May explained, "Even though our new record is much quieter than our image would suggest, we merely thought we'd prove that it was something we could do." The single was a minor U.K. hit, peaking at #28.

Based on their last single, any illusions fans might have had that the Pretty Things had mellowed were shattered that August when the group toured New Zealand. "Pretty Things' Shock Exhibition" screamed the headlines of the New Zealand *Truth*. "Shocked police found long-haired, drunken members of English pop group the Pretty Things swigging whiskey only minutes before their performance in New Plymouth last week. In scenes unprecedented in the 50-year-old history of the city's opera house, the long haired 'musicians' broke chairs, lit fires backstage and abused officials." The article went on to report, "Unshaven drummer Vivian Prince ruined heartthrob singer Eden Kane's act" by laying down shreds of carpet at Kane's feet and shouting at Kane to step on them, crawling around the stage with a lighted newspaper, setting fire to props, breaking furniture, interrupting headliner Sandie Shaw's act with various pranks, and swigging whiskey from his shoe, which Prince joked was "meths" (i.e. methylated spirits).

A Christchurch newspaper reported, "The Pretty Things' performance was anarchic. With their shabby clothing and their shaggy coiffures, they looked like five delegates at a nihilists' conference. This impression was reinforced by their stage antics. The drummer, Vivian Prince, jumped on balloons, terrorized the others with swipes from his king-size sword, and finally went berserk with a plastic machine gun which he eventually smashed on the edge of the stage and flung at his screaming audience."

Offstage, Prince insisted on carrying around a dead crayfish for several days. John Stax recalled his behavior to *Ugly Things:* "We'd been giving Viv a bit of a hard time because of his drinking. He was really bad news. We'd locked the dressing room and he tried to break into it with an axe. You could see the axe, just like you see in the movies! Anyway, he got over that, and that night he tried to set fire to the bloody stage. He was just rushing across stage with these firebrands, like lighted torches made of newspapers! The fire brigade were called out and they kept squirting him with all this stuff, chasing him across the stage!"

The orgy of tabloid headlines and lurid details shocked the conservative nation and earned the Pretty Things a lifetime ban on playing in New Zealand. At the end of the tour, Prince was kicked off the plane heading home—prior to takeoff, fortunately—after an altercation with the pilot. Prince defended himself to *Melody Maker,* telling the newspaper, "The reports about us being incapably drunk and ruining the shows are false. Five papers printed stories which completely contradicted these reports. They said we went down great and the audiences were raving with us." His comments were corroborated by an article in the New Plymouth *Daily News,* which reported, "The Pretty Things brought the house down. They did everything but provide for a lover of beautiful music—and there were none of those in the audience. Theirs was R&B at its raving best. Electric excitement, and an original stage style, plus good R&B drumming. Viv Prince's brandishing a flaming newspaper was in short a very original twist to their act."

Even with the quintet's acknowledged penchant for outrageousness, it was apparent that Prince was becoming a liability. Increasingly, Skip Alan, Mitch Mitchell or Twink (a.k.a. John Alder) had to substitute when the drummer was incapacitated or failed to show up for gigs. However, Prince stayed around long enough to complete most of the group's second album, *Get the Picture?,* released in December 1965. Ranging from the jangling pop of "You Don't Believe Me" to the folkishness of "London Town" to the savage R&B of "Gonna Find Me a Substitute," the album showed incredible diversity and marked the continuing emergence of May and Taylor as songwriters on the tracks "Buzz the Jerk," "Get the Picture" and the atmospheric "Can't Stand the Pain." *Record Mirror* gave the LP an enthusiastic review, noting that it "could shake up a few folk who think of the Things as being a bit of a musical joke."

By the time of the album's release, Viv Prince had officially left the band. As Phil May explained to *Disc Weekly,*

"We all like Viv but we had a disagreement over group policy." Prince responded to the official explanation by saying, "I agree it was a policy disagreement. Among other things they seemed to think that the personal publicity that I was getting was bad for the group." His replacement was 17-year-old Skip Alan (born Alan Skipper, June 11, 1948; Westminster, London, U.K.), who had previously played on sessions with Donovan and had fronted his own Skip Alan Trio. His first recording with the Pretty Things was "Midnight to Six Man," a single released at the end of the year right after the LP.

"We spent months trying to find something to record but there wasn't anything good enough about," Taylor told *Record Mirror* at the time. "We didn't want to push anything out, so we waited. Then we had to go to the studio and do something, so Phil and I sat down and wrote 'Midnight to Six Man' in half an hour. We got the idea from all these people who you never see during the day. Then spend all their lives down [at] clubs at night and that's the only sort of place they ever go." The group reportedly spent 16 hours in the studio recording this composition, which they felt certain would return them to the upper regions of the charts. Though propelled in part by recommendations from *Melody Maker* ("a hard swinging modern R&B record") and *New Musical Express* ("the general atmosphere is exciting and tingling"), the single barely scraped into the U.K. Top 50, spending one week at #46.

The following year, a short film called *The Pretty Things* featured the group as silent actors in several *Hard Day's Night*-type scenarios and in a live club segment. Four songs from the soundtrack—"Midnight to Six Man," "Can't Stand the Pain," "£.S.D." and "Me Needing You"— were released on the *On Film* EP in January. Their next single, the storming, fuzz-laden "Come See Me," followed in April. The record was too wild for some reviewers' tastes. *Disc Weekly* called it "too ugly," adding, "They've become identified with this rather anti-sound; it's rather a shame." *New Musical Express* wrote, "All the time, there's a storming insidious beat," and concluded that while the A-side had "virtually no melody, which may well prevent it from climbing high in the chart . . . it gets right down to the guts of r&b." The flip side, "£.S.D.," referred to English currency—pounds (£), shillings (s) and pence (d)—but the underlying drug theme wasn't hard to deduce and the band was once again the subject of controversy. Only this time, controversy failed to translate into sales; the single reached #43 for five weeks before dropping off the charts.

After the relative failure of their last few singles, Phil May publicly remained defiant and refused to compromise their approach, telling *Disc and Music Echo* at the time, "As far as records are concerned we keep to our sound because it's ours. People have come to us with some lovely stuff which is obviously a hit—in fact other people have done it and it has been a hit—but it's too pretty for us." May then added, "But we won't conform. I suppose you could say we do what we want and to hell with everyone else, but that's a bit strong. The way I'd put it is like this: we play what we want to play, every single number, and we won't conform with trends. That way we're happy. And it looks as though we're happy too."

Nevertheless, they tried a new approach for their next single, recording Ray Davies's "A House in the Country" released in June 1966. More restrained than its predecessors, *New Musical Express* called the song "bouncy and quite tuneful." In an interview in *Record Mirror*, May explained, "We just can't keep on fighting the rest of the world," referring to the difficulties the band had in getting TV bookings because of their well-earned reputation for trouble. He noted that although their stage act would remain the same, they would try different approaches for their singles "rather than churn out all the wild stuff."

Despite the lack of success of "A House in the Country," they continued with their new sound on their next release, "Progress," an upbeat, horn-driven pop number released in December 1966. Although the single garnered some attention from the press, it was essentially another commercial nonentity.

Around this time, Brian Pendleton left the group rather suddenly by failing to show up for scheduled gigs and disappearing from sight. Eventually, the group members discovered that he had suffered a nervous breakdown. The group elected not to replace him and continued as a four-piece; but by this time they were floundering.

For their next album, *Emotions*, they augmented their quartet with session players, often using the orchestrations of Reg Tilsley. A frustrated Stax left during the making of the album and May brought in his childhood friend, bassist Wally Allen (a.k.a. Alan Wally Waller, b. April 9, 1944; Barnehurst, Kent, U.K.), and keyboardist John Povey (b. August 20, 1942; London, U.K.), both ex-Fenmen. The two new members were key to the Pretty Things' changing sound, providing harmony vocals and, in Allen's case, quality songwriting.

Emotions was issued in May 1967 to disappointing reviews and poor sales as disillusioned fans eschewed the group's softer, more melodic approach. The band members themselves disliked the album, feeling their songs had been sabotaged by the overwhelming string and brass overdubs courtesy of arranger/orchestrator Reg Tilsley. Nonetheless, *Emotions* made for a vivid time capsule of mid- to late-1960s England. Tracks such as "Death of a Socialite," "Photographer" and "Tripping" were worthy, socially relevant pop songs, and the quiet ballads "The Sun" and "Growing in My Mind" showed a new sensitivity in May's vocal approach.

Meanwhile, as a supplemental income source in the late 1960s and early 1970s, the Pretty Things members recorded anonymously for the DeWolfe Music Library, who filed their tracks for future use in typically low budget movies whenever a suitably "swinging" or "groovy" scene was called for. Consequently, the Pretty Things' music can be heard in some unlikely places, including some late 1960s/early 1970s soft porn titles and such horror flicks as Michael Armstrong's *The Haunted House of Horror*. These music library records (usually comprised of one side of vocal and one side of instrumental versions of the same songs) were credited to the fictitious group "Electric Banana" and were never intended for official release, so when the records began surfacing credited to the Pretty Things, the group members were not pleased. DeWolfe originally issued five albums of these recordings: *Electric Banana* (1967), *More Electric Banana* (1968), *Even More Electric Banana* (1969), *Hot Licks* (1970) and *The Return of the Electric Banana* (1978).

With *Emotions,* the Pretty Things completed their Fontana contract and freed themselves to pursue their new musical direction—an experimental sound more in tune with London's nascent psychedelic underground. They then signed with EMI and in the summer of 1967 ensconced themselves at Abbey Road, where they found a more free-thinking, creative environment working alongside the Beatles and Pink Floyd.

Teaming up with producer Norman Smith (fresh from Pink Floyd's debut, *Piper at the Gates of Dawn*), they released their first EMI single, "Defecting Grey" backed with "Mr. Evasion," in November. "We took him [Norman Smith] our cut of 'Defecting Grey,' which at six minutes was considered too long for airplay," May told *Disc and Music Echo.* "By the time he'd worked it over it was still 5 1/2 minutes long but we all decided to stick to our guns," May recalled. The A-side has since become a British psychedelic classic, a radically ambitious, Middle Eastern-tinged piece that intertwined several musical themes to stunning effect.

The equally dazzling "Talkin' About the Good Times"—resplendent with swirling harmonies, economical yet essential guitar riffs and colorful Mellotron sonorities—followed in April 1968, backed with "Walking Through My Dreams." By this time, Skip Alan had left the group to marry a French woman he met while on tour. His replacement was Twink, who had most recently been a member of Tomorrow, a like-minded psychedelic outfit.

Sometime during July and August the group filmed *What's Good for the Goose,* a Norman Wisdom movie about a banker going through a midlife crisis. The group provided the music in the club scenes, and had small acting parts in the comedy.

Following the filming of the movie, the group continued sessions for their psychedelic masterpiece, *S.F. Sorrow,* a song cycle (or, as some preferred calling it, "rock opera") based on a Phil May short story. In November 1968, Derek Boltwood previewed the album in his *Record Mirror* column, "From the Underground": "The Pretty Things have just finished work on their new album, *S.F. Sorrow.* And I've just heard the finished article all the way through. And I'm more than impressed by it. I hope it doesn't sound too pompous when I say I think it's an important pop work." The group labored on the song cycle for over a year before releasing it in December 1968, preceded by the single "Private Sorrow" (backed with "Balloon Burning"). Reviews were almost unanimously glowing. *New Musical Express* wrote, "[The Pretty Things] have improved beyond all recognition and have produced an album which should rate as one of the best of 1968." *Disc and Music Echo* raved, "It doesn't sound like anything you've ever heard, the whole conception of the album is a mind-blower," and *Beat Instrumental* declared, "A very enterprising attempt by the Pretty Things at something new in pop music."

The group even planned to perform *S.F. Sorrow* in mime. "We'll use stereo tape backing tracks, with a backdrop and our own lights, with Twink miming the parts." *Melody Maker* reviewed a performance at the Roundhouse, musing, "It proved to be interesting and entertaining and gives the Pretty Things another dimension to their act." However, the group abandoned the idea after a couple of successful performances when it became apparent that the audience wanted live, not taped, music.

Things looked good for the band as 1969 began, and they continued to be a popular live draw. *Melody Maker* Features Editor Chris Welch declared, "As 1969 swings in, it is obvious that the Things have become one of the most important creative, playing groups on the club scene." May also expressed confidence in their latest project: "We've never enjoyed ourselves so much as we are now. I feel that we have got something to say and something to offer. We do all our own material. We kicked off our old image at last about four months ago and I think people are really impressed by us now. We all believe in what we are doing—we're all tuned in." In April, the group announced that they had signed a U.S. deal with the Rare Earth label (a Tamla Motown subsidiary) and that an American tour was in the works.

However, the Pretty Things' luck stayed true to form and by year's end things had begun to unravel. Rare Earth had delayed releasing *S.F. Sorrow,* so by the time it was out in the States, the Who's *Tommy* was already on the shelves. Ignorant of which came first—and of the fact that Pete Townshend had acknowledged the influence of the Pretty Things' rock opera on his own (which he later denied)—the U.S. music press was quick to dismiss *Sorrow* as a *Tommy* rip-off. *Rolling Stone* condemned the release, calling it "ultra-pretentious" and comparing it to "some grossly puerile cross between the Bee Gees, *Tommy* and the Moody Blues." May blamed the debacle on their U.S. record label. "The problem was with Tamla in the States. I called them a month before *Tommy* was due and asked them to get it moving but at that time they were pushing Rare Earth [the group] and everything else was a bad deal. It eventually appeared six weeks after *Tommy* and critics were saying things like 'a good pop record in the ilk of *Tommy*.' But we made it 12 months before *Tommy* appeared and when we pointed this out some of them apologized in print."

The failure of *S.F. Sorrow* to sell left May "sick and depressed." In the meantime, Twink had parted company with the group, recording a solo album before forming the Pink Fairies. The band replaced him on drums with the prodigal Skip Alan. Taylor also decided to throw in the towel, citing boredom as his main reason. He went into record production, working with Hawkwind among others, then dropped out of the music business for a while.

The Pretty Things recruited Victor Unitt from the Edgar Broughton Group as Taylor's replacement. Though disenchanted by the commercial failure of *S.F. Sorrow,* the band began work on a new album.

Parachute was released in June 1970. It embodied another crowning achievement for the group. The new songwriting alliance of Phil May and Wally Allen produced a flawless set of songs that ranged from the searing rocker "Miss Fay Regrets" to elegiac love ballads like "Grass," touching on superb vocal harmonies ("In the Square," "What's the Use"); bruising, heavy riffs ("Cries from the Midnight Circus"); and shimmering symphonic poetry ("Parachute").

By now, the group considered their past to be an albatross. "I have this terrible thought that people are going to expect 'Don't Bring Me Down' on stage. Six-year-old Pretty Things numbers, that kind of thing. It's a terrifying proposition," May told *Disc and Music Echo.* May even considered changing the group's name. "Originally people thought it would be a good idea if we changed our name . . . Maybe they were right, and if we had, it wouldn't have taken us such a long time to live down the past, but at the time I didn't think it was the correct course to take because it was like fooling the public."

Critically, *Parachute* was enthusiastically reviewed. *New Musical Express* called it "a most interesting album all through," while *Record Mirror* noticed its "often Beach Boy-like texture," writing, "The whole concept is clear and very attractive." Similarly, *Disc and Music Echo* chimed in with the comment, "Musically they sound very Beatley/Kinkish, with some lovely harmonies and that clever guitar sound." *Rolling Stone* named it their Album of the Year.

Praise alone was not enough to help *Parachute* emerge from the underground market. "The critical reception was a buzz. But you either sell or you don't. That's what it's all about, really. It's pointless making a good album if no one's going to hear it. You can't exist forever on critical acclaim," May explained afterward to writer Allan Jones. Further undermining the record's chance, their manager was involved in a near fatal car crash that left the band thrown into confusion and unable to capitalize on their critical stature.

In July, Victor Unitt returned to the Edgar Broughton Group and was replaced by Pete Tolson (b. September 10, 1951; Bishop's Stortford, Herts, U.K.), a teenage guitar whiz who'd previously played in Eire Apparent. Tolson's first single with the Pretty Things was "October 26" backed with "Cold Stone," which came out in November. *Melody Maker's* review predicted it would be "a huge hit," observing, "They have come up with some uncharacteristic vocal harmonies, almost of Beach Boys caliber." However, the single flopped, as did a three-track EP ("Stone Hearted Mama," "Summertime," "Circus Mind") released the following May. *New Musical Express* dubbed "Stone Hearted Mama" a "rocker with a bouncy beat, a catchy melody and a tingling jangle sound from the guitar backing." On a hopeful note, *Record Mirror* wrote that the EP was "more directly commercial than their last couple" and that they had "a good tight sound going."

At this point, the Pretty Things were in a state of disarray. When Wally Allen left to become an EMI house producer, the Pretty Things informally disbanded in June 1971. But, the Pretty Things' 1971 breakup proved temporary. They re-formed only five months later with a new bass player, Stuart Brooks, formerly of Black Cat Bones [see **Black Cat Bones**], and a new manager, Bill Shepherd, who promptly secured a record deal with Warner Brothers.

Breaking into the American market became the group's primary objective in the 1970s. Their Warner Brothers album, *Freeway Madness* (December 1972), set the stage. *Rolling Stone* said of it, "The great brilliance of *Freeway Madness*, a carefully conceived studio album, is its near perfect combination of seemingly disparate elements: neoclassic English white blues, alternating with a Crosby-Stills-Nash derived acoustic style wonderfully reworked in bracing off-harmonies."

Postscript

The Pretty Things toured the States in 1973, adding Gordon Edwards on keyboards and guitar, after which they were signed to Led Zeppelin's new label, Swan Song. They then replaced Brooks with Jack Green on bass and two albums followed—*Silk Torpedo* (1974) and *Savage Eye* (1976). Although these sold well, the Pretty Things' mainstream breakthrough never came. Amid immense turmoil, May walked out on the group in the summer of 1976, and the band was essentially finished.

In 1978, May met up with Waller again for one rather uneven album with the Fallen Angels. However, the Pretty Things refused to stay down. By late 1979, Taylor was again aboard, along with May, Povey, Wally Allen, Tolson and Skip Alan. They recorded 1980's *Crosstalk* (Warner Brothers), a strong, edgy album that sank without a trace due to poor marketing. The Pretty Things once again disappeared into the shadows.

May and Taylor continued working with various line-ups throughout the 1980s and 1990s, playing R&B in clubs and bars and recording occasional one-off projects for indie labels. These included *Live at Heartbreak Hotel* (1984), *Out of the Island* (1988) and two albums as the Pretty Things/Yardbird Blues Band—*The Chicago Blues Tapes* (1991) and *Wine, Women & Whiskey* (1993)—recorded in Chicago with Yardbirds drummer Jim McCarty and various Chicago blues musicians.

Concurrent with these activities was an ongoing album project with producer/drummer/lawyer/manager Mark St. John, which was finally released in 1999 as *Rage Before Beauty*. St. John was also actively engaged on the band's behalf pursuing unpaid back royalties—a complicated process that culminated in 1995 with the group's securing possession and ownership of their entire back catalog.

This accomplishment galvanized the re-formation of the Pretty Things' 1967–68 lineup: May, Taylor, Povey, Wally Allen and Skip Alan. Along with new guitarist Frank Holland, they resurfaced in 1998 to perform *S.F. Sorrow* live over the Internet from Abbey Road studios. This landmark concert, which also included guest appearances from Dave Gilmour and Arthur Brown, was released on CD soon afterward as *Resurrection*. It was followed in March 1999 by a powerful and well-received new album, *Rage Before Beauty*, which the group supported with a tour of America in September 1999.

Currently, this amazingly durable group is still fully engaged and fanning the flames of controversy. Fittingly, their latest single, "All Light Up," made headlines after it was discovered that they had used the voices of schoolchildren to chant the song's pro-drug message. In more than 35 years, not a lot has changed for the Pretty Things.

Discography

Release Date	Title	Catalog Number

U.S. Singles

1964	Rosalyn/Big Boss Man	Fontana 1916
1964	Don't Bring Me Down/We'll Be Together	Fontana 1941
1965	Honey I Need/I Can Never Say	Fontana 1508
1965	Cry to Me/I Can Never Say	Fontana 1518
1965	Cry to Me/Judgement Day	Fontana 1518
1965	Midnight to Six Man/Can't Stand the Pain	Fontana 1540
1966	Progress/Come See Me	Fontana 1550
1966	Judgment Day/Come See Me	Fontana 1550
1968	Talkin' About the Good Times/Walking Through My Dreams	Laurie 3458
1968	Private Sorrow/Balloon Bursting	Rare Earth 5005

U.S. Albums

1964	*The Pretty Things*	Fontana 67544

Honey I Need/Rosalyn/13 Chester Street/Unknown Blues/Moon Is Rising/Don't Bring Me Down/Roadrunner/We'll Be Together/Judgement Day/Big City/Pretty Things

1969	*S.F. Sorrow*	Rare Earth 506

S.F. Sorrow Is Born/Bracelets of Fingers/She Says Good Morning/Private Sorrow/Balloon Burning/Death/Baron Saturday/The Journey/I See You/Well of Destiny/Trust/Old Man Going/Loneliest Person

1970	*Parachute*	Rare Earth 515

Scene One/The Good Mr. Square/She Was Tall, She Was High/In the Square/The Letter/Rain/Miss Fay Regrets/Cries from the Midnight Circus/Grass/Sickle Clowns/She's a Lover/What's the Use/Parachute

1972	*Freeway Madness*	Warner Brothers BS 2680

Love Is Good/Havana Bound/Peter/Rip Off Train/Over the Moon/Religion's Dead/Country Road/All Night Sailor/Onion Soup/Another Bowl

U.K. Singles

1964	Rosalyn/Big Boss Man	Fontana TF 469
1964	Don't Bring Me Down/We'll Be Together	Fontana TF 503
1965	Honey I Need/I Can Never Say	Fontana TF 537
1965	Cry to Me/Get a Buzz	Fontana TF 585
1965	Midnight to Six Man/Can't Stand the Pain	Fontana TF 647
1966	Come See Me/£.S.D.	Fontana TF 688
1966	A House in the Country/Me Needing You	Fontana TF 722
1966	Progress/Buzz the Jerk	Fontana TF 773
1967	Children/My Time	Fontana TF 829
1967	Defecting Grey/Mr. Evasion	Columbia DB 8300
1968	Talkin' About the Good Times/Walking Through My Dreams	Columbia DB 8353
1968	Private Sorrow/Balloon Burning	Columbia DB 8494
1970	The Good Mr. Square/Blue Serge Blues	Harvest HAR 5016
1970	October 26/Cold Stone	Harvest HAR 5031

U.K. EPs

1964	*The Pretty Things*	Fontana TE 17434

Don't Bring Me Down/Big Boss Man/Rosalyn/We'll Be Together

1965	*Rainin' in My Heart*	Fontana TE 17442

Rainin' in My Heart/London Town/Sittin' All Alone/Get a Buzz

1966	*On Film*	Fontana TE 17472

Midnight to Six Man/Can't Stand the Pain/£.S.D./Me Needing You

1971	*Stone Hearted Mama*	Harvest HAR 5037

Stone Hearted Mama/Summertime/Circus Mind

U.K. Albums

1965 *The Pretty Things* Fontana TL 5329
Roadrunner/Judgement Day/Chester Street/Big City/Unknown Blues/
Mama, Keep Your Big Mouth Shut/Honey I Need/Oh Baby Doll/She's
Fine She's Mine/Don't Lie to Me/The Moon Is Rising/Pretty Thing

1965 *Get the Picture?* Fontana
TL 5280
You Don't Believe Me/Buzz the Jerk/Get the Picture?/Can't Stand the
Pain/Rainin' in My Heart/We'll Play House/You'll Never Do It Baby/I
Had a Dream/I Want Your Love/London Town/Cry to Me/Gonna Find Me
a Substitute

1967 *Emotions* Fontana TL 5425
Death of a Socialite/Children/The Sun/There Will Never Be Another
Day/House of Ten/Out in the Night/One Long Glance/Growing in My
Mind/Photographer/Bright Lights Big City/Tripping/My Time

1967 *Electric Banana* DeWolfe 3040
Walking Down the Street/If I Needed Somebody/Free Love/Cause I'm
a Man/Danger Signs/I See You/Street Girl/Grey Skies/I Love You/Love
Dance and Sing/A Thousand Ages from the Sun/Do My Stuff/Take Me
Home/James Marshall

1968 *S.F. Sorrow* Columbia
SCX 6306
1969 *More Electric Banana* De Wolfe 3069
I See You/Street Girl/Grey Skies/Love, Dance and Sing/A Thousand
Ages from the Sun/I See You (instrumental)/Street Girl (instrumen-
tal)/Grey Skies (instrumental)/I Love You (instrumental)/Love, Dance and
Sing (instrumental)/A Thousand Ages from the Sun (instrumental)

1969 *Even More Electric Banana* De Wolfe 3123
Alexander/It'll Never Be Me/Eagle's Son/Blow Your Mind/What's
Good for the Goose/Rave Up/Alexander (instrumental)/It'll Never Be
Me (instrumental)/Eagle's Son (instrumental)/Blow Your Mind (instru-
mental)/The Dark Theme (instrumental)

1970 *Parachute* Harvest SHVL 774
1970 *Hot Licks* DeWolfe 3284
Sweet Orphan Lady/I Could Not Believe My Eyes/Good Times/Walk
Away/The Loser/Easily Done/Sweet Orphan Lady (instrumental)/I Could
Not Believe My Eyes (instrumental)/Good Times (instrumental)/Walk
Away (instrumental)/The Loser (instrumental)/Easily Done (instrumental)

1972 *Freeway Madness* Warner Brothers
K 46190
1992 *On Air* (CD) Band of Joy
BOJ CD 003
Don't Bring Me Down/Hey Mamma/Midnight to Six Man/Buzz the
Jerk/£.S.D./Big Boss Man/Deflecting Grey/Cold Stone/Sickle Clowns/
She's a Lover/Cries from the Midnight Circus/Stone Hearted Mamma/
Summertime/Peter/Rip Off Train/Onion Soup

Savoy Brown

Originally called the Savoy Brown Blues Band, this group can rightly take credit for cutting the farewell anthem of the 1960s British blues boom in the form of a modern blues aptly titled "Train to Nowhere." Historically as well as musically, this song remains a sad reminder that by the time of its 1969 release as a single, most original blues were no longer commercially viable in Britain, as more and more blues clubs closed their doors for good.

Led by founder/guitarist Kim Simmonds (b. December 5, 1947; Newbridge, South Wales, U.K.), Savoy Brown became a major live act in America, although their popularity at home was limited and they were never able to break out of the club scene. Perhaps their domestic success was impeded by the constant turnover of musicians, as Simmonds was the band's only continuous member. However, these frequent lineup changes also led to some noteworthy ensembles. Many consider that the recordings featuring Chris Youlden's rich vocals and songwriting augmented by Kim Simmonds's jazz-tinged, fluent blues guitar were Savoy Brown's finest work; this being especially so on such late-1960s cuts as "She's Got a Ring in His Nose and a Ring on Her Hand" (a classy swing-blues) and the completely different and desolate groove of "Mr. Downchild." The early-1970s also saw some interesting personnel changes, including a collaboration with Chicken Shack's Stan Webb (when the band also was known as the Boogie Brothers).

Early in his life, Savoy Brown guitarist Kim Simmonds was heavily influenced by his older brother Harry (christened Henry). Harry Simmonds had started listening to music when he was about 13, especially to Bill Haley. He later became interested in R&B and blues, particularly the music of James Brown, Ike and Tina Turner, Jimmy Reed, Otis Rush and Muddy Waters. He often purchased American imports from the Swing Shop, a small record store located in Streatham, Southwest London, which was also a hangout for Dave and Jo Ann Kelly (see **Dave Kelly, Jo Ann Kelly**).

Kim became absorbed in the records in his older brother's collection. "My brother, Harry, used to come home with all these records and I used to hear nothing but blues," he told *Beat Instrumental*. "I was hooked straight away." Among Kim's influences were Howlin' Wolf (and his guitarist Hubert Sumlin), Earl Hooker, Freddy King, Matt Murphy, Otis Rush and Muddy Waters. At age 13, Kim purchased his first guitar and taught himself to play Chuck Berry riffs. By age 15 he was still playing the guitar, though by then he had dropped out of school and taken a clerical job at the Ministry of Defense in Whitehall.

While waiting outside Transat Imports, a record store located in London's Chinatown district, Kim met another blues enthusiast, harmonica player and neighbour John O'Leary. O'Leary was working for an American chemical company and had picked up the harmonica after seeing Cyril Davies perform with Alexis Korner's Blues Incorporated. O'Leary and Kim became friends and O'Leary invited Kim and his brother Harry to a jam session. "I went along not expecting very much, but Kim had got a really good thing going," Harry later observed.

He encouraged his brother to form a band and they all agreed that Harry would manage them. The initial lineup consisted of Kim Simmonds on guitar, O'Leary on harmonica, Leo Manning on drums, vocalist Brice Portius, and bassist Ray Chappell. Both Manning and Portius were black, while the other members were white, thus making Savoy Brown one of the first racially integrated groups to play in British clubs.

Their first pianist, Trevor Jeavons, was soon replaced by Bob Hall (who became one of Savoy Brown's longest-serving, albeit part-time, members) [see **Brunning Hall Sunflower Blues Band**]. Previously, Hall had been a member of John Lee's Groundhogs (later the Groundhogs), which had backed John Lee Hooker on his 1964 British tour. He had also played backup to Jimmy Reed and Little Walter. By the time of the Groundhogs' first recordings, however, Hall had departed because of time conflicts with his day job.

The new group decided to call themselves the Savoy Brown Blues Band to emphasize their Chicago Blues-style repertoire. They took Savoy from the U.S. blues label, Savoy Records, which they thought sounded elegant and "Brown" because they perceived it as being about as plain as you can get. Strung together, the words created a balance of opposites.

Like many bands, they found it tough to get bookings at first, but unlike other bands, the Simmonds brothers simply decided to open their own blues club, Kilroy's, in May 1966. Kilroy's was located in an upstairs room of Nag's Head Tavern on York Road in Battersea. Kim described the club to *Relix*: "They used to have a folk club one night a week and as folk was dying out by then we approached them about having a blues room on Monday nights. We'd take our gear down in a taxi or something like that. We used to rehearse there anyway. From what I can recall, we distributed flyers around London and the club came into being. At first only a few people came and then we played there every week and it built up, and eventually it became a bona-fide blues club. Fleetwood Mac played there, and Freddie King and all sorts of artists." The Nag's Head eventually became home to the Blue Horizon club—a place where future British blues talents such as Fleetwood Mac's Danny Kirwan (then with his first band, Boilerhouse) were discovered [see **Fleetwood Mac**].

As the Savoy Brown Blues Band 's manager, Harry landed a story about the group and their blues club in the pages of the local *Wandsworth Borough News*. At the time, Harry (who also worked as a London postman) would enterprisingly take the band to gigs in his Post Office van. Kilroy's became a local success and soon attracted the notice of Mike Vernon. Along with childhood friend Neil Slaven, Vernon published the blues and soul music magazine *R&B Monthly,* and was at the time a producer at Decca. Vernon had also established the Blue Horizon label along with his brother, Richard, which included two subsidiary labels, Purdah and Outa-Site.

As Vernon explained in the liner notes of *History of British Blues*, "I talked Harry Simmonds, their manager, into letting me record the band for a single to be released on my own Purdah label—that was the precedent to Blue Horizon." They recorded four tracks in August 1966 at London's Wessex Studios, with Vernon producing. Vernon issued two of the tracks, "I Tried" and the Willie Dixon-penned "I Can't Quit You Baby," as a single on Purdah to be distributed by mail order. The other two, "True Blue" (a.k.a. "True Story") and "Cold Blooded Woman" were assigned Purdah catalog numbers but not released. They eventually came out as part of the Immediate label's *Blues Anytime* series.

The band received a big break when Brian Wilcock, a deejay at Klook's Kleek R&B Club at the Railway Hotel (located in the West Hampstead area of London), and a friend of Harry Simmonds arranged for the band to play the interval for the Cream's appearance there on August 2, 1966. Since the Cream made their official debut at the 6th National Jazz and Blues Festival on July 31, this would be their first club engagement outside of a warmup gig held on July 29 at the Twisted Wheel in Manchester. Expectations were high for the Cream, which played two sets, but Savoy Brown created such a storm during their slot that they racked up enough gig offers to enable them to go full time. Wilcock eventually became their tour manager in September 1967.

The band started to expand their gig list to include engagements at the Tiles Club, the Flamingo, and at the Marquee in central London and the Metro in Birmingham. Kim once said about those early shows, "We started playing places like the Metro in Birmingham, which is like a big soul club, but we managed to please the people because we had Brice Portius, a black singer, and they would relate to him in the sense that they might relate to Geno Washington, even though we were playing blues. I mean we would play up-tempo stuff and bounce around a little." Several shows even found them backing Champion Jack Dupree. Altogether, their lineup remained stable except for pianist Hall, who once again had conflicts with his daytime job that caused him to drop out for awhile but return on a part-time basis when his replacement didn't work out. (Demos and acetates were recorded with this lineup prior to the sessions for their first album.) Ex-Stone's Masonry guitarist Martin Stone was added while O'Leary departed to become a member of John Dummer's Blues Band [see **John Dummer Band**]. Both Graham "Shakey Vick" Vickery and Steve Hackett auditioned to play harp during this period, but O'Leary was not replaced.

Decca signed the band on the recommendation of Slaven and Vernon, and by mid-1967 the group was at West Hampstead Studios, London, recording their first album with Mike Vernon again producing. In the excellent *Blue Horizon* CD set, Vernon discussed his rationale for signing the band to Decca rather than to one of his own labels: "Firstly, Blue Horizon was still, at the time, little more than a fanzine label and secondly, I must herein admit that I didn't care too much for Brice as a vocalist."

The Savoy Brown Blues Band's first Decca long player was recorded in just thirty hours spanning three consecutive days. *Shake Down* was a gritty collection of blues standards with just one original, Stone's "The Doormouse Rides the Rails." Among the tracks were B.B. King's "Rock Me Baby," John Lee Hooker's "It's All My Fault," three Willie Dixon songs and "Black Night" by Fenton Robinson. The standout track was the group-arranged "Shake 'Em on Down," a raucous workout extending to just over six minutes. *Shake Down* was released in the U.K. in September 1967, but for reasons unknown, the LP didn't appear at all in the U.S.

The Savoy Brown Blues Band continued to gig extensively while *Shake Down* was in production, doing a punishing 24 gigs in just 21 days as the backing band for John Lee Hooker. They also got a summer-long residency in Charlottenlund, north of Copenhagen, Denmark. At around the time of *Shake Down's* release, in an odd coincidence the band experienced a true drug-related "shake down" in Barnstaple, a town in Devon, England, during a short tour of the West Country. This incident led Harry to actually fire his brother Kim from the band after the dates in Denmark, although he was quickly let back in. Other changes ensued as Chappell and Portius left and were replaced by Bob Brunning on bass and Chris Youlden on vocals. Brunning had previously been Fleetwood Mac's bassist for a few weeks in August 1967.

Youlden had been in various outfits, including a band that had alternately called itself the Down Home Blues Band and Shakey Vick's Big City Blues Band, and another called the Cross Ties Blues Band.

Next, Manning quit and was replaced on drums by Hughie Flint, formerly of John Mayall's Bluesbreakers [see **John Mayall**] and Alexis Korner's band, Free at Last [see **Alexis Korner**]. Finally, Stone departed and Kim asked O'Leary to rejoin the band. O'Leary agreed at first, then changed his mind due to "unreasonable conditions." Stone was instead replaced by "Lonesome" Dave Peverett.

Dave Peverett (b. April 16, 1943; d. February 7, 2000) was born in Dulwich but grew up in Brixton, southwest London. He first got into music after hearing "Rock Around the Clock" by Bill Haley and the Comets. He then listened to Jerry Lee Lewis, Little Richard, Fats Domino, Chuck Berry and Elvis Presley before turning on to blues musicians Bo Diddley, Muddy Waters, Lightnin' Hopkins and John Lee Hooker. At age 16, he bought his first guitar and, with his brother on drums, gathered other musicians and formed a band that played their first party in 1963. After undergoing a series of name changes, the group (whose membership included Chris Youlden) eventually settled on the name the Cross Ties Blues Band. By 1966, they had become the Lonesome Jax Blues Band, named after Dave Peverett's first stage name. The band played the London club circuit and colleges.

Later, Peverett joined the Swiss blues group Les Questions, with whom he played until October 1967, at which point he returned to the U.K. with plans to start a band along with Youlden. Instead, he joined Savoy Brown.

With only Kim and Hall from the prior lineup, the group entered the studio to record their next single. Youlden emerged as a major creative force within the band, contributing the frantic "Taste and Try, Before You Buy," which became the A-side of their next release. Kim had written the flip side, "Someday People."

Record Mirror praised the band as playing "a style of Chicago blues which is both commercial and authentic" and observed that Youlden was "often rated in the same breath as Long John Baldry and Rod Stewart."

Shortly after the single was cut, the band underwent more member changes. Both Brunning and Flint left; Brunning has since cited the "creative accountancy" of the band's management as the main reason for walking. (Manager Harry used to pay band members a fixed weekly wage regardless of how many gigs they played and the money made from each gig. From a musician's point of view, this was a good incentive for *not* getting too successful). By 1968, Brunning formed the Brunning Hall Sunflower Blues Band with Bob Hall, and Flint went on to early-1970s pop-chart success in McGuinness-Flint, later settling with the Blues Band.

After the Savoy Brown Blues Band had tried out several replacements for drums (including drummer Bill Bruford) and bass, the band decided on Rivers Jobe and Roger Earle, respectively. Jobe had previously been a member of the Anon (from May 1965 to July 1966) with future Genesis founding members Anthony Phillips and Mike Rutherford.

Producer Mike Vernon arranged for sessions for the group's next album, *Getting to the Point*, which took place in March 1968. Alongside Kim, Youlden emerged as co-leader of the group, and jointly or separately the pair composed most of the material. While the U.K. version of the album had cover art depicting Kim wearing round glasses with the image of a black man in each lens, the U.S. cover

art depicted more innocuous and politically correct images of a maze breaking up a collage of artwork. Kim explained what the original cover design was trying to depict to *Melody Maker*: "Our cover tried to show that although we are white we see things the same ways as a Negro, but for some reasons it was changed."

With just two cover songs and seven originals, the album marked the Savoy Brown Blues Band's transition from being a blues covers outfit to a band that had asserted their own identity. Highlights included the moody "Mr. Downchild," "Stay with Me Baby" and the Willie Dixon-penned "You Need Love."

Getting to the Point was released in both the U.S. and the U.K. in July 1968 to positive reviews. *Disc Weekly* wrote approvingly that the album "showcases their fine instrumental ability (particularly guitarist Kim Simmonds) and clean, tight sound. An exciting LP—it's difficult to sit still while it's on, and that's what the blues is all about, after all." *Rolling Stone* observed, "Savoy Brown does not come on with complex technical artistry and does not attempt to overplay its music. Its strength lies in its group rapport and dynamics. Vocalist Chris Youlden is one of the better blues singers to emerge from England. His voice has the resonance and inflection so necessary to establish the power and emotion which is the blues."

In June 1968, the group had released the single "Walking by Myself" backed with "Vicksburg Blues." "Walking by Myself" was a strong ensemble piece showcasing Bob Hall on piano, the confident soloing of Simmonds and a vocal duet between Youlden and Peverett. The group had by now refined their name to just "Savoy Brown" for this and subsequent releases.

From October 7 through 9, 1968, the band recorded the seminal "Train to Nowhere," which one critic described as "droningly hypnotic in feel." Youlden turned in powerful vocals on the record, and the band utilized a brass section for the first time (reportedly this included five trombones). It was later released as a single, with *Rolling Stone* citing "Train to Nowhere" as "certainly one of 1969's real undiscovered single gems." The recording also exposed the refined production skills of producer Vernon, who managed to build tension throughout the song, which in essence was a primitive one-line melody or modern "field-holler." At the time, two days was an abnormally long period of time to spend in a studio recording and mixing just one track, but the results did, and still do, deserve far more critical and commercial acclaim. The flip side, the haunting

"Tolling Bells," was even more dynamic and, once again, the group succeeded in creating an insistent tension.

By late 1968, Savoy Brown's schedule was booked solid with never fewer than six gigs a week. Audience reaction was always enthusiastic, as Kim explained to *Beat Instrumental:* "Since we've got the new line-up together, the band has been working much better. Interest in our sort of music is on the upsurge, and we're doing very well now."

In November, the band discharged bassist Jobe and asked former member Brunning (who had recently filled in for some gigs) to join again permanently. Brunning declined, and so Tone Stevens (b. September 12, 1949) joined instead.

On December 6, 1968, the band performed at the City of Leicester College of Education. The performance was taped with Dave Peverett substituting for Chris Youlden, who was sick and couldn't sing well enough to perform. They recorded the set anyway, and three tracks, "May Be Wrong," "It Hurts Me Too" and "Louisiana Blues" appeared on their next album. "Louisiana Blues," a largely instrumental song, became a showstopper on their forthcoming U.S. tour. A fourth live track, "Sweet Home Chicago," appears to have been lost in the Decca vaults. All of Peverett's vocals were re-recorded in the studio.

In December, the band returned to the studio to record two more tunes, "She's Got a Ring in His Nose and a Ring on Her Hand" and "Don't Turn Me from Your Door." On January 22, 1969, they recorded "Grits Ain't Groceries (All Around the World)." "Grits" was composed by Titus Turner, and under the name "All Around the World," it had been a Top Ten R&B hit in 1955 as covered by Little Willie John. Little Milton then revived the song in 1969 as "Grits Ain't Groceries." The song featured an explosive horn section and was paired with "Ring" for the U.S. market. In spite of the high caliber of both sides of this release, the single never took off.

Savoy Brown began their first ten-week U.S. tour on January 24. They played both the Fillmore East and Fillmore West, and gigs in Chicago and Detroit along the way. At their first U.S. gig—a small New York club called the Scene (run by music veteran Steve Paul)—the audience reacted coolly. So there and then, Savoy Brown decided to liven up their stage act by giving Youlden more focus: he began taking the stage wearing a top hat and sporting a big cigar stuffed in his mouth. Velvet trousers and a black fur jacket completed the image. The band also added a long boogie to their set that, like "Louisiana Blues," turned out to be a crowd pleaser. Kim later recalled the tour to *Disc and Music Echo,* "Until we hit Detroit—about half-way through the first tour—things weren't all that great. Then suddenly we got a reaction that . . . well, even going back to Detroit now it couldn't be repeated." The tour proved to be a big success. Harry explained, "The good it's done them is enormous. They are inspired by the great audience reactions. Whereas in England they used to wear dirty old jeans and just play the music, they really put on a show now. Kim doesn't hide in the background on stage any more—he and Chris are right out in front."

In May 1969, the band released their next album, *Blue Matter.* Consisting of previously released singles, live tracks recorded at Leicester with Peverett on vocals, and a John Lee Hooker cover, *Blue Matter* was a dazzling effort. *Melody Maker* called it a "nice, meaty album and certainly the best we have had so far from this group," and *Record Mirror* said, "It represents a long jump from the twelve bar tribe and an immersion into what can be accomplished by stretching obsolete limits." Regardless of praise from the music press, the LP stalled at #182 on the U.S. charts and didn't even make the charts in the U.K.

Later that month, the band held studio sessions for their next album (the last to be produced by Mike Vernon), *A Step Further.* Originally called *Asylum,* the album was released in the U.S. to coincide with the band's second American tour, which was slated for four months commencing on June 17. One track, "I'm Tired," was released as a U.S. single and reached #74 on the charts. *Rolling Stone* emphasized Youlden's "marvellous vocal" and the song's "irresistible rhythm." The album continued the formula of the previous LP—one live side and one studio side. The best offerings were studio tracks: "I'm Tired," the moody "Life's One Act Play" and the upbeat Youlden composition "Made Up My Mind." The live side was an endless boogie that *Melody Maker* called "quite remarkably boring, consisting of one riff recorded 'live' at Cooks Ferry Inn," although it remains a favorite of Savoy Brown devotees. Kim himself was pleased with the result, telling *Beat Instrumental,* "I think the latest album, *A Step Further*, surprised a lot of people in that it was much heavier than anything we've done before." *A Step Further* peaked at #71 in the U.S.

During the studio sessions for *A Step Further*, Hall, Peverett, Stevens and Earle started jamming on some old rockabilly tunes. Unknown to them, the engineer recorded these informal and spontaneous jams. After hearing the results, the foursome decided to create a rockabilly album and recorded a few more songs in the same vein, including the classic rock'n'roll standards "Shake, Rattle and Roll," "Matchbox" and "Keep a Knockin'." These recordings were issued on 1969's *The World of Rock and Roll* album credited to Warren Phillips and the Rockets.

Savoy Brown's second U.S. tour consolidated their initial success. Crowds in Detroit were especially enthralled, and Savoy Brown became the biggest act there since the Cream.

Upon their arrival home, the band went on a U.K. tour with Jethro Tull and Terry Reid from September 25 to October 29, 1969. Harry again fired his brother Kim in December 1969, and the band actually played in BBC sessions without him. (Kim rejoined shortly thereafter.)

In late January 1970, Savoy Brown embarked on their third U.S. tour, after which they returned to England to record the tracks for their next album, *Raw Sienna* (produced jointly by Kim and Youlden). The album was more complex than its predecessors, and Kim expressed satisfaction with the final product. "*Raw Sienna* is a personal achievement for me," Kim told *Melody Maker*. "Both from the production side and musically. It's our best album to date partly because everyone had so much freedom while we were actually recording." Youlden's compositions once again provided the highlights; the album incorporated more brass, and jazzier arrangements such as "A Hard Way to Go," "Needle and Spoon" and "I'm Crying." *New Musical Express* thought highly of the LP, printing, "A rich deep blues sound, especially from the bass (Tone Stevens) . . . with Chris Youlden producing the right sound on the vocals . . . and Kim Simmonds a powerful lead guitar." Despite the press attention, *Raw Sienna* never caught fire, reaching only #121 on the U.S. charts.

Commercial indifference and creative issues, as well his being tired of standing around during Kim's guitar solos, led Youlden to leave Savoy Brown in May 1970. Kim tried to put the best spin on the key loss, telling *Melody Maker*, "It's been a healthy split . . . and Chris just wanted to go his own way. While he was in the group, he was finding it increasingly difficult to compromise, which you must [do] with[in] a group." Kim also discussed Youlden's departure with *Beat Instrumental:* "He's not the sort of person who finds it easy to make compromises—maybe that's what makes someone successful—and he and the band were progressing in very different

directions. I think he wrote his songs with a particular treatment in his head while the band gave them a different style altogether; he's nearer to people like Jimmy Witherspoon than a heavy band. I'd known for a while that he would be leaving."

Youlden was not replaced, and Peverett began handling lead vocals. Kim explained to *Record Mirror* that more changes were in store. "Now that our lead singer Chris Youlden has left the group, we must have got into a looser scene musically and in the future are planning to augment the band. At the moment we're appearing as a quartet and we seem to be doing well on all the gigs in Britain now."

The band played 14 British gigs between June and August, then returned to the studio to record their next album. With the loss of their chief songwriter, the other group members had to pick up the slack. "Since Chris left the group we've all been more involved in writing material," Tone Stevens told *Record Mirror*. "Our new single is a number I wrote called 'Poor Girl' and it's a kind of reflection on the tours of America, the girls I've met, the posers." The album, *Lookin' In* was released in October 1970, a mere four months after the band's previous release. *Lookin' In* offered a return to basics, eschewing the brass backing and complex arrangements in favor of more riff-oriented, heavier rock song structures. The best tracks were the lengthy "Leavin' Again," Stevens's hard-edged "Poor Girl" and the title track. Savoy Brown's most commercially successful album to date, *Lookin' In* reached #39 on the U.S. charts.

The band then asked Bob Hall, still only a part-time member at this point, to become a full-time member. But Hall, who continued his daytime job, refused and was not replaced. As Kim explained to *Beat Instrumental*, "At one time Bob could just come along to a gig and he'd been able to fit in perfectly. The time came when we were too complex for him to be able to do it anymore unless he'd become a full-time member." With Hall not replaced, Kim would sometimes fill in on piano during performances. They also brought in a conga player, Owen Finnegan, although his stint with the group was brief.

On November 18, 1970, the group began their fifth U.S. tour (except for Finnegan, who failed to obtain his visa on time). While the group was again favorably received in the States, Kim and the other band members mutually agreed that the group would break up upon their return to England. Kim discussed the break up with *New Musical*

Express: "I wish to broaden the band's musical scope and the present line-up is too restrictive." Kim elaborated his rationale to *Sounds:* "The old group wasn't happening in a spontaneous way and even on the last tour of America the kids were noticing our lack of enthusiasm." For their part, Peverett, Stevens and Earle were eager to strike out on their own, and by joining forces with Rod Price, they would soon achieve stardom in the rock'n'boogie band Foghat.

Even though he had discharged all the members, Kim decided not to disband Savoy Brown, but instead make a complete lineup change by bringing in drummer Ron Berg, keyboardist Paul Raymond, bassist Andy Pyle and singer Pete Scott. Berg was formerly of Blodwyn Pig, Raymond had been a member of Chicken Shack [see **Chicken Shack**] and Plastic Penny and Pyle had previously been in Blodwyn Pig and McGregor's Engine. The new members rehearsed from late December to early January, preparing for Savoy Brown's sixth U.S. tour. The band also recorded a four-song BBC session in January, which included a prototype of "Street Corner Talking."

From February 5 to April 2, 1971, the band toured the U.S., coheadlining with the Faces. Dissatisfied, Kim again decided to purge the lineup in order to rejuvenate the band, so at the end of the tour, Pyle and Berg left to join Juicy Lucy and Kim replaced them with Andy Silvester and Dave Bidwell, formerly bassist and drummer with Chicken Shack. Ex-Idle Race vocalist Dave Walker also joined as a replacement for Scott. (Scott surfaced on the 1975 Beggars Opera album, *Beggars Can't Be Choosers*). Kim explained the turnover to *Circus* magazine: "Our progression was nil and we weren't exactly getting favourable reviews, especially on the west coast. I wanted to stay as free as possible and instead I felt hemmed in." Kim also felt that the band "desperately needed a new direction" and decided that a return to basics was the best course to chart.

The group recorded the album *Street Corner Talking* in four 12-hour sessions. Produced by Neil Slaven, *Street Corner Talking* was a surprisingly coherent and accessible collection. The lead track, "Tell Mama," became the group's signature song and a minor hit (U.S. #83) when released in edited form. *New Musical Express* applauded the single, saying, "It's carefree and gay, makes for utterly compulsive listening, and is also tailor-made for the discos." Other standout tracks included the mid-tempo "Let It Rock" and a cover of the Temptations' hit "I Can't Get Next to You." *Street Corner Talking* was released in September 1971 and reached #75 on the U.S. charts.

Overall, the new LP's reviews were mostly positive. *Disc and Music Echo* wrote, "It's a good album—well thought-out, composed and produced. Numbers are varied, it rocks nicely, there's some blues guitar here and there like on the title track, but it's not tedious." *Rolling Stone* called it "the group's most comprehensively enjoyable record in ages," adding, "*Street Corner Talking* marks the rebirth of Savoy Brown. The personnel changes that brought the present group together is [sic] also responsible for Savoy Brown's new life as a rock band, which looks to be a long and profitable one."

The group made two more U.S. tours in 1971. In February 1972, the band released their seventh LP, *Hellbound Train*, again produced by Neil Slaven. Although not one of their better albums, *Hellbound Train* ironically became Savoy Brown's most successful LP by reaching #34 on the U.S. charts. *Rolling Stone* offered faint approval, describing the release as "a modest success by a pleasant-sounding band. This is a safe, low-keyed, enjoyable record through a side and a half. Then comes the title tune, an extended impressionistic piece. It tries to be dark, but it just gets murky."

The band toured Britain with Chicken Shack before starting their eighth U.S. tour in late February. In June 1972, Silvester left to replace Pyle in Juicy Lucy. Pyle in turn replaced Silvester in Savoy Brown. The lineup, thus revised, recorded a concert in the summer of 1972 in Central Park that was voted the best of New York's 1972 concert series by the *Village Voice*. The show was released in 1989 as *Live in Central Park*, a confident-sounding rock album showcasing four songs from their forthcoming *Lion's Share* project, along with "Tell Mama" and "Shot in the Head" from *Street Corner Talking*.

By the time *Lion's Share* was released in November 1972, Walker had left to join Fleetwood Mac for what mostly would be a short and unhappy stay. Savoy Brown replaced him with veteran musician Jackie Lynton. *Lion's Share* contained some memorable tracks, particularly "Shot in the Head," written by former Easybeats members Harry Vanda and George Young, and Kim's "Second Try," an excellent rocker. *Lions Share* just scraped the U.S. charts, reaching #151.

Postscript

Kim Simmonds continued to record and tour under the name Savoy Brown, releasing *Jack the Toad*

(1973, U.S. #84), *Boogie Brothers* with Stan Webb and Miller Anderson (1974, U.S. #101), *Wire Fire* (1975, U.S. #153), *Skin 'n' Bone* (1976), and *Savage Return* (1978). By 1979, Kim had moved to the U.S., where he continued to release records as Savoy Brown, including *Just Live* (1981, German, recorded in 1970), *Greatest Hits—Live in Concert* (1981), *Rock'n'Roll Warriors* (1981), *Slow Train* (1986), *Make Me Sweat* (1987), *Kings of Boogie* (1989, German), *Live 'n' Kicking* (1990, German), *Let It Ride* (1992), *Bring It Home* (1995), the solo acoustic *Solitaire* (1998) and *The Blues Keep Me Holding On* (1999). In 2000, Simmonds issued a second solo acoustic CD, *Blues Like Midnight*.

Chris Youlden recorded two solo albums, *Nowhere Road* (1973) and *City Child* (1974), then left the music business to return to school. He issued *Second Sight* in 1991.

Dave Walker stayed with Fleetwood Mac long enough to record *Penguin*. He joined Black Sabbath in 1978, staying for only a few months. He rejoined Savoy Brown in January 1987 and stayed through October 1991.

Jackie Lynton formed Jackie Lynton's Grande, which released one album. A second album was released in 1980 under the name of the Jackie Lynton Band.

Andy Pyle rejoined Blodwyn Pig and later was a member of the Kinks (from November 1976 to April 1978). He also played with Alvin Lee and Wishbone Ash.

Berg and Pyle again teamed up on the Alvin Lee album *Pump Iron* in 1975. Their next project together was a band they formed in 1978 called Network, which also included ex-Kink John Gosling.

Paul Raymond went on to join UFO and their spin-off, the Michael Schenker Group.

Discography

Release Date	Title	Catalog Number

U.S. Singles

1968	Shake 'Em on Down (Part 1)/ Shake 'Em on Down (Part 2)	Parrot 40034
1969	Grits Ain't Groceries/She's Got a Ring in His Nose and a Ring on Her Hand	Parrot 40037
1969	Train to Nowhere/Made Up My Mind	Parrot 40039
1969	I'm Tired/Stay with Me Baby	Parrot 40042
1970	A Hard Way to Go/The Incredible Gnome Meets Jaxman	Parrot 40046
1970	Poor Girl/Mr. Hare	Parrot 40057
1970	Sitting and Thinking/That Same Feeling	Parrot 40060
1971	Tell Mama/Rock and Roll on the Radio	Parrot 40066
1972	Coming Down Your Way/ I Can't Find You	Parrot 40075
1972	If I Could See an End/ Lost and Lonely Child	Parrot 45-362

U.S. Albums

1968   *Getting to the Point*   Parrot PAS-71024
Flood in Houston/Stay with Me Baby/Honey Bee/The Incredible Gnome Meets Jaxman/Give Me a Penny/Mr. Downchild/Getting to the Point/Big City Lights/You Need Love

1969   *Blue Matter*   Parrot PAS-71027
Train to Nowhere/Tolling Bells/She's Got a Ring in His Nose and a Ring on Her Hand/Vicksburg Blues/Don't Turn Me from Your Door/May Be Wrong/Louisiana Blues/It Hurts Me Too

1969   *A Step Further*   Parrot PAS-71029
Made Up My Mind/Waiting in the Bamboo Grove/Life's One Act Play/A. I'm Tired, B. Where Am I/Savoy Brown Boogie: Feel So Good-Whole Lotta Shakin' Goin' On-Little Queenie-Purple Haze-Hernando's Hideaway

1969   *Raw Sienna*   Parrot PAS-71036
A Hard Way to Go/That Same Feelin'/Master Hare/Needle and Spoon/A Little More Wine/I'm Crying/Stay While the Night Is Young/Is That So/When I Was a Young Boy

1970   *Lookin' In*   Parrot PAS-71042
Gypsy/Poor Girl/Money Can't Save Your Soul/Sunday Night/Looking In/Take It Easy/Sittin an' Thinking/Leavin' Again/Romanoff

1971   *Street Corner Talking*   Parrot PAS-71047
Tell Mama/Let It Rock (a.k.a. Rock and Roll on the Radio)/I Can't Get Next to You/Time Does Tell/Street Corner Talking/All I Can Do/Wang Dang Doodle

1972   *Hellbound Train*   Parrot PAS-71052
Doin' Fine/Lost and Lonely Child/I'll Make Everything Alright/Troubled by These Days and Times/If I Could See an End/I'll Make You Happy/Hellbound Train

1972   *Lion's Share*   Parrot PAS-71057
Shot in the Head/Second Try/The Saddest Feeling/I Can't Find You/Howling for My Darling/So Tired/Denim Demon/Love Me Please/I Hate to See You Go

1989   *Live in Central Park* (CD)   Relix RRCD 2014
Recorded in 1972.
Let It Rock/Shot in the Head/The Saddest Feeling/Can't Find You/Tell Mama/Love Me Please/Hip Shake

Miscellaneous U.S. Releases

1968   *An Anthology of British Blues Volume II*   Immediate 52014
Includes "I Can't Quit You Baby" and "True Blue."

1973   *History of British Blues*   Sire 3701
Includes "True Blue."

U.K. Singles

1966	I Tried/I Can't Quit You Baby	Purdah 3503
1967	Taste and Try, Before You Buy/ Someday People	Decca F 12702
1968	Walking by Myself/Vicksburg Blues	Decca F 12797
1969	I'm Tired/Stay with Me Baby	Decca F 12978
1969	Train to Nowhere/Tolling Bells	Decca F 12843
1970	A Hard Way to Go/Waiting in the Bamboo Grove	Decca F 13019
1970	Poor Girl/Master Hare	Decca F 13098
1971	Tell Mama/Let It Rock	Decca F 13247

U.K. Albums

1967   *Shake Down*   Decca LK-4883 (M)
                        Decca SKL-4883 (S)
Ain't Superstitious/Let Me Love You Baby/Black Night/High Rise/Rock Me Baby/I Smell Trouble/Pretty Woman/Little Girl/The Doormouse Rides the Rails/It's All My Fault/Shake 'Em on Down

1968   *Getting to the Point*   Decca LK-4935 (M)
                                 Decca SKL-4935 (S)
1969   *Blue Matter*   Decca LK-4994 (M)
                         Decca SKL-4994 (S)
1969   *A Step Further*   Decca LK-5013 (M)
                            Decca SKL-5013 (S)
1969   *Raw Sienna*   Decca LK-5043 (M)
                        Decca SKL-5043 (S)
1970   *Lookin' In*   Decca SKL-5066
1971   *Street Corner Talking*   Decca TXS-104
1972   *Hellbound Train*   Decca TXS-107
1972   *Lion's Share*   Decca SKL 5152
2000   *Looking from the Outside*   Mooncrest
        Live 1969/1970   CRESTCD051
I'm Tired/Hard Way to Go/A Little More Wine/Savoy Brown Boogie No. 2/I Want You to Love Me/Louisiana Blues/Memory Pain/Leaving Again/Many Can't Save Your Soul/Looking from the Outside

2000   *Jack the Toad—Live '70/'72*   Mooncrest
                                        CRESTCD052
So Tired/Let It Rock/The Saddest Feeling/Jack the Toad/I Hate to See You Go/Love Me Please/Tell Mama/Shake Rattle and Roll/Hellbound Train/All I Can Do

Warren Phillips and the Rockets
1969   *The World of Rock and Roll*   Decca SPA 43
Matchbox/Linda Lou/Blue Jean Boogie/Sweet Little Lucy/Keep a Knockin'/Blue Suede Shoes/High School Confidential/Mean Woman Blues/Money Honey/Whole Lotta Shakin' Goin' On/Be-Bop-A-Lula/Honey Don't/Shake, Rattle and Roll
        Lonesome Dave Peverett: vocals, guitar

Bob Hall: piano
Tone Stevens: bass
Roger Earle: drums

Miscellaneous U.K. Releases

1968   *Blues Anytime*   Immediate
                          IMLP 014
Various artists compilation including "I Tried" and "Cold Blooded Woman."

1968   *Blues Anytime Volume 2*   Immediate
                                    IMLP 015
Various artists compilation including "I Can't Quit You Baby" and "True Blue (True Story)."

Foreign Releases

1981   *Just Live* (German)   Line Records/
                                IMLP 4.001 46J
Recorded live in US 1970.
Poor Girl/Sunday Night/Leavin' Again/It Hurts Me Too/Louisiana Blues/You Gotta Run Me Down/Blue Jean Boogie/Choo-Choo-Ch-Boo-gie/Encore Blues

The Siegel-Schwall Band

While many of their contemporaries looked to Willie Dixon, Little Walter, Muddy Waters and Howlin' Wolf as exotic influences, the Siegel-Schwall Band played and learned from these men day in and day out at Pepper's Lounge, the legendary blues venue located at 43rd and Vincennes in Chicago. "These guys were so kind to us. They really took us under their wing," recalled Corky Siegel in a 2000 interview for *Blues-Rock Explosion.* Ironically, after having honed their sound with such renowned blues masters, another twist of fate brought the Siegel-Schwall Band to the public's attention not for their skillful country-blues, but because of a novel collaboration with renowned Japanese conductor Seiji Ozawa in a project that merged classical and blues music.

Rock'n'rollers Chuck Berry, Little Richard, Fats Domino and Elvis Presley were Corky Siegel's (b. October 24, 1943; Chicago, Illinois) earliest influences. In high school he played tenor saxophone in a group that also included future Siegel-Schwall drummer Russ Chadwick. Attending Roosevelt University in Chicago, Siegel studied classical saxophone and was a member of the University Jazz Big Band along with guitarist Jim Schwall, another university student. Around 1964, Siegel first became interested in blues harmonica and was influenced by such master harpists as Howlin' Wolf, Jimmy Reed and Muddy Waters. Siegel recalled his switch from sax to harp: "I would often tell people that the saxophone kept tearing at my vest pocket when I tried to force it in there and the harmonica fit perfect and I am a practical person so I decided to go for the harmonica instead of sax. In some ways this is true. My first interest in harmonica was evolved from the Bob Dylan recordings and some friends of mine that played harmonica in that style or even a more bluesy style. It just seemed like a cool instrument and the most amazing thing is that you can carry it wherever you go. When I finally heard the real blues guys play it, it blew my mind and I fell in love."

Jim Schwall (b. November 12, 1942; Evanston, Illinois) started playing guitar in high school, influenced by the folk revival of the late 1950s, particularly the Weavers. He later joined bluegrass bands, although he absorbed the music of folk-blues players such as Big Bill Broonzy, Lightnin' Hopkins and Brownie McGhee. As members of the University Jazz Band, Siegel and Schwall were only remotely aware of each other until, sometime in 1964, they became acquainted while sharing an elevator. Schwall's guitar was slung over his back and Siegel asked him if he played blues. Schwall replied that he played a little blues but mostly country and bluegrass and the pair went off to look for a place to jam. They went to a small beatnik coffeehouse off the Harper street strip, where they played together for the first time.

The pair soon began working as a blues duo calling themselves "Corky Siegel and Jim Schwall Two Man Blues Band," with Siegel on harp and Wurlitzer electric piano (with a bass drum and high-hat underneath the piano) and Schwall on amplified acoustic guitar. Remarkably, for two blues novices, one of their first engagements was on Chicago's South Side at Pepper's Lounge. Located at 503 E. 43rd Street, Pepper's was the weekend venue for Muddy Waters. Described by *Sing Out* as "a tough grind for the musicians," Pepper's featured the top blues talent of the day and was no place for untested players.

As Siegel later remarked, "We popped into Pepper's to audition and Johnny Pepper hired us to replace Buddy Guy and Junior Wells, who had just begun to go on the road and had to give up their Thursday spot—that's what Jim Schwall remembers. I think Johnny Pepper took us on because we were so innocent." One of the conditions of their Pepper's gigs was that they use a rhythm section. "He [Johnny Pepper] did not want us to perform as a two-piece group so he hired a bass player and a drummer for us—specifically Bob Anderson and Billy Davenport—so we could be a more normal four-piece group," Siegel said.

As the Thursday-night house band at Pepper's, Siegel-Schwall gained valuable experience backing the artists who dropped by to play. "Every night all these amazing blues masters would come by and sit in: Muddy Waters, Howlin' Wolf, Little Walter, Hound Dog Taylor, Willie Dixon, Otis Spann, and all the young guys too when they were in town like Buddy Guy and Junior Wells and James Cotton, Otis Rush, Johnny Twist." After a while, Jos Davidson (another Roosevelt student) and Russ Chadwick replaced Anderson and Davenport on bass and drums.

In 1966, after playing at Pepper's for a few months, the band got a gig at Big John's on Wells Street, on Chicago's North Side. The group had auditioned against three other acts to fill in for Paul Butterfield while he was on the road. Their first dates at Big John's ran from March 30 to April 3, 1966. This began a long relationship with Big John's and another club in Old Town called Mother Blues. Shortly after they started playing at Big John's, noted blues authority and Vanguard Records producer Sam Charters spotted the band and recognized their potential. He immediately signed them to Vanguard Records, a folk label that had recently started to issue blues records—including the highly successful Charters production *Chicago/The Blues/Today!*, a three-volume series of blues compilations.

During their engagement at Big John's, they also came into contact with another individual who changed the course of their career. Seiji Ozawa, a distinguished conductor who was then the summer-series conductor of the Chicago Symphony Orchestra, was persuaded to see the band's performance at Big John's by his friend, *Sun Times* music critic David Noble. Ozawa was fascinated by the blues band and talked to the group during their breaks. He eventually became a regular visitor when he was in town, exchanging musical ideas with the group and eventually suggesting the joint performance of a composition for blues group and orchestra.

Ozawa was born in Shenyang, China (September 1, 1935) to Japanese parents. He studied Western music as a child, attending the Toho School of Music in Tokyo, where he graduated with a first prize both in composition and conducting. Then in 1959, he took first place at the International Competition of Orchestra Conductors held in Besancon, France, which led to an invitation by Charles Munch, the conductor of the Boston Symphony Orchestra, to attend the Tanglewood Music Center, where he was awarded the Koussevitzky Prize for Outstanding Student Conductor in 1960. By 1961, he had come to the attention of Leonard Bernstein, who appointed him assistant conductor of the New York Philharmonic for the 1961–62 season. Not long after, he became the music director of the Chicago Symphony Orchestra's Ravinia Festival (1964–68) and of the Toronto Symphony (1965–1969). Thus the concept of merging two very divergent forms of music—blues and classical—was a radical idea posing great risk for the ambitious maestro, as all the critical attention would be placed on him. Undaunted, Ozawa pursued the intriguing idea, and his collaboration with Siegel and Schwall reached fruition within two years.

Meanwhile, the band went into the recording studio to record their first album, produced by Charters. The sessions went quickly, as they managed to record all the songs in only one take. Released in 1966, *The Siegel-Schwall Band* consisted of the band's readings of blues standards (such as Jimmy Reed's "Going to New York," Willie Dixon's "Hoochie Coochie Man" and Howlin' Wolf's "Down in the Bottom") alongside their own compositions. The album received a favorable write-up from influential *San Francisco Chronicle* critic Ralph Gleason, who said, "They have excitement and they swing, which is the raison d'être of it all." A review in *Broadside* magazine was similarly complimentary: "In a simple sentence, The Siegel-Schwall Band plays fine Chicago blues."

In mid-1967, the band went to San Francisco and played at the Avalon, sharing bills with the Youngbloods (June 15–18), Quicksilver Messenger Service (July 4) and the Steve Miller Blues Band (July 6–9). Avalon/Family Dog impresario Chet Helms was enthusiastic enough over the Siegel-Schwall Band to offer to manage them. As Siegel later said, "Chet and his people really loved the group. And the group really loved Chet and his people. At the time we were self-managed by my girlfriend and . . . we all agreed to go with Chet." However, legal conflicts with Vanguard forced Helms to terminate his relationship with the group. Siegel explained, "We had an ill-fated contract with Vanguard Records, and Chet and his lawyer, Brian

Rohan, were not able to resolve anything with Vanguard and this inevitably tied their hands . . . this took the wind out of the Family Dog sails regarding the high hopes they had for Siegel-Schwall and we were on our own again."

The band also appeared at the Newport Folk festival on July 16, 1967. Around this time, their second album, *Say Siegel-Schwall*, was released. By now, Davidson had left the band and had been replaced by Jack Dawson on bass. Highlights of the album included "Bring It with You When You Come," featuring some fine mandolin work by Schwall, as well as "Slow Blues in A" and "That's Why I Treat My Baby So Fine." Unfortunately, the release escaped commercial and critical notice.

Toward the end of the year, the group also played on the East Coast, appearing at the Bitter End and the Scene in New York City. Their Bitter End appearance received sharply contrasting reviews from the trade magazines. *Cashbox* effused, "If you do like Blues, the Siegel-Schwall Blues Band serves up some of the best that you're likely to find around town." However, *Variety* condemned them, observing that they had "nothing significant to add to the blues genre" and further advising them to "abandon [their] current direction . . . [and] develop contemporary pop sounds."

Their third effort, *Shake!*, was released in 1968. Distinguished jazz and blues critic Pete Welding reviewed the album in *Rolling Stone,* allowing that the quartet was "tight, together and, as a rule, unambitiously successful."

Meanwhile, jazz trombonist William Russo, a composer and arranger with Stan Kenton, was commissioned by the Illinois Arts Council to work closely with Siegel to write the blues/classical symphony score for the project with Ozawa. The finished product, "Three Pieces for Blues Band and Symphony Orchestra," provided a score for the symphony orchestra while allowing the Siegel-Schwall Band the freedom to improvise.

The 1968 premier of "Three Pieces for Blues Band and Symphony Orchestra," performed by Siegel-Schwall and the Chicago Symphony Orchestra under the wand of Seiji Ozawa, met with tremendous acclaim. *The Chicago Tribune* singled out Siegel, observing, "When [he] cupped his harmonica and the pavilion microphone together and began a half saxophone half blues trumpet wail, even the least conservative Chicago Symphony Orchestra member might have shivered at the hand-writing on the crumbling walls." *The Chicago Sun Times* said, "The work was a clear success, a result due in no small part to the excellence of the Siegel-Schwall group. Ozawa plainly was delighted with the work and with good reason. It moves, it has something to say, and it was exciting to hear."

Following the Chicago performance of "Three Pieces," the Siegel-Schwall Band temporarily disbanded. Schwall joined friends Jim and Kathy Post as a backing musician. The Posts performed under the name Friend and Lover, and had just put out a hit single, "Reach Out of the Darkness."

Siegel continued to perform "Three Pieces," appearing next with the New York Philharmonic at Lincoln Center on October 9, 1969. Guest conductor Seiji Ozawa led the orchestra while Siegel utilized an interim band with very young musicians who nonetheless gave a tremendous performance. Siegel again received rave reviews in the press. *The New York Times* critic Harold Schonberg described the work as "a fun piece on the whole, not very original, not particularly imaginative, but clear in outline and energetic in substance. At first the audience seemed to be amused. But when it was all over, cheers rang through Philharmonic Hall. The audience did not merely like it, the audience loved it." *Hi Fidelity* exclaimed, "Through sheer virtuosity and genuine feeling, Siegel soon silenced his opposition." According to the liner notes for the album that was released of a later performance, the then-president of the symphony has been credited with saying, "[It was] the longest and most intense standing ovation I have ever seen in Lincoln Center," adding that the only time he had heard a reaction that strong anywhere was after a performance given by Caruso.

Following the New York Philharmonic performance, Siegel formed another interim band to accompany him on future performances. The lineup consisted of Jim McCarty (of Mitch Ryder's Detroit Wheels), drummer Sam Lay (formerly with Paul Butterfield [see **Paul Butterfield**]) and bassist John Sauter.

In 1970, Seiji Ozawa became the artistic director of the Boston Symphony Orchestra and brought "Three Pieces" to Tanglewood. The performance received an impressive review from *Downbeat* magazine, which observed, "Corky Siegel's band delighted Tanglewood audiences [when] playing 'Three Pieces' under Seiji Ozawa's baton. The entire Boston Symphony served as side-men."

Schwall rejoined Siegel in December 1969 with the reformed band retaining Lay on drums and Sauter on bass. However, the lineup was short-lived, as Shelly Plotkin replaced Lay and Al Radford replaced Sauter. Although the group occasionally ventured to distant towns around the country, including San Francisco, they decided to keep most of their gigs within 250 miles of Chicago so they could return home the day after an engagement.

They recorded their final release for Vanguard, *Siegel-Schwall '70*, at Paragon Studios in Chicago, except for two tracks recorded live: "Angel Food Cake" and "A Sunshine Day in My Mind." The two live tracks captured an energy and intensity only hinted at on their studio sides and were the record's standout cuts.

While Charters produced their previous efforts, this release was produced by Bill Traut. The band's relationship with Vanguard had been rocky; clashes between the musicians on one side and producer Charters and label co-owner Maynard Solomon on the other ultimately caused the group to cease recording. The situation was finally resolved when Traut prevailed on Solomon to allow Siegel-Schwall to record the final album in their contract under his production. On the surface, Traut seemed like an unlikely choice. He was best known as a producer of garage rock, with credits including the Shadows of Knight, the Nazz, H.P. Lovecraft and the American Breed. However, Traut was a friend of the band, and their next venture would be with a new label that he cofounded.

The group continued to land outstanding press coverage while between contracts. A *Billboard* critique of the group's performance at the Fillmore West on March 13, 1971, dubbed the band, "One of the best visual acts in America."

The group next signed with Wooden Nickel Records, a new label founded by Bill Traut, Jim Golden and Jerry Weintraub, with manufacturing and marketing to be provided by RCA Records. Their first release for the label, issued in 1971, bore the same title as their first album of five years earlier: *The Siegel-Schwall Band*. Coproduced by Bill Traut and Peter Szillies, the album was recorded at RCA's Mid American Recording Center and at the Quiet Knight nightclub, both in Chicago. The set was highlighted by a 10-minute live version of Jimmy Reed's "Hush, Hush" and received positive critical notice. *Beat Instrumental* said, "Unlike most contemporary blues bands, they have resisted the temptation to become self-indulgent. Each track is allowed to have its own individual appeal." *Billboard* simply called it "an excellent album," adding, "It should be the biggest seller ever for the group."

Seiji Ozawa became Music Director of the San Francisco Symphony in 1970 and in 1971 invited Siegel-Schwall to join the orchestra for three performances of "Three Pieces" (with a fourth added due to demand). The performances again received widespread critical praise. *The Oakland Tribune* reported, "The audience at the opera house gave one of the most enthusiastic ovations we can ever recall on this side of the Atlantic, as Seiji Ozawa and the Corky Siegel Band introduced the color 'blues' to the palette of the San Francisco Symphony." *The San Francisco Chronicle* was equally enraptured: "The crowd went wild. Unquestionably Siegel was the star making the mouth organ sing, talk, howl and cry. It was improvisation with a flare."

One of the performances was documented by the Deutsche Grammophon label, which released "Three Pieces" on one side of an album issued in 1973. The LP reached #105 on the *Billboard* album charts. An extract from the performance, "Blues Band, Opus 50, Part 1," was even released as a single, which also reached #105 on the charts.

In 1972, the band issued *Sleepy Hollow*, which they had recorded at Paragon Recording Studios in Chicago. It consisted entirely of original material, with its best tracks including "I Wanna Love Ya," written and sung by Rollow Radford and "His Good Time Band."

Postscript

The group's lineup remained intact until 1974, as they continued playing gigs close to home. During this period, they issued *953 West* (1973), the aforementioned *Three Pieces for Blues Band and Orchestra* (1973) and *Last Summer* (1974). Following the release of *Last Summer*, the band broke up, although not before one final album, *R.I.P.* (1975), was released.

Siegel then went solo, issuing *Corky Siegel* on the small Dharma Records label in 1976 and collaborating with William Russo and Seiji Ozawa to produce "Street Music (A Blues Concerto)" in 1979. Performed jointly with the San Francisco Symphony directed by Seiji Ozawa, the performance was issued on the Deutsche Grammophon label.

Siegel led the Corky Siegel Band from 1981 to 1983 and released one album—*Out of the Blue* on Stuff Records (1983)—before going solo again.

In 1987, Siegel-Schwall reunited to help celebrate the fifteenth anniversary of radio station WXRT-FM. The resulting performance was released on Alligator Records as *The Reunion Concert*.

In 1994, Alligator Records issued Corky Siegel's *Chamber Blues,* featuring the artist performing with a classical sting quartet and a tabla player. In his long career, Siegel has since composed and performed works for Arthur Fiedler and the San Francisco Symphony, Chicago's Grant Park Symphony and the National Symphony Orchestra. His credits also include "Continuum," which he composed with Alwin Nikolias.

Corky Siegel's Chamber Blues' most recent recording, *Complementary Colors* (1998), was among *Billboard* magazine's Writers' and Editors' Top Ten Picks for 1998.

Following the breakup of Siegel-Schwall, Schwall formed the Jim Schwall Band. He has since earned a Ph.D. in music and continues to perform while holding down a Professorship of Music at the University of Michigan.

Seiji Ozawa became music adviser to the Boston Symphony Orchestra in 1972; in 1973, he was appointed music director of the orchestra, a position he still holds. His tenure with the Boston Symphony Orchestra is the longest of any musical director currently active with an American orchestra.

The Siegel-Schwall Band continues to perform with a lineup consisting of Siegel, Schwall, Radford and Lay.

Discography

Release Date	Title	Catalog Number
	U.S. Singles	
1971	Always Thinking of You Darling/ Sleepy Hollow	Wooden Nickel 0104
1972	Good Time Band/Hey Billie Jean	Wooden Nickel 0114
	U.S. Albums	
1966	*The Siegel-Schwall Band*	Vanguard VRS-9235 (M) Vanguard VSD-79235 (S)

Down in the Bottom/I Have Had All I Can Take/Boot Hill/When I Get the Time/I've Got to Go Now/Mama-Papa/I'll Be the Man/Little

Babe/Going to New York/Mary/So Glad You're Mine/Hoochie Coochie Man/Break Song

1967 *Say Siegel-Schwall*   Vanguard
                                             VRS-9249 (M)
                                             Vanguard
                                             VSD-79249 (S)

I'm a King Bee/Slow Blues in A/You Don't Love Me/I.S.P.I. Blues (Illinois State Psychiatric Institution)/Bring It with You When You Come/My Baby Thinks I Don't Love Her/That's Why I Treat My Baby So Fine/I Liked It Where We Walked

1968 *Shake!*   Vanguard
                                             VSD-79289

Shake for Me/My Starter Won't Start/Jim Jam/Louise, Louise Blues/Wouldn't Quit You/You Can't Run That Fast/Think/Rain Falling Down/Get Away Man/Yes I Love You

1970 *Siegel-Schwall '70*   Vanguard
                                             VSD-6562

Walk in My Mind/Do You Remember/Geronimo/Angel Food Cake/Song/Tell Me/A Sunshine Day in My Mind/I Don't Want You to Be My Girl

1971 *The Siegel-Schwall Band*   Wooden Nickel
                                             WNS 1002

Wish I Was on a Country Road/Devil/Leavin'/Corrina/I Won't Hold My Breath/Next to You/Hush Hush

1972 *Sleepy Hollow*   Wooden Nickel
                                             WNS 1010

I Wanna Love Ya/Somethin's Wrong/Hollow/Blues for a Lady/His Good Time Band/You Don't Love Me Like That/Sick to My Stomach/Always Thinkin' of You Darlin'/Hey, Billie Jean

1973 *Leonard Bernstein: Symphonic Dances*   Deutsche
      from Westside Story. William Russo: Grammophon
      Three Pieces for Blues Band   2530309
      (Siegel-Schwall Band) and Orchestra
Recordings made in 1971.
1st Part/2nd Part/3rd Part

2001 *The Complete Vanguard Recordings*   Vanguard 19092

Disc 1: *The Siegel-Schwall Band*
Howlin' for My Darlin' (previously unreleased)/I've Had All I Can Take (previously unreleased, instrumental)/Down in the Bottom/I Have Had All I Can Take/Boot Hill/When I Get the Time/I've Got to Go Now/Mama-Papa/I'll Be the Man/Little Babe/Going to New York/Mary/So Glad You're Mine/Hoochie Coochie Man/Break Song

Disc 2: *Say Siegel-Schwall*
I'm a King Bee/Slow Blues in A/You Don't Love Me/I.S.P.I. Blues (Illinois State Psychiatric Institution)/Bring It with You When You Come/My Baby Thinks I Don't Love Her/That's Why I Treat My Baby So Fine/I Liked It Where We Walked/Easy Rider (previously unreleased)/I Like the Way You Rock/Don't Want No Woman/Sneaky Pete (previously unreleased, take 2)

Disc 3: *Shake/Siegel Schwall '70*
Shake for Me/My Starter Won't Start/Jim Jam/Louise, Louise Blues/Wouldn't Quit You/You Can't Run That Fast/Think/334-3599/Rain Falling Down/Get Away Man/Yes, I Love You/I Don't Want You to Be My Girl/Do You Remember/Geronimo/Angel Food Cake/Walk in My Mind/Song/Tell Me/A Sunshine Day in My Mind

U.K. Albums

1968 *Shake*   Vanguard
                                  SVRL 19044
1972 *The Siegel-Schwall Band* RCA SF 8246

Ten Years After

Ten Years After emerged from the underground to become one of the top concert attractions in the world. As part of the second British Invasion of the late 1960s, they toured America 28 times between 1967 and 1973. They also notched an impressive five U.S. Top 40 albums, eight U.K. Top 40 albums, a U.S. Top 40 single and a U.K. Top Ten single. They built their reputation through constant touring, increasingly proficient and inventive LPs, and memorable live shows that in turn led to massive album sales, culminating with a half hour of electrifying entertainment at Woodstock that Michael Wadleigh captured in his film adaptation of the concert. His 1970 documentary film, *Woodstock,* provides 11 minutes of Alvin Lee's immaculate guitar-hero posturing as he and the band motored through their hit song, "I'm Going Home."

But the band was not without their critics, many of whom focused their ire on frontman Alvin Lee, whose playing, they complained, was excessive. Alvin Lee and Ten Years After always courted controversy and had a knack for generating resentment from certain quarters in the music world. From their very beginnings in 1967, the members of Ten Years After were mavericks who challenged everything about the music business. They became known for doing such seemingly snobbish and puzzling things as turning down offers to appear on *Top of the Pops,* a U.K. TV show that was an irresistible ticket to instant exposure and disposable fame (even for rock bands), as well as for riling *Rolling Stone* publisher Jan Wenner in an incident that many believe from then on caused the magazine (renowned for its maniacally exacting standards) to turn particularly vicious whenever it reviewed a Ten Years After album.

At their best, Ten Years After offered a high-energy fusion of blues, rock and jazz presented with style and excitement; at their worst, many groused that they were the originators of some of the most indulgent and protracted blues-rock soloing of the 1960s. Addressing the critics' comments directly, Alvin once told *Circus* magazine, "I've read a lot of good things. I've read a lot of bad things. The only conclusion I've ever come to is that I'm not going to please all the people all the time. I know some people are really down on my guitar style. Personally, I'm happy with what I do. I'm still striving. I realize I'm moving in the right direction and the fact that that direction has proved to be a successful one is a matter of chance more than anything else. That is, I mean what I happen to like to play, people happen to like to listen to. That, in a way, is luck."

Alvin Lee (b. December 19, 1944; Nottingham, U.K.) was exposed to the blues at an early age through his parents. His father played the guitar, his mother the ukulele, and both were avid record collectors who introduced Alvin to the blues. At 12, Alvin took up the clarinet, but then moved over to guitar soon after meeting Big Bill Broonzy, whom Alvin's parents had invited to their home for coffee after a concert in Nottingham. Alvin had also just recently heard and been inspired by Lonnie Donegan and skiffle music in general.

"I learnt [how to play] basically from a friend of the family," Alvin said to *Beat Instrumental*. "He taught me the major chords. But I didn't take playing too seriously until I was 16." His early influences included Scotty Moore, Chuck Berry, Lonnie Mack, John Lee Hooker, Muddy Waters and Chet Atkins.

At 13, Alvin joined his first band, Vince Marshall and the Squarecaps. Later, he teamed up with Alan Upton and the Jailbreakers, another local band that used to play at the Palace Cinema in Sandiacre, Nottingham.

In 1960, Alvin answered an ad in a local paper for a band called the Atomites that were looking for a guitar player. After auditioning, Alvin got the job. The drummer for the Atomites was Pete Evans and the bassist was Leo Lyons (b. David William Lyons, November 30, 1943; Mansfield, Nottingham, U.K.) They brought in singer Ivan Harrison, who went by the stage name Ivan Jay, and the band became Ivan Jay and the Jaymen in 1961. As the group evolved, Harrison was replaced by Faron Christie and the group shortened their name to the Jaycats and then the Jaybirds. The Jaybirds played local gigs and gained popularity both at home in Nottingham and abroad.

The group moved to London in 1961, and, according to Lyons, signed with legendary record producer Joe Meek—but nothing came of the relationship. As Lyons recalled in a *Record Mirror* article, "We lasted in London for about one year, by which time, in spite of small success, we found we could no longer stave off poverty and returned to Nottinghamshire. By this time, from five fresh-faced youths there were only three: Alvin, myself and a drummer. The others could not stand the failure."

In June 1962, they secured a residency at the Star Club in Hamburg, Germany, within a week of the Beatles playing the same stage. However, two of the members soon quit, forcing the group to return home to pick up new drummer Dave Quickmire. The band returned to Germany as a trio with Alvin assuming lead vocals. This became a formative time for the Jaybird's sound.

Encouraged by their local success, Alvin and the Jaybirds move to London once again to try to break into the scene. Yet again they met with failure in the big city and the group was forced to return home after nine months where, as one of the top local bands, they were able to get more gigs. In a 1964 article, *The Midland Beat* reported that Alvin was "considered by many [as] the best in the Midlands."

In August 1965, drummer Ric Lee (no relation to Alvin) joined the group. Ric (b. October 20, 1945; Mansfield, Nottingham, U.K.) had been raised listening to big bands and had been influenced by Gene Krupa, Buddy Rich, Louis Bellson and Duke Ellington. He had formerly been a member of a local group, the Mansfields, and had played with them a year before moving to London to work on sessions.

With their new drummer in tow, the threesome gigged all over northern England and in 1966 moved to London for a third time. They then spent six weeks providing the music for the stage production of *Saturday Night and Sunday Morning*.

After the show closed, they backed the pop group the Ivy League on tour until February 1967. Alvin talked about the experience to *Melody Maker:* "We started doing the backing for the Ivy League and I think they were quite an important little event in our careers because we learnt a lot while we were with them. All we had to do was to make noises behind them but it was very boring musically and when we split from them it took about six months to get our own things back again."

Lyons, too, recollected those initial gigs as less than pleasant. "We formed a band in our own right playing the music we wanted to and, of course, starved for four months," he told *Record Mirror.* "We did about four disastrous gigs as a band. No one could dance to what we played and at the time that was the kiss of death. I was supplementing my own earnings doing sessions playing jazz in a restaurant and even worked with a legitimated [sic] dance band. "

The Jaybirds expanded their lineup with the addition of keyboard player Chick Churchill (b. January 2, 1949; Flintshire, Scot.), who had studied classical piano for eight years. Churchill auditioned playing boogie-woogie piano and the rest of the group decided to bring him in as their organist. However, until a Hammond organ could be purchased, Churchill worked for three months in the less auspicious role of band roadie.

Leo Lyons managed the band from 1962–1967, but by the spring of 1967, the group had persuaded Chris Wright to represent them. Wright and his partner, Terry Ellis, had recently formed the Ellis-Wright Agency and were looking to take on new clients.

The band's first major step up came in the form of an audition at London's famed Marquee Club—an audition that turned out to be in front of the club's manager, John Gee. Alvin recalled the significance of the venue to *Melody Maker:* "Of all the clubs in London in those days, the Marquee was the most important. I remember Leo [Lyons] got us an audition there, and we were all very scared of John Gee. He was very strict you know. He'd tell all the bands they had to be in the dressing room a quarter of an hour before they were due on."

About the audition, Gee said, "I was working away in my office when suddenly I heard the strains of Woody Herman's 'Woodchoppers Ball.' Seized with curiosity, I entered the club and there on stage were these four guys obviously having a wild ball. To this day I've never discovered how they came to be there and I've never really bothered to ask. I was wildly excited with their playing and gave them a date at the Marquee."

Their first gig at the club—an intermission set following the Bonzo Dog Band—was on May 27, 1967. Seeking a hipper moniker than the Jaybirds, the group tried out "Blues Trip," but played their first gig at the Marquee as "Blues Yard" before adopting the name "Ten Years After." It was Lyons who found the name Ten Years After from a headline in a newspaper article about the end of conscription in the U.K. (Their second choice was the dreadful "Life Without Mother.")

Around this time, Lyons was invited to join a band that Jimi Hendrix was forming. As Lyons told *Blues-Rock Explosion,* "I was told about the Jimi gig by session player Mike O'Neil. I met Chas [Chandler] and Jimi down at the Cromwellian Club one afternoon and talked with them. They were offering to pay band members $20 per week. This would have been in 1966 when Jimi first came over. At that time I had never seen Jimi play, not that it would have made any difference. I decided that I had put far too much time into my own band and declined the offer."

Ten Years After quickly established a reputation—based largely on Alvin's mastery of the guitar—as one of Britain's leading blues-rock attractions. Their playing earned them a residency at the Marquee in the summer of 1967.

Then came a crucial showcase at the Seventh National Jazz & Blues Festival held at Windsor on August 11–13, 1967, about which *Record Mirror* reported that they "fairly stole the show"—quite an achievement when the likes of Pink Floyd and Zoot Money were further up the bill on the same day. A *Melody Maker* review of a performance in the October 6, 1967, issue was glowing: "Ten Years After are currently drawing huge applause and crowds at London's Marquee club on Friday nights and it is not difficult to see why . . . Here is hard blues in any language, played with skill and feeling."

Even with all the media attention and their surprise success at the Marquee, the group still managed to fail their initial audition for Decca. But three months later, the label offered them a recording contract on its subsidiary, Deram. Mike Vernon produced their self-titled first album, and Deram released it on October 27, 1967. Recorded over two days, the album showcased the band's live repertoire and included cover versions of such Chicago classics as Willie Dixon's "Spoonful" along with Alvin Lee originals. Highlights included "I Can't Keep from Crying Sometimes" and the ten-minute jam, "Help Me."

The album didn't sell right away, reportedly because in its first week of release, all pressings were accidentally shipped to Glasgow. However, promotional copies found their way to critics who were almost uniformly enthusiastic. A reviewer for *New Musical Express* remarked, "Their instrumental work is very absorbing and imaginative," and *Disc and Music Echo* found it "an impressive 'first' and a nice record to have around."

While the album effectively recreated the style of the Chess masters, the group didn't want to be pigeonholed as mere clones. As Alvin explained to *Melody Maker,* "We don't want to do a pure blues scene. We are aiming at a wider range of music. We have already had a few knocks from the purists. Not first-hand knocks, but rumors have reached us that we are not playing pure blues, and we are only pretending."

While it was unusual for an album to be released before a group had achieved some success with a single, the label still applied pressure on the group to produce a commercial-friendly 45. As Alvin explained to *Melody Maker*, "Getting a hit is something I have always been a bit unsure about. But I would like one now, as it is another medium to have a go at. I read in the MM [*Melody Maker*] that Eric Clapton doesn't want to make singles, but I think it is a challenge to try and do something in a three minute form."

Their first single, "Portable People," came out in February 1968, the same month they made their first appearance in Scandinavia. While Scandinavian audiences went wild over them, the single fell short of the mark. *New Musical Express* described the A-side favorably: "It's got a savoury country flavour, a delicious guitar figure and a jaunty rumbling rhythm." However, the melancholy B-side ("The Sounds") was a far more interesting track. Both songs were re-issued on the 1972 compilation LP, *Alvin Lee & Company.*

The first album sold steadily and was being played on the underground stations in San Francisco and New York, where it came to the attention of American concert promoter Bill Graham. He invited the group to perform at the Fillmores East and West during their first American tour. "We were all knocked out by that," Alvin told *Record Mirror* at the time. "We hadn't approached them or anything—the let-ter just arrived out of the blue. And when we got it, our manager framed it, and it's up on the wall of our office now! I think he's even more knocked out than we are."

Alvin also expressed concern that the group might be getting too indulgent on stage. "Another thing that worries me slightly is that I think we might be getting a bit too freaky on stage. Sometimes when we're playing, I go into a guitar solo that lasts about twenty minutes. And though the group's enjoying themselves, we tend to forget about the audience. If they don't understand what's going on, they might get bored—and they sometimes do."

With work on their second studio album still ongoing, their label was adamant in wanting a new album out before the U.S. tour. Lacking enough time to complete the studio effort, the group elected to record a live album for the U.S. market.

As Ric explained to *Beat Instrumental*, "We all know that live recordings can turn out pretty horrible. But we've got to have an LP to take to the States, and the one we're working on at the moment won't be finished in time. It's a complex, progressive album and we don't want to complete it in a panic—so we had to settle for the lesser of two evils, a live record or nothing at all. And it might turn out to be a fantastic record. You can't tell."

For the live album, producer Mike Vernon recorded a concert at Klook's Kleek, West Hampstead, London, on May 14, 1968. Decca and Deram were so pleased with the results that they decided to release the record on both sides of the Atlantic that summer. The album, *Undead,* was a better showcase for Alvin's remarkable dexterity on the fret board, particularly on the instrumental "At the Woodchopper's Ball" and the jazz-tinged "I May Be Wrong, But I Won't Be Wrong Always." The closing number, "I'm Going Home," became the band's signature song.

Undead met with unanimous accolades from the critics. *Melody Maker* called it "a remarkably rewarding 'live' set which should be circulated among all those who find some of the guts and swinging missing from contemporary jazz musicians," and the newspaper further felt that the album was "proof that British groups are achieving maturity." Not to be outdone, *Record Mirror* exclaimed, "'Excitement Unlimited' could easily be the overall title of this splendid LP."

On June 13, 1968, Ten Years After arrived in the U.S. to begin their first tour there, opening in Los Angeles.

The two-month tour included three dates at the Fillmore Auditorium on June 28–30. A bootleg recording of their first night at the Fillmore revealed the band in blazing form, performing "Help Me," "Rock Me Baby," "Spoonful," "I May Be Wrong, But I Won't Be Wrong Always," "No Title," "Summertime into Shantung Cabbage," "Spider in My Web," "Crossroads" and "At the Woodchoppers Ball." However, in what was possibly a fateful misstep, conflict erupted backstage between drummer Ric Lee and *Rolling Stone* publisher Jan Wenner, an argument that some feel adversely impacted future coverage of the band by the influential publication.

Alvin told *Beat Instrumental* about the effects their first American tour had on the group: "This tour was the biggest thing that's happened to us yet. When you know people are really liking the music you play, it's much easier to do justice to yourself. I felt as if I'd been standing still musically for about a year, but America has sparked me off again. I've learnt a lot and I think I've improved a lot in my playing. We've all come back a lot more self-confident about what we're doing."

By now, the fact that Alvin was becoming the focal point of the group was causing some internal strife. As Alvin said to *Record Mirror,* "It started in America where the businesslike publicist we had over there found people were picking up on me and decided to exploit the situation. There was a weird feeling in the band about it at the time and I kept saying, 'It's nothing to do with me, men,' and it really wasn't. Finally we all sat down together and discussed it and it was decided that if it was going to help the band we would let it go, but I've never really liked to think of the band as anything other than a band."

Upon their return home, Ten Years After appeared at the Eighth National Jazz & Blues Festival at Sunbury, Middlesex, on Saturday, August 10, 1968. Also appearing at the three-day festival were the Herd, T. Rex, Marmalade, Traffic, Al Stewart, Joe Cocker, Jethro Tull, Incredible String Band, the Nice, Taste and John Mayall. Even against a backdrop of such daunting players, Ten Years After once again triumphed on stage. *Beat Instrumental* wrote, "Last year's acknowledged heroes of the Festival, held at Windsor, were Ten Years After. They flew back specially from their very successful tour of America and brought the house down—well, the field—with their half-hour spot."

Buoyed by the success of their American tour and successful festival appearances at home, the band became major headliners in Britain. "Since we've returned home it's been tremendous," Alvin told *Record Mirror*. "Every gig has been a full house. We now find people in England will accept the lengthy numbers we like to play. We start our set by doing a set number, you know, and take it right from there as the audience responds. The better the audience, the better we play."

The band recorded their third album, *Stonedhenge*, at Britain's Decca Studios between September 3 and 15, 1968. Later in the month, the group returned to the U.S. for their second American tour, which was extended through December. Alvin explained that with the U.S. market responding so well, they were planning on spending a lot more time there: "We may possibly spend half our time here [in the U.S.] doing two-month gigs," he said.

Ten Years After had by now been labeled the "next big act." On September 27 and 28, 1968, they played at the Fillmore East along with Country Joe and the Fish and Procol Harum. *Billboard* commented, "Perhaps the biggest problem with the underground quintet [Country Joe] was following a superb set by Ten Years After—it was Ten Years After who supplied the evening's real excitement." *Esquire* magazine likewise said that Ten Years After was "by far the most exciting group since Big Brother."

In November 1968, the band released their second single, "I'm Going Home" backed with "Hear Me Calling." While the single did not even chart in the U.S. and Britain, it unexpectedly soared to #1 in France. Alvin's status continued to grow, as did the group's. An article in *Disc and Music Echo* on leading British guitarists (headlined "Britain's New Fab Four") placed Alvin in such illustrious company as Eric Clapton, Peter Green and Stan Webb.

Stonedhenge was released on February 22, 1969. The adventurous LP featured blues-rock boogie with psychedelic influences along with slower blues-based tracks. Alvin explained to *Disc and Music Echo*, "We felt that we had to do something different on this album because otherwise we wouldn't be progressing. And we didn't want to get too much into the blues scene because it's getting so commercial, with so many people just jumping on the bandwagon."

Critics fawned over the album, with *Melody Maker* proclaiming it nothing less than "one of the best albums of 1969," adding, "The group has moved on from blues into an area that is impossible to stick labels on. It's just magnificent music." *Record Mirror* was equally enamored:

"They are more than just a blues group—they represent the current situation in contemporary pop music."

Among the album highlights were a lengthy, spacey, guitar- and organ-driven track called "No Title"; the jam-happy "Hear Me Calling"; the darkly haunting "A Sad Song"; and the slow-building "Going to Try." An outtake from these sessions, "Boogie On," was included in the 1972 compilation *Alvin Lee & Company. Stonedhenge* became the band's first album to appear on the LP charts, shooting to #6 in the U.K., but only climbing to #61 in the U.S.

Riding on the album's success, the band members' individual reputations soared too. In an annual poll published in February, the readers of *Beat Instrumental* voted Alvin Lee at #5, Ric Lee at #18, Leo Lyons at #3 and Chick Churchill at #9 at their instruments for 1968. Fans voted Ten Years After as the eighth best group on stage.

Following a two-month trek across the U.K., Ten Years After kicked off another U.S. tour at New York's Fillmore East on February 28. This tour, the group's third in America, was extended through early May. They became the first British group to have a midweek engagement at the Fillmore East with four sell-out shows. They then began another U.K. tour with a performance at the Royal Albert Hall on May 6.

New Musical Express reviewed the Royal Albert Hall performance, observing, "[Alvin's] high-pitched sound almost broke the eardrum barrier!" and, "'I'm Going Home' gave the voices a chance to pierce the atmosphere and cause thousands of fans to rise to their feet stamping, clapping and whistling. A triumphant return for the group."

However, at a stopover at the Montreux Jazz Festival in Switzerland on June 20, tensions surfaced that spilled over into a backstage argument that fueled press speculation that the band might split up. Ric later told *Beat Instrumental*, "I think Montreux got blown up out of all proportion. We've had these sort of rows before but the difference with this one was that there happened to be a reporter there, that's all. What happened at Montreux sorted things out and it wasn't what it was cracked up to be in the press."

The emotionally charged tour ended on June 28, 1969, with an appearance at the Bath Festival of Blues, a high-profile event that also showcased Fleetwood Mac, John Mayall, Led Zeppelin, Chicken Shack, Savoy Brown, Taste, Blodwyn Pig, Colosseum and Clouds.

Ten Years After returned to the U.S. and appeared at the Newport Jazz Festival on the Fourth of July holiday. Also appearing on the bill were Jeff Beck; Jethro Tull; Roland Kirk; Steve Marcus; and Blood, Sweat and Tears. It was the first and last time that rock acts played at the prestigious jazz festival. Respected jazz critic Leonard Feather condemned Ten Years After's performance: "Ten Years After started out on a truly intriguing, fluent blues kick, but soon degenerated into heavy, distorted monotony." Alvin Lee said of the ill-fated concert, "Shall we say sometimes you get those days when you shouldn't have got up, and that was one of them." He blamed the difficulties on the fact that "the amps broke down and the P.A. system was crummy."

The band continued their tour of American festivals with the Seattle Pop Festival on July 25, the Newport Jazz and Blues Festival in Sunbury on August 8, the Woodstock Festival on August 17 and the Texas International Pop Festival on September 1.

Deram issued the band's fourth album, *Ssssh*, in August 1969. It became their biggest hit yet, reaching #4 in the U.K. and #20 in U.S. While Mike Vernon had produced their first three albums, Alvin had produced this latest release. Ric explained to *Record Mirror* how this album was different from the others: "We've gone on to a more hard rock thing without anyone saying we should. It's just a natural thing which has happened."

The top tracks on the release included the jazz- and psychedelia-accented "Stoned Woman"; the bluesy, hard hitting "I Woke Up This Morning"; and the controversial "Good Morning Little Schoolgirl." The last tune caused quite a stir with the lyric, "I wanna ball you, all night long," which was considered off-color enough for New York radio station WNEW-FM to ban the album from its playlist.

Beat Instrumental claimed that the record was "easily the best album Ten Years After have ever made," and *Disc and Music Echo* called it "absolutely gripping from beginning to end and a fine mixture of everything that's best about TYA—their blues, rock and driving beat, plus the organ of Chick Churchill, and of course Alvin's guitar."

However, *Melody Maker* offered a more cautious assessment, commenting, "[The] main problem seems to be finding good material, or rather distinctive material." And *Rolling Stone* slammed the album, insisting, "Ten Years After has become a practitioner of rock 'mood' music—the kind to be played loudly and not listened to. In its pursuit of a parochial approach to blues rock, and in its formal austerity, any real substance or personality has been avoided . . . Alvin Lee's only distinguishing feature is playing to excess." The reviewer's most cutting comment, "The music, in a peculiar way, is as passionless as Lawrence Welk—more strenuous of course, but equally tepid," caused some to wonder about the magazine's impartiality.

By then, Ten Years After had conquered all fronts except the singles charts. Alvin discussed the dilemma he faced to *Disc and Music Echo:* "There are some great problems in writing a single. It's got to be very short, and you've got to come to the main point within the first minute. It has to be reasonably repetitive and for me this means changing my whole style of writing."

In mid-October, the band began a tour of Europe that included stops in Belgium, Sweden, Germany, Austria and Denmark. In December, Ten Years After and Blodwyn Pig began a joint tour of the U.K. that included two dates at London's Royal Albert Hall. *Melody Maker* offered these comments about the performance: "There are only a handful of rock bands in the world who can generate enough excitement to get the whole of the Albert Hall onto their feet. Ten Years After are one of the select few." *Disc and Music Echo* confirmed the band's success, printing, "Their performance had everyone on their feet chanting 'We Want More' for nearly five minutes."

On February 11, 1970, with their fifth album completed but not yet released, Ten Years After left for another tour of America (their fifth in just two years) that included a show scheduled at the Fillmore East on February 26. When tickets went on sale, the line formed at 6:30 A.M. and by the time the box office closed, $20,000 worth of tickets had been sold, which was announced as record sales for a single day. Two more shows were added.

Ten Years After's next album, *Cricklewood Green,* marked a return to their blues roots. It was another very strong collection with several outstanding tracks, including the driving "Working on the Road," the mystic "50,000 Miles Beneath My Brain," the swinging blues of "Me and My Baby" and a lovely ballad, "Circles." *Melody Maker* called the tracks "heavy satisfying music," judging it "their best album to date." Despite another negative *Rolling Stone* review, *Cricklewood Green* became the band's highest charting American album (#14), while it matched the success of the previous LP in the U.K. (#4).

An edited track from the album, "Love Like a Man" was released as a single. For the British market, Deram paired a shortened version of "Love Like a Man" on the A-side with a seven-minute live version recorded at the Fillmore West on the flip side. Chick Churchill explained the reasons behind this unusual release to *Record Mirror:* "We've had a lot of pressure put on us over the past few years to issue a single, but we didn't want to compromise our own policy and must release the average 3-minute disc. After some thought we decided to issue 'Love Like a Man'. . . However, we wanted to give the people who buy our records value for money and also express what we feel about music. So we decided on using an 8 1/2 minute version of the number which was recorded during a stage performance in America."

"Love Like a Man" hit pay dirt in the U.K. where it made the Top Ten but stalled at #98 in America. *New Musical Express* described the song as "a moody atmospheric disc, with a thumping beat, reverberating guitar sound and an impassioned vocal by composer Alvin Lee . . . [with] a repetitive melody line that's instantly assimilated."

In April 1970, Ten Years After concluded their American tour and began a tour of Germany, followed in May by dates in England and Scotland. By now, the Woodstock movie and triple album had been released, both featuring Alvin's furious performance of "I'm Going Home," which had become one of the festival's highlights. The *Woodstock* release, combined with their recent hit single and increasingly sold-out shows, catapulted the group into superstardom.

Alvin regarded their new status as a mixed blessing. On the one hand very grateful, he nevertheless thought that an emphasis on the highly charged boogie of "I'm Going Home" only depicted a single dimension of what the band did and therefore was not really representative of the complete Ten Years After. He viewed the film as a double-edged sword, telling *Rolling Stone,* "It represented part of us, but that part was blown out of proportion to the other parts. It brought us to the attention of a wider audience; however, that wider audience wasn't particularly the right thing for the concerts. The whole FM underground feeling is one I've always been happy with. To play to the minority audience to me is better than playing to a mass audience that just came for the event."

Alvin's songwriting took on another dimension as he started to experiment with new sounds. He became interested in the music of electronic composer Tod Dockstader, saying to *Circus* magazine, "This is what interests me, the electronic sounds, as opposed to music. It still is music, but it's just taking another step. It could be the wrong direction, I don't know, but I'm interested in finding out. I hope to do a few experimental gigs with it and see what happens."

In June, the group began yet another American tour, one that included a performance at the Second Atlanta International Pop Festival in Gainsville, Georgia, on July 4, 1970. Others appearing included Jimi Hendrix, the Allman Brothers, Mountain, Procol Harum, Jethro Tull and the Chambers Brothers.

Following a July appearance at the Fillmore East, *Melody Maker* wrote, "The fuss and commotion that [Ten Years After] are causing is comparable to the Beatles or Stones, partly because they are the most exciting rock-blues band assembled and are four faultless musicians, and partly because of the exuberance and style of Alvin Lee."

The group returned to England in time to play the Isle of Wight Festival—an event that attracted over 600,000 people—on August 29, 1970. One track from their set, "I Can't Keep from Cryin' Sometimes," appeared on the *Isle of Wight and Atlanta* triple set released in 1971. *New Musical Express* commented, "Rarely in recent months have Ten Years After played better than they did on the festival's coldest night."

On September 4, 1970, the group was scheduled to play at what was billed as "Super Concert '70," held on the German island of Fehmarn. Also slated to perform were Jimi Hendrix, Taste, the Kinks, Procol Harum and Canned Heat. Ten Years After were waiting in the hotel, ready to perform, but due to earlier violent fighting in the crowd, the promoter canceled the headline acts.

Ten Years After continued to play in England and on the continent through mid-November, then returned to the U.S. to begin their eighth American tour, which lasted until December 1, 1970.

Their next album, *Watt,* was released at the end of the year to a wave of positive reviews, although it was a disappointment compared to the band's previous material. Perhaps it was the grinding concert schedule, or perhaps it was that they were contractually obligated to provide Deram with a last album, but the record captured the band bereft of ideas and just going through the motions. From a lack-

luster live version of "Sweet Little Sixteen" to some insipid studio tracks, the release clearly lacked unique material, yet the British music press held Ten Years After in such high regard that they continued to offer mostly praise. *Beat Instrumental* called the album "probably the band's best album to date"; *Disc and Music Echo* described it as "nice to listen to and musically sound"; and *New Musical Express* proclaimed that is was "a splendid effort designed to bring joy to their fans as they gather round the log fire digesting the Christmas pud." Only *Record Mirror* complained, "The riffs must be wearing a little thin by now."

Predictably, *Rolling Stone* lambasted the release as an "exceedingly dispensable album" and castigated Alvin as a "blushing apology for a songwriter, a singer and producer." While *Rolling Stone* may finally have been more accurate than other publications in its assessment of the album, such nasty, personalized rhetoric stung Alvin and the group. Fortunately for the band, the review had little impact commercially and the LP reached a respectable #21 on the U.S. charts and #5 in the U.K.

Reacting to the increasing criticism of their work, the band took some time off the road to write new material and change their stage act. Under the headline "TYA Get into a New Bag," Alvin explained the reasons behind the hiatus to *Melody Maker:* "The idea of having three months off was to enable us to look at our music in general and the objective [behind] what we do, and how to go about it. The three months' rest gave us the opportunity to develop new ideas which have sparked off a whole new fire, drawing us together and combining our energies."

The group returned to the road for a month-long tour of Europe beginning February 24. Alvin confessed to *New Musical Express* that his previous statements about their time supposedly spent working on new material were in fact misquotes. "I hope you haven't come here expecting to hear our new bag," the guitarist stated. "We were misquoted—we didn't have the three months off to do a new thing. I spent it getting everything that went before out of my head. I don't know what difference you'll notice."

In early April, the band began another American tour that lasted until mid-May, at which time they began work on their next album, breaking off in August to return to America yet again for their tenth U.S. tour.

The group then embarked on a British tour in mid-September that was a quick sellout. Alvin took the opportunity to lash out at his critics. "We've really enjoyed this current British tour," he told *Disc and Music Echo*. "The audiences here now listen much more attentively—the same as they do in the States. We've been putting more stress on the first part of our act, but we still get the odd freak judging us only on the rock'n'roll we do at the end and saying we're a load of rubbish. I can take criticism but it always seems to be 'The audience liked them but I, the reporter was the only one who really knew how bad they were.'"

Ten Years After's contract with Deram expired after *Watt* and they decided to sign new contracts with Columbia (United States) and Chrysalis (Europe). The first album for the new labels, *A Space in Time*, was released in October 1971 and featured fewer guitar-based pieces in favor of electronics and more reflective material.

The set was well received in the U.K., with *Disc and Music Echo* musing, "There is no getting away from the fact that when it comes to giving us exciting and extremely crisp rock-n-roll, they must be the band to turn to." *Record Mirror* asserted, "The familiar recipe of blues-cum-rock will strike home as rapidly and effectively as have previous albums."

In what had by now become expected, *Rolling Stone* attacked the album, charging, "The original material and arrangements are terribly lame. Vocal melodies and guitar lines are virtually indistinguishable from one song to the next and few arrangements highlight anything besides Alvin Lee and his two, three or four guitar parts."

A Space in Time nonetheless went gold in the U.S. and became the band's most commercially successful album. The LP also included their only Top 40 U.S. single, the atmospheric "I'd Love to Change the World." In the United States, the album reached #17, but in Britain—without the added promotion accruing from a hit single—it only reached #36 on the album charts.

In November 1971, the band started their twelfth American tour that brought them for the first time to New York's Madison Square Garden on November 18, 1971.

The following January, the band went on a tour of selected British universities. Supporting them was Jude, a group led by ex-Procol Harum guitarist Robin Trower. Ten Years After toured Europe in March and early April 1972 and by mid-April had started another North American tour.

In May, Decca released an album titled *Alvin Lee & Company*, which was a compilation of outtakes combined with both sides of their debut single and both sides of the export-only single "Rock Your Mama" backed with "Spider in My Web." This unauthorized release prompted Chrysalis to issue a statement: "We wish it to be known that neither Chrysalis or Ten Years After were in any way involved in the title and packaging of the album and had no controls over its release by Deram, the group's former label."

In late May, the group went on yet another American tour following some dates in Japan. On August 13, the group made their first U.K. appearance since January, when they topped the bill on the third and final day of the Eleventh National Jazz, Blues, Folk and Rock Festival.

Ten Years After returned to their U.S. tour in October in support of their latest release, *Rock & Roll Music to the World*. With the exception of "Choo Choo Mama," which became a concert favorite, the album (U.S. #43, U.K. #27) was another critically disappointing effort.

Postscript

Following the release of their next album, *Recorded Live* (1973), Ten Years After took six months off for solo projects. Alvin issued *On the Road to Freedom* (1972) with American vocalist Mylon LeFevre and some assistance from George Harrison (who used the pseudonym Harry Georgeson) as well as Ron Wood, Steve Winwood and Mick Fleetwood. Churchill issued *You and Me* the same year.

Ten Years After regrouped and issued *Positive Vibrations* (1974) before disbanding, playing their farewell U.K. concert on March 22, 1974, at the Rainbow in London. The group then reunited for a 40-date tour of the U.S. in July and August of 1975.

In 1983, Ten Years After reunited temporarily for the twenty-fifth anniversary of the Marquee Club and a couple of festival concerts. In 1988, they re-formed again for a series of summer festivals and a 1989 album release, *About Time*. In 1997, they toured Brazil and played three rock festivals in Scandinavia. The next year, the group performed at "A Day at the Garden," a three-day music festival held at the same Bethel, New York, site as the original Woodstock Festival. In 1999, they played the festival circuit in Europe and toured the United States.

Alvin Lee has been the group's most visible solo performer and has issued numerous albums, including *In Flight* (1975), *Pump Iron* (1975), *Rocket Fuel* (1978), *Ride On* (1979), *Free Fall* (1980), *Detroit Diesel* (1986), *Zoom* (1992), *1994* (1994, U.S. title: *I Hear You Rockin'*) and *Live in Vienna* (1996).

Churchill eventually went into the publishing business; Lyons became a producer with three albums by UFO to his credit; and Ric Lee worked in the publishing and management fields and joined Chicken Shack in 1979.

Discography

Release Date	Title	Catalog Number

U.S. Singles

1968	Portable People/The Sounds	Deram 85027
1968	I'm Going Home/Hear Me Calling	Deram 85035
1970	Love Like a Man/If You Should Love Me	Deram 7529
1970	I'd Love to Change the World/ Let the Sky Fall	Columbia 45457
1970	Baby, Won't You Let Me Rock 'n' Roll You/Once There Was a Time	Columbia 45530
1972	Choo Choo Mama/You Can't Win Them All	Columbia 45736

U.S. Albums

1968 *Ten Years After* Deram 18009
I Want to Know/I Can't Keep from Crying Sometimes/Adventures of a Young Organ/Spoonful/Losing the Dogs/Feel It for Me/Love Until I Die/Don't Want You Woman/Help Me

1968 *Undead* Deram 18016
I May Be Wrong, But I Won't Be Wrong Always/At the Woodchopper's Ball/Spider in My Web/Summertime into Shantung Cabbage/I'm Going Home

1969 *Stonedhenge* Deram 18021
Going to Try/I Can't Live without Lydia/Woman Trouble/Skoobly-Oobly-Doobob/Hear Me Calling/A Sad Song/Three Blind Mice/No Title/Faro/Speed Kills

1969 *Ssssh* Deram 18029
If You Should Love Me/Good Morning Little Schoolgirl/I Woke Up This Morning/Stoned Woman/The Stomp/Bad Scene/I Don't Know That You Don't Know My Name/Two Time Mama

1970 *Cricklewood Green* Deram 18038
Sugar the Road/Working on the Road/50,000 Miles Beneath My Brain/Year 3,000 Blues/Me and My Baby/Love Like a Man/Circles/As the Sun Still Burns Away

1970 *Watt* Deram 18050
I'm Coming On/My Baby Left Me/Think About the Time/I Said Yeah/The Band with No Name/Gonna Run/She Lies in the Morning/Sweet Little Sixteen

1971 *A Space in Time* Columbia 30801
Once of These Days/Here They Come/I'd Love to Change the World/Over the Hill/Baby, Won't You Let Me Rock 'n' Roll You/Let the Sky Fall/Once There Was a Time/Hard Monkeys/I've Been There Too

1972 *Alvin Lee & Company* Deram 18064
The Sounds/Rock Your Mama/Hold Me Tight/Standing at the Crossroads/Portable People/Boogie On/Spider in My Web (single version)/Hear Me Calling (single version)/I'm Going Home (single version)

1972 *Rock & Roll Music to the World* Columbia 31779
You Give Me Loving/Convention Prevention/Turned-Off TV Blues/Standing at the Station/Choo Choo Mama/You Can't Win Them All/Religion/Tomorrow I'll Be Out of Town/Rock and Roll Music to the World

Miscellaneous U.S. Releases

1970 *Woodstock* (3 LP) Cotillion SD 3-500
Includes "I'm Going Home."

1971 *The First Great Rock Festivals of the Seventies: Isle of Wight and Atlanta* Columbia G3X30805
Recorded at the Isle of Wight/Atlanta Pop Festival. Includes "I Can't Keep from Cryin' Sometimes" from Isle of Wight.

U.K. Singles

1968	Portable People/The Sounds	Deram DM 176
1968	Hear Me Calling/I'm Going Home	Deram DM 221
1970	Love Like a Man (studio)/ Love Like a Man (live)	Deram DM 299
1970	Love Like a Man (studio)/ Love Like a Man (live)	Deram DM 310

U.K. Albums

1968	*Ten Years After*	Deram DML 1015 (M)
		Deram SML 1015 (S)
1968	*Undead*	Deram DML 1023 (M)
		Deram SML 1023 (S)
1969	*Stonedhenge*	Deram DML 1029 (M)
		Deram SML 1029 (S)
1969	*Ssssh*	Deram DML 1052 (M)
		Deram SML 1052 (S)
1970	*Cricklewood Green*	Deram DML 1065 (M)
		Deram SML 1065 (S)

1970	*Watt*	Deram SML 1078
1971	*A Space in Time*	Columbia 30801
1972	*Alvin Lee & Company*	Deram SML 1096
1972	*Rock & Roll Music to the World*	Columbia 31779
2001	*Live at the Fillmore East*	Chrysalis 5332972

Recorded February 27–28, 1970.
Love Like a Man/Good Morning Little Schoolgirl/Working on the Road/The Hobbit/50,000 Miles Beneath My Brain/Medley: Skoobly-oobly-doobob-I Can't Keep from Crying-Sometimes-Extension on One Chord/Help Me/I'm Going Home/Sweet Little 16/Roll Over Beethoven/I Woke Up This Morning/Spoonful

Miscellaneous U.K. Releases

| 1970 | *Woodstock* (3 LP) | Atlantic 2663 001 |
| 1971 | *The First Great Rock Festivals of the Seventies: Isle of Wight and Atlanta* (3 LP) | CBS 66311 |

Foreign Releases

| 1968 | Rock Your Mama/ Spider in My Web (export only) | Deram DM 191 |

Johnny Winter

Johnny Winter (b. John Dawson Winter III; February 23, 1944) has made his mark by consistently delivering highly charged, gutsy blues guitar playing with a minimum of attention-getting embellishments. Although publications such as *Variety*, *Cash Box* and *Rolling Stone* have all at one time or another hailed him as "rock's next superstar," Johnny has always managed to play his own music, at his own pace, to his own appreciative audience.

Winter addressed the superstar hype in a 1971 letter to *Circus* magazine. "I was playing something different than was expected, not worse," he wrote. "I was playing rough, raw, loud country blues—not smooth city or English blues, psychedelic rock or whatever it is. That's what a lot of the public expected from me when they knew I was supposed to be the next superstar. I like my music a lot so I don't think the publicity or hype or whatever you choose to call it was unjustified. I sat on my ass for ten years

because nobody knew who I was so I was glad to have people saying good things about me. The things they said were so good that there was an unbelievable amount of pressure on me to live up to it, but I for one, think I did. Other people decided I should be the next superstar—not me. I just wanted to play good blues, and if by doing that I naturally became the next superstar, then great! The music business could use a few more real ones."

Alan Heineman, writing for *Downbeat*, put that phase of Winter's career in perspective: "Winter is worth hearing. You will be moved and sometimes exhilarated, but you're unlikely to be stunned or to discover anything really new. That's not necessarily a criticism of Winter, merely of the way he's being hyped."

The Texas guitar-slinger remains an enduring, respected talent on the blues scene. In 1988 he became the first white artist inducted into the Blues Foundation's Hall of Fame.

Johnny and his younger brother Edgar (b. December 28, 1946) were both born with albinism, a condition that left them with little or no pigment in their eyes, skin and hair. Because of this, they both had abnormally white skin and hair and poor vision. They were raised in Beaumont, Texas, in a household that provided a nurturing musical environment in which the brothers could blossom. As Johnny explained to *Downbeat*, "We sang regularly because Daddy loved to sing harmony. He sang in a barbershop quartet and in a church choir, so Edgar and I started singing as soon as we were born, almost." In addition to singing, their father played alto saxophone in the local swing band and their mother played classical piano. Johnny took up the clarinet at age five then switched to ukulele, finally settling on the guitar at around age 11. Edgar was even more musically versatile, playing ukulele, guitar, keyboards, electric bass, drums and saxophone by the time he reached high school.

The two brothers formed a duet with both of them singing accompanied by Johnny on the ukulele. At one of their first public performances in a talent contest broadcast on a local television station, they won a watch. They also appeared on the *Don Mahoney and Jeana Claire Show* (a children's television program) and unsuccessfully auditioned for Ted Mack's *Original Amateur Hour* as well.

Because of their albinism, the Winter brothers were often the subjects of schoolyard taunts. "[The] first part of my life was probably the lousiest because I was an albino and the kids in school were really cruel," Johnny told *Hit Parader*. "You can't rationalize with kids. People were rotten to me for no reason except that I had white hair. It really bothered me." At first, he responded to the insults with fistfights, later becoming more involved in his guitar as a means of escape. "I didn't study or anything," he once said in an interview with *Circus* Magazine. "I didn't give a damn. I just played the guitar. Before that, the big thing for acceptance was fighting. If somebody said something I didn't like, I'd fight 'em. I pretty much always won; I had so much hate in me."

Johnny's poor vision made classroom study difficult. "When the teacher would put something on the blackboard, I'd go up real quiet and ask if I could have a copy at my desk, cause I couldn't see," he recalled to *Look* magazine. "But she'd make me get a chair and sit up real close, in everybody's way. It was a drag, you know, because I was just a little kid and pretty sensitive."

In music, however, Johnny found the great equalizer. Although he couldn't drive a car or play sports because of his eyesight, he could play the guitar just fine. "You know the most popular guy is usually the star football player or a big baseball player, and lack of vision kept me from doing all those things," he once said thoughtfully to *Hit Parader*. "My eyesight is 20/200. I can't really see except real close up. But when I got into music, it didn't matter. I've never felt impaired at all."

Johnny grew up on a steady diet of 1950s rock'n'roll, but when he discovered the blues while listening to local disc jockey Clarence Garlow and his *Bon Ton Show* on radio station KJET, he started to acquire blues records and learned how to copy the styles and techniques of the masters. "I loved blues the minute I first heard it," he recalled to *Circus* magazine. "I didn't care who hated it or what, and it wasn't because it was black people's music or anything. I just loved it, loved the sound of it. Blues makes you feel groovy. You hear other people sing and you know they've got the same problems as you. When you sing it yourself, you're letting it all out, telling people how you feel."

Even though he loved the music and was uncommonly gifted with both singing and the guitar, Winter never planned on making the blues his livelihood. "Blues was always a personal thing for me. I never really considered making a living as a blues singer at the time. Nobody was liking it."

He formed his first band, Johnny Macaroni and the Jammers (later just "Johnny and the Jammers"), while in high school. The group featured Edgar on piano and Willard Chamberlan on saxophone. When Johnny was 15, he and his band landed a permanent gig at Tom's Fish Camp, where they performed the hits of the day on Fridays and Saturdays. Around this time, Johnny acquired a fake identification card and started to go to local clubs that played the blues (such as the Ten Acre Club in Cheek, Texas, and the Raven in Beaumont), where he would watch Junior Walker, Bobby "Blue" Bland and B.B. King perform to all-black audiences.

Johnny made his recording debut in 1959, playing guitar on two tracks recorded by the Coastaleers. Later that same year, he entered the Johnny Melody Contest, a local talent show sponsored by radio station KTRM in promotion of the movie *Johnny B. Goode*. Johnny and his group won first place and the contest prize was studio time at Bill Hall's Gulf Coast Recording Studios in Beaumont. "I brought the band in, and we played the two songs I had written, 'School Day Blues' and 'You Know I Love You,'" Winter recalled to *Downbeat*. "We thought it would be just an audition, but Bill said, 'Great. We'll cut it right now.' We cut the whole thing in an hour or two, and it came out a month later on Dart Records. I think it was number eight in Beaumont, which was great for us—it meant that we got a lot of school gigs, and we even started playin' club gigs."

By 1960, at the age of just 16, Johnny had become a session guitarist, often recording in the local Beaumont studio two or three times a week. He approached producer Ken Ritter, who owned the KRCO label, about recording in his own right. They struck a deal and Johnny recorded a pair of singles released on KRCO, the instrumental "Creepy" backed with the ballad "Oh My Darling," and "One Night of Love" backed with "Hey, Hey, Hey," the latter issued as Johnny Winter and the Crystaliers. Since both singles charted locally, Ritter signed Johnny to his newly formed FROLIC label. Johnny issued four singles on FROLIC, including a version of Johnny "Guitar" Watson's "Gangster of Love" backed with "Eternally," a balled featuring Edgar's horn arrangements. "Eternally" was then leased to Atlantic Records, and when paired with Johnny's composition, "You'll Be the Death of Me," it became a Top Ten regional hit in 1962. "'Eternally was a real big hit around Houston, Beaumont, and parts of Louisiana," Johnny recalled. "My price went way up, and I was doin' coliseum shows with the Everly Brothers and Jerry Lee Lewis."

In late 1962, Johnny and his brother went to the Raven to see B.B. King. "There were a few white blues fans about but they hardly ever came to that club, which was in quite a tough neighborhood," B.B. King later told *Melody Maker*. "That night it was crowded . . . 12 or 1300 people, all black. Around about 11 or 11:30, I saw this group of white people coming in and I remember thinking it's the Internal Revenue. 'Doggone it,' I thought, 'what didn't I pay this time?' But one of them came up and asked me if another of his party could sit-in and play. Now I have a policy in clubs; if I'm paid I do the playing, don't let anyone sit-in unless I know they can play. I'll get out of it, you understand, any way I can. So when this fellow came up I didn't jump at the idea. Anyway, they asked again and I thought about it, put myself in his place and thought if they were in a white club and refused to let me play, what would I be thinking? I asked Sonny Freeman, my drummer and bandleader, should we let him play . . . So we agreed to let him play one tune. We put him up and I asked him if he was sure he could play. Well, that was Johnny and he came up and called a blues and he really played well, and the black people gave him a standing ovation." King said that if he was jealous, it was for the standing ovation the crowd never gave him. "So he played another, and I joined him for that. Then I told him: 'If you keep going we'll meet on the road some time.' I can foresee talent, and I think I did that night."

Johnny entered LaMar Technical College in September 1962, only to drop out after one semester. Shelving the books, he went to Chicago in 1963, hoping to play with his idols Muddy Waters and Little Walter. While in the Windy City, he joined the Gents, a group led by former Johnny and the Jammers bassist Dennis Drugan. While he was making good money performing twist music and the hits of the day with the Gents, he still wanted to play blues music. He discovered a blues club on State Street called the Fickle Pickle (operated by Mike Bloomfield [see **Mike Bloomfield**]) and sat in during their Tuesday-night jam sessions. After eight months, he returned to Texas where he recorded one last single for Ritter and the FROLIC label, the Beatles-inspired "Gone for Bad" backed with "I Won't Believe It." For the next few years, Johnny continued to record singles both as a leader and as a sideman for local and regional labels such as Diamond Jim, Todd Records, Goldband, and Jin Records, often using fictitious group names. While three singles were picked up for national distribution on the Todd, Atlantic and MGM labels, none managed to chart nationally.

After awhile, Johnny decided to team up with his brother Edgar, who by then had met an Atlanta-based promoter who wanted to put a band on tour. From the end of 1964 through 1966, Johnny and Edgar toured the southern U.S. The band tried various names, including the Crystaliers, the Black Plague, It and Them, and the Great Believers. The core group consisted of Johnny on vocals and guitar, Edgar on keyboards, bassist Issac Peyton Sweat (b. 1945, Port Arthur, Texas; d. June 23, 1990, Richmond, Texas) and drummer Norman Samaha.

Johnny recalled this phase of his career to *Hit Parader:* "For two years we had an agent in Atlanta, Georgia and we played lounges, the GoGo circuit. We played R&B, ballads and things. You know a drinking type crowd. The response was kind of good; it was what they wanted to hear. But that scene just isn't—well it was just a way for us to stay alive."

Johnny returned to Houston in 1966 and secured an extended engagement at Houston's Act III nightclub. It was around this time that Roy Ames became his manager, promising to get Johnny recorded on Don Robey's label, Duke Records. Founded by Robey in Houston in 1949, Duke (with its sister labels, Peacock and Backbeat) was the most successful black-owned independent label in the South. Its roster included Johnny Ace, who had had three #1 R&B singles on Duke; Bobby Bland, who had also scored three #1 R&B singles for the label; Clarence "Gatemouth" Brown; Little Junior Parker; Roy Head, whose "Treat Her Right" had risen to #2 on both pop and R&B charts for Backbeat Records; and Willie Mae "Big Mama" Thornton, whose "Hound Dog" had spent seven weeks in the #1 spot on the R&B charts.

Ames arranged for a meeting with Robey, who agreed to sign Johnny. However, when Ken Ritter heard about it, he intervened, claiming that Johnny was still under contract to FROLIC—and that he had sold the contract to Bill Hall. After Hall sent Johnny a registered letter to that effect, Robey rescinded his offer.

With the deal with Duke Records scuttled, Ames sought another producer and soon enlisted the services of Huey Meaux. Meaux had produced several national hits, including Barbara Lynn's "You'll Lose a Good Thing," Roy Head's aforementioned "Treat Her Right," and the Sir Douglas Quintet's "She's About a Mover." Meaux produced a pair of singles for Johnny. The first was issued as being by "the Insight," and was a cover of Charles Brown's "Please Come Home for Christmas" (featuring a Johnny and Edgar duet on vocals) backed with James Brown's "Out of Sight." The other was "Leavin' Blues" backed with "Birds Can't Row Boats." "Leavin' Blues" featured Johnny's first recorded use of electric slide guitar and was the most convincing of the Meaux-produced tracks, while "Birds" featured surreal, psychedelic word-play and was perhaps the strangest (but most interesting) of all of Winter's early tracks.

When only two singles were released over a period of two years, Johnny ended his association with Ames and Meaux in 1967. However, a great amount of material had been recorded during his time with the pair, and many songs from this era were eventually released after Johnny gained prominence. To this day, Johnny contends that much of this material was never intended for release.

After breaking off relations with Ames and Meaux, Johnny briefly joined Roy Head's former backup group, the Traits, with whom he issued a single in 1967—a cover of Mose Allison's "Parchman Farm" backed with Lowell Fulsom's "Tramp" on Universal Records. Of more interest was a session Ames set up where Johnny backed Calvin "Loudmouth" Johnson on May 17, 1967. This session showed Johnny in fine form backing the bluesman and was an early indication of the direction his music would soon take.

In April 1968, Winter was persuaded by childhood friend "Uncle" John Turner (a.k.a. "Red" Turner), a drummer, to form a blues-based band. Turner had previously been a member of the soul cover band the New Breed, which later became the Young Lads. Both those bands also featured bassist Tommy Shannon. Shannon once reminisced about a time when Winter sat in with them at a Dallas club called the Fog: "Johnny sat in with the band, and I was blown away, I thought he was beautiful. He came in with long white hair, incredible stage presence. I'd never seen an albino before." Shannon was asked to join on bass, and the trio, which would call themselves "Winter," was complete.

"The whole idea of this group was we weren't going to play for anyone but ourselves," Johnny said to *Hit Parader*. "We had a good combination. They both gave up everything to do it right." But the new group discovered that the public, at the time, had little interest in the blues. "Right away we found out . . . [that we couldn't get] club dates. We started working head joints in the area. You gotta travel, but there are head places where teenagers and groovy people go. For months, we really just starved though."

Johnny found work playing locally at such places as the Love Street Circus and Feelgood Machine Club in Houston, and the Vulcan Gas Company, a nightclub located in Austin where their first gig was opening for Muddy Waters. Johnny signed a contract for an album and a single with Bill Josey, owner of the Austin-based Sonobeat Records. Josey recorded the band over two nights in August 1968 at the Vulcan Gas Company. The band sifted through their set during recording sessions held when the club was closed to the public. A single was issued, "Mean Town Blues" backed with "Rollin' and Tumblin'," and a couple hundred copies of a demo album were pressed to stimulate interest from the bigger labels.

Winter traveled to England because he had heard of the thriving blues scene there. "Edgar and I came over here [England] simply because I'd heard that most of the better blues things were coming out of England," Johnny recalled to *New Musical Express*. "We got really lost and very cold. We were based at Chris Willard's Record Shop, and slept just in one room, mainly on the floor. The only other people we knew over here lived in Bexhill-on-Sea. At the time I didn't have a work permit and so I couldn't play. I had the acetates of the Liberty album [Sonobeat demo album] and played them to quite a few people, including Mike and Richard Vernon."

Mike Vernon was a producer who with his brother, Richard, operated the Blue Horizon label. Blue Horizon had been very successful in the U.K., releasing albums by both American blues artists and homegrown talent, including Fleetwood Mac and Chicken Shack. The Vernon brothers told Johnny that they'd record him for Blue Horizon on his next visit. So Johnny went home and continued working out songs, preparing for his sessions with Vernon.

As it turned out, he was ready to leave for the U.K. again when a highly favorable write-up appeared in *Rolling Stone* magazine, setting in motion a stunning chain of events. The *Rolling Stone* article, "Texas," written by Larry Sepulvado and John Burks, appeared in the December 2, 1968 issue. Covering the Texas music scene, the article noted, "The hottest item outside of Janis Joplin, though, still remains in Texas. If you can imagine a hundred and thirty pound cross-eyed albino with long fleecy hair playing some of the gutsiest fluid blues guitar you have ever heard, then enter Johnny Winter."

The notoriety he received from the article caused Johnny's career to take off like a rocket and completely altered his immediate plans. "I was originally going to come back to England to record an album for their [Mike and Richard Vernon's] Blue Horizon label. But as fate would have it, when I returned to the States it all happened for me. I sometimes wonder what would have happened to me had I come back [to the U.K.]," Johnny said to *New Musical Express*.

The article came to the attention of New York entrepreneur Steve Paul, who headed directly to Texas to try to sign Johnny to a management contract. Paul was the owner of the Scene, a very hip Greenwich Village nightclub. Steve Paul's Scene was a club where the top musicians would stop to meet and play the night away. The jams were legendary and allegedly included the Monkees with Frank Zappa, Janis Joplin with Eric Burdon, Tiny Tim with the Doors, Jimmy Page with Jeff Beck, Jimi Hendrix with B.B. King, and Hendrix with Jim Morrison. The jam with Hendrix and Morrison was taped and eventually became a record. (It's been rumored that Johnny was also a participant in the session, although he was living in Texas when the actual jam took place and claims never to have met Jim Morrison. It is more likely that the McCoys, who were the house band at the Scene and would figure prominently in Johnny's future, may have sat in on the jam session.)

Johnny initially resisted having Paul—a fast-talking New Yorker—as his manager. "I was prejudiced against him—he talked too much, and I told him I didn't want a manager," Johnny later told *Look* magazine. So instead, before signing with Paul, he went to San Francisco at the invitation of Mercury Records, where he cut some demo tracks that included a cover of Robert Johnson's "When You Got a Friend." While in the Bay Area, he sat in with the Quicksilver Messenger Service, Magic Sam, and Big Brother during Janis Joplin's final appearance with the group at the Avalon, and also played a set at the Fillmore during a Tuesday night audition. Still, Paul persisted. "He called me every day man, every day, no matter where I was," Johnny recalled to *Rolling Stone*. "Somehow, he found out where I was. I could be anywhere—a club, a restaurant eating—where nobody in the world would know where I was, and there was a call from Steve Paul. I still don't know how he did it."

Paul persuaded Johnny to come to New York and sent him a free round-trip ticket. Johnny arrived in New York on December 13, and the next day Paul arranged for Johnny to perform at the Fillmore East. Mike Bloomfield introduced him to the crowd, calling him "a great motherfucker." Johnny proceeded to bring the house down. An article appearing in *The New York Times* on January 7 praised Johnny's abilities. "On guitar, he is a fountain of vintage blues. His moves are fast, and his playing is stac-

cato and harsh. He captures the agony of the blues." Winter explained his approach to the newspaper: "I think we're more black and more into simple things than most blues bands. We don't want to make it more modern, we want to make it funkier."

Johnny then played the Fillmore East on January 10–11 with his own trio on the same bill as B.B. King and Terry Reid. He also participated in some jams at the Scene with Stephen Stills and Jimi Hendrix. Interest in Johnny from the record labels intensified.

With label interest high, Paul announced he would accept "sealed bids" from select record companies interested in Johnny's talent. "It was really strange, you know, really strange, because a month ago none of them would have even bothered to listen to me, and all of a sudden, they're offering me thousands of dollars and anything I wanted . . . It was really strange, really weird, for no reason. It makes you realize how much bullshit the whole thing is," Johnny told *Rolling Stone*. Spirited bidding between Columbia Records, RCA and Atlantic ensued, with *Time* magazine reporting in its February 28, 1969, issue that Columbia Records signed Johnny to a five-year contract that could pay him $600,000. While former Columbia Records president Clive Davis states in his biography that the figure was $50,000 per album for six albums over a three-year period, with an additional two-year option for four more albums, the hype accompanying the signing generated tremendous publicity for Johnny.

When reporting on the deal, *Rolling Stone* predicted, "It is expected that Johnny Winter will be 'the next super star' if the hype isn't too heavy." Johnny's increase in stature enabled him to command upwards of $7,500 a night for bookings, while only a few months prior, he was sometimes earning as little as $50 a week playing Texas bars and dance halls.

However, Atlantic was threatening to take legal action. Atlantic vice-president Jerry Wexler stated that Roy Ames held a valid legal contract with Johnny that predated the Columbia signing and that Ames assigned the contract along with enough masters and tapes for two albums to Atlanta. "We have the only valid contract on Johnny Winter," Wexler told *Rolling Stone*. "And therefore any contract which Winter may have entered into with anybody else can have no validity if this contract is good—and we believe that it is." However, the threatened legal maneuvering never took place and Wexler backed out from issuing the masters after Johnny requested that they not be released.

The hype generated from the signing and subsequent press placed considerable pressure on Johnny. "You could feel it just walking out on the stage," he complained to *Rolling Stone*. "I definitely felt pressure from everybody in the business, people who just came to watch, because there was so much shit out on me. We played as good as we could, but we had a lot of problems," Winter admitted. "We just didn't know what we were doing. We'd never played for large groups of people like that; we'd always done club work. We made a lot of mistakes. We started playing with too many amps, using crazy equipment people, and, you know, we had to listen to those people, because we didn't know what we were doing."

For his highly anticipated debut on Columbia, Johnny brought in legendary bassist Willie Dixon and harpman Walter Horton to assist with the recordings. At the same time, Imperial, which had bought the rights to the Sonobeat album, rushed to release the record to capitalize on the publicity surrounding Johnny's performances. The reissued *The Progressive Blues Experiment* made the LP charts on April 12, 1969—one month before the release of the Columbia album. *Rolling Stone* wrote highly of Johnny's performance on the Imperial LP, noting, "There's an urgency and bite to every track, even the ones that don't work. As an electric guitarist, Winter is explosive, fluid, percussive and driving." However, the magazine was critical of his rhythm section: "Winter fights an uphill battle against one of the stiffest, raggediest rhythm sections this side of the Rio Grande."

When *Hit Parader* asked Johnny about this criticism of his band, he responded, "I understand why it is. But we don't have a Cream-type group. It would never work in the first place. I want guys that are primarily following me. I think they're excellent for that."

With expectations high for his first Columbia release, *Johnny Winter*, Winter delivered a solid record with several standout tracks, most notably "Be Careful with a Fool," "Mean Mistreater" and "I'm Yours and I'm Hers." However, press reviews were mixed, with *Rolling Stone* actually preferring the demo recordings over the Columbia LP. "It hasn't the looseness, excitement, intensity . . . the real power and urgency of the best stuff on the earlier Sonobeat session. Most of the music on the Columbia set sounds tired, fussy, too worked-over and worried out of any real vitality." *Beat Instrumental* observed, "If anyone ever needed evidence of albino Johnny Winter's prodigious technique on guitar, this album is a good showcase, although his vocals are rather weak." *New Musical Express,* on the other hand, extolled Johnny's "fine voice full of feeling coupled with an often exciting blues guitar." Both albums cracked the U.S. charts, with *The Progressive Blues Experiment* reaching #40 and *Johnny Winter* reaching #24.

To promote the album, Johnny played several major rock festivals across the country during the summer of 1969, starting with the Toronto Pop Festival held during the weekend of June 21–22 at Varsity Stadium and Arena. *Rolling Stone* reported, "Highlights of the festival included appearances by Johnny Winter (who, some said, played one of his finest sets since leaving Houston)." That same weekend, Johnny appeared at Newport '69, held at Devonshire Downs, Northridge, California. The next week, he played at the Denver Pop Festival held on June 27–28 at Mile High Stadium in Denver, Colorado. (The festival was marred by violence). Johnny then performed at two festivals the following week—the two-day Atlanta Pop Festival held at the Atlanta International Speedway on July 4–5 (Johnny played on the first day), and the Newport Jazz Festival held from July 3–6 at Newport, Rhode Island (Johnny played on the last day, as did B.B. King, who joined Johnny during his set). *Downbeat* was not impressed with his Newport performance, complaining, "Winter is a guitarist of limited imagination . . . [his singing is a] parody of the black country blues singers. Some of his chanting sounded like a desperately ill person in a hospital ward."

Johnny continued his rigorous festival tour with stops at the Laurel Pop Festival in Baltimore, the Forest Hills Music Festival, the Atlantic City Pop Festival, the Memphis Blues Festival, and Woodstock, culminating with the Texas International Pop Festival held from August 30 to September 1. One track from Johnny's Sunday-night Woodstock performance, "Mean Town Blues," was released on the CD *Woodstock Diary* and the boxed set *Woodstock: The Twenty-Fifth Anniversary Collection*. His appearance at the Texas International Pop Festival was bootlegged on the Oh Boy label and issued on Thunderbolt as *White Lightning*.

While Johnny's first album for Columbia had to compete for sales against just one other unauthorized album, his second effort on the label, *Second Winter,* had to compete with three unauthorized releases that each contained material recorded years before. The first one, *The Johnny Winter Story*, released in August by GRT Records, contained material recorded for Ken Ritter from about 1961 to 1964. Johnny protested to *Rolling Stone*, "It's early material that they dubbed other musicians on. Some of the cuts—they dubbed in a whole new band—drums, guitars, bass, piano, everything. They had the first track our band had done and cut it way down and cut the second band that they'd done way up. You can hear parts where the old band is in the background and the two drummers are hitting the beat at different times." *Rolling Stone* condemned the release as "an unmitigated abortion, an offal-heap of very early tries for the top 40 . . . that it was released at all is a travesty, and a triumph of the recording industry's undying tradition of greedy entrepreneurship." More albums of older material followed—and have plagued Johnny ever since.

In October 1969, Buddah Records released *First Winter*, a set of tapes acquired from Huey Meaux. A month later, Janus (which was half-owned by GRT) released *About Blues*, made from tracks acquired from former manager Roy Ames. These old recordings hurt Johnny's reputation, and some magazines mistakenly reviewed them as "new products," deceiving Johnny's fans. "Every once in a while someone will come up and say, 'I don't like your new record; it doesn't seem as good as your other one,'" Winter lamented in 1970. "You ask him about it, and you find it's one of these. Most of the tunes weren't even released, weren't even good enough to be put out on local labels." Winter concluded, "It's just bad music."

Second Winter was a three-sided album (the fourth side was blank) recorded in Nashville with his brother Edgar on keyboards and saxophone. A transitional effort mixing rock'n'roll standards with blues-rock numbers, *Second Winter* remains a favorite with many fans. Highlights included a cover of Bob Dylan's "Highway 61 Revisited," "Memory Pain" and "Hustled Down in Texas." *Second Winter* garnered universal critical acclaim and showed that for the moment, Johnny was living up to his hype. *Beat Instrumental* called the album "very strong," adding, "This should please electric blues fans." Meanwhile *Melody Maker* reported, "He is injecting new excitement into the blues while retaining a genuine blues feel . . . B.B. King himself has called Winter 'one of the greatest singers I ever heard.'" *Rolling Stone* applauded the release as a "solid advance over his first set for the label—an unrelenting floodtide of throbbing, burning sound, a work of folk art which captures the tradition of blues and rock from the prehistoric Delta bottleneck sundown moans to the white-hot metal pyrotechnics of today and tomorrow." Released at the end of the year, *Second Winter* reached #55 on the LP charts.

By this time, Winter had decided that his existing rhythm section should be replaced with other musicians. Before touring Europe in May 1970, he met with both Turner and Shannon to discuss their status and, as he told *Rolling Stone*, "We came to the conclusion that we couldn't possibly do anything, couldn't get any further, there was just nowhere we could go except the same way we'd been going, and all of us were tired of that. We'd done it for two years." The group disbanded upon their return from Europe. Johnny went to New York; Shannon and Turner went to San Francisco to start a new group. Shannon eventually joined Stevie Ray Vaughan's Double Trouble.

In search of new players, Steve Paul recommended the McCoys, who were the house band at the Scene. The McCoys were struggling to shed a bubblegum image that was based largely on their 1965 #1 single "Hang On Sloopy." The McCoys consisted of guitarist/vocalist Rick Zehringer (b. August 5, 1947; Celina, Ohio), his brother Randy Zehringer on drums, and bassist Randy Jo Hobbs (b. March 22, 1948, Randolph County, Indiana; d. August 5, 1993, Dayton, Ohio). Hailing from Ohio, the group had been known at various times as the Rick Z Combo, Rick and the Raiders, and the McCoys. They had issued their first single in late 1962 as Rick and the Raiders and by 1965 were performing throughout Ohio. During one gig in Dayton where they opened for the Strangeloves, they were invited to return to New York to record "Hang On Sloopy." The Strangeloves—who were the songwriting and production team of Bob Feldman, Jerry Goldstein and Richard Gottehrer—produced the McCoys' version of "Sloopy." Following its release on the Bang label, the single rose to #1 in the United States. The McCoys' next release, the Little Willie John-penned "Fever," reached #7 later in the year. Several minor hits followed before the group switched to Mercury in 1968, hoping to adopt a more progressive sound. They recorded two highly experimental albums for Mercury, *Infinite McCoys* (1968) and *Human Ball* (1969). Neither generated much interest and the group slipped into obscurity.

To many, the pairing seemed ridiculous. Winter was a heavy guitarist being groomed to become America's next superstar while the McCoys were considered a lightweight band with the pop hit "Sloopy" to their credit. However, Johnny liked the idea. He wanted a band with another frontman to share the spotlight—a situation wherein everybody could contribute something. At the same time, the McCoys were looking for a good guitarist and frontman as well as a way to establish a new, hipper identity. Guitarist Rick Zehringer—who changed his professional name to Derringer for his first collaboration with Johnny—acted as the perfect foil. "It helped both of us," Johnny told *Circus* magazine, "because my spontaneity raised the energy level of what they were doing and their order and planning helped out my spontaneity and gave it some kind of continuity. It just worked very nicely."

For their first album together, the ensemble was billed as Johnny Winter And, which became the title of Johnny's third Columbia release issued in October 1970. The album, an excursion into heavier rock, contained many excellent tracks, most notably Rick Derringer's "Rock and Roll, Hoochie Koo," "Prodigal Son" and the Hendrix-influenced "Guess I'll Go Away." *Sounds* magazine endorsed Johnny's new approach: "This new dimension in Winter's music may have made the difference between Johnny being an expensive hype or one of the world's outstanding rock musicians and fortunately the latter seems to be true." *Rolling Stone* was even more generous when taking note of the new lineup: "The soul of the album is the interplay between Johnny Winter and Rick Derringer . . . Together, they sound like Hendrix playing behind Clapton. In fact, the album will remind you of the best moments of early Hendrix and early Cream." Others, however, argued that there was little variety from song to song. Johnny responded to the criticism to the *The Los Angeles Free Press:* "That's true; it does sound a lot the same. That's why we're trying to change it around a little bit. I'm still trying man; give me a chance. I'm still learning stuff. You're limited when you're playing blues. We're working on it." The LP stalled at #154 on the album charts.

Health problems caused drummer Randy Zehringer to drop out of the band, and Johnny replaced him with Bobby Caldwell, who broke up his own group, Noah's Ark, to join. The band toured extensively, including embarking on a British tour through January and February 1971. In April, Columbia released a live album—*Johnny Winter And Live*—that was recorded at Bill Graham's Fillmore East in New York and Pirate's World in Dania, Florida. *Johnny Winter And Live* was a powerful recording highlighted by some incredible guitar interplay between Johnny and Derringer on "Mean Town Blues" and the bluesy, slow burning "It's My Own Fault," as well as in the raucous old rock'n'roll standards that made up a medley. The live album sold well, reaching #40 on the album charts.

Postscript

The pressure of constant touring took a toll on Johnny. At the end of 1971, he checked into a hospital to be treated for heroin addiction and suicidal depression. After spending almost a year in rehabilitation, he emerged in 1973 to record what was perhaps his finest album to date, the aptly titled *Still Alive and Well*.

He continued his recording activity into the decade with *Saints and Sinners* (1974), *John Dawson Winter III* (1974), *Captured Live* (1976) and *Together* (with Edgar Winter, 1976).

In addition to his own recording activity, Johnny played on and produced four albums for Muddy Waters, of which the first three won Grammy awards: *Hard Again* (1977), *I'm Ready* (1978), *Muddy "Mississippi" Waters Live* (1979) and *King Bee* (1980). As a result of the collaboration with Waters, Johnny rededicated himself to the blues as reflected in *Nothin' but the Blues* (1977), *White Hot and Blue* (1978) and *Raising Cain* (1980). Still, some purists claimed that Johnny was using Waters to exploit a genre traditionally identified with black Americans. In an interview with the *The Los Angeles Times*, Johnny countered, "I didn't know if people would put down my work with Muddy . . . that attitude of 'Here's just another white guy trying to take advantage of Muddy Waters.' But we got along great . . . he told me he didn't want anyone else producing him. To gain that kind of respect . . . from someone like Muddy . . . is just incredible."

In 1984, after a four-year recording hiatus, Johnny signed with Alligator Records, a Chicago-based independent label for which he made three highly acclaimed albums: *Guitar Slinger* (1984), *Serious Business* (1985) and *3rd Degree* (1986). On *3rd Degree* he reunited with Tommy Shannon and Uncle John Turner.

Subsequent releases—including *Winter of 1988* (1988), *Let Me In* (1991), *Hey Where's Your Brother?* (1992) and *Johnny Winter Live in New York City '97* (1998)—have appeared on different labels.

In 1992, Johnny's version of "Highway 61 Revisited" provided one of the highlights of Bob Dylan's thirtieth anniversary tribute CD and video.

Discography

Release Date	Title	Catalog Number

U.S. Singles

1959	School Day Blues/You Know I Love You[1]	Dart 131
1960	Creepy/Oh My Darling	KRCO 106
1961	One Night of Love/Hey, Hey, Hey[2]	KRCO 107
1962	That's What Love Does/ Shed So Many Tears	Frolic 45-501
1962	Voodoo Twist/Ease My Pain	Frolic 45-503
1963	Gangster of Love/Eternally	Frolic 45-509
1963	Gone for Bad/I Won't Believe It	Frolic 45-512
1963	Broke & Lonely/Crying in My Heart[3]	Diamond Jim 204
1963	Broke & Lonely/Crying in My Heart[3]	Jin Records 174
1963	Roadrunner/The Guy You Left Behind	Todd 1084
1963	Jole Blon/Bring It on Home[4]	Diamond Jim 206
1964	Eternally/You'll Be the Death of Me	Atlantic 2248
1965	Gone for Bad/I Won't Believe It	MGM 13380
1965	Comin' Up Fast (Part 1)/(Part 2)[5]	Cascade 365
1965	Please Come Home for Christmas/ Out of Sight[6]	Cascade 364
1965	Reeling & Rocking/Rocking Pneumonia[7]	Hallway 1206
1966	Leavin' Blues/Birds Can't Row Boats	Pacemaker 243
1967	Parchman Farm/Tramp[8]	Universal 30496
1968	Mean Town Blues/Rollin' and Tumblin'	Sonobeat 107
1969	Gangster of Love/Roadrunner	GRT 9
1969	Forty-Four/Rollin' & Tumblin'	Imperial 66376
1969	I'm Yours and I'm Hers/ I'll Drown in My Tears	Columbia 44900
1969	Johnny B. Goode/I'm Not Sure	Columbia 45058
1970	Out of Sight/Bad News	Buddah 168
1970	Rock and Roll Hootchie Koo/ Twenty-First Century Man	Columbia 45260
1971	Good Morning Little Schoolgirl/ Jumpin' Jack Flash	Columbia 45368

[1] Johnny and the Jammers
[2] Johnny Winter and the Crystaliers
[3] Texas Guitar Slim
[4] The Party Boys
[5] The Great Believers
[6] The Insight
[7] Neal & the Newcomers
[8] With the Traits

U.S. Albums

1968 *The Progressive Blues Experiment*   Sonobeat RS-1002
Rollin' and Tumblin'/Tribute to Muddy/I Got Love if You Want It/Bad Luck and Trouble/Help Me/Mean Town Blues/Broke Down Engine/Black Cat Bone/It's My Own Fault/Forty-Four

1969 *The Progressive Blues Experiment*   Liberty LBR 1001 / Imperial 12431

1969 *Johnny Winter*   Columbia CS-9826
I'm Yours and I'm Hers/Be Careful with a Fool/Dallas/Mean Mistreater/Leland Mississippi Blues/Good Morning Little School Girl/When You Got a Good Friend/I'll Drown in My Tears/Back Door Friend

1969 *The Johnny Winter Story*   GRT 10010
Ease My Heart/That's What Love Does/Crying in My Heart/The Guy You Left Behind/Shed So Many Tears/Creepy/Gangster of Love/Road Runner/Leave My Woman Alone/I Can't Believe You Want to Leave/Broke and Lonely/Oh My Darling/By the Light of the Silvery Moon/Five After Four A.M.

1969 *First Winter*   Buddah BDS-7513
Recordings made between 1960 and 1968 produced by Huey P. Meaux.
Bad News/Leavin' Blues/Take a Chance on My Love/Easy Lovin' Girl/ I Had to Cry/Birds Can't Row Boats/Out of Sight/Coming Up Fast, Part I/ Coming Up Fast Part II/Parchman Farm/Please Come Home for Christmas

1969 *About Blues*   Janus 3008
Parchment Farm/Livin' in the Blues/Leavin' Blues/Thirty-Eight, Twenty-Two, Twenty/Bad News/Kind Hearted Woman/Out of Sight/Low Down Gal of Mine/Going Down Slow/Avocado Green

1969 *Early Times*   Janus 3023
Stay by My Side/I Had to Cry/Kiss Tomorrow Goodbye/Harlem Nocturne Instrumental/Easy Lovin' Girl/Bad News/Spiders of the Mind/My World Turns All Around Her/Take a Chance on My Love/Please Come Home for Christmas

1970 *Before the Storm* (2 LP)   Janus 3056
Parchman Farm/Livin' in the Blues/Leavin' Blues/Thirty-Eight, Twenty-Two, Twenty/Bad News/Kind Hearted Woman/Out of Sight/Low Down Gal of Mine/Going Down Slow/Avocado Green/Stay by My Side/I Had to Cry/Kiss Tomorrow Good Bye/Harlem Nocturne (instrumental)/Easy Lovin' Girl/Spiders of the Mind/My World Turns All Around Her/Take a Chance on My Love/Please Come Home for Christmas

1970 *Second Winter* (2 LP)   Columbia CS-9947
Memory Pain/I'm Not Sure/The Good Love/Slippin' and Slidin'/Miss Ann/Johnny B. Goode/Highway 61 Revisited/I Love Everybody/Hustled Down in Texas/I Hate Everybody/Fast Life Rider

1970 *Johnny Winter And*   Columbia KC-30221
Guess I'll Go Away/Ain't That a Kindness/No Time to Live/Rock and Roll, Hoochie Koo/Am I Here?/Look Up/Prodigal Son/On the Limb/Let the Music Play/Nothin' Left/Funky Music

1971 *Johnny Winter And Live*   Columbia KC-30425
Good Morning Little School Girl/It's My Own Fault/Jumpin' Jack Flash/Rock and Roll Medley: Great Balls of Fire-Long Tall Sally-Whole Lotta Shakin' Goin' On/Mean Town Blues/Johnny B. Goode

1988 *Birds Can't Row Boats* (CD)   Relix RRCD 2034
Don't Drink Whiskey/Suicide Won't Satisfy/Goin' Down Slow/Blue Suede Shoes/I Wonder If I Care/Easy Lovin' Girl/Take My Choice/Coming Up Fast/Living in the Blues/Birds Can't Row Boats/Ice Cube/Gone for Bad/Tramp/The Mistress/Avocado Green

1990 *A Lone Star Kind of Day*   Relix RRCD 2042
Louie, Louie/We Go Back Quite a Ways/Busted in Austin/Ease My Pain/Don't Hide It/You'll Be the Death of Me/Fallin' in Love/Stay by My Side/A Jack Daniel's Kind of Day/Shed So Many Tears/Gangster of Love/Oakie Doakie Stomp/Who Dunnit/Come Back Baby/The Guy You Left Behind/Bad News/Broke and Lonely

1991   *Nightrider* (CD)   Relix RRCD 2045
Hook You/Hello My Lover/Half a Pint/Careful with a Fool/Bad News
(unissued take)/Bad News (issued take)/Bad News (alternate version)/Eternally/Parchman Farm (unissued version)/Voo Doo Twist/I Had
to Cry/Night Ride/Kind Hearted Woman/Leaving Blues (unissued
take)/How Do You Live a Lie/Lost Without You/Rockin' Pneumonia

1997   *Ease My Pain*   Sundazed Records
                                             CD: SC 6071
Ease My Heart/That's What Love Does/Crying in My Heart/The Guy You
Left Behind/Shed So Many Tears/Creepy/Gangster of Love/Road Run-
ner/Leave My Woman (Wife) Alone/I Can't Believe You Want to
Leave/Broke and Lonely/Oh My Darling/By the Light of the Silvery
Moon/Five After Four A.M.

1997   *Livin' in the Blues*   Sundazed Records
                                             CD: SC 6071
Livin' in the Blues/Leavin' Blues/Parchman Farm/Bad News/Birds Can't
Row Boats/The World Turns All Around Her/Take a Chance on My
Love/32-20 Blues/Kindhearted Woman Blues/Going Down Slow/Low
Down Gal of Mine/Out of Sight/I Had to Cry/Avocado Green

Miscellaneous U.S. Releases

1994   *Woodstock: The Twenty-Fifth*   Atlantic 82636-2
        Anniversary Collection (4 CD)
Includes "Mean Town Blues" by Johnny Winter.

1994   *Woodstock Diary*   Atlantic 82634
Contains "Mean Town Blues" by Johnny Winter.

With Calvin "Loudmouth" Johnson
1995   *Blues to the Bone*   Relix RRCD 2054
Recorded May 17, 1967.
Late on Blues/Loudmouth/Lien on Your Body (Mortgage on Your
Soul)/Once I Had a Woman/Take My Choice/Unwelcome in Your
Town/Gangster of Love/Alone in My Bedroom/Hootchie Cootchie
Man/Moth Balls/She's Mine/Dissatisfied Mind/Rock Me Baby

U.K. Singles

1969	I'm Yours and I'm Hers/	CBS 4386
	I'll Drown in My Tears	
1969	Rollin' and Tumblin'/	Liberty LBF 15219
	Bad Luck and Trouble	
1970	Johnny B. Goode/I'm Not Sure	CBS 4795
1970	Rock and Roll, Hoochie Koo/	CBS 5358
	21st Century Man	
1971	Jumping Jack Flash/	CBS 7227
	Good Morning Little School Girl	

U.K. Albums

1969	*Johnny Winter*	CBS 63619
1969	*The Progressive Blues Experiment*	Liberty
		LBL 83240E (M)
		Liberty LBS
		83240E (S)
1970	*Second Winter* (2 LP)	CBS 66231
1970	*First Winter*	Buddah 2359 011
1970	*Johnny Winter And*	CBS 64117
1971	*Johnny Winter And Live*	CBS 64289

1984   *Early Winter*   Target Records
                                             PRCV 116
Ease My Pain/That's What Love Does/Crying in My Heart/Guy You Left
Behind/Shed So Many Tears/Creepy/Gangster of Love/Roadrunner/Leave
My Woman Alone/I Can't Believe You Want to Leave/Broke and
Lonely/Oh My Darling/By the Light of the Silvery Moon/Five After
Four A.M.

1986   *Livin' in the Blues*   Castle SHLP 132
Goin' Down Slow/Kind Hearted Woman/38-20-30 Blues/Low Down
Gal of Mine/Avocado Green/My World Turns Around Her/Coming Up
Fast/Living in the Blues/Bad News/I Had to Cry/Kiss Tomorrow Good-
bye/Parchman Farm/Tramp/Harlem Nocturne

1989   *Five After Four A.M.*   Thunderbolt
                                             THBL 073
Oh My Darling/Five After Four A.M./That's What My Love Does/Shed
So Many Tears/Road Runner/Guy You Left Behind/Gangster of Love/By
the Light of the Silvery Moon/Leave My Woman Alone/I Can't Believe
You Want to Leave

1990   *Living the Blues* (CD)   Thunderbolt
                                             CDTB 083
Coming Up Fast/Living in the Blues/Suicide Won't Satisfy/Easy Loving
Girl/Gone for Bad/Reeling and Rocking/Tramp/Ice Cube/Birds Can't Row
Boats/Blue Suede Shoes/Out of Sight/You'll Be the Death of Me/Night
Ride/Leaving Blues/Ease My Pain/Broke and Lonely/Goin' Down Slow

1991   *Blue Suede Shoes* (CD)   Thunderbolt
                                             CDTB 108
Don't Drink Whiskey/Hook You/Blue Suede Shoes/I Wonder If I Care
as Much/Voodoo Twist/How Do You Live a Lie/Lost Without You/Jole
Blon/Bring It on Home/Hello My Lover/Ice Cube/Rockin' Pneumo-
nia/Gangster of Love/Parchman Farm/Bad News/Bad News (alternate version)/Road Runner

1992   *Jack Daniel's Kind of Day* (CD)   Thunderbolt
                                             CDTB 142
Sloppy Drunk/The Mistress/Careful with a Fool/Shed So Many
Tears/Eternally/Raining Teardrops/Jack Daniel's Kind of Day/Going
Down Slow/Stay by My Side/We Go Back Quite a Ways/Low Down Gal
of Mine/Thirty-Two Twenty Blues/Silvery Moon/I Had to Cry/Gonna
Miss Me When I'm Gone/Crazie Baby

1993   *White Lightning* (CD)   Thunderbolt
                                             CDTB 149
Recorded at the Texas International Pop Festival at the Dallas International Motor Speedway, Lewisville, September 1, 1969.
Introduction/Mean Town Blues/Black Skin Bone/Mean Mistreater/Talk
to Your Daughter/Look Up/I Can Love You Baby

Caveat Emptor
During his relationship with Huey Meaux, Ken Ritter and Roy Ames, Winter recorded several hours of material that was not intended for release.
These unauthorized recordings have surfaced in countless configurations through the years, much to Winter's chagrin. On his official Web
site, Winter wrote in 2000, "You see, there are many people out there who
claim to have some releases of mine, that are, actually, not mine—and it
sickens me to have my name attached to these albums that are a waste
of your time and money because they don't sound good and are just plain
rip-offs!"

The Yardbirds

"**B**old innovators" is the phrase that best describes the legacy of the Yardbirds. While most articles about this fabled group focus on the three legendary lead guitarists who passed through their ranks—Eric Clapton, Jeff Beck and Jimmy Page—the group's music should not be overlooked. The Yardbirds were a revolutionary band and adventure-seekers who seemingly broke new ground with each release. Perhaps due to their unlikely mixture of inspired brilliance and frustrating inconsistency, the Yardbirds were never able to elevate themselves into the stratosphere of pop royalty, despite several hit singles. The members were more often than not frustrated with their lack of publicity (nowadays called "buzz") and at their seeming inability to become the music press's "new pet darlings" or even obtain greater recognition for their individual accomplishments. These issues, combined with their failure to properly handle their business affairs and generate income commensurate with their successes, all led to the group's premature demise. Still, the Yardbirds' legacy was finally recognized with their induction into the Rock and Roll Hall of Fame in 1992.

The Yardbirds' origins can be traced back to the late 1950s with the formation of the Strollers, a band comprised of several schoolboys attending Hampton Grammar School. The lineup included future Yardbird bassist Paul Samwell-Smith (b. May 8, 1943; Twickenham, Middlesex, U.K.) on guitar and drummer Jim McCarty (b. July 25, 1943; Liverpool, Lancashire, U.K.). With the addition of Chet Atkins-devotee Brian Smith (Paul Samwell-Smith's brother) on guitar, the group changed their name to the Country Gentlemen, after Smith's Gretsch Country Gentlemen guitar. Sean Newcome on vocals and Paddy Kirwin on bass rounded out the group. Based in Richmond, just west of London, the Country Gentlemen played locally in pubs and at school dances. Performing mostly rock'n'roll covers of popular artists of the day—such as the Everly Brothers, Buddy Holly, Ricky Nelson, and Cliff Richard and the Shadows—the Country Gentlemen lasted until early 1962 when the members went their own ways following graduation. Samwell-Smith temporarily put down his guitar and went to work for his father as an electrical contractor.

Meanwhile, in late 1962, an R&B group was taking shape in Surbiton, Surrey, featuring two future Yardbirds, Chris Dreja (b. November 11, 1945; Surbiton, Surrey, U.K.) and Tony "Top" Topham (b. July 3, 1947; Southall, Surrey, U.K.). While attending classes at the Hollyfield Road School in Surbiton, the two met and became close friends during their third-year art class. Another musician, guitarist Eric Clapton [see **Eric Clapton**], was also attending the Hollyfield Road School at the time. Dreja and Topham would spend hours listening to Topham's father's blues albums and practicing the songs they heard. Topham and Dreja assembled an R&B group and secured their first public engagement at the Crown Pub in Kingston. After a few changes, the group stabilized somewhat and consisted of Dreja and Topham plus Jamie Langston on guitar, Robin Wayne on drums and sometimes Perry Foster on vocals and harmonica. Together they practiced at Foster's home in Putney, South London, and eventually managed to get a gig during the intermission spot at the Railway Tavern and Hotel in Norbiton near Kingston. Their repertoire consisted mostly of covers of songs associated with Muddy Waters, Jimmy Reed, and others like them. These players stayed together until May 1963, when they merged with members of another local group, the Metropolis Blues Quartet (MBQ).

Formed in late 1962, the MBQ featured Samwell-Smith (who had switched to bass), Keith Relf (b. March 22, 1943, Richmond, Surrey, U.K.; d. May 14, 1976) on vocals and harp, Laurie Gains on guitar and "Bumsie" Lloyd (replaced by Brian Ripley) on drums. Relf, who had attended the Kingston Art College at the same time as Clapton, learned to play guitar—but it was on the harmonica that he really excelled, strongly influenced by bluesmen Little Walters, Jimmy Reed and Cyril Davies [see **Cyril Davies and the R&B All-Stars**]. The MBQ, which played acoustic country blues, had a regular engagement in Kingston on the Jazz Boat and also played frequently at the Railway Tavern and Hotel.

In May 1963, Dreja and Topham joined forces with the MBQ's Relf and Samwell-Smith plus drummer McCarty, whom Samwell-Smith brought to the meeting. McCarty, who had a day job working at a stockbroker's office, had run into Samwell-Smith again after the breakup of the Country Gentlemen. When Samwell-Smith turned him on to the album *Jimmy Reed at Carnegie Hall*, McCarty started to delve deeply into other American blues artists, such as Bo Diddley, Slim Harpo, Howlin' Wolf and Billy Boy Arnold.

The new, revitalized MBQ consisted of Dreja (rhythm guitar), Topham (lead guitar), Samwell-Smith (bass), McCarty (drums) and Relf (harp and vocals). In short order, the new unit decided to change their name, and Relf suggested the "Yardbirds," a term meaning "hobos who hang around railroad yards." The newly christened group practiced at the Railway Hotel, Norbiton, before moving on to the South Western Hotel in Richmond, which became their main rehearsal site. They worked mainly on material gleaned from various American blues albums, including those of Howlin' Wolf, Bo Diddley and Jimmy Reed.

Shortly after the group formed, Relf and Samwell-Smith approached Cyril Davies after one of his gigs and persuaded him to allow the Yardbirds to play the intermission spot for him at the Eel Pie Island Hotel, located on a small island in the River Thames. The band went over well in their first gig, and Davies offered them another the following week at the Railway Hotel in Harrow. Again, the band was well received and the Harrow engagement—within weeks of the group's forming—evolved into a Friday-night residency. This in turn led to a regular gig at Studio 51, Ken Colyer's club on Great Newport Street in central London, where they were often paired with the Downliners Sect [see **Downliners Sect**]. These Studio 51 engagements were sometimes all-nighters, and since the band had only a limited repertoire, they had to extend the length of the songs they knew. The group began to hone their improvisational skills, performing blues material with a much looser, open-ended approach instead of rigidly adhering to a song's structure. This allowed for extended instrumental improvisations that incorporated the radical crescendos of sound (known as "rave-ups") that would become their trademark. A three-minute song might be stretched for up to 20 minutes and, when it worked, the audience would be whipped into a frenzy.

Next, in a stroke of good fortune, the Yardbirds took over the Rolling Stones' Sunday-night residency at the Craw Daddy (also spelled Crawdaddy) Club in Richmond. Largely due to the efforts of local promoter Giorgio Gomelsky, the Craw Daddy Club had become a hotbed of R&B activity. By day the premises were used as a clubhouse by the Rugby Athletic Grounds and served as headquarters for the Richmond Rugby Club and the London Scottish Rugby Club. On Sunday nights, though, this athletic club was transformed into the Craw Daddy Rhythm and Blues Club with a capacity of nearly seven hundred.

The colorful Gomelsky was born in Italy in 1934 and was brought up in France and Switzerland. As a teenager, he became intensely interested in jazz, particularly the bebop he heard on the American Forces Network Radio in Europe. His interest widened to include the blues and films. Around 1954 or 1955, he emigrated to England with the intention of becoming a jazz and film critic. He made a film of the Chris Barber Band performing at the First Richmond Jazz Festival in August 1961, and by mid-1962 was promoting his own Sunday trad jazz concerts in the back room of the Station Hotel. One of the first bands to which he gave a residency was the Confederates, led by Dave Hunt (and featuring future Kinks legend Ray Davies). When Hunt's band gave up the gig in February 1963, the Rolling Stones became the resident band. In June 1963, Gomelsky leased the larger facilities at the Richmond Athletic Club, where he promoted the Sunday night concerts featuring the Stones as house band. The Rolling Stones were packing the joint, but with the release of their first single, "Come On," in June 1963, it became clear that they would soon outgrow the venue, and they gave their last Craw Daddy performance on September 22, 1963.

Gomelsky gave his right-hand man, Hamish Grimes, the assignment of finding a suitable replacement act. Grimes scouted several bands, including Them. Meanwhile, the Yardbirds introduced themselves to Gomelsky and invited him to one of their rehearsals at an upstairs room in the South Western Hotel located across from the Richmond Station. Gomelsky was impressed with their energy and the expressive way they played and offered them the Sunday night residency.

While their Craw Daddy appearances had helped launch the Rolling Stones into stardom, Gomelsky did not have a contract with them, so he lost the band to teenage publicist Andrew Oldham. Determined not to make the same mistake twice, he put the Yardbirds on salary and insisted that they sign a management contract with him. The band played their first gig at the Craw Daddy on September 29, 1963, and suffered their first personnel casualty after just three dates. At 16, Topham was the youngest in the group; his parents had planned for him to attend Epson Art School that autumn. Concerned about the impact a musician's lifestyle would have on their son's studies, they forced him to quit the band.

Topham's replacement, Eric Clapton, joined the Yardbirds after an audition at the band's rehearsal space in the South Western Hotel. His first gig with them was at the Craw Daddy on October 20, 1963. As an acquaintance of Relf's from Kingston Art College, Clapton was a veteran of the Roosters and Casey Jones and the Engineers (which he had been with just briefly when Relf invited him to audition). Clapton was already building a reputation as a formidable guitarist on the blues circuit, and he assimilated the Yardbirds' repertoire quickly, further helping the group establish their reputation. A local newspaper, the *Daily Mail,* reported on a Craw Daddy performance: "What a sound! With kinky fluorescent blue and scarlet light picking them out, the group unleash a throbbing explosion of sound which frequently blasts the electric bulb filaments."

Meanwhile, Gomelsky was also busy in October organizing the American Folk Blues Festival (AFBF) to be held at Fairfield Halls, Croydon. The AFBF was part of a European tour of American blues artists organized by German impresarios Horst Lippman and Fritz Rau. The 1963 tour featured Muddy Waters, Victoria Spivey, Big Joe Williams, Memphis Slim, Lonnie Johnson, Willie Dixon and Sonny Boy Williamson II (Rice Miller). While in Croydon, Lippman and Sonny Boy Williamson went to see the Yardbirds perform at the Star Club. Williamson sat in with the band and was so enthusiastic about their new guitarist that Lippman decided that as soon as the tour was over Williamson would return to England to record and tour with the Yardbirds. Gomelsky convinced Lippman that the Craw Daddy Club would provide the best means of showcasing Williamson supported by the Yardbirds. So on December 7 and 8, 1963, both the Yardbirds' own performance and their set backing up Williamson were recorded at the Craw Daddy. Nine of the tracks recorded with Williamson were released in the U.S. in mid-1966 as *Sonny Boy Williamson and the Yardbirds*; five tracks recorded during the Yardbirds' set were first released on a German label in 1981 as *The First Recordings.*

At the end of the year, Clapton took a two-week vacation to visit his mother in Germany. In his absence, the band decided to continue working and used Roger Pearce, a fine guitarist and Relf's friend, to fill in on lead guitar (Pearce had occasionally sat in with the band). Upon his return, Clapton was surprised and piqued to learn that the band had carried on without him. Pearce became the guitarist for the Grebbels, which began to support the Yardbirds frequently at the Craw Daddy.

In addition to the regular Craw Daddy gig, the band kept busy with a Saturday night residency at the Star Club in Croydon and various other engagements in and around London. The excitement generated by their live performances led directly to their next break—a Thursday-night residency at the Marquee. The Marquee was a jazz-oriented club on Oxford Street that had started to present R&B acts just as the style of music had begun to overtake traditional and modern jazz in popularity. (Long before he considered forming a group himself, Relf had gone to the Marquee to watch Cyril Davies perform.)

The Yardbirds first performed at the Marquee on January 23, 1964. The club moved to a larger venue—90 Wardour Street—on March 13, 1964, and the Yardbirds played the new room's opening night in a show that was also Sonny Boy Williamson's final performance in Britain. The gig took place on a Friday and the Yardbirds switched to a Friday-night residency beginning with this date.

On February 28, 1964, the group appeared at the First Rhythm & Blues Festival, held at the Town Hall in Birmingham, on a bill that also included Sonny Boy Williamson, the Spencer Davis Rhythm and Blues Quartet, and Long John Baldry's Hoochie Coochie Men (with Rod Stewart). The Yardbirds backed Williamson on three songs that were first issued in 1972 on a French various artists LP, *Rock Generation Volume 5.* The Repertoire CD *The Steampacket/The First R&B Festival* also included these tracks plus an additional Williamson/Yardbirds track.

The Yardbirds' first studio recording sessions took place in December 1963 and January 1964 at the R. G. Jones Studio. They recorded three tracks that were intended as demos: Jimmy Reed's "Baby What's Wrong" (which appeared on Sire's *History of British Blues*); John Lee Hooker's "Boom Boom"; and a Relf composition, "Honey in Your Hips." (The last two tracks were mysteriously released as a German and Dutch single in 1966.) Gomelsky hawked the tapes to various record companies and ended up signing the band to EMI.

EMI released the Yardbirds' first single, "I Wish You Would" backed with "A Certain Girl," on the Columbia label in May 1964. "I Wish You Would," first recorded by Billy Boy Arnold in 1955, was uncompromising R&B, while "A Certain Girl" was a cover of Ernie K. Doe's pop-R&B classic accented by a wicked Clapton solo. "We try to vary the styles of numbers—tempo and so on," Clapton told *Melody Maker* a couple of months after the single was issued. "What would we call ourselves? Well, a sort of R&B group, I suppose, when you come down to it."

On August 9, the band was booked to play at the Fourth National Jazz and Blues Festival in Richmond, Surrey. It was their most important gig to date, and disaster struck. Relf, a chronic asthma sufferer, had been ailing all week. On August 7, the Grebbels opened up the Festival and after their set, vocalist Tony Carter (a.k.a. Tony Russell) was dispatched to the Marquee to substitute for Relf. The next night, Relf collapsed and was rushed to a hospital, where he nearly died on the operating table as doctors repaired a collapsed lung. He later recalled the incident to *Record Mirror:* "First thing I remember was being told that I'd never be able to sing again. I just had to get used to the idea of never returning to the group. And of course I had this feeling that I was letting the boys down—though I knew it was just one of those things that couldn't be helped."

The group played at the festival the closing night with Mick O'Neill, lead singer with the Authentics, taking over the vocals. At the end of their set, Georgie Fame, Graham Bond, Ginger Baker and Mike Vernon joined them onstage for a jam session. Following the festival, the band had a two-week tour of Switzerland booked in August that they could not get out of, so they met their commitments using O'Neill on vocals.

Meanwhile, doctors ordered Relf to spend the next three months in strict convalescence as the group contemplated their future. With the status of their lead singer in doubt, the Yardbirds went into the recording studio later that month to lay down the instrumental track for their next single, "Good Morning Little Schoolgirl." After only two weeks, Relf insisted on being released from the hospital to rejoin the group. Concerned with his health, the others pleaded with him not to return so quickly, but Relf was determined. As Samwell-Smith told *Rave* magazine a short time later, "If Keith had not returned we would have packed it in. The Yardbirds without Keith is unthinkable." The band, accompanied by Relf, returned to the studio in September. Relf added the vocals to "Schoolgirl" and the band recorded "I Ain't Got You" for the flip side. While the A-side was generally lackluster, Clapton again distinguished himself on the flip side with his excellent guitar work. The BBC banned the single on the grounds that the lyrics of the A-side were too suggestive, something Relf took exception to. "I don't think they're suggestive at all," he told *Melody Maker.* "And I don't think the record could be banned or anything like that. You can have

an 18-year-old schoolgirl, don't forget." In spite of the ban, the single rose to #44 on the strength of the band's concert performances.

On September 19, 1964, the band embarked on their first package tour that also featured headliner Billy J. Kramer and the Dakotas, Cliff Bennett and the Rebel Rousers, and the Nashville Teens. Relf saw the supporting role as less physically taxing than their normal gigs. "The doctor told me to take it easy for a while, and I shall be able to do so," he told *Disc Weekly.* "A 15-minute stage spot will be less tiring than the long stints we have done." Then, from mid-November through early December, they were part of a package tour headlined by Jerry Lee Lewis.

With one moderately successful single behind them, the Yardbirds needed to score a hit. Returning to the studio sometime in November to take part in a session produced by Manfred Mann, the band was offered a Paul Jones composition, "The One in the Middle." Declining to record the song, the group instead elected to record a Major Lance B-side called, "Sweet Music," with Paul Jones providing backup vocals. The soft soul number was totally unsuitable for the band and was not issued as a single (although it did appear on the American compilation album *For Your Love*).

Since their first two singles had failed to capture the excitement of their concert performances, the band decided that their debut LP would be recorded live at the Marquee. Recorded in March 1964, *Five Live Yardbirds* consisted entirely of covers of songs from American black artists (such as Chuck Berry's "Too Much Monkey Business," the Isley Brothers' "Respectable," Howlin' Wolf's "Smokestack Lightning," John Lee Hooker's "Louise" and Slim Harpo's "I Got Love if You Want It"). *Five Live Yardbirds* has since been recognized as a seminal live album. Lester Bangs, writing for *Rolling Stone,* called it "without a doubt one of the four or five most exciting rock concerts ever recorded." He continued, "The early Yardbirds were loose and raw and played with a breathtaking natural energy that has never been matched by any of their progeny." Looking back from 1973, Relf commented, "It had the feel of the Yardbirds' sweaty nights in the club packed to the brink. Exciting days." Released in December 1964, the album did not make the British charts, but it established their reputation as an up-and-coming band.

The Yardbirds closed out the year by appearing as the opening act on the Beatles' Christmas concerts held at London's Hammersmith Odeon Cinema. The Christmas shows were held from December 24 to January 16 and featured Freddie and the Dreamers, Sounds Incorporated, and Elkie Brooks in addition to the Fab Four. It was during these shows that a publisher named Ronnie Beck approached the Yardbirds. Beck had a demo of "For Your Love," a tune penned by an unknown Manchester songwriter named Graham Gouldman. As a teenager, Gouldman had spent three years with a local group called the Whirlwinds. They had released one single for HMV in 1964 before splitting up and reconfiguring as the Mockingbirds. The group was signed to Columbia, which had rejected their demo of "For Your Love" as "too uncommercial." Gouldman later found fame as a member of 10 CC.

While Samwell-Smith immediately saw the potential in "For Your Love," Clapton wanted to record an Otis Redding song, "Your One and Only Man," as the group's next single. Samwell-Smith, whom Gomelsky had designated as "musical director," got his way and supervised the recording of "For Your Love" with the band augmented by Denny Piercy on bongos, Brian Auger on harpsichord, and an unknown bassist. Clapton initially refused to play on the track "For Your Love," then relented, but only to play the blues-based bridge. While "For Your Love" charted new territory for the band, the flip side was a blues instrumental, "Got to Hurry," on which Clapton gave another fine performance. Reaction to the new single was immediate and favorable. *Disc Weekly* declared, "This is definitely the best record the Yardbirds have ever made and . . . a very welcome change." Clapton's reservations aside, "For Your Love" was an innovative, strong single that gave the group the hit they so desperately needed in both the U.S. (#6) and the U.K. (#3).

After the single, the group wasted little time in moving away from their blues foundation. Samwell-Smith explained to *Melody Maker*, "We used the harp[sichord] and bongo because the R&B sound is a bit dated now—it really is. Although on club sessions you still can't beat R&B, which is a lovely, exciting sound. I love the harpsichord sound, though."

Meanwhile, Relf told *Record Mirror,* "We're getting away from the old twelve-bar bit and doing other things. We may include a Dylan number and more pop stuff. . . . We give the public what they want to hear. If they want more pop numbers, we'll play them."

Despite the commercial breakthrough, Clapton was becoming more and more isolated from the rest of the group. He was particularly resentful of Samwell-Smith's growing influence over the choice of material they recorded. The guitarist's dissension had widened with the band's latest single and their apparent willingness to try more commercial forms of music. In March 1965, Clapton announced that he was leaving the Yardbirds. "They are going too commercial," he complained to *Melody Maker*. Relf shot back, "He [Clapton] loves the blues so much I suppose he did not like it being played badly by a white shower like us."

Clapton's immediate plans were to "take up management of a record shop" and join a new outfit, Mike O'Neill Junior and the Soul Brothers. During his 16-month tenure with the Yardbirds, he had become England's first "guitar hero." It was a reputation he would solidify with his next move, a stint in John Mayall's Bluesbreakers [see **John Mayall**].

Needing to fill the vacant lead guitar slot, the band turned to session guitarist Jimmy Page. Gomelsky told Page that Clapton wasn't willing to "expand," and he asked Page if he would like to join the Yardbirds. Page declined and instead recommended his friend Jeff Beck, a guitarist with the Tridents.

Beck was born on June 24, 1944, in Wallington, Surrey, U.K. As a young man, he learned to play piano, violin and cello, then decided to take up the guitar after having been influenced by American guitar pioneer Les Paul and such rockers as Buddy Holly and Gene Vincent. At 16 he joined a local band, the Deltones, which mostly covered songs by the Shadows. By 1962, captivated by Chicago blues artists—particularly Buddy Guy, Muddy Waters and Otis Rush—Beck founded an R&B group, the Nightshift. The Nightshift played at Eel Pie Island and other venues, such as Palais (located in Wimbledon) and the Tolworth Co-Op in Surrey.

The Nightshift recorded two singles, "Stormy Monday Blues" (backed with "That's My Story") and "Corrina Corrina" (backed with "The Lavender Tree"). It's doubtful that Beck played on either of the singles, as they were released after he joined the Yardbirds. Beck found time to appear on other recordings, though, including a single with Screaming Lord Sutch ("Dracula's Daughter" backed with "Come Back Baby," 1962) and a single with Chris Andrews ("Yesterday Man" backed with "Too Bad You Don't Want Me"). The Andrews single reached the Top Three in the U.K. and went to the top of the German singles charts.

In late 1963, while playing with the Nightshift, Beck was approached by Paul Lucas and his brother John. They asked him if he would be interested in becoming part of their R&B band, the Tridents. Beck agreed to join and while with the Tridents played regularly at the 100 Club, Studio 51 and Eel Pie Island. Also, four studio tracks were recorded but not released until two of them appeared on the 1991 boxed set, *Beckology,* that also included a live recording of Bo Diddley's "Nursery Rhyme" cut at Eel Pie Island.

Following up on Page's recommendation, Gomelsky and Grimes went to see the Tridents perform at the 100 Club. After their set, the two approached Beck and declared, "You're gonna be in a top fucking band!" They instructed him to be at the Marquee Club the next day to audition. Beck turned out to be an ideal replacement for Clapton. While Beck was a fine blues guitarist, he was more experimentally inclined, already dabbling in feedback and distortion techniques.

The Yardbirds' first release with Beck was an EP, *Five Yardbirds,* issued in April 1965. The EP consisted of three tracks: an insipid cover of the Vibrations' "My Girl Sloopy" (which would be a #1 U.S. hit when covered by the McCoys as "Hang On Sloopy"), "I'm Not Talking," and "I Ain't Done Wrong." *New Musical Express* reported that the group was also at work on a new LP, *A Yardbird's View of Beat,* which would be "a compendium of rhythm and blues, gospel and spiritual styles." While this set never materialized, many of the tracks they recorded were included in the *Train Kept A-Rollin'* boxed set.

In April, the group appeared on the British TV show *Top of the Pops* to promote "For Your Love." They also linked up with the Kinks, Goldie and the Gingerbreads, the Mickey Finn, and lesser acts for a nationwide U.K. package tour from April 30 to May 20. For a short while, Beck felt the initial going a bit rough as Clapton still had a large following. "Eric was very popular," he told *Beat Instrumental.* "Now I honestly find I can't look directly at audiences. I've got this feeling, you know, that they're all there just waiting for me to make a mistake, so they can stand shouting out to get Eric back in the group." He was compelled during one performance to walk up to the microphone and announce, "Don't be so fucking rude. Don't you read the papers? Eric's left." Nevertheless, he quickly became a crowd favorite, playing the guitar behind his back and using controlled feedback.

Before Beck's arrival, the group had been working on an arrangement of another Gouldman composition, "Heart Full of Soul." The group had recorded a version using a sitar, but the exotic instrument ended up sounding thin and reedy, and the Indian musician couldn't get a handle on the 4/4 meter. However, the versatile Beck was able to emulate the sitar parts effectively on his guitar using a Tonebender fuzz box, and the song became the A-side of their next single. With Ron Prentice as guest on double bass, Samwell-Smith was free to supervise the recording. The flip side, "Steeled Blues," was a blues instrumental featuring Beck's astonishing slide guitar and Relf's harmonica.

Issued in June 1965, "Heart Full of Soul" received immediate critical acclaim and became another Top Ten hit on both sides of the Atlantic (U.S. #9, U.K. #2). Influential *Record Mirror* writer Norman Jopling praised the "tremendously powerful sound that this group generates," further noting, "A smooth, yet powerful beat and some rather interesting lyrics. . . . Great guitar work and, of course, a chart success."

On August 6, the Yardbirds appeared at the Fifth National Jazz & Blues Festival held at the Richmond Athletic Association Grounds at Richmond, U.K. The Yardbirds appeared on Friday, the first night of the three-day festival, and the excited crowds broke through the barriers to mob them on stage. "The reception they received was similar to that which greeted the Stones last year," reported *Beat Instrumental.* "People jumped up and down on the seats that were available; the dancers raved on the grass."

That same month, the group's American label, Epic Records, released a compilation album titled *For Your Love* consisting of both sides of their first three singles; the three tracks included on the *Five Yardbirds* EP; and two innocuous outtakes, "Sweet Music" and "Putty (In Your Hands)"—which poached the melody from Barrett Strong's "Money (That's What I Want)." *For Your Love* only managed to reach #96 on the U.S. LP charts.

To promote their first American album, the Yardbirds set off for the United States at the beginning of September for two weeks of radio and TV appearances. But labor union officials at the American Federation of Television and Radio Artists (AFTRA), combined with work permit problems with the U.S. Department of Immigration, conspired to limit their performances to a handful of dates. The group was booked to appear on such programs as *Shindig!* and *Where the Action Is,* but upon their arrival, union officials told them that they would not be allowed to perform. When manager Giorgio Gomelsky asked the union official for some type of explanation, he was told, "We don't have to give any reason." The group ended up appearing on the TV program *Hullabaloo* after protracted negotiations, and filmed an episode of *Where the Action Is* that was never aired due to the work visa situation. To add insult to injury, the Yardbirds were not allowed to register at a Sunset Strip hotel where they had reservations, as a hotel clerk refused to check them in and ordered them to leave. They were even denied admission to Disneyland.

The trip was not a complete disaster, however, as they were able to record in two of the nation's most famous recording studios—Sam Phillips Recording Service (the relocated Sun Studios) and Chess. For their session at Phillips, they recorded a manic version of a rockabilly tune associated with Johnny Burnette's Rock and Roll Trio, "The Train Kept A-Rollin'," and a protest song penned by Manfred Mann's Mike Hugg called "You're a Better Man Than I." While at Chess, they cut "I'm a Man." They also recorded "New York City Blues" at CBS studios in New York City.

The band's next single, issued when they returned to their homeland in October, contained two A-sides: "Still I'm Sad" and "Evil Hearted You." With a melody derived from a 13th-century Gregorian chant, "Still I'm Sad" was penned by Samwell-Smith and McCarty and utilized six-string guitar, high-hat, triangle and seven voices (including manager Gomelsky's). "Evil Hearted You," another Gouldman composition, was less distinguished than his previous songs for the Yardbirds. Relf told *Melody Maker*, "We took a big risk when we released 'Still I'm Sad' as an A-side with 'Evil Hearted You,' but we felt that 'Evil' wasn't really strong and we wanted to put a really unusual, experimental thing on the other side." The release was another critical success, with *New Musical Express* describing "Evil Hearted You" as "extremely forceful . . . [with] tremendous impact, and there's a great guitar interlude," while a *Beat Instrumental* reviewer said of the flip side, "The boys have really tried for something different with this number and after hearing it, I think they've certainly achieved it." Commercially, the single with two A-sides reached #3 on the British charts.

Melody Maker reported on October 30 that the Yardbirds hoped to record an album titled *Yardbirds, I View,* and release it by Christmas. One side was to consist of five original numbers—one from each member of the band—and the other was to be "typical Yardbirds arrangements of classic numbers." This album never arrived.

As the months rolled on, the group began to feel that they were not receiving the recognition they deserved, even with three adventurous Top Three singles behind them. Keith Relf complained to *Melody Maker*, "People now expect each of our records to be different. But as far as publicity is concerned, it's completely up the spout, and I don't even know if it exists for us. We need publicity of a certain kind—about the music we are trying to do." He went on to explain, "The present mood of the group is frustration." Jeff Beck echoed this sentiment, adding, "The Yardbirds have been going for about 18 months now and nobody has been saying they are going to be the next thing, like they do for other groups. We get very despondent when we try so hard."

In October 1965, Epic Records in the U.S. released the single "I'm a Man" coupled with "Still I'm Sad." Recorded at Chess Studios during their first U.S. tour, "I'm a Man" took Bo Diddley's song into overdrive, greatly accelerating the song's tempo. Beck's guitar work was stunning, particularly during the song's final moments when he and Relf exchanged guitar and harp riffs until Beck took over for the frenzied, hyper-charged finale. "I'm a Man" became their third straight U.S. hit, reaching #17 on the singles charts. It also became a showstopper in concert as a fierce, ever-evolving jam that would last up to 30 minutes while Beck played behind his back or experimented with feedback.

On November 18, the Yardbirds started a major tour with co-headliners Manfred Mann that was scheduled to last until December 5. The bill also included the Mark Leeman Five, Paul and Barry Ryan, the Scaffold, and Gary Farr and the T-Bones [see **Mark Leeman Five**]. The plan was for Manfred Mann and the Yardbirds to take part in satirical sketches with Scaffold, a group that included Paul McCartney's brother, Mike McGear. As Giorgio Gomelsky told *New Musical Express,* "There will be no compére. The Scaffold will perform sketches between the musical acts, and everyone on the bill will be involved in them." *New Musical Express* predicted of the tour, "It could be the flop of the year—or it could be the biggest thing in package shows since the invention of the electric guitar." Chris Dreja acknowledged the group's exposure at such an undertaking: "No doubt about it, we are taking a risk. This has never been done before, and we don't know if the fans will take to the idea of having satirical sketches as well as beat." Unfortunately, the package tour lacked adequate publicity and the performers ended up playing to half-empty houses on many nights.

In late December, the band returned to the United States for a second tour to promote their latest U.S. release, *Having a Rave Up with the Yardbirds*. Like the *For Your Love* LP, *Having a Rave Up* was a hodgepodge consisting of miscellaneous U.S. and U.K. singles combined with four live tracks lifted from the U.K.-only *Five Live Yardbirds* album, as well as the previously unreleased "The Train Kept A-Rollin'" and "You're a Better Man Than I." The album fared little better than its predecessor, reaching only #53 on the LP charts. Over the holidays, the group managed a return visit to Chess studios on December 21, where they recorded the magnificent "Shapes of Things."

Upon their return to Britain, the Yardbirds flew to Italy to participate in the San Remo Song Festival. As part of the festival, they were required to record two songs: "Questa Volta," which Relf sang in Italian, and "Paff . . . Bum." Both tracks were terribly banal and Beck refused to contribute to "Questa Volta," leaving Dreja to play lead. The band was poorly received at the festival, where the audience slow-clapped and hissed during their performance.

The band's first release of 1966 was another classic single, "Shapes of Things," which was issued in the U.K. in February and a month later in the U.S. Written by Relf, Samwell-Smith and McCarty, the single was again lauded by the music press and became yet another worldwide smash, charting high in both the U.S. (#11) and the U.K. (#3). *Melody Maker* singled out Beck's stupendous guitar work: "A great big group sound and some quite fantastic guitar from Jeff Beck make this a big, big hit. Beck achieves a sitar effect on guitar and contributes much to the group's very individual noise. The boys deserve full marks for coming up with something different."

Beck himself was recognized individually by readers of *Beat Instrumental,* in which he finished a close second in the lead guitarist category to Hank Marvin of the Shadows, a remarkable achievement for someone who had only been in the public eye for a few months.

In March, the music press reported that several members of the Yardbirds were working on solo records: Dreja and McCarty were writing "an abstract comedy number together"; Samwell-Smith was set to make his vocal debut recording a Jackie DeShannon number, "Green Trees"; Beck was planning to record an instrumental version of George Gershwin's "Summertime"; and Relf was planning to record Bob Lind's "Mr. Zero" with orchestral backing. The strategy behind these solo projects was to try to give the individual members of the group greater exposure.

"All the members of other leading groups are known individually to the fans—but not us," Relf explained to *Beat Instrumental*. "So, it seemed a good idea to try some solo discs." Relf then elaborated on these changes to *Record Mirror:* "We're going to wear suits and promote individual people in the group—we're all going to be 'faces' if the policy works out. Yes, this is our go-ahead period." Only Relf's project saw the light of day, however, as he issued his first solo single, "Mr. Zero" backed with "Knowing," in May. Relf told *New Musical Express* at the time of the release, "This does not mean I'm leaving the group—just that I want to develop my singing in other fields." The record received positive reviews, but reached just #50 on the British charts.

Despite the band's commercial success, they were becoming increasingly dissatisfied with their financial arrangements with their manager. Agreeing that a change was in order, the band fired Gomelsky in April and replaced him with Simon Napier-Bell. Napier-Bell was a film producer who had become interested in pop management the prior year when he managed a minor act, Diane Ferraz and Nicky Scott. He achieved greater success when he teamed up with Vicki Wickham to write English lyrics to an Italian ballad discovered by Dusty Springfield that became "You Don't Have to Say You Love Me"—Springfield's biggest international hit.

That same month, Beck fell ill after a performance at Marseilles in France and was admitted to a hospital. The rest of the group continued on to Copenhagen with Dreja taking over on lead guitar while Beck flew back to London, where he was diagnosed with meningitis (he rejoined the group later that month).

The band went into the studio to record their long awaited second album that spring. The first track to appear was a single issued a month later in May 1966, "Over Under Sideways Down" backed with "Jeff's Boogie." The A-side was modeled after the boogie rhythm of Bill Haley's "Rock Around the Clock." Beck came up with the opening riff and Napier-Bell thought of the title. "The overall feel is infectious and absorbing," commented *New Musical Express*. *Disc and Music Echo* was similarly impressed, printing, "It's fascinating and all very splendid." The B-side was an instrumental tour de force for Beck. The single reached #13 in the U.S. and #10 in the U.K.

In July, Columbia released the group's first true studio LP in Britain. Taking only a week to record, the LP was simply called *The Yardbirds*. It later became known as

"Roger the Engineer" due to Dreja's cover art depicting a caricature of engineer Roger Cameron. While each composition was credited jointly to all five band members, the group typically laid down the basic tracks without Beck, and the lead guitarist then overdubbed his part to complete the track. Produced by Samwell-Smith and Napier-Bell, *The Yardbirds* was an eclectic release with selections ranging from blues-oriented material ("Lost Woman," "Rack My Mind") to more adventurous tracks, such as the gospel-tinged "Ever Since the World Began"; "The Nazz Are Blue," a blues boogie based on Elmore James's "Dust My Broom" featuring vocals by Beck; and "The Hot House of Omagararshid." This last was a particularly strange number in which the group chanted repetitive nonsensical phrases over an instrumental backing featuring some snarling guitar by Beck and exotic percussive effects (including the sound of Beck striking a beer bottle with a drumstick and Dreja shaking of a flimsy board to create a wobbly sound).

The U.S. version of the album was issued in August with some changes: It was retitled *Over Under Sideways Down* and a picture of the group was used in lieu of the drawing. In addition, two tracks were deleted from the U.S. release ("The Nazz Are Blue" and "Rack My Mind"), and "stereo" copies featured an electronically re-channeled remix of both single tracks. "Mono" copies included an additional scorching guitar solo on "The Hot House of Omagararshid." While an ambitious effort, the album only managed to reach #52 on the U.S. album charts and #20 in the U.K. Nevertheless, *Disc and Music Echo* said of the album, "The boys prove themselves one of our best AND most original groups."

Before the album was released, the group experienced another major loss when Samwell-Smith left the group to become a freelance producer. While Samwell-Smith was not integral to them with regard to his bass playing (he had only played on half the tracks on their latest album, leaving the rest to "Mick" of Simon's Triangle), his role as musical director was critical and his departure was a major loss for the Yardbirds. He gave his reasons for leaving to *Hit Parader:* "I'm a bit too old at twenty-three for all those screaming kids leaping about. I don't really think I'll be missed in the group—no one really noticed me on stage. I might as well have been a dummy . . . Keith and Jeff are really the only two faces that matter in the Yardbirds."

The final straw for Samwell-Smith came during a performance at one of the Oxford Colleges, where Relf's drunken behavior required Beck and Samwell-Smith to fill in on vocals. As soon as they all left the stage, Samwell-Smith informed the group that he was leaving the band.

As fate would have it, Jimmy Page, who had previously declined Gomelsky's offer to be their guitarist, was there at the show. His friend Beck had driven him to the performance, and on the ride back, Page volunteered to sit in for a few months on bass, although he had never played the bass guitar before. He then became a "temporary" member of the Yardbirds until a permanent bassist could be found. Instead, eventually they all decided that Dreja would learn the instrument and as soon as he became proficient, he would take over for Page, who would then switch over to second lead guitar. Shortly after joining, Page told *Melody Maker,* "At the moment I'm playing bass guitar but maybe I'll do a few things with a second guitar. Jeff Beck and I have had a lot of very interesting talks about using two lead guitars."

At the time he joined the band, Page was in constant demand as a session guitarist, appearing on numerous releases, including records by Them, Dave Berry, Lulu and the Luvvers, P.J. Proby, and Jackie DeShannon. But he was no longer content working sessions. "I was drying up as a guitarist," he told *Hit Parader.* "I played a lot of rhythm guitar, which was very dull and left me no time to practice."

James Patrick Page was born on January 9, 1944, in Heston, Middlesex, U.K. Inspired by Elvis Presley's "Baby Let's Play House," he first started to play the guitar in the late 1950s. By 1960 he had joined his first band, Neil Christian and the Crusaders. The Crusaders toured heavily with an R&B repertoire that included covers of Chuck Berry and Bo Diddley numbers. Page dropped out of the band in 1962 when a bout of glandular fever weakened him severely. He enrolled at Croydon Art College, but continued to jam at night at various jazz and blues clubs around Richmond. An invitation to play at the Marquee with Cyril Davies's Interval Band led to his first studio session with ex-Shadows members Jet Harris and Tony Meehan. The session yielded the instrumental single "Diamonds," released in January 1963, which became an instant smash, taking just four weeks to reach the top of the British charts. This led to more sessions for Page and by the end of 1964 he was doing as many as ten a week. Page also found time in 1964 for a short stint with Mickey Finn and the Bluemen, and he played blues harmonica on at least two of their earlier singles.

In 1965, Page produced some sessions for Andrew Loog Oldham's Immediate label, most notably the one yielding John Mayall's single, "I'm Your Witchdoctor" backed with "Telephone Blues." He also produced some jam sessions with Clapton and Beck that originally appeared on the *Blues Anytime* series of albums (and have since been reissued countless times). He issued his own first solo single in early 1965, "She Just Satisfies" backed with "Keep Movin'" (U.K./Fontana TF 533), but it couldn't muster an impression on the charts, even with *Record Mirror's* glowing review: "One of the finest guitarists in the business, now in the personal spotlight. Furious beat, with vocal touches almost vanishing in a welter of amplified backing. Right for dancing, right for listening, just right!"

With Page in tow, the Yardbirds left for their third U.S. tour in August 1966. Unfortunately, while on their way to play at the Carousel Ballroom in San Francisco on August 25, Beck came down with tonsillitis and Page had to take over the lead guitar slot with Dreja prematurely moving over to bass. Dreja must have been ready enough; the gig went off without a hitch and the unit continued performing as a four-piece for the rest of the tour. "Jeff's missed about seven dates so far—but Jimmy has been doing great . . . leaping about all over the place," Keith Relf told *Disc and Music Echo*. "It's the first time I have seen him really blow out onstage."

Beck reunited with the group following the tour, at which point they then had two lead guitarists. "I think that it will move more to free-form," Page told *Beat Instrumental*. "Mind you, it will be highly organized. The whole thing must be done tastefully otherwise the Yardbirds' sound would be ruined."

When the band returned to the U.K., they recorded their next single, the marvelous "Happenings Ten Years Time Ago" and "Psycho Daisies." "Happenings" was arguably the most adventurous recording the group ever issued, with a staggering twin solo and dueling lead guitars emulating police sirens and a nuclear explosion. For the recording, Beck and Page shared lead guitar, and session man John Paul Jones sat in on bass. They recorded "Psycho Daisies" at the same time. It was another combustible if less memorable number that also featured Beck on double-tracked leads, Page on bass and McCarty on drums. In the U.S., "Happenings" was coupled with "The Nazz Are Blue" and reached #30; in the U.K., paired with "Psycho Daisies," it reached #43.

In September, the Yardbirds returned to the studio to record five tracks for director Michelangelo Antonioni's film *Blow-Up*. Antonioni originally wanted the Who to appear in the film, but when they proved to be unavailable, he booked the Yardbirds instead. The band planned to perform "Train Kept A-Rollin'," but when copyright restrictions prevented them from using the song, they rewrote it as "Stroll On." In the film, the band is seen performing the song on a set that reconstructed Windsor's Ricky Tick Club. "Stroll On" was first released on the *Blow-Up* soundtrack album.

On September 23, 1966, the five-piece lineup featuring both Page and Beck on lead guitars embarked on a package tour with the Rolling Stones headlining and Ike and Tina Turner second-billed. The Yardbirds' "dream team" lineup, described by *New Musical Express* as featuring "the two more creative guitarists in Britain," was not always successful on stage. When the combination worked, it was extraordinary to witness Page and Beck trading solos on opposite sides of the stage or playing leads in unison. But the teamwork frequently disintegrated into what Norrie Drummond of *New Musical Express* described as an "outrageous cacophony which completely drowned out Keith Relf's voice," causing Drummond to suggest, "Perhaps if Jeff Beck cut out the gymnastics with his guitar, the group might find some semblance of music!" While Page was consistent, Beck's playing was notoriously erratic. Rather than working in tandem with Page, he would frequently try to overshadow him. Rumors started to appear in the press that Beck was going to be ousted from the group.

The package tour ended on October 9, and the band next planned to fly to the United States for another package tour. Just before they left, a *Melody Maker* front-page story headlined "Keith Relf to Quit Yardbirds?" reported, "Strong rumors suggest Keith is planning to leave the group due to continued poor health." Relf vehemently denied the rumors in the next issue of the magazine, telling the music weekly, "I don't understand why somebody would want to continually make trouble for me in my relationship with the group. I have no intention of leaving now or in the future."

While in the United States, the band went on a "Dick Clark Caravan of Stars" package tour, sharing the program with Brian Hyland ("Itsy Bitsy Teenie Weenie Yellow Polka Dot Bikini," "Sealed with a Kiss") and Gary Lewis and the Playboys. The tour was exceptionally grueling, requiring the band to give two performances daily while touring the South over a four-week period. In November, Beck reached a breaking point and in a fit of anger, smashed his Gibson Les Paul on the floor and dropped out of the tour while in Texas. The band elected to continue as a quartet with Page as the group's sole lead guitarist.

November also heralded Relf's second solo single, "Shapes in My Mind" backed with "Blue Sands," which sank without a trace. The A-side was written and produced by Napier-Bell, while, strangely, Relf was not involved in the recording of the B-side, which was an instrumental track by a little-known group called the Outsiders.

After the Texas debacle, rumors were flying in the press about not only Beck's imminent departure from the group but about Page's potential departure as well. Simon Napier-Bell disclosed to the press that Beck was leaving because of ill health. "There is no question of his being sacked," Napier-Bell said. But then Beck denied that he was leaving, telling *Disc and Music Echo*, "It's not true. I'm still with the group. Rumors were circulating in the States that I was letting the Yardbirds down and that I was leaving. It was just that I was ill again." However, Relf confirmed the departure, telling the music magazine, "Jeff has left. There won't be a replacement. We find we're working better as four—with Jimmy on lead guitar." One source close to the group told *Beat Instrumental*, "The Yardbirds just disagreed with him [Beck] because they felt that while he had mental and physical problems, 'the show must go on.' That sort of thing. The other members of the group put their personal problems aside and they felt that Jeff was not holding up his side of it."

Finally, Beck explained his perspective of the split in a column for *Beat Instrumental:* "It all really boiled down to my relationship with the rest of the group as a person, Jimmy Page excepted, of course. You wouldn't believe the stupid bickering which went on between some of us. That smashed Gibson incident arose out of something Keith said to me. You see, I was never really fully accepted into the group and when things got a little rough, as they did on the last American tour, most of the moans were directed at me. Trouble was, it never worked the other way round. I wasn't really allowed to pass an opinion on the other guys' playing or group policy. There are so many incidents which helped to cause the separation. I can't say much about the money side of things, but I'll just say this, you'd laugh if you knew how much I came away with when I left the group."

Upon their return to the U.K., the band returned to the studio on December 22, 1966, for their first session with-out Beck. They recorded the instrumental "L.S.D." and the backing track for "You Stole My Love," another Gouldman composition. Producer Samwell-Smith had already recorded the Mockingbirds' version of the song and was none to happy about having to record it with the Yardbirds as well. Although 15 takes of the backing track were recorded, a dispute between Samwell-Smith and Page resulted in the producer storming out of the sessions before the vocals were recorded. Both songs were included in the 1993 CD boxed set, *Train Kept A-Rollin'.*

As Beck had alluded, the band's financial situation had not improved under the stewardship of Napier-Bell, so the band opted to change managers again. Peter Grant, an ex-road manager and professional wrestler, took over and things improved immediately. Grant arranged for the group to go on a successful package tour of Singapore and Australia with Roy Orbison and the Walker Brothers during January and February of 1967.

With the disappointing showing of their last single, the group needed to rejuvenate their careers with a hit. Relf acknowledged to *Melody Maker*, "We tried to be much too clever on our last single," and added, "The whole scene seems to be one of artistic confusion with nobody knowing which way to turn." On the other hand, Page concluded that the problem was one of time: "The trouble is we aren't allowed to record in the States, and that means we must do everything in a terrible rush when we are here [in Britain]."

The group turned to producer Mickie Most to reverse their fortunes. Most had a reputation as a top producer of hit singles by the Animals, Herman's Hermits, Lulu, the Nashville Teens ("Tobacco Road"), and, significantly, their Epic labelmate Donovan, who was at the time enjoying massive popularity in the States. Page had previously worked with Most on numerous sessions, including two of the producer's own solo singles, "The Feminine Look" (U.K./Columbia DB 7117) and "Money Honey" (U.K./Columbia DB 7245), released in 1963 and 1964, respectively. While Most may have seemed like the best choice for a producer at the time, with hindsight his selection turned out to be ill-fated. The problem was that he ended up dominating much of the Yardbirds' final recordings, sometimes forcing lightweight material on them that was the antithesis of their image as a predominantly experimental, blues-based recording group.

The Yardbirds' first single produced by Most, recorded on March 5, was "Little Games" coupled with the group-penned "Puzzles." The topside was a bouncy pop number highlighted by Page's stellar guitar work. Released in April 1967, the single flopped, reaching just #51 on the U.S. singles charts while going absolutely nowhere in the U.K. Competing against this release was the first solo single from Jeff Beck, "Hi-Ho Silver Lining," which Most also produced (U.K./Columbia DB 8151). Beck's single climbed to #14 on the British charts.

Meanwhile, in America, Epic released a Yardbirds *Greatest Hits* album, which would become their biggest seller, reaching #28 on the charts. The spring was a busy time for them as they toured Europe during March and April. On March 16 they appeared on the German TV show *Beat Beat Beat,* where four songs were recorded that were eventually issued in audio and video on the 2000 CD *Cumular Limit.*

The Yardbirds' second Most-produced single, "Ha Ha Said the Clown" backed with "Tinker, Tailor, Soldier, Sailor," was issued in July in the U.S., but was not released in the U.K. since Manfred Mann had already scored a hit there with the song. The topside was pure bubblegum with disposable and repetitive lyrics and a short instrumental solo. Relf was the only member of the group to even appear on this track, as session players provided the backing. "Tinker, Tailor, Soldier, Sailor" was just as abysmal, though it was partially salvaged by Page's magnificent, distorted guitar work, which included his second recorded use of a violin bow ("Puzzles" was the first).

In August, the group released their last studio album, *Little Games*, in the U.S. The album was not deemed strong enough to issue in their homeland. They had recorded it in just three days between April 28 and May 1. In 1977, Page told *Trouser Press*, "It was just so bloody rushed. Everything was done in one take because Mickie Most was basically interested in singles and didn't believe it was worth the time to do the tracks right on the album."

Little Games contained an interesting mishmash of material that varied widely in style and quality. From the experimental "Glimpses" featuring Relf's heavily distorted intonation over an instrumental backing, to the vaudeville of "Stealing Stealing," only "Smile on Me," written by the group, and "Drinking Muddy Water," a thin rewrite of Muddy Waters's "Rollin' and Tumblin'," contained any traces of the Yardbirds' blues roots. The most interesting track on the album was the Indian-sounding "White Summer," a showcase for Page on acoustic guitar. Adopted from a traditional folk song, "She Moved Through the Fair," which Page picked up from a Davey

Graham record issued in 1963, "White Summer" would be carried over into the live sets of Page's next group, Led Zeppelin. Surprisingly, *Downbeat* gave *Little Games* the thumbs up, calling it "an album as exciting as their earlier ones and a good deal more ordered," even going so far as to say, "The range is wide and the writing is improved." The album reached #80 on the U.S. album charts.

In September, the Yardbirds began another U.S. tour with McCarty replaced temporarily due to a breakdown. Fortunately, he was able to join the tour after just two missed gigs. While in New York, McCarty went to the Village Theater where he saw folk singer Jake Holmes perform "Dazed and Confused," a song about a troubled relationship and which had a captivating, descending bass line. The group appropriated the bass line and Relf rewrote the lyrics. (Contrary to popular belief, the tune was known as "I'm Confused." Epic staff was unaware of Jake Holmes's original version and mistitled it after being unable to determine the title after listening to their live version.) The song, which they first performed at the Village Theater in New York in November 1967, became the band's most powerful number for the final months of their existence.

Their next single, "Ten Little Indians" backed with "Drinking Muddy Water," came out in October 1967 and continued the downward spiral of their latest releases. The topside, recorded on September 25, 1967, was not one of Harry Nilsson's finest compositions and was likely to alienate any remaining Yardbirds fans expecting more substantial output. Barely scraping the Top 100 of the U.S. charts (#94), the single was mercifully not issued in the U.K.

The group toured France, Belgium and Germany toward the end of the year. One newspaper reported that the band had written music for an hour-long ballet to be performed at the Paris Olympic on December 13 and 14. The event was canceled, though, when the backers pulled out.

Between November 1967 and January 1968, the Yardbirds returned to the studio to record "Think About It" and two versions of "Goodnight Sweet Josephine." "Josephine" was an insignificant sing along about a prostitute. The B-side, on the other hand, was incredibly powerful due to Page's psychedelic-tinged guitar pyrotechnics. The American and British single releases contained the second version of "Josephine" on the A-side. In the U.K., the single was only pressed on acetates (one for each version of the A-side and the same B-side) and was not commercially released. "Josephine" managed a dismal #127 on the U.S. charts.

Page summarized the Mickie Most period to *Hit Parader*: "We had done 'Happenings Ten Years Time Ago,' on our own and then our manager decided to turn us over to a producer. We thought it was a great idea because the producer just had tremendous success with 'Sunshine Superman.' We had tremendous confidence in him. So we did 'Little Games' and it didn't do very well, but that was all right. It was a reasonable number to do. Then he gave us 'Ha Ha Said the Clown,' which we didn't like, but we still had confidence in him. Over a period of time, his ideas started to kill us off."

From late March to June 1968, the group toured the United States. By now the Yardbirds had become divided into factions as Relf and McCarty wanted to perform soft, folk-oriented material while Page wanted to continue playing hard rock. In addition, Relf's and McCarty's drug problems created friction within the band.

On March 30, their show at the Anderson Theater in New York was recorded with the intention of releasing a live album. In early April, the band listened to the tapes and rejected them all. The material subsequently came out as *Live Yardbirds! Featuring Jimmy Page* in September 1971 to capitalize on Page's enormous popularity with Led Zeppelin. It was quickly withdrawn from the market, however, at the insistence of Jimmy Page. While the album was poorly recorded and contained irritating, obviously dubbed-in applause, the power of the lineup was still clearly present in these live recordings, particularly on "Dazed and Confused" and "The Train Kept A-Rollin."

Unable to generate a satisfactory album from the Anderson Theater tapes, the Yardbirds began rehearsing new material and their U.S. label, Epic, assigned Manny Kellem to produce them. Kellem was an unlikely choice as he was best known for easy-listening music. Sessions took place between April 3 and April 5, 1968, yielding five tracks: "Taking a Hold on Me," "Knowing That I'm Losing You" (an early version of Led Zeppelin's "Tangerine"), "Spanish Blood" (a spoken word track), "Avron Knows," and a cover of the Garnet Mimms soul number "My Baby." "Avron Knows" was a strong rocker and "Spanish Blood" was a particularly interesting track that pitted McCarty's recitation of a poem against Page's acoustic guitar accompaniment. However, Epic decided not to release any of these tracks as singles, and they were shelved until their inclusion on *Cumular Limit*, with the

exception of "Knowing That I'm Losing You," which was omitted out of fear of litigation by Jimmy Page.

Following the sessions, the Yardbirds returned home and gave their final performance at the Luton Technical College on July 7, 1968. After the split, Relf and McCarty formed a new band (Together) while Page and Dreja tried to reform the Yardbirds. Ultimately, Page found other musicians who became the members of Led Zeppelin, although for their first dates they performed as the Yardbirds to honor some Scandinavian gigs that were already booked. After a couple of British club dates as the Yardbirds, they changed their name to Led Zeppelin after Dreja threatened legal action.

Postscript

Following his departure from the Yardbirds, Topham released a solo single in 1969, "Christmas Cracker" backed with "Cracking Up Over Christmas," and a solo album the following year titled *Ascension Heights*. Topham also appeared on Blue Horizon albums by Christine Perfect, Gordon Smith and Duster Bennett. In 1987, he reunited with McCarty to form a new band that played the London pub circuit.

Topham's successor, Clapton, went on to join John Mayall's Bluesbreakers before forming Cream and the excellent if short-lived Blind Faith [see **Cream, Blind Faith**]. He has since had an enormously successful solo career.

Beck released two Top 20 British singles in 1967, "Hi-Ho Silver Lining" (U.K. #14) and "Tally Man," a Gouldman composition (U.K. #30). In 1968, he enjoyed further British single success with the release of the instrumental "Love Is Blue." The single's flip side, "I've Been Drinking" (featuring Rod Stewart on vocals), was issued as an A-side in 1973 and reached #27 on the singles charts. In 1968, Beck assembled a band consisting of himself, Ron Wood on bass, Mickey Waller on drums and Rod Stewart on vocals for his first album, *Truth* (U.S. #15). In 1969, he recorded one more album with Stewart, *Beck-Ola*, with new drummer Tony Newman and pianist Nicky Hopkins (U.S. #15, U.K. #39) before the group disbanded. In 1971, a new lineup released *Rough and Ready* and in 1972 the group released *The Jeff Beck Group* (U.S. #19). Beck formed Beck, Bogert and Appice with Tim Bogert and Carmine Appice, both formerly of Vanilla Fudge, in 1973. Beck, Bogert and Appice released one self-titled album in

1973 before disbanding (U.S. #12, U.K. #28). In 1975, Beck revived his solo career with the release of the tremendous, all-instrumental *Blow by Blow* produced by George Martin. The following year, he collaborated with keyboardist Jan Hammer for the sophisticated *Wired* (U.S. #16, U.K. #38). His successful string of albums continued with *Jeff Beck and the Jan Hammer Group Live* (1977, U.S. #23), *There and Back* (1980, U.S. #21, U.K. #38), *Flash* (1985, U.S. #39, U.K. #83) and *Jeff Beck's Guitar Shop* (1989, U.S. #49). In 1993, he released the soundtrack to the film *Frankie's House* with Jed Leiber, and *Crazy Legs* as Jeff Beck and the Big Town Playboys. In 1999, he released *Who Else?* and in 2000 issued *You Had It Coming*.

Relf and McCarty—under the moniker Together—issued "Henry's Coming Home" backed with "Love Mum and Dad" in 1968. Another A-side written but not performed by the duo, this time under the group name Reign, was issued in 1970: "Line of Least Resistance" backed with "Natural Lovin' Man." Together evolved into Renaissance with the addition of John Hawken (keyboards), Louis Cennamo (bass) and Relf's sister, Jane (vocals). The Relf-McCarty lineup released two albums, *Renaissance* (1969) and *Illusion* (1970) before Relf and McCarty went their separate ways.

Relf next pursued production work and his credits included Medicine Head, Saturnalia and Hunter Muskett. He then joined Armageddon and played on their self-titled album released in 1975. Tragically, he died in his home on May 14, 1976, after being electrocuted by a defective amplifier.

McCarty went on to form Shoot, which released one album, *On the Frontier* (1973). While with Shoot, McCarty switched to keyboards and vocals. McCarty released two albums with Illusion, *Out of the Mist* (1977) and *Illusion* (1978), the latter produced by Samwell-Smith. An incomplete third album was released in 1989 under the title *Enchanted Caress*.

In 1982, McCarty and Dreja performed on a Spanish TV show as the Yardbirds and Friends. In 1983, Samwell-Smith joined his old comrades for two shows celebrating the twentieth anniversary of the Marquee Club. Joining the trio were singer John Fiddler (formerly of Medicine Head), guitarist John Knightsbridge and harmonica player Mark Feltham.

After their acclaimed Marquee performance, the three ex-Yardbirds and vocalist Fiddler formed the Box of Frogs. The quartet's first album, *Box of Frogs* (1984), included

guest appearances by Beck (four tracks, including the radio hit "Back Where I Started") and guitarist Rory Gallagher (two tracks). The album became a minor hit, reaching #45 on the LP charts. A follow-up album, *Strange Land,* was less successful, reaching number #177 on the U.S. charts despite the guest appearance of Page on one track and a remake of "Heart Full of Soul" that featured Gouldman on guitar. McCarty has since participated in recordings questionably issued as the Yardbirds and the Pretty Things/Yardbird Blues Band, the latter of which features McCarty as the sole Yardbird. Chris Dreja joined Jim McCarty on the album *Yardbirds Reunion Concert* (later reissued as *Reunion Jam)*, even though the concert series was billed as the McCarty Band.

Following the 1992 induction of the Yardbirds into the Rock and Roll Hall of Fame, Dreja and McCarty decided to reform the Yardbirds. The present line-up consists of Gypie Mayo on lead guitar and backing vocals; John Idan on bass and lead vocals; and Alan Glen on harmonica, backing vocals and percussion in addition to Dreja and McCarty.

After leaving the Yardbirds, Samwell-Smith went into production, with credits including the first Renaissance album (featuring Relf and McCarty), Jethro Tull (*The Broadsword and the Beast* LP) and Carly Simon (*Spoiled Girl*). Samwell-Smith's biggest successes were producing most of Cat Stevens's 1970s albums, including *Mona Bone Jakon* (1970), *Tea for the Tillerman* (1970), *Teaser and the Firecat* (1971), *Catch Bull at Four* (1972) and *Buddah and the Chocolate Box* (1974). Samwell-Smith also joined Dreja and McCarty in Box of Frogs between 1984 and 1986.

Dreja remained with Page for a short while following the breakup of the Yardbirds. Page attempted to recruit vocalist Terry Reid and Procol Harum drummer B.J. Wilson (among others), and, although both declined, Reid recommended Robert Plant who in turn recommended a drummer, John Bonham. Bassist John Paul Jones replaced Dreja before the new unit—which assumed the name Led Zeppelin—began recording.

The blues-based, hard-rocking Led Zeppelin became phenomenally successful. Their ten albums all achieved gold status and their last three studio albums—*Presence* (1976), *In Through the Out Door* (1979) and *Coda* (1983)—each went platinum within a year of release. Eight of Zeppelin's albums reached the top of the U.K. charts, while six topped the U.S. charts. Led Zeppelin disbanded in 1980 following the death of John Bonham.

In 1982, Page contributed to the soundtrack of the Charles Bronson bloodbath film, *Death Wish II*. In 1985, he formed the Firm with ex-Free vocalist Paul Rodgers. The Firm released two albums, *The Firm* (U.S. #17, U.K. #15) and *Mean Business* (U.S. #22) in 1985 and 1986, respectively, before splitting up. In 1988, Page released his first solo album, *Outrider* (U.S. #26, U.K. #27). In 1993, he collaborated with David Coverdale (formerly the vocalist with Whitesnake) on *Coverdale/Page* (U.S. #5, U.K. #4).

In 1994, Page reunited with Robert Plant for an appearance on the television show *MTV Unplugged*, which resulted in the release of the album *No Quarter—Unledded* (U.S. #4, U.K. #7). In the summer of 2000, he collaborated with the Black Crowes on a tour. A two-CD set, *Live at the Greek*—featuring a heavy dose of Zeppelin classics and additional blues covers—came out of the tour.

Discography

Release Date	Title	Catalog Number

U.S. Singles

The Yardbirds

1965	I Wish You Would/A Certain Girl	Epic 5-9709
1965	For Your Love/Got to Hurry	Epic 5-9790
1965	Heart Full of Soul/Steeled Blues	Epic 5-9823
1965	I'm a Man/Still I'm Sad	Epic 5-9857
1966	Shapes of Things/I'm Not Talking	Epic 5-9881
1966	Shapes of Things/New York City Blues	Epic 5-10006
1966	Over Under Sideways Down/Jeff's Boogie	Epic 5-10035
1966	Happenings Ten Years Time Ago/ The Nazz Are Blue	Epic 5-10094
1967	Little Games/Puzzles	Epic 5-10156
1967	Ha Ha Said the Clown/ Tinker, Tailor, Soldier, Sailor	Epic 5-10204
1967	Ten Little Indians/Drinking Muddy Water	Epic 5-10248
1968	Goodnight Sweet Josephine/ Think About It	Epic 5-10303

Keith Relf

1966	Mr. Zero/Knowing	Epic 5-10044
1967	Shapes in My Mind/Blues Sands	Epic 5-10110

U.S. Albums

1965	*For Your Love*	Epic LN24167 (M)
		Epic BN26267 (S)

For Your Love/I'm Not Talking/Putty (In Your Hands)/I Ain't Got You/Got to Hurry/I Ain't Done Wrong/I Wish You Would/A Certain Girl/My Girl Sloopy/Sweet Music/Good Morning Little Schoolgirl

1966	*Having a Rave Up with the Yardbirds*	Epic LN24177 (M)
		Epic BN26177 (S)

You're a Better Man Than I/Evil Hearted You/I'm a Man/Still I'm Sad/Heart Full of Soul/The Train Kept A-Rollin'/Smokestack Lightning/Respectable/I'm a Man (Live)/Here 'Tis

1966	*Over Under Sideways Down*	Epic LN24210 (M)
		Epic BN26210 (S)

Lost Woman/Over Under Sideways Down/I Can't Make Your Way/Farewell/Hot House of Omagararshid/Jeff's Boogie/He's Always There/Turn into Earth/What Do You Want/Ever Since the World Began

1967	*Little Games*	Epic LN24313 (M)
		Epic BN26313 (S)

Little Games/Smile on Me/White Summer/Tinker, Tailor, Soldier, Sailor/Glimpses/Drinking Muddy Water/No Excess Baggage/Stealing Stealing/Only the Black Rose/Little Soldier Boy

1971	*Live Yardbirds! Featuring Jimmy Page*	Epic EG-30135

The Train Kept A-Rollin'/You're a Better Man Than I/Heart Full of Soul/Dazed and Confused/My Baby/Over Under Sideways Down/Drinking Muddy Water/Shapes of Things/White Summer/I'm a Man

1992	*Little Games Sessions and More* (2 CD)	EMI 0777-7-98213-2 7

Little Games (stereo mix)/Smile on Me/White Summer/Tinker, Tailor, Soldier, Sailor (vocal version)/Glimpses (version 1)/Drinking Muddy Water/No Excess Baggage/Stealing Stealing/Only the Black Rose/Little Soldier Boy/Puzzles/I Remember the Night/Ha Ha Said the Clown/Ten Little Indians (vocal)/Goodnight Sweet Josephine (version 1)/Think About It/Little Games (mono mix)/You Stole My Love/White Summer (acoustic version)/Tinker, Tailor, Soldier, Sailor (instrumental)/L.S.D./Drinking Muddy Water (mono mix)/De Lane Lea Lee/Glimpses (version 2)/Never Mind/Ten Little Indians (instrumental)/Goodnight Sweet Josephine (version 2)/Henry's Coming Home[1]/Love Mom and Dad[1]/Together Now[1]/Shining Where the Sun Has Been[2]/"Great Shakes" U.S. commercial spot

    [1] Performed by Together.
    [2] Performed by Jim McCarty and Keith Relf.

Miscellaneous U.S. Releases

1966	*Sonny Boy Williamson and the Yardbirds*	Mercury MG21071 (M) Mercury SR61071 (S)

Bye Bye Bird/Mr. Downchild/23 Hours Too Long/Out on the Water Coast/Baby Don't Worry/Pontiac Blues/Take It Easy Baby/I Don't Care No More/Do the Weston

1967	*Blow-Up* (movie soundtrack)	MGM E-4447 ST (M) MGM SE-4447 ST (S)

Contains one Yardbirds track, "Stroll On."

1973	*History of British Blues*	Sire SAS 3701

Contains one Yardbirds track, "Baby What's Wrong," cut at their first recording session in 1963.

U.K. Singles

1964	I Wish You Would/A Certain Girl	Columbia DB 7283
1964	Good Morning Little Schoolgirl/ I Ain't Got You	Columbia DB 7391
1965	For Your Love/Got to Hurry	Columbia DB 7499
1965	Heart Full of Soul/Steeled Blues	Columbia DB 7594
1965	Still I'm Sad/Evil Hearted You	Columbia DB 7706
1966	Shapes of Things/You're a Better Man Than I	Columbia DB 7848
1966	Over Under Sideways Down/Jeff's Boogie	Columbia DB 7928
1966	Happenings Ten Years Time Ago/ Psycho Daisies	Columbia DB 8024
1967	Little Games/Puzzles	Columbia DB 8165
1968	Goodnight Sweet Josephine/ Think About It[1]	Columbia DB 8368

[1] Unreleased; acetates only.

U.K. EPs

1964   *Five Yardbirds*   Columbia SEG8421
My Girl Sloopy/I'm Not Talking/I Ain't Done Wrong

1967   *Over Under Sideways Down*   Columbia SEG8521
Over Under Sideways Down/I Can't Make Your Way/He's Always There/What Do You Want

U.K. Albums

1964   *Five Live Yardbirds*   Columbia SX1677
Too Much Monkey Business/I Got Love if You Want It/Smokestack Lightning/Good Morning Little Schoolgirl/Respectable/Five Long Years/Pretty Girl/Louise/I'm a Man/Here 'Tis

1966   *The Yardbirds*   Columbia
                                          SX6063 (M)
                                          Columbia
                                          SCX 6063 (S)
Same tracks as U.S. *Over Under Sideways Down* plus "Rack My Mind" and "The Nazz Are Blue."

1984   *Shapes of Things* (7 CD boxed set)   Charly BOX 104
Contains five tracks (outtakes) not appearing on albums released during the lifetime of the band.

Disc 1: *The First Recordings*
Smokestack Lightning/You Can't Judge a Book By Its Cover/Take It Easy Baby/Talkin' 'Bout You/Let It Rock/I Wish You Would/Boom Boom/ Honey in Your Hips/Who Do You Love

Disc 2: *Sonny Boy Williamson and the Yardbirds*
Bye Bye Bird/Mr. Downchild/The River Rhine/23 Hours Too Long/A Lost Care/Pontiac Blues/Take It Easy Baby/Out on the Water Coast/I Don't Care No More/Honey in Your Hips/Western Arizona

Disc 3: *Five Live Yardbirds*
Too Much Monkey Business/I Got Love If You Want It/Smokestack Lightning/Good Morning Little Schoolgirl/Five Long Years/Pretty Girl/Louise/I'm a Man/Here 'Tis

Disc 4: *For Your Love*
For Your Love/I'm Not Talkin'/I Ain't Got You/Putty (In Your Hands)/Got to Hurry/I Ain't Done Wrong/I Wish You Would/A Certain Girl/Sweet Music/Good Morning Little Schoolgirl/My Girl Sloopy

Disc 5: *Having a Rave Up with the Yardbirds*
I'm a Man/You're a Better Man Than I/Evil Hearted You/Still I'm Sad/Heart Full of Soul/The Train Kept A-Rollin'/Smokestack Lightning/Respectable/Here 'Tis

Disc 6: *Shapes of Things*
What Do You Want/Jeff's Blues/Like Jimmy Reed Again/Someone to Love (Part One)/Shapes of Things/Steeled Blues/Someone to Love (Part Two)/New York City Blues/Stroll On/For RSG

Disc 7: *Odds and Sods*
Good Morning Little Schoolgirl (3 takes)/Heart Full of Soul (2 takes)/Chris' Number/Pounds and Stomps/Got to Hurry (3 tracks)/Without You[1]/Climbing Through[1]

[1] Performed by the Authentics.

1989   *First Recordings: London 1963*   Decal LIK 58
Smokestack Lightning[1]/Honey in Your Hips[1]/You Can't Judge a Book By Its Cover[1]/I'm Talkin' 'Bout You[2]/Honey in Your Hips[2]/Let It Rock[1]/I Wish You Would[1]/Who Do You Love[1]/Boom Boom[2]

[1] Recorded live at the Craw Daddy Club, Richmond, U.K., December 7–8, 1963.
[2] Recorded at R. G. Jones studio, Morden, Surrey, U.K., December 1963.

1991   *Yardbirds . . . On Air* (2 LP)   Band of Joy
                                          BOJLP 20 (LP)
                                          Band of Joy
                                          BOJCD 20 (CD)
I Ain't Got You/For Your Love/I'm Not Talking/I Wish You Would/Heart Full of Soul/I've Been Wrong/Too Much Monkey Business/Love Me Like I Love You/I'm a Man/Evil Hearted You/Still I'm Sad/Hang on Sloopy/Smokestack Lightning/You're a Better Man Than I/The Train Kept A-Rollin'/Shapes of Things/Dust My Blues/Scratch My Back/Over Under Sideways Down/The Sun Is Shining/Shapes of Things (version 2)/Most Likely You Go Your Way (And I'll Go Mine)/Little Games/Drinking Muddy Water/Think About It/Goodnight Sweet Josephine/My Baby

1993   *Train Kept A-Rollin'* (4 CD)   Charly Records
                                        CD LIK BOX 3
Disc 1
Smokestack Lightning/You Can't Judge a Book by Its Cover/Let It Rock/I Wish You Would/Who Do You Love/Honey in Your Hips/Bye Bye Bird/Mister Downchild/The River Rhine/23 Hours Too Long/A Lost Care/Pontiac Blues/Take It Easy Baby (version 1)/Out on the Water Coast/I Don't Care No More/Western Arizona/Take It Easy Baby (version 2)/Baby What's Wrong/Boom Boom/Honey in Your Hips

Disc 2
Talkin' About You/I Wish You Would (alternate take, long version)/A Certain Girl (alternate take)/Slow Walk/Highway 69/My Little Cabin/Too Much Monkey Business/I Got Love if You Want It/Smokestack Lightning/Good Morning Little Schoolgirl/Respectable/Five Long Years/Pretty Girl/Louise/I'm a Man/Here 'Tis/I Wish You Would/A Certain Girl/Good

Morning Little Schoolgirl (backing track)/Good Morning Little School-girl (backing track and harmonica)/Good Morning Little Schoolgirl (master)/I Ain't Got You

Disc 3
For Your Love/Got to Hurry (take 2, false start)/Got to Hurry (take 3)/Got to Hurry (take 4)/Putty (In Your Hands)/Sweet Music (take 3)/Sweet Music (take 4)/I'm Not Talking/I Ain't Done Wrong/My Girl Sloopy/Heart Full of Soul (sitar version)/Heart Full of Soul/Steeled Blues/Evil Hearted You/Still I'm Sad/Shapes of Things/You're a Better Man Than I/I'm a Man/New York City Blues/The Train Kept A-Rollin'/Paff . . . Bum (version 1)/Questa Volta/Paff . . . Bum (version 2)/Mr. Zero/Knowing/Without You[1]/Climbing Through[1]

   [1] Performed by the Authentics.

Disc 4
Jeff's Blues (take 1)/Jeff's Blues (take 2)/Someone to Love, Part One (take 2, instrumental)/Someone to Love, Part One (take 4, instrumental)/Some-one to Love, Part One (take 14, instrumental)/Someone to Love, Part One (take 15, vocal)/Someone to Love (Part Two)/Like Jimmy Reed Again/Chris' Number (take 1)/Pounds and Stomps (XYZ)/Pounds and Stomps/What Do You Want (take 1)/What Do You Want (take 2)/What Do You Want (take 3)/What Do You Want (take 4)/Here 'Tis (stereo instru-mental version)/Here 'Tis (version "For R.S.G.")/Crimson Curtain (edit of take 1 and insert)/Stroll On/I'm a Man[1]/Shapes of Things[1]

   [1] Live in Germany 1967.

1997	*. . . Where the ACTION Is!* (2 CD)	New Millennium Communications PILOT 10

Disc 1
Same tracks as *Yardbirds . . . On Air.*

Disc 2
Recorded in Stockholm, 1967.
Shapes of Things/Heart Full of Soul/You're a Better Man Than I/Most Likely You Go Your Way (And I'll Go Mine)/Over Under Sideways Down/Little Games/My Baby/I'm a Man

2000	*Cumular Limit*	Burning Airlines/ New Millennium Communications PILOT 24

Disc 1
Tinker, Tailor, Soldier, Sailor (alternate mix)/Shapes of Things (live)/Hap-penings Ten Years Time Ago (live)/Over Under Sideways Down (live)/I'm a Man (live)/Ten Little Indians (alternate version)/Glimpses (alternate mix)/You Stole My Love (alternate version)/Avron Knows/Spanish Blood/My Baby/Taking a Hold on Me/Dazed and Confused (live)

Disc 2
Shapes of Things/Happenings Ten Years Time Ago/I'm a Man/Over Under Sideways Down (video of same live performances as on Disc 1)/WOR-FM Interview

Miscellaneous U.K. Releases

1966   *Sonny Boy Williamson and the Yardbirds*   Fontana TL5277

Foreign Releases
Singles

1966	Questa Volta/Paff . . . Bum (Italy)	Ricordi SIR 20-010

Albums

1972	*Rock Generation Volume 5* (French)	BYG 529.705

Various artists LP including live versions of "Slow Walk," "Highway 69," "My Little Cabin" backing Sonny Boy Williamson, plus "Got My Mojo Working"—a live jam including other artists.

1981	*The First Recordings* (German)	L&R 44.001

Smokestack Lightning[1]/You Can't Judge a Book by Its Cover[1]/Take It Easy Baby[2]/Talkin' 'Bout You[3]/Let It Rock[1]/I Wish You Would[1]/Boom Boom[3]/Honey in Your Hips[3]/Who Do You Love[1]

   [1] Recorded December 8, 1963, at the Craw Daddy Club during the Yardbirds' set.
   [2] Recorded December 7, 1963, at the Craw Daddy Club while backing Sonny Boy Williamson.
   [3] Recorded December 10, 1963, at R.G. Studios, Morden, Surrey.

1991	*The Steampacket: The First R&B Festival* (German)	Repertoire RR 4090-WZ

Same tracks as *Rock Generation Volume 5* plus "Bye Bye Bird" (Sonny Boy Williamson solo).

1993	*The Live Saga, "1963–1967"* (Belgium CD)	Backtrack BT 9301

Shapes of Things[1]/Heart Full of Soul[1]/You're a Better Man Than I[1]/Most Likely You Go Your Way (And I'll Go Mine)[1]/Over Under Sideways Down[1]/Little Games[1]/My Baby[1]/I'm a Man[1]/I Wish You Would[2]/Honey in Your Hips[3]/Too Much Monkey Business[4]/I Got Love if You Want It[4]/Pretty Girl[4]/Respectable[4]/Smokestack Lightning[4]/Good Morning Lit-tle Schoolgirl[4]/Shapes of Things[5]/Happenings Ten Years Time Ago[5]/Over Under Sideways Down[5]/I'm a Man[5]

   [1] Live studio recordings in Stockholm, Sweden, April 4, 1967.
   [2] Recorded live at Palais Des Sports, Paris, France, June 20, 1965.
   [3] Recorded live in Richmond, U.K., at the Craw Daddy Club, December 8, 1963.
   [4] From the *Five Live Yardbirds* LP.
   [5] Recorded live in Hamburg, Germany, March 15, 1967.

1993	*Rare Concerts, "1964–1968"* (Belgium CD)	Backtrack BT 9302

The Train Kept A-Rollin'[1]/You're a Better Man Than I[1]/Dazed And Con-fused[1]/My Baby[1]/Over Under Sideways Down[1]/Drinking Muddy Water[1]/Shapes of Things[1]/White Summer[1]/I'm a Man[1]/I Wish You Would[2]/You're a Better Man Than I[3]/The Train Kept A-Rollin'[3]/Dust My Broom[3]/Scratch My Back[3]/Over Under Sideways Down[3]/The Sun Is Shining[3]/Shapes of Things[3]

   [1] From the *Live Yardbirds! Featuring Jimmy Page* LP.
   [2] Recorded live at Palais Des Sports, Paris, France, June 20, 1965.
   [3] Recorded live in London, U.K., 1966.

Selected Bibliography

Magazines Consulted

Beat, Beat Instrumental, Blues Access, Blues Revue, Blues Revue Quarterly, British Blues Review, Circus, Crawdaddy, Disc, Discoveries, Disc and Music Echo, Disc Weekly, Downbeat, Guitar Player, Goldmine, Hit Parader, Hullabaloo, Jazz & Pop, Jazz News & Review, The Los Angeles Free Press, The Los Angeles Times, Mojo, Mojo Navigator, Music Echo, New Musical Express, The New York Times, Record Collector, Record Mirror, Rolling Stone, Sounds, Ugly Things, Vintage Guitar and *Zig Zag*.

General Reference Books

Brunning, Bob. *Blues in Britain* (Blandford Press, 1995)

Fancourt, Leslie. *British Blues on Record 1957–1970* (Retrack Books, 1992)

Fancourt, Leslie. *Blue Horizon Records 1965–1972* (Retrack Books, 1992)

Frame, Pete. *The Complete Rock Family Trees* (Omnibus Press, 1993)

Frame, Pete. *More Rock Family Trees* (Omnibus Press, 1998)

Frame, Pete. *The Beatles and Some Other Guys* (Omnibus Press, 1998)

Hounsome, Terry. *Rock Research 6* (Record Researcher Publications, 1994)

Neely, Ted. *Goldmine Price Guide to 45 RPM Records* (Krause Publications, 1999)

Neely, Ted. *Goldmine Record Album Price Guide* (Krause Publications, 1999)

Record Collector, Rare Record Guide 2000 (Parker Mead Limited, 1998)

Rice, Tim, et al. Guinness British Hit Singles (GRRR Books, 1985)

Rice, Tim, et al. Guinness British Hit Albums (GRRR Books, 1986)

Whitburn, Joel. *Top Pop Singles 1955–1990* (Record Research, 1991)

Whitburn, Joel. *Top Pop Albums 1955–1996* (Record Research, 1991)

Artist Specific Magazine Articles and Book

A complete listing of all of the sources consulted during the preparation of this book would encompass over 70 pages. We have therefore elected to list only selected sources below and post the complete bibliography to the following URL: http://www.sixtiesrock.com/

Allman Brothers

Crowe, Cameron. "The Allman Brothers Story," *Rolling Stone*, December 6, 1973, pp. 46, 47, 50, 52, 54

Freman, Scott. *Midnight Riders* (Little, Brown & Company, 1995)

Nolan, Tom. *The Allman Brothers Band: A Biography in Words and Pictures* (Chappel Music Company, 1976)

Obrecht, Jas. "Duane Allman Remembered," *Guitar Player*, October 1981, pp. 68–70, 76, 78–81, 84

Artwoods

Artwoods. "How to Make It with Two Misses," *Melody Maker*, April 24, 1965, p. 8

Craine, Don. "The Artweeds—An Art History Lesson," *Ugly Things*, #14, 1995, pp. 25–27

Rawlings, Terry. "The Artwoods," *Record Collector*, May 1992, pp. 115–122

Uncredited. "'We Aim to Excite!' . . . Say the Artwoods," *Record Mirror*, June 5, 1965, p. 5

Bakerloo

Sanders, Rick. "Bakerloo," *Beat Instrumental*, March 1969, p. 27

Uncredited. "Player of the Month: Clem Clempson," *Beat Instrumental*, January 1970, p. 6

Uncredited. "Colosseum's Guitarist Has Roots in Classical Sounds," *Disc & Music Echo*, February 14, 1970, p. 25

Walsh, Alan. "Bakerloo Blues Line—Bringing the Beatles to Blues," *Melody Maker*, January 11, 1969, p. 10

Bishop, Elvin

Dupree, Tom. "Elvin Bishop: Gettin' Loose Down South," *Rolling Stone*, July 4, 1974, p. 24

Fiofori, Tom. "Elvin Bishop," *Guitar Player*, October 1969, pp. 20–22

Fiofori, Tom. "Blossoming Blues: The Elvin Bishop Group," *Downbeat*, February 5, 1970, pp. 12–13, 29

Glover, Tony. "Elvin Bishop Cops a Coat," *Rolling Stone*, December 24, 1970, pp. 24–25

Black Cat Bones

Dawbarn, Bob. "There's Been a British Blues Scene for Sixty Years," *Melody Maker*, January 4, 1969, p. 12

Tiller, Paul. "From Souls to Bones," *Ugly Things*, Issue 16, pp. 71–71

Tiller, Paul. "The Black Cat Bones Story, Part 2," *Ugly Things*, Issue 17

Uncredited. "Black Cat Bones Recording L.P.," *Beat Instrumental*, November 1968

Blind Faith

Christgau, Robert. "Are the 'Blind' Keeping Faith?," *The New York Times*, July 20, 1969, pt. 3, page 4

Goodman, Pete. "Blind Faith in the States," *Beat Instrumental*, September 1969, pp. 42–43

Laine, Wesley. "Super Album? Well Here Are Some Interesting Things from Blind Faith," *Record Mirror*, August 23, 1969, p. 8

Welch, Chris. "Inside Blind Faith," *Melody Maker*, October 4, 1969, p. 17

Bloomfield, Mike

Bloomfield, Mike. *Me and Big Joe* (RE/Search, 1980)

Brooks, Michael. "Michael Bloomfield—'Straight Stone City Blues,'" *Guitar Player*, June 1971, August 1971

Ward, Ed. *Mike Bloomfield: The Rise and Fall of an American Guitar Hero* (Cherry Lane Books, 1983)

Wolkin, Jan Mark and Keenom, Bill. *Michael Bloomfield: If You Love These Blues* (Miller–Freeman Books, 2000)

Blues Project

Blues Project. *The Sound: An Autobiography* (McGraw-Hill, 1968)

Kooper, Al and Edmonds, Ben. *Backstage Passes* (Stein and Day, 1977)

Uncredited. "Blues Project," *Hit Parader*, November 1966, pp. 19, 40, 42

Uncredited. "Inside the Blues Project—Part II," *Hit Parader*, December 1966, pp. 35, 45, 46

Bond, Graham

Heckstall-Smith, Dick. *The Safest Place in the World* (Quartet Books, 1989)

Hogg, Brian. "The Graham Bond Organisation," *Record Collector*, October 1982, pp. 29–34

Shapiro, Harry. *Graham Bond: The Mighty Shadow* (Guinness, 1992)

Uncredited. "Graham Bond—A Revolution in Group Sound," *Melody Maker*, August 7, 1965, p. 7

Butterfield Blues Band, Paul

C. P. "Paul Butterfield," *Beat Instrumental*, December 1966, p. 12

Demicheal, Don. "Father and Son: An Interview with Muddy Waters and Paul Butterfield," *Downbeat*, August 7, 1969, pp. 12–13, 32

Ellis III, Tom. "Paul Butterfield," *Blues Access*, Parts 1–4, Fall 1995, Spring 1996, Fall 1996, Summer 1997

Paulsen, Don. "After Hours with the Butterfield Blues Band," *Hit Parader*, December 1967, pp. 14–15

Canned Heat

Davis, Rebecca. "Child Is Father to the Man," *Blues Access*, Fall 1998, pp. 40–43

Diehl, Digby. "The Canned Heat's Obsession with the Blues," *The Los Angeles Times*, December 8, 1968, Calendar Section, p. 12

Parra, Fito de la. *Living the Blues* (Record Grafix, 1999)

Welding, Pete. "Look Back to the Future—An Interview with Canned Heat's Al Wilson," *Downbeat*, June 13, 1968, pp. 21–23, 44, 47

Chicken Shack

Clifford, Mike. "Chicken Shack," *Beat Instrumental*, March 1969, pp. 18–20

Eldridge, Royston. "Shocks from the Shack," *Melody Maker*, December 27, 1969, p. 9

Goddard, Lon. "The Chicken Shack—A Big Underground Breakthrough?" *Record Mirror*, May 17, 1969, p. 7

Logan, Nick. "Chicken Shack's Christine a Surprising Girl," *New Musical Express*, July 20, 1968, p. 11

Clapton, Eric

Coleman, Ray. *Survivor: The Authorized Biography of Eric Clapton* (Sidgwick & Jackson, 1985)

Hilburn, Robert. "Clapton Finds the Right Combination," *The Los Angeles Times*, November 17, 1970, Part IV, p. 12

Roberty, Marc. *Eric Clapton: The Complete Recording Sessions, 1963–1992* (St. Martin's Press, 1993)

Shapiro, Harry. *Eric Clapton: Lost in the Blues* (De Capo, 1992)

Climax Blues Band

Boucher, Caroline & Shipston, Roy. "Their Name Gives Climax the Blues," *Disc & Music Echo*, December 19, 1970, p. 17

Hollingworth, Roy. "Climax Chicago," *Melody Maker*, September 12, 1970, p. 40

Uncredited. "Climax: Set to Beat the Blues," *New Musical Express*, December 23, 1972, p. 33

Watts, Michael. "Climax Chicago—Back to Blues," *Melody Maker*, August 1, 1970, pp. 28

Cream

Altham, Keith. "Cream Are the Very End," *New Musical Express*, October 28, 1966, p. 10

Johnson, Pete. "Cream Guitarist a Reluctant Idol," *The Los Angeles Times*, October 13, 1968, Calendar Section, p. 1, 37

Platt, John. *Disraeli Gears* (Schirmer Books, 1998)

Welch, Chris. *Cream: The Legendary Sixties Supergroup* (Miller-Freeman Books, 2000)

Davies and the R&B All-Stars, Cyril

Dawbarn, Bob. "Cyril Was the Man on Harmonica," *Melody Maker*, January 18, 1964, p. 12

Uncredited. "R&B at the Marquee," *Jazz News & Review*, January 2, 1963

Uncredited. "Rhythm & Blues to Record," *Jazz News & Review*, February 14, 1963

Vickery, Graham. "Cyril Davies: Preaching the Blues," *British Blues Review*, December 1988, pp. 10–11

Downliners Sect

Clayson, Alan. "Downliners Sect," *Record Collector*, March 1992, pp. 48–51

Green, Richard. "Latest Sect—Downliners!," *New Musical Express*, June 19, 1964, p. 9

Jones, Peter. "The Sect Maniacs," *Record Mirror*, June 27, 1964, p. 11

Shute, Bill and Stax, Mike. "The Downliners Sect Story," *Ugly Things*, Parts 1–3; #5 undated; #6 Summer 1987; #8, 1989

Dummer Band, John

Clifford, Mike. "John Dummer Blues Band," *Beat Instrumental*, February 1969, p. 4

Dawbarn, Bob. "Going Backwards into Blues with the John Dummer Band," *Melody Maker*, January 18, 1969, p. 12

Uncredited. "McPhee Joins Dummer," *Beat Instrumental*, August 1968, p. 29

Uncredited. "Don't Let the Short Hair Fool You," *Melody Maker*, February 21, 1970, p. 11

Dunbar Retaliation, Aynsley

Clifford, Mike. "Aynsley Dunbar Retaliation," *Beat Instrumental*, December 1968, p. 12

Clifford, Mike. "Player of the Month: John Morshead," *Beat Instrumental*, February 1969, p. 8

M. H. "Profile: Victor Brox," *Beat Instrumental*, April 1969, p. 39

Middleton, Ian. "Aynsley Dunbar: 'When You Play You've Got to Feel It,'" *Record Mirror*, September 28, 1968, p. 6

Electric Flag

Delehant, Jim. "Mike Bloomfield: Leader of the Band," *Hit Parader*, April 1968, pp. 44–45

Uncredited. "Electric Flag Is Busted: 'The Lenny Bruce Riff,'" *Rolling Stone*, November 9, 1967, p. 6

Wenner, Jan. "The Rolling Stone Interview: Mike Bloomfield," *Rolling Stone*, April 6, 1968, pp. 11–14

Wenner, Jan. "The Rolling Stone Interview: Mike Bloomfield (Part 2)," *Rolling Stone*, April 20, 1968, p. 11

Fleetwood Mac

Brunning, Bob. *Fleetwood Mac: Behind the Masks* (New English Library, 1990)

Celmins, Martin. *Peter Green: Founder of Fleetwood Mac* (Castle Communications, 1995)

Fleetwood, Mick and Davis, Stephen. *Fleetwood: My Life and Adventures in Fleetwood Mac* (Morrow, 1990)

Shapiro, Harry. "Peter Green's Blues," *Record Collector*, July 1993, pp. 82–86

Gallagher, Rory (Taste)

Clifford, Mike. "Taste," *Beat Instrumental*, March 1969, p. 8

D.J.M. "Player of the Month—John Wilson," *Beat Instrumental*, May 1970

Gallagher, Rory. "Me and My Music," *Disc & Music Echo*, July 25, 1970, p. 17

Powers, Vincent. *Send 'Em Home Sweatin': The Showbands Story* (Kildanore, Dublin, 1990)

Goldberg, Barry

Gabriel, Paul. "Sweet Home Chicago," *Discoveries*, June 1997, pp. 44–48

Johnson, Pete. "Barry Goldberg—On Making It!," *Hit Parader*, April 1969, pp. 46–47

Manno, George. "Barry Goldberg—Michael's Best Friend," *Vintage Guitar Magazine*, pp. 80–82

Uncredited. "Hullabaloo for the Blues—The Goldberg-Miller Blues Band," *Hit Parader*, May 1966, pp. 50–51

Gravenites, Nick

Case, Greg. "Born in Chicago," *Hit Parader*, October 1969, pp. 22–25

Gravenites, Nick. "Bad Talkin' Bluesman," *Blues Revue*, Issues #18–26; July/August 1995 through December/January 1996–7

Grissam, John. "Nick Gravenites Quits Commuting," *Rolling Stone*, March 15, 1973, p. 18

Robble, Andrew. "Gettin' Down with Nick Gravenites," *Relix*, October 1993, pp. 18–19

Kelly, Dave

Bainton, Roy. *Talk to Me Baby (The Story of the Blues Band)* (Firebird Books, 1994)

Gilbert, Jeremy. "New Roads for Brother Dave," *Melody Maker*, December 6, 1969, p. 12

Kelly, Jo Ann

Dawbarn, Bob. "Jo-Ann, Cringing at that Mother Figure Image," *Melody Maker*, November 30, 1968, p. 14

Grossman, Stefan. "Jo-Ann Kelly—British Queen of 6- and 12-String Country Blues," *Guitar Player*, August 1978, pp. 28, 94, 96

Moody, Pete. "Jo Ann Kelly—Parts 1–3," *British Blues Review*, April, June and October 1988

Tobler, John. "Jo Ann Kelly," *Zig Zag*, April 1970, p. 28

Korner, Alexis

Abrahams, Derek. "'Stop Reliving the Past and Enjoy Now,' Says Alexis Korner," *Beat Instrumental*, November 1971, pp. 18–19

Dawbarn, Bob. "Good Luck to the Boys on the Bandwagon Says Alexis Korner," *Melody Maker*, August 22, 1964, p. 15

James, Patrick. "Alexis Explains His Sound," *Record Mirror*, July 4, 1964, p. 10

Shapiro, Harry. *Alexis Korner* (Bloomsbury, 1996)

Leeman Five, Mark

Uncredited. "Dead Singer's Tapes Are Refused," *Melody Maker*, July 17, 1965, p. 1

Uncredited. "Leeman Five Will Try a Change," *Beat Instrumental*, August 1966

Uncredited. "Mark Leeman Dies in Road Accident," *Melody Maker*, July 3, 1965, p. 4

Uncredited. "Rave Night for Mark's Benefit," *Melody Maker*, July 24, 1965, p. 12

Mahal, Taj

Delehant, Jim and Mahal, Taj. "The Mind of a Modern Bluesman—Taj Mahal," *Hit Parader*, September 1969, pp. 19–21

Hansen, Barret. "The Rise and Fall of the Rising Suns," *Goodphone*, December 3, 1979

Mahal, Taj with Foehr, Stephen. *Taj Mahal: Autobiography of a Bluesman* (Sanctuary Publishing, 2001)

Robbins, Paul. "Sound of Sunlight Rising," *The Los Angeles Free Press*, July 2, 1965, p. 6

Mandel, Harvey

Forte, Dan. "Harvey Mandel: The Best Unknown in Pop Guitar," *Guitar Player*, May 1977, pp. 20, 21, 58, 60, 62, 64, 68

Isola, Gregory. "Harvey Mandel: Snake Still Blazing His Own Trail," *Blues Revue*, July/August 1995, pp. 18–19

Skelly, Richard. "Harvey Mandel: The Snake Strikes Back," *Goldmine*, August 19, 1994, pp. 64, 66, 68, 146

Uncredited. "Harvey Mandel," *Hit Parader*, May 1969, p. 61

Mayall, John

Carpenter, John. "Free Press Interview with John Mayall," *The Los Angeles Free Press*, June 13, 1969, pp. 60–61

Feather, Leonard. "John Mayall—Still a Blues Crusader," *The Los Angeles Times*, October 27, 1969, Part IV, p. 21

Kirkham, Clive. "Living the Blues Bluesbreakers Style," *Melody Maker*, July 15, 1967, p. 4

K. S. "John Mayall—Blues Purist," *Beat Instrumental*, September 1967, p. 13

Musselwhite, Charlie

Branning, Dan. "Charlie Plays the Blues," *The San Francisco Examiner*, March 15, 1973

Robble, Andrew. "Blues from the Heart," *Blues Revue Quarterly*, Issue 13, Summer 1994, pp. 19–27

Seigal, Buddy. "Charlie Musselwhite's Souvenir of Chicago," *The Los Angeles Times*, October 27, 1995, pp. F1, F21

Vernon, Mike. "Blues at the Golden Bear," *Melody Maker*, August 9, 1969, p. 10

Nelson, Tracy (Mother Earth)

Berg, Karin. "Eye, Eye It's Miss Nelson," *Disc & Music Echo*, February 5, 1972, p. 13

Cohodas, Nadine. "Tracy Nelson," *Blues Access*, Fall 1995, pp. 20–24

Morris, Phil. "Mother Earth: Home Cooking," *Circus*, June 1970, pp. 30–31, 48

Nelson, Tracy. "Tracy Nelson—Head of Mother Earth," *Hit Parader*, June 1969, pp. 52–53

Piazza, Rod

Boehm, Mike. "Mighty Long Flight Up to Good Times," *The Los Angeles Times,* August 13, 1992, Calendar Section, p. F-1

Kaufman, Eileen. "DBS Rocks At Genesis IX," *The Los Angeles Free Press,* August 11, 1967, p. 17

Means, Andrew. "Enigmatic Bacon Fat," *Melody Maker,* November 21, 1970, p. 26

Powell, Bryan. "Flyin' High in the Here and Now," *Blues Access,* Fall 1999, pp. 32–36

Power, Duffy

Erskine, Peter. "Power to the People," *Disc and Music Echo,* April 21, 1973, p. 25

Means, Andrew. "Power Blasts from the Past," *Melody Maker,* February 27, 1971, p. 28

Power, Duffy. "Why Names Change," *New Record Mirror,* March 30, 1963, p. 7

Power, Duffy. "Verbal Power: Duffy's Story in His Own Words," *Record Collector,* March 1995, pp. 97–101

Pretty Things

Clayson, Alan. "The Pretty Things," *Discoveries,* May 1997, pp. 36–40

Clifford, Mike. "Pretty Things: Evolution Rather Than Revolution," *Beat Instrumental,* December 1968, p. 4

Jones, Peter. "Adults Hate Us More Than Stones," *Record Mirror,* September 18, 1964, p. 15

Stax, Mike. "Interview with a Legend: Phil May," *Ugly Things* #4, Spring 1985

Savoy Brown

Pratt, Tim. "Savoy Brown: Parts 1–3," *BBR Boogie,* March 1991, May 1991, March 1992

Roeser, Steve. "Savoy Brown—The Kim Simmonds Interview," *Discoveries,* October 1999, pp. 38–46

Salvo, Patrick. "Savoy Brown Surviving Socially," *Circus,* October 1972, pp. 32–33, 36–38

Sanders, Rick. "Savoy Brown at Last," *Beat Instrumental,* November 1968, p. 8

Siegel-Schwall Band

Ransom, Kevin. "If Brahms Ever Heard a Blues Harmonica . . . ," *The Detroit News,* September 28, 1995

Schonberg, Harold C. "Music: Blues at the Philharmonic," *The New York Times,* October 10, 1969, p. 39

Stilley, Brenn. "Siegel-Schwall Play the Opera," *Rolling Stone,* May 27, 1971, p. 18

Uncredited. "Siegel-Schwall, 'Happy Group,' Call It Quits," *Rolling Stone,* March 14, 1974, p. 22

Ten Years After

Boltwood, Derek. "The Fastest Guitarist Alive!," *Record Mirror,* March 30, 1968, p. 6

Green, Richard. "Hit Album Different from Live Shows," *New Musical Express,* March 8, 1969, p. 2

Harris, David. "Ten Years After: Breakin' the Blues," *Circus,* May 1970, pp. 17–20

Staehr, Herb. *Alvin Lee & Ten Years After Visual History* (Free Street Press, 2001)

Winter, Johnny

Carr, Roy. "Music's for Fun It's Absurd to Be So Serious!," *New Musical Express,* May 16, 1970, p. 11

Jahn, Mike. "Blues Guitar Sound of Johnny Winter Comes North," *The New York Times,* January 7, 1969, p. 30:6

Jones, Max. "Johnny—A Winter of Content," *Melody Maker,* October 17, 1970, pp. 20–21

Kahn, Ashley. "Johnny Winter: Back to the Blues—His Early Years (Part 1)," *Goldmine,* March 28, 1986, 10, 16, 18, 24

Yardbirds

Dreja, Chris; McCarty, Jim; and Platt, John. *Yardbirds* (Sidgwick & Jackson, 1983)

Carson, Annette. *Crazy Fingers* (Creda Communications, 1998)

Hjort, Christopher and Hinman, Doug. *Jeff's Book: A Chronology of Jeff Beck's Career, 1965–1980* (Rock'n'Roll Research Press, 2000)

Russo, Greg. *Yardbirds: The Ultimate Rave-Up* (Crossfire Publications, 2000)

Index